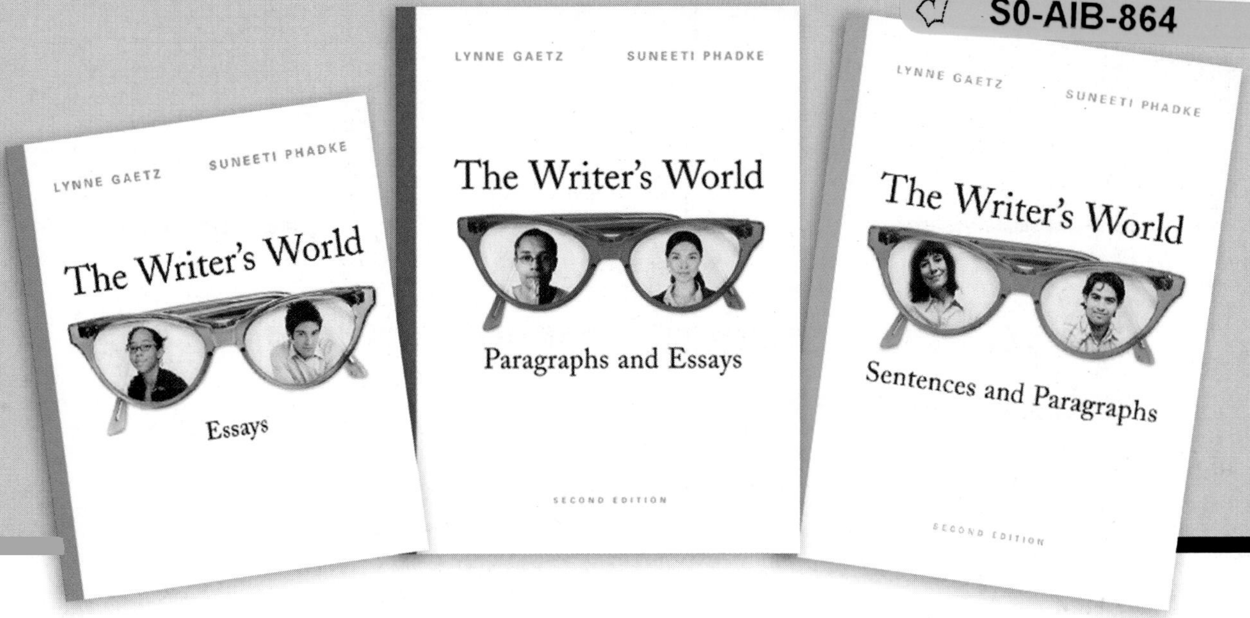

What are the diverse needs of your students?

- For *many of my students, English is a second language.*
- *I have many visual learners in my classes.*
- *My students have varying skill levels.*

Students differ in many ways, and each brings his or her own set of needs to the writing classroom. It is the great variety of those needs that poses a major challenge for writing instructors. Lynne Gaetz and Suneeti Phadke, the authors of *The Writer's World*, understand this dynamic from their numerous years of teaching students how to improve their writing. They understand that there are many types of writers, all with unique strengths and weaknesses, circumstances, and goals. Therefore, *The Writer's World* is designed to help you reach as great a number of students as possible by meeting the needs of those students. The following pages detail how *The Writer's World* helps learners with varying needs come together and excel at becoming stronger, more consistent, and more creative writers.

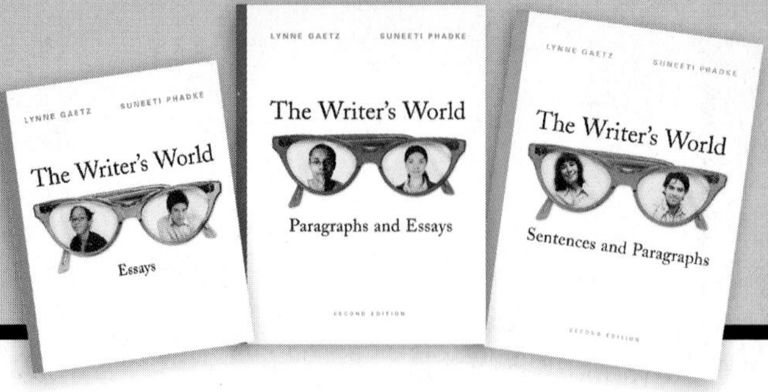

Do you have students for whom English is a second language?

> *"For my ESL students I find the chapters in the grammar section are what I use the most. I REALLY appreciate the box "Hints" that I can refer my students to as a reminder of something that often pertains to their writing."*
>
> —Patrice Plummer, *Bakersfield College*

With Lynne Gaetz and Suneeti Phadke's expertise in teaching nonnative speakers of English, ESL material is a strength of *The Writer's World* texts.

- **ESL Teaching Tips:** *The Writer's World: Essays* contains 88 ESL Teaching Tips in the margins of the Annotated Instructor's Edition. Many of these teaching tips are derived from the authors' first-hand experience teaching nonnative speakers in their classrooms, while others have been suggested by users of *The Writer's World* and experts in the field of English language training.

ESL Teaching Tip:
Nonnative speakers may not know the difference between the simple and progressive verb forms; therefore, draw their attention to this rule.

- **Seamless Integration of ESL Topics:** *The Writer's World* weaves traditional ESL topics throughout the text, often in a "Hint" box. By identifying them as ESL topics only in the Annotated Instructor's Edition (and not the student edition), this important material can benefit both native and nonnative speakers

- **Vocabulary Boost:** One important skill for nonnative speakers is improved vocabulary. *The Writer's World* author team has introduced Vocabulary Boost throughout the text to prompt students to review and improve their own writing. Designed to help enhance student vocabulary, Vocabulary Boost helps ESL and non-ESL students alike!

vo•cab•u•lar•y BOOST

Writers commonly overuse the same vocabulary. To make your writing more vivid and interesting, look at your first draft and underline at least ten repeated nouns and verbs. (Remember that a noun is a person, place, or thing.) Then add details or specific descriptions to five of the nouns. Here is a brief example of how you might avoid repetition of nouns and verbs.

Dull, repetitive: Patrice likes cycling. Patrice often cycles to work at his bookstore. Often Patrice is reckless and cycles without a helmet.

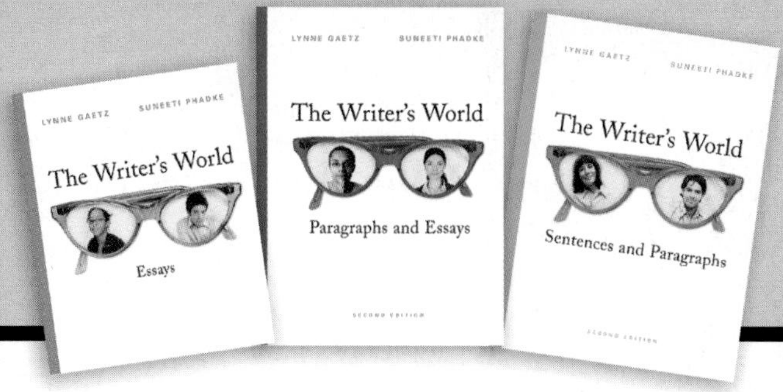

Do you have visual learners?

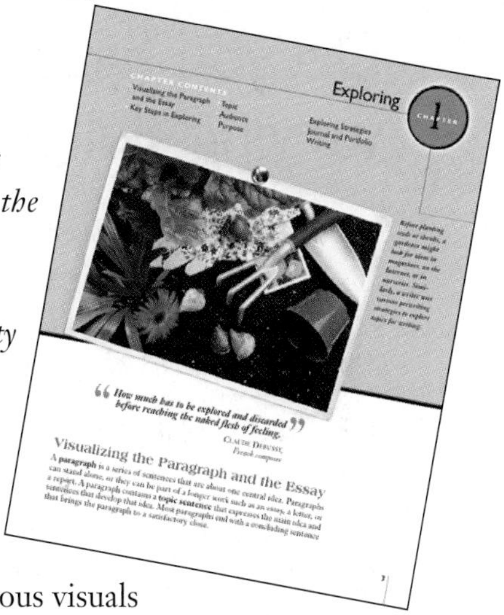

"My students appreciate how the beginning of each chapter includes a photo and the overview of each chapter. I tell them that those are the ideas they need to grasp from each chapter. The visual appeal of the text is a great motivator for my students."

—Karin Russell, *Keiser University*

The authors have utilized visuals throughout the text to illustrate key writing concepts. These visual cues help students retain information by providing it to them in an additional format.

- **Visuals to Illustrate Concepts:** *The Writer's World* uses numerous visuals throughout the text to illustrate concepts, including tables and charts, chapter opening photos, and ". . . at Work" boxes.

- **Visual Writing Prompts:** Topics and ideas for essay writing can come from a number of different sources. In addition to reading essays, *The Writer's World* encourages students to take inspiration from examining photos and watching popular movies. These visual prompts, found at the end of each writing chapter and thematic unit, give students varied and engaging options for finding an essay topic.

Writing Activity 2: Film Writing

1. *Remember the Titans* is about racial conflicts in small-town Virginia. In *The Fight Club*, a young man deals with his inner demons. Choose one of those films and describe the steps the main character takes to overcome adversity.
2. In *The Departed*, two young men become police officers in a department where they must play vastly different roles. Officer Billy Costigan goes undercover to infiltrate the mob, while mobster Colin Sullivan becomes a police officer. Compare and contrast the main characters.
3. View a film that deals with conflict such as *Crash*, *Clueless*, *Taxi Driver*, *Friday Night Lights*, *The DaVinci Code*, or *The Shawshank Redemption*, and discuss the causes or effects of the main character's decisions.

- **Open and Inviting Text Design:** *The Writer's World* layout grabs students' attention and draws them into the material. The text has just the right mix of exciting visual and design elements to help stimulate readers' interest without being cluttered.

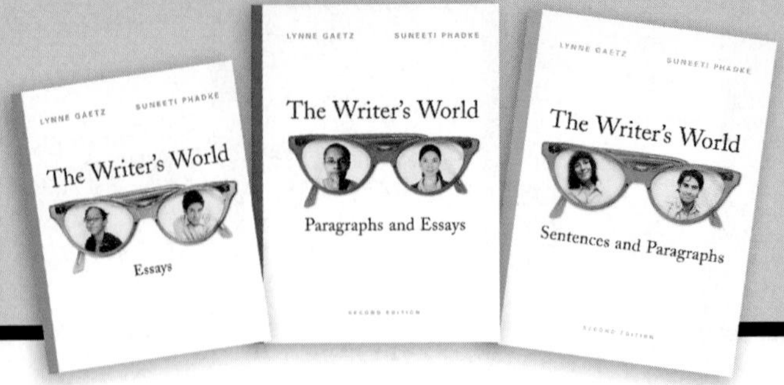

Do you have students with varying skill levels?

> *"I use the Final Review exercises of the grammar chapters as homework, group practice, or in-class exercises to check student's understanding before they take an assessment of the material. The thing I like the most about these reviews is that they are in passages rather than in individual sentences . . . so this format gives them more authentic practice."*
>
> —Lory Conrad, *University of Arkansas, Fort Smith*

- **Thematic Grammar Chapters:** This unique way of presenting grammar concepts thematically makes the material more engaging. The more engaging grammar is, the more likely students will retain key concepts.

- **MyWritingLab™ ships automatically with every copy of *The Writer's World.*** It is the first complete learning system that will truly help students become better writers.

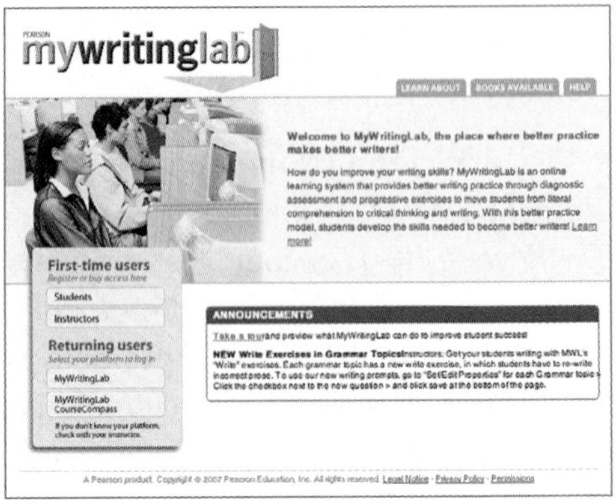

  - ***A Comprehensive Writing Program.*** MyWritingLab houses over 9,000 exercises in grammar, writing process, essay development, and research.

  - ***Diagnostic Testing.*** MyWritingLab includes groundbreaking diagnostic testing that thoroughly assesses students' skills in grammar. Based on the results, students receive a study plan that reflects the areas where they need help the most and those areas that they have mastered.

  - ***Recall, Apply, and Write Exercises.*** These activities, the heart of MyWritingLab, are designed to move students from literal comprehension to critical comprehension to demonstrating concepts in their own writing. This recursive learning process, not available in any other online resource, enables students to master the skills and concepts they need to be successful writers.

For tips on integrating MyWritingLab into your course, see pages I–9 through I–12.

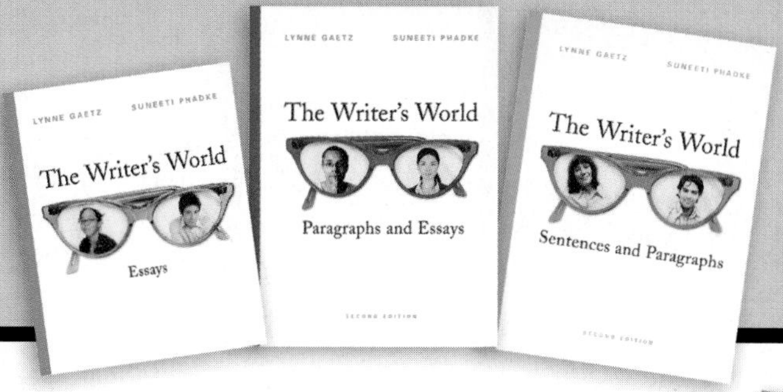

What are the diverse needs of instructors?

The Writer's World: Essays

INSTRUCTOR SUPPORT:

- **Annotated Instructor's Edition.** The AIE contains the answers to all of the exercises in the text and over 150 teaching tips in the margins for instructors. (ISBN: 0-13-243723-6)

- **Instructor's Resource Manual.** For each chapter in the text, this resource provides PowerPoint slides, summaries, and additional chapter quizzes. Also included are sample syllabi and a textbook answer key for those instructors who wish to distribute exercise answers to their students. (ISBN: 0-13-243724-4)

STUDENT SUPPORT:

Instructors can choose to package any of these student supplements. Consult your local Pearson representative for desk copies and the correct package ISBNs. You can also call 1-800-526-0485.

The Prentice Hall Grammar Workbook, Second Edition
(ISBN: 0-13-194771-0)

The Prentice Hall Editing Workbook
(ISBN: 0-13-189352-1)

Applying English to Your Career
(ISBN: 0-13-192115-0)

The Prentice Hall ESL Workbook, Second Edition
(ISBN: 0-13-194759-1)

The Prentice Hall Writer's Journal
(ISBN: 0-13-184900-X)

The Prentice Hall Florida Exit Test Study Guide for Writing
(ISBN: 0-13-111652-5)

The Prentice Hall THEA Study Guide for Writing
(ISBN: 0-13-041585-5)

The New American Webster Handy College Dictionary, Third Edition
(ISBN: 0-13-032870-7)

The New American Roget's College Thesaurus
(ISBN: 0-13-045258-0)

A Prentice Hall Pocket Reader: Patterns
(ISBN: 0-13-144352-6)

A Prentice Hall Pocket Reader: Themes
(ISBN: 0-13-144355-0)

A Prentice Hall Pocket Reader: Argument
(ISBN: 0-13-189525-7)

A Prentice Hall Pocket Reader: Writing Across the Curriculum
(ISBN: 0-13-194210-7)

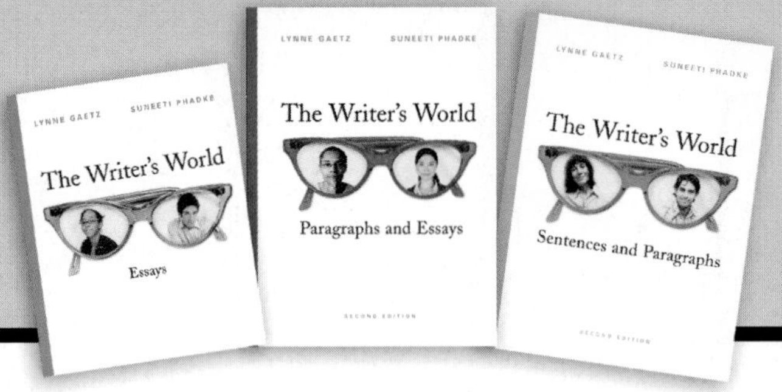

The growing *Writer's World* community

With over 250 colleges and 40,000 students using *The Writer's World* in its first year alone, *The Writer's World* community is growing rapidly. We rely on that community to continually improve the series, and those improvements can be seen here and in the revisions of the *Paragraphs and Essays* and *Sentences and Paragraphs* texts.

The authors and Pearson-Prentice Hall would like to thank the following instructors who reviewed the completed first editions and not only told us what they liked, but made specific comments for improvements. Some of these reviewers were asked to provide specific feedback on an entire text, others responded specifically to the ESL material, and others were asked how best to use *The Writer's World* in the classroom. We are most grateful for their comments.

Linda S. Anderson, Washington University*
Maria Assif, Truman College
Linda Austin, Glendale Community College
Craig Bartholomaus, Metropolitan Community College—Penn Valley
Scott Bauman, Orangeburg-Calhoun Technical College
Timothy Benell, Hunter College*
Sandra Block, Century College
Kay Blue, Owens Community College
Christian Blum, Bryant and Stratton College
Frances Boyd, Columbia University*
Nellie Boyd, Texas Southern University
Christina Bumgardner, Minnesota School of Business
Lorraine Caplan, IADT Pittsburgh
Karen Carlson, Jamestown Business College
Sharon Cavusgil, Georgia State University*
Cynthia Clark, Belmont Technical College
Lory Conrad, University of Arkansas—Fort Smith
Jodi Crandall, University of Maryland—Baltimore County*
Jonathan Dewberry, Gibbs College
Candace Dismuke, Texas Southern University
Kevin Dvorak, Keiser University
Crystal Echols, Sinclair Community College
Donna Estill, Alabama Southern Community College
Beth Flanagan, Tennessee Career College
Sally Gearhart, Santa Rosa Junior College*
Jennifer Georgen, Missouri College
Anne Gervasi, DeVry University
Charles Gonzalez, Central Florida Community College
Lois Gould, Kaplan Career Institute
Martha Hall, The New England School of English*
Carin Halper, Fresno City College
Beth Hammett, College of the Mainland
Carrie Harrison, Pittsburgh Technical Institute
Laraine Herring, Yavapai College
Amy Hickman, Collins College
Sara K. Holzberlein, Spring International Language Center*
Steve Horowitz, Central Washington University*
Greg Jewell, Drexel University*
Doreen Johnson, Rochester Community and Technical College
Aleyenne Johnson-Jonas, The Art Institute of California
Teresa Kozek, Housatonic Community College
Julie Kratt, Cowley County Community College
Trudy Krisher, Sinclair Community College
Deonne Kunkel, City College of San Francisco
Michael Lackey, William R. Harper College
Michelle Lockett, Lincoln College of Technology

***ESL Expert**

Carole MacClennan, Sinclair Community College
Elizabeth McCaffrey, St. Francis College
Alice McDonough, College of Technology
Sara McLaughlin, Texas Tech University
Christine Foster Meloni, Northern Virginia Community College*
Tara Mills, DeVry University
Mary Needle, Cuyahoga Community College
Caryn Newburger, Austin Community College
Sarah Nichter, Sullivan University
David Norman, South University
Angela Parrino, Hunter College School of Continuing Education*
Jeff Partridge, Capital Community College
Patrice Plummer, Bakersfield College
Kim Rickard, Sinclair Community College
Doug Rigby, Lehigh Carbon Community College
Esther Robbins, Prince George's Community College*
Nina Rosen, Santa Rosa Junior College*
Marybeth Ruscica, St. John's University
Karin Russell, Keiser University
Lynn Saul, Pima Community College
Basudha Sengupta, Diablo Valley College
Kathy Sherak, San Francisco State University*
Theresa Sternat, Eastfield College
Sharon Tash, Saddleback Community College
Roseann Torsiello, Berkeley College
James Trick, Newport Business Institute
Chris Twiggs, Florida Community College at Jacksonville
Mary Verbout, Yavapai College
Rhonda Wallace, Cuyahoga Community College
Arlene Weaver, Wilbur Wright College
Dale Weinbach, Miami International University of Art and Design
Tunya Whitaker, Westwood College
George Q. Xu, Clarion University of Pennsylvania*

***ESL Expert**

We also would like to remember the original members of *The Writer's World* community—those who reviewed manuscript and attended focus groups before the original publication of the series in August 2005.

Karin Alderfer, Miami Dade College
Paul Bellwoar, Harper College
Nellie Boyd, Texas Southern University
Beverly Braniff, Carl Sandburg University
Donald Brotherton, DeVry University
Lina Brotherton, Oakton Community College
Barbara Brown, Olive Harvey College
Mary Coleman, San Diego Community College
David Critchett, Community College of Rhode Island
Sandra Cusak, Heald University
Robin Daniel, Broward Community College
Patsy Daniels, Lane College
Nancy Davies, Miami Dade College
Rita Delude, New Hampshire Technical College
Curt Duffy, Los Angeles Pierce College
Bettie Estes, Ozarka College
Ray Foster, Scottsdale Community College
Maria Garcia-Landry, Palm Beach Community College
Anne Gervasi, DeVry University
Casey Gilson, Broward Community College
Kate Gleason, Interboro Institute
Joyce Henna, Honolulu Community College
Todd Heyden, Pace University
Lorena Horton, San Jacinto College
Cari Kenner, Texas State Technical College
Deonne Kunkel, Diablo Valley College
Paulette Longmore, Essex County Community College
Teri Maddox, Jackson State Community College
Robin Madieros, Community College of Rhode Island
Peter Marcoux, El Camino College
Sara McLaughlin, Texas Tech University
Alpha McMath, Triton College
Caryn Newburger, Austin Community College

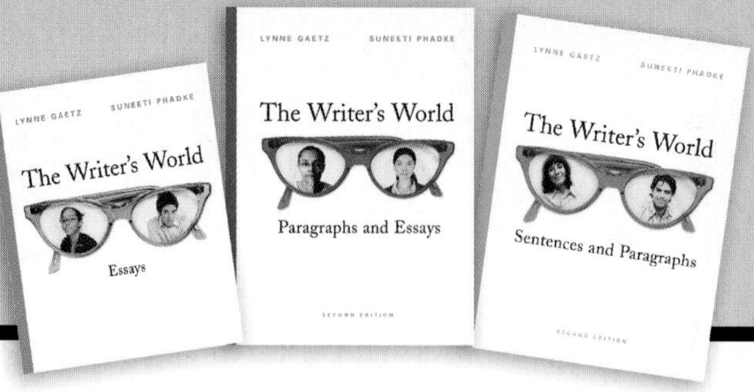

Virginia Nugent, Miami Dade College
Patrick Parks, Elgin Community College
Bruce Peppard, El Camino College
Dara Perales, Palomar College
Patricia Pullenza, Mesa Community College
Marcia Rogers, Orange Coast College
Bonnie Ronson, Hillsborough Community College
Harvey Rubenstein, Hudson County Community College
Anna Marie Schlender, Austin Community College
Jeffrey Siddal, College of DuPage
Karen Sidwell, St. Petersberg College
Marcie Sims, Green River Community College
Virginia Smith, Carteret Community College
Marc Sonnenfeld, Broward Community College
Carmen Subryan, Howard University
Mitchell Summerlin, Calhoun Community College
Lisa Tittle, Harford Community College
Danielle True, Florida Gulf Coast University
Donald Weasenforth, Collin County Community College
Sally Wheeler, Georgia Perimeter College
Evelyn Wilson, Tarrant County Community College
David Winsper, Springfield Technical College
Beverly Winters, Florida Community College
Arnold Wood, Florida Community College
Wendy Wright, El Camino College
Gary Zacharias, Palomar College
Donna Accardo, Los Angeles Pierce College
Jeanette Adkins, Tarrant County College
Pam Arterburn, Mount San Antonio College
Michelle Banks, Pasadena City College
Nicholas Bekas, Valencia Community College
Jennifer Black, McLennan Community College
Frank Cronin, Austin Community College
Patricia Dungan, Austin Community College
Joan Eberle, Shasta College
Heather Elko, Brevard College
Karen Feldman, Seminole Community College
Linda Fields, Broward Community College
Chriss Foster, Merrit College
Laura Foster-Eason, Collin County Community College
Gladys Garcia, California State University—Long Beach
Maria Garcia-Landry, Palm Beach Community College
Casey Gilson, Broward Community College
Barbara Goldberg, Humboldt State University
Sally Good, South Plains College
Traci L. Gourdine, American River College
Liza Greenberg, Miami Dade College
Dr. Susan Guzman-Trevino, Temple College
Carmen Hall, St. Petersburg College
Carin Halper, Fresno City College
Judy Harris, Tomball College
Gisela Herrera, East Los Angeles College
Alex Immerblum, East Los Angeles College
Diana Jones, Anglo-American University
Catherine Lally, Brevard Community College
Rebecca Loya, El Camino College
Alexandra Maeck, Los Angeles City College
Mimi Markus, Broward Community College
Karen McCafferty, Fresno City College
Joseph McDade, Houston Community College
Suzanne Morales, Central Texas College
Linda Nugent, San Joaquin Delta College
Sandra Offiah-Hawkins, Daytona Beach Community College
Cindy Okamura, Riverside Community College
Joan Perillo, Hillsborough Community College
Neil Plackcy, Broward Community College
Patricia Plasket-Oslerman, Palm Beach Community College
Valerie Russell, Valencia Community College
Margaret Rustick, California State University—Hayward
Mickey Schafer, University of Florida
Marjorie Smith, Ventura College
Marie Theodore-Pharel, Broward Community College
Stacey Thompson, Austin Community College
Denton Tulloch, Miami Dade College
Wendy Ward, Miami Dade College
Donna Willingham, Tomball College
Anne Ysunza, Santa Rosa Junior College

PEARSON mywritinglab™

MyWritingLab™ and Your Course: The Basics

Results Show That Students Overwhelmingly Support MyWritingLab

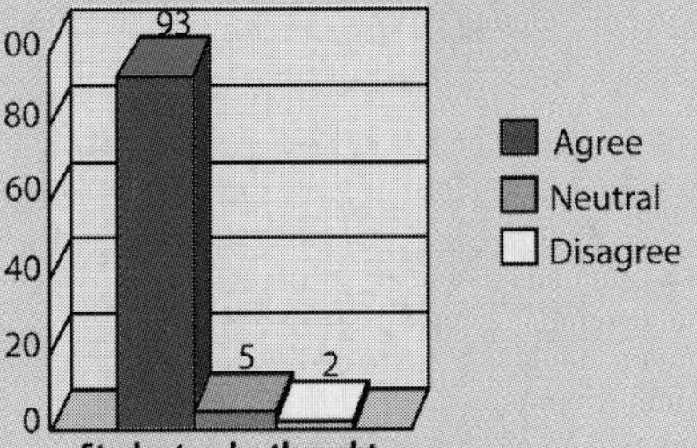

Students who thought MyWritingLab was easy to use

What do students think of MyWritingLab?

A recent survey of 531 students who used MyWritingLab for at least one semester (3/2007) revealed extremely positive results. The graph at left shows how easy students found the system to use.

What is MyWritingLab?

MyWritingLab from Pearson Education is the first online learning system built from the ground up to help low-literacy learners improve their writing skills. MyWritingLab combines established pedagogy with an easy-to-use online platform.

The Pedagogy

- **Diagnostics:** MyWritingLab first diagnoses students on their writing strengths and weaknesses.
- **Study Plan:** The diagnostics lead to a Study Plan that is unique to each student. The Study Plan provides access to the exercises students need to work on to improve their skills.
- **Step-by-Step Exercises:** A team of educators created exercises — Recall, Apply, and Write — to challenge students at the Knowledge, Application, and Synthesis levels of the cognitive domain. More than ten thousand questions help your students move beyond the recall of grammatical facts to the ability to express themselves in written form.

The Platform

The best pedagogy in the world is worthless if hidden behind confusing Web pages. A team of instructional designers, writing teachers, and students worked together tirelessly to put all this pedagogy behind an intuitive, easy-to-use platform. Our guiding principles:

- **The "3 Tab Rule":** Devoid of confusing drop down menus, busy pages, or unnecessary images, the pages include 3 simple tabs at the top to guide students.
- **Most Important Information Up Front:** The content in the four panels on the homepage changes depending on what the student needs to do next.
- **Use the Simplest Language at All Times:** Every word of instruction has been carefully scrutinized for reading comprehension.

www.mywritinglab.com

MyWritingLab™ and Your Course: Student Success

Did students find the exercises in MyWritingLab useful? Take a look.

Recall exercises test students on the basics of good writing skills.

"I could learn at my own pace, jumping ahead of the class, or spend more time on my weak areas without holding up the class."

—*Clint Kropp, Portland Community College*

How Useful Are the Recall Exercises?

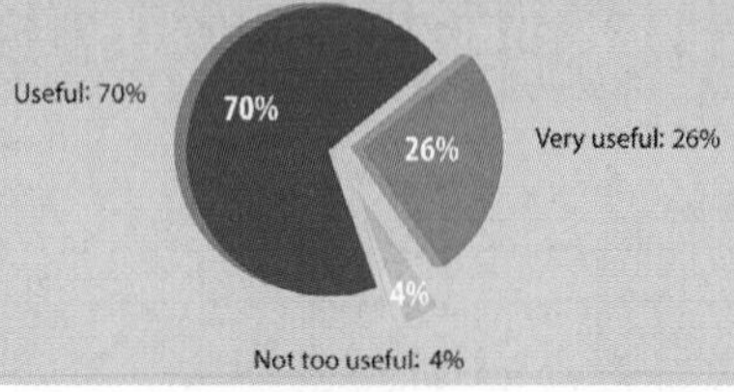

Apply exercises test students' ability to improve others' writing.

"I like to work on the 'apply' exercises. They help me look for mistakes in my own papers."

—*Irene Vu, CSU, Dominguez Hills*

How Useful Are the Apply Exercises?

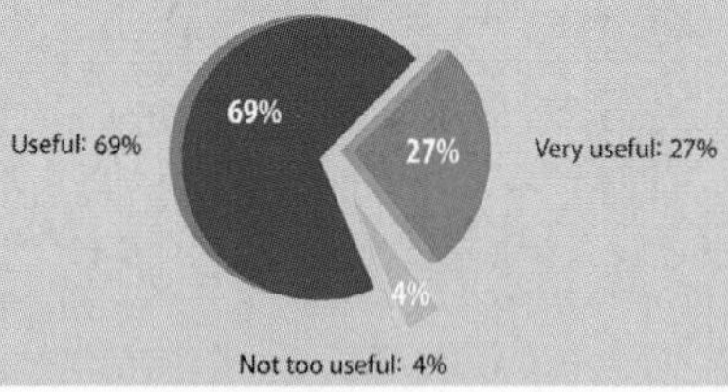

Write exercises challenge students to create their own well-written responses to open-ended questions.

"Since English is my second language, I needed to put in extra effort to write better essays. MyWritingLab ... definitely helped my writing."

— *Jung-ah Lee, West Valley College*

How Useful Are the Write Exercises?

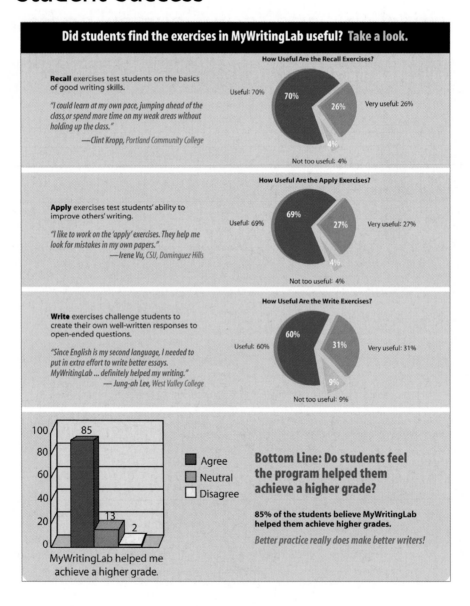

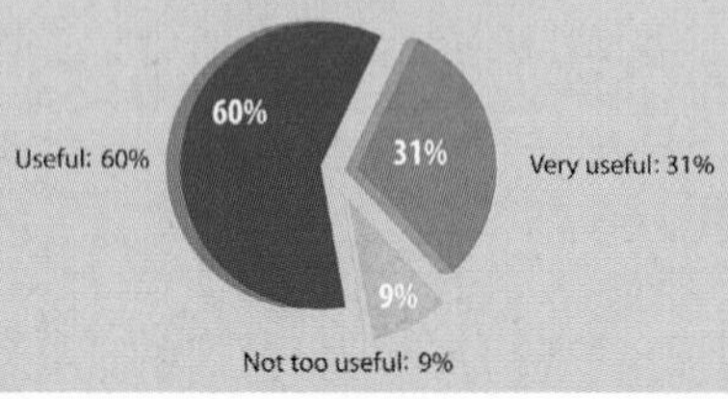

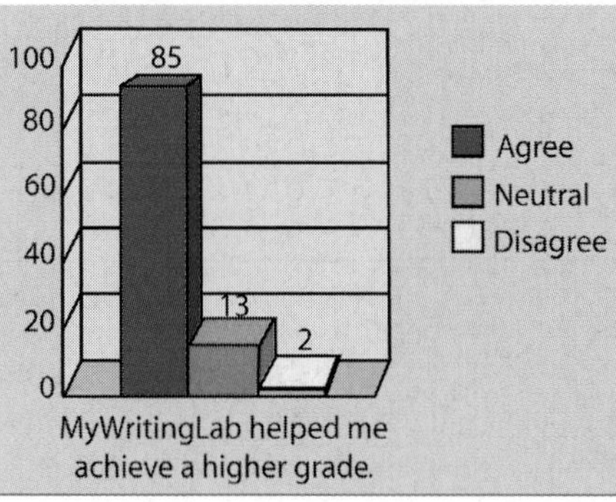

Bottom Line: Do students feel the program helped them achieve a higher grade?

85% of the students believe MyWritingLab helped them achieve higher grades.

Better practice really does make better writers!

www.mywritinglab.com

MyWritingLab™ and Your Course: Assessment

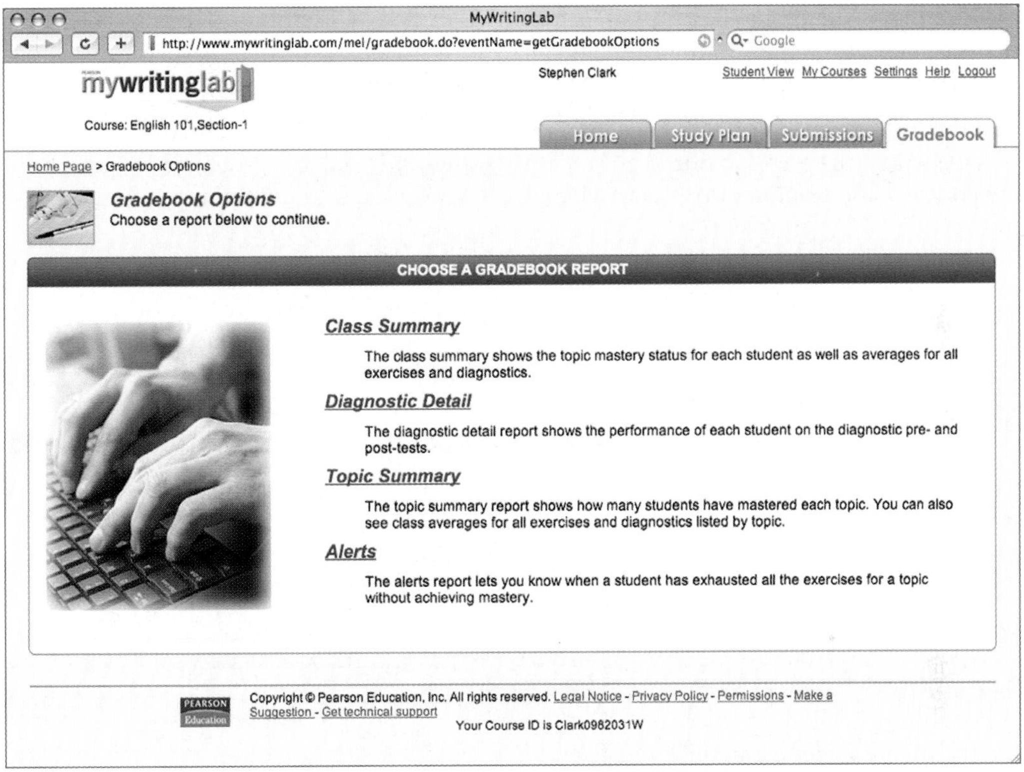

Comprehensive, detailed reporting provides both instructors and students with progress tracking for the skill work in MyWritingLab. At a glance, an instructor can see details such as student mastery, individual progress, time on task, topic averages, diagnostic details, alerts to indicate students who are struggling, and more!

PEARSON TUTOR SERVICES:

With MyWritingLab, students receive complimentary access to Pearson Tutor Services, powered by SMARTTHINKING, Inc. Students can submit a specified number of papers or essays each semester to Smartthinking's highly qualified e-structors™, who provide detailed feedback on how to improve the essay. Feedback is usually returned within 24 hours.

www.mywritinglab.com

MyWritingLab™ and Your Course: Integration

MyWritingLab is incredibly flexible and can be used in several useful ways in your classroom. Students can use it to focus on their individual areas of weakness, or the instructor can choose the MWL course that matches the table of contents of *The Writer's World*.

To find out how other instructors have integrated MyWritingLab into their course, visit our Faculty Advocate page on our Web site at www.mywritinglab.com/facultyadvocates.html. There you will find teaching tips, their syllabi with MyWritingLab integrated, and more!

Here are what some of the Faculty Advocates have to say . . .

"In order to avoid slowing the whole class down, I have found it very useful to assign elements of MWL to those students who are having particular ESL difficulties other students are not experiencing. MWL has also helped in reinforcing comments I make on students' papers."

Ona Seaney,
Southern Methodist University

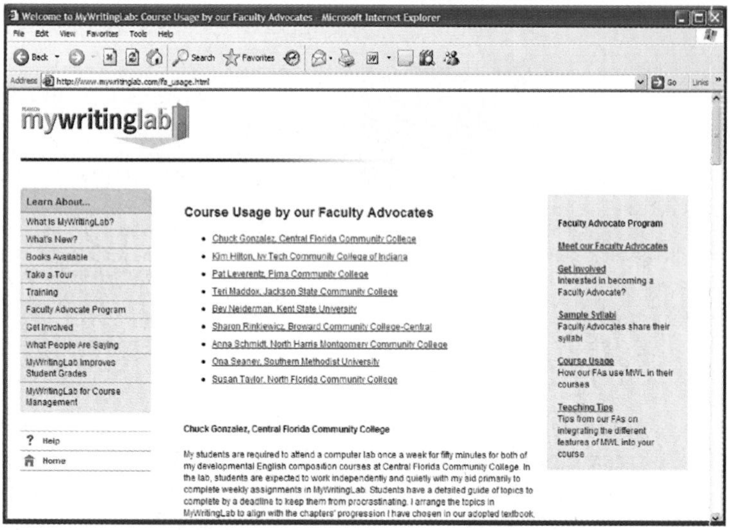

"We use the Watch feature in class as we study select areas of grammar and editing and engage in discussion to clarify with examples and verbal explanations. Some practices are then assigned to the whole class, but much of the value of MyWritingLab is its accessibility to students for individualized grammar and editing exercises. After each final paper is graded, I assign each student a MyWritingLab topic to practice based on needs assessed from the graded paper."

Pat Leverentz,
Pima Community College

www.mywritinglab.com

ANNOTATED INSTRUCTOR'S EDITION

LYNNE GAETZ
Lionel Groulx College

SUNEETI PHADKE
St. Jerome College

The Writer's World

Essays

PEARSON
Prentice Hall

Upper Saddle River, New Jersey 07458

Editorial Director: Leah Jewell
Editor in Chief: Craig Campanella
Editorial Assistant: Deborah Doyle
Director of Marketing: Brandy Dawson
Marketing Manager: Lindsey Prudhomme
Marketing Assistant: Jessica Muraviov
Text Permissions Specialist: Jane Scelta
Development Editor in Chief: Rochelle Diogenes
Development Editor: Leslie Taggart
Permissions Assistant: Peggy Davis
Senior Operations Supervisor: Sherry Lewis
Director, Image Resource Center: Melinda Patelli
Manager, Image Rights and Permissions: Zina Arabia
Manager, Visual Research: Beth Brenzel
Image Permissions Coordinator: Ang'John Ferreri
Image Researcher: Beth Brenzel
Interior Designer: Laura Gardner
Cover Designer: Anne DeMarinis
Cover art: Judith Miller Archive/Dorling Kindersley Media Library/Getty Images
Full-Service Project Management: Karen Berry, Pine Tree Composition, Inc.
Copyeditor: Laura Patchkofsky
Composition: Pine Tree Composition, Inc.
Printer/Binder: Courier Companies, Inc.
Cover Printer: Phoenix Color Corporation
Text Font: 10.5/12 Janson

For permission to use copyrighted material, grateful acknowledgment is made to the copyright holders on pages 653–655, which are considered an extension of the copyright page.

Pearson Education LTD.
Pearson Education Singapore, Pte. Ltd
Pearson Education, Canada, Ltd
Pearson Education–Japan
Pearson Education Australia PTY, Limited
Pearson Education North Asia Ltd
Pearson Educación de Mexico, S.A. de C.V.
Pearson Education Malaysia, Pte. Ltd
Pearson Education, Upper Saddle River, NJ

PEARSON
Prentice Hall

10 9 8 7 6 5 4 3 2 1

ANNOTATED INSTRUCTOR'S EDITION

LYNNE GAETZ
Lionel Groulx College

SUNEETI PHADKE
St. Jerome College

The Writer's World

Essays

PEARSON
Prentice Hall

Upper Saddle River, New Jersey 07458

Editorial Director: Leah Jewell
Editor in Chief: Craig Campanella
Editorial Assistant: Deborah Doyle
Director of Marketing: Brandy Dawson
Marketing Manager: Lindsey Prudhomme
Marketing Assistant: Jessica Muraviov
Text Permissions Specialist: Jane Scelta
Development Editor in Chief: Rochelle Diogenes
Development Editor: Leslie Taggart
Permissions Assistant: Peggy Davis
Senior Operations Supervisor: Sherry Lewis
Director, Image Resource Center: Melinda Patelli
Manager, Image Rights and Permissions: Zina Arabia
Manager, Visual Research: Beth Brenzel
Image Permissions Coordinator: Ang'John Ferreri
Image Researcher: Beth Brenzel
Interior Designer: Laura Gardner
Cover Designer: Anne DeMarinis
Cover art: Judith Miller Archive/Dorling Kindersley Media Library/Getty Images
Full-Service Project Management: Karen Berry, Pine Tree Composition, Inc.
Copyeditor: Laura Patchkofsky
Composition: Pine Tree Composition, Inc.
Printer/Binder: Courier Companies, Inc.
Cover Printer: Phoenix Color Corporation
Text Font: 10.5/12 Janson

For permission to use copyrighted material, grateful acknowledgment is made to the copyright holders on pages 653–655, which are considered an extension of the copyright page.

Pearson Education LTD.
Pearson Education Singapore, Pte. Ltd
Pearson Education, Canada, Ltd
Pearson Education–Japan
Pearson Education Australia PTY, Limited
Pearson Education North Asia Ltd
Pearson Educación de Mexico, S.A. de C.V.
Pearson Education Malaysia, Pte. Ltd
Pearson Education, Upper Saddle River, NJ

PEARSON
Prentice Hall

10 9 8 7 6 5 4 3 2 1

Contents

CHAPTER 11 Classification 175

CHAPTER 12 Comparison and Contrast 198

CHAPTER 13 Cause and Effect 217

CHAPTER 14 Argument 236

Appendices

Appendices

Readings Listed by Rhetorical Mode

ILLUSTRATION

NARRATION

PROCESS

Preface

About the First Edition of *The Writer's World: Essays*

The Writer's World can help students produce writing that is technically correct and rich in content. The book's unique features will appeal to both native and nonnative students with varying skill levels. Additionally, visual learners will find much to provoke thought in the eye-catching image program.

A Research-Based Approach

From the onset of the development process, we have comprehensively researched the needs and desires of current developmental writing instructors. We personally met with scores of instructors from around the country, asking for their opinions and insights regarding (1) the challenges posed by the course, (2) the needs of today's ever-changing student population, and (3) the ideas and features we were proposing in order to provide a more effective teaching and learning tool. Prentice Hall also commissioned dozens of detailed manuscript reviews from instructors, asking them to analyze and evaluate each draft of the manuscript. These reviewers identified numerous ways in which we could refine and enhance our key features. Their invaluable feedback was incorporated throughout *The Writer's World*, making this book the product of a successful and interactive partnership between the authors, publisher, and well over 200 developmental writing instructors.

How We Organized *The Writer's World*

The Writer's World presents essay development in five parts.

Part I: The Writing Process teaches students (1) how to formulate ideas (Exploring); (2) how to expand, organize, and present those ideas in a piece of writing (Developing); and (3) how to polish writing so that students convey their message as clearly as possible (Revising and Editing). Students will find the step-by-step approach clear and easy to follow.

Part II: Essay Patterns gives students a solid overview of the patterns of development. Using the same easy-to-understand process (Exploring, Developing, and Revising and Editing), each chapter explains how to convey ideas using specific writing patterns.

Part III: More College and Workplace Writing covers topics ranging from the letter and résumé to the research essay. This section also explains how to respond to films and literary works, and a chapter gives students tips on studying and preparing for essay exams.

Part IV: The Editing Handbook is a thematic grammar handbook. In each chapter, the exercises correspond to a section theme, such as The Forces of Nature or Human Development. As students work through the chapters, they hone their grammar and editing skills while gaining knowledge about a variety of topics. In addition to helping retain interest in the grammar practices, the thematic material provides a spark that ignites new ideas that students can apply to their writing.

Part V: Reading Strategies and Selections offers tips, readings, and follow-up questions. Additionally, students are given visual prompts in the photo and film writing sections. Students learn how to write by observing and dissecting what they read. The readings contain themes that also are found in Part IV: The Editing Handbook, thereby providing more fodder for generating writing ideas.

How *The Writer's World* Meets Students' Diverse Needs

You will find many unique elements in *The Writer's World* including our visual program, our coverage of nonnative speaker material, and strategies for addressing students' varying skill levels.

To meet your students' diverse needs, we asked reviewers to critique features that would enhance the learning process of their students. The result has been the integration of the following items.

The Visual Program

A stimulating, full-color book, *The Writer's World* recognizes that we live in a visually oriented world, and it encourages students to become better communicators by responding to images. In Parts I, II, and III, **chapter opening images use similes, analogies, and metaphors** to help students to think about each chapter's key concept in a new way. For example, in the Chapter 11 opener, a photograph of a shoe store sets the stage for classification. Shoes are grouped according to style, which helps students understand the premise of classification.

Providing variety and acting as visual cues and writing prompts, Part IV's **chapter-opening photos** reflect the themes in the grammar handbook. Colored tabs at the sides of the pages are designed to guide students through the six separate sections of Part IV. Part V's readings have been made visually engaging for students by including **photo and film writing prompts**.

The Writer's World completes its visual program by offering students and instructors full access to *MyWritingLab*—one of the most highly regarded writing applications available today. The program includes diagnostic pretests; hundreds of recall, apply, and write practices; ESL units; and posttests for evaluation. Also included are audio and animated "mini-lectures" that act as refreshers and additional support for visual and auditory learners.

Seamless Coverage for Nonnative Speakers

Instructors in our focus groups noted the growing number of nonnative/ESL speakers enrolling in the developmental writing courses. To meet the challenge of this rapidly changing dynamic, we have carefully implemented and integrated content throughout to assist both native and nonnative speakers.

The Writer's World does not have separate ESL boxes, ESL chapters, or tacked-on ESL appendices. Instead, information that traditionally poses a challenge to nonnative speakers is woven seamlessly throughout the book. In our extensive experience teaching writing to both native and nonnative speakers of English, we have learned that both groups learn best when they are not distracted by ESL labels. With the seamless approach, nonnative speakers do not feel self-conscious and segregated, and native speakers do not tune out detailed explanations that may also benefit them. Many of these traditional problem areas receive more coverage than you would find in other developmental writing textbooks, arming the instructor with the material to effectively meet the needs of nonnative speakers. Moreover, the Annotated Instructor's Edition provides 88 ESL Teaching Tips designed specifically to help instructors better meet the needs of their nonnative speaking students.

Issue-Focused Thematic Grammar

In our survey of the marketplace, many of you indicated that one of your primary challenges is finding materials that are engaging to students in a contemporary context. This is especially true in grammar instruction. **Students come to the course with varying skill levels**, and many students are simply not interested in grammar. To address this challenge, we have introduced **issue-focused thematic grammar** into *The Writer's World*.

Each section in Part IV revolves around a common theme. These themes include **Conflict, Urban Development, International Trade, Forces of Nature, Plants and Insects,** and **Human Development**. Each chapter within a section addresses issues related to the theme. The thematic approach enables students to broaden their awareness of important subjects, allowing them to infuse their writing with reflection and insight. Also, we believe (and our students concur) that the themes make grammar more engaging. And the more engaging grammar is, the more likely students will retain key concepts.

To emphasize the importance of teaching grammar in the context of the writing process, we open each grammar chapter with a **Grammar Snapshot** activity. To further highlight that grammar is not isolated from the writing process, in each of the six grammar sections we offer writing prompts and links to the readings in Part V that relate to the chapter theme.

Key Learning Aids in *The Writer's World*

Overwhelmingly, reviewers asked that both a larger number and a greater diversity of exercises and activities be incorporated into the book. In response to this feedback, we have developed and tested the following learning aids in *The Writer's World*. These tools form the pedagogical backbone of the book, and we are confident they will help your students become better writers.

Hints In each chapter, **Hint** boxes highlight important writing and grammar points. Hints are useful for all students, but many will be particularly helpful for nonnative speakers. For example, in Chapter 8: Description, there is a hint about how to create a dominant impression, and in Chapter 21: Sentence Combining, there is a hint about how to recognize Compound Sentences.

The Writer's Desk Parts I, II, and III include **The Writer's Desk** exercises to help students practice all stages and steps of the writing process. Students begin with prewriting and then progress to developing, organizing (using paragraph and essay plans), drafting, and, finally, revising and editing to create a final draft.

Essay Patterns "at Work" To help students appreciate the relevance of their writing tasks, Chapters 6–14 begin with an authentic writing sample. Titled **Illustration at Work, Narration at Work,** and so on, this feature offers a glimpse of the writing patterns people use in different types of workplace writing.

Vocabulary Boost In Chapters 6–14, the vocabulary boost is a collaborative activity that helps students to broaden their vocabulary. For example, in Chapter 10, the Vocabulary Boost helps students understand *connotation*.

Checklist Major points in each chapter are reviewed in the checklist box, which appears at the end of the chapter.

Writers' Exchanges Students who learn best by collaborating and sharing ideas will appreciate the discussion and group work activities that open each chapter in **Part II: Essay Patterns**. Each Writers' Exchange activity introduces the students to the writing pattern in a fun and nonintimidating way.

The Writer's Room These writing activities correspond to general, academic, and workplace topics. Some prompts are brief to allow students to form ideas freely while others are expanded to give students more direction. Students who respond well to visual cues will appreciate the photo writing exercises in **The Writer's Room**. In Part II: Essay Patterns, students can respond to thought-provoking quotations. To help students see that grammar is not isolated from the writing process, there are also **The Writer's Room** activities in each chapter in Part IV: The Editing Handbook. In Part V, **The Writer's Room** is enhanced with photo and film prompts.

Acknowledgments

Many people have helped us produce *The Writer's World*. First and foremost, we thank our students for inspiring us and providing us with invaluable feedback. Their words and insights pervade this book.

We also benefited greatly from the insightful comments and suggestions from over 200 instructors across the nation, many of whom are listed in the opening pages of the Annotated Instructor's Edition. Our colleagues' feedback was invaluable and helped shape *The Writer's World* series' content, focus, and organization.

We are indebted to the team of dedicated professionals at Pearson-Prentice Hall who have helped make this project a reality. They have boosted our spirits and have believed in us every step of the way. Special thanks to Leslie Taggart for her magnificent job in polishing this book and to Craig Campanella for trusting our instincts and enthusiastically propelling us forward. Lindsey Prudhomme worked tirelessly to ensure we were always meeting the needs of instructors. We owe a deep debt of gratitude to Yolanda de Rooy, whose encouraging words helped ignite this project. Karen Berry's attention to detail in the production process kept us motivated and on task and made *The Writer's World* a much better resource for both instructors and students. We also thank Laura Gardner for her brilliant design, which helped keep the visual learner in all of us engaged.

Finally, we dedicate this book to our husbands and children who supported us and who patiently put up with our long hours on the computer. Manu, Octavio, and Natalia continually encouraged us. We especially appreciate the help and sacrifices of Diego, Becky, Kiran, and Meghana.

A Note to Students

Your knowledge, ideas, and opinions are important. The ability to communicate those ideas clearly is invaluable in your personal, academic, and professional life. When your writing is error-free, readers will focus on your message, and you will be able to persuade, inform, entertain, or inspire them. *The Writer's World* includes strategies that will help you improve your written communication. Quite simply, when you become a better writer, you become a better communicator. It is our greatest wish for *The Writer's World* to make you excited about writing, communicating, and learning.

Enjoy!

Lynne Gaetz & Suneeti Phadke
thewritersworld@prenhall.com

Call for Student Writing!

Do you want to be published in *The Writer's World*? Send your paragraphs and essays to us along with your complete contact information. If your work is selected to appear in the next edition of *The Writer's World*, you will receive an honorarium, credit for your work, and a copy of the book!

Lynne Gaetz & Suneeti Phadke
thewritersworld@prenhall.com

Lynne Gaetz and family in Mexico.

Suneeti Phadke and family in Turkey.

PART I

The Writing Process

The writing process is a series of steps that most writers follow to advance from thinking about a topic to preparing the final draft. Generally, you should follow the process step by step. However, sometimes you may find that your steps overlap. For example, you might do some editing before you revise, or you might think about your main idea while you are prewriting. The important thing is to make sure that you have done all the steps of the process before preparing your final draft.

Before you begin the next chapters, review the steps in the writing process.

Exploring

Chapter 1

Step 1 Think about your topic.

Step 2 Think about your audience.

Step 3 Think about your purpose.

Step 4 Try exploring strategies.

Developing

Chapters 2, 3, 4

Step 1 Express your main idea.

Step 2 Develop your supporting ideas.

Step 3 Make a plan or an outline.

Step 4 Write your first draft.

Revising and Editing

Chapter 5

Step 1 Revise for unity.

Step 2 Revise for adequate support.

Step 3 Revise for coherence.

Step 4 Revise for style.

Step 5 Edit for technical errors.

Exploring

CHAPTER 1

CONTENTS

Before planting seeds or shrubs, a gardener might look for ideas in magazines, on the Internet, or in nurseries. Similarly, a writer uses various prewriting strategies to explore topics for writing.

Visualizing the Paragraph and the Essay

A **paragraph** is a series of sentences that are about one central idea. Paragraphs can stand alone, or they can be part of a longer work such as an essay, a letter, or a report. A paragraph contains a **topic sentence** that expresses the main idea and **body sentences** that develop that idea. Most paragraphs end with a **concluding sentence** that brings the paragraph to a satisfactory close.

Sample Paragraph

The **topic sentence** introduces the subject of the paragraph and shows the writer's attitude toward the subject. ➢

The **body of the paragraph** contains details that support the topic sentence. ➢

The paragraph ends with a **concluding sentence.** ➢

People learn negotiation skills through sports. Children playing informally at recess must decide what game to play and what rules to follow. They must negotiate with the other children about game boundaries. Every day, my daughter comes home from school telling me that she and her friends have invented a new game. The children make up the rules of the new game by bargaining with each other. In team sports, athletes must make choices about who will play a certain position or which player will play for how much time. Such decisions require negotiation skills, which help people in other areas of their lives.

An **essay** contains several paragraphs that revolve around one central idea. The introductory paragraph includes a **thesis statement** expressing the main idea of the essay. **Body paragraphs** support the thesis statement. Finally, the essay closes with a **concluding paragraph** that wraps up the main ideas the writer has presented throughout the paper.

Sample Essay

The **title** gives a hint about the essay's topic. ➢

The **introductory paragraph** introduces the essay's topic and contains its thesis statement. ➢

The **thesis statement** contains the essay's topic and its controlling idea. ➢

Each **body paragraph** begins with a topic sentence that supports the thesis statement.

Sports: A Vital Necessity

Humans have been playing sports since the beginning of civilization. Cave art in France and Africa depicts people playing archery, wrestling, and horse racing. Indigenous North Americans engaged in team sports such as lacrosse or running. The ancient Greeks, Romans, Chinese, and Egyptians also enjoyed many physical activities. Similarly, most people enjoy sports today. Young girls and boys play in soccer leagues, or they may play a baseball game during recess. Adults, too, play or watch sports. Athletic activities are very necessary to people's well-being. In fact, sports help people to develop good character because they learn many skills.

First, when people play games, they learn how to make friends. In the United States, according to the National Center for Health Statistics, 24 percent of adults engage in some form of physical activity three or more times a week and approximately 67 percent of high school students participate in some type of physical activity. Whether it is exercising informally or playing a team sport, people interact with strangers. Going to the gym, participating in a hiking club, and playing in a team sport bring different people into close personal contact with each other. These strangers all have something in common. They like to engage in the same activity, so most people end up developing friendships.

People learn negotiation skills through sports. Children playing informally at recess must decide what game to play and what rules to follow. They must negotiate with the other children about game boundaries. Every day, my daughter comes home from school telling me that she and her friends have invented a new game. The children make up the rules of the new game by bargaining with each other. In team sports, athletes must make choices about who will play a certain position or which player will play for how much time. Such decisions require negotiation skills, which help people in other areas of their lives.

Each **body paragraph** contains details that support the topic sentence.

Players learn how to deal with disappointments and pressure. Disappointment about the level of play or an important loss is common for most people involved in sports. For example, many Olympic athletes are very discouraged when they lose, but most continue training to become even better. Players on high school and college teams also learn to win and lose. For example, my neighbor's son plays on the volleyball team. His team had a winning streak, but the team lost in the semi-finals. All the players on the team were extremely disappointed but vowed to play better in the next season. Sports teach people how to win and lose gracefully. Such a lesson is invaluable in life.

People build character through sports. In fact, they learn many valuable life lessons, including social skills. They learn practical skills such as how to negotiate. As Jeff Kemp, in his article "A Lesson in Humility," says, "In fact, sports teach important moral lessons that athletes can apply on and off the playing field." So don't just sit around at home; go participate in a sport.

The **concluding paragraph** brings the essay to a satisfactory close.

Essay-length prose is the backbone of written communication in and out of college. Throughout your life, you will use principles of essay writing in various formats, including research papers, emails, reports, formal letters, newsletters, and Web pages. Essays help you explore ideas and share those thoughts with others. By reading through this text and completing the many helpful writing practices in it, you will significantly improve your chances of getting more out of your courses and jobs. Enjoy the journey!

Key Steps in Exploring

Perhaps you have been given a writing assignment and then stared at the blank page, thinking, "I don't know what to write." Well, it is not necessary to write a good essay immediately. There are certain things that you can do to help you focus on your topic.

> *"How much has to be explored and discarded before reaching the naked flesh of feeling."*
> CLAUDE DEBUSSY, *French composer*

Understand Your Assignment

As soon as you are given an assignment, make sure that you understand your task. Answer the following questions about the assignment.

- How many words or pages does the assignment require?
- What is the due date for the assignment?
- Are there any special qualities my writing should include? For example, should my writing be double-spaced? Should I include a list of works cited?

After you have considered your assignment, consider the following four key steps in the exploring stage of the writing process.

EXPLORING

STEP 1 ➤ **Think about your topic.** Determine what you will write about.

STEP 2 ➤ **Think about your audience.** Consider your intended readers and what interests them.

STEP 3 ➤ **Think about your purpose.** Ask yourself why you want to write.

STEP 4 ➤ **Try exploring strategies.** Experiment with different ways to generate ideas.

Teaching Tip: If you prefer, you can substitute the word "subject" for "topic."

Teaching Tip: The Essay Pattern chapters contain Vocabulary Boost activities to help students improve their vocabulary.

Teaching Tip: To help your students understand the concept of audience, ask them what tone they would adopt for the following cases: a children's television show, a cookbook, an electric razor advertisement for men, or a political speech.

Topic

Sometimes your topic has been assigned and is already very specific. At other times, it may be very general. For example, if your assigned topic is "food," narrow it down so that you can focus on something specific about food. You might write about the dangers of diets or how to cook a certain type of cuisine. You might describe the symbolism of food in a literary work or try to explain the chemical makeup of a specific food. When you are given a general topic, find an angle that interests you and make it more specific.

To find a focus for your topic, ask yourself the following questions.

- What about the topic interests me? Will it interest other readers?
- Do I have special knowledge about the topic?
- Does anything about the topic arouse my emotions?

Audience

Your **audience** is your intended reader. In your personal, academic, and professional life, you will often write for a specific audience; therefore, you can keep your readers interested by adapting your tone and vocabulary to suit them.

Tone is your general attitude or feeling toward a topic. You might write in a tone that is humorous, sarcastic, serious, friendly, or casual. For example, imagine you are preparing an invitation to an event. To determine the design, phrasing, and format, you need to know some important information about your recipients. What are their ages and lifestyles? Are they mostly males or females?

Would they prefer printed invitations or e-mail invitations? Questions like these can help you connect with your audience.

Knowing your readers is especially important when preparing academic or workplace documents. When you consider your audience, ask yourself the following questions:

- Who will read my assignment—an instructor, other students, or people outside the college?
- Do the readers have a lot of knowledge about my topic?
- How will I need to adjust my vocabulary, writing style, or tone to appeal to my readers?

In academic writing, your audience is generally your instructor or other students, unless your instructor specifically asks you to write for another audience such as the general public, your employer, or a family member.

Hint **Instructor as the Audience**

Your instructor represents a general audience. Such an audience of educated readers will expect you to reveal what you have learned or what you have understood about the topic. Your ideas should be presented in a clear and organized manner. Do not leave out information because you assume that your instructor is an expert in the field. Also, you should write in standard English. In other words, try to use correct grammar, sentence structure, and vocabulary.

PRACTICE 1 As you read the following messages, consider the differences in both the tone and the vocabulary the writer uses. Then answer the questions that follow.

Teaching Tip: Group Work
Students can do Practice 1 in pairs or groups, and they can compare answers.

A

yo, :)

im in ur english class on 2sday. how ru? can u help with my essay? >:o b4 i write, i need 2 know what the topic is? what is # of words? plz check my plan cuz i don't no if i'm on the rite track... :'(is it ok? btw, will c u in class.

gtg Andrea :)

B

Dear Professor Gonzales,

I am in your Tuesday morning English class. I have started working on my essay and have prepared an essay plan, but I am not sure if my thesis statement is appropriate and focused enough. Could you please look at my plan and let me know if I am on the right track? Also, could you please remind me of the length of the assignment?

Thank you,

Reginald Harper

Teaching Tip:
Give students a scenario that they can write about. For example, they have to cancel an important appointment or outing. Ask groups of students to write a letter of apology for different audiences. One team can write to a child, another can write to a boss, a third can write to a friend or spouse, and so on.

1. Why is the language inappropriate in the first instant message?

   The instructor might not understand the abbreviations and might not appreciate the symbols. It is too informal.

2. What judgments might the instructor make about the two students based on the messages?

   Andrea doesn't show respect. She treats the instructor like a peer. Reginald writes his message using proper English, which shows that he is serious and knows about the importance of using appropriate language with a particular audience.

Purpose

Teaching Tip:
Bring in different types of writing samples such as a business letter, a postcard, a letter to the editor, and so on. In small groups, students can discuss the audience and purpose of each selection.

Your **purpose** is your reason for writing. Keeping your purpose in mind will help you focus your writing.

When you consider your purpose, ask yourself the following questions.

- Is my goal to **entertain**? Do I want to tell a story?
- Is my goal to **persuade**? Do I want to convince readers that my point of view is the correct one?
- Is my goal to **inform**? Do I want to explain something or give information about a topic?

It is possible to write for a combination of reasons. In fact, most essays have more than one purpose. For example, an essay describing a personal experience with fraud could also inform readers about protecting themselves from identity theft, or an essay describing how the heart pumps blood could simultaneously persuade readers to reconsider smoking.

Hint **General and Specific Purpose**

Your **general purpose** is to entertain, to inform, or to persuade. Your **specific purpose** is your more precise reason for writing. For example, imagine that you have to write about an election. You can have the following general and specific purposes.

General purpose: to inform
Specific purpose: to compare platforms of two different candidates

Teaching Tip:
Group Work
Students can do Practice 2 in pairs or groups. Discuss how the language style is adapted for the different audiences.

PRACTICE 2 The following selections are all about food; however, each excerpt has a different purpose, has been written for a different audience, and has been taken from a different source. Read each selection carefully. Then underline any language clues (words or phrases) that help you identify its source, audience, and purpose. Finally, answer the questions that follow each selection.

EXAMPLE:

I just made my very first dessert. It looks awesome. I hope it tastes alright. I almost freaked out when I realized I forgot to turn the oven on. My instructor is super, and he's got a great sense of humor with me and the other students. Next, I am going to try to make a more complicated dessert.

← slang
← slang
← slang, informal tone

What is the most likely source of this paragraph?

a. Web site article (b. personal letter) c. textbook d. memoir

What is its primary purpose? *to inform*

Who is the audience? *friend or family member*

Teaching Tip:
The paragraphs in Practice 2 came from the next sources:
1) *Meatless Days* by Sara Suleri. University of Chicago Press, 1989, p. 39;
2) http://www.eufic.org/en/quickfacts/adult_nutrition.htm;
3) *Sociology* (11th editon) by John J. Macionis. Upper Saddle River, NJ: Prentice Hall, 2007, p. 95.

1. I went out with my old friends Nuzhat Ahmad and Ayla, as the three of us often did, in a comradeship of girlhood. We went driving to Bagh-e-Jinnah, formerly known as Lawrence Gardens, located opposite the Governor's House along the Mall in Lahore. We were trying to locate the best *gol guppa* vendor in town and stopped by to test the new stand in Lawrence Gardens. Gol guppas are a strange food: I have never located an equivalent to them or their culinary situation. They are an outdoor food, a passing whim, and no one would dream of recreating their frivolity inside his or her own kitchen. A gol guppa is a small hollow oval of the lightest pastry that is dipped into a fiery liquid sauce made of tamarind and cayenne and lemon and cold water. It is evidently a food invented as a joke, in a moment of good humor.

What is the most likely source of this paragraph?

a. Web site article b. personal letter c. textbook (d. memoir)

What is its primary purpose? *to entertain*

Who is the audience? *general readers of fiction*

2. Eat regularly. Eating is one of life's great pleasures, and it is important to take time to stop, relax, and enjoy mealtimes and snacks. Scheduling eating times also ensures that meals are not missed, resulting in missed nutrients that are often not

compensated for by subsequent meals. This is especially important for school-age children, adolescents, and elderly people.

What is the most likely source of this paragraph?

(a. Web site article) b. personal letter c. textbook d. memoir

What is its primary purpose? *to persuade*

Who is the audience? *a general audience who is interested in health and nutrition*

3. About 5,000 years ago, another revolution in technology was taking place in the Middle East, one that would end up changing the entire world. This was the discovery of agriculture, large-scale cultivation using plows harnessed to animals or more powerful energy sources. So important was the invention of the animal-drawn plow, along with other breakthroughs of the period—including irrigation, the wheel, writing, numbers, and the use of various metals—that this moment in history is often called "the dawn of civilization."

What is the most likely source of this paragraph?

a. Web site article b. personal letter (c. textbook) d. memoir

What is its purpose? *to inform*

Who is the audience? *students who are learning about human civilization*

Exploring Strategies

After you determine your topic, audience, and purpose, try some **exploring strategies**—also known as **prewriting strategies**—to help get your ideas flowing. Four common strategies are *freewriting*, *brainstorming*, *questioning*, and *clustering*. It is not necessary to do all of the strategies explained in this chapter. Find the strategy that works best for you.

You can do both general and focused prewriting. If you have writer's block, and do not know what to write about, use **general prewriting** to come up with possible writing topics. Then, after you have chosen a topic, use **focused prewriting** to find an angle of the topic that is interesting and that could be developed in your essay.

Hint **When to Use Exploring Strategies**

You can use the exploring strategies at any stage of the writing process:

- To find a topic
- To narrow a broad topic
- To generate ideas about your topic
- To generate supporting details

Narrow Your Topic

An essay has one main idea. If your topic is too broad, you might find it difficult to write a focused essay about it. For example, imagine that you are given the topic "mistakes." If the topic is not narrowed, it will lead to a meandering and unfocused essay. To narrow the topic, think about types of errors, examples of errors, or people who make errors. A more focused topic could be "mistakes newlyweds make" or "mistakes first-year college students make." Find one angle of the topic that you know a lot about and that you personally find interesting. If you have a lot to say, and you think the topic is compelling, chances are that your reader will also like your topic.

Review the following examples of general and narrowed topics.

Topic	Narrowed Topic
jobs	preparing for a job interview
music	protest songs from the past and present

To help narrow and develop you topic, you can use the following exploring strategies.

Freewriting

Freewriting gives writers the freedom to write without stopping for a set period of time. The goal of this exercise is to record the first thoughts that come to mind. If you run out of ideas, don't stop writing. Simply fill in the pause with phrases like "blah blah blah" or "What else can I write?" As you write, do not be concerned with word choice, grammar, or spelling. If you use a computer, let your ideas flow and do not worry about typing mistakes. You could try typing without looking at the screen.

Teaching Tip:
Reassure students that their freewriting (and other exploring strategies) can be messy and will not necessarily be marked for points.

Alicia's Freewriting

College student Alicia Parera thought about mistakes college students make. During her freewriting, she wrote down everything that came to mind.

> Mistakes students make? Not doing the homework. Not asking for help when they need it? I sometimes feel shy to speak up when I don't understand something. What else? Some college students leave college early. Why do they leave? Tim. He only stayed for one semester. I don't think he was ready for college life. He treated college like high school and always came late. Goofed off. Cut class. What else? What about Amanda who had that family crisis? She had to leave when her mother was sick. Of course, finances. It's tough. Sometimes I go crazy trying to keep up with my job, friends, schoolwork . . . it's really hard.

Brainstorming

Brainstorming is like freewriting, except that you create a list of ideas, and you can take the time to stop and think when you create your list. As you think about the topic, write down words or phrases that come to mind. Do not worry about grammar or spelling; the point is to generate ideas.

Alicia's Brainstorming

Topic: Mistakes that college students make

- party too much
- not doing homework
- feeling too shy to speak with instructors when they have problems
- getting too stressed
- choosing the wrong career path
- don't know what they want to do
- feeling intimidated in class

Questioning

Another way to generate ideas about a topic is to ask yourself a series of questions and write responses to them. The questions can help you define and narrow your topic. One common way to do this is to ask yourself *who, what, when, where, why*, and *how* questions.

Alicia's Questioning

Who makes the most mistakes? — first-year students because they aren't always prepared for college life

Why do some students miss classes? — feel like there are no consequences, don't feel interested in their program

When do most students drop out? — administrators say that November is the most common month that students drop out

How should colleges encourage students who are at risk of dropping out?
— give more financial aid
— offer career counseling

Where can students get help? — guidance counselors, instructors, friends, family, professionals doing student's dream job

Why is it an important topic? — new students can learn about pitfalls to avoid, administrators can develop strategies for helping students

Clustering

Clustering is like drawing a word map; ideas are arranged in a visual image. To begin, write your topic in the middle of the page and draw a box or a circle around it. That idea will lead to another, so write the second idea and draw a line connecting it to your topic. Keep writing, circling, and connecting ideas until you have groups or "clusters" of them on your page.

Alicia's Clustering

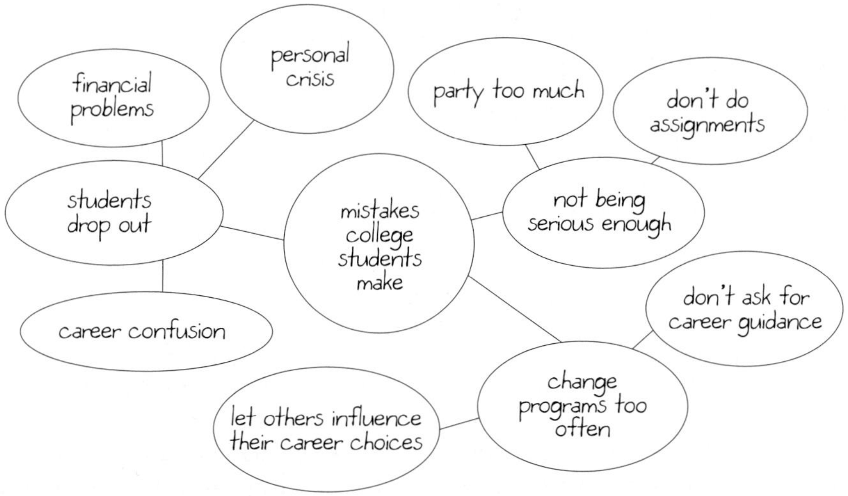

Writer's Desk Exploring

Explore the next three topics. Use a different exploring strategy for each topic. You can choose to do freewriting, brainstorming, questioning, or clustering.

stereotypes mistakes volunteer work

Teaching Tip: For this pen-pal activity, ask students to prewrite about a topic such as career goals, college life, or current events. Then collect their writing and shuffle them. Ask students to take a random notebook or sheet and to write questions or comments about what has been written. They do not have to edit the student's writing. They simply respond to what they find interesting. This activity provides students with informal writing practice, and it gives them a chance to reflect on the ideas that they are reading about. Or if you are teaching the same course to two groups, you might want to exchange one class set with another.

Journal and Portfolio Writing

Keeping a Journal

You may write for work or school, but you can also practice writing for pleasure. One way to practice your writing is to keep a journal. A **journal** can be a book, computer file, or even a blog where you record your thoughts, opinions, ideas, and impressions. Journal writing gives you a chance to practice your writing without worrying about the audience and what they might think about it. It also gives you a source of material when you want to write about a topic of your choice.

In your journal, you can write about any topic that appeals to you. Here are some possible topics for journal writing.

- Anything related to your personal life, such as your feelings about your career goals, personal problems and solutions, opinions about your college courses, reflections about past and future decisions, or feelings about your job
- Your reactions to controversies in your family, neighborhood, college, city, country, or world
- Your reflections on the opinions and philosophies of others, including your friends or people whom you read about in your courses

Keeping a Portfolio

A **writing portfolio** is a place (a binder or an electronic file folder) where you keep samples of all of your writing. The purpose of keeping a portfolio is to have a record of your writing progress. In your portfolio, keep all drafts of your writing assignments. When you work on new assignments, review your previous work in your portfolio. Identify your main problems and try not to repeat the same errors.

The Writer's Room Topics to Explore

Writing Activity 1

Choose one of the following topics, or choose your own topic. Then generate ideas about the topic. You may want to try the suggested exploring strategy.

General Topics

1. Try freewriting about people who have helped you succeed.
2. Brainstorm a list of thoughts about different types of fear.
3. Create a cluster diagram about a useful invention.
4. Ask and answer questions about voting.

College and Work-Related Topics

5. Try freewriting about an unforgettable day at work or college. Include any emotions or details that come to mind.
6. Brainstorm a list of ideas about career goals.
7. Ask and answer questions about bosses.
8. Create a cluster diagram about the pressures students face.

Teaching Tip: Appendix 4 offers grammar, spelling, and vocabulary logs that students can keep in their portfolios.

Teaching Tip: Students can use their favorite exploring strategy in the Writer's Room activities. They do not have to use the suggested strategy.

Writing Activity 2

Use questioning to generate ideas about the following image. Ask and answer *who*, *what*, *when*, *where*, *why*, and *how* questions.

EXPLORING

When you explore a topic, ask yourself these questions.

- What is my **topic**? Consider what you will write about.
- Who is my **audience**? Think about your intended reader.
- What is my **purpose**? Determine your reason for writing.
- Which exploring strategy will I use? You could try one of the next strategies, or a combination of strategies.
  - **Freewriting** is writing without stopping for a limited period of time.
  - **Brainstorming** is making a list.
  - **Clustering** is drawing a word map.
  - **Questioning** is asking and answering a series of questions.

How Do I Get a Better Grade?

PEARSON mywritinglab

Visit www.mywritinglab.com for audio-visual lectures and additional practice sets for prewriting strategies. ***Get a better grade with MyWritingLab!***

Developing the Main Idea

CHAPTER 2

CONTENTS

Faced with so many plant and flower varieties, a gardener narrows down which ones are most appropriate for his or her garden. Similarly, a writer considers many ideas before choosing a main idea for an essay.

Key Steps in Developing the Main Idea

In Chapter 1, you learned how to consider your reading audience and your purposes for writing. You also practiced using exploring strategies to formulate ideas. In this chapter, you will focus on developing a main idea that can be expanded into a complete essay. There are two key steps in this process.

> *"The skill of writing is to create a context in which other people can think."*
>
> EDWIN SCHLOSSBERG, *cultural historian*

DEVELOPING THE MAIN IDEA

STEP 1 → **Write a thesis statement.** Write a statement that expresses the main idea of the piece of writing.

STEP 2 → **Develop the supporting ideas.** Find facts, examples, or anecdotes that best support your main idea.

Writing a Thesis Statement

The **thesis** is your main idea that you want to express. A clear thesis statement presents the topic of the essay, and it includes a **controlling idea** that expresses the writer's opinion, attitude, or feeling about the topic. The controlling idea can appear at the beginning or end of the thesis statement.

topic — controlling idea

Art courses should be compulsory in all high schools.

controlling idea — topic

School districts should stop funding **art courses.**

Teaching Tip: Discuss the types of essays the thesis statements could develop. If your students are already familiar with writing patterns (rhetorical modes), you might ask them what pattern the thesis statements suggest. Possible answers are (1) process, (2) narration, (3) argument, (4) argument, (5) cause and effect, (6) definition, (7) description, and (8) classification.

PRACTICE 1 Circle the topic and underline the controlling idea in each thesis statement.

EXAMPLE: (Insomnia) is caused by several factors.

1. Three strategies can help you become (a better public speaker.)
2. (Moving to a new country) was a traumatic experience for me.
3. There should not be (racial profiling at borders.)
4. (School uniforms) should be compulsory in public schools.
5. There are several reasons for (Australia's compulsory voting system.)
6. (Phishing) is a dangerous Internet scam.
7. (My office) is an obstacle course.
8. There are three types of (annoying office workers.)

Writing an Effective Thesis Statement

When you develop your thesis statement, ask yourself the following questions to help you avoid thesis statement errors.

1. **Is my thesis a complete statement?**
Ensure that your thesis does not express an incomplete idea or more than one idea. A thesis statement should reveal one complete thought.

Incomplete:	Allergies: so annoying. (This is not a complete statement.)
More than one idea:	There are many types of allergens, and allergies affect people in different ways. (This statement contains two distinct ideas. Each idea could become an essay.)
Thesis statement:	Doctors suggest several steps people can take to relieve symptoms related to pet allergies.

2. **Does my thesis statement have a controlling idea?**
Rather than announcing the topic, your thesis statement should make a point about the topic. It should have a controlling idea that expresses your attitude or feeling about the topic. Avoid phrases such as *My topic is* or *I will write about*.

Announces:	I will write about computers. (This sentence says nothing relevant about the topic. The reader does not know what the point of the essay is.)
Thesis statement:	When Microsoft develops a new operating system, there are political, financial, and environmental consequences.

3. **Can I support my thesis statement in an essay?**
Your thesis statement should express an idea that you can support in an essay. If it is too narrow, you will find yourself with nothing to say. If it is too broad, you will have an endless composition.

Too broad:	There are many childless couples in our world. (This topic needs a more specific and narrow focus.)
Too narrow:	The average age of first-time mothers is approximately twenty-six years old. (It would be difficult to write an entire essay about this fact.)
Thesis statement:	Many couples are choosing to remain childless for several reasons.

Teaching Tip:
Demonstrate that the thesis statement about couples who remain childless can be supported with several points. Ask students to brainstorm reasons that people choose not to have children.

4. **Does my thesis statement make a valid and interesting point?**
Your thesis statement should make a valid point. It should not be a vaguely worded statement or an obvious and uninteresting comment.

Vague: Censorship is a big problem.
(For whom is it a big problem?)

Obvious: The Internet is important.
(So what? Everyone knows this.)

Invalid: The Internet controls our lives.
(This statement is difficult to believe or prove.)

Thesis statement: The Internet has become a powerful presence in our personal, social, and working lives.

Teaching Tip:
You can give students the next examples and ask them to explain why the sentences are invalid. Examples:

No one can afford to attend college anymore.

Republicans and Democrats will never agree on issues.

Children are becoming too violent.

Teaching Tip:
Pair Work
You could ask students to do Practice 2 with a partner. They can then choose three weak statements and create better thesis statements.

PRACTICE 2 Examine each statement.

- Write **TS** if it is an effective thesis statement.
- Write **I** if it is an incomplete idea.
- Write **M** if it contains more than one complete idea.
- Write **A** if it is an announcement.

EXAMPLE: This essay is about spousal abuse. A

1. The high price of oil. I
2. My college has a great sports stadium, but it needs to give more help to female athletes. M
3. Nursing is extremely demanding. TS
4. In this paper, I will discuss global warming. A
5. My subject is the torture of war prisoners. A
6. There are many excellent commercials on television, but some are too violent. M
7. The loss of a job can actually have positive effects on a person's life. TS
8. The problem of negative election advertisements. I

PRACTICE 3 Examine each statement.

- Write **TS** if it is a complete thesis statement.
- Write **V** if it is too vague.
- Write **O** if it is too obvious.

EXAMPLE: Americans are more nationalistic. V

1. New York has a large population. O

2. We had a major problem. ___V___
3. Some adult children have legitimate reasons for moving back into their parents' homes. ___TS___
4. The roads are very crowded during holiday periods. ___O___
5. There are several ways to do this. ___V___
6. Children in our culture are changing. ___V___

PRACTICE 4 Examine each pair of sentences.

- Write **B** if the sentence is too broad.
- Write **TS** if the sentence is an effective thesis statement.

EXAMPLE: ___B___ Plants can help people.

___TS___ Learning to care for plants gave me unexpected pleasure.

1. ___B___ Music is important around the world.

   ___TS___ Some simple steps can help you successfully promote your music.
2. ___TS___ My neighborhood is being transformed by youth gangs.

   ___B___ Violence is a big problem everywhere.
3. ___B___ My life has been filled with mistakes.

   ___TS___ My jealousy, insecurity, and anger ruined my first relationship.
4. ___TS___ The car accident transformed my life.

   ___B___ Everybody's life has dramatic moments.
5. ___TS___ Good e-mail manners are important in the business world.

   ___B___ Good manners are important.

PRACTICE 5 Examine each pair of sentences.

- Write **N** if the sentence is too narrow.
- Write **TS** if the sentence is an effective thesis statement.

EXAMPLE: ___N___ I grow coriander in my garden.

___TS___ Learning to care for plants gave me unexpected pleasure.

1. ___N___ My poodle's name is Short Stop.

   ___TS___ Owning a pet taught me how to be more responsible.
2. ___N___ Our roads are very icy.

   ___TS___ Driving in the winter requires particular skills.

3. __N__ Carjacking rates have increased by 20 percent in our city.

__TS__ You can avoid being a carjacking victim by taking the next steps.

4. __TS__ I hurt myself in various ways during my three days on the beach.

__N__ There are many sharp pieces of shell on the local beach.

5. __TS__ Identical twins who are raised together have distinct personalities.

__N__ My twin sisters have similar birthmarks on their necks.

Revising Your Thesis Statement

A thesis statement is like the foundation that holds up a house. If the thesis statement is weak, it is difficult to construct a solid and compelling essay. Most writers must revise their thesis statements to make them strong, interesting, and supportable.

When you plan your thesis, ask yourself if you can support it with at least three ideas. If not, you have to modify your thesis statement. To enliven a dead-end statement, ensure that your thesis can answer the *why*, *what*, or *how* questions. Sometimes, just by adding a few words, a dead-end statement becomes a supportable thesis.

Poor thesis: Many students drop out of college.
(How could you develop this into an essay? It is a dead-end statement.)

Better thesis: Students drop out of college **for several reasons**.
(You could support this thesis with at least three ideas. This thesis statement answers the question "Why?")

Teaching Tip:
Ask students to generate three ideas to support the statement "Students drop out of college for several reasons." Possible answers include financial problems, confusion about career goals, life-changing events such as death or childbirth, inability to integrate into college life, and commuting problems.

After students have brainstormed reasons, ask them how they could restate the thesis to list the specific details, as advised in the Hint box. An example could be *Students may drop out of college because they have academic, emotional, or financial problems.*

Hint **Writing a Guided Thesis Statement**

Give enough details to make your thesis statement interesting. Your instructor may want you to guide the reader through your main points. To do this, mention your main and supporting ideas in your thesis statement. In other words, your thesis statement provides a map for the readers to follow.

Weak: My first job taught me many things.

Better: My first job taught me about the importance of responsibility, organization, and teamwork.

PRACTICE 6 The next thesis statements are weak. First, identify the problem with the statement (write *vague*, *incomplete*, and so on) and ask yourself questions to determine how you might be able to revise it. Then revise each statement to make it more forceful and focused.

EXAMPLE: Spousal abuse is a big problem.

Comments: *Obvious. Vague. For whom is it a problem? How is it a problem?*

Revision: *Our state government should provide better support for victims of spousal abuse.*

1. I will explain how the family is falling apart.

   Comments: *Announces. Whose family is falling apart?*

   Revision: Answers will vary.

2. I made a difficult decision.

   Comments: *Vague. What decision? Why was it difficult?*

   Revision: Answers will vary.

3. The media is essential in our lives.

   Comments: *Broad. Which form of the media? Is it really essential?*

   Revision: Answers will vary.

4. I am an environmentalist.

   Comments: *No controlling idea. So what? How is this important?*

   Revision: Answers will vary.

5. Fashions are too impractical.

   Comments: *Broad. Why? Male or female fashions? What age group is this about?*

   Revision: Answers will vary.

Overview: Writing a Thesis Statement

To create a forceful thesis statement, you should follow the next steps.

Step 1

Find your topic. You can use exploring strategies to get ideas.

General topic: Traditions

Brainstorming:
- Commercialization of holidays
- My family traditions
- Important ceremonies
- Why do we celebrate?
- Benefits of traditions
- Initiation ceremonies

Step 2

Narrow your topic. Decide what point you want to make.

Narrowed topic: Initiation ceremonies

Point I want to make: Initiation ceremonies can help people make the transition from childhood to adulthood.

Step 3

Develop a thesis statement that you can support with specific evidence. You may need to revise your statement several times.

Initial thesis statement: Initiation ceremonies serve a valuable function.

Revised thesis statement: Meaningful initiation ceremonies benefit individuals, families, and communities.

Writer's Desk Write Thesis Statements

Write a thesis statement for each of the next topics. If you explored these topics in Chapter 1, you can use those ideas to help you write your thesis statement. If you have not explored these topics yet, then spend a few minutes exploring them. Brainstorm some ideas for each topic to help you define and narrow them. Then develop a thesis statement that makes a point and is not too broad or too narrow.

stereotypes about beauty   mistakes in relationships   value of volunteer work

EXAMPLE Topic: Mistakes students make   Narrowed topic: *reasons students drop out*

Thesis statement: Students may drop out of college because they are unprepared, have financial problems, or experience an emotional crisis.

1. ______________________________

____

2. ______________________________

____

3. ______________________________

____

Developing the Supporting Ideas

The next step in essay writing is to plan your supporting ideas. Support is not simply a restatement of the thesis. The body paragraphs must develop and prove the validity of the thesis statement.

Each body paragraph has a **topic sentence** that expresses the main idea of the paragraph. Like a thesis statement, a topic sentence must have a controlling idea. Details and examples support the topic sentence. In the following illustration, you can see how the ideas flow in an essay. Topic sentences support the thesis statement, and details bolster the topic sentences. Every idea in the essay is unified and helps to strengthen the essay's thesis.

Teaching Tip:
Explain that ideas in an essay must support the thesis just as the legs support a table or pillars support a bridge. Everything in the essay must develop the idea presented in the thesis statement.

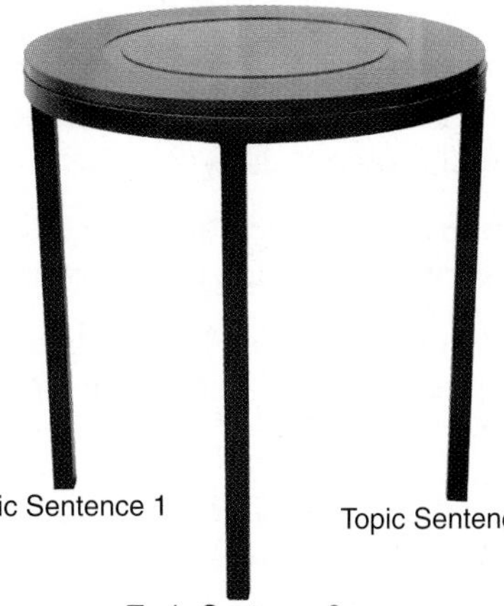

PRACTICE 7 Write a thesis statement for each group of supporting ideas. Ensure that your thesis statement is clear, makes a point, and is not too broad or too narrow. Answers will vary.

Teaching Tip:
Draw students' attention to the supporting ideas in Practice 7. Point out that supporting ideas develop and prove the thesis. They do not simply restate it.

EXAMPLE: Thesis: *When you buy a car, make an informed decision.*

a. Ask family members what type of car they would prefer.

b. Research on the Internet or in car guides to find information about specific models that interest you.

c. Keeping your budget in mind, compare new and used cars.

1. Thesis: *To make an outstanding sales presentation, you should know your sales pitch, use appropriate body language, and involve the customer.*

   a. First, internalize and believe in your sales pitch.

   b. Speak softly, and do not scare the customer with a commanding voice or aggressive mannerisms.

   c. Finally, involve the customer in your sales presentation.

2. Thesis: To dramatically improve school success rates, educators should seriously consider dividing students according to gender.
   a. When boys are in all-male classrooms, teachers can modify their activities to keep the boys' attention.
   b. All-female classrooms permit the female students to focus on the material and show their intelligence.
   c. Unlike co-education classrooms, same-gender classrooms are easier for teachers to control.

3. Thesis: The voting age should be raised to 25 years.
   a. Most people under twenty-five years of age simply mimic how their parents or friends vote.
   b. To make an informed choice during an election, people need to have life experiences, which include paying rent and bills.
   c. Twenty-five-year-olds are also less likely to be manipulated by a politician because they have a stronger sense of what they want.

Teaching Tip:
Group Work
Students can work in teams. Ask teams to write their thesis statement and topic sentences on the board. You can ask them to decide which statements are most appropriate.

PRACTICE 8 Read the full essay in this practice and then do the following. Answers will vary.

1. Determine the topic of each body paragraph. Then write a topic sentence for each body paragraph. Your topic sentence should have a controlling idea and express the main point of the paragraph.
2. Ask yourself what this essay is about. Then compose a thesis statement that sums up the main point of the essay. You might look in the concluding paragraph to get some ideas.

(Introduction) When I was a child, we had a daily routine. My parents both worked, but they got home at about 5 p.m. They spent about half an hour unwinding over a cup of coffee. Then they worked together to cook the meal, and by 6:30 they called us children to dinner. We ate and talked together. The same thing cannot be said about many families today.

Thesis Statement: Several factors have contributed to the disappearance of the family dinner hour.

(Body 1) Topic Sentence: Because of busy and conflicting schedules, family members can't find the time to sit down together.

Overtime was not so common in the past, but today many employers expect their workers to spend an extra hour or two in the workplace, so employees don't get home until 7 or 8 p.m. Also, children's lives are filled with more activities than they were in past decades. For example, my daughter takes dance class at 7 p.m., and my son gets together with friends for band practice every evening. They dash through the door at different times, throw a frozen pizza in the microwave, and eat alone.

(Body 2) Topic Sentence: *The television is replacing dinner conversations among family members.*

The little box certainly is entertaining, but people won't talk about their daily experiences when the television is on. According to the Census Bureau, a growing number of families have placed televisions in the kitchen. "It keeps the sofas and carpets much cleaner if everybody just watches TV in the kitchen," says Sylvie Labelle, a mother of four. Thirteen-year-old Jeremy Labelle mentions, outside his mother's hearing, that he doesn't really talk to anybody in the family. Daily communication, which is an important staple for healthy family life, is disappearing and being replaced by a television set.

(Body 3) Topic Sentence: *Packaged and frozen foods make it easy for family members to prepare their own meals.*

Even a seven-year-old child can heat up his own dinner. Most parents don't want to cook from scratch after a long workday. Our grocery stores and specialty markets understand this need and provide families with a wide variety of frozen meals. Brigitte Lofgren says that the microwave oven is the most useful appliance in her house: "We all heat up our own meals. Nobody has to cook." When family members heat up their own meals, one after another, it is less likely that they will bother to eat together.

(Conclusion) Most families recognize that they are losing communication time. They watch in frustration as the family dinner disappears. They assure themselves that because of hectic lifestyles, they have no choice but to stagger eating times. Televisions on the kitchen counter provide something to focus on during meals. And the quality of prepackaged and frozen meals is improving, so who really needs to cook? Yet it is tragic that the family meal, a simple and effective way to keep family members linked together, is no longer a priority in many people's lives.

Generating Supporting Ideas

When you develop supporting ideas, ensure that they all focus on the central point that you are making in the thesis statement. To generate ideas for body paragraphs, you could use the exploring strategies (brainstorming, freewriting, clustering, or questioning) that you learned in Chapter 1.

Review the process that student Alicia Parera went through. First, she created a list to support her thesis statement. Then she reread her supporting ideas and removed ideas that she did not want to develop in her essay. She also grouped together related ideas.

Teaching Tip: Ask students to discuss why Alicia crossed out the last idea Point out that college can be useful for students who want to start a business. Also, it is not a common reason for students to drop out.

Initial Ideas

Draft thesis statement: Students drop out of college for many reasons.

Supporting ideas:

- can't adapt to college life
- feel confused about career goals
- don't have study skills
- can't afford tuition
- part-time job takes time away from schoolwork
- financial problems
- lose a family member
- undergo an emotional crisis such as a breakup
- ~~want to start their own businesses~~

After critically examining her supporting ideas, Alicia chose three that could become body paragraphs. She evaluated each set of linked ideas and summarized the connection between them. These sentence summaries then became her topic sentences. Alicia also reworked her thesis statement.

Revised Thesis and Supporting Points

Thesis Statement: Students may drop out of college because they are unprepared, have financial problems, or experience an emotional crisis.

Topic Sentence: Many students are unable to adapt to college life.

Topic Sentence: Some students face overwhelming financial burdens.

Topic Sentence: Furthermore, they may undergo an emotional crisis.

Hint **Look Critically at Your Supporting Ideas**

After you have made a list of supporting ideas, look at it carefully and ask yourself the next questions.

- **Which ideas could I develop into complete paragraphs?** Look for connections between supporting ideas. Group together ideas that have a common thread. Then create a topic sentence for each group of related ideas. In Alicia's example, three of her ideas became topic sentences.
- **Does each idea support my thesis?** Choose ideas that directly support the thesis statement and drop any ideas that might go off topic. In Alicia's example, the last idea, "Want to start their own businesses" didn't support her thesis, so she crossed it out.

PRACTICE 9 Brainstorm three supporting ideas for the next thesis statements. Find ideas that do not overlap, and ensure that your ideas support the thesis. (You can brainstorm a list of ideas on a separate sheet of paper, and then add the three best ideas here.) Answers will vary.

EXAMPLE: Driving in the city is very stressful.

– pedestrians and cyclists are careless

– poor street planning has led to larger traffic jams

– other drivers act in dangerous and erratic ways

1. Losing a job can have some positive consequences.

____

____

____

2. There are several concrete steps that you can take to help preserve the environment.

____

____

____

3. When young people move away from home, they quickly learn the next lessons.

____

____

____

Teaching Tip:
If you have started to discuss writing patterns with your students, discuss what types of essays the statements in Practice 9 would generate.

Teaching Tip:
Pair Work
Students can do Practice 9 in pairs. You might ask them to brainstorm a large list of supporting ideas for each topic on a separate paper. Then they can group the ideas and create three topic sentences that can support each thesis.

Writer's Desk Generate Supporting Ideas

Brainstorm supporting ideas for two or three of your thesis statements from the previous Writer's Desk. Look critically at your lists of supporting ideas. Ask yourself which supporting ideas you could expand into body paragraphs, and then drop any unrelated ideas.

The Writer's Room Topics to Develop

Writing Activity 1

Choose one of the Writer's Room topics from Chapter 1 and write a thesis statement. Using an exploring strategy, develop supporting ideas for your thesis.

Writing Activity 2

Narrow one of the following topics. Then develop a thesis statement and some supporting ideas.

General Topics

1. good hygiene
2. annoying rules
3. delaying childbirth
4. traditions
5. allergies

College and Work-Related Topics

6. pressures students face
7. credit cards
8. creative teaching
9. improving services
10. benefits of extracurricular activities

THESIS STATEMENT AND TOPIC SENTENCES

When you write a thesis statement, ask yourself these questions.

- Is my thesis a complete sentence?
- Does it contain a narrowed topic and a controlling idea?
- Is my main point clear and interesting?
- Can the thesis be supported with several body paragraphs? (Ensure that the topic is not too narrow, or you will hit a dead end with it. Also ensure that the topic is not too broad. Your essay requires a clear focus.)
- Can I think of details, examples, and other ideas to support the thesis?
- Is my thesis forceful and direct, and not too vague or obvious?
- Does my thesis make a valid point?
- Do I have good supporting ideas?
- Does each topic sentence have a controlling idea and support the thesis statement?

How Do I Get a Better Grade?

CHAPTER 3

Developing the Essay Plan

CONTENTS

- Key Steps in Developing the Essay Plan
- Organizing Supporting Ideas
- Developing an Essay Plan

Like gardens, essays require careful planning. Some ideas thrive among each other while others do not. Writers develop essay plans to help them decide which ideas support the main idea most effectively and where to place those ideas so that readers can understand them.

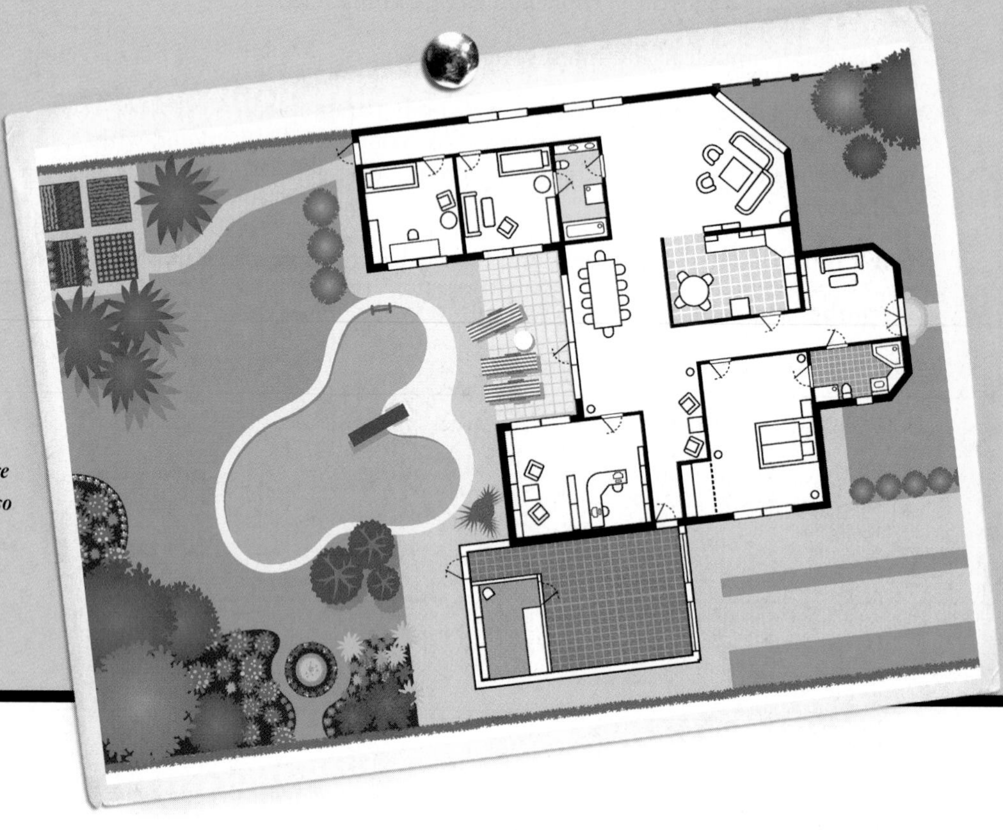

Key Steps in Developing the Essay Plan

In the previous chapters, you learned how to use exploring strategies to formulate ideas and narrow topics. You also learned to develop main ideas for essays. In this chapter, you will focus on the third stage of the essay writing process: developing the essay plan. There are two key steps in this process.

DEVELOPING THE ESSAY PLAN

STEP 1 ➤ **Organize your supporting ideas.** Choose an appropriate method of organization.

STEP 2 ➤ **Write an essay plan.** Place your main and supporting ideas in an essay plan.

"Good plans shape good decisions."

LESTER R. BIDDLE, *Management Consultant*

Organizing Supporting Ideas

Once you have a list of main ideas that will make up the body paragraphs in an essay, you will need to organize those ideas in a logical manner using time, space, or emphatic order.

Time Order

To organize an essay using **time order (chronological order)**, arrange the details according to the sequence in which they have occurred. Time order can be effective for narrating a story, explaining how to do something, or describing an event.

When you write essays using time order, you can use the following transitional expressions to help your readers understand when certain events happened. (There is a more extensive list of transitions on page 68 in Chapter 5.)

after that	first	last	next
eventually	in the beginning	meanwhile	suddenly
finally	later	months after	then

PRACTICE 1 The supporting ideas for the following thesis statement are organized using time order.

THESIS STATEMENT: My one and only ferry ride was a disaster.

1. To begin with, the only available seat was in a horrible location near the back of the boat.
2. Next, the rain began, and the passengers on deck rushed inside.
3. After that, the ferry began to rock, and some passengers became ill.

One paragraph from the essay also uses time order. Underline any words or phrases that help show time order.

Next, the rain began, and the passengers on deck rushed inside. Suddenly, a sprinkle became a downpour. I was in the middle of the crowd, and water was running in rivulets down my face and down the back of my collar. Then, those behind me got impatient and began to shove. The doorway was narrow, and many people were jostling for position. I was pushed to the right and left. Meanwhile, I was soaked, tired, and cranky. The crowd squeezed me more and more. Finally, I was pushed through the door; I stumbled and tried not to fall. The inner seating room was so crowded that I had to stand in the aisle holding on to the back of one of the seats.

Emphatic Order

To organize the supporting details of an essay using **emphatic order**, arrange them in a logical sequence. For example, you can arrange details from least to most important, from general to specific, from least appealing to most appealing, and so on.

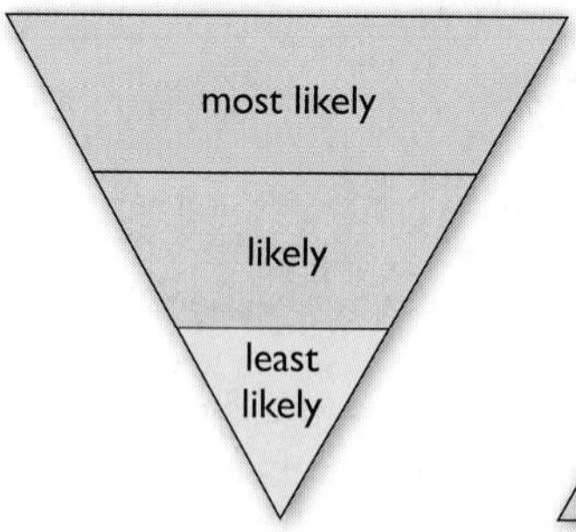

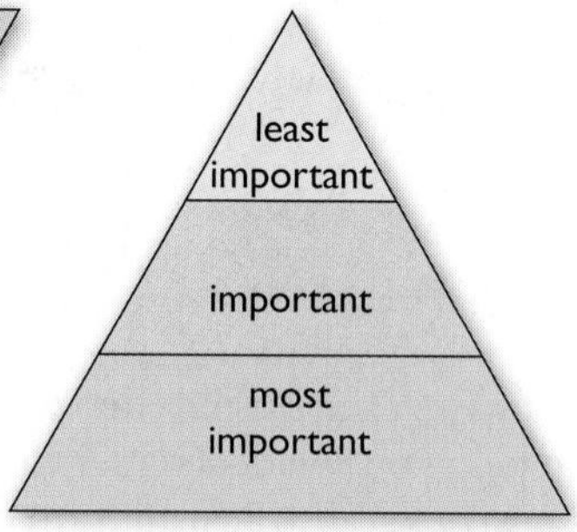

Teaching Tip: Remind students that transitional words and expressions are not necessary in every sentence. They should only use transitions when the reader might not see the connection between ideas.

Here are some transitional expressions that help readers understand which ideas you want to emphasize the most or the least in the body paragraphs of an essay.

above all	first	moreover	principally
clearly	in particular	most importantly	the least important
especially	last	of course	the most important

PRACTICE 2 The supporting ideas for the following thesis statement are organized using emphatic order.

THESIS STATEMENT: In our city, some types of public transportation are more dependable and pleasant than others.

1. First, subways can be uncomfortable and even frightening.
2. Bus trips can have certain drawbacks.
3. The most pleasant and reliable way to travel seems to be the suburban train.

One paragraph from the essay also uses emphatic order. Underline any words or phrases that help show emphatic order.

First, subways can be uncomfortable and even frightening. Above all, subway riders must deal with crowds. In front of the tracks, there is very little seating room, so people line the walls. Of course, the lighting is usually terrible, so ordinary people look sad and even sinister under the fluorescent tubes. Feeling uncomfortable and unattractive, they avoid eye contact. Moreover, for those who feel claustrophobic, being in a subway can feel like being in a grave. There is no sunlight, no sky, and no outdoors for the entire duration of the journey. Passengers can only stare at the sullen faces of the other travelers. Clearly, the entire subway experience can be unpleasant and disturbing.

Hint **Using Emphatic Order**

When you organize details using emphatic order, use your own values and opinions to determine what is most or least important, upsetting, remarkable, and so on. Another writer may organize the same ideas in a different way.

Space Order

Organizing ideas using **space order** helps the reader to visualize what you are describing in a specific space. For example, you can describe someone or something from top to bottom or bottom to top, from left to right or right to left, or from far to near or near to far.

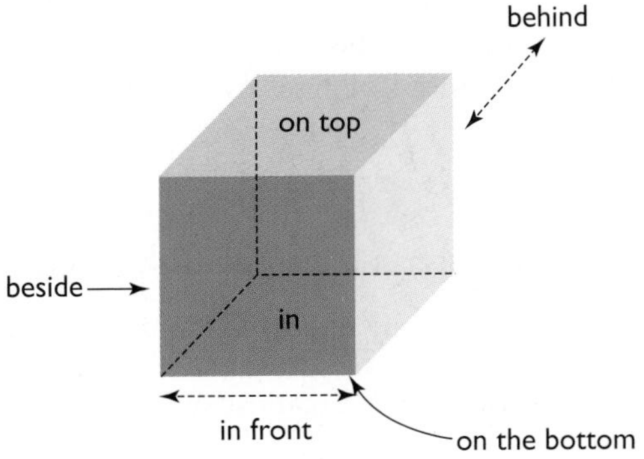

Help readers find their way through your essay by using the following transitional expressions.

above	beneath	nearby	on top
behind	closer in	on the bottom	toward
below	farther out	on the left	under

PRACTICE 3 The supporting ideas for the following thesis statement are organized using space order.

THESIS STATEMENT: With very little money, local students helped turn a tiny old house into a vibrant youth center.

1. Working outdoors, two students cleared the yard.
2. Focusing on the exterior surfaces of the building, a second team of students painted and made minor repairs.
3. Inside the house, some students turned the living room into a recreation and meeting place.

One paragraph from the essay also uses space order. Underline any words or phrases that indicate space order.

Inside the house, some students turned the living room into a recreation and meeting place. First, they washed and then painted the walls. At the far end of the room, next to the fireplace, there was an old bar with an orange counter and frayed yellow bar stools. The students stripped and varnished the counter of the bar and cleaned the sink. They turned the space into an art corner. Local teenagers who like to paint and sculpt now have a nice workspace. In the center of the room, there was an area rope rug that had seen better days. They removed the rug and replaced it with woven straw matting. Beside the rug was a stained and smelly pink and green sofa. The students discarded the sofa. Rather than purchase a new one, which would have cost hundreds of dollars, they used the center's funds to buy large blue cushions at a discount department store. When the renovations were finished, the room looked like a new and fresh space.

Hint **Combining Time, Space, or Emphatic Order**

You will likely use more than one type of organizational method in an essay. For example, in a time order essay about a journey, one paragraph might be devoted to a particular place that you visited, and in that paragraph, you might use space order to describe the scene.

Teaching Tip: As an additional activity, ask students to add transitional words or phrases to the topic sentences in Practice 4. Their transitions should help clarify the type of order.

PRACTICE 4 Read each list of supporting ideas, and number the items in a logical order. Then write time, space, or emphatic to indicate the organization method. Answers will vary.

EXAMPLE: Thesis Statement: Painting a basic picture can be a rewarding experience.

__1__ Choose a location that you find particularly peaceful.

__3__ Add colors to your sketch that best represent the mood you are feeling.

__2__ Settle in and make a preliminary sketch of the place.

Order: __time__

1. Thesis Statement: Overexposure to the sun can have terrible consequences.

   __1__ The skin cells lose elasticity and wrinkles set in earlier.

   __3__ Some people develop cancers that can lead to premature death.

   __2__ Brown spots can develop on parts of the face.

   Order: __emphatic__

2. Thesis Statement: We encountered many problems during our trip from Mexico City to Guadalajara.

   __3__ We arrived late at night and had a lot of trouble finding our friend's house.

   __1__ We didn't have enough money for the first tollbooth, so we took the side roads.

   __2__ On a small road halfway there, an accident completely blocked our route.

   Order: __time__

3. Thesis Statement: For an important interview, dress conservatively.

   __3__ Employers may notice every detail, so pay attention to your footwear.

   __1__ If possible, invest in a good haircut a few days before the interview.

   __2__ Wear a suit jacket and matching pants or a skirt.

   Order: __space__

4. Thesis Statement: Harold Roos should win the citizen's award for three reasons.

   __1__ Every Sunday, Mr. Roos does volunteer work at the hospital.

   __3__ Last September, Mr. Roos saved Eduardo Borsellino's life when he pulled the young man out of a submerged car.

   __2__ Mr. Roos employs many local citizens in his downtown clothing store.

   Order: __emphatic__

Teaching Tip:
Pair Work
Ask students to work in pairs and create an essay plan for one of the readings in Chapter 40.

Developing an Essay Plan

A contractor would never build a house without making a drawing or plan of it first. In the same way, an **essay plan** or an **outline** can help you to organize your thesis statement and supporting ideas before writing your first draft. Planning your essay actually saves you time because you have already figured out your supporting ideas and how to organize them so your readers can easily follow them. To create an essay plan, follow the next steps.

- Looking at the list of ideas that you created while prewriting, identify the ones that most effectively support your thesis statement.
- Next, write topic sentences that express the main supporting ideas.
- Finally, add details under each topic sentence.

A formal essay plan uses Roman numerals and letters to identify main and supporting ideas. A formal plan also contains complete sentences. The basic structure looks like this:

Thesis statement: ______________________________

I. ______________________________

A. ______________________________

B. ______________________________

II. ______________________________

A. ______________________________

B. ______________________________

Concluding Idea: ______________________________

In the planning stage, you do not have to develop your introduction and conclusion. It is sufficient to simply write your thesis statement and an idea for your conclusion. Later, when you write your essay, you can develop the introduction and conclusion.

Teaching Tip:
Before you assign essay plans, specify whether you prefer informal or formal essay plans. Explain that an informal plan can include phrases instead of complete sentences, and it doesn't require Roman numerals.

Alicia's Essay Plan

Alicia Parera wrote topic sentences and supporting examples and organized her ideas into a plan. Notice that she begins with her thesis statement, and she indents her supporting ideas.

THESIS STATEMENT: Students may drop out of college because they have financial problems, experience an emotional crisis, or are unprepared for college life.

I. Some students face overwhelming financial burdens.

A. They may have a part-time job to pay for such things as tuition and rent.

B. Moreover, a part-time job leaves no time for studying and homework.
C. Also, transportation may be expensive and beyond a student's means.

II. Furthermore, some students are faced with life-changing events and must leave college to cope.
A. A pregnancy and childbirth consume energy and attention.
B. Also, a serious illness or death in the family can cause a student to miss classes, and it becomes too difficult to catch up.
C. Of course, a broken relationship can cause a student to feel emotionally fragile and unable to concentrate.

III. They may be unprepared for college life.
A. They might have poor study skills.
B. Furthermore, some students cannot respect schedules.
C. The increased freedom in college causes some students to skip too many classes.
D. Additionally, many students feel confused about career goals and decide to leave college.

PRACTICE 5 Read the thesis statement and the list of supporting ideas and details. First, highlight three supporting ideas (topic sentences) and number them 1, 2, and 3. Then, using numbers such as *1a, 1b, 1c, 2a, 2b, 2c,* etc., organize the details that could follow each topic sentence. On a separate piece of paper, place the ideas in an essay plan. Answers will vary.

Teaching Tip:
Pair Work
Students could do this practice with a partner.

THESIS STATEMENT: *Men have disadvantages at home and in the workplace.*

- High-tower construction work, which is mainly done by males, is very risky. 2a
- In family court, men do not get custody of children as often as women do. 3
- According to journalist Ian McArthur, most boys are told to "take it like a man" so they learn to rein in their emotions. 1c
- More men do work that puts their lives at risk than women do. 2
- Sheila Siskel, a lawyer, acknowledges that many judges still consider the woman as the child's primary caregiver. 3a
- Men are more likely to repair roofs, scale electrical poles, and operate heavy machinery. 2b
- Greg Chu says, "It is unsatisfying and heartbreaking when I am reduced to visiting my own children twice a month!" 3c
- Over ninety percent of workplace deaths happen to men, according to the U.S. Department of Labor Web site. 2c
- Some men are ridiculed when they show emotion. 1 ▶

- Manuel Figuera, a graphic designer, says, "Some believe a crying man is an emotional weakling or a wimp." 1a
- Men's groups, including Divorced Dads, protest the attitudes of the courts toward fathers in their fight for parental rights. 3b
- Movies such as *Saving Private Ryan* reinforce the stereotype that men must be stoic and control their emotions. 1b

Teaching Tip: You might ask students to create this essay plan in pairs or groups.

PRACTICE 6 On a separate sheet of paper, create an essay plan for the next thesis statement. Answers will vary.

THESIS STATEMENT: Women have disadvantages at home and in the workplace.

Teaching Tip: If Practice 7 and 8 are done in class, ask students to work together to come up with supporting ideas. Students can do this on a separate sheet of paper and provide specific evidence for each detail.

PRACTICE 7 Read the following essay plan. Brainstorm and develop three supporting ideas for each topic sentence. Answers will vary.

THESIS STATEMENT: Common fairy tales follow a certain model.

Topic Sentence: Fairy tales never mention a real date or place.

Supporting ideas:

- The tales usually begin with "once upon a time."
- The stories often include phrases like "in a land far away."
- Cinderella, Snow White, and the others are from magical kingdoms.

Topic Sentence: The main character must overcome great obstacles to achieve his or her goal.

Supporting ideas:

- Red Riding Hood has to make her way through a dark forest and face the wolf.
- The prince in Sleeping Beauty must slay a dragon.
- Hansel and Gretel must survive on their own in the forest and kill the wicked witch.

Topic Sentence: The main character accomplishes his or her goals with the help of magic or some other unnatural phenomena.

Supporting ideas:

- Cinderella's fairy godmother turns a pumpkin into a stagecoach so the pretty young girl can arrive at the ball in style.

- The genie in the lamp helps Aladdin by giving him three wishes.

- The prince awakens Sleeping Beauty when he kisses her and breaks the magic spell.

PRACTICE 8 Read the following essay plan. Brainstorm and develop three supporting ideas for each topic sentence. Answers will vary.

THESIS STATEMENT: I learned valuable lessons during my years in grammar school and high school.

Topic Sentence: First, I learned how to get along with others.

Supporting ideas:

- I learned to share my food, magazines, and games.

- By playing interactive sports such as soccer, I learned how to work as a team player and how to lose gracefully.

- In class and during recess periods, I learned to talk rather than fight.

Topic Sentence: I learned to organize my time.

Supporting ideas:

- After missing the school bus a few times, I learned to be punctual.

- I got penalized for handing in homework late, which taught me to respect deadlines.

- Because I had large amounts of homework, I made myself a study schedule.

Topic Sentence: Most importantly, I learned about respect, compassion, and gratitude.

Supporting ideas:

- After a student teacher left the classroom in tears, I realized that teachers are human and deserving of respect.
- When a classmate was humiliated, I felt his pain and showed him I care.
- I felt grateful for our educational system when I met a girl from another nation who was so happy to be going to school.

Writer's Desk Write an Essay Plan

Brainstorm ideas for an essay on a separate piece of paper. You can choose ideas that you developed in Chapter 2. Then do the following.

1. Highlight at least three ideas from your list that you think are most compelling and most clearly illustrate the point you are making in your thesis statement. These three ideas will make up your body paragraphs.
2. Group together any related ideas with the three supporting ideas.
3. Organize your ideas for the body paragraphs using time, space, or emphatic order.
4. Create a complete essay plan.

The Writer's Room Topics to Develop

Writing Activity 1

Choose one of the Writer's Room topics from Chapter 2, and create an essay plan. Using an exploring strategy, develop supporting ideas for your thesis.

Writing Activity 2

Create a list of supporting ideas for one of the next thesis statements. Then develop an essay plan.

General Topics

1. Single people should (or should not) have the right to adopt children.
2. The three talents I would most like to have are . . .
3. Noise pollution is increasing in our homes and neighborhoods.
4. There are good reasons to postpone marriage.

College and Work-Related Topics

5. New employees make three types of common mistakes.
6. An elected official should have the following characteristics.
7. I do (or do not) vote for the following reasons.
8. (Choose a story, novel, or film) has important lessons for all of us.

CHECKLIST: ESSAY PLAN

When you develop an essay plan, ask yourself these questions.

- Does my thesis statement express the main idea of the essay?
- In my plan, does each body paragraph contain a topic sentence?
- Does each topic sentence support the thesis statement?
- In each body paragraph, do the sentences support the topic sentence?
- Are my ideas well organized?

How Do I Get a Better Grade?

PEARSON mywritinglab

Visit www.mywritinglab.com for audio-visual lectures and additional practice sets about essay planning.
Get a better grade with MyWritingLab!

CHAPTER 4

Developing the First Draft

CONTENTS

By preparing the soil and planting seeds and shrubs, a gardener creates a landscape's basic foundation. In the same way, a writer plans the main idea, develops the plan, and then prepares the first draft of a writing assignment.

Key Steps in Developing the First Draft

In previous chapters, you learned how to develop a thesis statement, support it with ideas, and create an essay plan. To develop a first draft, follow the next five steps.

DEVELOPING THE FIRST DRAFT

STEP 1	**Write an introduction.** Try to attract the reader's attention in the first paragraph of your essay.
STEP 2	**Write complete body paragraphs.** Expand each supporting idea with specific details.
STEP 3	**Write a conclusion.** Bring your essay to a satisfactory close.
STEP 4	**Title your essay.** Sum up your essay topic in a few words.
STEP 5	**Write the first draft.** Tie the introduction, body paragraphs, and conclusion into a cohesive essay.

> ***"Detail makes the difference between boring and perfect writing. It's the difference between a pencil sketch and a lush oil painting. As a writer, words are your paint. Use all the colors."***
>
> RHYS ALEXANDER, *Author*

Writing an Introduction

The **introductory paragraph** introduces the subject of your essay and contains the thesis statement. A strong introduction will capture the reader's attention and make him or her want to read on. Introductions may have a lead-in, and they can be developed in several different ways.

The Lead-In

The point of writing an essay is to have people read it and to entertain, inform, or persuade them. So, try to grab your readers' attention in the first sentence. There are three common lead-ins that you can try:

- a quotation
- a surprising or provocative statement
- a question

Introduction Styles

You can develop the introduction in several ways. Experiment with any of the following introduction styles.

- **Give general or historical background information** that gradually leads to your thesis. For example, in an essay about movie violence, you might begin by discussing some classic films.
- **Tell an interesting anecdote** or a story that leads to your thesis statement. For example, you might begin your essay about film violence by describing how aggressive your younger brother and his friends became after they watched the movie *Fight Club*.
- **Describe something in vivid detail,** and then state your thesis. For example, you might begin your essay about movie violence by describing a particularly gory film scene.
- **Define a term,** and then state your thesis. For example, in an essay about ways to avoid marital conflicts, you can begin by defining a happy marriage.

- **Present a contrasting position,** which is an idea that is the opposite of the one you will later develop, and then offer your thesis. Your readers will not expect you to present one side and then to argue for the other side. For example, in an essay about abortion, you might begin by presenting the arguments of those who would not agree with your particular point of view on the debate.
- **Pose several questions,** and end with a thesis statement. The purpose may be to engage your readers by inviting them to think about the topic. You might also ask questions that you will answer in your essay. For instance, in an essay about lotteries, you might ask: *Have you ever bought a lottery ticket? Why do so many people play lotteries?*

The next example presents the structure of a typical introduction.

Lead-in ➢
Historical background information ➢
Thesis statement ➢

Have good manners disappeared? In past centuries, a gentleman would spread his cloak over a muddy road so that his lady wouldn't dirty her feet. Twenty years ago, an elderly man or woman would never have to stand in a bus because other passengers would offer up their seats. Times have certainly changed. Today, many people lack consideration for others. **Parents and schools should teach children basic good manners.**

ESL Teaching Tip: For the benefit of nonnative speakers, remind students that the main point should be very clearly stated in the introductory paragraph.

PRACTICE 1 Read the following introductions. Underline each thesis statement and determine what introduction style the writer used.

1. I got out of bed as usual. I shaved, showered and put on a clean shirt. Trotting out to the kitchen where my wife, Nadine, was standing, I looked at her and asked, "Now what?" The day before, I had accepted a generous buyout offer at Verizon Corp., effectively ending my thirty-year career there as a midlevel manager. I was fifty-one. With the papers in front of me, I listened patiently as my financial adviser cautioned me that some people in my position are not mentally prepared to retire, but I never dreamed that his advice would apply to me. I was wrong. <u>Retirement left a void in my life that I filled in some odd ways</u>.

Peter Borghesi, "I Was Out of a Job and an Identity," *Newsweek*

a. Underline the thesis statement.

b. What is the introduction style? Indicate the best answer.

_____ general background   __X__ anecdote

_____ definition   _____ questions

2. Adolescent males are dangerous. They join gangs, and they are responsible for most of the crime in our society. They drive too fast, causing accidents on our highways. They all experiment with drugs, and they annoy others with their loud music. But is such a portrayal of our nation's young men really fair? In fact, most stereotypes about adolescent males are incorrect and misleading.

   Abeer Hamad, student

   a. Underline the thesis statement.

   b. What type of lead-in did the writer use?

   _____ quotation _____ question __X__ surprising statement

   c. What is the introduction style? Indicate the best answer.

   _____ historical background _____ anecdote

   _____ definition __X__ contrasting position

3. Where did you buy that blouse? I heard the question every time I wore it. It was a truly lovely designer model that had been marked down to $40. It was pale blue with swirling tiny flower buds running down each front panel. The little buttons were topped with imitation pearls. Unfortunately, the middle button kept coming undone. People at a certain angle to my left could peek in and view the lace eyelets on my brassiere. When I wore the blouse, my head kept bobbing down, looking to see if I was exposing myself. Over the years, I have had several humorous and embarrassing wardrobe and makeup malfunctions.

   Catalina Ortega, student

   a. Underline the thesis statement.

   b. What type of lead-in was used?

   _____ quotation __X__ question _____ surprising statement

   c. What is the introduction style? Indicate the best answer.

   _____ general background _____ anecdote

   _____ definition __X__ description

4. Nationalism is the sometimes angry belief in the independence of one's people. It often includes resentment or even hatred of alien rulers or threatening foreigners: "No foreigners will push us

around!" It is the strongest and most emotional of the world's ideologies. Most of the world's people—including Americans—are nationalistic.

Michael G. Roskin and Nicholas O. Berry, *The New World of International Relations*

a. Underline the thesis statement.

b. What is the introduction style? Indicate the best answer.

_____ historical background _____ anecdote

__X__ definition _____ contrasting position

5. "Men only." A century ago, the campuses of colleges and universities across the United States might as well have hung out that sign. Almost all of the students and faculty were male. There were a small number of women's colleges, but many more schools—including some of the best-known American universities, such as Yale, Harvard, and Princeton—barred women outright. Since then, women have won greater social equality. By 1980, the number of women enrolled at American colleges finally matched the number of men. In a surprising turn of events, women now outnumber men on college campuses for several reasons.

Adapted from John J. Macionis, "The Twenty-First-Century Campus: Where Are the Men?" *Sociology*

a. Underline the thesis statement.

b. What type of lead-in was used?

__X__ quotation _____ question _____ surprising statement

c. What is the introduction style? Indicate the best answer.

__X__ historical background _____ anecdote

_____ definition _____ questions

6. Why do some hip-hop artists embed jewels and gold in their teeth? Are the grills meant to impress others, or do the grills fit some deep need on the part of the artists to show that they matter? Is the hip-hop artist who shows off his "bling" any different than the accountant who buys a BMW to show that she has succeeded, or the corporate executive who marries a beautiful trophy wife?

Showing off one's wealth is not new. In fact, throughout history, people have found extravagant ways to flaunt their wealth.

Jamal Evans, student

a. Underline the thesis statement.

b. What is the introduction style? Indicate the best answer.

_____ general background _____ anecdote

_____ definition __X__ questions

PRACTICE 2 Write interesting lead-ins (opening sentences) for the next topics. Use the type of lead-in that is indicated in parentheses.
Answers will vary.

EXAMPLE: Bicycle helmet laws (question)

How many cyclists have needlessly died this year from head injuries?

1. dangerous dogs (a surprising or controversial statement)

____

____

2. ridiculous fashions (a question)

____

____

3. the junk food nation (a surprising fact or idea)

____

____

PRACTICE 3 Choose *one* of the next thesis statements. Then write three introductions using three different introduction styles. Use the same thesis statement in each introduction. Answers will vary.

It's important to know more than one language.

Famous musicians generally make poor (or good) role models.

Computers have made our lives more complicated.

You can choose any three of the following introduction styles:

- Anecdote
- Description
- Definition
- Contrasting position
- Series of questions
- General or historical background

Teaching Tip:
As an additional activity, write a thesis statement on the board such as "There are three common mistakes people make on the first date." and then place students in teams. Ask each team to prepare an introduction using a different style. Team members can read their introductions out loud. Then the class can show, with applause, which introductions are the most powerful.

Writer's Desk Write Two Introductions

In Chapter 3, you prepared an essay plan. Now, on a separate piece of paper, write two different styles of introductions for your essay. Use the same thesis statement in both introductions. Later, you can choose the best introduction for your essay.

Teaching Tip: Many students have problems providing sufficient examples and details in their body paragraphs. After students read this section, ask them to evaluate one of their previous essays and analyze whether or not they included well-supported paragraphs.

Writing Complete Body Paragraphs

In your essay plan, you developed supporting ideas for your topic. When you prepare the first draft, you must flesh out those ideas. As you write each body paragraph, ensure that it is complete. Do not offer vague generalizations, and do not simply repeat your ideas. Provide evidence for each topic sentence by inserting specific details. You might include examples, facts, statistics, anecdotes, or quotations.

Examples are people, places, things, or events that illustrate your point. To support the view that some local buildings are eyesores, the writer could give the following examples.

> The car dealership on Labelle Boulevard is run-down.
>
> The gray block apartment buildings that line Main Street are monotonous.
>
> The Allen Drive mini-mall has tacky signs and cracked store windows.

Teaching Tip: Point out the difference between an opinion or observation and a fact. Give students these examples.

Opinion: The children are too young to be left alone. Fact: Evan is nine, and Tracy is just six.

Observation: The local economy is booming. Fact: The local employment center reports that fewer people are looking for work this year.

Facts are objective details that can be verified by others. **Statistics** are facts that are expressed in percentages. (Make sure that your statistics are from reliable sources.) To support the view that transportation costs are too high for students, the following facts and statistics could be given as evidence.

> A one-way bus ticket now costs $3.50 for students.
>
> The monthly subway pass just increased to $260 for students.
>
> In a college survey of four hundred students, 70 percent expressed concern about the recent rate increases in public transportation.

Anecdotes are true experiences that you or someone else went through. An anecdote expresses what happened. **Quotations** are somebody's exact words, and they are set off in quotation marks. To support the view that lack of sleep can have dangerous consequences, the following anecdote and quotation could be included as evidence.

> When Allen Turner finished his nightshift, he got into his car and headed home. On Forest Drive, he started to nod off. Luckily, a truck driver in another lane noticed that Turner's car was weaving and honked.

Turner said, "My eyes snapped open and I saw a wall growing larger in front of me. I slammed on my brakes just before smashing into it."

Essay with Sample Body Paragraphs

Read the next body paragraphs. Notice how they are fleshed out with specific evidence.

Teaching Tip: Ask students to look again at Alicia's essay plan in Chapter 3 on pages 38–39. Ask students to brainstorm what type of specific evidence could help make the essay more complete. A draft of the essay about college dropouts appears in Chapter 5.

Thesis Statement:

For personal and financial reasons, a growing number of adult children are choosing to live with their parents.

Body Paragraphs

The cost of education and housing is very high, so it is more economical to live at home. First, rents have increased dramatically since the 1990s. In The Daily Journal, Anna Reinhold states that rents tripled in the past ten years. (≺ fact) During the same period, student wages have not risen as much as the rents. In fact, the minimum wage is still $6.15 an hour. (≺ fact) Also, college fees are increasing each year. Tuition and fees at four-year public colleges rose $344, or 6.3 percent this year, to an average of $5,836, according to the College Board's annual "Trends in College Pricing" report. (≺ statistic)

Many young people want to build a nest egg before moving out of the family home. When they remain at home, they can save income from part-time jobs. "I've saved $14,000 by staying in my parents' place," says Kyle Nehme, a twenty-four-year-old student at the University of Texas. (≺ quotation) Such students do not need to worry about student loans. According to financial analyst Raul Gomez, "Students who stay in the family home reap significant financial benefits." (≺ quotation)

Students who remain in their parents' home have a much more relaxed and comfortable lifestyle. Often, the parents do the shopping and housework. For example, Liz Allen, a twenty-six-year-old marketing student, moved back in with her parents last May. She discovered how much more convenient it was when someone else did the vacuuming, laundry, and cooking. (≺ anecdote) Moreover, such students feel more secure and safe in the cocoon of home. In a Daily Journal survey of ninety adults who live at home, 64 percent cited "comfort" as their major reason. (≺ statistic)

Hint **Using Research to Support Your Point**

Your instructor might ask you to back up your ideas with research. You can look in several resources, including books, magazines, and the Internet, for relevant quotations, statistics, and factual evidence. For more information about doing research, see Chapter 16, The Research Essay.

Teaching Tip:
If Practice 4 is done in class, ask students to use anecdotes, facts, and examples as support. If you assign this practice as homework, you could ask students to do some research and find statistics or quotations to support the topic.

PRACTICE 4 Make the next body paragraphs more complete by adding specific examples. You can include the following:

- examples
- anecdotes from your own life or from the lives of others
- quotations (for this exercise, you can make up punchy quotations)
- facts, statistics, or descriptions of events that you have read about or seen

Do not add general statements. Ensure that the details you add are very specific.
Answers will vary.

THESIS STATEMENT: Prospective pet owners should become informed before buying an animal.

Body Paragraph 1 First, when families choose a dog, they should consider the inconvenience and possible dangers. Some breeds of dogs can become extremely aggressive. *Rottweilers and pit bulls, for example, have been known to act erratically. There have been many documented cases of dog attacks on humans. Last year a Michigan pet owner expressed shock and sadness when her beloved pit bull suddenly attacked her grandson. "My dog is usually so gentle," the owner said.* Moreover, dog owners must accept that dogs require a lot of time and attention. *Dogs need to be walked daily, so owners should expect to devote at least half an hour per day to that activity. Dogs also require attention. New Jersey pet owner Susan Dover said, "My dog chews the arms of my sofa when I leave her alone for too long."* Furthermore, it is very expensive to own a dog. *Vaccinations can cost thousands of dollars. Dog food is costly, and large dogs require a lot of food.*

Teaching Tip:
If your student essays lack well-supported body paragraphs, suggest that students prepare a very detailed essay plan before they write their next essay. They can add specific quotations, examples, statistics, and other references directly into their plan.

Body Paragraph 2 Some new pet owners decide to buy exotic pets. However, such pets come with very specific problems and require particular environments. *Snakes require terrariums with particular heat and light requirements. Lizards* *can die if they are not kept in the proper conditions. Other exotic pets such as lion cubs require outdoor enclosures that provide them with the room to roam.* Also, some exotic pets seem interesting when they are young, but they can become distinctly annoying or dangerous when they reach maturity. *Sarah Jorba bought a cute baby chimpanzee, but said her animal became "very aggressive and destructive" when it reached maturity. Owners of baby alligators end up with animals that they cannot maintain.*

Hint Making Detailed Essay Plans

You can shorten the time you spend developing the first draft if you make a very detailed essay plan. In addition to writing main ideas, your plan can include details for each supporting idea. Notice the detailed evidence in the following excerpt from an essay plan.

Thesis Statement: For personal and financial reasons, a growing number of adult children are choosing to live with their parents.

I. **Topic Sentence:** The cost of education and housing is very high.
   A. Rents have increased dramatically in the past ten years.
      Evidence: The Daily Journal states that rents tripled in the past ten years. ← fact
   B. Student wages have not risen as much as the rents.
      Evidence: The minimum wage is still $6.15 an hour. ← fact
   C. Tuition fees are very high.
      Evidence: Tuition and fees at four-year public colleges rose $344, or 6.3 percent this year, to an average of $5,836, according to the College Board's annual "Trends in College Pricing" report. ← statistic

Writer's Desk Make Complete Body Paragraphs

In Chapter 3, you prepared an essay plan. Now write complete body paragraphs for your essay. Ensure that each body paragraph contains specific details.

Writing a Conclusion

The **concluding paragraph** gives you one last chance to impress the reader and to make your point clear. A good conclusion makes the essay seem complete. One common and effective way to conclude a composition is to summarize the main ideas. The essay then comes full circle, and you remind the reader of your strongest points.

To make your conclusion more interesting and original, you could also close with a prediction, a suggestion, a quotation, or a call to action.

Hint **Linking the Conclusion to the Introduction**

One effective way to conclude an essay is to continue an idea that was introduced in the introduction.

- If you began an anecdote in the introduction, you can finish it in the conclusion.
- If you posed some questions in the introduction, you can answer them in the conclusion.
- If you highlighted a problem in the introduction, you might suggest a solution in the conclusion.

Look at the concluding paragraph to an essay about etiquette in our technological age.

> Do not hide behind technology as your excuse for displaying rude or annoying behavior. You can turn off your cell phone when you are with someone you care about. If someone is writing an e-mail, do not read over his or her shoulder. Also, never send nor accept chain e-mails that promise wealth, happiness, or cures for cancer.

The last sentence in the essay could be one of the following.

Prediction: If you follow the basic rules of etiquette, you will ensure that your friends and colleagues maintain their respect for you.

Suggestion: The next time someone forwards you a nasty chain letter asking you to send it to at least ten people or else, return it to the sender ten times.

Quotation: As the French author Colette once said, "It is wise to apply the oils of refined politeness to the mechanism of friendship."

Call to Action: To help the next generation learn good manners, offer to teach a class to local high school students about etiquette in the technological age.

PRACTICE 5 Read the following conclusions and answer the questions.

Teaching Tip:
For a fun activity, ask students to print out the introductions and conclusions to one of their essays. Mix up the selections and then give either an introduction or a conclusion to each student. Ask students to wander around the class matching the introductions with the conclusions.

A. Laws designed to spook such scammers may be on the way, in the same way legislators tried to wipe out spam a few years ago. California Governor Arnold Schwarzenegger has approved legislation specifically outlawing such scams, giving prosecutors another tool to pursue the fraudulent. But it's still too early to measure whether such laws will be effective at curbing phishing attacks. Until then, consumers should continue to click carefully and be cautious about how and where they hand over personal information.

Mike Musgrove, "Phishing," *The Washington Post*

1. What method does the author use to end the conclusion? suggestion

B. Just as a peacock spreads its tail feathers to attract the opposite sex, human beings flaunt their wealth to impress their mates and to establish their power over others. The grills on the teeth of hip-hop artists are simply modern versions of the Taj Mahal, the pyramids, or the elaborate castles of kings and queens. As Mel Brooks said in *The Producers*, "When you've got it, baby, flaunt it."

Jamal Evans, student

2. What method does the author use to end the conclusion? quotation

C. In this new millennium, let's put the concept of IQ to rest, once and for all. Stop giving IQ tests. Stop all the studies on IQ and birth order, IQ and nutrition, or IQ and Mozart. Let's find newer, more fluid, and more fair ways to debate and enable human potential. Let's use our heads for a change.

Dorothy Nixon, "Let's Stop Being Stupid About IQ"

3. What method does the author use to end the conclusion? call to action

Hint **Avoiding Conclusion Problems**

In your conclusion, do not contradict your main point, and do not introduce new or irrelevant information. Also, avoid ending your essay with a rhetorical question, which is a question that cannot be answered, such as "When will humans stop having wars?"

Writer's Desk Write a Conclusion

Write a conclusion for the essay you've been preparing in the previous Writer's Desk exercises.

Choosing an Essay Title

Think of a title *after* you have written your essay because you will have a more complete impression of your essay's main point. The most effective titles are brief, depict the topic and purpose of the essay, and attract the reader's attention.

Grammar Hint Capitalizing Titles

Place your title at the top center of your page. Capitalize the first word of your title, and capitalize the main words except for prepositions (*in, at, for, to,* etc.) and articles (*a, an, the*). Leave about an inch of space between the title and the introductory paragraph.

Descriptive Titles

Descriptive titles are the most common titles in academic essays. They depict the topic of the essay clearly and concisely. Sometimes, the writer takes key words from the thesis statement and uses them in the title. Here are two examples of descriptive titles.

Etiquette in the Technological Age

Avoiding Mistakes in the First Year of College

Titles Related to the Writing Pattern

You can also relate your title directly to the writing pattern of your essay. Here are examples of titles for different writing patterns.

Illustration:	Problems with Internet Dating
Narration:	My Worst Nightmare
Description:	The Anniversary Party
Process:	How to Handle a Workplace Bully
Definition:	The Meaning of Tolerance
Classification:	Three Types of Fathers
Comparison and Contrast:	Fads Versus Timeless Fashions
Cause and Effect:	The Reasons People Pollute
Argument:	Why Writing Matters

Hint **Avoiding Title Pitfalls**

When you write your title, watch out for problems.

- Do not view your title as a substitute for a thesis statement.
- Do not write a really long title because it can confuse readers.
- Do not put quotation marks around the title of your essay.

PRACTICE 6 Read the next introductions and underline the thesis statements. Then write titles for each essay. Answers will vary.

1. Some people fear mistakes more than others fear snakes. Perfectionism refers to self-defeating thoughts and behaviors aimed at reaching excessively high unrealistic goals. Unfortunately, nobody is perfect. In fact, there are many problems associated with the desire to be perfect.

   Title: ______________________________

2. Gang life, once associated with large urban centers in the United States, has become a common part of adolescent experience in towns and rural areas. Many of the gang members have no strong role models at home, and their gang affiliation makes them feel like part of a powerful group. To combat the problems associated with youth gangs, adolescents need to be given more responsibilities in our society.

   Title: ______________________________

3. "A person who is not initiated is still a child," says Malidoma Somé. Somé is from the Dagara Tribe in West Africa, and he underwent a six-week initiation ceremony. Left alone in the bush with no food or clothing, he developed a profound appreciation of nature and of magic. When he returned to his village, everyone welcomed him and other initiates with food and dancing. Somé had passed from childhood into adulthood and was expected to assume adult responsibilities. The ceremony helped Somé and the other initiates feel like valued participants in village life. Our culture should have formal initiation ceremonies for adolescents.

   Title: ______________________________

PRACTICE 7 Read the next body paragraphs of a short essay. First, highlight the topic sentence in each body paragraph. Then, on a separate sheet of paper, develop a title, a compelling introduction, and a conclusion. Answers will vary.

Add a title

Add an introduction

Body 1 First, family communication suffers when a television is present. The TV is turned on from morning to night. Families install televisions in the kitchen, living room, and bedrooms. Thus, in locations where families traditionally congregated to talk, they now sit mutely—sometimes next to each other—staring at the screen. Instead of reading a bedtime story together, families deposit children in front of the television to watch a bedtime video. Fourteen-year-old Annie Wong says, "When I get home from school, I head straight for my bedroom. I watch my shows in my room, and my brother watches the TV in the living room. I never have to talk to him."

Body 2 Too often, when people do communicate, their discussions revolve around television shows. It is common to hear people quoting Dr. Phil or Oprah, and water cooler conversations often revolve around the latest hot series. Thirty-year-old William and his friend Jay love nothing more than to reminisce about their favorite programs. When *Lost* was at its peak, they discussed each episode in detail. They also love theme songs. "I know the songs for about fifteen television shows," William says, as he proceeds to do the *Fresh Prince of Bel-Air* rap. Jay admits that his conversations with William rarely stray beyond the lightness of the television world.

Body 3 Most importantly, the health of children has changed since the introduction of television. Before televisions existed, children played outdoors and spent most of their free time doing physical activities. Today, most children pass hours sitting or lying down as they stare at the television screen. According to Anna Franklin, a researcher at the Mayo Clinic, such inactivity is contributing to the obesity epidemic in our nation. Ben Tyler, a 10-year-old from Fort Lauderdale, admits that he watches between six and eight hours of television each day. "I can watch whatever I want," he says proudly. But Ben is also overweight and suffers from asthma.

Add a conclusion

Writing the First Draft

After creating an introduction and conclusion, and after arranging the supporting ideas in a logical order, you are ready to write your first draft. The first draft includes your introduction, several body paragraphs, and your concluding paragraph.

Writer's Desk Write the First Draft

In the previous Writer's Desk exercises, you wrote an introduction, a conclusion, and an essay plan. Now write the first draft of your essay.

The Writer's Room Topics to Develop

Writing Activity 1

Choose an essay plan that you developed for Chapter 3, and write the first draft of your essay.

Writing Activity 2

Write the first draft of an essay about one of the following topics.

General Topics

1. In divorce cases, grandparents should receive visitation rights.
2. Movies and television shows glorify crime and criminals.
3. Lying is appropriate in certain situations.
4. I would like to improve three of my traits.

College and Work-Related Topics

5. People go to college for the following reasons.
6. Getting fired can be a liberating experience.
7. Compare learning from experience versus learning from books.
8. I do (or do not) have the skills to be a salesperson.

CHECKLIST: FIRST DRAFT

When you develop the first draft, ask yourself these questions.

- Do I have a compelling introduction?
- Does my introduction lead into a clear thesis statement?
- Do my body paragraphs contain interesting and sufficient details?
- Do the body paragraphs support the idea presented in the thesis statement?
- Do I have an interesting title that sums up the essay topic?
- Does my conclusion bring my essay to a satisfactory close?

Revising and Editing

CHAPTER 5

CONTENTS

The revising and editing stage of the writing process is similar to adding the finishing touches to a garden. Like a gardener, a writer considers what he or she needs to add or trim to make it the best creation possible.

Key Steps in Revising and Editing

Revising and editing is the final step in the writing process. When you **revise**, you modify your writing to make it stronger and more convincing. To revise, read your first draft critically, and look for faulty logic, poor organization, or poor sentence style. Then reorganize and rewrite it, making any necessary changes. When you **edit**, you proofread your final draft for errors in grammar, spelling, punctuation, and mechanics.

> *"Mistakes obviously show us what needs improving. Without mistakes, how would we know what we had to work on?"*
>
> PETER MCWILLIAMS, *American author*

There are five key steps to follow during the revising and editing stage.

REVISING AND EDITING

STEP 1	**Revise for unity.** Ensure that all parts of your work relate to the main idea.
STEP 2	**Revise for adequate support.** Determine that your details effectively support the main idea.
STEP 3	**Revise for coherence.** Verify that your ideas flow smoothly and logically.
STEP 4	**Revise for style.** Ensure that your sentences are varied and interesting.
STEP 5	**Edit for technical errors.** Proofread your work and correct errors in grammar, spelling, mechanics, and punctuation.

Teaching Tip: Explain that every idea in an essay must move in the same direction just as this road goes straight ahead. There should be no forks in the road.

Revising for Unity

Unity means that the ideas in an essay clearly support the focus of the essay. All information heads in the same direction, and there are no forks in the road. If an essay lacks unity, then some ideas drift away from the main idea a writer has expressed in the essay. To check for unity in an essay, consider the following:

- Ensure that all topic sentences in the body paragraphs support the thesis statement of the essay.
- Ensure that all sentences within a body paragraph support the topic sentence of that paragraph.

Essay Without Unity

The next essay plan looks at the reasons for deforestation. The third topic sentence veers away from the writer's central focus that deforestation has implications for the quality of life.

Thesis Statement: Deforestation in the Amazon has tremendous implications for people's quality of life.

Topic Sentence 1: First, logging, mining, and agriculture displace indigenous peoples in the Amazon.

Topic Sentence 2: Also, scientists believe that deforestation in the Amazon will lead to a rapid increase in global climate change, which will affect people worldwide.

Topic Sentence 3: Many development experts are trying to find methods to have sustainable development in the Amazon.

This topic sentence strays from the thesis of this essay.

PRACTICE 1 The following thesis statements have three supporting points that can be developed into body paragraphs. Circle the point that does not support the thesis statement.

1. Thesis Statement: North America is developing a culture of victimization.
   a. First, many people blame their personal and professional problems on addiction.
   b. Furthermore, the increase in personal injury lawsuits suggests that more people see themselves as victims.
   (c.) In addition, lobbyists are petitioning on behalf of special interest groups.
2. Thesis Statement: International adoptions should be banned.
   a. An internationally adopted child will often lose contact with his or her culture.
   (b.) Too many celebrities have adopted internationally.
   c. By adopting from poor countries, westerners are complicit in the exploitation of poor people forced to give up their babies due to poverty.

Teaching Tip: Ask students to think of three points that argue in favor of international adoptions.

Paragraph Without Unity

Not only must your essay have unity, but each body paragraph must have unity. The details in the paragraph must support the paragraph's topic sentence. The next paragraph is part of a larger work. In it, the writer drifted away from his main idea. Some sentences do not relate to the topic sentence. If the highlighted sentences are removed, then the paragraph has unity.

> Americans should not fear the practice of outsourcing by businesses. First, outsourcing is the same practice as subcontracting. In the past, many companies subcontracted work to companies within the same country. Now, businesses simply subcontract to other nations. Furthermore, outsourcing usually leads to higher profits because the product or service is produced more cost effectively. Therefore, the head company's profit margin increases, allowing it to reinvest in domestic markets. In addition, when a company increases its profit, not only do the stockholders benefit, but so do the employees of the

The writer detours here. ➢

company. The stockholders receive more value for their stock, and the employees receive more salaries and benefits. My sister worked in computers and her job became obsolete when her company outsourced the work to India. Now my sister is devastated. She has lost her house and car, and she cannot find another job in her field. Thus, with more disposable incomes, people can help the domestic economy by buying more products.

Teaching Tip: Remind students that the topic sentence must be supported by everything else in the paragraph.

PRACTICE 2 Paragraphs A and B contain problems with unity. In each paragraph, underline the topic sentence and cross out any sentences that do not support the controlling idea.

Paragraph A

<u>The gated community is an attempt to create a modern utopia.</u> First, many people are buying property in gated communities because they want to feel more secure. Gated communities are surrounded by fences and guarded entrances. Therefore, tenants feel that crime will stop at the gate. People also buy homes in gated communities because they do not want to spend time maintaining the yard. Most gated communities have lawn mowing or snow clearing services available. ~~In fact, home maintenance services are becoming very popular in all types of neighborhoods. Such services are not only meant for the elderly, but they are also meant for busy young families.~~ For some people, gated communities give them a lifestyle choice. Since there are rules to follow in a gated community, some homeowners feel that they will be able to live in a community with likeminded neighbors. For example, people with similar religious values may want to live in one community. Thus, gated communities seem to be an attempt at creating utopian living conditions.

Paragraph B

<u>The electric car is not as good for the environment as many people think</u>. First, many people buy electric cars thinking that such vehicles produce no carbon dioxide emissions. Consumers forget how electricity is produced. Most electricity plants generate power by burning coal, oil, or diesel fuel. In fact, burning coal releases many contaminants into the air, which create a great deal of air pollution. Moreover, electric car batteries contain toxic ingredients. If these are not properly recycled, they could contaminate landfill sites. ~~My friend is in the market for a car, and we are going to test-drive a few on the weekend. He is considering both new and used cars.~~ So think carefully about environmental concerns before buying your next car.

Revising for Adequate Support

An arch is built using several well-placed stones. Like an arch, an essay requires **adequate support** to help it stand on its own.

When revising an essay for adequate support, consider the following:

- Ensure that your thesis statement is broad enough to develop several supporting points. It may be necessary to revise the thesis statement to meet the length requirements of the essay.
- When you write the body paragraphs of the essay, insert specific details and try to include vivid descriptions, anecdotes, examples, facts, or quotations.

ESL Teaching Tip: In many cultures, people use circular reasoning because they believe that stating a point directly is rude or aggressive. Explain to the class that it is important to express a point upfront and to support it with clear evidence.

Avoid Circular Reasoning

Circular reasoning means that a paragraph restates its main point in various ways but does not provide supporting details. Like driving aimlessly around and around a traffic circle, the main idea never seems to progress. Avoid using circular reasoning by directing your paragraph with a clear, concise topic sentence and by supporting the topic sentence with facts, examples, statistics, or anecdotes.

Paragraph with Circular Reasoning

The following paragraph contains circular reasoning. The main point is repeated over and over. The writer does not provide any evidence to support the topic sentence.

> Traveling is a necessary educational tool. Students can learn a lot by visiting other countries. Many schools offer educational trips to other places for their students. Students may benefit from such cultural introductions. Clearly, traveling offers students an important educational opportunity.

This writer leads the reader in circles.

In the second version of this paragraph, the paragraph contains specific examples that help to illustrate the main point.

Revised Paragraph

Anecdotes and examples provide supporting evidence. ➢

Traveling is a necessary educational tool. Students can learn a lot by visiting other places. Many schools and colleges offer educational trips. On such trips, students visit museums, art galleries, and historical sites. For example, the art department of our college sponsored a trip to Washington, D.C., and the students visited the Smithsonian. Other travel programs are work programs. Students may travel to another region or country to be involved in a community project. Students in the local high school, for example, helped build a community center for children in a small town in Nicaragua. The students who participated in this project all said that they learned some very practical lessons, including organizational and construction skills. Clearly, traveling offers students an important educational opportunity.

PRACTICE 3 Read the following paragraphs and write OK next to the ones that have adequate support. Underline the specific details in those paragraphs. Then, to the paragraphs that lack adequate support, add details such as descriptions, examples, quotations, or anecdotes. Use arrows to indicate where you should place specific details. Answers will vary.

The next example is from an essay. In the first paragraph, the writer was repetitive and vague. After the writer added specific examples and vivid details, the paragraph was much more interesting.

Weak Support

To become a better dresser, follow the next steps. First, ask friends or family members what colors suit you. Also, don't be a slave to the latest fashion. Finally, spend money on a few good items rather than filling your closet with cheap outfits. My closet is half-full, but the clothing I have is of good quality.

Better Support with Details

To become a better dresser, follow the next steps. First, ask friends or family members what colors suit you. *I love green, for instance, but when I wore an olive green shirt, a close friend said it brought out the green in my skin and made me look ill.* Also, don't be a slave to the latest fashion. *Although tank tops and low-waist jeans were popular for several years, I didn't have the right body type for that fashion because my belly spilled over the tops of my jeans. Instead, I wore longer shirts with my jeans, so I looked stylish but not ridiculous.* Finally, spend money on a few good items rather than filling your closet with cheap outfits. My closet is half-full, but the clothing I have is of good quality.

1. **Many cyclists are inconsiderate.** Some think that they don't have to obey traffic rules and that traffic signs are just for car drivers. Also, some cyclists are pretty crazy and do dangerous things and risk their lives or the lives of others. People have ended up in the hospital after a run-in with these two-wheeled rebels. Cyclists should take safety courses before they ride on public roads.

   Write OK or add details

   Cyclists don't stop at stop signs. Last week I saw a rider just miss a head-on collision with a car because she was cycling the wrong way on a one-way street.

   They weave in and out of slow or stopped traffic. Half a dozen times I have been nearly run off the sidewalk by frantic bicycle couriers late for their deliveries.

2. **During my first job interview, I managed to overcome my fright.** I sat in a small, brightly lit room in front of four interviewers. A stern woman stared at me intently and curtly asked me why I wanted the job. Perspiration dripped into my eyes as I stammered that I had seen an advertisement. She smirked and asked me to be more specific. Feeling that I didn't have a chance anyway, I relaxed and stopped worrying about the faces gazing at me. I spoke about my first experience in a hospital, and I described the nurses who took care of me and the respectful way the orderlies treated me. I expressed my heartfelt desire to work as an orderly, and I got the job.

   Write OK or add details

   OK

3. **Hollywood producers should stop making movies based on old television shows.** Many of the original series were on television in the 1960s or 1970s, and younger audiences cannot relate to movies based on those television shows. Even when those programs were first on the air, they were mediocre. The remakes are boring for young people even when studios hire stellar actors and spend fortunes on special effects. Then the studio bosses are surprised when the remakes are not successful. Hollywood studios should realize that the public doesn't want any more remakes of old television shows.

   Write OK or add details

   Starsky and Hutch, The Dukes of Hazzard, and Charlie's Angels were dull shows in their original versions.

   The expense of hiring Will Ferrell and Nicole Kidman did not help Bewitched at the box office.

Revising for Coherence

Make your writing as smooth as possible by using expressions that logically guide the reader from one idea to the next. When revising an essay for **coherence**, consider the following:

- Ensure that sentences within each body paragraph flow smoothly by using transitional expressions.
- Ensure the supporting ideas of an essay are connected to each other and to the thesis statement by using paragraph links.

Transitional Expressions

Just as stepping stones can help you cross from one side of the water to the other, **transitional expressions** can help readers cross from idea to idea in an essay.

Here are some common transitional expressions.

Function	Transitional Word or Expression
Addition	again, also, besides, finally, first (second, third), for one thing, furthermore, in addition, in fact, last, moreover, next, then
Comparison and contrast	as well, equally, even so, however, in contrast, instead, likewise, nevertheless, on the contrary, on the other hand, similarly
Concession of a point	certainly, even so, indeed, of course, no doubt, to be sure
Effect or result	accordingly, as a result, consequently, hence, otherwise, then, therefore, thus
Emphasis	above all, clearly, first, especially, in fact, in particular, indeed, least of all, most important, most of all, of course, particularly, principally
Example	for example, for instance, in other words, in particular, namely, specifically, to illustrate
Reason or purpose	because, for this purpose, for this reason, the most important reason
Space	above, behind, below, beneath, beside, beyond, closer in, farther out, inside, near, nearby, on one side/the other side, on the bottom, on the left/right, on top, outside, to the north/east/south/west, under
Summary or conclusion	in conclusion, in other words, in short, generally, on the whole, therefore, thus, to conclude, to summarize, ultimately
Time	after that, at that time, at the moment, currently, earlier, eventually, first (second, etc.), gradually, immediately, in the beginning, in the future, in the past, later, meanwhile, months after, now, one day, presently, so far, subsequently, suddenly, then, these days

Teaching Tip:
Remind students that transitional expressions are followed by a comma. If they are placed between two independent clauses, then they are preceded by a semicolon. Read the following examples:

Therefore, fast-food chains should list product ingredients.

I love eating fast food; however, I haven't gone to a fast-food restaurant in months.

Hint **Use Transitional Expressions with Complete Sentences**

When you add a transitional expression to a sentence, ensure that your sentence is complete. Your sentence must have a subject and a verb, and it must express a complete thought.

Incomplete: For example, violence on television.

Complete: For example, violence on television is very graphic.

ESL Teaching Tip:

Group Work

Ask nonnative speakers to underline transitions they do not understand. Then, in groups with native speakers, students can discuss those terms. Those who understand a term can teach the others by using that term in a sentence.

Adding Transitional Words Within a Paragraph

The next paragraph shows transitional words linking sentences within a paragraph.

> Learning a new language provides invaluable benefits to a person's life. **First**, researchers have found that learning a foreign language is a kind of exercise for the brain. It improves the area in the brain that processes information. Such people display better problem-solving abilities. **Furthermore**, people who know a second language can communicate with more people. **Therefore**, they can use this skill to acquire greater understanding of different cultures. **For example**, knowing a foreign language may give them more personal satisfaction when they are traveling because it allows them more opportunities to communicate with other people. **In addition**, bilingual people are more competitive in the job market. Because they know another language, they may be more mobile in their careers. They may **also** be able to take advantage of more job opportunities. In their spare time, people should learn a second language. They won't regret it.

GRAMMAR LINK

For more practice using transitions in sentences, see Chapter 17, Compound Sentences, and Chapter 18, Complex Sentences.

PRACTICE 4 Add appropriate transitional expressions to the following paragraph. Choose from the following list, and use each transitional word once. There may be more than one correct answer. Answers will vary.

in addition	therefore	in fact	for instance
first	then	for example	moreover

Counterculture is a pattern of beliefs and actions that oppose the cultural norms of a society. ____First,____ hippies are the best-known counterculture group in the recent past, and they are known for rebelling against authority. ____For instance,____ they rejected the consumer-based capitalist society of their parents in favor of communal living arrangements.

___Moreover,___ the hippie generation valued peace and created a massive antiwar movement. ___In fact,___ there were mass protests against the Vietnam War. ___Also,___ small religious groups belong to the countercultural current. These groups live with other like-minded people and turn away from widely accepted ideas on lifestyle. ___For example,___ the Amish are pacifists, and they reject modern technology. ___In addition,___ militant groups and anarchist groups reject conventional laws. Some of these groups want to eliminate legal, political, and social institutions. Countercultural social patterns will always remain part of the mainstream society.

PRACTICE 5 The next paragraph lacks transitional expressions. Add appropriate transitional expressions wherever you think they are necessary. Answers will vary.

People in our culture tend to idolize notorious gangsters. First, Al Capone operated during Prohibition, selling alcohol and building a criminal empire. He became infamous and his name is instantly recognizable. Then, The Gotti family's patriarch was the head of a large and vicious crime family in New Jersey. The family members are celebrities and one of the daughters, Victoria Gotti, had her own reality television show. Moreover, Filmmakers contribute to the idealization of criminals. For example, Movies such as *The Godfather* and *Live Free or Die Trying* celebrate gangsters and criminals. Gangsters appear to have exciting and glamorous lives. It is unfortunate that our culture elevates criminals to heroic status.

Making Links in Essays

To achieve coherence in an essay, try the following methods to transition from one idea to the next.

1. **Repeat words or phrases from the thesis statement in the topic sentence of each body paragraph.** In this example, *giftedness* and *ambiguity* are repeated words.

Thesis Statement:	Although many schools offer a program for gifted children, there continues to be ambiguity concerning the definition of gifted.
Body Paragraph 1:	One ambiguity is choosing the criteria for assessing the gifted.
Body Paragraph 2:	Another ambiguity pertains to defining the fields or areas in which a person is gifted.

2. **Refer to the main idea in the previous paragraph, and link it to your current topic sentence.** In the topic sentence for the second body paragraph, the writer reminds the reader of the first point (*insomnia*) and then introduces the next point.

Thesis Statement:	Sleeping disorders cause severe disruption to many people's lives.
Body Paragraph 1:	Insomnia, a common sleep disorder, severely limits the sufferer's quality of life.
Body Paragraph 2:	The opposite condition of insomnia, narcolepsy also causes mayhem as the sufferer struggles to stay awake.

3. **Use a transitional word or phrase to lead the reader to your next idea.**

Body Paragraph 3:	Moreover, when sufferers go untreated for their sleep disorders, they pose risks to the people around them.

Teaching Tip: Students may overuse transitional words. Remind students to use transitions only when they think a reader might need further guidance to navigate from one idea to the next.

Revising for Style

When you revise for sentence **style**, you ensure that your essay has concise and appropriate language and sentence variety. You can ask yourself the following questions.

- Have I used a variety of sentence patterns? (To practice using sentence variety, see Chapter 22.)
- Are my sentences parallel in structure? (To practice revising for parallel structure, see Chapter 25.)
- Have I used exact language? (To learn about slang, wordiness, and overused expressions, see Chapter 33.)

Alicia's Revision

In Chapter 3, you read Alicia's essay plan about college dropouts. After writing her first draft, she revised her essay. Look at her revisions for unity, support, coherence, and style.

Add title. ➢ Dropping Out of College

I live in a small coastal town on the Atlantic. The town attracts tourists from all over the country. Because of its beautiful beach. My college roommate, Farrad, works as a cook at the local pizza stand. Last year, Farrad started working a few hours per week, but then because of his efficiency, his boss increased Farrad's hours. My roommate then joined a growing group of people. He became a college dropout. **Students may drop out of college because they lack financial support, experience an emotional crisis, or are unprepared.**

Thesis statement ➢

Add transition. ➢ *First*

~~S~~some students drop out because they face overwhelming financial burdens. Like Farrad, they may have a part-time job to help pay for tuition and rent. If the job requires students to work for many hours, they might not have time to study or to do homework.

Add detail. ➢ *According to an Indiana government Web site, Investment Watch, "Teenagers and young adults often find themselves in high debt with little knowledge of basic savings and budgeting concepts. About 40 percent of Americans spend 110 percent of their income."*

Nadia, for exemple, works in the computer lab four nights a week.

Add detail. ➢ *The number of hours is overwhelming and she may drop out of college.*

Clarify pronoun. ➢ *Some students*

~~They~~ also drop out because they live far from campus, and transportation may be too expensive or inconvenient.

events, and they

Furthermore, some students undergo life-changing events~~. They~~ must leave college. A college student may get married or a

Combine sentences. ➢

In an interview with CNN, Dr. William Pepicello, President of the University of Phoenix, stated that one reason that students drop out is "life gets in the way."

female student may become pregnant and taking care of a baby may consume all of her time and energy. ~~There are public and private daycare centers. But parents must choose very carefully.~~

Revise for unity. ➢

Add transition. ➢ *In addition, an*

~~An~~ illness in the family may cause a student to miss too many classes. A student may feel emotionaly fragile because of a broken relationship. The student may not be able to cope with their feelings and wanted to leave college.

adapt to
Moreover, some students may be unable to ~~get into~~ college life. Some have poor study skills and fall behind in homework assignments. Students may not be able to organize there time. Or a student might be unused to freedom in college and skip too many classes. For instance, my lab partner has missed about six classes this semester. *In addition, not* ~~Not~~ every student has clear career goals. *According to the National Academic Advising Association (NACADA) Web site, 75 percent of first-year students do not have clear career goals.* Those who are unsure about their academic futur may drop out rather than continue to study in a field they do not enjoy. *For instance, my cousin realized she did not want to be an engineer, so she left school until she could figure out what she really wanted to do.*

Even though students drop out of college for many good reasons, some decide to return to college life. *For example,* Farrad hopes to finish his studies next year. *He knows he would have to find a better balance between work and school to succeed, but he is motivated to complete his education.*

< Find better word.

< Add transition.

< Add detail.

< Add detail.

< Add transition.

< Improve conclusion.

Hint **Enhancing Your Essay**

When you revise, look at the strength of your supporting details. Ask yourself the following questions.

- Are my supporting details interesting and will they grab my reader's attention? Should I use more vivid vocabulary?
- Is my concluding sentence appealing? Could I end the paragraph in a more interesting way?

Editing for Errors

When you **edit**, you reread your writing and make sure that it is free of errors. You focus on the language, and you look for mistakes in grammar, punctuation, mechanics, and spelling.

There is an editing guide on the inside back cover of this book. It contains some common error codes that your instructor may use. It also provides you with a list of errors to check for when you proofread your text.

GRAMMAR LINK

To practice your editing skills, try the practices in Chapter 39.

Editing Tips

The following tips will help you to proofread your work more effectively.

- Put your text aside for a day or two before you do the editing. Sometimes, when you have been working closely with a text, you might not see the errors.
- Begin your proofreading at any stage of the writing process. For example, if you are not sure of the spelling of a word while writing the first draft, you could either highlight the word to remind yourself to verify it later, or you could immediately look up the word in the dictionary.
- Use the grammar and spelling checker that comes with your word processor. However, be vigilant when accepting the suggestions. Do not always choose the first suggestion for a correction. For example, a grammar checker cannot distinguish between when to use *which* and *that*. Make sure that suggestions are valid before you accept them.
- Keep a list of your common errors in a separate grammar log. When you finish a writing assignment, consult your error list and make sure that you have not repeated any of those errors. After you have received each corrected assignment from your instructor, you can add new errors to your list. For more information about a grammar and spelling log, see Appendix 5.

Teaching Tip: If your students are familiar with grammatical terms, you might ask them to identify the types of errors in the paragraph. (Types are: fragment, spelling, run-on, tense shift, pronoun shift, and punctuation.)

Alicia's Edited Essay

Alicia edited her essay about college dropouts. She corrected errors in spelling, punctuation, and grammar.

Dropping Out of College

I live in a small coastal town on the Atlantic. The town attracts tourists from all over the country~~. Because~~ *country because* of its beautiful beach. My college roommate, Farrad, works as a cook at the local pizza stand. Last year, Farrad started working a few hours per week, but then because of his efficiency, his boss increased Farrad's hours. My roommate then joined a growing group of people, and he became a college dropout. Students may drop out of college because they lack financial support, experience an emotional crisis, or are unprepared.

First, some students drop out because they face overwhelming financial burdens. Like Farrad, they may have a part-time job to help pay for tuition and rent. According to an Indiana government Web site, <u>Investment Watch</u>, "Teenagers and young adults often find themselves in high debt with little knowledge of basic savings and budgeting concepts. About 40 percent of Americans spend 110 percent of their income." If the job requires students to work for many hours, they might not have time to study or to do homework. Nadia, for ~~exemple~~ *example*, works in the computer lab four nights a week. The number of hours is overwhelming, and she may drop out of college. Some students also drop out because they live far from campus, and transportation may be too expensive or inconvenient.

Furthermore, some students undergo life-changing events, and they must leave college. In an interview with CNN, Dr. William Pepicello, President of the University of Phoenix, stated that one reason that students drop out is "life gets in the way." A college student may get married or a female student may become pregnant *, [add comma]* and taking care of a baby may consume all of her time and energy. In addition, an illness in the family may cause a student to miss too many classes. A student may also feel ~~emotionaly~~ *emotionally* fragile because of a broken relationship. The student may not be able to cope with ~~their~~ *his or her* feelings and ~~wanted~~ *want* to leave college.

Moreover, some students may be unable to adapt to college life. Some have poor study skills and fall behind in homework assignments. Also, students may not be able to organize ~~there~~ *their* time. Or a student might not be used to freedom in college and skip too many classes. For instance, my lab partner has missed about six classes this semester. In addition, not every student has clear career goals. According to the National Academic Advising Association (NACADA) Web site, 75 percent of first-year students do not have clear career goals. Those who are unsure about their academic ~~futur~~ *future* may drop out rather than continue to study in a field they do not enjoy. For instance, my cousin realized she did not want to be an engineer, so she left school until she could figure out what she really wanted to do.

Even though students drop out of college for many good reasons, some decide to return to college life. Farrad, for example, hopes to finish his studies next year. He knows he ~~would~~ *will* have to find a better balance between work and school to succeed, but he is motivated to complete his education.

Writer's Desk Revise and Edit Your Paragraph

Choose an essay that you have written for Chapter 4, or choose one that you have written for another assignment. Carefully revise and edit the essay. You can refer to the Revising and Editing checklists on the inside covers.

Peer Feedback

After you write an essay, it is useful to get peer feedback. Ask a friend, family member, or fellow student to read your work and give you comments and suggestions on its strengths and weaknesses.

Hint **Offer Constructive Criticism**

When you peer edit someone else's writing, try to make your comments useful. Phrase your comments in a positive way. Look at the examples.

Instead of saying ...	You could say ...
You repeat the same words.	Maybe you could find synonyms for some words.
Your paragraphs are too short.	You could add more details here.

Teaching Tip:
Draw attention to this hint. Students should encourage each other by offering constructive criticism.

You can use this peer feedback form to evaluate written work.

Peer Feedback Form

Written by ______________________ Feedback by ______________________

Date: ______________________

1. What is the main point of the written work? ______________________

____

____

2. Which details effectively support the thesis statement? ______________________

____

____

3. What, if anything, is unclear or unnecessary? ______________________

____

____

4. Give some suggestions about how the work could be improved. ______________________

____

____

5. What is the most interesting or unique feature of this written work? ______________________

____

____

Writing the Final Draft

When you have finished making revisions on the first draft of your essay, write the final draft. Include all the changes that you have made during the revising and editing phases. Before you submit your final draft, proofread it one last time to ensure that you have caught any errors.

Writer's Desk Write Your Final Draft

You have developed, revised, and edited your essay. Now write the final draft.

Hint Spelling, Grammar, and Vocabulary Logs

- **Keep a Spelling and Grammar Log.** You probably repeat, over and over, the same types of grammar and spelling errors. You will find it very useful to record your repeated grammar mistakes in a Spelling and Grammar Log. You can refer to your list of spelling and grammar mistakes when you revise and edit your writing.
- **Keep a Vocabulary Log.** Expanding your vocabulary will be of enormous benefit to you as a writer. In a Vocabulary Log, you can make a list of unfamiliar words and their definitions.

See Appendix 5 for more information about spelling, grammar, and vocabulary logs.

The Writer's Room Essay Topics

Writing Activity 1

Choose an essay that you have written for this course or for another course. Revise and edit that essay, and then write a final draft.

Writing Activity 2

Choose any of the following topics, or choose your own topic, and then write an essay. Remember to follow the writing process.

General Topics

1. online shopping
2. heroes in sports
3. a problem in politics
4. unfair gender roles
5. making the world better

College and Work-Related Topics

6. something you learned in college
7. bad work habits
8. reasons to accept a job
9. unpleasant jobs
10. a funny co-worker

Teaching Tip:
To verify that students understand the essay-writing process, you can suggest that they write an essay explaining the essay-writing process.

CHECKLIST: REVISING AND EDITING

When you revise and edit your essay, ask yourself the following questions.

- Does my essay have **unity**? Ensure that every paragraph relates to the main idea.
- Does my essay have **adequate support**? Verify that there are enough details and examples to support your main point.
- Is my essay **coherent**? Try to use transitional expressions to link ideas.
- Does my essay have good **style**? Check for varied sentence patterns and exact language.
- Does my essay have any errors? **Edit** for errors in grammar, punctuation, spelling, and mechanics.
- Is my **final draft** error-free?

How Do I Get a Better Grade?

PEARSON mywritinglab

Visit www.mywritinglab.com for audio-visual lectures and additional practice sets about revising and editing. ***Get a better grade with MyWritingLab!***

PART II

Essay Patterns

What Is an Essay Pattern?

A pattern or mode is a method used to express one of the three purposes: to inform, to persuade, or to entertain. Once you know your purpose, you will be able to choose which writing pattern to use.

Patterns may overlap. You can combine writing patterns. You may use one predominant pattern, but you can also introduce other patterns as supporting material.

Illustration
to illustrate or prove a point using specific examples

Narration
to narrate or tell a story about a sequence of events that happened

Process
to inform the reader about how to do something, how something works, or how something happened

Description
to describe using vivid details and images that appeal to the reader's senses

Definition
to explain what a term or concept means by providing relevant examples

Classification
to classify or sort a topic to help readers understand different qualities about that topic

Comparison and Contrast
to present information about similarities (compare) or differences (contrast)

Cause and Effect
to explain why an event happened (the cause) or what the consequences of the event were (the effects)

Argument*
to argue or to take a position on an issue and offer reasons for your position

*Argument is included as one of the nine patterns, but it is also a purpose in writing.

Illustration

CHAPTER 6

CONTENTS

If vendors simply advertised "great" or "new and improved" products, but did not show examples to support their claims, they would not sell very much at all. In the same way, writers have a better chance of informing, entertaining, or persuading readers when they illustrate their ideas using examples.

Writers' Exchange

Work with a partner. You have three minutes to list as many words as you can that are examples of the following. For example, bungee jumping is a dangerous sport.

dangerous sports   bad fashion fads   sticky food

Teaching Tip:
The Writers' Exchange activity can help your students understand illustration. List some of the students' ideas on the board.

> *"Sports serve society by providing vivid examples of excellence."*
>
> GEORGE F. WILL, *editor and columnist*

Teaching Tip: Ask students to think of types of writing that include examples such as advertisements, rental leases, brochures, real estate ads, and instruction manuals.

EXPLORING

What Is Illustration?

Illustration writing includes specific examples that help readers acquire a clearer, deeper understanding of an essay's subject. You illustrate or give examples each time you explain, analyze, narrate, or express an opinion. Examples might include something that you have experienced or observed, or they may include factual information, such as a statistic.

Here are some examples people give every day to explain or clarify what they mean.

Audience: Family or roommates

The house is becoming a pigsty.

- There are piles of shoes and boots in the entrance.
- Newspapers and letters are on the kitchen table.
- Dishes are piled in the sink.

Audience: Classmate

Our instructors give us too much homework.

- Our science lab is due tomorrow.
- We must submit a five-page research essay on Monday.
- We must study for our history exam, which is also on Monday.

Audience: Coworker

Financial cutbacks are hurting productivity.

- Each employee must do the work of several people.
- Jobs are not completed properly.
- Employees are stressed and suffering from burn-out.

The Illustration Essay

There are two effective ways to exemplify your main point and support your body paragraphs in an illustration essay.

1. Use a **series of examples**. When writing an essay about innovative commercials, you might list things that some directors do such as using bizarre camera angles, introducing hilarious scenarios, adding fun jingles, or creating catchy slogans.
2. Use an **extended example**, such as an anecdote or a description of an event. When writing about problems faced by first-year college students, you might tell a story about a specific student's chronic lateness.

Illustration at Work

Portland Bolt and Manufacturing Company requires a large sales force. In the following excerpt from a job announcement on their Web site, there is a list of examples showing what a sales associate must do.

Sales Associate Duties

- Estimating the costs associated with manufacturing bolts.
- Assigning appropriate profit margins to estimates.
- Selling bolts and fasteners primarily via the telephone to an established customer base made up of contractors, steel fabricators, and other construction-related companies.
- Tracking and following up a small quantity of specific construction projects.
- Making sales order entries.
- Doing a limited amount of prospecting.
- (Optional) Limited selling in both the local and regional marketplace.

A Student Essay

Read the student essay and answer the questions that follow.

Priceless Euphoria

by Lisa Monique

1 The Beatles recorded a song satirically titled *Money*, in which they sing, "The best things in life are free." Undoubtedly, the best things in life *are* free. Although costs might be associated, these "things" are not purchased items. The best things are a common thread among all people regardless of sex, race, religion, or nationality. In fact, the best things in life are not things but are precious segments in time involving and engaging us in experiences, emotions, and various states of being.

2 Nature provides us with many priceless treasures of breathtaking scenery. We might view a cascading waterfall, a brilliant sunset casting a serene, pink glow on the mountain jags and peaks, or the glistening beauty of a fresh, undisturbed snowfall. Each location we visit stimulates the senses. A day at the beach allows us to listen to crashing waves, watch a school of dolphins play, splash in the shallow water, or bury our feet in the gushy, wet sand. The desert is also a smorgasbord of sensations.

Marvels include the mighty Saguaro cacti, the ethereal haze of the Palo Verde trees, and the grace and gentleness of a passing butterfly.

3 Emotional experiences, as well, are often the best "things" in life. Falling in love, viewing the birth of a child, having the first kiss, laughing and conversing with an old friend, and watching the klutzy steps of a puppy are some simple delights in life. Emotional experiences can occur with loved ones, but they can also be kindled in natural environments. A day at the beach is renewing and refreshing. Hiking and observing the desert help us to feel wild, free, and reckless. The purity of a fresh snowfall makes us feel childlike and innocent.

4 Similarly, states of being bring great satisfaction, which is, yet again, a great thing. Good health after a prolonged illness or even after a short bout of the flu is a greatly appreciated state of being. Invaluable gratification is derived from meeting a deadline, winning a race, nurturing a garden, sculpting a creation, giving a gift, receiving a gift, dispensing good advice, accepting good advice, planning a successful event, helping someone in need, and achieving a well-earned goal.

5 Money does directly buy cars, jewelry, furs, vacations, large homes, designer clothing, or French perfume. Purchases are not the best "things" in life. It is true that crayons and paper are purchased, but coloring is free. Writing, dancing, laughing, loving, and learning are all beneficial activities with peripheral costs. The value is found in each experience. Consequently, "the best things in life are free" is not just a simple song lyric, but also a rather complex and admirable human philosophy.

Teaching Tip:
The Writer's Desk activities, the first of which appears on the next page, provides students with an opportunity to develop a topic through all stages of the writing process using the illustration rhetorical mode. In the Warm Up, they begin by exploring various topics and examples for illustration. Those topics then carry on throughout the chapter.

PRACTICE 1

1. Who is the intended audience? *General audience*
2. Highlight the essay's thesis statement.
3. Highlight the topic sentence in each body paragraph.
4. In the body paragraphs 2, 3, and 4, what does the writer use?
   (a.) series of examples b. extended examples
5. In paragraph 4, what does the writer mean by *states of being*? Using your own words, explain her point.

   She means having good health or doing activities that make a person feel satisfied.
6. What organizational strategy does the writer use?
   a. time order b. space order (c.) emphatic order

7. Add one more example to each body paragraph. Answers will vary.

nature ______________________________

____

emotional experiences ______________________________

____

states of being ______________________________

____

Explore Topics

In the Writer's Desk Warm Up, you will try an exploring strategy to generate ideas about different topics.

Writer's Desk Warm Up

Read the following questions, and write the first ideas that come to your mind. Think of two to three ideas for each topic.

EXAMPLE: What can go wrong when you rent an apartment?

—hard to find a landlord who will rent to a student

—can't find a good apartment in a decent area on a student budget

—roommate problems

1. What are some things you would like to accomplish in the near future?

____

____

2. What are some professions that make useful or worthwhile contributions to society?

____

____

3. What are some status symbols in today's society?

____

____

DEVELOPING

The Thesis Statement

The thesis statement of the illustration essay is a general statement that expresses both your topic and your controlling idea. To determine your controlling idea, think about what point you want to make. Remember to express an attitude or point of view about the topic.

topic — controlling idea

Newlyweds often have misconceptions about married life.

controlling idea — topic

I am unable to control **the mess in my work space.**

Writer's Desk Write Thesis Statements

Write a thesis statement for each of the following topics. You can look for ideas in the Warm Up on page 85. Each thesis statement should express your topic and controlling idea. Answers will vary.

EXAMPLE:

Topic: apartment rental problems

Thesis Statement: *Students who want to rent an apartment may end up frustrated and disappointed.*

1. Topic: future accomplishments

   Thesis Statement: ______________________________

2. Topic: valuable professions

   Thesis Statement: ______________________________

3. Topic: status symbols in our society

   Thesis Statement: ______________________________

The Supporting Ideas

After you have developed an effective thesis statement, generate supporting ideas.

- Use prewriting strategies to generate a list of examples. Brainstorm a series of examples and extended examples that will best illustrate your main point.
- Choose the best ideas. Use either a series of examples or extended examples.
- Organize your ideas. Choose the best organizational method for this essay pattern.

Teaching Tip:
For extra practice, ask students to develop supporting ideas for all three Writer's Desk topics. The topics are listed in the previous Writer's Desk.

Writer's Desk Generate Supporting Ideas

Choose one of your thesis statements from the previous Writer's Desk. List three or four examples that support the thesis statement.

EXAMPLE:

Thesis Statement: *Students who want to rent an apartment may end up frustrated and disappointed.*

Supports: *—can't find an affordable place*

—landlords might be hesitant to rent to them

—roommates may be immature

—not enough housing for students

—only available housing is in dangerous neighborhood

Thesis Statement: ______________________________

____

Supports: ______________________________

____

____

____

The Essay Plan

When writing an outline for an illustration essay, ensure that your examples are valid and relate to the thesis statement. Also, include details that will help clarify your supporting examples and organize your ideas in a logical order.

Teaching Tip:
Ask students to generate specific details that could flesh out the first draft of the sample essay. For example, under II A, "They have limited choices," details could be *The student housing on Maple Street has only fifty units.*

Teaching Tip:
Ask students to keep their essay plans and attach them to the final draft. You can then determine how the students have developed their ideas.

ESL Teaching Tip:
Encourage students from other countries to discuss culture-specific status symbols. Ask them to share thesis statements and ensure that the statement expresses a point and an attitude or point of view. For instance, you could ask them to compare the following two thesis statements. Discuss how the second statement is more specific and expresses a point of view.

There are many status symbols in our culture.

In the business world, status symbols are very superficial.

THESIS STATEMENT: Students who want to rent an apartment may end up frustrated and disappointed.

I. Landlords often hesitate to rent to students.
  A. Young people might be irresponsible.
  B. They don't have credit ratings.
II. Students have money problems.
  A. They have limited choices.
  B. They cannot apply for nicer apartments because many are too expensive.
  C. They must settle for dives and dumps.
III. Sharing a place with another student can end badly.
  A. The roommate might be very messy.
  B. The roommate might be a party guy or girl.
  C. There could be financial disputes over unpaid rent and bills.
IV. Some students choose to rent alone but have other problems.
  A. They may feel lonely.
  B. Girls living alone may feel unsafe.
  C. They may be unable to pay all of the bills.

Writer's Desk Write an Essay Plan

Refer to the information you generated in previous Writer's Desks, and prepare a detailed essay plan. Consider the order in which you list details.

The First Draft

After outlining your ideas in a plan, write the first draft using complete sentences. Also, include transitional words or expressions to help your ideas flow smoothly. Here are some transitional expressions that can help you introduce an example or show an additional example.

To introduce an example		To show an additional example	
for example	namely	also	in addition
for instance	specifically	first (second)	in another case
in other words	to illustrate	furthermore	moreover

vo•cab•u•lar•y BOOST

Here are some ways to vary sentences, which will help you avoid boring readers with repeated phrases.

1. Underline the opening word of every sentence in your first draft. Check to see if some words are repeated.
2. If you notice every sentence begins the same way, try introducing the sentence with an adverb, such as *usually, generally,* or *luckily,* or a prepositional phrase such as *With his help* or *Under the circumstances*. In the following example, *They* is repeated too many times.

Repeated first words

People make many mistakes with their finances. They want luxuries that they cannot afford. They buy items on credit. They do not consider the high interest rates that credit card companies charge.

Variety

People make many mistakes with their finances. Desiring luxuries that they cannot afford, consumers buy items on credit. Sadly, many do not consider the high interest rates that credit card companies charge.

Writer's Desk Write the First Draft

In the previous Writer's Desk, you developed an essay plan. Now write the first draft of your illustration essay. Remember to include details such as specific names, places, facts, or statistics to flesh out each body paragraph.

REVISING AND EDITING

Revise and Edit an Illustration Essay

When you finish writing an illustration essay, review your work and revise it to make the examples as clear as possible to your readers. Ensure that the order of ideas is logical, and remove any irrelevant details. Before you work on your own essay, practice revising and editing a student essay.

Teaching Tip: The activity of revising and editing a student essay should help your students understand the important link between the writing process and the grammar chapters.

A Student Essay

Read the essay, and then answer the questions that follow. As you read, correct any errors that you find, and make comments in the margins.

Finding an Apartment

by Shannon Nolan

1 Renting an apartment for the first time is one of the defining rites of passage that marks the transition from adolescence to young adulthood. Many young people have a dream of what their first apartment will be like, whether it is the boho chic flat in a trendy neighborhood, the immaculate penthouse in the heart of downtown, or the ultimate party pad with a gang of best friends for roommates. Unfortunately, it is often harder to find that perfect apartment than it is to daydream about it. Students who want to rent an apartment may end up frustrated and disappointed.

2 Finding an apartment—any apartment—can be hard enough. Landlords are often hesitant to rent to students for the very reasons students want an apartment. Young renters do not have credit ratings with banks, and they haven't proved that they're capable of handling responsability. They throw parties, make noise, and never stay in one place very long. Landlords usually require a reference from a former landlord and a security deposit, if not the co-signature of a parent or relative. ~~However, landlords are far from the sainted beings their high standards might indicate. The ones who don't ask for references are usually equally lax about fixing blocked drains or leaking ceilings, and the ones who do demand references aren't necessarily any better.~~

3 Money is another common issue when renting a place. A student budget in most cases is fairly limited. Rent, bills, and tuition must be paid, on a part-time salary at best. The cost of renting an apartment larger than a refrigerator box is usually too much for one person alone. Often after one weekend of apartment hunting, the dream of the perfect apartment goes up in smoke. The place advertised as a "spacious studio" turns out to be a sort of basement mausoleum with grime-covered slats for windows, more appropriate as the setting for a horror movie than a romantic year of independence. "One bedroom" means "walk-in closet." A trend emerges—if the price is right, everything else is wrong.

4 To reduce expenses, many people opt to share a place, but the joys of shared housekeeping can turn overnight into a disaster. Students quickly wonder why did they want a roommate in the first place. A certain amount of messiness can be expected from first-time renters, but some people take this to an extreme. No one wants to end up rooming with the guy who starts a biology lab in the kitchen—studying the growth patterns of breakfast cereal mold (especially when he is a sociology major). Similarly, students who are serious about their studies do not want to live with a party-guy or -girl who is out all night, every night, and who seems to come home only for about five minutes at a time to puke in the sink.

5 Some students, unhappy with their experiences sharing a closet-sized bedroom in a dorm decide to rent a bachelor or studio apartment, prefering to pay a little more in exchange for peace of mind. Sandra, a second-year student, took this route and found that a whole new problem confronted her. "I couldn't believe how lonely I was the first few months," she said. "Even though I hated my roommate, I actually missed her. I spent so much time studying in coffee shops that I might as well have stayed in res." Besides loneliness, safety is another problem for those living alone. Many students, especially girls, are worried about the risks of walking home alone.

6 The first year or so of independence can be a vulnerable time, and not just emotionally. Finding apartments is tough, and renting can be expensive. Sharing can be a solution—unless roommates become a nightmare. Then there is the dangers of being lonely and depressed or of having something bad happen with no one there to offer support. It might seem like the pitfalls of apartment renting outweigh the benefits. But the first step into true independence has its rewards as well, and after all, it's a step everyone must take.

PRACTICE 2

Revising

1. Highlight the thesis statement.
2. Highlight the topic sentence in paragraphs 2 and 4.
3. In paragraph 2, the writer veers off course. Cross out the sentences that do not support the topic sentence.
4. Paragraph 3 is missing a topic sentence. Which sentence best sums up the main point of paragraph 3?
   a. Many apartments are small and ugly.
   b. Landlords do not rent to students easily.
   c. Because students have limited budgets, they must settle for small, run-down apartments.
   d. Apartments are often not as nice as they are described in the advertisements.
5. Paragraph 5 is also missing a topic sentence. Which sentence best sums up the main point of paragraph 5?
   a. Furthermore, students who can afford to live alone might have problems.
   b. There are safety issues when renting an apartment.
   c. Sandra had her own studio apartment.
   d. Sometimes students who live alone feel lonely.
6. Which paragraph contains an extended example? 5

GRAMMAR LINK

See the following chapters for more information about these grammar topics:
Embedded Questions, Chapter 22
Commas, Chapter 35
Spelling, Chapter 34
Subject–Verb Agreement, Chapter 27

Editing

7. Paragraph 4 contains an embedded question error. (For information about embedded questions, see the Grammar Hint following this practice.) Underline and correct the error.

   Correction: *Students quickly wonder why they wanted a roommate in the first place.*

8. Paragraph 5 contains a comma error. Underline and correct the error.

   Correction: *bedroom in a dorm, decide*

9. This essay contains misspelled words in paragraphs 2 and 5. Underline and correct them.

   corrections *responsibility* *preferring*

10. Underline and correct a subject–verb agreement error in paragraph 6.

    Correction: *There are the dangers*

Grammar Hint **Writing Embedded Questions**

When a question is part of a larger sentence, do not use the question word order. View the next examples.

Error: I wondered how would I pay the rent.
Correction: I wondered how I would pay the rent.

See Chapter 22 for more information about writing embedded questions.

Writer's Desk Revise and Edit Your Essay

Revise and edit the essay that you wrote for the previous Writer's Desk. You can refer to the revising and editing checklists at the end of this chapter and on the book's inside covers.

A Professional Essay

Eric Gall is a freelance writer based in Toronto. His articles have appeared in *The National Post*, *The Queen's Journal*, and various other publications. In the next essay, he examines the power of intrusive technology.

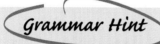

Little Brother Is Watching

by Eric Gall

1 In late 2006, Michael Richards, Seinfeld's shock-haired neighbor Kramer, found out the hard way that messing up in public is now a whole lot messier. Thanks to the cell phone video camera and the Internet's latest **killer app**—YouTube.com—Richards' racist meltdown at a heckler during a standup routine in L.A. was viewed by millions. As Richards discovered, Little Brother is watching, again and again, and he is emailing the link to all his friends.

2 Back in 2005, when Chad Hurley, Steve Chen, and Jawed Karim founded YouTube, they thought they were building a place where ordinary people could share their favorite camcorder movies, TV moments and, yes, cell phone clips. And share they did. One would have to have been living on one of the more desolate craters on Pluto not to have seen the Backstreet Boys' "I Want It That Way" as lip-synched by two Chinese pranksters. Arguably the site's tipping point, their dorm-made video spawned a million imitations and clicked YouTube to the top of every browser bookmark list.

3 What Chad, Steve, and Jawed couldn't have predicted was that they were bringing George Orwell's dystopic *1984* to life in a way no one saw coming. While Orwell's protagonist, Winston Smith, lived a miserable existence, at least he knew he was being watched as he carried out life's mundane tasks. It was not the same case with University of Missouri quarterback Chase Daniel, whose moment of fame came during a game on November 4, 2006. He didn't anticipate being filmed as he sat on the bench performing his own digital download—from nose to mouth—and having his little picnic uploaded onto the World Wide Web. Students worldwide have also happily uploaded cell phone videos of teachers "losing it" in class—some actually hitting their students. Many of these educators, it is alleged, were pushed to the brink by their pupils for the very purpose of being **surreptitiously** filmed.

4 Beyond the facility to humiliate, there is a positive side to the power of YouTube. Two Los Angeles cops were caught on a cell phone camera "subduing" an alleged **perp** (another of the site's recent top hits). While their YouTube moment now has them slapping their own foreheads, it demonstrates that "the whole world is in fact watching." So what better way is there to blow the whistle than to use the powers of online video blogs, especially if you've tried and failed by every other means? That's what Michael DeKort, former Lockheed Martin engineer on the US Coastguard's "Deepwater" project, did when nobody would listen to his concerns about serious security flaws the company and the coastguard were determined to ignore. His ten-minute "kitchen confidential" shot on grainy home video finally caught

Teaching Tip: Like many essays, "Little Brother Is Watching" includes elements of other writing patterns such as cause and effect and comparison and contrast. If you are planning to show other modes, you might ask students to identify what the essay compares and contrasts. (The answer is the predictions in Orwell's *1984* and the current reality.) Students can also look for the positive and negative effects of online video. (Some positive effects include making people more conscientious of how they act in public. Some negative effects are the destroyed careers and humiliation of those caught in embarrassing videos.)

killer app: a very useful computer application or program

surreptitiously: secretly

perp: perpetrator

the eye of the navy, congress and, crucially, other Lockheed and coastguard personnel eager to corroborate his story—not to mention the media and two dozen lawyers eager to help him advance and defend his case.

5 Other "good" causes are also getting their fifteen minutes of infamy via the site. Take the Canadian-made Dove commercial that shows an ordinary woman being transformed through the magic of technology into an impossibly beautiful billboard model in just ninety seconds. Within hours of its arrival on the site, the ad was on its way to becoming a global phenomenon—selling soap and reinforcing the idea that images, especially digitally produced ones, can't be trusted.

6 Orwell's Big Brother and YouTube's Little Brother both have potent methods of exerting thought control over those who mess up in public. For his crimes against the Party, *1984*'s protagonist Winston Smith faced compulsory re-education (also known as torture and brainwashing) courtesy of the Thought Police. For Michael Richards, the L.A. police, and anyone else caught in an embarrassing scenario, there is "voluntary" cultural sensitivity training, along with anger management classes and public apologies, which ironically are also available on—you guessed it—YouTube.

7 But if we're smart, we won't wait until our "Kramer moment" is being endlessly replayed by sniggering surfers from Moose Jaw to Mogadishu. We'll just make sure we never do anything embarrassing, illegal, or stupid ever again. Right?

8 Yeah, sure. See you on YouTube.

Teaching Tip: Engage students in a discussion about the online video phenomenon. Also, if they ask, point out that the last sentence in paragraph 6 does not have a subject–verb agreement error. The "along with" phrase is not equivalent to an "and." They can find details about this rule in Chapter 27, Subject–Verb Agreement.

PRACTICE 3

1. Highlight the thesis statement.
2. Highlight the topic sentence in body paragraphs 4, 5, and 6.
3. Which of the following would make an effective topic sentence for paragraph 3?
   a. Chase Daniel was humiliated by an online video blog.
   b. There are many Internet sites that contain video blogs.
   c. Today, people are caught off guard when their embarrassing moments are uploaded and viewed by millions.
   d. The World Wide Web has images of teachers who have abused their students.
4. How many examples does Gall use to show the positive power of YouTube?
   a. one
   b. two
   c. three
   d. four

5. How is the "little brother is watching" phenomenon positive? Provide your own examples to show that it benefits society. Answers will vary.

Teaching Tip:

Pair Work

Ask students to work in pairs and develop other examples of how new technology has changed our lives. They could also brainstorm extra examples for the body paragraphs in "Little Brother Is Watching."

The Writer's Room Topics for Illustration Essays

Writing Activity 1

Write an illustration essay about one of the following topics, or choose your own topic.

General Topics

1. mistakes that parents make
2. annoying holidays
3. mistakes that newlyweds make
4. great or horrible films
5. bad habits

College and Work-Related Topics

6. things people should know about my college
7. examples of successful financial planning
8. qualities of an ineffective manager
9. mistakes students make
10. examples of obsolete jobs

READING LINK

More Illustration Readings

"Weird Weather" by Pamela D. Jacobsen (page 607)

"Songs of Insects" by Sy Montgomery (page 621)

WRITING LINK

More Illustration Writing Topics

Chapter 20, Writer's Room topic 1 (page 332)

Chapter 24, Writer's Room topic 1 (page 379)

Chapter 34, Writer's Room topic 1 (page 507)

Chapter 37, Writer's Room topic 1 (page 544)

Writing Activity 2

Choose a quotation you agree or disagree with, and then write an illustration essay based on it.

> If the only tool you have is a hammer, you tend to see every problem as a nail.
>
> Abraham Maslow, psychologist

> A photograph is a secret about a secret.
>
> Diane Arbus, photographer

The squeaky wheel gets the grease.

Proverb

Obstacles are those frightful things you see when you take your eyes off your goal.

Henry Ford, businessman

Writing Activity 3

Imagine that you must create an essay for a time capsule. In one hundred years, your descendants will read what you have written. How would you describe the world you are living in today? Give examples to show that our world has positive or negative points.

CHECKLIST: ILLUSTRATION ESSAY

After you write your illustration essay, review the essay checklist on the inside front cover. Also ask yourself the following questions.

- Does my thesis statement include a controlling idea that I can support with examples?
- Do I use a series of examples or an extended example in each body paragraph?
- Does each body paragraph support the thesis statement?
- Does each body paragraph focus on one idea?
- Do I have sufficient examples to support my thesis statement?
- Do I logically and smoothly connect paragraphs and supporting examples?

Teaching Tip:

Writer's World Competition

Please advise students that they can submit their essays for possible publication to: <thewritersworld@prenhall.com>.

How Do I Get a Better Grade?

Visit www.mywritinglab.com for audio-visual lectures and additional practice sets about illustration writing. ***Get a better grade with MyWritingLab!***

7 CHAPTER

Narration

CONTENTS

When investigating a story, a reporter must try to find answers to the questions who, what, when, where, why, *and* how. *You answer the same questions when you write a narrative essay.*

Teaching Tip: The Writers' Exchange activity can help your students understand narration. This activity helps students loosen up and start thinking of ideas. As an alternate activity, ask students to describe what happened during a recent newsworthy event.

Writers' Exchange

Try some nonstop talking. First, sit with a partner and come up with a television show or movie that you have both seen. Then, starting at the beginning, describe what happened in that episode or film. Remember that you must speak without stopping. If one of you stops talking, the other must jump in and continue describing the story.

EXPLORING

What Is Narration?

> *"Everyone is necessarily the hero of his or her own life story."*
> JOHN BARTH, *author*

Narrating is telling a story about what happened. You generally explain events in the order in which they occurred, and you include information about when they happened and who was involved in the incidents.

The next examples show how you might use narration in everyday situations.

Audience: Neighbor

The car accident was really my fault.

- When I left the house, I was late for work, so I was driving too fast.
- My cell phone, which was in my pocket, rang.
- As I reached into my pocket to get the phone out, I crashed into the stop sign.
- Luckily, I wasn't hurt, but my car needs major repairs.

Audience: Instructor

My homework isn't ready because of events beyond my control.

- My binder containing the instructions was in my basement when it flooded.
- I called a classmate to give me the instructions, but he gave me the incorrect information.
- I then tried to contact you, but you were not available during your office hours.

Audience: Clients

Our marketing campaign will work like a puzzle to pique the consumers' interest.

- The first billboard will not have any words—just a stunning photograph of the product with a question mark.
- Two weeks later, we will include variations of the brand name with the letters mixed up and a giant question mark.
- In four weeks, consumers will view the completed image with the brand name.

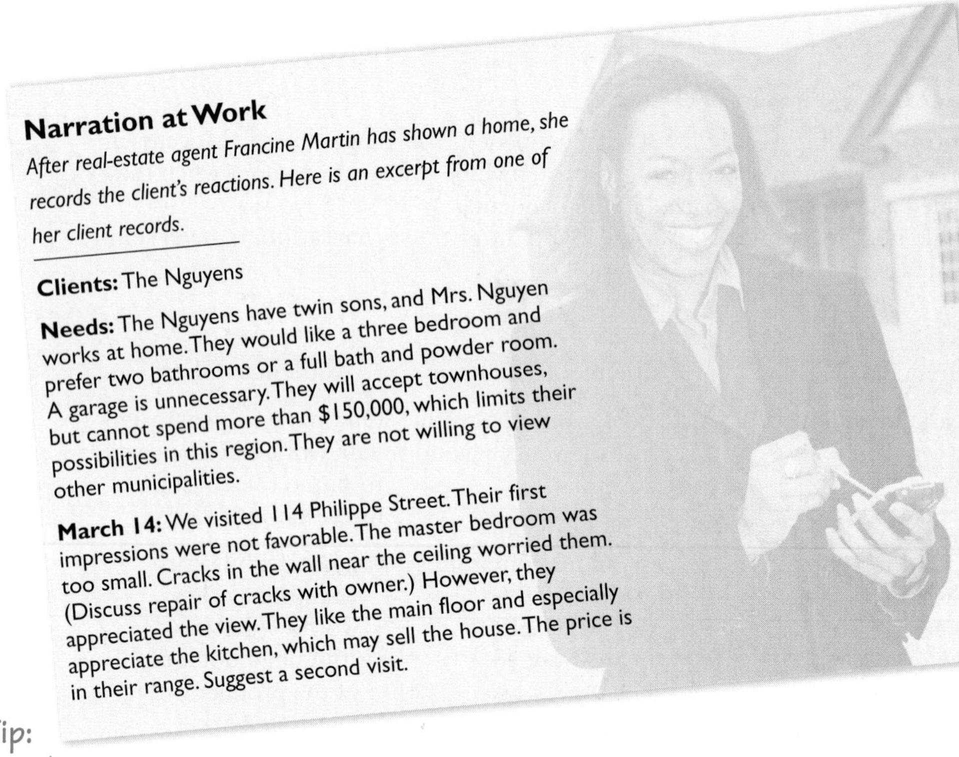

Narration at Work

After real-estate agent Francine Martin has shown a home, she records the client's reactions. Here is an excerpt from one of her client records.

Clients: The Nguyens

Needs: The Nguyens have twin sons, and Mrs. Nguyen works at home. They would like a three bedroom and prefer two bathrooms or a full bath and powder room. A garage is unnecessary. They will accept townhouses, but cannot spend more than $150,000, which limits their possibilities in this region. They are not willing to view other municipalities.

March 14: We visited 114 Philippe Street. Their first impressions were not favorable. The master bedroom was too small. Cracks in the wall near the ceiling worried them. (Discuss repair of cracks with owner.) However, they appreciated the view. They like the main floor and especially appreciate the kitchen, which may sell the house. The price is in their range. Suggest a second visit.

Teaching Tip:
Ask students to read the Narration at Work and answer *who, what, when, where, why*, and *how* questions about the text.

The Narrative Essay

When you write a narrative essay, consider your point of view.

Use **first-person narration** to describe a personal experience. To show that you are directly involved in the story, use *I* (first-person singular) or *we* (first-person plural). This is an example of first-person narration: "When I got on the tiny plane, I tried to calm myself. I strapped myself in beside the pilot. As the plane lurched down the runway, I screamed."

Use **third-person narration** to describe what happened to somebody else. Show that you are simply an observer or storyteller by using *he*, *she*, *it* (third-person singular), or *they* (third-person plural). This is an example of third-person narration: "Every morning, Joe cut out pieces of cardboard and placed them in his shoes. Then Joe buttoned up his only good shirt, and smoothed down his hair. He was going to look for a job, and he had to look his best."

Hint **Combining Essay Patterns**

Narration is not only useful on its own; it also enhances other types of writing. For example, student writer Omar Hakim had to write an essay about the effects of gambling. His essay was more compelling than it might otherwise have been because he included an anecdote about his uncle's gambling addiction.

A Student Essay

Read the essay and answer the questions that follow.

Teaching Tip: If your students have studied description, ask them to highlight examples of descriptive imagery in the student essay.

My Journey Down the Grand Canyon

by Andrew Wells

1 Twenty years old, on a break from studies, I decided to set out backpacking to see where it would take me. Having found myself in a youth hostel in Flagstaff, Arizona, I spontaneously decided to see the Grand Canyon. My plan was to hike right from the top of the canyon, down to the Colorado River, and then back up. What I didn't realize was that this sort of hiking is not a simple test of aerobic fitness or personal desire. No, it's a type of brutal self-destruction. The next two days hiking in the canyon left me dazed and depleted.

2 On the first day, I walked and hitchhiked the seventy-three miles from Flagstaff and descended five miles before nightfall. I set out the next morning toward the river, and my physical condition rapidly deteriorated. First, the soles of my boots gave out, partially tearing from the seams and flapping against the pads of my feet with every step I took. My blisters ached continuously. The straps from my backpack tore into my shoulder blades and pain ran down my spine. But the dull pounding of my boots against the rocky terrain drowned out my thoughts. My focus remained on the path in front of me. I knew that if I lost concentration, at any point I could trip and fall over the edge. At least the awe-inspiring surroundings made it easier to forget the pain.

3 In the canyon, my surroundings were ever changing. At one moment, I was following a winding dirt path under light tree cover, with deer roaming, birds chirping, and small mammals scurrying about. Then suddenly I was on a sandy ledge following a stream that cut between towering walls of red rock. I could see nothing but the three feet in front of me where the wall curved with the stream. Then when I turned a corner, the walls opened up into a majestic gorge one mile across; it was green, lush,

and lightly snow-covered. A little farther, as I looked down below me, I could trace the trail winding down the gorge and gradually disappearing.

4 Eventually I reached Phantom Ranch at the bottom of the canyon. It serves as a rest stop for die-hard hikers and is so popular that people have to reserve years ahead of time. At the ranch I encountered two types of people. There are retired couples who are passionate hikers and who wait a year and a half for reservations. Some that I met had scaled Mount Everest. And then there are those who work at the ranch. Most of them don't leave the canyon for months on end because the only way out is a grueling fifteen-mile trek or a rather expensive ride on the back of a mule. To further their isolation, the media is virtually nonexistent. The ranger has a radio, and there's one emergency telephone.

5 I spoke with the man working the canteen desk. He was a calm slow talker in his early thirties, tall and thin, with ear-length tangled hair and a dull, emotionless expression. While poking at a block of wood with a steel pick, he droned on and on about all the people he knew about who had died in the canyon. "Once, some parents let their three-year-old girl walk alone, and she just walked right off the edge. Another time a couple tried to hike in from the far west, ran out of water, and expired." He kept tapping the wood with his pick. "Then there was the guy who was knocked off the edge by one of the sheep." In my head, I begged for him to stop.

6 If a hiker is tired at the bottom of the canyon, he's in serious trouble. Trouble was what I came face-to-face with. Climbing back up, I encountered a big-horned sheep on a narrow ledge. It wanted to go where I was, and I wanted to go where it was, but there was no room to pass. For minutes on end the sheep and I engaged in a stare-down. Then all of a sudden, it got bored with me and climbed up an 85-degree sheer rock face! I was dumbfounded. It was so smart, and as soon as I passed, it climbed back down, turned, looked at me, and walked on. It understood perfectly what was going on.

7 After several hours of nonstop hiking, I had absolutely no drive left. The rock face kept getting steeper and the air significantly thinner. Each layer of the canyon above me was hidden behind the nearest sheet of towering sandstone. So when I thought I had gotten to the top, to my great dismay, a whole new area opened up above me. Then a woman in at least her late seventies plowed past me on her way uphill out of the canyon. She was no more than five feet tall, with short gray hair and a hunched back. I was honestly in pretty good hiking shape from all the heavy walking I had done. I passed just about everyone else, but this woman was unbelievable. (I was carrying a twenty-pound pack, though, so I call it a no-contest and want a rematch.)

8 At certain points, I felt like saying, "That's it. I'm living the rest of my life on this ledge. I'm not moving." And then I started making deals with myself, planning what I was going to do with my life once I got out, just to motivate myself to keep going. When I reached the top, I looked down into the bowels of the canyon and felt relieved that I had done it. It's something that does not need to be done more than once. I can retain the knowledge of what I have accomplished. I have come out believing that there's nothing that can stop me, and there's no greater feeling.

Teaching Tip: If your students have descended the Grand Canyon, they might have very different experiences from Andrew's. You can discuss how a narrative essay can be a very personal writing form.

PRACTICE 1

1. Highlight the thesis statement.
2. Highlight the topic sentence in paragraphs 2 and 3. Remember, the topic sentence is not necessarily the first sentence in the paragraph.
3. Using your own words, sum up what happened in each body paragraph. Begin with paragraph 4.

   Paragraph 4: *He met two types of people at Phantom Ranch: retired passionate hikers and the ranch workers.*

   Paragraph 5: *A strange fellow at the canteen desk described people who had died in the canyon.*

   Paragraph 6: *Climbing back up, a bighorn sheep blocked his path.*

   Paragraph 7: *During the last part of the journey, when he felt exhausted, an old woman rushed past him.*

4. In paragraph 5, Wells describes a man he met. Which images help you visualize the man?

   Possible answers: tangled hair, dull expression, poked at a block of wood, droned on

5. Why did the writer write about his experience? You will need to make a guess based on the information in the essay.

   He feels proud that he has accomplished such a difficult task.

Teaching Tip: The Writer's Desk activities, such as the one on the next page, provide students with an opportunity to develop a topic through all stages of the writing process using the narrative rhetorical mode. In the Warm Up, they begin by exploring various topics for narration. Those topics then carry on throughout the chapter.

Explore Topics

In the Writer's Desk Warm Up, you will try an exploring strategy to generate ideas about different topics.

Writer's Desk Warm Up

Read the following questions, and write the first ideas that come to your mind. Think of two to three ideas for each topic.

EXAMPLE: What difficult realizations have you made?

My choice to stay in college was hard. Leaving home was difficult. When I broke up with my girlfriend. What else? My friend told me that I interrupt others too much. When I let my brother take the blame for something I did, I realized that I have a dark side.

1. What are some disagreements or misunderstandings that you have had with someone you love?

____

____

____

2. What were some significant moments in your childhood?

____

____

____

3. Think about some stressful situations that brought out the best or worst in you. List some ideas.

____

____

____

DEVELOPING

The Thesis Statement

When you write a narrative essay, choose a topic that you personally find very interesting, and then share it with your readers. For example, very few people would be interested if you simply list what you did during your recent vacation. However, if you write about a particularly moving experience during your vacation, you could create an entertaining narrative essay.

Ensure that your narrative essay expresses a main point. Your thesis statement should have a controlling idea.

topic / controlling idea

The day I decided to get a new job, my life took a dramatic turn.

controlling idea / topic

Sadie's problems began **as soon as she drove her new car home.**

Hint **How to Make a Point**

In a narrative essay, the thesis statement should make a point. To help you find the controlling idea, you can ask yourself the following questions:

- What did I learn?
- How did I change?
- How did it make me feel?
- What is important about it?

For example:

Topic: *ran away from home*

Possible controlling idea: *learned the importance of family*

topic / controlling idea

When I ran away from home at the age of fifteen, I discovered the importance of my family.

PRACTICE 2 Practice writing thesis statements. Complete the following sentences by adding a controlling idea. Answers will vary.

1. During my sister's wedding, she realized ______________________________
____
2. Because my family is large, I know ______________________________
____
3. When I graduated, I discovered ______________________________
____

Writer's Desk Write Thesis Statements

Write a thesis statement for each of the following topics. You can look for ideas in the Warm Up on page 104. Each thesis statement should mention the topic and express a controlling idea.

EXAMPLE: Topic: A difficult realization

Thesis statement: *When I betrayed my brother, I made an unpleasant discovery about myself.*

1. Topic: A disagreement with a loved one

   Thesis statement: ______________________________

   ____

2. Topic: A significant moment in childhood

   Thesis statement: ______________________________

   ____

3. Topic: A stressful situation

   Thesis statement: ______________________________

   ____

The Supporting Ideas

A narrative essay should contain specific details so that the reader understands what happened. To come up with the details, ask yourself a series of questions and then answer them as you plan your essay.

- **Who** is the essay about?
- **What** happened?
- **When** did it happen?
- **Where** did it happen?
- **Why** did it happen?
- **How** did it happen?

When you orally recount a story to a friend, you may go back and add details, saying, "Oh, I forgot to mention something." However, you do not have this luxury when writing narrative essays. When you write, clearly organize the sequence of events so that your reader can follow your story easily.

Hint **Narrative Essay Tips**

Here are some tips to remember as you develop a narrative essay.

- Do not simply recount what happened. Try to indicate why the events are important.
- Organize the events in chronological order (the order in which they occurred). You could also reverse the order of events by beginning your essay with the outcome of the events, and then explaining what happened that led to the outcome.
- Use some descriptive language. For example, you could use images that appeal to the senses. For more information on using descriptive imagery, see page 120 in Chapter 8.

Writer's Desk **Develop Supporting Ideas**

Choose one of your thesis statements from the previous Writer's Desk on page 106. Then generate supporting ideas. List what happened.

EXAMPLE: A difficult realization	Topic: ______________________
—about four years old	______________________
—broke sister's glass ornaments	______________________
—blamed brother	______________________
—Mark was scolded	______________________
—didn't admit the truth, kept denying it	______________________
—felt extremely guilty	______________________

The Essay Plan

Before you write a narrative essay, make a detailed essay plan. Write down main events in the order in which they occurred. To make your narration more complete, include details about each event.

Teaching Tip: For extra practice, ask students to develop supporting ideas for all three Writer's Desk topics. The topics are listed in the previous Writer's Desk.

THESIS STATEMENT: When I betrayed my brother, I made an unpleasant discovery about myself.

I. I wanted to touch my sister's glass ornaments.
   A. I snuck into her room.
   B. I climbed her dresser.
   C. My brother watched me climb.

II. The dresser fell forward.
   A. I jumped off.
   B. A glass deer crashed to the floor and broke.
III. Our mother asked who did it, and I blamed my brother.
   A. My brother was scolded.
   B. He was confined to his bedroom.
   C. I heard him crying.
IV. I never admitted that I had done it.
   A. My brother was sad more than angry.
   B. I felt really guilty, but I still couldn't confess.
   C. I realized that my actions made me a liar and a coward.

Teaching Tip:
Ask students to keep their essay plans and then attach them to the final draft. You can then determine how the students have developed their ideas.

Writer's Desk **Write an Essay Plan**

Refer to the information you generated in previous Writer's Desks, and prepare a detailed essay plan. Include details for each supporting idea.

The First Draft

After you outline your ideas in a plan, you are ready to write the first draft. Remember to write complete sentences and to use transitions to help readers understand the order in which events occur or occurred. Here are some transitions that are useful in narrative essays.

To show a sequence of events

afterward	finally	in the end	meanwhile
after that	first	last	next
eventually	in the beginning	later	then

Enhancing Your Essay

One effective way to enhance your narrative essay is to use dialogue. A **direct quotation** contains the exact words of an author, and the quotation is set off with quotation marks. When you include the exact words of more than one person in a text, you must make a new paragraph each time the speaker changes.

> "Who did this?" my mom shrieked, as my brother and I stood frozen with fear.

"Mark did it," I assured her shamelessly, as my finger pointed at my quivering brother.

An **indirect quotation** keeps the author's meaning but is not set off by quotation marks.

As Mark and I stood frozen with fear, our shrieking mother asked who did it. I assured her shamelessly that Mark did it, as my finger pointed at my quivering brother.

Grammar Hint **Using Quotations**

When you insert a direct quotation into your writing, capitalize the first word of the quotation, and put the final punctuation inside the closing quotation marks.

- Place a comma after an introductory phrase.

  Zsolt Alapi said, "Everyone was terrified."

- Place a colon after an introductory sentence.

  Zsolt Alapi described the atmosphere: "Everyone was terrified."

See Chapter 37 for more information about using quotations.

Writer's Desk **Write the First Draft**

In the previous Writer's Desk, you developed an essay plan. Carefully review your essay plan, make any necessary changes to the details or chronology, and then write the first draft of your narrative essay.

REVISING AND EDITING

Revise and Edit a Narrative Essay

When you finish writing a narrative essay, carefully review your work and revise it to make the events as clear as possible to your readers. Check that you have organized events chronologically, and remove any irrelevant details. Before you revise and edit your own essay, practice revising and editing a student essay.

Teaching Tip: The activity of revising a student essay should help your students understand the important link between the writing process and the grammar chapters.

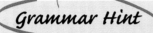

A Student Essay

Read the essay, and then answer the questions that follow. As you read, correct any errors that you find, and make comments in the margins.

Crashing Glass Deer

by Adele Berridge

1 My brother and I grew up in a suburban bungalow near a freeway. Built in the 1950s, my house boasted a living room with a picture window, three bedrooms, and a bathroom. My older sister and I shared the middle bedroom, and my younger brother Mark, as the only boy, was given his own room next to ours. He was my fraternal twin and my best friend. On the day that I betrayed Mark, I made an unpleasant discovery about myself.

2 Sherry, my sister, had just turned eight, and my brother and I were both four. We had celebrated my sister's birthday a few days before, and some of her prized possessions were on display in our shared bedroom. Most impressive of all was a set of glass deer. My sister placed the three fragile deer on top of her dresser, well out of reach of my grubby little hands. Those deer fascinated me, and I thought they represented Bambi's family. I longed to hold them, but I can't reach them.

3 That morning, my sister had gone to school, and my mother was doing laundry at the opposite end of the house. I brought my brother into my room and told him that we would play with Sherry's deer. We would be carefull, I assured him. He didn't want to proceed, but he watched me as I pulled out each drawer on my sister's dresser, starting with the bottom drawer, then the middle, and then the top, until I made a series of steps.

4 I had my slippers on, and I climbed up, carefully stepping on the edge of each drawer. I reached the second drawer from the top, and was just reaching for the deer when the dresser started to tip toward me. I leapt off the drawer to safety just as the large piece of furniture crashed to the ground. The glass ornaments smashed on the hardwood floor. My brother and I stared in stunned silence as hard footsteps clomped down the hall.

5 "Who did this?" my mom shrieked, as my brother and I stood frozen with fear. "He did it," I assured her shamelessly, as my finger pointed at my quivering brother. My brother denied it, of course.

6 Peering closely at us both, my mother's eyes rested on her son. The next minutes were a torrent of shouting and loud wailing as my brother was punished for the act. I remained perfectly still, numb. Noises and colors swirled around me, the occasional image registering like a snapshot. Then, as I backed out of the room and slunk down the hall to the living room, I heard the distant sound of my brother's muffled sobs. At the time, I knew that I was being *really, really bad,* but there was no turning back.

7 That incident haunted me for years to come. As a child, I thought that the human soul was a round white pie plate and that sins were like black specks of dirt on it. In my mind's eye, my soul was stained with the mud of sin. I knew what I was: a liar and a coward. My brother's tear-streaked face burned into my brain, I saw his disappointed eyes staring at me not with anger but with bewilderment. I was his sister and best friend, and I had betrayed him in order to save myself. The guilt wouldn't go away, nor would my sense that I was inherently bad. Occasionaly my brother would remind me of the incident, and I pretended that I couldn't remember that time, yet I couldn't forget it. Denying it only intensified the guilt, of course.

8 I wish I could say I changed overnight, but I'm a slow learner. I lied again and again. However, that incident planted a seed in me that budded and grew with time. I would have to overcome my own inherent cowardice and learn to take responsibility for my actions. It had to feel better than lying and living with horrible guilt.

9 Today, I get it. On that day all those years ago, if I had simply told the truth and taken the punishment, most likely I would'nt even remember the incident today. Because I lied, I've never forgotten it.

PRACTICE 3

Revising

1. Write down the two parts of the thesis statement.

   topic + controlling idea

   On the day that I betrayed Mark, I made an unpleasant discovery about myself.

2. What type of order do the specific details follow? Circle your response.

   a. space   (b.) time   c. emphatic

3. What type of narration is this?

   (a.) first person   b. third person

4. Paragraph 4 lacks a topic sentence. An appropriate topic sentence for paragraph 4 could be

   a. The glass deer was on top of the dresser.
   (b.) I concentrated on my goal of getting my hands on those glass deer.
   c. My brother didn't move.
   d. The glass deer were fragile.

5. Underline a dialogue problem in paragraph 5, and then write a rule regarding quotations and dialogue.

   There should be a new paragraph when the speaker changes.

GRAMMAR LINK

See the following chapters for more information about these grammar topics:
Run-Ons, Chapter 24
Verb Consistency, Chapter 29
Spelling, Chapter 34
Apostrophes, Chapter 36

Editing

6. Underline a tense consistency error in paragraph 2. The tense shifts for no apparent reason. Write the correction on the line below.

   Correction: *I couldn't reach them.*

7. This essay contains misspelled words in paragraphs 3 and 7. Underline and correct them.

   Corrections: *careful* *occasionally*

8. Paragraph 7 contains a run-on sentence. Underline the error, and show three ways to correct the sentence

   Corrections: *. . . burned into my brain, and I saw his disappointed eyes . . .*

   . . . burned into my brain. I saw his disappointed eyes . . .

   . . . burned into my brain; I saw his disappointed eyes . . .

9. Underline an apostrophe error in paragraph 9. Write the correct word on the line below.

   Correction: *wouldn't*

ESL Teaching Tip: Pair nonnative speakers with native speakers to do the vocabulary boost. You might suggest that each pair use a thesaurus. They can peer edit each other's essays.

vo•cab•u•lar•y BOOST

Writers commonly overuse words. To make your writing more vivid and interesting, identify five common and overused verbs in your essay. Replace each verb with a more vivid and specific verb.

First draft: We walked to the edge of the cliff and looked at the sea.

Revision: We strolled to the edge of the cliff and gazed at the sea.

Writer's Desk **Revise and Edit Your Essay**

Revise and edit the essay that you wrote for the previous Writer's Desk. You can refer to the revising and editing checklists at the end of this chapter and on this book's inside covers.

A Professional Essay

In his memoir, *Cockeyed*, Ryan Knighton, an author and teacher, describes his slow descent into blindness. In the following excerpt from an article, he narrates what happened.

Out of Sight

by Ryan Knighton

1 On my 18th birthday, my first retina specialist, a man who delivered his bedside manner like napalm, informed me that I would be blind within a few years. "No cure," he said. "Sorry." The specialist told me the name of the condition, retinitis pigmentosa. He described how it would soon **eradicate** my remaining night vision, limit me to tunnel vision, and eventually blinker me altogether. The whole scene took less than ten minutes.

eradicate: remove completely

2 For four years, I had exhibited clumsy behaviour nobody could account for. As a warehouse worker during summer vacations, I drove a forklift and ran over nearly everything possible, including one of my co-workers. True, I hated him and his insistence that we play nothing but Iron Maiden on the shipping area stereo, but it wasn't in my character to crush him.

3 But the real giveaway came when I drove my father's Pontiac into a ditch. Lots of friends crashed their parents' cars, but my accident stood out. I did my teenaged duty at roughly five miles per hour. How do you miss a turn at that speed unless your eyes are closed? After sundown, mine might as well have been.

4 When I reported to my mother that, as a new driver, I was having trouble on rainy nights, she said they gave everybody trouble and told me not to worry. I was on my way out the door, about to drive to work. "But do you use the cat's eyes sometimes?" I asked.

5 "Sure," she said. "That's what they're for, reflecting light when it's hard to see the yellow line."

6 "No, I mean do you use them? Do you drive on them?"

7 When I couldn't see the yellow line, I had taken to steering onto the cat's eyes. This, I found, helped position me on the road. I was a little close to the middle, maybe, but better than anything I could determine on my own. The clunk clunk clunk of the reflectors under my tires let me know where I was. I suppose I drove Braille.

8 "You drive on the cat's eyes?" my mother asked.

9 "Well, only at night." I would wager my mother called for my first ophthalmological appointment by the time I had shut the front door behind me.

10 Retinitis pigmentosa is the loss of photoreceptors associated with pigmentary changes in the retina. Another way to put it is that my retina is scarring itself to death. I've enjoyed the slow loss of all peripheral and night vision. By my own estimate, I have a year to go until that tiny pinhole of clarity in which I live will consume itself, and the lights will go out. To know what's filling up my little tunnel, I rely mostly on context.

11 Once I asked a red-headed waitress for directions to the washroom. I didn't know she was a waitress by the colour of her hair, of course—the bit

of it I saw—but by the smell of coffee, which was quickly overwhelmed by a perfumy fog.

12 "Would you like more coffee?"

13 "I'd love coffee," I said, "but I'd love to be in the men's room even more."

14 "Um, okay, the men's room is over that way."

15 I stared vacantly ahead while she, I imagine, continued to point "that way." Then I heard the pleasant sound of coffee being poured.

16 "I'm sorry," I said, "but I don't know what *that way* means." I plucked my white cane from the bag beside me. "I guess it wasn't obvious, and I forgot to—"

17 "Oh my God, I'm sorry, I didn't know you're blind! You didn't look—you don't look—not at all—I mean really."

18 I smiled with that warm sensation you get when you are sixteen and someone says you look like you're in your twenties. "Thanks. That is very kind. Where did you say the washroom is?"

19 "At the back."

20 "Which way is back?"

21 "It's over there," she said, and walked away.

22 All I wanted were specific directions. Instead, my waitress gave me a demonstration of the fact that, along with vision, parts of language disappear into blindness. The capacity of language to guide me has atrophied. Not even Braille can substitute for some words. *This way. Right here, in front of you. No, there. Right there, under your nose.* Such directional cues have lost their meaning. Who would have guessed that a disease can alter language as it alters the body, disabling parts of speech—that language is, in this way, an extension of the body and subject to the same pathologies.

23 "EXCUSE ME."

24 My waitress was back, not a second too soon. I really did need to use the facilities.

25 "I don't mean to intrude," she said, "but didn't you go to Langley Secondary School?"

26 "Yes, I did."

27 "It's Ryan, right? I'm Danielle! We were in drama class together. God, I didn't recognize you at all. You look so different now," she said.

28 I braced myself. "I'm not sure what it is. Maybe it's—" *The fierce squint? The white cane? The expression of perpetual disorientation?*

29 "It's—well. I know!" She put a hand on my head with daring compassion. "You shaved your hair off. When did you do that?"

30 Now I was free to burn with embarrassment at my self-centeredness. Just because it's a sighted world doesn't mean blindness is the first thing people notice about me, nor the first thing that comes to mind. Along with

mutant celebrity and meaningless words, I suppose paranoia is another side effect. "A couple of years ago, I guess," I replied.

31 "Looks cool."

32 "Thanks."

33 "I remember in high school your hair used to be long," she said. "Really long. It was down to here, right?"

PRACTICE 4

1. What type of narration is this text?

   (a.) first person   b. third person

2. The thesis of this essay is not stated directly, but it is implied. Using your own words, write the thesis of this essay.

   Answers will vary. *When I became blind, it impacted my life in various ways.*

3. Describe how Knighton introduces his topic. What introduction style does he use? Circle the letter of the best answer.

   a. definition   b. general   (c.) anecdote   d. historical

4. Knighton divides his essay into two time periods. What are they?

   before his diagnosis of blindness   *after his diagnosis*

5. How does Knighton realize that he is losing his sight? In two or three sentences, explain what happens.

   He drives on the cat's eyes because he can't see well at night. He mentions this fact to his mother, and she gets him an appointment with an eye specialist.

6. In which paragraph is there a definition of a term? *Paragraph 10*

7. Describe what happens during Knighton's encounter with the waitress. Use your own words.

   Knighton asks the waitress for directions to the men's room. Her directions are only useful for someone with sight. She points and says, "Over there." Eventually he realizes that he went to high school with the waitress.

8. Write down one example of an indirect quotation from the essay.

   I asked a red-haired waitress for directions to the men's room.

9. Write down one example of a direct quotation from the essay.

   Answers will vary.

Teaching Tip:
Point out that Ryan Knighton uses the "definition" writing pattern in paragraph 10. He also explains the cause and effects of his blindness. You can discuss how an essay with one overall pattern can still incorporate elements of other writing patterns.

10. Narrative writers do more than simply list a series of events. Knighton explains why the events were meaningful. What did he learn?

    He learned that losing sight also entails losing language. Many words became meaningless. He also learned to feel less paranoid about the way people perceive him.

The Writer's Room Topics for Narrative Essays

Writing Activity 1

Choose any of the following topics, or choose your own topic, and write a narrative essay.

General Topics

1. a breakup
2. a risky adventure
3. a personal ritual
4. a thrilling or frightening moment
5. a news event that affected you

College and Work-Related Topics

6. an interesting encounter
7. a sudden realization at school or work
8. an uncomfortable incident at work
9. a positive or negative job interview
10. a difficult lesson at work or school

Writing Activity 2

Choose a quotation you agree or disagree with, and then write a narrative essay based on it.

> Youth would be an ideal state if it came a little later in life.
>
> —Herbert Henry Asquith, politician

> Always do what you are afraid to do.
>
> —Ralph Waldo Emerson, essayist

> There's always one who loves and one who lets himself be loved.
>
> —W. Somerset Maugham, author

> Blind belief is dangerous.
>
> —Kenyan proverb

Writing Activity 3

Write about a physical or spiritual journey that you have been on. Describe what happened.

READING LINK

More Narrative Readings

"I Telemarketer" by Eugene Henry (page 596)

"Into Thin Air" by Jon Krakauer (page 614)

WRITING LINK

More Narrative Writing Topics

See the next grammar sections for more narrative writing topics.

Chapter 21, Writer's Room topic 1 (page 344)

Chapter 31, Writer's Room topic 1 (page 470)

Chapter 35, Writer's Room topic 2 (page 521)

CHECKLIST: NARRATION ESSAY

After you write your narration essay, review the checklist on the inside front cover. Also ask yourself these questions.

- ☐ Does my thesis statement clearly express the topic of the narration?
- ☐ Does my thesis statement contain a controlling idea that is meaningful and interesting?
- ☐ Does my essay answer most of the following questions: who, what, when, where, why, how?
- ☐ Do I use transitional expressions that help clarify the order of events?
- ☐ Do I include details to make my narration more vivid?

Teaching Tip:

Writer's World Competition

Please advise students that they can submit their essays for possible publication to: <thewritersworld@prenhall.com>.

How Do I Get a Better Grade?

Visit www.mywritinglab.com for audio-visual lectures and additional practice sets about narrative writing.

Get a better grade with MyWritingLab!

CHAPTER 8

Description

CONTENTS

Sculptors chisel features and other details in their work to express their artistic vision. Similarly, writers use the tools of descriptive writing to create images that readers can visualize in their mind's eye.

Teaching Tip: The Writers' Exchange activity can help your students understand description. Write some of their ideas on the board. As an extra activity, you could ask students to choose three of the words and construct a paragraph.

Writers' Exchange

Choose one of the objects from the following list. Then, brainstorm a list of descriptive words about the object. Think about the shape, texture, smell, taste, color, and so on. List the first words that come to your mind.

For example: cake *gooey, sweet, chocolate, smooth, pink icing, layered*

panther old car sweater baby apple

EXPLORING

What Is Description?

Description creates vivid images in the reader's mind by portraying people, places, or moments in detail. Here are some everyday situations that might call for description.

Audience: Roommate

The apartment we will rent is close to the campus.

- The north side of the campus has student housing.
- Our apartment is in the middle of Grove Street, which is still a dusty, unpaved road.
- The building is next to the wooded lot.

Audience: Classmate

The experiment in chemistry class went well.

- We dissolved Epsom salts on construction paper.
- Crystals of many different shapes formed as the paper dried.
- The crystals were mainly bright coral and sunny yellow.

Audience: Intern

Our company has renovated the front lobby.

- The walls are painted in warm browns and beiges.
- There are two overstuffed chairs and a soft leather couch.
- There are oil paintings on the walls and dried flowers in ceramic vases on the tables.

> ***"The greatest honor that can be paid to the work of art, on its pedestal of ritual display, is to describe it with sensory completeness. We need a science of description."***
>
> CAMILLE PAGLIA, *writer*

Teaching Tip: Ask students to think of types of writing that include description, such as tourist brochures, medical pamphlets, and so on.

Description at Work

To help hikers plan camping trips effectively, the Web site http://www.americansouthwest.net describes hiking trails in Zion National Park.

The trail descends quite steeply, close to the course of the South Fork of Taylor Creek, and soon reaches the main stream. Here, the canyon is deep but wide and V-shaped, with red rocks and sandy soils, quite densely covered by trees, bushes, and cacti. The path follows the valley upstream, at first on the south side but later on either side as it crosses the creek several times. The water is fast flowing but shallow and easily forded.

Teaching Tip: Ask students which details appeal to the reader's senses.

Teaching Tip: Write a topic on the board such as "the neighborhood." Ask students to brainstorm sentences that would depict a positive or negative attitude about the topic.

The Descriptive Essay

When you write a descriptive essay, focus on three main points.

1. **Create a dominant impression.** The dominant impression is the overall atmosphere that you wish to convey. It can be a strong feeling, mood, or image. For example, if you are describing a casual Sunday afternoon party, you can emphasize the relaxed ambience in the room.
2. **Express your attitude toward the subject.** Do you feel positive or negative toward the subject? For instance, if you feel pleased about your last vacation, then the details of your essay might convey the good feelings you have about it. If you feel tense during a business meeting, then your details might express how uncomfortable the situation makes you feel.
3. **Include concrete details.** Details will enable a reader to visualize the person, place, or situation that you are describing. You can use active verbs and adjectives so that the reader imagines the scene more clearly. You can also use **imagery,** which is description using the five senses. Review the following examples of imagery.

ESL Teaching Tip: Encourage your nonnative speakers to use a thesaurus or a dictionary to find vivid vocabulary. To practice making lists of descriptive words and phrases, divide students into groups and give each group a photograph to describe. (You could use any of the photos in this book.) Place nonnative speakers with native speakers.

Sight: A Western Tiger Swallowtail dipped by my face. About three inches across, its lemon yellow wings were striped improbably and fluted in black. They filliped into a long forked tail with spots of red and blue.
(Sherman Apt Russell, "Beauty on the Wing")

Sound: The tree outside is full of crows and white cranes who gurgle and screech.
(Michael Ondaatje, *Running in the Family*)

Smell: I think it was the smell that so intoxicated us after those dreary months of nostril-scorching heat, the smell of dust hissing at the touch of rain and then settling down, damply placid on the ground.
(Sara Suleri, *Meatless Days*)

Touch: The straps from my backpack tore into my shoulder blades and pain ran down my spine.
(Andrew Wells, "My Journey Down the Grand Canyon")

Taste: Entirely and blessedly absent are the cloying sweetness, chalky texture, and oily, gummy aftertaste that afflict many mass-manufactured ice creams.
(R.W. Apple Jr., "Making Texas Cows Proud," *The New York Times*)

A Student Essay

Read the following student essay and answer the questions that follow.

The Wake-Up Call

by Jennifer Alvira

1 My hands were covered in flavored syrup, and my hair sat in a messy bun on the top of my head. I cringed at the sight of last-minute customers. I had had enough of people for one day and was ready to close the shop for the night.

2 I picked up the dingy mop from an old pail and started mopping the chocolate encrusted tiles. Our milkshake machine had splattered the checkerboard walls in a vanilla mess while the eight glass jars of candies had spilled out over the marble countertop. After five long minutes of hard scrubbing, the black and white of the wall started to shine through. I swept up the broken candies from the floor. When the stressful day finally came to an end, I grabbed my purse and headed for the door. Little did I know that in the next hour, I was about to destroy my car and my self-confidence as a driver.

3 The air grew heavy with storm clouds, and a thin layer of car oil residue coated the road. If driving in the dark was not terrifying enough, it was pouring rain. I climbed into my silver '92 Dodge Spirit, the car given to me on my sixteenth birthday. The interior was a deep burgundy red and emanated a distinct aroma of wet tennis shoes and old carpet. The exterior had its own collection of dents and scratches but remained beautiful to me. It was my personal dream car despite what anyone else said; it always started and never gave me any real problems.

4 Night blanketed the roads, and my nerves started to twist in knots. I hated driving at night. I arrived about a half a mile from the intersection at Eber and Dairy Road. An abandoned white chapel sat peacefully to the right, and a humble section of mysterious houses thrived in a community called Little Oak Creek further up the road. It appeared to me that I was the only car on the road at this hour. As I neared the intersection, I pressed on the gas pedal to make sure I would fly through before the light turned yellow.

5 I had just made it past the light when the glare of a pair of headlights caught the corner of my left eye. I slammed on the brakes only to feel my tires lose traction and slide across pavement. The abrupt impact barely gave me enough time to close my eyes. I gripped the steering wheel so tightly that my palms stung when I finally let go. The two-ton weight of my car shoved the other car completely off the road into a patch of trees in front of Little Oak Creek.

6 My air bag deployed with a loud bang and burst with white powder. I pushed open the door and stumbled out. The smell of burnt tires and exhaust smoke permeated the night. The accident seemed like a nightmare.

7 By then, I couldn't hold back fear anymore. Tears smeared my stunned face, while cars passed by with none stopping to assist me. I hyperventilated, and my entire body shook. Everything happened so quickly; I didn't have a chance to feel the throbbing in my wrist from the sprain or the enormous bruise from where my knee had slammed into the dashboard.

8 Finally, a young woman and her son appeared in the warm rays of the streetlamp. The woman clutched a small blue jacket, with her son closely behind.

9 "Darling, are you okay?"

10 She draped a light jacket over my frail shoulders and proceeded to cup my trembling hands within hers. I noticed a metallic taste in my mouth, and I could barely form a coherent sentence. "I'm alive and can feel all my limbs. I'm okay."

11 The young lady rubbed my shoulders, and made sure to stand next to me in case my body gave way to the shock. "What's your mom's phone number so that I can tell her you're fine?" Her sweet voice eased my terror, and I could finally take a deep breath. I looked over at her son, who stood quietly beside his mother. His eyes widened as he stared at my now nonexistent source of transportation.

12 The police showed up after two hours of waiting for their arrival. I found out that the sixteen-year-old girl driving the other vehicle jumped out of her car in a bout of panic. Her knees bled from the rough impact of asphalt. Her boyfriend and mother were at the scene and stayed close to her side. The police ticketed the girl with failure to yield to passing cars while making a left turn. The accident was not my fault, and I welcomed the flood of relief.

PRACTICE 1

1. Look in the opening paragraphs and highlight the thesis statement.
2. The writer describes in detail the events of the fateful night. Find examples of imagery from the essay. Answers will vary.
   a. Sight *Our milkshake machine had splattered the checkerboard walls in a vanilla mess.*
   b. Sound *My air bag deployed with a loud bang.*
   c. Taste *I noticed a metallic taste in my mouth.*
   d. Touch *I gripped the steering wheel so tightly that my palms stung.*

e. Smell *. . . a distinct aroma of wet tennis shoes and old carpet.*

3. What dominant impression does the writer create in this essay? Underline examples in the essay to support your answer.

   Answers will vary. Possible answers are "fear" and "shock."

Teaching Tip: Encourage all students to use a thesaurus to enhance their vocabulary when writing descriptions.

Explore Topics

In the Writer's Desk Warm Up, you will try an exploring strategy to generate ideas about different topics.

Writer's Desk Warm Up

Read the following questions, and write the first ideas that come to your mind. Think of two or three ideas for each topic.

EXAMPLE: List some memorable trips you have taken.

—my trip to Africa

—the time I stayed with my grandmother in Seattle

—a field trip to the Natural History Museum

1. Who are your best friends?

2. What are some unattractive fashion trends?

3. List some memorable trips that you have taken.

Teaching Tip:
The Writer's Desk activities provide students with an opportunity to develop a topic through all stages of the writing process using the descriptive rhetorical mode. In the Warm Up, they begin by exploring various topics. Those topics then carry on throughout the chapter.

ESL Teaching Tip:
Encourage your nonnative speakers to write about culture-specific topics. Let them know that others in the class will appreciate descriptive details about an unfamiliar topic.

DEVELOPING

When you write a descriptive essay, choose a subject that lends itself to description. You should be able to describe images or objects using some of the five senses. To get in the frame of mind, try thinking about the sounds, sights, tastes, smells, and feelings you would experience in certain places, such as a busy restaurant, a hospital room, a subway car, a zoo, and so on.

The Thesis Statement

In the thesis statement of a descriptive essay, you should convey a dominant impression about the subject. The dominant impression is the overall impression or feeling that the topic inspires.

topic / controlling idea

The photograph of me as a ten-year-old has an embarrassing story behind it.

controlling idea / topic

Feeling self-satisfied, **Odysseus Ramsey started his first day in public office.**

Hint **How to Create a Dominant Impression**

To create a dominant impression, ask yourself how or why the topic is important.

Poor: Land developers have built homes on parkland.
(Why should readers care about this statement?)

topic / controlling idea

Better: **The once pristine municipal park** has been converted into giant estate homes that average families cannot afford.

Writer's Desk Thesis Statements

Write a thesis statement for each of the following topics. You can look for ideas in the Warm Up on page 123. Each thesis statement should state what you are describing and contain a controlling idea.

EXAMPLE: Topic: a memorable trip

Thesis Statement: *My first day in Ghana left me enthralled but exhausted.*

1. Topic: a close friend

   Thesis Statement: ____

   ____

2. Topic: unattractive fashion trends

   Thesis Statement: ____

   ____

3. Topic: a memorable trip

   Thesis Statement: ____

   ____

The Supporting Ideas

After you have developed an effective thesis statement, generate supporting details.

- Use prewriting strategies such as freewriting and brainstorming to generate ideas.
- Choose the best ideas. Most descriptive essays use imagery that describes the person or scene.
- Organize your ideas. Choose the best organizational method for this essay pattern.

Show, Don't Tell

Your audience will find it more interesting to read your written work if you show a quality or an action of a place or person rather than just state it.

Example of Telling: Mr. Leon was a very kind man.

Example of Showing: Our neighbor, Mr. Leon, a grim-faced, retired seventy-year-old grandfather, always snapped at the neighborhood children, telling us not to play street hockey, not to make so much noise, and not to throw the ball near his roses. When it came to important matters, however, he was always supportive of us. Mr. Leon taught all the local youths to ride bikes. He used to walk along beside us holding on to the cycle as we wobbled down the sidewalk. One day, we learned that Mr. Leon had been donating fifty bicycles to the local children's charity annually for many years.

ESL Teaching Tip:

Pair Work

If your nonnative speakers have trouble using descriptive imagery, ask them to work with a partner and brainstorm some ideas. Because nonnative speakers may choose inappropriate words from a thesaurus, ask pairs (which should include a native speaker) to verify that all descriptive words are used correctly.

Teaching Tip:
Give your students a list of one-line sentences of a characteristic or quality. For example, *Mrs. Smith was very grumpy, The building was run-down,* or *The park was crowded.* They can expand on the description by writing paragraphs that show the characteristic or quality.

ESL Teaching Tip:
If you have nonnative speakers in your class, ensure that they are teamed with native speakers when doing Practices 2 and 3.

Teaching Tip:
Group Work
Ask students to do Practices 2 and 3 in groups because they are somewhat difficult.

PRACTICE 2 Choose one of the following sentences, and write a short description that shows—not tells—the quality of the person or place. Answers will vary.

1. Today was a perfect day.
2. I was frightened as I walked down the street.
3. The weather did not cooperate with our plans.

Use Different Figurative Devices

When writing a descriptive essay, you can use other figurative devices (besides **imagery**) to add vivid details to your writing.

- A **simile** is a comparison using *like* or *as*.

  My thoughts ran as fast as a cheetah.

  Let us go then you and I,
  When the evening is spread out against the sky
  Like a patient etherised upon a table;
  (from "The Love Song of J. Alfred Prufrock" by T.S. Eliot).

- A **metaphor** is a comparison that does not use *like* or *as*.

  Life is sweet-and-sour soup.
  You need a blue sky holiday
  (from "Bad Day" by Daniel Powter)

- **Personification** is the act of attributing human qualities to an inanimate object or animal.

  The chocolate cake winked invitingly at us.
  Life has a funny way of helping you out.
  (from "Ironic" by Alanis Morrissette).

PRACTICE 3 Practice using figurative language. Use one of the following to describe each item: simile, metaphor, or personification. If you are comparing two things, try to use an unusual comparison. Answers will vary.

EXAMPLE: toddler: *The toddler climbed like a monkey out of his crib. (simile)*

1. mountain: *Overcoming my shyness was like climbing the highest mountain.*
2. hair: *Her hair was cotton candy pink.*
3. ocean: *On that scorching day, the ocean generously invited us in.*

vo•cab•u•lar•y BOOST

Use Vivid Language

When you write a descriptive essay, try to use **vivid language**. Use specific action verbs and adjectives to create a clear picture of what you are describing.

My boss was ~~angry~~ livid. Use a more vivid, specific adjective.

The child ~~cried~~ whimpered. Use a more vivid, specific verb or image.

Think about other words or expressions that more effectively describe these words: *laugh, talk, nice, walk.*

Teaching Tip: The Vocabulary Boost activity helps all students, especially nonnative speakers, expand their vocabulary. Ask students to brainstorm words that are overused. Examples are *nice, beautiful, good, bad,* and *happy.*

Writer's Desk List Sensory Details

Choose one of your thesis statements from the previous Writer's Desk and make a list of sensory details. Think about images, impressions, and feelings that the topic inspires in you.

EXAMPLE: Topic: a memorable trip

—colorful clothes

—bright, warm sand

—appetizing smell of food

—putrid odor of sewers

—a cool breeze

—powerful drumbeat of music

—bodies moving to a beat

Your topic: ______________________________

Your list of sensory details: ______________________________

____

____

____

____

The Essay Plan

An essay plan helps you organize your thesis statement, topic sentences, and supporting details before writing a first draft. When you make an essay plan, remember to include concrete details and to organize your ideas in a logical order. If you want to emphasize some descriptive details more than others, arrange them from least affecting to most affecting. If you want your readers to envision a space (a room, a park, and so on), arrange details using spatial order.

Teaching Tip: Ask students to keep their essay plans and then attach them to their final draft. You can then determine how the students have developed their ideas.

THESIS STATEMENT: My first day in Ghana left me enthralled but exhausted.

I. I was overwhelmed by my surroundings.
   A. People wore traditional African clothing.
   B. Some walked balancing objects on their heads.
   C. Mothers carried babies tied to their backs.
   D. I could smell different types of food.
II. The beach was unlike any other beach I'd seen.
   A. I felt a cool breeze and saw orange sand.
   B. I sat in the shade and had a cold beverage.
   C. People were swimming and dancing.
III. The scenery of the countryside was breathtaking.
   A. There were mud huts with straw roofs.
   B. People were cooking on open fires.
   C. Many animals roamed, including dogs and goats.
   D. I saw immense anthills.

Teaching Tip: To give students more practice, you can ask them to develop supporting ideas for all three Writer's Desk topics, which are listed in the Warm Up.

Writer's Desk Write an Essay Plan

Choose one of the ideas that you have developed in previous Writer's Desks and prepare an essay plan. Remember to use vivid details and figurative language to help create a dominant overall impression.

Teaching Tip: Remind students to avoid using slang. Instead of writing *The meal is awesome*, students should try to find more specific descriptive vocabulary. Point out that slang changes often and confuses readers. It is also too informal.

The First Draft

After you outline your ideas in a plan, you are ready to write the first draft. Remember to write complete sentences. Also, as you write, think about which transitions can effectively help you lead your readers from one idea to the next. Descriptive writing often uses space order. Here is a list of transitions that are useful for describing the details of a person, place, or thing.

To show place or position

above	beyond	in the distance	outside
behind	closer in	nearby	over there
below	farther out	on the left/right	under
beside	in front	on top	underneath

Writer's Desk Write the First Draft

In the previous Writer's Desk, you developed an essay plan. Now write the first draft of your descriptive essay. Before you write, carefully review your essay plan and make any necessary changes.

REVISING AND EDITING

Revise and Edit a Descriptive Essay

When you finish writing a descriptive essay, review your work and revise it to make the description as vivid as possible to your readers. Check that you have organized your ideas, and remove any irrelevant details. Before you work on your own essay, practice revising and editing a student essay.

Teaching Tip: The activity of revising a student essay should help your students understand the important link between the writing process and the grammar chapters.

Grammar Hint Using Adjectives and Adverbs

When you revise your descriptive essay, check that you have used adjectives and adverbs correctly. For example, many people use *real* when the adjective is actually *really*.

Incorrect use of an adjective: My brother, Magnus, is real tall and powerful.

Correct use of an adjective: My brother, Magnus, is really tall and powerful.

See Chapter 32 for more information about adjectives and adverbs.

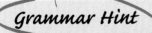

A Student Essay

Read the essay, and then answer the questions that follow. As you read, correct any errors that you find, and make comments in the margins.

African Adventure

by Natalia MacDonald

1 My trip to Africa began with a twenty-hour journey filled with boring flights and long layovers. When I finaly arrived in Ghana, it was 9:00 P.M. local time, and I was exhausted. I went straight to my hotel to get some rest for the long day I had ahead of me. My first day in Ghana left me enthralled but exhausted.

2 On waking, Kwame, the coordinator of my volunteer program picked me up to accompany me for the day. As I left the hotel, I was overwhelmed by the heat and the surroundings. Although many people dressed in Western-style clothing, the majority wore traditional African dress. The colors were incredibly vibrant: bright blues, purples, and yellows. Men, women, and children alike walked by carrying incredible amounts of goods balanced on their heads with such amazing grace and poise. Mothers also carried their babies in a way you had never seen before, tied to their backs with colorful scarves in almost a piggy-back position with their little feet sticking out at either side. As we hurried through the center, I noticed the strong smells of food being cooked by street vendors, fruit being sold in baskets, and of course the not-so-pleasant smell of the open sewers lining the roads. After getting to the bank and cashing my traveler's checks, it was off to the beach.

3 Everything from the sand to the activities people were doing was unique. The first thing I felt was the much-needed cool breeze from the ocean brush against my face as I approached. After being in the hustle and bustle of the capital, feeling the rich, dark orange sand between my toes felt very relaxing. I then took a seat in the shade to enjoy a cold beverage and observe my surroundings. Some people were swimming and sunbathing, and others were dancing. There was a particular group of young boys dressed in colorful loincloths dancing to traditional music. The powerful drumbeat of the music was moving. The boys moved their bodies with such a natural fluidity along with the music that I was completely captivated. I was thoroughly enjoying myself, but it was time to catch my bus.

4 The bus was a large white van that left from a station not too far from the beach. As we drove out of the city and on to the dirt road, the scenery was breathtaking. We drove past many different types of villages along the way. Some of the villages were large and had schools, stores, and houses while others were much smaller and more basic and consisted of a

circle of around twenty little mud huts with straw roofs with people cooking over an open fire in the middle. Along the road there were many animals walking around such as dogs and mules, but mostly there were small goats. ~~A month later I went to visit a national park to see wild animals~~. The road itself was the same rich, dark orange color that the sand had been at the beach. One of the most incredible sights were the numerous huge anthills that were formed from the dark orange dirt. They stood about four feet high! After driving through some rain, we finally arrived in Manya Krobo, my new home.

5 My first full day in Ghana was one filled with new discoveries and adventure. In a mere matter of hours, I saw things that I had only read about in books and seen in movies. In one day, I had gone from the snowy minus 18-degree weather of Montreal to the humid 90 degrees of Ghana. My long planned and awaited adventure in Africa was finally a reality.

PRACTICE 4

Revising

1. Highlight the thesis statement.
2. Highlight the topic sentences in paragraphs 2 and 4.
3. Paragraph 3 lacks a topic sentence. One possible topic sentence could be:
   a. I went to the beach that evening.
   (b.) La Pleasure beach was unlike any other beach I had ever seen.
   c. There were many people at La Pleasure beach.
   d. Everyone goes to La Pleasure beach in Ghana.
4. What overall dominant impression does the writer convey in the essay? Underline examples in the essay to support your answer.

   Surprise and awe. Answers will vary.

5. In paragraph 4, cross out the sentence that does not support the topic sentence.

Editing

6. Paragraph 1 contains a spelling mistake. Underline and correct the mistake.

   Correction: *finally*

7. Paragraph 2 contains a pronoun shift. Underline and correct the error.

   Correction: *Mothers also carried their babies in a way I had never seen before . . .*

GRAMMAR LINK

See the following chapters for more information about these grammar topics:
Subject-Verb Agreement, Chapter 27
Spelling, Chapter 34
Commas, Chapter 35

8. Underline and correct a comma error in paragraph 2. *On waking, Kwame, the coordinator of my volunteer program, picked me up . . .*

Teaching Tip: For question 9, explain that the subject is "one," thus the verb must be singular.

9. Underline and correct one subject–verb agreement error in paragraph 4. Correction: *One of the most incredible sights was the numerous huge anthills that were formed from the dark orange dirt.*

Writer's Desk Revise and Edit Your Essay

Revise and edit the essay that you wrote for the previous Writer's Desk. You can refer to the revising and editing checklists at the end of this chapter and on this book's inside covers.

A Professional Essay

Lucie L. Snodgrass, a regular contributor to *Vegetarian Times*, is a passionate gardener and a college teacher. She is also the author of *Green Roof Plants: A Resource and Planting Guide*. In the following essay, she reflects on the importance of bees.

Living Among the Bees

by Lucie L. Snodgrass

1 Scattered along a gently sloping hill on our farm is a series of white wooden boxes that resemble fallen tiles from a game of giant dominos. The boxes arrived one spring six years ago in an old pickup truck driven by Ed Yoder, a longtime neighbor and beekeeper who sells his honey at local supermarkets. Always searching for open land in this county of dwindling farms, Ed approached my husband and me, asking whether we would mind having some hives on our property. Since we didn't, twenty of them—home to about a million bees—came to share our 135 acres. At least that's how we described it initially. In reality, we've come to understand, it is the bees who have consented to share their workspace with us, and we, clumsy and often inadvertently destructive humans, are the better for it.

2 Our coexistence did not get off to an auspicious start. Shortly after the bees moved in, I began, as I always do in spring, spending most of my free time in the vegetable garden—tilling the raised beds, pulling early weeds, and carrying out flats of plants started in the greenhouse some fifty feet away. The bees, I quickly learned, disapproved of my activity. They had

claimed this formerly quiet area as their own. They had chosen well, packed as the garden was with nectar-dripping flowers and fruit trees in brilliant bloom, a veritable juice bar that they frequented from early to late.

3 Each of my trips into the garden brought an angry protest as dozens of them dive-bombed my head, just as barn swallows do to cats when their territory is encroached upon. I had always found that funny, but being the victim myself was eminently less amusing. I tried varying the hours that I gardened; I tried apologizing to the bees each time I walked in; I even tried singing to them—all to no avail. Whether I was early or late, contrite or in song, the bees were piqued to see me, a fact made clear by the number of welts on various parts of my body. After six stings, I'd had enough.

4 "Ed," I complained on the beekeeper's next visit, "every time I go into the vegetable garden, your bees sting me. Something's got to give." He returned my gaze, his sympathy evident. "Of course they sting you," he said after a long silence. "You're walking right into their flight path."

5 And so my real experience began of living with the bees and their fiercely protective keeper. I quickly learned that Ed's devotion was complete, his concern solely for them. Implicit in his reply was the suggestion that I, and not the bees, was at fault for getting stung. Only after I pointed out that the garden had been there longer than the hives and that it wasn't feasible to move the orchard did he agree to move the hives that were closest to the garden—a concession I'm sure he secretly regrets even today.

6 That was the only disagreement we've ever had, and perhaps if I had avoided the garden for a while, as Ed bluntly suggested, the problem would have resolved itself. In retrospect, perhaps the bees, like people moving into a new neighborhood, needed some time to settle in without the threat of interference. In any event, they have long since accepted my presence, whether I am picking raspberries, walking on the road back to our nursery—a trip that takes me within ten feet of some of the hives—or simply sitting beside a hive for long stretches, watching the bees come and go. I've never again been stung, not when I've scooped some into my hand to rescue them from drowning in the birdbath or when I've picked them up, so covered with pollen they couldn't fly, to avoid someone trampling them. Ed says that the bees have come to trust me, and I believe that I, in turn, have given them my trust.

7 As wonderful as watching the bees is watching Ed, who is an old-fashioned suitor. He visits the bees almost every day, wooing them with presents, fixing things, delighting in the offerings they give back to him. When he has to disturb the bees, he calms them first, moving among them with his smoker like a priest with incense burners. **Loquacious** by nature, Ed can spend the day talking about his charges: waxing on about their

loquacious: talkative

cleanliness, their loyalty to their queen, and their industriousness. Ed's love is infectious. We felt no small amount of pride when he told us after the first year's harvest that their honey production increased dramatically after the bees moved to our farm, certain that our unsprayed fields and flower gardens were responsible. We mourned with him when he lost many of his colonies to mites several years ago and others to a harsh winter. And we have done things that we would never have contemplated, like plowing up a few acres to plant clover because Ed told us that the bees would love it.

8 As with any good teachers, the bees have made me see things in a new light. About a half a mile from the hives is a small, perpetually muddy bog with a boardwalk of old heart pine running through it. In early spring, when the skunk cabbage blooms, I find bees there by the thousands, humming happily and drinking greedily. It is, I now know, their first source of nectar in spring. I am glad, and wiser, to know that the skunk cabbages, which always make my nose wrinkle, are to bees what poached strawberries are to me: both a delectable perfume and a welcome harbinger of spring.

9 The bees' contributions to the farm are everywhere. Berry bushes that bore modestly before the bees' arrival now hang heavy with fruit; my vegetable plants produce an embarrassing abundance of heirloom squash, cucumbers, and runner beans. Even seemingly barren fruit trees, far from the house and orchard in what were once cow pastures, have suddenly begun producing again. And, of course, there is the honey itself, velvety brown and perfectly sweet, dissolving in my tea and rippling across my bread. None of this is my work; it is all the bees' doing, and in their labor I have found wonder, gratitude, and a welcome sense of my own very modest place in the world.

PRACTICE 5

1. What is the writer's attitude toward the subject? Circle the best answer.
   (a.) positive   b. negative   c. neutral
2. Highlight the thesis statement.
3. How has the relationship between the writer and the bees changed? Explain, using your own words. *The bees and the writer have learned to trust each other. The bees no longer sting her.*
4. The writer describes her life with the bees. Highlight some of the most effective examples of imagery. Answers will vary.

5. A simile is a comparison using *like* or *as*. Highlight one simile in paragraph 6 and another in paragraph 7.

6. Circle some examples where the writer personifies or attributes human qualities to the bees. Answers will vary.

7. Throughout the essay, the writer shows how the bees have had a positive influence on her life. In your own words, give some examples of how the bees have helped the writer.

Answers will vary.

The bees have produced more honey after moving to the writer's farm. The bees teach her to appreciate things in nature that she has not appreciated before, like the skunk cabbage. The bees have helped pollinate her orchard and vegetable garden. They have produced quality honey that she likes to eat.

The Writer's Room Topics for Descriptive Essays

Writing Activity 1

Write a descriptive essay about one of the following topics, or choose your own topic.

General Topics

1. a music concert
2. the day _____ went to the ________
3. a family meal
4. a night out
5. an exciting sports event

College and Work-Related Topics

6. a beautiful building or area on campus
7. a frustrating day
8. an eccentric professor
9. a new person I have met
10. an exciting event

WRITING LINK

More Descriptive Writing Topics

Chapter 21, Writer's Room topic 1 (page 344)
Chapter 23, Writer's Room topic 1 (page 367)
Chapter 25, Writer's Room topic 1 (page 387)
Chapter 28, Writer's Room topic 1 (page 429)
Chapter 29, Writer's Room topic 1 (page 444)
Chapter 31, Writer's Room topic 1 (page 470)
Chapter 38, Writer's Room topic 1 (page 552)

READING LINK

More Descriptive Readings

"Into Thin Air" by Jon Krakauer, page 614
"Monsoon Time" by Rahul Goswami, page 617

Writing Activity 2

Choose a quotation that you agree or disagree with, and then write a descriptive essay based on it.

> Everything has its wonders, even darkness and silence, and I learn whatever state I am in to be content.
>
> —Helen Keller, blind & deaf educator

> Every artist dips his brush in his own soul and paints his own nature into his pictures.
>
> —Henry Ward Beecher, abolitionist and clergyman

> A few days ago I walked along the edge of the lake and was treated to the crunch and rustle of leaves with each step I made. The acoustics of this season are different, and all sounds, no matter how hushed, are as crisp as autumn air.
>
> —Eric Sloane, artist

> Train up a fig tree in the way it should go, and when you are old sit under the shade of it.
>
> —Charles Dickens, novelist

Teaching Tip:
For Writing Activity 3, you could ask students to discuss in groups a strange or unusual event that they have seen or heard.

Teaching Tip:
Have students read one of the essays in the Reading Link. They could discuss the effectiveness of the imagery.

Writing Activity 3

Have you or someone you know ever seen an unusual event or been in an unusual situation? Describe the scene or event. Include vivid details.

CHECKLIST: DESCRIPTIVE ESSAY

After you write your descriptive essay, review the essay checklist on the inside front cover. Also ask yourself these questions.

- ☐ Does my thesis statement clearly show what I will describe in the essay?
- ☐ Does my thesis statement have a controlling idea that makes a point about the topic?
- ☐ Does my essay have a dominant impression?
- ☐ Does each body paragraph contain supporting details that appeal to the reader's senses?
- ☐ Do I use vivid language?

Teaching Tip:
Writer's World Competition
Please advise students that they can submit their essays for possible publication to: <thewritersworld@prenhall.com>.

How Do I Get a Better Grade?

PEARSON mywritinglab

Visit www.mywritinglab.com for audio-visual lectures and additional practice sets about description writing. ***Get a better grade with MyWritingLab!***

CHAPTER 9

Process

CONTENTS

Every industry uses processes. For example, dressmakers need to study designs, cut fabric, sew pieces, and so on. Along similar lines, writers not only have to follow the writing process, but sometimes they need to be able to explain processes to their readers as well.

Teaching Tip:
The Writers' Exchange activity can help your students understand process. Write some of their ideas on the board. Each step could be developed into a paragraph for a process essay.

Writers' Exchange

Choose one of the following topics and have a group or class discussion. Describe the steps you would take to do that process.

- How to become an annoying neighbor
- How to write an essay
- How to get rich quickly
- How to parallel park

EXPLORING

What Is Process?

A **process** is a series of steps usually done in chronological order. In process writing, you explain how to do something, how an incident took place, or how something works. Take a look at the following examples of processes that people discuss in everyday life.

> ***"I am always doing that which I cannot do, in order that I may learn how to do it."***
>
> PABLO PICASSO, *Cubist painter*

Audience: Family member

Cook pasta in the following way.

- Boil a pot of water.
- Add a pinch of salt.
- Put pasta into boiling water.
- Cook for 8 minutes.
- Drain water.
- Serve pasta hot.

Audience: Classmate

Follow the next steps to become a tutor.

- Decide what subject you want to tutor.
- See the person responsible for hiring a tutor.
- Find out the number of hours you need to tutor.

Audience: Intern

Take the customer's order by following these procedures.

- First, check to see the order form is filled out correctly.
- Next, call our warehouse to verify stock.
- Then, send the order form to the warehouse manager.

Teaching Tip: Ask students to identify the steps in the process.

Process at Work

Frank Morelli is a mechanic who specializes in repairing Toyotas and Volvos. In this pamphlet excerpt, he advises customers on how to buy a car.

First, decide if you want a new or used car. There are some advantages and disadvantages for both. A new car will be more expensive, but you can buy an extended warranty, and a new car will likely not incur expensive repairs. A used car is, of course, more economical. However, if the previous owner has not properly maintained the car, you may have to pay for costly repairs, and the car may not last for very long.

Next, research the safety record of the car that you want to buy. Some types of cars offer extensive safety features such as dual airbags and a reinforced frame. To find information about the safety statistics of the car you want to buy, consult the car insurance Web sites or read some consumer magazines that deal with cars.

The Process Essay

Before planning a process essay, you need to determine your purpose. Do you want to tell readers how to complete a process or how to understand a process?

1. **Complete a process.** This type of essay contains directions for completing a particular task. For example, a writer might explain how to change a flat tire, how to decorate a room, or how to use a particular computer program.
2. **Understand a process.** This type of essay explains how something works or how something happens. For example, a writer might explain how the admissions process at a college works or how food goes from the farm to the table.

A Student Essay

Read the essay and answer the questions that follow.

Learning Good Finances

by Tony Ruiz

1 Every year, when you apply for more student aid, it takes a toll on your fiscal confidence. If you are anything like I am, no matter how well you think you have curbed your spending, you always find yourself staring at your W-2 tax return form in disbelief. Your humble living standards do not reflect the overwhelming discrepancy between your alleged total earnings and your most recent bank statement. Students can begin making smart financial decisions today and help reduce the financial burden they are likely to experience after graduation.

2 Students should avoid spending money on unnecessary gadgets. For example, the iPod is a terrible investment for students who are trying to save money. Besides paying at least $199 for the iPod nano or $269 for the iPod Video, consumers end up buying crucial trendy accessories. An FM transmitter that will let listeners wire their iPod through a car's sound system costs $29.95. For those who want to listen to FM radio while walking to class, the FM Radio Remote costs another $49.95. And before long, the iPod's dead battery will have to be replaced for $59 (plus shipping and handling). Some students might even be tempted to buy a newer model of iPod. Meanwhile, an impressive iTunes library costs $0.99 for every song and $1.99 for every episode of *Lost* that could be watched Wednesday nights at no cost.

3 Another common mistake students make is adopting expensive daily regimens. They should reduce "treat" spending by half. For the sluggish, a $4.50 personalized Starbucks coffee is the only way to function. Jamba Juice is the formidable, health-conscious counterpart. Replacing the

designer drink every day with generic coffee or fruit juice would amount to substantial savings. Skipping the Chai Latte or the Mocha Cappuccino Delight three days out of five is painless but effective.

4 Students can earn more money by investing carefully. Setting aside even as little as $500 every year toward student debt means that after a four-year period, they will have $2,000 less to worry about paying off. The elimination of interest charges will generate pocket change in the long term as well. Furthermore, student loans also offer a unique advantage since the cost to students will not be felt until graduation, so they should make that money work for them. Those who are absolutely sure that they will not need a certain amount of money until graduation can lock up the money with a certificate of deposit and let it earn interest yields typically higher than those of savings and money market accounts.

5 Nobody expects students to invest all of their time and money in scholarly endeavors. Everybody needs to have some leisure activities. But they should be reasonable. New gadgets and expensive habits are unnecessary indulgences.

PRACTICE I

1. Highlight the thesis statement.
2. Highlight the topic sentence in each body paragraph.
3. Who is the audience for this essay? *College students*
4. For each of the body paragraphs, list some supporting details the writer gives.

   Paragraph 2: *iPod nano = $199. iPod video = $269; FM Radio Remote = $49.95*

   Paragraph 3: *Starbucks coffee; Jamba Juice; $4.50 per specialized drink*

   Paragraph 4: *Saving $500 a year will lead to $2,000 after two years. Lock the money into a certificate of deposit.*

Teaching Tip: The Writer's Desk activities, such as the one on the next page, provide students with an opportunity to develop a topic through all stages of the writing process using the process rhetorical mode. In the Warm Up, they begin by exploring various topics. These topics then carry on throughout the chapter.

Explore Topics

In the Writer's Desk Warm Up, you will try an exploring strategy to generate ideas about different topics.

Writer's Desk Warm Up

Read the following questions, and write the first ideas that come to your mind. Think of two or three ideas for each topic.

EXAMPLE: Imagine that you are choosing a college to begin your higher education. What are some steps that you should follow to choose an appropriate college?

—find out the programs the college offers

—find out the cost

—think about the size of the college

1. How can you become a better friend?

____

____

____

2. What can you do to fall out of love?

____

____

____

3. How can someone become competent in another language?

____

____

____

ESL Teaching Tip: Encourage your nonnative speakers to write about culture-specific topics because other students will enjoy learning something new or exotic.

DEVELOPING

When you write a process essay, choose a process that you know something about. For example, you might be able to explain how to become more environmentally conscious; however, you might not know how to reduce nuclear waste.

The Thesis Statement

In a process essay, the thesis statement states what process you will be explaining and what readers will be able to do after they have read the essay.

topic — controlling idea

Remaining attractive to your spouse can help keep your relationship exciting.

controlling idea — topic

Consistency, patience, and time are essential **to becoming a good parent**.

Writer's Desk Thesis Statements

Write a thesis statement for each of the following topics. You can look for ideas in the Warm Up on page 142. Each thesis statement should state the process and contain a controlling idea.

EXAMPLE: Topic: how to choose an appropriate college

Thesis Statement: *The next steps are important when choosing an appropriate college.*

1. Topic: how to become a better friend

   Thesis Statement: ______________________________

2. Topic: how to fall out of love

   Thesis Statement: ______________________________

3. Topic: how to learn another language

   Thesis Statement: ______________________________

The Supporting Ideas

A process essay contains a series of steps. When you develop supporting ideas for a process essay, think about the main steps that are necessary to complete the process.

- Use prewriting strategies such as freewriting and brainstorming to generate ideas.
- Choose the best ideas. Clearly explain the steps of the process.
- Organize your ideas. Choose the best organizational method for this essay pattern. Process essays generally use chronological or time order.

Teaching Tip: Go over these examples with students. Ensure that they see the difference between a list of examples of an interesting vacation and a process explaining how *to plan* an interesting vacation.

Hint: Give Steps, Not Examples

When you explain how to complete a process, describe each step. Do not simply list examples of the process.

Topic: How to Plan an Interesting Vacation

List of Examples	Steps in the Process
• go to a tropical island	• decide what your goal is
• ride a hot air balloon	• research possible locations
• swim with the sharks	• find out the cost
• tour an exotic city	• plan the itinerary according to budget

Writer's Desk List the Main Steps

Choose one thesis statement from the previous Writer's Desk. List the main steps to complete the process.

EXAMPLE:

Thesis Statement: *The next steps are important when choosing an appropriate college.*

1. *Ask about programs.*
2. *Find out the cost.*
3. *Consider the size of the college.*
4. *Ask about student housing.*

Thesis Statement: ____________________

____

Steps to complete the process:

____

____

____

____

____

The Essay Plan

An essay plan helps you organize your thesis statement, topic sentences, and supporting details before writing a first draft. Decide which steps and which details your reader will really need to complete the process or understand it.

Teaching Tip: For extra practice, ask students to develop supporting ideas for all three Writer's Desk topics. The topics are listed in the Warm Up.

THESIS STATEMENT: The next steps are important for choosing an appropriate college.

I. Find out which programs the college offers.
   A. Look for different options like majors and minors.
   B. Make note of the number of years to complete the program.
   C. Figure out the prerequisites necessary to get accepted.

II. Determine what you can afford to spend on your education.
   A. Ask the administration for details on tuition and other expenses.
   B. Research the available student loans and grants.
   C. Find out about other sources of financial aid, including scholarships.

III. Consider the size of the college.
   A. A smaller college may have smaller class sizes and more individualized attention.
   B. It may be easier to make friends in smaller classes.
   C. A bigger college may have more programs, a more heterogeneous student population, and more student services.

Writer's Desk Write an Essay Plan

Refer to the information you generated in previous Writer's Desks, and prepare a detailed essay plan. Add details and examples that will help to explain each step.

Teaching Tip: Ask students to keep their essay plans and then attach them to their final draft. You can then determine how the students have developed their ideas.

The First Draft

As you write your first draft, explain the process in a way that would be clear for your audience. Address the reader directly. For example, instead of writing, "You should scan the newspaper for used cars," simply write, "Scan the newspaper for used cars." Also, remember to use complete sentences and transitions to smoothly string together the ideas from your essay plan. Here are some time–order transitions that are useful for explaining processes.

To begin a process	To continue a process		To end a process
(at) first	after that	later	eventually
initially	afterward	meanwhile	finally
the first step	also	second	in the end
	furthermore	then	ultimately
	in addition	third	

Grammar Hint **Avoid Sentence Fragments**

Ensure that you do not use sentence fragments to list the steps of the process. A sentence must have a subject and a verb to express a complete idea.

> Consider your airline's carry-on luggage requirements. First, ^check^ the weight of your suitcase.

See Chapter 23 for more information about sentence fragments.

Writer's Desk **Write the First Draft**

In the previous Writer's Desk, you developed an essay plan. Now, carefully review your essay plan, make any necessary changes, and write the first draft of your process essay.

Teaching Tip:
The activity of revising a student essay should help your students understand the important link between the writing process and the grammar chapters.

REVISING AND EDITING

Revise and Edit a Process Essay

When you finish writing a process essay, carefully review your work and revise it to make the process as clear as possible to your readers. Check to make sure that you have organized your steps, and remove any details that are not relevant to being able to complete or understand the process. Before you revise and edit your own essay, practice revising and editing a student essay.

A Student Essay

Read the essay, and then answer the questions that follow. As you read, correct any errors that you find, and make comments in the margins.

The Right College

by Jose Luis Fonseca

1 When I first thought about a college to attend, I really did not know what to do. It was very lucky that Dave Hunt, my good friend, was more organized than me and could help me make such an important decision. One Sunday afternoon, very close to the deadline, we sat in a café, and he proceeded to explain exactly what I should think about when choosing a college. The next steps are crucial for finding an appropriate college.

2 Learn about the programs different colleges offer. Some important factors to consider are the number of years to complete the program that interests you. You need to know about different program options like major and minor subjects. It is necessary to know the prerequisite courses or experience necessary to get accepted into a program. If you want to pursue social work, perhaps you need some experience working with people. If you are interested in bookkeeping, maybe you need a particular high school math course to get accepted into the program. For instance, when I applied to our college's nursing program, I needed my Grade 12 science credit.

3 Also, the cost. Education is very expensive. When determining which college to go to, find one where you can afford to spend several years studying. For example, a college in the next city with a great reputation might cost a lot for tuition, housing, and transportation. ~~I live far from the campus. The traffic is incredibly heavy, and it takes me a long time to get there.~~ The local college might not be as well known or respected, but perhaps you will be able to afford the tuition, or you may be able to live at home, and your transportation costs might be much lower. For example, Trang Hoang, a mechanical engineering student, saved money by going to our local college. "My decision to study locally has never hurt my career prospects," she says.

4 You may not know what you want to study. In such a case, it is advisable to take a variety of courses to see where your interests lie. When Dave Hunt was eighteen, he started out majoring in art, but after one term, he worried about earning a good living, and he switched to administration. He realized that he loves working with numbers, so he is very happy about his decision. Keep your mind open to different subjects.

5 A smaller college will have smaller class sizes and more individualized attention. It is easier to make friends in smaller classes. But a larger college may have more programs. It may also have a more heterogeneous student

population, which would enable you to meet students with different backgrounds. A larger college may also provide more student services, clubs, and other activities, you may find such experiences enriching.

6 So think very carefully when choosing a college. The right college will provide you with innumerable advantages such as a good education, the right career opportunity, and long-lasting friendships. Take advantage of different sources and become informed. You will never regret it.

PRACTICE 2

Revising

1. Highlight the thesis statement.
2. Highlight the topic sentences for paragraphs 2 and 3.
3. Which of the following would make an effective topic sentence for paragraph 5? Circle the best answer.
   a. It is easy to make friends at college.
   b. Participate in different activities at a bigger college.
   c. Small colleges are not as interesting as big colleges.
   (d.) Keep the size of the college in mind when making your decision.
4. Which paragraph is unnecessary for the development of ideas? _4_ Explain why. _Taking a variety of courses has nothing to do with choosing a college._
5. In paragraph 3, cross out the sentence that does not support the topic sentence.
6. Paragraph 5 lacks adequate support. Think of a detailed example that would help flesh out the paragraph. Answers will vary.

   ____

   ____
7. Paragraph 2 lacks transitions. Add at least three transitions to link the sentences. Answers will vary.

   __________ __________ __________

GRAMMAR LINK

See the following chapters for more information about these grammar topics:
Run-Ons, Chapter 24
Pronouns, Chapter 31
Fragments, Chapter 23

Editing

8. Underline a pronoun problem in the introductory paragraph. Write the correction in the following space.

   Correction: _Dave was more organized than I (was)._

   ____

9. Underline the sentence fragment in paragraph 3. Then correct it here.

   Correction: *Also, consider the cost of your education.*

10. Underline the run-on sentence in paragraph 5. Then correct it here.

    Correction: *A bigger college may also provide more student services, clubs, and other activities. You may find such experiences enriching.*

vo•cab•u•lar•y BOOST

Look at the first draft of your process essay. Underline the verb that you use to describe each step of the process. Then, when possible, come up with a more evocative verb. Use your thesaurus for this activity.

Writer's Desk **Revise and Edit Your Process Essay**

Revise and edit the essay that you wrote for the previous Writer's Desk. You can refer to the revising and editing checklists at the end of this chapter and on this book's inside covers.

A Professional Essay

Journalist Stacey Colino specializes in health and family issues and has written for *The Washington Post*, *Parenting*, and *Shape*. In the next essay, she writes about how to become a happier person.

Do You Have What It Takes to Be Happy?

by Stacey Colino

1 If you add up money, beauty, fame and admiration, you've got the formula for a lifetime of bliss, right? Wrong. The truth is, your financial status, external circumstances, and life events account for no more than 15 percent of your happiness quotient, studies show. What elements do make a difference? Surprisingly simple internal factors such as having healthy

self-esteem, a sense of optimism and hope, gratifying relationships, and meaning and purpose in your life have the most influence, according to recent studies on what researchers call "subjective well-being."

2 If that sounds like a tall order, here's the good news: Even if they don't come naturally, many of the attitudes and thought patterns that influence happiness can be cultivated, which means you can boost your capacity for happiness today—and in the future. "Studies with twins reveal that happiness is somewhat like a person's cholesterol level—it's genetically influenced, but it's also influenced by some factors that are under our control," explains David Myers, Ph.D., a social psychologist at Hope College in Holland, Michigan, and author of *The Pursuit of Happiness* (Harper-Collins, 1993). In other words, while your genetically determined temperament has a fairly strong influence on your happiness quotient, you can nudge it upward with the attitudes and approaches you bring to your life. To develop a sunnier disposition, use the simple strategies outlined in the following essay, and you'll be on your way to a richer, more satisfying life, starting now!

3 Develop an upbeat attitude. No, you don't want to become a Pollyanna who overlooks problems and thinks everything is peachy even when it isn't. But you do want to consciously focus on what's positive in your life because this can engender a sense of optimism and hope. And research has found that happy people are brimming with these key ingredients. In one study at Southern Methodist University in Dallas, happy subjects were more hopeful about their wishes than their less **sanguine** peers. It's not that their wishes came true more often, but the happy people expected them to come true. How? They do it by expecting to have a joyful summer every day, not just when they're on vacation, by identifying negative thoughts and countering them with positive or neutral ones, and by embracing challenges (such as parasailing or public speaking) instead of fearing them. Such people realize that challenges will help them grow as a person.

sanguine: optimistic

4 Hang out with your favorite people. It's as simple as this: Carving out as much time as you can to spend with people you value gives you a sense of connection, as well as a support system for when your luck heads south. Research at the University of Illinois at Urbana–Champaign found that people who are consistently very happy have stronger romantic and social relationships than unhappy people. "We're social creatures by nature," says Louis H. Janda, an associate professor of psychology at Old Dominion University in Norfolk, Virginia. "When you're involved with others, it gives you a sense of belonging and lets you engage in mutually enjoyable activities, all of which can buffer you from stress."

5 Infuse your life with a sense of purpose. If you want to be happy, it is important to give your life meaning: Research at Middle Tennessee State University in Murfreesboro found that having a sense of purpose is a significant predictor of happiness and life satisfaction. To create a vision of what's meaningful to you, ask yourself, "What activities make me feel excited or enthusiastic? What do I want to be remembered for? What matters most to me?" If you can articulate these desires to yourself, you can set specific goals to help you fulfill them. If you realize that your strongest desire is to become an influential teacher and role model, for example, you might set a goal of volunteering to help disadvantaged kids or of going back to school to get your teaching degree.

6 Count your blessings, not your burdens. When people keep a gratitude journal, in which they jot down a daily list of what they appreciate in their lives, they experience a heightened sense of well being, according to research at the University of California, Davis, and the University of Miami in Florida. "There's a natural tendency to take things for granted, but if you stop and think of all the ways you are blessed, it doesn't take long for the mind to use that as the new baseline for perceiving how happy you are," explains study co-author Michael E. McCullough, Ph.D., an associate professor of psychology and religious studies at the University of Miami.

7 Recharge your energy and your spirits. Sure, exercise can work wonders in keeping your mood buoyant, but so can getting some simple **R & R.** "Happy people lead active, vigorous lives yet reserve time for restorative sleep and solitude," Myers says. Short-change yourself of the shut-eye you need, and it's hard to enjoy much of anything when you're exhausted. In a recent study involving more than nine hundred women, researchers assessed how happy women were based on their daily activities and found that sleep quality had a substantial influence over how much the women enjoyed life, even when they engaged in plenty of pleasurable activities like sex and socializing.

R & R: rest and relaxation

8 Put on a happy face! If you act as if you're on cloud nine—by smiling with your mouth and eyes, speaking in a cheerful voice, and walking confidently—going through the motions can trigger the actual emotion. There's even science to prove it: A study at Fairleigh Dickinson University in Teaneck, New Jersey, found that when people forced themselves to smile or laugh, they experienced a substantial boost in mood afterward.

9 So start off by acting as if you're walking on the sunny side of the street—even if it's cloudy. Chances are, you'll begin to feel a little happier after just a few steps!

PRACTICE 3

1. What is the writer's specific purpose? *to show people how to be happy*
2. Highlight the thesis statement. It may not be in the first paragraph.
3. Read the topic sentence of each body paragraph. Highlight the verbs in each topic sentence.
4. In each topic sentence, the subject is implied but not stated. What is the subject?

   The subject is "you."
5. In paragraph 5, list the examples the writer gives to support the topic sentence.

   Give your life meaning, ask yourself questions to find your life meaning, and set goals to achieve that meaning.
6. The writer supported her main ideas with many specific examples. Identify and underline six research studies that the writer refers to.
7. Circle the names of three experts that the writer quotes.
8. The writer uses no transitional words or phrases to link the steps of the process. Add a transitional word or expression to the beginning of at least four body paragraphs.
   Answers will vary.

The Writer's Room Topics for Process Essays

Writing Activity 1

Write a process essay about one of the following topics or choose your own topic.

General Topics

How to . . .

1. buy a used car
2. become a good driver
3. communicate more effectively with family members
4. win a ______________
5. live on a budget

College and Work-Related Topics

How to . . .

6. look for a new job
7. assemble a ______________
8. become a better manager or supervisor
9. change a law
10. make a good impression at an interview

Writing Activity 2

Choose a quotation that you agree or disagree with, and then write a process essay based on it.

> The first step to getting the things you want out of life is this: Decide what you want.
>
> —Ben Stein, writer

> We now accept the fact that learning is a lifelong process of keeping abreast of change. And the most pressing task is to teach people how to learn.
>
> —Peter Drucker, writer

> There was a definite process by which one made people into friends, and it involved talking to them and listening to them for hours at a time.
>
> —Rebecca West, journalist

> Civilization is a slow process of adopting the ideas of minorities.
>
> —Anonymous

WRITING LINK

More Process Writing Topics

Chapter 21, on page 344, see Writer's Room Topic 2.
Chapter 25, on page 387, see Writer's Room Topic 2.
Chapter 26, on page 396, see Writer's Room Topic 1.
Chapter 30, on page 454, see Writer's Room Topic 1

READING LINK

More Process Readings

"The Rich Resonance of Small Talk" by Roxanne Roberts (page 599)
"The Rules of Survival" by Laurence Gonzales (page 610)

Teaching Tip: Have students read one of the essays in the Reading Link and discuss the main ideas. Also ask students what characterisics the reading has to classify it as a process essay.

Writing Activity 3

What are some steps people can take to have an enduring personal relationship?

Teaching Tip: You could ask students to brainstorm together and come up with ways to achieve wealth, happiness, notoriety, education, or love.

CHECKLIST: PROCESS ESSAY

As you write your process essay, review the checklist on the inside front cover. Also ask yourself these questions.

- Does my thesis statement make a point about the process?
- Do I include all of the steps in the process?
- Do I clearly explain each step so my reader can accomplish the process?
- Do I mention all of the supplies that my reader needs to complete the process?
- Do I use transitions to connect all of the steps in the process?

Teaching Tip:
Writer's World Competition
Please advise students that they can submit their essays for possible publication to: <thewritersworld@prenhall.com>.

How Do I Get a Better Grade?

Definition

CHAPTER 10

CONTENTS

Exploring
- What Is Definition?
- The Definition Essay
- Explore Topics

Developing
- The Thesis Statement
- The Supporting Ideas
- The Essay Plan
- The First Draft

Revising and Editing
- Revise and Edit a Definition Essay
- A Professional Essay: "On Genius" by Dorothy Nixon

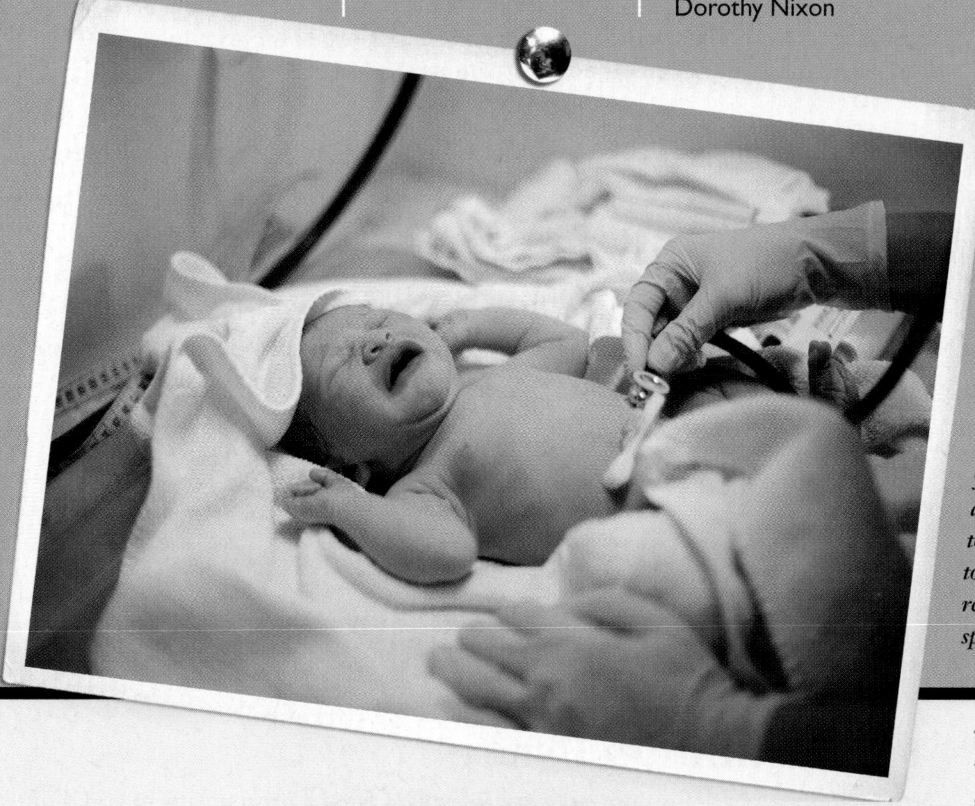

To help patients understand a diagnosis, doctors may define the illness itself or explain related medical terms. Similarly, you may write an entire essay in which you define a term. Or, you may need to define only a few terms within an essay to ensure that your readers understand specific concepts.

Writers' Exchange

Brainstorm some common slang expressions. Think about words you use to express pleasure or disgust. You can also consider words describing a specific type of person. Choose one expression and define it without using a dictionary. Make your definition clear so that a nonnative speaker will understand the word.

Teaching Tip:
The Writers' Exchange activity can help your students understand definition. This activity can be done in small groups or as a class discussion. Write some slang words on the board that students will then define. You might draw their attention to the types of definitions students use (definition by synonym, category, or negation). Place nonnative speakers with native speakers.

> ***"Freedom's just another word for nothing left to lose."***
>
> KRIS KRISTOFFERSON, *actor and singer*

EXPLORING

What Is Definition?

When you define, you explain the meaning of a word. Some terms have concrete meanings, and you can define them in a few words. For example, a *town* is "a small city." Other words, such as *values*, *faith*, or *human rights*, are more abstract and require more detailed definitions. It is possible to write a paragraph, an essay, or even an entire book about such concepts. Here are some examples of terms people regularly define in different situations.

Audience: Children

I expect you to be *reliable*.

- Phone if you are going to be late.
- Do your chores to help out.
- Do your homework every night.

Audience: Classmate

In my sociology class we are discussing the term *poverty*.

- Poverty means different things to different cultures.
- In this country, the government always talks about low-income families.
- Some countries, like China, define poverty by the minimum caloric intake of an individual.

Audience: Colleague

My supervisor said my presentation "needs improvement."

- I spoke too quickly.
- I relied too heavily on my PowerPoint slides.
- My presentation was too long.

The Definition Essay

When you write a definition essay, try to explain what a term means to you. For example, if someone asks you to define *overachiever*, you might give examples of overachievers and what you think those people do that goes beyond the limits. You may also explain what an overachiever is not. Also, remember the next two points.

1. **Choose a term that you know something about.** You need to understand a term to say something relevant and interesting about it.
2. **Give a clear definition.** Write a definition that your reader will easily understand, and support your definition with examples.

Teaching Tip:
Ask students to identify the various ways the writer defines a great teacher.

Definition at Work

In the following excerpt, Michigan's 2004 Teacher of the Year, Heidi Capraro, defines what makes a great teacher.

We have a passion for teaching. We care about our students, parents, and the communities in which we work and teach. We celebrate the positive accomplishments in the field of teaching and look for brighter possibilities for the future.

I think teachers have to be sensitive to each student's tolerance for frustration and recognize that each one handles this kind of stress differently. We want to engage and motivate students, not force them to shut down and quit. This applies to students at every age. I think people assume that as children grow up, they don't need the same support and understanding. In reality, they have more difficulties to face as they reach their teenage years. Kindness, empathy, opportunities for success, modifications, and adults with a personal interest in them—these are what every child needs.

Hint **Consider Your Audience**

Consider your audience when you write a definition essay. You may have to adjust your tone and vocabulary, depending on who will be reading the essay. For example, if you write a definition essay about cloning for your political science class, you may have to explain concepts using basic, nontechnical terms. If you write the same essay for your biology class, you may be able to use more technical terms.

A Student Essay

Read the student essay and answer the questions that follow.

Journalists Are History's Record Keepers

by Lindsey Davis

plethora: a large amount

Fourth Estate: the entire press, including newspapers, television news programs, magazines, etc.

1 When you want to find research for that paper on World War II for class, you hit the books in the library, looking for the historian who summed up the events or the political scientist who offered critical insight as to why it happened. But when you want to find out what is happening in the world right now, you pick up the *Los Angeles Times* or log onto your computer and browse the **plethora** of news sites. Journalists play multiple roles in society. From the **Fourth Estate** as the check on government and business to the responsibility of creating a forum for debate and free speech, the job of journalists is crucial to society's progress. But beyond this role, journalists are historians. They are the note takers and storytellers who document today's activities and events to safeguard their accuracy and preserve the record of history.

2 First, different types of media are crucial for preserving historical records. Newspapers, news websites, and television news programs are the only place you can turn to find the latest breaking developments of what is happening in Washington, what reforms Governor Schwarzenegger is planning, the status of the war in Iraq, and the crucial stats of the last NFL playoff game. Before it goes in the history books, it goes in the newspaper. Before you can find it in the library, you can find it in the news.

3 Moreover, journalists are the record keepers for the community. They will give you the plain and simple facts. They will find out how much those tickets were selling for at the Rose Bowl. They will tell you who won the basketball games and what the upcoming baseball season looks like. But beyond simple facts, they will record the emotions of a Rose Bowl defeat. How about those new movies and CDs that are coming out next week? They will give you the scoop of what's good and what's bad. They will tell you what you can't miss in Los Angeles. You can find the thoughts and analyses of a vast array of differing voices.

4 Furthermore, journalists are also crucial to preserving the spirit of the times. It is within the media that you'll find the record of the year's events. But this history won't be complete unless it includes your voice, your opinion, and your perspective on events. Tell the journalists what's going on and what you would like to see covered. Send them an e-mail. Talk to reporters and tell them what you think. The media will never be able to create an accurate record of history unless you help gather all the facts by saying what you know or what you saw. Do you think something was wrongly covered? Let the media know. Do you disagree with a column you

have read? Send a letter to the editor and make sure your viewpoint is printed and recorded as well.

5 Journalists are committed to ensuring that whatever happens is recorded forever. Some people say that journalists write the rough draft of history. But they strive to report accurately enough that it will be the final draft. Their dedication ensures that you get the news and ensures that history is recorded. All they ask is that you read to keep the history alive.

PRACTICE 1

1. What is the specific purpose of this essay? *It is to inform the reader about the importance of the press for recording history.*
2. Highlight the thesis statement.
3. Highlight the topic sentence of each body paragraph.
4. What introductory style is used? Circle the best answer.
   a. anecdote
   b. historical
   c. contrasting position
   (d.) general background
5. In your own words, list some of the specific examples in each body paragraph. Answers will vary.
   Paragraph 2: newspapers, television, Web sites give latest development in news and sports
   Paragraph 3: cost of tickets, who won game, new CDs
   Paragraph 4: record of year's events, letters to the editor, interactions between the public and the media
6. Circle the transitional links in this essay.

Teaching Tip:
The Writer's Desk activities, such as the one on the next page, provide students with opportunities to develop a topic through all stages of the writing process using the definition rhetorical mode. In the Warm Up, they begin by exploring various topics. Those topics then carry on throughout the chapter.

ESL Teaching Tip:
If you have a majority of nonnative speakers in the class, you may want to brainstorm some ideas for the Warm Up on the next page with the entire group because nonnative speakers may not know the connotations of *house* versus *home*.

Explore Topics

In the Writer's Desk Warm Up, you will try an exploring strategy to generate ideas about different topics.

Writer's Desk Warm Up

Read the following questions, and write the first ideas that come to your mind. Think of two or three ideas for each topic.

EXAMPLE: What is a volunteer? Think of some characteristics of a volunteer.

—is involved in charitable causes

—wants to help people

—has love for humankind

1. What is a home?

____

____

____

2. What is the American dream?

____

____

____

3. What is a religion?

____

____

____

DEVELOPING

The Thesis Statement

A clear thesis statement for a definition essay introduces the term and provides a definition. There are three basic ways to define a term.

Definition by Synonym

Providing a definition by synonym is useful if the original term is difficult to understand, and the synonym is a more familiar word.

term +	synonym
He is a neophyte,	which means he is a beginner or novice.

Definition by Category

When you define by category, you determine the larger group to which the term belongs. Then you determine what unique characteristics set the term apart from others in that category.

term +	category +	detail
A forest ranger	is a worker	who is trained to protect wildlife in national parks.

Definition by Negation

When you define by negation, you explain what a term does not mean. You can then include a sentence explaining what it does mean.

term +	what it is not +	what it is
Obsession	is not an eccentricity;	it is a mental illness.

Grammar Hint **Using Semicolons**

You can join two related and complete ideas with a semicolon, as the writer has done in this example of a definition.

EXAMPLE: Marriage is not the end of your freedom; it is the beginning of a shared journey.

See Chapter 21 for more information about using semicolons.

Making a Point

Defining terms by synonym, category, and negation are only guidelines for writing thesis statements for a definition essay. Keep in mind that your essay will be more interesting if you express your attitude or point of view in your thesis statement.

No point: Avarice means greed.

Point: Human avarice, or greed, invariably leads to tragedy.

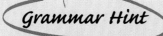

Teaching Tip:
Ask students to compare the following examples. Which sentence in each pair clearly indicates a point of view or attitude?
(1) He is a critic, which means he states his opinion; He is a controversial critic, stating opinions that jar people from their comfort zone;
(2) Westerns are films set in the North American frontier; Set in the North American frontier, Westerns are films that raise audience passions and longings;
(3) A statesman is not a politician but a leader; A statesman is not an ordinary politician but a skilled and farsighted leader.

ESL Teaching Tip:
Group Work
For Practice 2, pair nonnative speakers with native speakers. Students should also discuss if they have defined the term using a synonym, category, or negation. If they do not remember the types of definitions, refer them to pages 160–161.

PRACTICE 2 Write thesis statements by defining the following terms using your own words. Try to make definitions by synonym, category, and negation. Remember to indicate your controlling idea in the thesis statements. Answers will vary.

EXAMPLE: Road rage *is not a momentary lapse of judgment; it is serious criminal behavior.*

1. A misfit ______________________________

2. A jock ______________________________

3. B-list actors ______________________________

4. Rush-hour traffic ______________________________

5. A mentor ______________________________

Hint — Be Precise!

When you write a definition essay, it is important to use precise words to define the term. Moreover, when you define a term by category, make sure that the category for your term is correct.

Anorexia nervosa is the inability to eat.
(Anorexia nervosa is not an ability or an inability.)

Anorexia nervosa is when you want to be thin.
(*When* refers to a time, but anorexia nervosa is not a time.)

Anorexia nervosa is where it is hard to eat properly.
(*Where* refers to a place, but anorexia nervosa is not a place.)

Now look at a better definition of this illness.

Anorexia nervosa is a tragic **eating disorder** characterized by the desire to become very thin.

PRACTICE 3 Revise each sentence using precise language.

Answers will vary.

EXAMPLE: Multitasking is when you do many activities at once.

Multitasking is doing many activities at once.

1. A blacklist is when a list of people comes under suspicion.

   A blacklist is an inventory or a record of people who come under suspicion.

2. A poor loser is the inability to accept defeat graciously.

   A poor loser is a person who is unable to accept defeat graciously.

3. A twixter is overdependence on parents by adult children.

   A twixter is an adult child who is overdependent on his or her parents.

4. Feedback is when you get constructive criticism.

   Feedback is constructive criticism.

5. Networking is where you keep in contact with people to help your career.

   Networking is a system by which an individual keeps in contact with people to help his or her career.

vo•cab•u•lar•y BOOST

Some words have neutral, positive, or negative associations. Look at each set of words and categorize each as neutral, positive, or negative. Do this with a partner.

1. thin, cadaverous, lean, emaciated, wiry, skinny, slender
2. home, shack, cottage, slum, stomping ground, dump, sanctuary
3. dainty, delicate, finicky, fussy, prissy, fragile, elegant, frail
4. honest, coarse, crude, open, gross, straightforward
5. brat, child, sweetheart, cutie, munchkin, delinquent, heir, mama's boy

Teaching Tip:
Pair Work
Have students compare their answers with a partner to ensure that they have defined each term correctly.

ESL Teaching Tip:
Ask nonnative speakers to define a word or expression from their own language that has been appropriated by English speakers. Ask them if the term in their language has a different connotation than it does in English. Some examples are *macho*, *karma*, *guru*, *mensch*, *mandarin*, *raj*, or *outcaste*.

Teaching Tip:
Explain to students that word connotations are important to reveal their attitude toward the subject of their text.

ESL Teaching Tip:
Pair native and nonnative speakers in mixed groups to do the Vocabulary Boost. Nonnative speakers may not understand all of the connotations.

Writer's Desk Write Thesis Statements

Write a thesis statement in which you define each of the following topics. You can look for ideas in the previous Writer's Desk. Remember to make a point in your thesis statement.

EXAMPLE: Topic: a volunteer

Thesis Statement: *A volunteer is a necessary and generous person who is emotionally invested in the betterment of humankind.*

1. Topic: home

   Thesis statement: ____________________

   ____

2. Topic: the American dream

   Thesis statement: ____________________

   ____

3. Topic: a religion

   Thesis statement: ____________________

   ____

Teaching Tip:
You can make the Writer's Desk activity more challenging by asking students if they have defined by synonym, category, or negation.

The Supporting Ideas

After you have developed an effective thesis statement, generate supporting ideas. In a definition essay, you can give examples that clarify your definition. To develop supporting ideas follow these three steps:

- Use prewriting strategies to generate ideas. Think about facts, anecdotes, and examples that will help define your term.
- Choose the best ideas. Use examples that clearly reveal the definition of the term.
- Organize your ideas. Choose the best organizational method for this essay pattern.

Writer's Desk Generate Supporting Ideas

Choose one of your thesis statements from the previous Writer's Desk. List three or four ideas that most effectively illustrate the definition.

EXAMPLE: Thesis statement: *A volunteer is a necessary and generous person who is emotionally invested in the betterment of humankind.*

—offers to help others

—brings attention to charitable causes

—is selfless

—is important for society

Thesis statement: ______________________________

____

Supports: ______________________________

____

____

____

The Essay Plan

An essay plan helps you organize your thesis statement and supporting details before writing the first draft. A definition essay includes a complete definition of the term and provides adequate examples to support the central definition. When creating a definition essay plan, ensure that your examples provide varied evidence and do not just repeat the definition. Organize your ideas in a logical sequence.

Teaching Tip: As an additional activity, ask students to develop supporting ideas for all three Writer's Desk topics. The topics are listed in the Warm Up.

THESIS STATEMENT: A volunteer is a necessary and generous person who is emotionally invested in the betterment of humankind.

I. Volunteers do not earn money; they gain a sense of personal satisfaction.
   A. Donne wrote Meditation XVII: No man is an island.
   B. He believed that people are not isolated, but interconnected.
   C. Donne's philosophy influenced people such as Martin Luther King, Jr.

II. Many people of all types are volunteers.
    A. Extremely rich people contribute to charity.
    B. Ordinary people donate their time.
III. By giving their time and money, volunteers are crucial for charities to function.
    A. Nonprofit organizations help develop public awareness of different issues and problems.
    B. International organizations rely on volunteers.
    C. Volunteers also work at local community churches and schools.

Teaching Tip: Ask students to keep their essay plans and then attach them to their final draft. You can then determine how the students have developed their ideas.

Writer's Desk Write an Essay Plan

Refer to the information you generated in previous Writer's Desks and prepare a detailed essay plan.

The First Draft

Your essay plan is the backbone around which you can craft your first draft. Use it to write your first draft. As you write, remember to vary your sentence structure and to write complete sentences. Also include transitional words or expressions to help your ideas flow smoothly. Here are some transitional expressions that can help you show different levels of importance in a definition essay.

To show the level of importance

clearly	next
first	one quality . . . another quality
most important	second
most of all	undoubtedly

Writer's Desk Write the First Draft

Carefully review the essay plan you prepared in the previous Writer's Desk. Make any necessary changes to the definition or its supporting details, and then write your first draft.

REVISING AND EDITING

Revise and Edit a Definition Essay

When you finish writing a definition essay, carefully review your work and revise it to make the definition as clear as possible to your readers. You might have to adjust your definition and supporting ideas to suit their knowledge. Also keep in mind the tone of your essay. Certain words have either negative or positive connotations. Finally, check that you have organized your ideas logically and remove any irrelevant details. Before you revise and edit your own essay, practice revising and editing a student essay.

Teaching Tip: The activity of revising a student essay should help your students understand the important link between the writing process and the grammar chapters.

A Student Essay

Read the essay, and then answer the questions that follow. As you read, correct any errors that you find, and make comments in the margins.

Volunteers

by Michael Newberg

1 "What do we live for, if it is not to make life less difficult for each other"? wrote the English writer George Eliot. This question has been discussed throughout history during times of prosperity and poverty. Human beings need to be kind and giving to each other. Volunteers are the backbone of a kind world, and we desperately need their acts of charity. A volunteer is a necessary and generous person who is emotionally invested in the betterment of humankind.

2 Volunteers do not work to earn money; they work to gain a sense of personal satisfaction. One of the English poets, John Donne (1572–1631), believed that humanity has a collective responsibility. In a powerful poem, *Meditation XVII*, Donne wrote, "No man is an island, entire of itself . . . any man's death diminishes me, because I am involved in mankind." According to Donne, people must care for each other. His philosophy has influenced many people such as Martin Luther King, Jr. Volunteers want to help people because they want to make the world a more just society.

3 Some very wealthy people donate tremendous amounts of time and money to help others. Oprah, for example. She spends a lot of time and money with her girls' school in South Africa. Many middle-class and poor people also volunteer and help those in need. Soup kitchens, for instance, could not function without the service of many unpaid workers. Bae Kim is a cook in our college cafeteria, but he also volunteers once a week for the Meals on Wheels program in our district.

4 By giving their time and money, volunteers are crucial for charities to function. Nonprofit organizations, such as Doctors Without Borders or the Red cross, help raise public awareness about different issues, including the AIDS epidemic, war, political injustices, and so on. Most of these organizations rely on large numbers of volunteers from all walks of life. ~~Doctors Without Borders won the Nobel Peace Prize several years ago.~~ Volunteers not only work in large international organizations, but they also donate their own time and money to local churches, schools, and youth centers. Our community refugee help center could not function without the local high school students who regularly volunteer there.

5 Volunteers are increasingly necessary to create a kinder world. With powerfull communication technology, we see tragedy every day in our living rooms. Those volunteers from all walks of life who give their time and skills help to alleviate the suffering of others. As Martin Luther King Jr. said, "Life's most persistent and urgent question is, what are you doing for others?"

PRACTICE 4

Revising

1. Highlight the thesis statement.
2. What type of definition does the thesis statement have? Circle the best answer.
   a. synonym   (b.) category   c. negation
3. Highlight the topic sentences in paragraphs 2 and 4.
4. What type of definition is in the topic sentence for paragraph 2? Circle your answer.
   a. synonym   b. category   (c.) negation
5. Paragraph 3 does not have a topic sentence. Which sentence would be an effective topic sentence for that paragraph? Circle the best answer.
   a. Oprah Winfrey is one of the most generous people in America.
   b. Many people reflect on the act of giving.
   c. Many poor people donate their time to charitable organizations.
   (d.) Volunteers are found in all social classes.
6. Cross out the sentence in paragraph 4 that does not support the topic sentence.

Editing

7. The quotation in the introductory paragraph is incorrectly punctuated. Underline and correct the error.

   "What do we live for, if it is not to make life less difficult for each other?" wrote the English writer George Eliot.

8. Paragraph 3 has a fragment. Underline and correct the error.

   Correction: *Oprah, for example, is very generous.*

9. There is an error in capitalization in paragraph 4. Underline and correct the error.

   Correction: *Red Cross*

10. There is one spelling mistake in paragraph 5. Underline and correct the mistake.

   Correction: *powerful*

GRAMMAR LINK

See the following chapters for more information about these grammar topics:
Fragments, Chapter 23
Spelling, Chapter 34
Capitalization, Chapter 37
Quotations, Chapter 37

Writer's Desk Revise and Edit Your Essay

Revise and edit the essay that you wrote for the previous Writer's Desk. You can refer to the revising and editing checklists at the end of this chapter and on this book's inside covers.

A Professional Essay

Dorothy Nixon, a freelance writer, has written for *Salon.com*, *Chatelaine*, and *Today's Parent* magazine. In the following article, Nixon ponders the meaning of genius.

On Genius

by Dorothy Nixon

1 When Albert Einstein was chosen as *Time* magazine's Man of the Century, I was not surprised. Our society is simply obsessed with the idea of genius, and no man embodies that concept in this scientific age better than Albert Einstein, with his godlike grasp of mathematics and his messy mad-scientist hair.

2 Around the same time, a group of Canadian researchers were grabbing headlines. The researchers, while analyzing Einstein's brain, had discovered some extra connections in the famous physicist's grey matter. They theorized that Einstein's brain held the secret to the man's genius. "I held Einstein's brain, and I was in awe," said a researcher, revealing the fact that the research was not entirely objective on his part. After all, *awe* is usually a feeling reserved for religious experiences.

3 Rationally speaking, holding Einstein's brain cannot feel too differently from holding a chimp's brain or a Vegas chorus girl's brain.

Still, everyone understood what he meant: he was moved by the idea of Einstein's genius, which seems almost mystical in nature and therefore something to be "in awe of." The question remains, why were the scientists trying to quantify Einstein's genius by locating it somewhere in his brain in the first place? Genius is not quantifiable. Genius cannot be captured in a butterfly net or put in a bottle. Genius is not even that mysterious, really: it exists all around us, almost always in unrecognized form.

4 Societies tend to value some forms of genius over others. In the Renaissance, artists, sculptors, and architects were esteemed above all; in sixteenth century Vienna, musicians were revered; today, mathematicians and scientists are lauded. Da Vinci, Mozart, and Einstein arose from these environments.

nurtured: encouraged

5 Genius has to be given a chance; it has to be **nurtured.** It has to be rigorously trained, too. (Remember, genius is one percent inspiration and ninety-nine percent perspiration, according to Thomas Edison.) Genius has to have good timing, or it is liable to be labeled lunacy. Above all, it has to be recognized for what it is.

6 A while back, I was sitting on the Montreal–Toronto train. To my dismay, the grandmotherly woman beside me wanted to talk. I don't normally like talking on trains, but within minutes I was truly mesmerized by the old woman's story. In broken English, the old woman told me about her life; how she had grown up in a poor country and spent only a few years in school; how she had eloped to Canada with a hardworking young man from her village; how she had helped out her husband with his landscaping business "doing the money part" until they had enough cash scraped together to buy a small apartment building. She told me how her husband had died soon thereafter and left her with three young boys, and how, with good business "luck" (for she had never remarried), she made enough money to put all her boys through graduate school. Indeed, she was on her way this minute to visit her youngest son and his wife, both law school professors.

7 She felt sorry for young people these days, she said. They were all so busy juggling careers and kids that they found it so hard to cope. That is why she often visited her sons' homes to help out. While there, she cooked all the meals, mostly Italian specialties (as she described them my mouth watered uncontrollably), and even whipped up some outfits for the kids.

8 By modern definitions, this woman was not a genius: she did not discover a new element or the reason the stars stay up in heaven. She had not even been to high school. But as I got off the train, I felt that I had been in the presence of someone very special; someone with extraordinary gifts who had lived and was continuing to live a full and balanced life.

9 If that is not pure genius, what is?

PRACTICE 5

1. Highlight the thesis statement of the essay.
2. According to the writer, what four things does genius need to flourish?

   It needs to be given a chance, to be nurtured, to be trained, and to be recognized.

3. According to the writer, how has the definition of genius changed over time?

   Today's society values science, whereas in previous eras, society recognized arts and music.

4. Highlight the topic sentence of paragraph 6. Remember that it may not always be the first sentence of the paragraph.
5. The old woman tells the writer her life story. What can you infer (conclude) about the old woman's personality from this tale?

   She is hardworking, caring, loyal, and persevering.

6. The writer acknowledges that society recognizes Einstein as a genius. But why does the writer think that the old woman is also a good example of genius?

   The old woman has led a well-balanced and responsible life. She has taken care of her children, and she also helps to take care of her grandchildren. She has made a positive contribution to society through her actions.

7. In paragraph 6, why does the author place quotation marks around "doing the money part" and "luck"?

   The author is indicating that she doesn't really believe the woman simply had luck. She thinks the woman worked very hard.

ESL Teaching Tip: Go over the terms in Writing Activity 1 with the class. Your nonnative speakers may not understand what some of them mean.

The Writer's Room Topics for Definition Essays

Writing Activity 1

Write a definition essay about any of the following topics, or choose your own topic.

General Topics

1. a soul mate
2. meltdown
3. a saint
4. family
5. a good sport

College and Work-Related Topics

6. teamwork
7. poor workplace communication
8. equal opportunity
9. good education
10. healthy competition

Writing Activity 2

Choose a quotation that you agree or disagree with, and then write a definition essay based on it.

> The deepest definition of youth is life as yet untouched by tragedy.
>
> —Alfred North Whitehead, mathematician

> The absence of flaw in beauty is itself a flaw.
>
> —Havelock Ellis, sexual psychologist

> The fearless are merely fearless. People who act in spite of their fear are truly brave.
>
> —James A. LaFond-Lewis, restaurateur

> Leadership is a combination of strategy and character. If you must be without one, be without strategy.
>
> —H. Norman Schwarzkopf, general

Writing Activity 3

The Irish writer Oscar Wilde once said that all art is useless. Is art only paintings and sculptures, or does it also include folk art, advertising, music, writing, theater, dance, and so on? Does art have to be original, or can it include something that is copied? Does the definition of art depend on a person's background, such as his or her ethnicity? Write an essay in which you define what art means to you.

Teaching Tip:

Pair Work

Have students read one of the suggested definition readings in the Reading Link. Then, in pairs, they can list the main examples that help explain the definition.

READING LINK

More Definition Readings

"Raunch Culture" by Ariel Levy (p. 629)
"Twixters" by Betsy Hart (p. 632)

WRITING LINK

More Definition Writing Topics

Chapter 29, Writer's Room topic 2 (page 444)
Chapter 33, Writer's Room topic 1 (page 493)
Chapter 36, Writer's Room topic 2 (page 530)

CHECKLIST: DEFINITION ESSAY

As you write your definition essay, review the checklist on the inside front cover. Also ask yourself the following set of questions.

- ☐ Does my thesis statement contain a definition by synonym, category, or negation?
- ☐ Do I use concise language in my definition?
- ☐ Do I make a point in my thesis statement?
- ☐ Do all of my supporting paragraphs relate to the thesis statement?
- ☐ Do the body paragraphs contain enough supporting details that help define the term?

Teaching Tip:
Writer's World Competition
Please advise students that they can submit their essays for possible publication to: <thewritersworld@prenhall.com>.

How Do I Get a Better Grade?

PEARSON mywritinglab

Visit www.mywritinglab.com for audio-visual lectures and additional practice sets about definition writing.
Get a better grade with MyWritingLab!

Classification

CHAPTER 11

CONTENTS

To make it easier for shoppers, many shoe stores display footwear according to different styles and purposes, such as sandals, sneakers, and boots. Similarly, when writing a classification essay, you divide a topic into categories to help your readers understand your ideas.

Writers' Exchange

Work with a partner or group. Divide the next words into three or four different categories. What are the categories? Why did you choose those categories?

art	studio	medicine
construction	stethoscope	workshop
doctor	paintbrush	hospital
hammer	welder	sculptor

Teaching Tip:
The Writers' Exchange activity can help your students understand classification. Students might classify the words in different ways. Ask them what unites their three categories (the classification principle).

> *Seeing much, suffering much, and studying much are the three pillars of learning.*
>
> BENJAMIN DISRAELI, *politician*

EXPLORING

What Is Classification?

When you classify, you sort a subject into more understandable categories. For instance, if a bookstore simply put books randomly on shelves, you would have a hard time finding the book that you need. Instead, the bookstore classifies according to subject area.

In classification writing, each of the categories must be part of a larger group, yet they must also be distinct. For example, you might write an essay about the most common types of hobbies and sort those into board games, sports, and crafts. Take a look at some ways people use classification in common situations.

Audience: Family member

Your dirty laundry should be sorted in the following way.

- Put the colored clothing in the red basket.
- Put your whites in the beige basket.
- Put all bath towels in the green bin by the door.

Audience: Classmate

Different labs on our campus are high-tech, quaint, and outdated.

- Our science lab has the latest technology.
- The music lab is old, but quite beautiful and quaint.
- The language lab is outdated, and the audio needs to be upgraded to digital.

Audience: Customer

Our beds come in three categories.

- Innerspring mattresses have a variety of coil gauges and numbers of springs.
- Air mattresses can be pumped for a softer or firmer feel.
- Foam beds may be made from polyurethane foam, memory foam, or latex.

Teaching Tip:
Ask students to list other types of writing that include categories. Some examples are inventories, advertisements, medical reports, and report cards.

The Classification Essay

To find a topic for a classification essay, think of something that you can sort or divide into different groups. Also, determine a reason for classifying the items. When you are planning your ideas for a classification essay, remember the following points.

1. **Use a common classification principle.**
   A **classification principle** is the overall method that you use to sort the subject into categories. To find the classification principle, think about one common characteristic that unites the different categories. For example, if your subject is "jobs," your classification principle might be any of the following:
   - jobs in which people work with their hands
   - dangerous jobs
   - outsourced jobs

Teaching Tip:
Ask students to brainstorm categories for each classification principle. For example, "outsourced jobs" might include those in textiles, those in telephone technical support, and those in toy manufacturing.

2. **Sort the subject into distinct categories.**
A classification essay should have two or more categories.

Topic: jobs

Classification principle: dangerous jobs

Category 1
public security jobs

Category 2
construction jobs

Category 3
hazardous materials jobs

Hint **Categories Should Not Overlap**

When sorting a topic into categories, make sure that the categories do not overlap. For example, you would not classify *roommates* into aloof, friendly, and messy because a messy roommate could also be aloof or friendly. Although the categories share something in common, each category should be distinct.

Teaching Tip:
Ask students to identify the categories of the Web site.

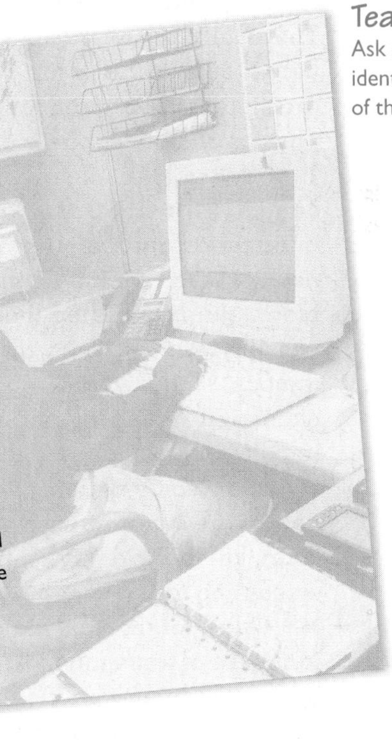

Classification at Work

Ahmad Bishr is a Web design consultant. In the next excerpt from an e-mail to a client, he makes suggestions about classifying a Web site.

The second thing you need to do is decide how to divide your site. The opening page should contain only the most pertinent information about the cottage you are trying to rent. For instance, include the number of rooms, the location, the most spectacular traits of the cottage, and so on. Each subcategory will become a link. Because you are trying to rent your cottage, I suggest that one link contain photos of the interior, with details about each room. You will also need a link that includes a rental calendar and rates. A fourth section might contain information about local attractions. Remember that too many categories will confuse the viewer. You'll want a simple, uncluttered site. Keep the divisions down to four or five pages at the most.

ESL Teaching Tip: The essay looks at heroes from a North American perspective. Engage students in a discussion of how notions about heroism may vary among different cultures.

A Student Essay

Read the student essay and answer the questions that follow.

Heroes

by Diego Pelaez

1 The word "hero" comes from the Greek word *heros*, which means a person of superhuman ability. *Webster's Dictionary* defines a hero as a person "admired for courage, fortitude, prowess, nobility, etc." Certainly, heroes come in many forms throughout a person's life. Somewhere out there, there is always a model, real or fictional, that drives people to better themselves and gives them the dream of being heroic. The three general ideas of a hero that most people embrace are the fictional superhero, the sports or media hero and, finally, the practical hero.

2 The dominant heroes of childhood are fictional superheroes. Action figures represent these titans and are the absolute blueprint for the average young person. Be they on television, in comic books, or in children's movies, characters such as Batman, Superman, and Spiderman usually dominate the imaginations of youngsters. It is common to see children blazing down the street wearing the capes of their idols. Thankfully, the female crowd has gotten away from Barbie; female action heroes such as Buffy the Vampire Slayer and Sydney Bristow from *Alias* are models of strength for young girls. These heroes defy the laws of physics and are capable of superhuman feats that any child dreams of.

3 However, as time wears on, children outgrow the superhero phase and idolize another form of superior humans: celebrities. With the information age, celebrities are **ubiquitous**. The Internet, television, newspapers, and magazines feature images of athletes, singers, and movie stars, providing them with more exposure than they could have ever possibly wanted. Thus, the superhero stage is followed by the "I want to be famous" stage, where adolescents start trying to shoot like Michael Jordan, act like Al Pacino, or sing like Mariah Carey. A good example is the unbelievable amount of worldwide acclaim for soccer player David Beckham; some nations have even erected statues in his image. These people are superheroes who make the game-winning shot on a basketball court, kill the bad guy on film, or perform on stage in front of thousands of screaming fans.

ubiquitous: everywhere

4 Alas, for the vast majority of people, there will come a day when fantasies of fame must give way to more realistic goals. Along with these goals come more practical, real-life heroes. Teachers, although they sometimes get a bad reputation, are heroes to far more people than they realize. Many teachers become mentors to their pupils, providing guidance

and inspiration. Young adults also look to inspirational figures in their field; thus, an aspiring journalist might idolize a writer from the local paper. Of course, most people, as they grow older, realize that the most potent figures in their lives are those family members—parents, grandparents, siblings, aunts, or uncles—who have guided them and been compelling role models.

5 Heroes fill people with a sense of their own possibilities. Children think they are indestructible, and this attitude is reflected in larger-than-life heroes who always seem to achieve the impossible. However, with the passage of time, goals become more realistic and so do definitions of heroes. Heroes drive children to dream of the impossible, and heroes encourage young adults to strive toward an ideal.

Teaching Tip: Point out that the student writer uses specific examples such as the names of some heroes to bolster his main points. Remind your students to include very specific details in their essays.

PRACTICE 1

1. Highlight the thesis statement.
2. Highlight the topic sentence in each body paragraph.
3. State the three categories that the writer discusses and list some details about each category.
   a. *fictional superheroes*
   Details: *They perform superhuman feats. Examples: Batman, Superman, Buffy the Vampire Slayer.*
   b. *celebrities*
   Details: *Famous people, such as athletes (David Beckham), movie stars (Al Pacino), and singers (Mariah Carey).*
   c. *practical, real-life heroes*
   Details: *These people include teachers, inspirational people in a student's field of study, and family members.*
4. Which introductory style does this essay use? Circle your answer.
   a. anecdote
   (b.) definition
   c. historical
   d. opposing position

Teaching Tip: The Writer's Desk activities, such as the one on the next page, provide students with opportunities to develop a topic through all stages of the writing process using the classification rhetorical mode. In the Warm Up, they begin by exploring various topics that can be divided for a classification essay. Those topics then carry on throughout the chapter.

Explore Topics

In the Writer's Desk Warm Up, you will try an exploring strategy to generate ideas about different topics.

Writer's Desk Warm Up

Read the following questions, and write the first ideas that come to your mind. Think of two to three ideas for each topic.

EXAMPLE: What are some types of lawbreakers?

—petty thieves (pickpockets, scam artists)

—people who break traffic laws

—violent criminals like carjackers and terrorists

1. What are some different categories of families?

____

____

____

2. What are some different types of shoppers?

____

____

____

3. When an election comes around, people act in different ways. What are some categories of political responses?

____

____

____

Making a Classification Chart

A **classification chart** is a visual representation of a main topic and its categories. Making a classification chart can help you to identify the categories more clearly so that you will be able to write more exact thesis statements.

When you classify items, remember to use a single method of classification and a common classification principle to sort the items. For example, you could classify friends according to the length of time you have known them. You could also classify friends according to the activities you do with them or the places where you met them.

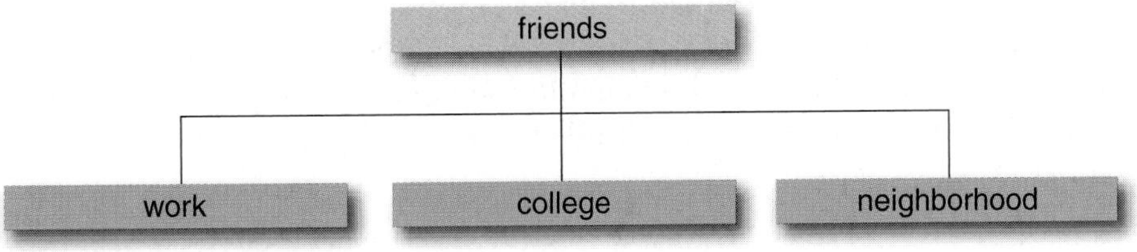

Classification Principle: places to make friends

You can also use a pie chart to help you classify items.

Places to Meet Friends

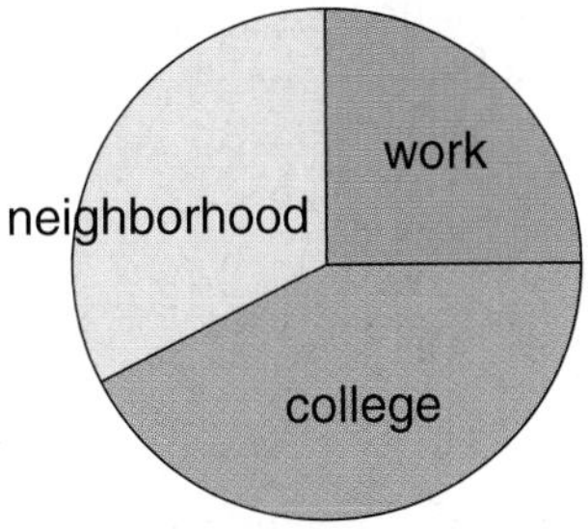

Hint Categories Versus Examples

When you are trying to find a topic for a classification essay, don't simply list examples. Each category of items should have subcategories. The following lists are for an essay about the physical and psychological benefits of playing certain sports. In the list of examples, the sports are all active team sports, so the advantages in each sport would be similar. In the second list of categories, each type of sport has particular benefits.

Topic: sports
Classification principle: physical and psychological benefits

List of examples	Categories
football	solo sports
baseball	pair sports
hockey	team sports

Teaching Tip:
If students need some guidance for topic 3 in the Writer's Desk Warm Up, engage them in a brief discussion of the ways they react during an election campaign. Are they bored and uninterested? Do they vote like other family members and treat voting simply as a duty? Are they passionately involved in the political campaign?

Teaching Tip:
Pair Work
Ask students to do this practice in pairs. Then review the answers with them.

PRACTICE 2 In the following classification charts, a subject has been broken down into distinct categories. The items in the group should have the same classification principle. Cross out one item in each group that does not belong. Then write down the classification principle that unites the group.

EXAMPLE:

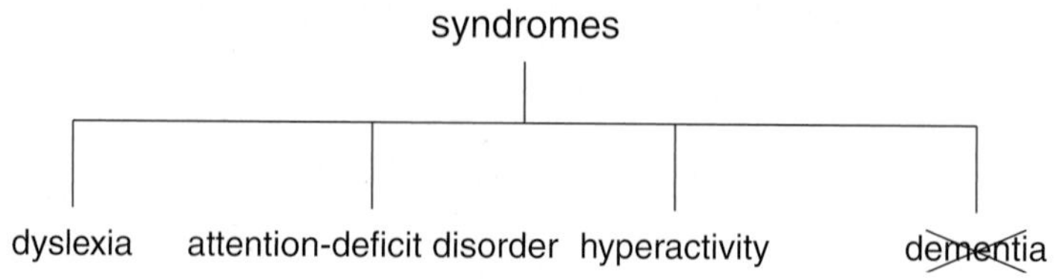

Classification principle: *childhood learning disorders*

1.

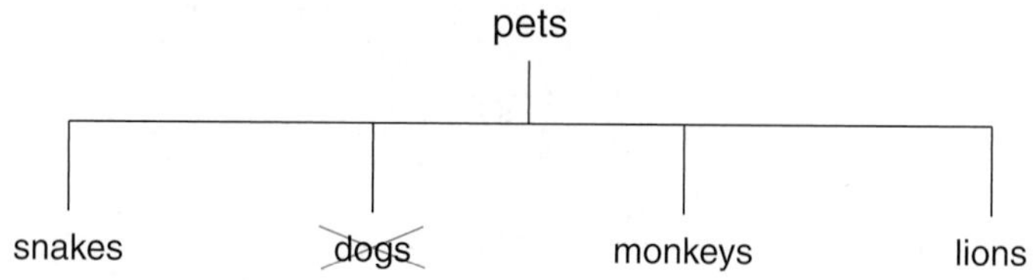

Classification principle: *exotic pets*

2.

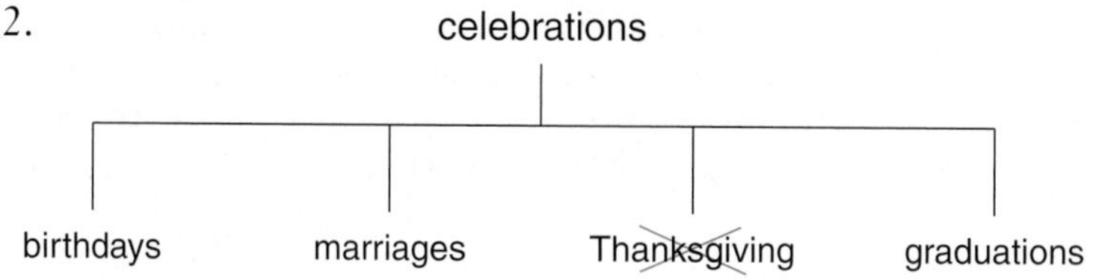

Classification principle: *life passages*

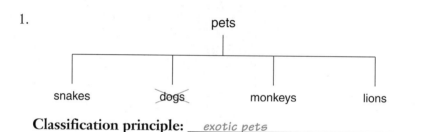

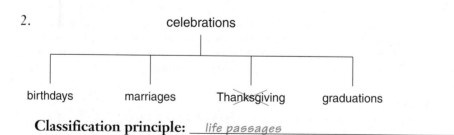

3. co-workers

~~friendly~~ | lazy | know-it-all | nosy

Classification principle: *annoying co-workers*

4. workplaces

cockpit | ~~garden~~ | toll | cubicle

Classification principle: *claustrophobic or tiny work spaces*

5. relationships

husband–wife | parent–child | brother–sister | boss–~~employee~~

Classification principle: *family relationships*

Hint **Make a Point**

To make interesting classification essays, try to express an attitude, opinion, or feeling about the topic. For example, in an essay about discipline, your classification principle might be types of discipline methods; however, the essay needs to inform readers of something specific about those methods. You could write about discipline methods that are most effective, least effective, ethical, unethical, violent, nonviolent, and so on.

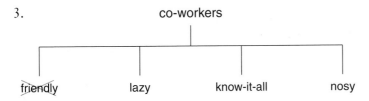

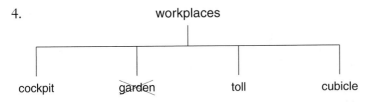

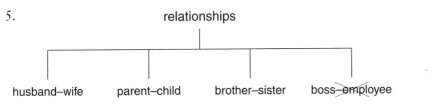

Writer's Desk Find Distinct Categories

Break down the following topics into three distinct categories. Remember to find categories that do not overlap. You can look for ideas in the Writer's Desk Warm Up on page 180.

EXAMPLE:

lawbreakers

pedestrians | cyclists | drivers

Classification principle: *people who break traffic laws*

1. families

Classification principle: ______________________________

2. shoppers

Classification principle: ______________________________

3. political responses

Classification principle: ______________________________

DEVELOPING

The Thesis Statement

The thesis statement in a classification essay clearly indicates what you will classify. It also includes the controlling idea, which is the classification principle that you will use.

> Several types of coworkers can completely destroy a workplace environment.

You can also mention the types of categories in your thesis statement.

> Nosy, lazy, and know-it-all coworkers can completely destroy a workplace environment.

Teaching Tip: Remind students not to list just types, but to list three distinct categories. For example, ask what is wrong with the following. Topic: *unhealthy foods* Categories: *sugary snacks, fried foods,* and *ice cream.* Students should notice that ice cream is also a sugary snack.

Grammar Hint **Parallel Structure**

Use parallel structure when words or phrases are joined in a series.

> Some annoying sales methods include calling customers on the phone, putting popup ads on the Internet, and ~~when people leave~~ leaving flyers on car windows.

See Chapter 25 for more information about parallel structure.

Writer's Desk Write Thesis Statements

Write clear thesis statements. You can refer to your ideas in previous Writer's Desks. Remember that your thesis statement can include the different categories you will be discussing.

EXAMPLE: Topic: lawbreakers

Thesis Statement: *Pedestrians, cyclists, and drivers regularly break the rules of the road.*

1. Topic: family

   Thesis statement: ______________________________

   ____

2. Topic: shoppers

   Thesis statement: ______________________________

   ____

3. Topic: political responses

   Thesis statement: ______________________________

   ____

The Supporting Ideas

After you have developed an effective thesis statement, generate supporting ideas. In a classification essay, you can list details about each of your categories.

- Use prewriting strategies to generate examples for each category.
- Choose the best ideas.
- Organize your ideas. Choose the best organizational method for this essay pattern.

One way to visualize your categories and your supporting ideas is to make a detailed classification chart. Break down the main topic into several categories, and then list supporting ideas for each category.

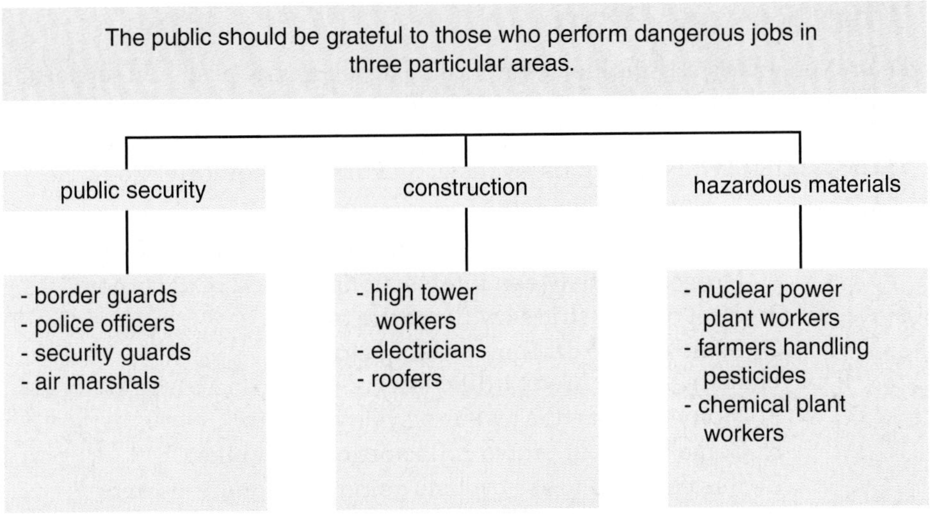

Teaching Tip:
For extra practice, ask students to develop supporting ideas for all three Writer's Desk topics. The topics are listed in the Warm Up.

Writer's Desk Develop Supporting Ideas

Choose one of the thesis statements from the previous Writer's Desk on page 186, and list supporting ideas.

Thesis statement: ______________________________

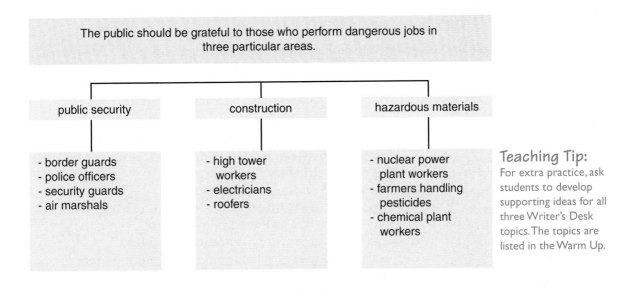

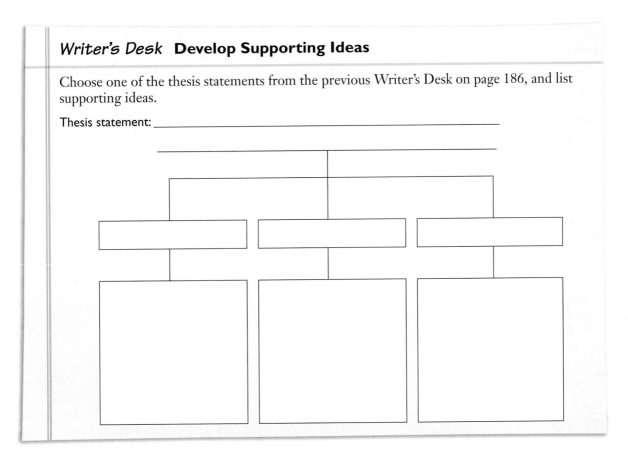

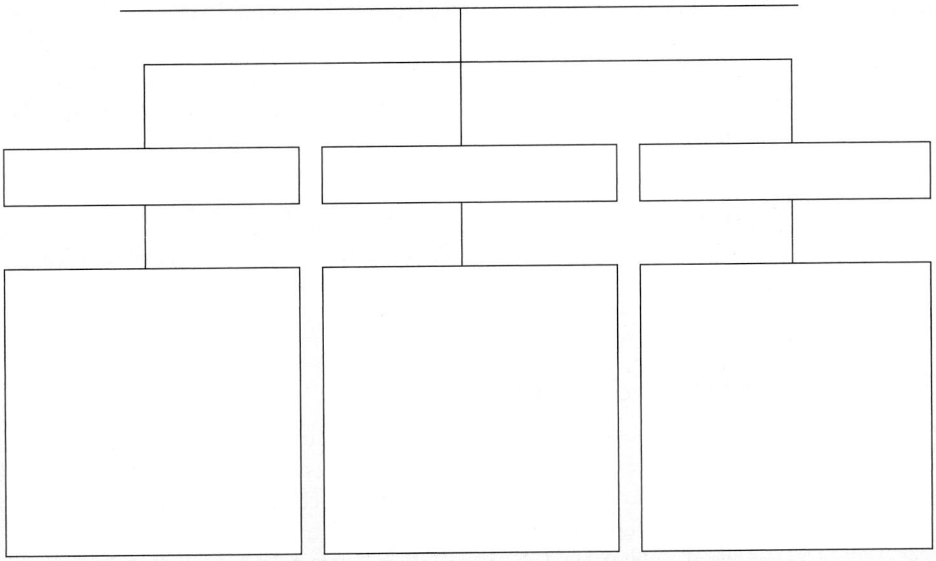

The Essay Plan

Before you write a classification essay, make a detailed essay plan. Add supporting details for each category.

THESIS STATEMENT: Pedestrians, cyclists, and drivers regularly break the rules of the road.

I. Pedestrians are supposed to obey traffic rules, but most do not.
   A. Many cross between intersections instead of at corners.
   B. A lot of pedestrians walk on the road.
   C. Some people disobey walking signals.

II. Cyclists regularly break traffic laws.
   A. Many cyclists don't wear bicycle helmets.
   B. Some don't put proper reflectors on their bikes.
   C. It is common to see cyclists going through lights and stop signs.

III. Drivers are the most dangerous lawbreakers.
   A. Speeding is common on roads and highways.
   B. Some people drive on the shoulders of roads.
   C. Many drivers disobey traffic signs.
   D. There are even drivers who go the wrong way on one-way streets.

Teaching Tip: You can ask students to keep their essay plans and then attach them to their final draft. You can then determine how the students have developed their ideas.

Writer's Desk Make an Essay Plan

Refer to the information you generated in previous Writer's Desks, and prepare a detailed essay plan. Arrange the supporting details in a logical order.

The First Draft

After you outline your ideas in a plan, you are ready to write the first draft. Weave together the ideas you have in your essay plan. Remember to write complete sentences and to include transitional words or expressions to help your ideas flow smoothly. Here are some transitions that can help you express which category is most important and to signal a movement from one category to the next.

To show importance
above all
clearly
most of all
the most important
particularly

To show types of categories
one kind . . . another kind
the first/second kind
the first/second type
the last category

Writer's Desk Write the First Draft

Carefully review the classification essay plan you prepared in the previous Writer's Desk and make any necessary changes. Then, write the first draft of your classification essay.

REVISING AND EDITING

Revise and Edit a Classification Essay

When you finish writing a classification essay, carefully review your work and revise it to make sure that the categories do not overlap. Check to make sure that you have organized your essay logically, and remove any irrelevant details. Before you work on your own essay, practice revising and editing a student essay.

Teaching Tip: The activity of revising a student essay should help your students understand the important link between the writing process and the grammar chapters.

A Student Essay

Read the essay, and then answer the questions that follow. As you read, correct any errors that you find, and make comments in the margins.

Breaking Traffic Laws

by Lonzell Courtney

1 Ask most people, and they will insist they are law-abiding. Dig a little deeper, though, and the hidden criminal emerges. Stand on any street corner for a few hours, and you probably will observe all types of people breaking traffic laws. Pedestrians, cyclists, and drivers regularly break the rules of the road.

2 There are many traffic laws that pedestrians ignore. For example, jaywalking. When people arrive at a crossing with traffic lights, they are supposed to wait for the walk signal. They should also cross the street at corners and proper crossings, and they should not walk on the road. Yet most people be breaking these rules. Armando Guzman, an exterminator

from Florida, is an unapologetic jaywalker. When him and I go for a walk, he crosses between intersections rather than make the long walk to the corner. Kate Shapiro, a hairdresser, admits that she always crosses when the "Don't Walk" signal is blinking if there is no traffic. "It is ridiculous to wait when I know I can cross safely," she argues. ~~Some pedestrians are also very rude. They push through crowds, knock people over, and are basically very unpleasant.~~

3 Cyclists also disrespect traffic laws. For example, many municipalities have bicycle helmet laws, but citizens regularly flout the law and drive with bare heads. In some states, bicycles must be equipped with reflectors, but many cyclists do not bother getting them. Other rules of the road apply to cyclists, yet they regularly plow past stop signs or zoom through red lights. Most unpleasant are the cyclists who speed along busy sidewalks even though that is illegal. Thus, most cyclists are lawbreakers, too.

4 Drivers, of course, are the worse offenders. They can harm or even kill others, yet virtually every driver has occasionally broken a traffic law. Who hasn't gone over the speed limit, for example? Many people believe that the maximum speed limit sign generally means, "I can go ten or fifteen miles per hour over that limit." Drivers also change lanes without signaling, they drive on the shoulder to pass slow traffic, and they allow children to ride without seatbelts. In 2006, Britney Spears famously placed her infant on her lap while driving. Of course, if she would have known about the subsequent scandal, she might have acted differently.

5 Most lawbreakers are unrepentant, and some of them have original excuses for ignoring traffic rules. They claim that everyone else does it. Some people condemn seatbelt and helmet laws as infringements on their rights.

PRACTICE 3

Revising

1. Highlight the thesis statement.
2. In paragraph 2, one of the examples is not a valid support. Cross it out.

   Explain why it is not valid. *The example is not about lawbreakers. Being rude is not breaking the law.*
3. This essay does not have a concluding sentence. Write a concluding sentence in the space. Answers will vary.

   ____

   ____

Editing

4. A fragment lacks a subject or a verb and is an incomplete sentence. Underline one fragment in paragraph 2. Then write a correct sentence here.

   Correction: *For example, many people are jaywalkers.*

5. Paragraph 2 contains a verb-tense error. Underline the error and correct it.

   Correction: *Yet most people break these rules.*

6. The writer uses a pronoun incorrectly in paragraph 2. Underline and correct the error.

   Correction: *he and I*

7. In paragraph 4, there is an error with the superlative form of an adjective. Underline the error and correct it.

   Correction: *worst*

8. In paragraph 4, there is an error with conditional forms (*if . . . would*). Underline the error and correct it.

   Correction: *If she had known*

GRAMMAR LINK

See the following chapters for more information about these grammar topics:
Fragments, Chapter 23
Verb Tenses, Chapter 28
Conditionals, Chapter 29
Pronouns, Chapter 31
Adjectives, Chapter 32

vo•cab•u•lar•y BOOST

Writers commonly overuse the same vocabulary. To make your writing more vivid and interesting, look at your first draft and underline at least ten repeated nouns and verbs. (Remember that a noun is a person, place, or thing.) Then add details or specific descriptions to five of the nouns and write more vivid verbs. Here is a brief example of how you might avoid repetition of nouns and verbs.

Dull, repetitive: Patrice likes cycling. Patrice often cycles to work at his bookstore. Often Patrice is reckless and cycles without a helmet.

Detailed, uses synonyms: **Patrice** likes **cycling** and **commutes** to work on his **bike**. Although **the 30-year-old bookstore owner** knows better, **he** often **recklessly rides** without a helmet.

Writer's Desk Revise and Edit Your Essay

Revise and edit the essay that you wrote for the previous Writer's Desk. You can refer to the revising and editing checklists at the end of this chapter and on this book's inside covers.

A Professional Essay

Frank Schmalleger is director of the Justice Research Association, a private consulting firm that focuses on issues relating to crime and justice. The following excerpt is from his book *Criminal Justice Today*.

Types of Correctional Officers

by Frank Schmalleger

1 Prison staff culture, in combination with naturally occurring personality types, gives rise to a diversity of officer types. Correction staff can be classified according to certain distinguishing characteristics. Among the most prevalent types are the dictator, the friend, the merchant, the turnkey, the climber, and the reformer.

The Dictator

2 Some officers go by the book; others go beyond it, using prison rules to reinforce their own brand of discipline. The guard who demands signs of inmate subservience, from constant use of the word *sir* or *ma'am* to frequent free shoeshines, is one type of dictator. Another goes beyond legality, beating or "macing" inmates even for minor infractions or perceived insults. Dictator guards are bullies.

3 Dictator guards may have sadistic personalities and gain ego satisfaction through feelings of near omnipotence, which come from the total control of others. Some may be fundamentally insecure and employ a false bravado to hide their fear of inmates. Officers who fit the dictator category are the most likely to be targeted for vengeance should control of the institution temporarily fall into the hands of the inmates.

The Friend

4 Friendly officers try to fraternize with inmates. They approach the issue of control by trying to be "one of the guys." They seem to believe that they can win inmate cooperation by being nice. Unfortunately, such guards do not recognize that fraternization quickly leads to unending requests for special favors—from delivering mail to bending "minor" prison rules. Once a few rules have been bent, the officer may find that inmates have the upper hand through the potential for blackmail.

5 Many officers have amiable relationships with inmates. In most cases, however, affability is only a convenience that both sides recognize can quickly evaporate. "Friendly officers," as the term is being used here, are *overly* friendly. They may be young and inexperienced. On the other

hand, they may simply be possessed of kind and idealistic personalities built on successful friendships in free society.

The Merchant

6 Contraband could not exist in any correctional facility without the merchant officer. The merchant participates in the inmate economy, supplying drugs, pornography, alcohol, and sometimes even weapons to inmates who can afford to pay for them.

7 Probably only a very few officers consistently perform the role of merchant, although a far larger proportion may occasionally turn a few dollars by smuggling some item through the gate. Low salaries create the potential for mercantile corruption among many otherwise "straight-arrow" officers. Until salaries rise substantially, the merchant will remain an institutionalized feature of most prisons.

The Turnkey

8 The turnkey officer cares little for what goes on in the prison setting. Officers who fit this category may be close to retirement, or they may be alienated from their jobs for various reasons. Low pay, the view that inmates are basically "worthless" and incapable of changing, and the monotonous ethic of "doing time" all combine to numb the professional consciousness of even young officers.

9 The term *turnkey* comes from prison argot where it means a guard who is there just to open and shut doors and who cares about nothing other than getting through his or her shift. Inmates do not see the turnkey as a threat, nor is such an officer likely to challenge the status quo in institutions where merchant guards operate.

The Climber

10 The climber is apt to be a young officer with an eye for promotion. Nothing seems impossible to the climber, who probably hopes eventually to be warden or program director or to hold some high-status position within the institutional hierarchy. Climbers are likely to be involved in schooling, correspondence courses, and professional organizations. They may lead a movement toward unionization for correctional personnel and tend to see the guard's role as a profession that should receive greater social recognition.

11 Climbers have many ideas. They may be heavily involved in reading about the latest confinement or administrative technology. If so, they will

suggest many ways to improve prison routine, often to the consternation of complacent staff members. Like the turnkey, climbers turn a blind eye toward inmates and their problems. They are more concerned with improving institutional procedures and with their own careers than they are with the treatment or day-to-day control of inmates.

The Reformer

12 The reformer is the "do-gooder" among officers, the person who believes that prison should offer opportunities for personal change. The reformer tends to lend a sympathetic ear to the personal needs of inmates and is apt to offer armchair counseling and suggestions. Many reformers are motivated by personal ideals, and some of them are highly religious. Inmates tend to see the reformer guard as naive but harmless. Because the reformer actually tries to help, even when help is unsolicited, he or she is the most likely of all the guard types to be accepted by prisoners.

13 Correctional officers have generally been accorded low occupational status. Historically, the role of prison guard required minimal formal education and held few opportunities for professional growth and career advancement. Such jobs were typically low paying, frustrating, and often boring. Growing problems in our nation's prisons, including emerging issues of legal liability, however, increasingly require a well-trained and adequately equipped force of professionals. As correctional personnel have become better trained and more proficient, the old concept of guard has been supplanted by that of correctional officer. Thus, many states and a growing number of large-city correctional systems make efforts to eliminate individuals with potentially harmful personality characteristics from correctional officer applicant pools.

PRACTICE 4

1. What is the topic of this essay? _types of prison guards_
2. What are the main characteristics of the following types of guards?
   a. the dictator _bossy, demands subservience, intimidating, bullying, may be sadistic_
   b. the friend _naive, tries to be one of the guys, may bend prison rules, usually young and inexperienced_
   c. the merchant _out to make a profit, supplies contraband, corrupt_

d. the turnkey *indifferent, only there to do the job, not personally invested in the job*

e. the climber *has goals and wants to be promoted, probably takes courses, gets involved, may try to change things*

f. the reformer *idealistic, sympathetic and listens to inmates, may have strong personal ideals or religious beliefs*

3. What is the writer's purpose? Circle your answer.

   a. to entertain b. to persuade (c.) to inform

4. Consider the order in which the guards are listed. Think of another effective way to organize the guards, and list them in order here.
   Answers will vary.

   Organizational method: ____________________

   a. __________ c. __________ e. __________

   b. __________ d. __________ f. __________

Teaching Tip:
Brainstorm ideas for question 4 with students. For instance, they might organize guards according to their level of naiveté, helpfulness to prisoners, or level of corruption.

Teaching Tip:
Pair Work
Have students read one of the essays in the Reading Link. In pairs, they can discuss what the classification principle is. Also, discuss if the categories overlap or are distinct.

The Writer's Room Topics for Classification Essays

READING LINK

More Classification Readings

"Types of Rioters" by David Locher (page 575)
"Living Environments" by Avi Friedman (page 592)

Writing Activity 1

Choose any of the following topics, or choose your own topic, and write a classification essay. Determine your classification principle and ensure that your categories do not overlap.

General Topics

Types of . . .

1. computer games
2. politicians
3. living arrangements
4. siblings
5. punishment

College and Work-Related Topics

Types of . . .

6. electronic modes of communication
7. procrastination techniques
8. success
9. risks
10. work spaces

WRITING LINK

More Classification Writing Topics

Chapter 22, Writer's Room topic 1 (page 356)
Chapter 26, Writer's Room topic 2 (page 396)
Chapter 30, Writer's Room topic 2 (page 454)
Chapter 37, Writer's Room topic 2 (page 544)

Writing Activity 2

Choose a quotation that you agree or disagree with, or one that inspires you, and then write a classification essay based on it.

> The four stages of life are infancy, childhood, adolescence, and obsolescence.
>
> —Art Linkletter, entertainer

> There are really only three types of people: those who make things happen, those who watch things happen, and those who say, "What happened?"
>
> —Ann Landers, advice columnist

> The wit makes fun of other persons; the satirist makes fun of the world; the humorist makes fun of himself.
>
> —James Thurber, author

> I'll keep it short and sweet—family, religion, and friendship. These are the three demons you must slay if you wish to succeed in business.
>
> —Matt Groening, creator of *The Simpsons*

Writing Activity 3

Examine this photo of the man doing tai chi, and think about some classification topics. For example, you might write about types of athletes, attitudes toward exercise, fitness programs, places to work out, or healthy activities. Determine a classification principle and then follow the writing process to write a classification essay.

CHECKLIST: CLASSIFICATION ESSAY

After you write your classification essay, review the checklist on the inside front cover. Also, ask yourself these questions.

- Does my thesis statement explain the categories that I will discuss?
- Do I use a common classification principle to unite the various items?
- Do I offer sufficient details to explain each category?
- Do I arrange the categories in a logical manner?
- Does all of the supporting information relate to the categories that I am discussing?
- Do I include categories that do not overlap?

Teaching Tip:
Writer's World Competition
Please advise students that they can submit their essays for possible publication to: <thewritersworld@prenhall.com>.

How Do I Get a Better Grade?

PEARSON mywritinglab

Visit www.mywritinglab.com for audio-visual lectures and additional practice sets about classification writing. ***Get a better grade with MyWritingLab!***

CHAPTER 12

Comparison and Contrast

CONTENTS

When you plan to move to a new place, you compare the features of different houses or apartments to help you make a decision. When you write a comparison and contrast essay, you examine two or more items or issues to help yourself and your readers make conclusions about them.

Teaching Tip:
The Writers' Exchange activity can help your students understand comparison and contrast. When students write some ideas on the board, you can demonstrate point-by-point or topic-by-topic comparisons.

Writers' Exchange

What were your goals as a child? What are your goals as an adult? Think about work, money, and family. Compare your answers with a partner, and discuss how childhood goals are different from adult goals.

EXPLORING

What Is Comparison and Contrast?

When you want to decide between options, you compare and contrast. You **compare** to find similarities and **contrast** to find differences. The exercise of comparing and contrasting can help you make judgments about things. It can also help you to better understand familiar things. The following examples show comparisons and contrasts people might use in everyday situations.

Audience: Family member

A laptop is more sensible than a desktop computer.

- The desk is small and a laptop takes less space than a desktop computer.
- Modern laptops have screens that are just as large and clear as many desktop monitors.
- Unlike a clunky desktop computer, we can easily transport a laptop to other rooms or to school or work.

Audience: Another student

The summer course is easier than the fall course.

- The summer course lasts for three weeks and the material is condensed, so there is less homework.
- The fall course has more reading and writing homework.
- The summer course has fewer students, so you can get more help if you need it.
- The fall course has large groups, so if you don't understand something, it is difficult to get help.

Audience: Customer

Our product is better than the competitor's product.

- Our product is less expensive than the competitor's.
- Our product is smaller and easier to use.
- The competition does not offer a rebate.
- The competition does not offer a variety of colors and sizes.

"I know not anything more pleasant, or more instructive, than to compare experience with expectation, or to register from time to time the difference between idea and reality. It is by this kind of observation that we grow daily."

SAMUEL JOHNSON, *writer*

The Comparison and Contrast Essay

In a comparison and contrast essay, you can compare and contrast two different subjects, or you can compare and contrast different aspects of a single subject. When you write using this essay pattern, remember to think about your specific purpose.

- Your purpose could be to make judgments about two things. For example, you might compare and contrast two cars to convince your readers that one is preferable.
- Your purpose could be to describe or understand two familiar things. For example, you might compare two movies to help your readers understand their thematic similarities.

Teaching Tip: Tell students that instructors sometimes use *compare* to mean both compare and contrast.

Comparison and Contrast at Work

Eric Hollymead works in public relations. In the next memo, he compares two job candidates. To respect each person's privacy, he has numbered the candidates.

Although both candidates have the required education, I suggest that we go with Candidate 1. Her experience is more relevant to this industry. I also believe she will be a better fit for the sales department because her energy level is high, and she seems like a real team player. Candidate 2, although highly competent, is less experienced in sales. He was quite nervous in the interview, and I sense he may be less at ease with clients. On the other hand, his questions were thoughtful, and he seemed interested in the business. I also appreciated his sense of humor. Perhaps we should keep his résumé on file should we have future positions that are more suitable to his skills.

Teaching Tip: Ask students to identify other instances in the workplace where people would use comparison and contrast.

Comparison and Contrast Patterns

Comparison and contrast essays follow two common patterns.

Point by Point Present one point about Topic A and then one point about Topic B. Keep following this pattern until you have a few points for each topic. Go back and forth from one side to the other like tennis players hitting a ball back and forth across a net.

Topic by Topic Present all of your points about one topic, and then present all of your points about the second topic. Offer one side and then the other side, just as opposing lawyers would do in the closing arguments of a court case.

Marina's Example

Marina is trying to decide whether she would prefer a part-time job in a clothing store or in a restaurant. Marina can organize her information using a topic-by-topic pattern or a point-by-point method.

THESIS STATEMENT: The clothing store is a better place to work than the restaurant.

Point-by-Point Comparison

Topic sentence: Salaries
- Job A
- Job B

Topic sentence: Working hours
- Job A
- Job B

Topic sentence: Working environments
- Job A
- Job B

Topic-by-Topic Comparison

Topic sentence: Job A
- salary
- hours
- working environment

Topic sentence: Job B
- salary
- hours
- working environment

A Student Essay

Read the student essay and answer the questions that follow.

Working Life

by Alfonso Castillo Zavas

1 My uncle Cayetano spent the first thirty years of his life in Mexico City. When he moved to the United States, he rented a room in our house, and he tried to get used to life in Boston. Many evenings, my uncle told stories about his workplace, and he reminisced about his younger days when he was an office worker in Mexico City. We realized that the workplace culture is more relaxed in the United States than it is in Mexico.

2 One noticeable difference between the two nations is the attitude about arrivals and departures of employees. In the 1980s, my uncle Cayetano worked as an accountant for a company in Mexico City. He was supposed to arrive at 8:00 a.m. each morning, but he was often late. He ran from the subway station to the door of the office building, hoping to arrive before 8:30 a.m., which was the time that the doors were locked for the day. Guards at the door ensured that employees arrived and left at the proper time. Local street vendors encouraged my uncle, yelling "Correle" when they saw him sprinting past. Every three months, his pay was docked because three late days counted for an absence. When my uncle came to Boston in 1992, he found a job with a computer company. The first thing he noticed was that there were no guards at the doors of his workplace. Attendance at work depended on an honor system. Employees were only accountable to their immediate superiors. My uncle learned to be punctual

not because of a guard locking a door, but because he wanted to complete his work in the amount of time allotted to him.

3 Another major difference in work cultures is mealtimes. In Mexico, there is no concept of lunch. Instead, most people eat the main meal, the "comida," at around 2:00 p.m. When my uncle worked for a Mexican company, he took a two-hour break for his main meal. In the cafeteria, he often had a plate filled with meat, rice, beans, avocados, and chili peppers, and a side dish filled with warm tortillas. After his meal, he returned to work from 4:00 to 6:00 p.m. Later, when he arrived at home, he ate a small snack. In his Boston job, he became acquainted with the lunch hour, which was earlier than he was used to. He learned that lunch is not the time to have a large meal; instead, most employees just have a bland sandwich or soup. He also learned that Americans finish work by 4:00 or 5:00 p.m. and then eat their main meal between 6:00 and 8:00 p.m. So Americans have a longer and more relaxed evening. In Mexico, my uncle had to work much later in the day and was quite tired when he finally got home from the office.

4 The most visible distinction between Mexican and American workplaces is the level of formal dress in the workplace. Although Mexican dress codes are becoming slightly more relaxed, men in most offices and banks wear suits and ties, and women wear suit jackets, skirts, pantyhose, and heels. My aunt Lucia, who lives in Mexico City, never goes to work without manicured nails, makeup, and a very nice outfit. When my uncle Cayetano received his job in Boston, he starched his shirt collar, put on a tie, and ensured that his shoes were shiny. He was surprised to see that some of his co-workers wore baggy casual trousers and even sneakers. Very few co-workers wore dress shirts, with most wearing polo shirts. He quickly learned that people dress nicely at his office in the United States, but much less formally than workers at his Mexican workplace.

5 When immigrants come to a new country, they must get used to food, eating times, dress codes, and workplace rules that may be very different from those they encountered in their native countries. While they adjust to the differences, they are sometimes judged. My uncle said that co-workers didn't understand why he always shined his shoes, and for a while his nickname was "shiny." When a new immigrant arrives in your workplace, show tolerance and respect for cultural differences.

PRACTICE 1

1. Highlight the thesis statement.
2. Highlight the topic sentence in each body paragraph.
3. What pattern of comparison does the writer follow in the entire essay?

   (a.) point by point   b. topic by topic

4. What pattern of comparison does the writer follow in body paragraphs 2, 3, and 4?
   a. point by point   (b.) topic by topic
5. Using your own words, sum up the main subjects in this essay.
   Paragraph 2: *work schedule in each country*
   Paragraph 3: *lunch break versus comida*
   Paragraph 4: *level of formal dress*
6. What does this essay mainly focus on? Circle the correct answer.
   a. similarities   (b.) differences
7. Underline transitional words or phrases that link ideas between body paragraphs.
8. How does the writer organize his arguments?
   a. time order   b. space order   (c.) emphatic order

Teaching Tip:
This Vocabulary Boost can help to expand your students' vocabulary.

ESL Teaching Tip:
Nonnative speakers may not be aware that many different prefixes mean *not*, including *il*, *im*, *in*, *dis*, *un*, and *non*. Also, remind students to be careful with their spelling when they add prefixes and suffixes to words. You might give them the following rules. Use *il* before words beginning with *l* (*illogical*). Use *ir* before words beginning with *r* (*irresponsible*). Use *im* before words beginning with *m* or *p* (*improbable*). Students can learn more about spelling of prefixes and suffixes in Chapter 34.

vo•cab•u•lar•y BOOST

In the student essay "Working Life," the writer uses the terms *accountable* and *accountant* in paragraph 2. The root word—or base word — for those terms is *count*. Prefixes and suffixes alter a word's meaning and are added to the root word. Prefixes appear at the beginning of a root word; suffixes appear at the end. Here are some examples.

Prefixes	Examples	Suffixes	Examples
anti = against	antiwar	*able* = ability	understandable
bi = two	bilingual	*al* = pertaining to	physical
hyper = excessive	hypersensitive	*dom* = a quality or state	freedom
il = not	illegal	*ful* = filled with	respectful
inter = between	interfaith	*ism* = belief	communism
mis = wrong	misspell	*ist* = practitioner	scientist
multi = many	multifunctional	*ive* = tends toward	regressive
pre = before	prenatal	*less* = without	helpless
re = again	rebirth	*ment* = condition	argument
un = not	unfaithful	*ness* = state of being	happiness

Brainstorm at least three variations of the following root words by using various prefixes and suffixes. Keep in mind that the previous list is not complete. There may be other prefixes or suffixes that you can think of.

1. use   *useful, useless, misuse, useable*
2. act   *react, interact, active, hyperactive, actual, reactive*
3. social   *socialist, socialism, antisocial, sociable*

Explore Topics

In the Writer's Desk Warm Up, you will try an exploring strategy to generate ideas about different topics.

Writer's Desk Warm Up

Read the following questions, and write the first ideas that come to your mind. Think of two to three ideas for each topic.

EXAMPLE: What are some key differences between girls' and boys' toys?

girls' toys	boys' toys
—pastel colors	*—noisy*
—stuffed animals	*—toy cars, trucks, fire engines*
—dolls with clothes	*—action figures*

1. What were your fears when you were a child? What are your current fears?

childhood fears	current fears
____________________	____________________
____________________	____________________
____________________	____________________

2. What are the key features of your generation and your parents' generation?

your generation	your parents' generation
____________________	____________________
____________________	____________________
____________________	____________________

3. How are your actions and appearance different in your public and private life?

public life	private life
____________________	____________________
____________________	____________________
____________________	____________________

DEVELOPING
The Thesis Statement

In a comparison and contrast essay, the thesis statement indicates what you are comparing and contrasting, and it expresses a controlling idea. For example, the following thesis statement indicates that the essay will compare the myths and reality of mold to prove that it does not seriously threaten human health.

Common household mold is not as dangerous as many people believe.

PRACTICE 2 Read each thesis statement, and then answer the questions that follow. State whether the essay would focus on similarities or differences.

1. The weather in our region is more extreme than it was in the past.
   a. What is being compared? *weather in the past and today*
   b. What is the controlling idea? *weather is more extreme today*
   c. What will the essay focus on? _____ similarities __X__ differences
2. Students need technical courses as well as academic courses for a well-rounded education.
   a. What is being compared? *technical and academic courses*
   b. What is the controlling idea? *both are useful*
   c. What will the essay focus on? __X__ similarities _____ differences
3. Before marriage, people expect to feel eternally lustful toward their "soul mate," but the reality of married life is quite different.
   a. What is being compared? *ideals and reality of marriage*
   b. What is the controlling idea? *expectations or situations change after marriage*
   c. What will the essay focus on? _____ similarities __X__ differences

Teaching Tip: The Writer's Desk activities, like the one on the previous page, provide students with an opportunity to develop a topic through all stages of the writing process using the comparison and contrast rhetorical mode. In the Warm Up, they begin by exploring various topics. Those topics then carry on throughout the chapter.

Grammar Hint — Comparing Adjectives and Adverbs

When comparing or contrasting two items, ensure that you have correctly written your comparative forms. For instance, never put *more* with an adjective ending in *-er*.

City life is ~~more~~ better than country life.

If you are comparing two actions, remember to use an adverb instead of an adjective.

Children learn lessons ~~easier~~ more easily when they are treated with respect.

See Chapter 32 for more information about making comparisons with adjectives and adverbs.

ESL **Teaching Tip:** This Grammar Hint is especially relevant for your nonnative speakers. They may transfer word structures from their own languages.

Writer's Desk Write Thesis Statements

For each topic, write a thesis statement that includes what you are comparing and contrasting and a controlling idea.

EXAMPLE: Topic: girls' and boys' toys

Thesis statement: *Both girls' and boys' toys reinforce gender stereotypes.*

1. Topic: childhood fears and adult fears

   Thesis statement: ______________________________

   ____

2. Topic: two generations

   Thesis statement: ______________________________

   ____

3. Topic: public versus private life

   Thesis statement: ______________________________

   ____

The Supporting Ideas

After you have developed an effective thesis statement, generate supporting ideas. In a comparison and contrast essay, think of examples that help to clarify the similarities or differences, and then incorporate some ideas in your final essay plan.

To generate supporting ideas, you might try using a Venn diagram. In this example, you can see how the writer draws two circles to compare traditional boys' and girls' toys and how some ideas fall into both categories.

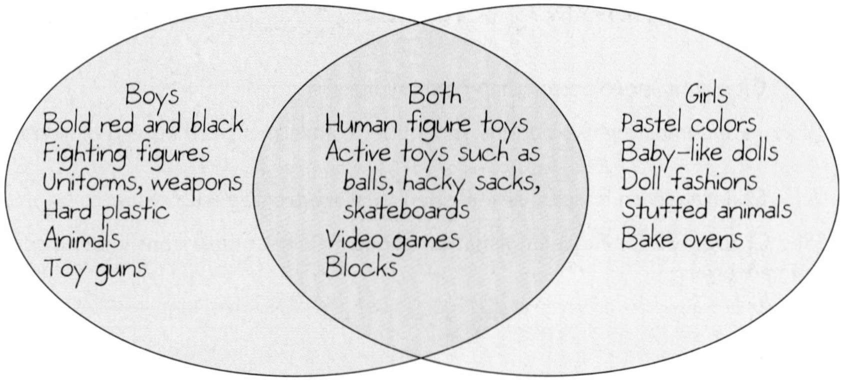

Writer's Desk Develop Supporting Ideas

Choose one of your thesis statements from the previous Writer's Desk. List some similarities and differences.

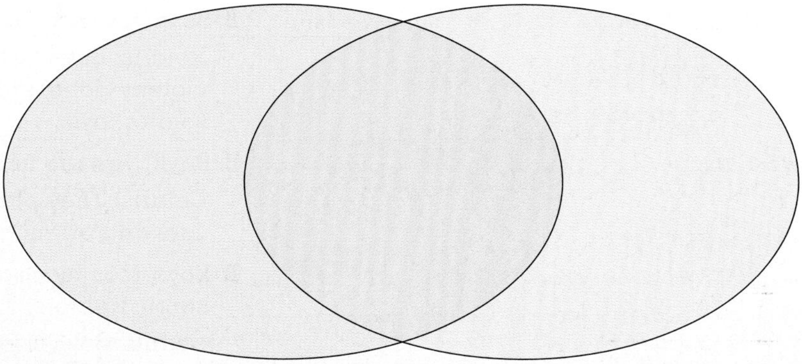

The Essay Plan

Before you write a comparison and contrast essay, make a detailed essay plan. Decide which pattern you will follow: point by point or topic by topic. Then add supporting details. Make sure that each detail supports the thesis statement. Also think about the best way to organize your ideas.

Thesis Statement: Both girls' and boys' toys reinforce gender stereotypes.

Point by Point

A/B Girls' toys focus on activities in the home, whereas boys' toys focus on outside activities.

Details: Girls have dollhouses and baking ovens whereas boys have carpenter sets and racecars.

A/B Colors are different in girls' and boys' toys.

Details: Girls' toys are pastel colors and boys' toys are bold colors.

Topic by Topic

A Girls' toys reinforce the importance of looks, body image, and fashion.

Details: They receive fashion dolls with clothing, shoes, and other accessories.

A Girls' toys are in soft pastel colors.

Details: They play with pink ponies and hug pale blue stuffed animals.

Teaching Tip:
As an additional activity, ask students to develop supporting ideas for all three Writer's Desk topics, which are listed in the Warm Up. They can try using Venn diagrams when they develop ideas for the other two Warm Up topics.

Point by Point (cont.)

A/B Girls' toys focus on nurturing, and boys' toys focus on heroic fighters.

Details: Girls have baby dolls and boys have GI Joes and guns.

Topic by Topic (cont.)

A Girls' toys encourage nurturing by focusing on home and the family.

Details: They have dolls with baby bottles, baking ovens, toy vacuums, and shopping carts.

B Boys' toys are more violent.

Details: Boys have toy guns, violent video games, and soldier toys.

B Boys' toys are in bold colors.

Details: They play with red toy cars and bright green soldiers.

B Boys' toys focus on activities and heroic fighters.

Details: Boys are given carpenter's tools, car racing, and service station play sets.

Teaching Tips:
You might ask students to keep their essay plans and then attach them to the final draft. You can then determine how the students have developed their ideas.

Writer's Desk Write an Essay Plan

Refer to the information you generated in previous Writer's Desks and prepare a detailed essay plan using a point-by-point or topic-by-topic pattern. You can use the letters A and B to indicate which side you are discussing in your plan. Include details about each supporting idea.

The First Draft

After you outline your ideas in an essay plan, you are ready to write the first draft. Remember to follow the topic-by-topic or the point-by-point pattern you used in your plan. Write complete sentences and use transitions to help your ideas flow smoothly. The following transitions can be helpful for guiding readers through a comparison and contrast essay.

To show similarities		To show differences	
additionally	in addition	conversely	nevertheless
at the same time	in the same way	however	on the contrary
equally	similarly	in contrast	then again

Writer's Desk Write the First Draft

Write the first draft of your comparison and contrast essay. Before you write, carefully review your essay plan to see if you have enough support for your points and topics. Flesh out each body paragraph with specific details.

REVISING AND EDITING

Revise and Edit a Comparison and Contrast Essay

When you finish writing a comparison and contrast essay, carefully review your work and revise it to make sure that the comparison or contrast is as clear as possible to your readers. Check that you have organized your essay logically, and remove any irrelevant details. Before you work on your own essay, practice revising and editing a student essay.

Teaching Tip: The activity of revising a student essay should help your students understand the important link between the writing process and the grammar chapters.

A Student Essay

Read the essay, and then answer the questions that follow. As you read, correct any errors that you find, and make comments in the margins.

Gender and Toys

by Ashley Lincoln

1 As a young mother, I am trying to avoid the pitfalls that parents so easily fall into. I try not to call my daughter cute and my son strong, thus reinforcing any cultural notions about their self-worth. I encourage my five-year-old daughter to play sports, and I bought my son a baby doll when he asked for one. My friends been saying they have the same concerns about gender roles. But insulating children against male or female role expectations is almost impossible. Most parents, in spite of their best efforts, reinforce gender stereotypes every time they shop for toys.

2 Girls' toys reinforce the importance of looks, body image, and fashion. Parents can buy their daughters makeup sets that include child-friendly lipstick, blush, and eye shadow. Fashion dolls of all shapes and sizes abound. Barbies, Bratz, and other teenage dolls stare at the buyer. Hanging next to the dolls are rows of clothing, shoes, hats, and tiny doll necklaces and bracelets. Girls can also play with a large doll head,

changing and curling the hair and adding makeup. Of course, none of the dolls are pudgy, pimply, large-boned, or just plain unattractive. When girls play with these toys, they quickly learn that beauty and the right clothes and makeup are very important.

3 If a little girl does not like fashion toys, they will surely enjoy baby dolls with their fake bottles of milk, soft little blankets, and strollers. Girls' toys encourage nurturing by focusing on the home and the family. At a very young age, girls learn to be competent mothers when they change the little diapers of their dolls. Girls can learn to cook with their Easy-Bake ovens, and they learn to shop with tiny shopping carts and cash registers. My daughter and her friends love playing "house" with one child acting as the mother. They shop, pull the "cry" strings on their dolls, and feed their "babies."

4 Boys' toys, on the other hand, stress jobs and activities outside the home. My son begged for, and received, a miniature workshop complete with a plastic saw, drill, screwdriver, and wrench. Lego sets prepare boys for creative occupations such as architecture and auto design. Computer and video games prepare boys for jobs in the high-tech industries. Finally, there is a lot of toy cars, trucks, and racetracks to remind boys that cars are very important to their identities.

5 Toys aimed at young males also permit boys to be the heroes in their fantasy games. In the boys' aisle of the toy store, there are rows of action figures. The GI Joes fight soldiers from other armies. Batman, Superman, and the X-Men fight fantasy villains. Curiously, the X-Men figures include female characters such as Storm, but the toys are not call "X-People." Aimed predominantly at boys, fighting action figures bolster ideas boys have about rescuing others. In their fantasy lives, boys learn early on that they are the heroes and the saviors.

6 Some suggest that it is useless to fight against the male and female roles. They point out that girls in previous centuries made their own dolls out of straw and rags, and boys made cars out of tin cans and wood. While that is true, toy stores take the stereotyping to extremes. One solution is to try to buy gender-neutral toys such as modeling clay, painting supplies, or balls and other sporting equipment.

PRACTICE 3

Revising

1. Highlight the thesis statement.
2. Highlight the topic sentence in each body paragraph.

3. Circle a transitional word or phrase in the topic sentence of paragraph 4. Then add transitional words or phrases to the other topic sentences.
   Answers will vary.

4. What pattern does the writer use to organize this essay? Circle your response.
   a. point by point (b.) topic by topic

5. The student writer uses the word "reinforce" at the end of the introduction and in the first sentence of the second paragraph. To avoid repeating the same word, what synonym could the student use?
   Answers will vary. *emphasize, strengthen, bolster, highlight*

Editing

6. Underline the verb error in the introduction. Write the correction on the line.
   Correction: *have been saying*

7. Underline and correct the pronoun shift in paragraph 3.
   Correction: *little girls/they*

8. Underline and correct the subject–verb agreement error in paragraph 4.
   Correction: *there are a lot of toy cars*

9. Underline and correct the passive verb that has been incorrectly formed in paragraph 5.
   Correction: *are not called*

GRAMMAR LINK

See the following chapters for more information about these grammar topics:
Subject–Verb Agreement, Chapter 27
Passive Voice, Chapter 28
Verbs, Chapter 29
Pronouns, Chapter 31

Writer's Desk Revise and Edit Your Essay

Revise and edit the essay that you wrote for the previous Writer's Desk. You can refer to the revising and editing checklists at the end of this chapter and on this book's inside covers.

A Professional Essay

Writer and translator Naomi Louder has published poetry in *The Fiddlehead Review* and *The New Quarterly*, among others. In the following essay, she uses the comparison and contrast pattern. Read the essay and answer the questions that follow.

The Dating World

by Naomi Louder

1 Dating has changed a lot over the years. Many people, post millennium, can't help associating the word "date" with a more innocent time and scenarios involving ice-cream sodas, varsity jackets, and drive-in movies. In smaller and more traditional communities, vestiges of this remain, and high school sweethearts who paired up early on wind up getting married straight out of school. Compared to previous generations, today's singles have a new dating ethic that involves flying straight into a whirlwind affair.

2 The most obvious difference between the past and the present is in dating methods. In the 1950s and 1960s, potential sweethearts met at school dances, the lunch-line at the school cafeteria, or at school sports events. There were certain formal rules of etiquette to be followed, down to the "base" system, dictating when, where, and how the relationship was to progress to its logical conclusion. People were concerned, after a date, with whether "first base"—a kiss—was attained. Nowadays, it is more common to obsess over the other party's sexual history, his or her expectations, and whether a relationship might be a possibility. The "base" system has been supplanted, in junior high or even elementary school, by the "gummy" trend, where cheap rubber bracelets, coded by color, announce the sexual experience or willingness of the wearer.

3 In a traditional dating context, couples worried primarily about pregnancy, and—mainly in the case of the girls—about losing their reputations. An ill-timed boast on the part of a boy could jeopardize a girl's dating career, while a pregnancy could result in the ultimate shame to the girl and her family or a rushed and gossiped-over wedding. In a contemporary urban center, these worries seem naïve. Early sexual relationships are more the norm than before, and the concerns are sexually transmitted infections, date rape, and abortion or adoption versus single parenthood. Certainly, some young people have reacted to these threats by rejecting the ethic of sexual freedom popularized in the 1960s. The revival of traditional religious values has influenced many young Americans, and chastity rings and church events make even the dating system of a more innocent era seem fraught. However, the majority of teens and young adults are more determined than ever to fulfill their sexual and emotional needs, sometimes before they are clearly aware of the consequences.

4 Both the traditional and the new dating methods have downsides. The new generation, with all its scorn of traditional and prudish dating

etiquette, finds itself lost and lonelier than ever. The old-fashioned courtship ritual has been condensed to a witty remark, a compliment or two, and an animal assault on a balcony, on a street corner, or in a taxi. Once the deed is done, people often find that they have no idea who they're dating. On the other hand, some would argue that when a mutual attraction is felt, holding back from intimacy is counter-productive. For instance, using the traditional method, people may try to represent themselves dishonestly, behaving with courtesy, unselfishness, or generosity that they would never bother with if they weren't trying to impress. The person's true personality—perhaps that of a slob or a diva—may only be unveiled when a commitment has been made. Advocates of casual encounters argue that when the formalities are dispensed with, people show themselves as they truly are.

5 There are pitfalls to both of these ways of dating, but the fact is, most people are looking for a partner in life, and the only way to find one is to trust somebody. A high school sweetheart or the best-looking person at a party is not necessarily the ideal partner. For the most part, relationships succeed because there is a sounder basis to them than passion or romance. If a true friendship is possible between two people, when passion and excitement fade, there will still be a reason to stay together.

PRACTICE 4

1. Highlight the thesis statement.
2. Highlight the topic sentence in paragraphs 2 and 4.
3. Paragraph 3 does not have a topic sentence. Which sentence best expresses the implied point?
   a. In the past, women worried about losing their reputations.
   b. Courtship rituals have changed.
   (c.) Dating concerns have also transformed since the 1950s.
   d. Today, there is a revival of religious values among young people.
4. In this essay, what pattern of comparison does the writer follow? Circle the correct answer.
   (a.) point by point   b. topic by topic
5. Using your own words, sum up the main subjects in this essay.

   Paragraph 2: *dating rules*

   Paragraph 3: *dating concerns*

   Paragraph 4: *disadvantages of both methods*

6. Does this essay mainly focus on similarities or differences? Circle the correct answer.
   a. similarities b. differences
7. What is the writer's purpose?
   a. to make a judgment b. to understand two things

The Writer's Room Topics for Comparison and Contrast Essays

Writing Activity 1

Choose any of the following topics, or choose your own topic, and write a comparison and contrast essay.

General Topics

Compare or contrast . . .

1. team sports versus solo sports
2. an early bird and a night owl
3. a true friend and an acquaintance
4. a watcher versus a doer
5. living near family versus living away from family

College and Work-Related Topics

Compare or contrast . . .

6. courage versus recklessness
7. living on campus versus living off campus
8. being self-employed versus working for others
9. work and drudgery
10. expectations about a job versus the reality of the job

Writing Activity 2

Choose a quotation that you agree or disagree with, or one that inspires you, and then write a comparison and contrast essay based on it.

> A wise man can see more from the bottom of a well than a fool can from a mountaintop.
>
> —Unknown

It seemed the world was divided into good and bad people. The good ones slept better while the bad ones seemed to enjoy the waking hours much more.

—Woody Allen, filmmaker

Imagination is more important than knowledge.

—Albert Einstein, physicist

People who work sitting down get paid more than people who work standing up.

—Ogden Nash, poet

Writing Activity 3

Examine the photo, and think about things that you could compare and contrast. You can focus on something in the photo, or use it to spark ideas about related topics. Some ideas might be two homes that you lived in, two buildings that you have worked in, two architectural styles, two neighborhoods, the city versus the countryside, or your dream home versus your actual home. Then write a comparison and contrast essay.

READING LINK

More Comparison and Contrast Readings

"My African Childhood" by David Sedaris (page 585)
"The Untranslatable Word 'Macho'" by Rose del Castillo Guilbault (page 635)

WRITING LINK

More Comparison and Contrast Writing Topics

Chapter 20, Writer's Room topic 2 (page 332)
Chapter 23, Writer's Room topic 2 (page 367)
Chapter 27, Writer's Room topic 1 (page 410)
Chapter 32, Writer's Room topic 1 (page 482)
Chapter 38, Writer's Room topic 2 (page 552)

Teaching Tip:

Pair Work

Have students read one of the essays in the Reading Link. Then, in pairs, they can list the main comparisons or contrasts.

CHECKLIST: COMPARISON AND CONTRAST

After you write your comparison and contrast essay, review the checklist on the inside front cover. Also, ask yourself the following set of questions.

- ☐ Does my thesis statement explain what I am comparing and contrasting?
- ☐ Does my thesis statement make a point about the comparison?
- ☐ Does my essay have a point-by-point or topic-by-topic pattern?
- ☐ Does my essay focus on similarities or on differences?
- ☐ Do all of my supporting examples clearly relate to the topics that I am comparing or contrasting?

Teaching Tip:
Writer's World Competition
Please advise students that they can submit their essays for possible publication to: <thewritersworld @prenhall.com>.

How Do I Get a Better Grade?

Visit www.mywritinglab.com for audio-visual lectures and additional practice sets about comparison and contrast writing.
Get a better grade with MyWritingLab!

Cause and Effect

CHAPTER 13

CONTENTS

When a flood occurs, people ask themselves, "How did this happen?" and "What is the extent of the damage?" Writers use the cause and effect pattern to explain the answers to these types of questions.

Writers' Exchange

Work with a group of students. Each group has two minutes to brainstorm as many reasons as possible to explain why people eat fast food. Then, each team will have two minutes to explain the effects of eating fast food. The team with the most causes and effects wins.

Teaching Tip:
Group Work
The Writers' Exchange activity can help your students understand cause and effect. Try this activity as a class discussion, and list ideas on the board.

> *“We cannot live only for ourselves. A thousand fibers connect us with our fellow men; and among those fibers, as sympathetic threads, our actions run as causes, and they come back to us as effects.”*
>
> Herman Melville, *novelist and sailor*

EXPLORING

What Is Cause and Effect?

Cause and effect writing explains why an event happened or what the consequences of such an event were. A cause and effect essay can focus on causes, effects, or both.

You often analyze the causes or effects of something. The next examples show you causes and effects of decisions in your home, college, and work.

Audience: Family member

My car accident happened for a few reasons.

- The fog had reduced visibility.
- The driver behind me was following too closely.
- There was a sudden traffic jam, and I had to stop quickly.

Audience: College administrator

Several events have caused a lack of student housing.

- There has been an increase in enrollment in our college.
- One student residence burned down during the summer.
- Another student residence was converted into condominiums.

Audience: Colleague

My company is downsizing for the following reasons.

- There is too much competition.
- We rely more on machines than on manpower.
- The owners want to retire soon.

The Cause and Effect Essay

When you write a cause and effect essay, focus on two main tasks.

Teaching Tip: Ask students to think of types of writing that include causes or effects such as medical pamphlets, report cards, and magazine ads.

1. **Indicate whether you are focusing on causes, effects, or both.** If you do decide to focus on both causes and effects, make sure that your thesis statement indicates your purpose to the reader.
2. **Ensure that your causes and effects are valid.** You should determine real causes and effects and not simply list things that happened before or after the event. Also, verify that your assumptions are logical.

Illogical: Our furnace stopped working because the weather was too cold. (This is illogical; cold weather cannot stop a furnace from working.)

Better: Our furnace stopped working because the filters needed replacing and the gas burners needed adjusting.

Teaching Tip:
Ask students to list causes and effects in these paragraphs.

Cause and Effect at Work

In this community newsletter about safety, the writer explains about the causes and effects of computer-related injuries.

Musculoskeletal disorders (MSDs) are a family of painful disorders affecting tendons, muscles, nerves, and joints in the neck, upper and lower back, chest, shoulders, arms, and hands. They include repetitive strain injuries (RSIs), which may take years to develop. Recovery can be difficult and may even require surgery in extreme cases.

MSDs are the scourge of the computerized workplace. Workers can develop chronic pain if their workstations are set up without proper attention to ergonomics. A small change, such as repositioning the screen or keyboard or using an adjustable chair, can often eliminate the problem.

A Student Essay

Read the student essay and answer the questions that follow.

The Causes of Aggressiveness in Ordinary People

by Catherine Belisle Prevost

1 During World War II, many German citizens behaved in an inhuman manner toward the people who were put in concentration camps. In 1961, in an effort to understand how people could behave so callously, Stanley Milgram conducted a series of experiments. He wondered how ordinary people could be led to commit aggressive and horrible acts. A few years later, another researcher named Philip Zimbardo conducted his own tests to determine how social roles influence behavior. The experiments led to some astounding conclusions. Ordinary people can be persuaded to commit cruel acts when they are in submissive or dominant positions.

2 Many idealistic young men and women join the military. These ordinary soldiers and marines, who are in a submissive relationship with superior officers, sometimes have no choice but to act violently. During

previous wars, soldiers have shot others, set fire to villages, and terrorized civilians because they had to do what their commanders asked. Thomas Brinson and Vince Treanor, in an article for *Veteran*, wrote, "In military training, soldiers are taught to react when threatened with aggressive, even violent behavior. In Vietnam there were no rules. Violence was sanctioned, rewarded, and reinforced as crucial to survival." Furthermore, soldiers feel powerless because those who refuse orders can be charged with desertion. During the American Civil War and during previous world wars, many soldiers who deserted were imprisoned or sent before firing squads. Richard Norton Taylor, in an article for *The Guardian*, says that more than three hundred British soldiers were executed for desertion during World War I. Thus, many ordinary people who join the military may feel compelled to act in cruel and inhuman ways.

3 Even when people have the option of disobeying orders, they can still be persuaded to act cruelly. In Stanley Milgram's experiment, a professor asked ordinary volunteers to give electric shocks to another human. Although no shocks were actually given, the subjects in the experiment believed that they were hurting someone. In that case, the participants could easily have disobeyed and left the room with no consequences. Yet, as Joseph Dimow, the author of "Resisting Authority," says, "Of forty participants in Milgram's first experiment, fifteen refused to continue at some point, while twenty-five went all the way to 450-volt shocks." In a more recent case, managers of fast-food restaurant chains were telephoned by someone pretending to be a police officer. The "officer" said that a female employee was guilty of theft, and he convinced several restaurant managers in different locations across the nation to strip-search young employees. Donna Jean Summers, an assistant manager at McDonald's, received one of those calls on April 9, 2004. She obeyed the caller and strip-searched eighteen-year-old employee Louise Ogborn. Summers could easily have disobeyed the person on the phone, yet she did as she was told. Therefore, dominated people can commit cruel acts even when they simply think they are obeying orders.

4 People in submissive positions are not the only ones who can be persuaded to act aggressively. A lot of people in dominant positions also act in horrible ways. The news is filled with stories of prison guards, police officers, and others in authoritarian roles who abuse their power. When some people are in powerful positions, they can become filled with a sense of superiority and strength, and they may end up seeing those under their authority as objects. In Philip Zimbardo's Stanford Prison Experiment, students were randomly selected to be guards or prisoners. According to Kathleen O'Toole, in her article "The Stanford Prison

Experiment," guards "increased their coercive aggression tactics, humiliation, and dehumanization of the prisoners. For example, the student guards forced prisoners to clean out toilet bowls with their bare hands." Christina Maslach, the woman credited with stopping the experiment, describes the change in one of the participants. When she first spoke with the student who was nicknamed "John Wayne," she thought that he was charming. Later, she saw him in the experiment; she was shocked by his transformation into a sadistic and cruel guard: "He was talking in a different accent, a Southern accent, which I hadn't recalled at all. He moved differently. [. . .] It was like Jekyll and Hyde," said Maslach. The experiment demonstrated that some ordinary people in authoritarian positions can become cruel and aggressive toward those under their command.

5 Ordinary people in controlling or submissive positions have the capacity to become tyrants. Perhaps those in positions of power should get leadership training, and those who are dominated should be taught that there are logical and legal limits they must not cross. As George Eliot, the English novelist, once wrote, "Cruelty, like every other vice, requires no motive outside of itself; it only requires opportunity."

Teaching Tip: This type of essay would normally be followed by a Works Cited page. If you plan to give students research essays, ask them to identify the sections in the essay that must be properly cited. You can find more information about citing and documenting sources in Chapter 16.

PRACTICE 1

1. Highlight the thesis statement.
2. Does the thesis statement express causes, effects, or both? *Only causes*
3. What introductory style does the writer use?
   a. anecdote b. contrasting position (c.) historical background
4. Highlight the topic sentences in paragraphs 2, 3, and 4.
5. Using your own words, sum up the causes that contribute to tyrannical behavior.
   — People who are expected to obey orders, such as soldiers, may be convinced to commit horrible acts.
   — Ordinary citizens may commit atrocious acts if they think they are obeying authority.
   — People in dominant positions may abuse their power.
6. The writer concludes her essay by which of the following?
   a. suggestion b. call to action c. prediction (d.) quotation

Explore Topics

In the Writer's Desk Warm Up, you will try an exploring strategy to generate ideas about different topics.

Writer's Desk Warm Up

Read the following questions, and write the first ideas that come to your mind. Think of two or three ideas for each topic.

EXAMPLE: Why are reality television shows so popular?

—voyeurism

—people are bored with sitcoms and other regular television programs

—a large variety for every taste

1. Why do people get into debt?

___

___

___

2. What are some causes and effects of addictions? Specify the type of addiction.

___

___

___

3. Why do people want to be famous? What are the effects of fame?

___

___

___

DEVELOPING

The Thesis Statement

When writing a thesis statement for a cause and effect essay, clearly demonstrate whether the focus is on causes, effects, or both. Also, make sure that you state a controlling idea that expresses your point of view or attitude.

controlling idea (causes) topic

There are many reasons for **global warming.**

topic controlling idea (effects)

Global warming may have a profound influence on our lifestyles.

topic controlling idea (causes and effects)

Global warming, which has developed for many reasons, may have a profound influence on our lifestyles.

PRACTICE 2 Look carefully at the following thesis statements. Decide if each sentence focuses on the causes, effects, or both. Look at the key words that give you the clues and circle the best answer.

1. Poverty persists in developing countries because of lack of education, scarcity of jobs, and political corruption.
   (a.) causes b. effects c. both
2. In our college, the high student dropout rate, which is triggered by the tourist industry, results in long-term problems for the community.
   a. causes b. effects (c.) both
3. The Asian tsunami has created many problems for the environment, as well as in people's mental and physical health.
   a. causes (b.) effects c. both

Grammar Hint — Affect and Effect

Use *affect* as a verb and *effect* as a noun. *Affect* means "to influence or change" and *effect* means "the result."

verb

How does the ban on fast food in public schools affect children's health?

noun

What effects will the ban on fast food in public schools have on children's health?

You can also use *effect* as a verb that means "to cause or to bring about a change or implement a plan."

verb

Health care professionals lobbied to effect changes in public school lunch menus.

See Chapter 34 for more information about commonly confused words.

Teaching Tip:
The Writer's Desk activities, such as the one on the next page, provide students with opportunities to develop a topic through all stages of the writing process using the cause and effect rhetorical mode. In the Warm Up, they begin by exploring various topics. Those topics then carry on throughout the chapter.

ESL Teaching Tip:
Pair Work
Ask students to discuss their answers with a partner to encourage collaboration between native and nonnative speakers.

Writer's Desk Write Thesis Statements

Write a thesis statement for each of the following topics. You can look for ideas in the previous Writer's Desk. Determine if you will focus on the causes, effects, or both in your essay.

EXAMPLE: Topic: popularity of reality shows

Thesis Statement: *Reality television shows have become increasingly popular for several reasons.*

1. Topic: getting into personal debt

   Thesis Statement: ______________________________

   ____

2. Topic: having an addiction

   Thesis Statement: ______________________________

   ____

3. Topic: having fame

   Thesis Statement: ______________________________

   ____

Teaching Tip:
Pair Work
After students write thesis statements, ask them to exchange books with a partner. The partner should analyze each sentence and determine if the focus is on causes, effects, or both.

The Supporting Ideas

After you have developed an effective thesis statement, generate supporting ideas. In a cause and effect essay, think of examples that clearly show the causes or effects. To develop supporting ideas follow these three steps:

- Use prewriting strategies such as freewriting and brainstorming to generate ideas.
- Choose the best ideas. Use examples that clearly reveal the causes and effects.
- Organize your ideas. Choose the best organizational method for this essay pattern.

Hint **Do Not Oversimplify**

Avoid attributing a simple or general cause to a very complex issue. When you use expressions such as *it appears that* or *a possible cause is,* it shows that you are aware of the complex factors involved in the situation.

Oversimplification: Global warming is caused by cars.

Better: One possible cause of global warming is the CO_2 emissions from cars.

Identifying Causes and Effects

Imagine that you had to write a cause and effect essay on gambling. You could brainstorm and think of as many causes and effects as possible.

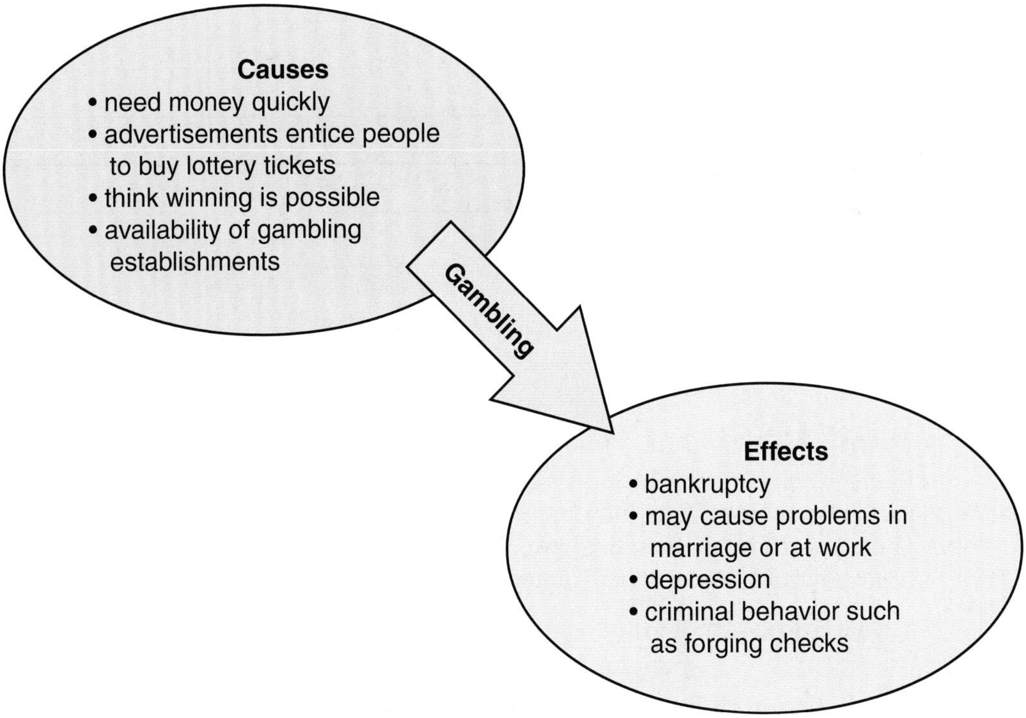

Causes
• need money quickly
• advertisements entice people to buy lottery tickets
• think winning is possible
• availability of gambling establishments
Gambling
Effects
• bankruptcy
• may cause problems in marriage or at work
• depression
• criminal behavior such as forging checks

Writer's Desk Identify Causes and Effects

Choose the topic of one of the thesis statements from the previous Writer's Desk. Then write some possible causes and effects.

EXAMPLE: Topic: *Popularity of reality television programs*

Causes	Effects
new television concept	*become TV junkie*
empathize with the contestants	*contestants become famous*
each episode has a hook ending	*take pleasure in others' humiliation*
feel superior to contestants	*live vicariously through others*

Focus on: *causes*

Topic: ____________________

Causes	Effects
______	______
______	______
______	______
______	______

Focus on: ____________________

Teaching Tip:
Pair Work
Ask students to discuss their answers for the Writer's Desk activity with a partner. Together, they will help each other come up with more ideas.

Teaching Tip:
As an additional activity, ask students to develop supporting ideas for all three Writer's Desk topics. The topics are listed in the Warm Up.

The Essay Plan

In many courses, instructors ask students to write about the causes or effects of a particular subject. Take the time to plan your essay before you write your first draft. Also, think about how you would logically arrange the order of ideas. As you make your plan, ensure that you focus on causes, effects, or both.

THESIS STATEMENT: Reality television shows have become increasingly popular for several reasons.

I. Many situation comedies and movies of the week are no longer innovative, so people turn to reality shows.
   A. Some television comedies retell old jokes.
   B. Characters are often stereotypical.
   C. Many shows have predictable endings.

II. Reality television programs cater to a variety of tastes.
    A. Some shows focus on family dynamics.
    B. Some shows focus on romance.
    C. Other shows focus on extreme situations.
III. Home audiences live vicariously through contestants.
    A. Audiences may feel superior to contestants.
    B. An audience member can empathize with a contestant.
    C. Audience members think they can become famous like the contestants.

Writer's Desk Write an Essay Plan

Choose one of the ideas that you have developed in previous Writer's Desks and prepare an essay plan. If you think of new details that will explain your point more effectively, include them in your plan.

The First Draft

After you have developed and organized your ideas in your essay plan, write the first draft. Remember to write complete sentences and to use transitional words or expressions to help your ideas flow smoothly. Most writers arrange cause and effect essays using emphatic order, which means that they place examples from the most to the least important or from the least to the most important. The following transitional expressions are useful for showing causes and effects.

To show causes	To show effects
for this reason	accordingly
the first cause	as a result
the most important cause	consequently

Teaching Tip: Ask students to keep their essay plans and then attach them to their final draft. You can then determine how the students have developed their ideas.

Writer's Desk Write the First Draft

Carefully review and, if necessary, revise your essay plan from the previous Writer's Desk, and then write the first draft of your cause and effect essay.

ESL
Teaching Tip:
Pair nonnative speakers with native speakers when doing the Vocabulary Boost. Possible answers are: friend, man, child, relax, items or products, criminal.

vo•cab•u•lar•y BOOST

If you use inappropriate vocabulary in a particular context, it can affect the way people respond to you. For example, you would not use street language in a business meeting. Replace the following words with terms that can be used in academic or professional writing.

buddy guy kid chill stuff crook

REVISING AND EDITING

Teaching Tip:
The activity of revising a student essay should help your students understand the important link between the writing process and the grammar chapters.

Revise and Edit a Cause and Effect Essay

When you finish writing a cause and effect essay, review your work and revise it to make the examples as clear as possible to your readers. Check that you have organized your ideas logically and remove any irrelevant details. Before you work on your own essay, practice revising and editing a student essay.

A Student Essay

Read the essay, and then answer the questions that follow. As you read, correct any errors that you find, and make comments in the margins.

Reality Television Is Here to Stay

by Ivan Pogrebkov

1 Matt is a twenty-one-year-old college student. Each Thursday evening, he and his friends get together to watch television. They are hooked on reality shows, which have changed the television landscape since they first arrived on the screen a few years ago. These television shows have become increasingly popular for several reasons.

2 First, the traditional situation comedies have become repetitive; therefore, bored viewers are looking for more innovative programming that will hold their attention. For example, many weekly comedy programs have the same mind-numbing plot in which the parents have to deal with their children getting into superficial trouble. The jokes are the same and the endings are predictable. The parents help the children solve the problem, and everybody learn a valuable life lesson. Most viewers are tired of this format where family problems can be solved in thirty minutes. ~~Some comedies in the past were very good, though. *Seinfeld* was a great situation comedy that was very popular and ran for a decade.~~ Reality

television is more interesting than run-of-the mill television shows because ordinary people can react in unexpected ways.

3 There are reality shows that focus on family dynamics, shows concentrating on romance, and on extreme situations. Although reality shows are scripted to some degree, they do provide viewers with a degree of suspense and unpredictability. One never knows who is going to loose the competition. This factor attracts audiences to keep watching to find out the outcome for each participant.

4 Finally, reality shows are all the rage because audiences can relate to the situations and participants on some level. Most of the people appearing on reality shows are ordinary citizens as opposed to glamorous stars with expensive hairdos and clothes. Spectators' emotions may range from empathy for the participants to feeling superior to them. Because they are just like the participants, viewers enjoy envisioning themselves doing the same things and achieving fifteen minutes of fame. And, if the reality show is a contest, the winner usually wins money, prizes, and some amount of recognition.

5 People are loyal to reality shows because they offer variety, humor, and suspense. In fact, these programs are today's new soap operas. Although many critics find reality shows uninspiring, those programs are probably going to continue to be popular for a long time.

PRACTICE 3

Revising

1. Does the essay focus on causes, effects, or both? *causes*
2. Each body paragraph lacks adequate details. List some examples that could support the main idea of each body paragraph.
   Answers will vary. *Students should give examples from specific reality shows.*

   Paragraph 2 ______________________________

   ____

   Paragraph 3 ______________________________

   ____

   Paragraph 4 ______________________________

   ____

3. Highlight the topic sentence in paragraph 2, and then cross out any sentences that do not support the topic sentence.

Teaching Tip: Encourage students to list examples of particular reality shows. Discuss how examples would strengthen the essay.

4. An appropriate topic sentence for paragraph 3 is
   (a.) Reality programs, unlike most sitcoms, soap operas, and made-for-TV movies, cater to a variety of tastes.
   b. Contestants of reality shows must follow a script, so they are not "real."
   c. Reality shows are unpredictable.
   d. Not everyone likes reality shows because their premises are often tedious.
5. What is the introductory style of this essay? *anecdote*
6. How does the writer conclude the essay?
   a. with an observation (b.) with a prediction c. with a suggestion

Editing

7. In paragraph 2, there is a subject–verb agreement error. Underline and correct the error.

   Correction: *everybody learns*
8. In paragraph 3, a sentence has faulty parallel structure. Underline and rewrite the sentence.

   Correction: Answers will vary. *There are shows that focus on family dynamics, on romance, and on extreme situations.*
9. Underline and correct the misspelled word in paragraph 3.

   Correction: *lose*
10. Change a slang expression or cliché in paragraph 4 into standard English.

    Correction: *all the rage = very popular*

GRAMMAR LINK

See the following chapters for more information about these grammar topics:
Parallel Structure, Chapter 25
Subject–Verb Agreement, Chapter 27
Exact Language, Chapter 33
Spelling, Chapter 34

Writer's Desk Revise and Edit Your Essay

Revise and edit the essay that you wrote for the previous Writer's Desk. You can refer to the revising and editing checklists at the end of this chapter and on this book's inside covers.

A Professional Essay

Ellen Goodman is a Pulitzer Prize–winning columnist for the *Boston Globe*, and her articles appear in over 370 newspapers. She has also written several books, including *Value Judgments* and *Keeping in Touch*. In the next essay, she examines why North Americans are becoming more isolated socially.

Friendless in North America

by Ellen Goodman

1 Lynn Smith-Lovin was listening in the back seat of a taxi when a woman called the radio talk-show hosts to confess her affairs with a new boyfriend and a not-yet-former husband. The hosts, in their best therapeutic voices, offered their on-air opinion, "Give me an S, give me an L, give me a U," You can spell the rest. It was the sort of exchange that would leave most of us wondering why anyone would share her intimate life story with a radio host. Didn't she have anyone else to talk with? Smith-Lovin might have been the only one in the audience with an answer to the question: Maybe not.

2 The Duke University sociologist is co-author of one of those blockbuster studies that makes us look at ourselves. This one is labeled "Friendless in America." A face-to-face study of 1,467 adults turned up some disheartening news. One-fourth reported that they have nobody to talk to about "important matters." Another quarter reported they are just one person away from nobody. But this was the most startling fact. The study is a replica of one done twenty years ago. In only two decades, from 1985 to 2004, the number of people who have no one to talk to has doubled. And the number of confidants of the average person has gone down from three to two.

3 The people to whom we are closest form our own informal safety net. They're the ones who see us through a life crisis, lend us their spare bedroom, or pick up our kids at school in a pinch. Social isolation is as big a risk factor for premature death as smoking. Robert Putnam has already chronicled the erosion of the ties that bind in *Bowling Alone*. But we've paid less attention to "coping alone" or "suffering alone." Imagine if some other piece of the social safety net had frayed that furiously. Imagine if income had gone down by a third or divorce doubled or the medical system halved. We would be setting up commissions and organizing rallies.

4 Not everything in the study was gloomy. Deep in the data is the suggestion that families—husbands and wives, parents and adult children—might be closer. Spouses who call each other "my best friend" might be right. We might have fewer intimates but we're more intimate with them. On average, we see them more than once a week and have

known them seven years. Nevertheless, the big news is that circles have tightened, shrunk, and gone nuclear. As Smith-Lovin says, "Literally nothing takes the place of family." The greatest loss has been in neighbors and friends who will provide help, support, advice, and connections to a wider world.

5 There is no shortage of speculation about why our circle of friends is eroding. The usual suspect is the time crunch. It's knocked friendship off the balancing beam of life as we attend to work and family. It's left less time for the groups and associations that bind us. But in the past twenty years, technology has changed the way we use our "relationship time." Walk along any city street and people talking on cell phones are more common than pigeons. Go into Starbucks and a third of the customers are having coffee dates with their laptops. "It could be that talking to people close to us on cell phones has caused our social circle to shrink," says Smith-Lovin. It could be that we are both increasingly in-touch and isolated. It's become easier to keep extensive relationships over time and distance but harder to build the deep ones in our backyard. In the virtual neighborhood, how many have substituted email for intimacy, contacts for confidants, and Facebook for face to face?

6 A few years ago, when my friend Patricia O'Brien and I wrote a book on the power of friendship in women's lives, we noted that there was no official status for friends, no pro-friendship movement, no cultural or political support system for friends. Yet this voluntary relationship can be the most sustaining one of life.

7 Now we are living in smaller, tighter circles. We are ten degrees of separation from each other and one or two people away from loneliness. And many now outsource intimacy from friends to professional therapists and *gawd* help us, talk shows. Who can we talk to about important matters? Who can we count on? As we search for tools to repair this frayed safety net, we can take poor, paradoxical comfort from the fact that if we are feeling isolated, we are not alone.

PRACTICE 4

1. Who is the audience for this essay? *General audience*
2. The thesis of this essay is not stated directly, but it is implied. Using your own words, write the thesis of this essay. Answers will vary.

   The increasing use of technology is leading North Americans to become more and more isolated.

3. Circle the type of introduction Goodman uses.
   a. historical background   (b.) anecdote   c. general background
4. In your own words, how have the socialization habits of North Americans changed in the past twenty years?
   The circle of intimates has become smaller. We have lost closeness with neighbors and friends.
5. What specific reasons does Goodman give for this social change?
   Goodman says technology, such as cell phones and online communications, have contributed to social change.
6. Goodman writes, "It could be that we are both increasingly in-touch and isolated." What does she mean?
   New technology gives us the means to communicate with people who are far from us, but it also discourages us from having face-to-face meetings with those near us.

Teaching Tip:
Discuss Goodman's essay with your students. Suggest that they write a response. They can discuss the reasons they have certain friends or the effects of friendship on their lives.

ESL Teaching Tip:
Encourage your nonnative speakers to write about the causes or effects of moving to the United States.

Teaching Tip:
Pair Work
Ask students to read one of the suggested essays in the Reading Link. Then, in pairs, they can outline the essay and list the main causes or effects.

The Writer's Room Topics for Cause and Effect Essays

Writing Activity 1

Write a cause and effect essay about one of the following topics, or choose your own topic.

General Topics

Causes and/or effects of

1. a good/bad sports parent
2. getting married
3. a fear of ______________
4. road rage
5. a natural phenomenon

College and Work-Related Topics

Causes and/or effects of

6. a public policy
7. becoming successful
8. giving somebody a second chance
9. learning a skill
10. a hostile workplace

READING LINK

More Cause and Effect Readings

"The CSI Effect" by Richard Willing (page 572)
"Weird Weather" by Pamela D. Jacobson (page 607)

WRITING LINK

More Cause and Effect Writing Topics

Chapter 20, Writer's Room topic 1 (page 332)
Chapter 22, Writer's Room topic 2 (page 356)
Chapter 28, Writer's Room topic 2 (page 429)
Chapter 33, Writer's Room topic 2 (page 493)

Writing Activity 2

Choose a quotation that you agree or disagree with, and then write a cause and effect essay based on it.

> Usually when people are sad, they don't do anything. They just cry over their condition. But when they get angry, they bring about a change.
>
> —Malcolm X, political activist

> Human beings, by changing the inner attitudes of their minds, can change the outer aspects of their lives.
>
> —William James, psychologist

> Those who can make you believe absurdities can make you commit atrocities.
>
> —Voltaire, satirist

> Fire and swords are slow engines of destruction, compared to the tongue of a gossip.
>
> —Richard Steele, essayist

Writing Activity 3

Why do nations go to war? What are some causes and effects of war? Write about war.

CHECKLIST: CAUSE AND EFFECT ESSAY

As you write your cause and effect essay, review the checklist on the inside front cover. Also, ask yourself the following questions.

- Does my thesis statement indicate clearly that my essay focuses on causes, effects, or both?
- Do I have adequate supporting examples of causes and/or effects?
- Do I make logical and valid points?
- Do I use the terms *effect* and/or *affect* correctly?

How Do I Get a Better Grade?

Visit www.mywritinglab.com for audio-visual lectures and additional practice sets about cause and effect writing. ***Get a better grade with MyWritingLab!***

Teaching Tip:

Writer's World Competition

Please advise students that they can submit their essays for possible publication to: <thewritersworld @prenhall.com>.

14 CHAPTER

Argument

CONTENTS

Exploring
- What Is Argument?
- The Argument Essay
- Explore Topics

Developing
- The Thesis Statement
- The Supporting Ideas
- The Essay Plan
- The First Draft

Revising and Editing
- Revise and Edit an Argument Essay
- A Professional Essay: "Keep Your Roses" by Melonyce McAfee

Medical practitioners often use argument to convince colleagues about the best treatment for a patient. In the same way, you use argument writing to convince readers to see things from your point of view.

Teaching Tip:
The Writers' Exchange activity can help your students understand argument. Give them 30 seconds to speak, and then ring a bell or flick the lights to indicate when students should switch speakers. Another idea is to ask students to argue both sides of the issue. For example, they can debate for 30 seconds, and then they must switch sides and debate the opposing view.

Writers' Exchange

For this activity, you and a partner will take turns debating an issue. To start, choose which one of you will begin speaking. The first speaker chooses one side of any issue listed below, and then argues about that issue, without stopping, for a set amount of time. Your instructor will signal when to switch sides. After the signal, the second speaker talks nonstop about the other side of the debate. If you run out of ideas, you can switch topics when it is your turn to speak. Possible topics:

Technology has improved our lives.	Technology has hurt our lives.
It is better to be an only child.	It is better to have brothers and sisters.
Adolescence is the best time of life.	Adolescence is the worst time of life.
Our college needs improvements.	Our college does not need improvements.

EXPLORING

What Is Argument?

When you use **argument**, you take a position on an issue, and you try to prove or defend your position. Using effective argument strategies can help you convince somebody that your point of view is a valid one.

Argument is both a writing pattern and a purpose for writing. In fact, it is one of the most common aims, or purposes, in most college and work-related writing. For example, in Chapter 10, there is an essay called "On Genius," in which the author uses definition as the predominant pattern. At the same time, the author uses argument to convince the reader that true genius exists all around us. Therefore, in most of your college and work-related writing, your purpose is to persuade the reader that your ideas are compelling and legitimate.

The next examples show arguments people might make every day.

> "*Fear not those who argue but those who dodge.*"
>
> MARIE EBNER VON ESCHENBACH, *writer*

Audience: Mate

We need to move to a larger home.

- My home office space in the corner of our bedroom is not adequate.
- Our son and daughter are approaching ages where they will need separate bedrooms.
- We can have a larger apartment or duplex for the same cost if we are just willing to relocate slightly north of the city.

Audience: College dean

The Graphic Arts Department needs new computers.

- The department has grown, and there are not enough computers.
- The existing computers do not support new graphics programs.
- To make our education relevant, students must understand current high-tech tools.

Audience: Customer

Our company has the best cell-phone package.

- We have the lowest rates.
- We give more free daytime minutes than the competitors.
- We include call display and voice messaging in all of our packages.

Teaching Tip: You may wish to explain how argument can be both a writing pattern (rhetorical mode) and a purpose.

Teaching Tip: Ask students if they can think of other places where they might see, read, or hear argument being used. Examples: letters of protest, political campaigns, commercials, pop-up ads, promotional flyers, and editorials.

The Argument Essay

When you write an argument essay, remember four key points.

1. **Consider your readers.** What do your readers already know about the topic? Will they likely agree or disagree with you? Do they have specific concerns? Consider what kind of evidence would be most effective with your audience.

2. **Know your purpose.** In argument writing, your main purpose is to persuade the reader to agree with you. Your specific purpose is more focused. You may want the reader to take action, you may want to support a viewpoint, you may want to counter somebody else's argument, or you may want to offer a solution to a problem. Ask yourself, What is my specific purpose?

Teaching Tip: If you teach your students about ethos, logos, and pathos, you could point out that point 3 is about logos and point 4 is about ethos. Information about logos and pathos appears in "The Supporting Ideas" section.

3. **Take a strong position and provide persuasive evidence.** The first thing to do in the body of your essay is to prove that there is, indeed, a problem. Then back up your point of view with a combination of facts, statistics, examples, and informed opinions.
4. **Show that you are trustworthy.** Respect your readers by making a serious argument. If you are condescending, or if you try to joke about the topic, your readers may be less inclined to accept your argument. You can also help your readers have more respect for your ideas when you choose a topic that you know something about. For example, if you have been in the military or know people in the military, you might be able to make a very convincing argument about the lack of proper equipment for soldiers.

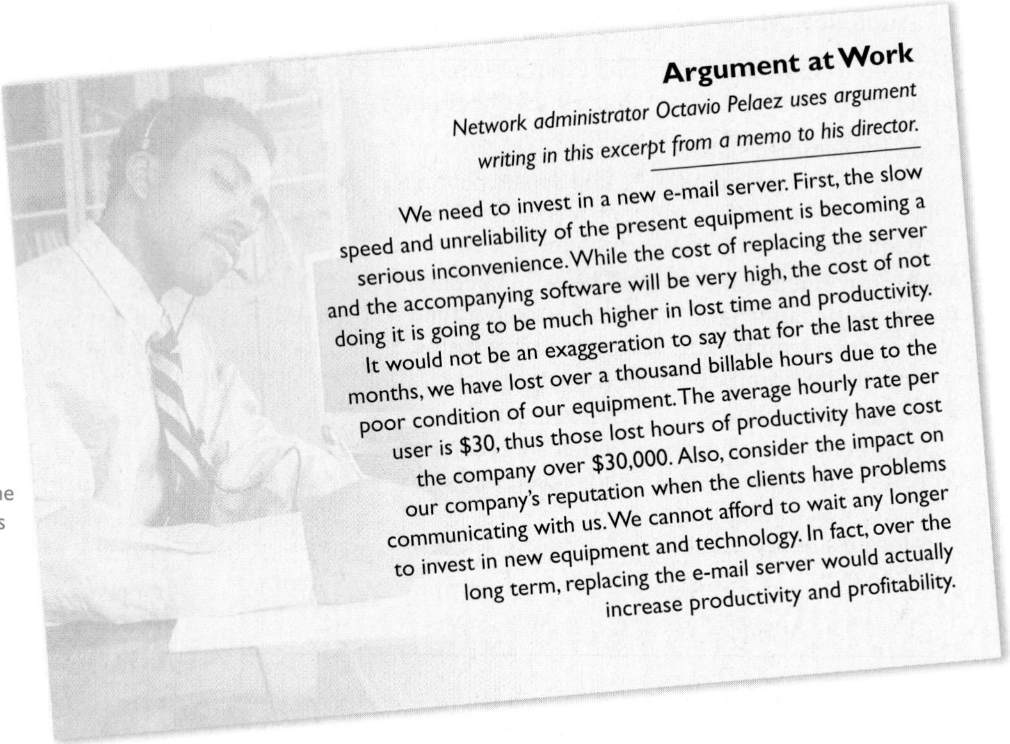

Argument at Work

Network administrator Octavio Pelaez uses argument writing in this excerpt from a memo to his director.

We need to invest in a new e-mail server. First, the slow speed and unreliability of the present equipment is becoming a serious inconvenience. While the cost of replacing the server and the accompanying software will be very high, the cost of not doing it is going to be much higher in lost time and productivity. It would not be an exaggeration to say that for the last three months, we have lost over a thousand billable hours due to the poor condition of our equipment. The average hourly rate per user is $30, thus those lost hours of productivity have cost the company over $30,000. Also, consider the impact on our company's reputation when the clients have problems communicating with us. We cannot afford to wait any longer to invest in new equipment and technology. In fact, over the long term, replacing the e-mail server would actually increase productivity and profitability.

Teaching Tip: Ask students to list the main point and the supporting arguments in this excerpt.

A Student Essay

Read the student essay and answer the questions that follow.

Changing Face of Cosmetic Surgery

by Kate Howell

1 Many people who undergo cosmetic surgery are regarded as vapid, shallow, and lacking in self-esteem. The phrases "Be happy with who you are" and "God made you perfect as is" are thrown around to provide assurance. For instance, a woman who attempts to change her appearance is told that such an act signals a level of dishonesty toward herself, her family and, possibly, her creator. The stigma associated with plastic surgery clearly exists—note the negative connotation of the word "plastic." However, such attitudes ignore reality. Anyone who uses cosmetic surgery to enhance his or her appearance should be applauded, not condemned.

2 "It is better to look good than to feel good." This line was made famous in the 1980s by Billy Crystal's "Fernando" character on *Saturday Night Live*, but few would have imagined that it was more than a catchphrase. It was actually an indication of a cultural phenomenon that exploded shortly thereafter. Cosmetic surgery has become popular on TV, in the office, and all around campus. TV shows such as *Extreme Makeover* have become hits. Prices for all kinds of procedures, from eyelifts to liposuction, have gone down, so more and more people can afford them. The age of plastic surgery recipients has also gone down, with college-aged girls opting for breast implants and nose jobs.

3 It is not just women who are body-obsessed. According to *HealthDay News*, men are the newest arrivals to the cosmetic surgery party. In 2000, there was a 16 percent increase in body-altering procedures performed on males. Competition in the business world is fierce, and men are looking for any advantage they can find. Bags under the eyes and a weak chin just won't cut it when there is an army of young bucks with MBAs gunning for every job. The idea that men are not supposed to care or show interest in their personal appearance is outdated and unfortunate. We do not live in a society of cattle ranchers and frontier explorers anymore. The beaten-up faces and callused hands of yore are no longer necessary tools of the trade; in today's society, they have been replaced by cheek lifts and palm scrubs, and that is not necessarily a bad thing.

4 There remains a degree of disapproval of plastic surgery, yet the importance of personal appearance is everywhere. Consumers spend billions of dollars each year on makeup, haircuts, tanning salons, manicures, and pedicures. Studies show that good-looking people tend to get hired for jobs. In the movies, some distinct qualities belong to the majority of the stars: trim bodies, immaculate grooming, and gleaming teeth. Yet nobody likes to acknowledge the fact that looks matter. Science tells us we are attracted to certain features, and it is ridiculous to deny

that fact. Appearance certainly isn't everything, but to downplay its importance is self-righteous hypocrisy.

5 If, as is widely believed, it is what is on the inside that matters, then people should not get in such a huff about altering one's outside. If a person feels unattractive, he or she should not be held back from making a change because friends or family cling to some half-hearted notion of "playing the cards one has been dealt." If people desire to remake their body as they see fit, then more power to them. In this time of laziness and apathy, at least these people are taking steps to try to improve their lot in life. As humans, we adapt to our society, and ours is now one of aesthetics. To borrow an oft-used phrase from hip-hop: Don't hate the player, hate the game.

PRACTICE 1

1. Highlight the thesis statement.
2. What introduction style does the author use?
   a. an anecdote
   b. a definition
   (c.) a contrasting position
   d. a description
3. Highlight the topic sentence in paragraphs 2 and 4. Be careful because the topic sentence may not be the first sentence.
4. The topic sentence in paragraph 3 is implied but is not stated directly. Choose the most effective topic sentence for this paragraph.
   a. Men are obsessed about their bodies.
   b. In 2000, the percentage of males getting cosmetic surgery increased.
   c. Men no longer want to have wrinkled, beaten-up faces and callused hands.
   (d.) To gain an advantage in the competitive workplace, men are increasingly opting to have cosmetic surgery.
5. What is the author's specific purpose? *To counter the idea that plastic surgery is bad*
6. The writer supports her point of view with specific evidence. Underline a quotation and a statistic.
7. In your own words, sum up the writer's main point about cosmetic surgery. Answers will vary.

   She points out that cosmetic surgery has become a standard part of our culture. She also conveys that looks are important and that they help people succeed in the workplace.

Teaching Tip: The Writer's Desk activities, such as the one on the next page, provide students with an opportunity to develop a topic through all stages of the writing process using the argument mode. In the Warm Up, they begin by exploring various controversial topics. Those topics then carry on throughout the chapter.

Explore Topics

In the Writer's Desk Warm Up, you will try an exploring strategy to generate ideas about different topics.

Writer's Desk Warm Up

Read the following questions, and write the first ideas that come to your mind. Think of two to three ideas for each topic.

EXAMPLE: Should alcohol advertising be banned?

Yes, I think so. It doesn't make sense that cigarette advertising is banned, when alcohol is much more dangerous. The ads make drinking seem glamorous.

1. Are some laws invalid, irrational, or unfair? To find ideas, you might think about laws related to drinking, driving, cycling, smoking, and voting.

2. Should the custom of tipping for service be abolished? Why or why not?

3. What are some of the major controversial issues in your neighborhood, workplace, college, state, or country? List some issues.

DEVELOPING

The Thesis Statement

In the thesis statement of an argument essay, state your position on the issue.

topic — controlling idea (the writer's position)

Many corporate executives are overpaid for very substandard work.

A thesis statement should be debatable, not a fact or a statement of opinion.

Fact: Some car companies have produced electric cars.
(This is a fact. It cannot be debated.)

Opinion: I think that people should buy electric cars.
(This is a statement of opinion. Nobody can deny that you feel this way. Therefore, do not use phrases such as *In my opinion, I think*, or *I believe* in your thesis statement.)

Argument: To address global warming and energy shortages, the automobile industry should focus on the production of electric cars.
(This is a debatable statement.)

ESL

Teaching Tip:
Some nonnative speakers may feel reluctant to share their thoughts in a forceful and direct manner. In many cultures, it is considered rude or arrogant to question elders or those in authority or to debate.

Hint **Be Direct**

Many students feel reluctant to take a stand on an issue. They may feel that it is too personal or impolite to do so. However, in academic writing, it is perfectly acceptable, and even desirable, to state an argument in a direct manner and then support it.

Teaching Tip:
Pair Work
Because Practice 2 is somewhat difficult, students could support each other by completing the practice in pairs.

PRACTICE 2 Evaluate the following statements. Write F for a fact, O for an opinion, or A for an argument.

1. The United States should impose a standard three-week vacation for all workers. _A_
2. Many colleges permit soft-drink companies to sell their products on campus. _F_
3. I disagree with advertising on college campuses. _O_
4. The city's major art gallery spent millions of dollars on an abstract painting. _F_
5. In my point of view, abstract art is ridiculous. _O_

6. Japanese animé should be recognized as an influential art form. ___A___
7. I think that no one should use racial profiling at borders. ___O___
8. Racial profiling at borders is a legitimate way to defend the nation. ___A___
9. In our state, art is not taught in most high schools. ___F___
10. Art education should be compulsory in our high schools. ___A___

Hint **Making a Guided Thesis Statement**

Your instructor may want you to guide the reader through your main points. To do this, mention your main and supporting ideas in your thesis statement. In other words, your thesis statement provides a map for the readers to follow.

> Art education should be compulsory in high schools because it encourages creativity, it teaches culture, and it develops students' analytical skills.

Writer's Desk Write Thesis Statements

Write a thesis statement for the next topics. You can look for ideas in the Warm Up on page 241. Make sure that each thesis statement clearly expresses your position on the issue.

EXAMPLE: Topic: alcohol advertising

Thesis statement: *Advertisements for alcoholic beverages should be prohibited on television or in any form of mass media.*

1. Topic: unfair laws

   Thesis statement: ______________________________

2. Topic: tipping customs

   Thesis statement: ______________________________

3. Topic: a controversial issue

   Thesis statement: ______________________________

The Supporting Ideas

To make a logical and reasoned argument, support your main point with facts, examples, and statistics. (For details about adding facts, examples, and statistics, see page 50 in Chapter 4.)

You can also include the following types of support.

- **Quote informed sources.** Sometimes experts in a field express an informed opinion about an issue. An expert's thoughts and ideas can add weight to your argument. For example, if you want to argue that people are becoming complacent about AIDS, you might quote an article published by a respected national health organization.
- **Consider logical consequences.** When you plan an argument, think about long-term consequences of a proposed solution to a problem. Perhaps you want to argue that alternative energy sources should be used to fuel automobiles. You could point out that the country will be less reliant on oil imports. As a result, consumers will not be subject to rising gas prices caused by conflicts in other areas of the world.
- **Acknowledge opposing viewpoints.** Anticipating and responding to opposing views can strengthen your position. For instance, if you argue that school uniforms should be mandatory, you might address those who feel that students need freedom to express themselves. Try to refute some of the strongest arguments of the opposition.

Teaching Tip: Ask students to think about the opposing viewpoints for the following arguments: *The sale of cigarettes should be banned. Daycares should be closed.*

Making an Emotional Appeal

Generally, an effective argument appeals to the reader's reason, but it can also appeal to his or her emotion. For example, you could use certain words or descriptions to encourage a reader's sense of justice, humanity, or pride. However, use emotional appeals sparingly. If you use **emotionally charged words** such as *wimp* or *thug*, or if you appeal to base instincts such as fear or cowardice, then you may seriously undermine your argument. Review the next examples of emotional appeals.

Overemotional:	A ferocious, bloodthirsty pit bull broke free of its leash and attacked a defenseless, fragile boy named Jason. The child, who will suffer from lifelong psychological trauma, is disfigured with irreparable facial scars.
Reasonable and more neutral:	Pit bulls can be unpredictable. The pit bull attack on nine-year-old Jason caused significant facial scarring and psychological trauma.

Hint **Avoid Common Errors**

When you write your argument essay, avoid the following pitfalls.

Do not make generalizations. If you begin a statement with *Everyone knows* or *It is common knowledge*, then the reader may mistrust what you say. You cannot possibly know what everyone else knows or does not know. It is better to refer to specific sources.

Generalization: Everyone knows that our nation is too dependent on oil.

Better: Prominent senators have stated that our nation's dependence on oil is a serious problem.

Do not make exaggerated claims. Make sure that your arguments are plausible.

Exaggerated: If marijuana is legalized, drug use will soar in schools across the nation.

Better: If marijuana is legalized, drug use may increase in schools across the nation.

Teaching Tip:
Ask students to brainstorm lists of arguments for or against a highly controversial issue such as abortion or war, and write their arguments on the board, which they can then read and evaluate to decide whether their arguments are generalizations, emotional appeals, exaggerated claims, or valid arguments.

PRACTICE 3 You have learned about different methods to support a topic. Read each of the following thesis statements and think of a supporting idea for each item. Use the type of support suggested in parentheses. Answers will vary.

1. Volunteer work should be mandatory in all high schools.

   (Logical consequence) ______________________________

   ____

2. Online dating is a great way to meet a potential mate.

   (Acknowledge an opposing view) ______________________________

   ____

3. Children should not be spanked.

   (Emotional appeal) ______________________________

   ____

4. The college dropout rate is too high in our state.

   (Logical consequence) ______________________________

   ____

5. Pointy-toed stilettos are unattractive, uncomfortable, and potentially harmful. (Acknowledge an opposing viewpoint) ____________________

____

ESL
Teaching Tip:
Pair native and nonnative students to do the Vocabulary Boost.

vo•cab•u•lar•y BOOST

Some words can influence readers because they have positive or negative connotations, which are implied or associated meanings. The meaning often carries a cultural value judgment with it. For example, *macho* may have negative connotations in one country and positive connotations in another country. For the word *thin*, synonyms like *skinny* or *skeletal* have negative connotations, while *slender* and *svelte* have positive ones.

Using a thesaurus, try to come up with related terms or descriptions that have either positive or negative connotations for the words in bold. Answers will vary.

Gloria is **large.** *big boned, fat, overweight, plump, curvy, robust, a "real" woman*

Calvin is **not assertive.** *weak, a wimp, girly, shy, sweet, attentive*

Mr. Wayne **expresses his opinion.** *is loud-mouthed, overbearing, strong-willed, forceful, confident*

Franklin is a **liberal.** *left-wing nut, bleeding heart, open-minded, inclusive*

Identify terms you chose that might be too emotionally loaded for an argument essay.

Consider Both Sides of the Issue

Once you have decided what issue you want to write about, try to think about both sides of the issue. Then you can predict arguments that your opponents might make, and you can plan your answer to the opposition. Here are examples.

Teaching Tip:
As an extra activity, you can give students a selection of topics and ask them to brainstorm *for* and *against* arguments.

Arguments for Banning Alcohol Advertisements

- Ads encourage drinking among adolescents.
- Ads are aimed at young males who can become aggressive.
- Alcohol kills more people than cigarettes.

Arguments Against Banning Alcohol Advertisements

- Print advertisers will lose significant income from magazine ads.
- Sporting events rely on advertising dollars.
- Advertisers should have freedom of speech.

Writer's Desk Consider Both Sides of the Issue

Choose one of the topics from the previous Writer's Desk, and write arguments showing both sides of the issue.

Topic: ____

For	Against
______________________	______________________
______________________	______________________
______________________	______________________
______________________	______________________
______________________	______________________
______________________	______________________

Hint Strengthening an Essay with Research

In some courses, your instructors may ask you to include supporting ideas from informed sources to strengthen your essays. You can find information in a variety of resources, including textbooks, journals, newspapers, magazines, or the Internet. When researching, make sure that your sources are from legitimate organizations. For example, for information about the spread of AIDS, you might find statistics on the World Health Organization Web site. You would not go to someone's personal rant or conspiracy theory site.

For more information about evaluating and documenting sources, refer to Chapter 16, The Research Essay.

Teaching Tip:
To give students more practice, you can ask them to develop supporting ideas for all three Writer's Desk topics, which are listed in the Warm Up.

The Essay Plan

Before you write your argument essay, outline your ideas in a plan. Include details that can help illustrate each argument. Ensure that every example is valid and relates to the thesis statement. Also think about your organization. Many argument essays use emphatic order and list ideas from the least to the most important or compelling.

THESIS STATEMENT: Advertisements for alcoholic beverages should be prohibited on television or in any form of mass media.

I. Banning alcohol ads would reduce excessive drinking and alcohol-related assaults and injuries among youths.
   A. Drinking is like a rite of passage, and ads encourage that belief.
   B. Many binge drinkers die from alcohol poisoning.
   C. Many rapes and assaults are blamed on excessive drinking.

II. Alcohol advertising targets young impressionable males who are the most dangerous drivers.
   A. Beer ads reinforce he-man attitudes.
   B. Young males are more likely to drink and drive than any others.
   C. Drunk driving rates are very high among young men.

III. It is hypocritical to ban cigarette advertising but not alcohol advertising.
   A. Cigarette packages carry warnings, but alcohol bottles don't.
   B. Alcohol is addictive.
   C. Alcohol causes many diseases such as cirrhosis of the liver.

Teaching Tip: Ask students to keep their essay plans and then attach them to the final draft. You can then determine how the students have developed their ideas.

Writer's Desk **Write an Essay Plan**

Choose one of the ideas that you have developed in the previous Writer's Desk, and write a detailed essay plan.

The First Draft

Now that you have a refined thesis statement, solid supporting details, and a roadmap of your arguments and the order in which you will present them, you are ready to write the first draft. Remember to write complete sentences and to include transitional words or expressions to lead readers from one idea to the next. Here are some transitions that introduce an answer to the opposition or the supporting ideas for an argument.

To answer the opposition	To support your argument
admittedly	certainly
however	consequently
nevertheless	furthermore
of course	in fact
on one hand/on the other hand	obviously
undoubtedly	of course

Grammar Hint **Keeping Pronouns Consistent**

In argument writing, ensure that your pronouns do not switch between *they*, *we*, and *you*. If you are writing about specific groups of people, use *they* to refer to those people. Only change pronouns when the switch is logical.

Many hunters argue that they need large collections and varieties of guns. Yet why would ~~you~~ *they* need a semi-automatic to go hunting?

See Chapter 31 for more information about pronoun usage.

Writer's Desk **Write the First Draft**

Write the first draft of your argument essay. Include an interesting introduction. Also, add specific details to flesh out each body paragraph.

REVISING AND EDITING

Revise and Edit an Argument Essay

When you finish writing an argument essay, carefully review your work and revise it to make the supporting examples as clear as possible to your readers. Check that the order of ideas is logical, and remove any irrelevant details. Before you revise and edit your own essay, practice revising and editing a student essay.

Teaching Tip: The activity of revising a student essay should help your students understand the important link between the writing process and the grammar chapters.

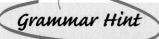

A Student Essay

Read the essay, and then answer the questions that follow. As you read, correct any errors that you find, and make comments in the margins.

Alcohol Advertising

by Kayin Jacobs

1 Magazines feature glossy vodka advertisements. During television sporting events, viewers see one beer ad after another. Alcohol, while society's most accepted drug, is considerably more dangerous than some other substances that cannot be advertised. The current massive promotion of alcoholic beverages has several negative side effects that are ignored because of the cultural significance of alcohol. Advertisements for alcoholic beverages should be prohibited on television or in any form of mass media.

2 Binge drinking is a common pass-time for students entering their first week of college. Eliminating alcohol ads would reduce excessive drinking and alcohol-related assaults and injuries among youths. While some may see drinking as a rite of passage for young people entering adulthood, the reality is that the practice doesn't have no positive benefits. The Web site *College Drinking: Changing the Culture*, which was created by the National Institute on Alcohol Abuse and Alcoholism (NIAAA), states that 1,400 college students between the ages of eighteen and 24 die every year in alcohol-related incidents, while 500,000 students suffer alcohol-related injuries each year. The East Tennessee State University School of Nursing site mentions that 600,000 college students are physically attacked by a student who has been drinking, while another 70,000 students are raped or sexually assaulted as a result of alcohol. Alcohol is the only recreational drug that is still actively advertised on television, and this is a large part of the reason why so many young people binge on the drug. Elimination of the advertising could result in a lower number of young people who drink, just as removing cigarette advertising from television has helped reduce the number of young smokers.

3 Alcohol advertising targets young impressionable males who are the most dangerous drivers. Beer ads, for example. These advertisements usually allude to a connection between drinking a certain beer and getting attractive females. Yet statistics about drunk driving fatalities indicate that young males are more likely to drink and drive than any other group. In the United States, 17,419 people died in alcohol-related traffic accidents in 2002, accounting for 41 percent of all traffic deaths, according to the Center for Disease Control Web site. It stands to reason

that the elimination of alcohol advertising would result in fewer drunk driving fatalities, as young men are both the primary target of these advertisements and the primary cause of most drunk driving deaths.

4 Cigarette packages contain warnings about negative health effects. Alcohol cans and bottles should also have warning labels explaining the addictive qualities of the product and the long-term effects of excessive drinking. Certainly, both cigarettes and alcohol are highly addictive. A lifetime drinker has health problems that could be compared to a lifetime smoker. Some of the potential health problems that could await an alcoholic include brain cell damage, inflammation and ulcers in the stomach, and cirrhosis, hepatitis, or cancer of the liver. According to the Center for Disease Control website, in 2003 there were 12,207 deaths from chronic liver disease caused by alcohol.

5 Now, don't get the wrong message. This is not an argument for the prohibition of alcohol but for a pause in the incessant marketing of this product to young people, young males in particular. Let's face it: young guys can become idiots when they have a bottle in their hands. Advertising promotes our alcohol culture, which results in many preventable deaths every year. Those who want alcohol can buy it, but it should not be actively marketed. A lesson society seems to have learned with cigarettes. Now let's hope the holocaust of people's lives is curbed with the ban of alcohol advertising.

Teaching Tip:
Point out that this type of essay would normally include a Works Cited page. You can ask students to identify sources that should be properly cited.

PRACTICE 4

Revising

1. Highlight the thesis statement.
2. Highlight the topic sentence in each body paragraph.
3. a. How does the topic sentence in paragraph 4 fail to support the thesis statement?

   Paragraph 4 is about warning labels and health consequences. It does not mention advertising, yet the essay is about alcohol advertising.

   b. Create a topic sentence for paragraph 4 that more effectively links the paragraph to the thesis statement.

   Companies should not advertise alcohol because the health consequences are as severe as those for cigarettes.

4. In the concluding paragraph, the writer uses emotionally charged words and exaggerates. Give examples of each of these problems.

   Emotionally charged language _young guys are idiots, holocaust_

   Exaggeration _comparing alcohol deaths to the holocaust_

5. Does the writer acknowledge the opposing viewpoint? _____ Yes __X__ No

Editing

6. Underline and correct a spelling mistake in paragraph 2.

   Correction: _pastime_

7. In paragraph 2, there is an inconsistency in the way the numbers are written. Underline and correct the error.

   Correction: _between eighteen and twenty-four_

8. In paragraph 2, there is a double negative. (Two negative words cancel each other out.) Underline the error and write the correct phrase in the space.

   Correction: _The practice doesn't have any positive benefits._

9. Identify fragments in paragraphs 3 and 5, and write correct sentences on the lines below.

   Paragraph 3: _Beer ads, for example, are aimed at males._

   Paragraph 5: _It is a lesson society seems to have learned with cigarettes._

GRAMMAR LINK

See the following chapters for more information about these topics:
Fragments, Chapter 23
Double Negatives, Chapter 29
Spelling, Chapter 34
Numbers, Chapter 38

***Writer's Desk* Revise and Edit Your Essay**

Revise and edit the essay that you wrote for the previous Writer's Desk. You can refer to the revising and editing checklists at the end of this chapter and on this book's inside covers.

A Professional Essay

Melonyce McAfee is an editorial assistant at *Slate* magazine. She has written for a variety of publications including the *San Diego Union-Tribune*. In this essay, she argues for the abolition of Administrative Professionals Day. Read the essay and answer the questions that follow.

Keep Your Roses

by Melonyce McAfee

1 Here's a plot line for the writers at NBC's *The Office*: It's April 26. Paper salesman Jim presents a bouquet of tulips to his office crush, Pam, the receptionist. The accompanying card reads, "For all you do. Happy Secretaries Day." Competitive and cringe-inducing boss Michael, until now oblivious to the holiday, sees the card and orders a garish bouquet, large enough to blot out Pam's head and overshadow Jim's arrangement. The bouquet arrives at 4:49 p.m. Eyes roll. Administrative Professionals Day is the Hallmark holiday that leads to interoffice jealousy, discomfort, and not much else.

2 The National Secretaries Association got the ball rolling with Professional Secretaries Week in 1952. The holiday was renamed Administrative Professionals Week in 2000, but I prefer the tell-it-like-it-is Secretaries Day. The **NSA** (now, naturally, the International Association of Administrative Professionals) claims the day is meant to enhance the image of administrative workers, promote career development, and encourage people to enter the field. But does it really do any of the above?

NSA: National Secretaries Association

3 In my first job out of college, I worked as a typist at a title company, a job akin to cryptography. I pecked my way toward carpal tunnel syndrome to turn chicken scratch into property reports. Typists served the entire office, but title officers also had personal secretaries. On Secretaries Day, we typists sucked our teeth at the bouquets on the secretaries' desks. At my next corporate job, I had gained an "assistant" title. But along with the other assistants, I was still left empty-handed. The office professionals chipped in for a bouquet for the division secretary, who regularly pawned off duties on us assistants and huffed when asked to, well, work. "I can't believe they got *her* flowers," we hissed.

4 My mother, a former hospital administrative assistant, was surprised with three greeting cards and a gorgeous scarf last Secretaries Day. She wasn't aware of the holiday and was touched that the nurses in her department took the opportunity to thank her for working hard on special projects. But she also had to listen to a chorus of "*I* didn't get anything" from other administrators. She says that didn't diminish her pleasure,

but it does prove my point. When the holiday makes someone feel appreciated, it almost invariably leaves others out in the cold.

5 Maybe part of the problem is that in the fifty years since the holiday began, the duties of a secretary have been farmed out across the office, and the job definition is no longer clear. A secretary used to be the woman who answered phones, took dictation, typed, picked up dry cleaning, and stole your husband, if she was really good. Now she (or he) might give PowerPoint presentations or build a Web site. Meanwhile, someone else might do the typing and filing.

6 The confusion over who qualifies as a secretary creates social anxiety about either overcelebrating the holiday or undercelebrating it. One Secretaries Day, a former advertising-sales assistant and co-worker of mine got lovely plants from colleagues who rushed to point out that they'd gotten her a gift even though she wasn't really a secretary. She got the impression they thought she might be offended by being lumped in with the administrative staff. The holiday forces workers, like it or not, to evaluate how they stack up. Mail-room guy, copy clerk, typist, receptionist, administrative secretary, executive assistant—are you low enough on the totem pole to merit a gift? Or are you too low?

7 In some industries, Secretaries Day is less apt to cause confusion. Schools, for example, have it easy—it's obvious that the lady in the front office with her glasses hanging by a chain is the secretary. But in many workplaces, administrative positions are rife with ambiguity. What about legal clerks at law firms and sales assistants at magazines—when you cut them, do they not bleed Wite-Out? In the media business, assistant positions are often a stepping-stone to greater glory. Still, assistants perform the same duties as secretaries. And even if most assistants don't do it for long, every publication has a guy who's been an editorial assistant for fifteen years. He can write a dozen screenplays and freelance hundreds of album reviews for the local indie paper, but he's still going to be an assistant ten years from now. Does he deserve the same Benihana gift certificate that the publisher's secretary gets? Of course he does. He just lacks the magic title.

8 Perhaps my impatience with Secretaries Day springs from job dissatisfaction, as an executive assistant at a New York–based magazine suggested when we mused about why the holiday creates bitterness. True—in my mind, I should be the boss. And I resent being reminded of my slow progress up the chain of command every April 26. Those of us who yearn to be professionals, not administrative professionals, tend to bristle at the idea that we're just boosters for the big boys and girls.

9 Some bosses feel compelled to take their secretary, assistant, or whoever out to lunch on Secretaries Day. It's a nice gesture, but who wants to sit through that awkward meal? Anyone who has seen the *Curb Your*

Enthusiasm episode in which Larry David takes his maid on a squirm-worthy lunch date at his country club knows the potential disaster of forced boss–employee **conviviality.** Instead of Secretaries Day, why not just chip in for a big cake on the Friday before Labor Day and toast everyone in the office. Wouldn't that be kinder, not to mention easier? I'd much prefer that to a holiday that's a catch-all for "attagirl," "I'm sorry for being an insufferable employer," and "we should talk about that raise."

conviviality: friendliness

PRACTICE 5

1. Highlight the thesis statement.
2. What technique does the writer use to introduce the topic?
   a. historical background (b.) anecdote c. a definition
3. What synonyms does McAfee use for "secretary" in this essay?
   Possible answers: *executive assistant, administrative assistant, administrative professional, typist*
4. In which paragraph does the writer acknowledge an opposing viewpoint? *2*
5. Which sentence best sums up the writer's implied argument in paragraph 3?
   a. Typists and assistants are secretaries.
   b. The writer worked as a typist in a small company for many years, and then she became an executive.
   c. Typists do a lot of hard work but are not appreciated.
   (d.) Many people in offices, such as typists and assistants, feel resentful when they are not rewarded on Secretaries Day.
6. Underline the topic sentence in paragraph 5.
7. Which sentence best sums up the writer's implied argument in paragraph 8?
   a. Administrative assistants really do the work of the bosses.
   b. Honestly, most administrative assistants dislike their jobs.
   (c.) Secretaries Day reminds administrative assistants that they have not advanced on the career ladder.
   d. Most administrative assistants want to be professionals.
8. Using your own words, sum up McAfee's main supporting arguments.
   Secretaries Day is not fair to other employees.
   In many workplaces, it is difficult to know who the secretary is.
   It reminds the secretary of his or her lowly status.

The Writer's Room Topics for Argument Essays

Writing Activity 1

Choose any of the following topics, or choose your own topic, and write an argument essay. Remember to narrow your topic and to follow the writing process.

General Topics

1. graffiti
2. gun laws
3. labor unions
4. home schooling
5. same-sex marriage

College and Work-Related Topics

6. usefulness of college programs
7. working while going to college
8. minimum wage
9. parental leave
10. working at home

Writing Activity 2

Choose a quotation that you agree or disagree with, and then write an argument essay based on it.

> Many would be cowards if they had courage enough.
>
> —Thomas Fuller, historian

> Advertising is the modern substitute for argument.
>
> —George Santayana, philosopher

> Of all forms of caution, caution in love is perhaps the most fatal to true happiness.
>
> —Bertrand Russell, author and philosopher

> Everything on the earth has a purpose, every disease an herb to cure it, and every person a mission.
>
> —Mourning Dove Salish, author

Writing Activity 3

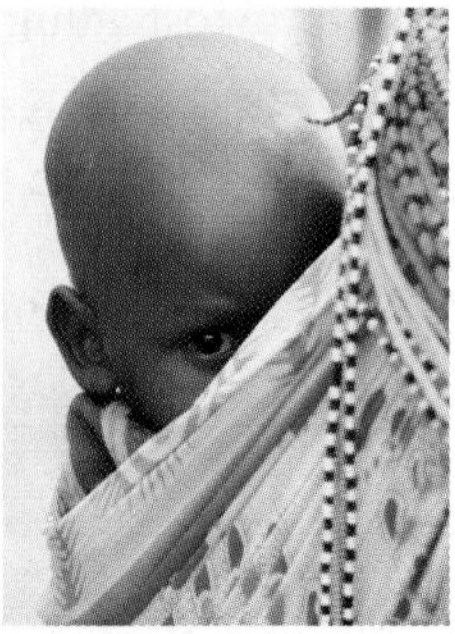

Examine the photo and think about arguments that you might make, such as controversies related to sex selection, sperm donors, international adoptions, foster care, and celebrity adoptions. For instance, you could argue that the children of sperm donors should or should not receive information about their biological fathers. Then write an argument essay.

CHECKLIST: ARGUMENT ESSAY

After you write your argument essay, review the checklist on the inside front cover. Also, ask yourself the following set of questions.

- Does my thesis statement clearly state my position on the issue?
- Do I make strong supporting arguments?
- Do I include facts, examples, statistics, and logical consequences?
- Do my supporting arguments provide evidence that directly supports the thesis statement?
- Do I acknowledge and counter opposing arguments?
- Do I use valid arguments? (Do I avoid making broad generalizations? Do I restrain any emotional appeals?)
- Do I use a courteous tone?

Teaching Tip:
Writer's World Competition
Please advise students that they can submit their essays for possible publication to: <thewritersworld@prenhall.com>.

Teaching Tip:
Suggest that students read one of the essays in the Reading Link. They can analyze the writer's arguments.

How Do I Get a Better Grade?

Visit www.mywritinglab.com for audio-visual lectures and additional practice sets about argument writing.
Get a better grade with MyWritingLab!

READING LINK

Argument

"Google's China Web" by Frida Ghitis (page 603)
"Medicating Ourselves" by Robyn Sarah (page 638)

WRITING LINK

See the next grammar sections for more argument writing topics.

Chapter 24, Writer's Room topic 2 (page 379)
Chapter 26, Writer's Room topic 1 (page 396)
Chapter 31, Writer's Room topic 1 (page 470)
Chapter 32, Writer's Room topic 2 (page 482)
Chapter 34, Writer's Room topic 2 (page 507)
Chapter 35, Writer's Room topic 2 (page 521)

PART III

More College and Workplace Writing

In the next chapters, you will learn about additional writing skills. Chapter 15, Paraphrasing and Summarizing, provides you with details about these important skills. Chapter 16 leads you through the process of writing a research essay.

When you apply for a job, the ability to present yourself in a professional manner is important. Thus, Chapter 17, The Résumé and the Letter of Application, provides you with information for writing succinctly.

Chapter 18, Responding to Film and Literature, leads you through the process of interpreting creative works.

Finally, essay exams are perhaps the most common type of writing that you will do in college. Chapter 19, Becoming a Successful Student, provides information about study skills and guides you through the exam writing process.

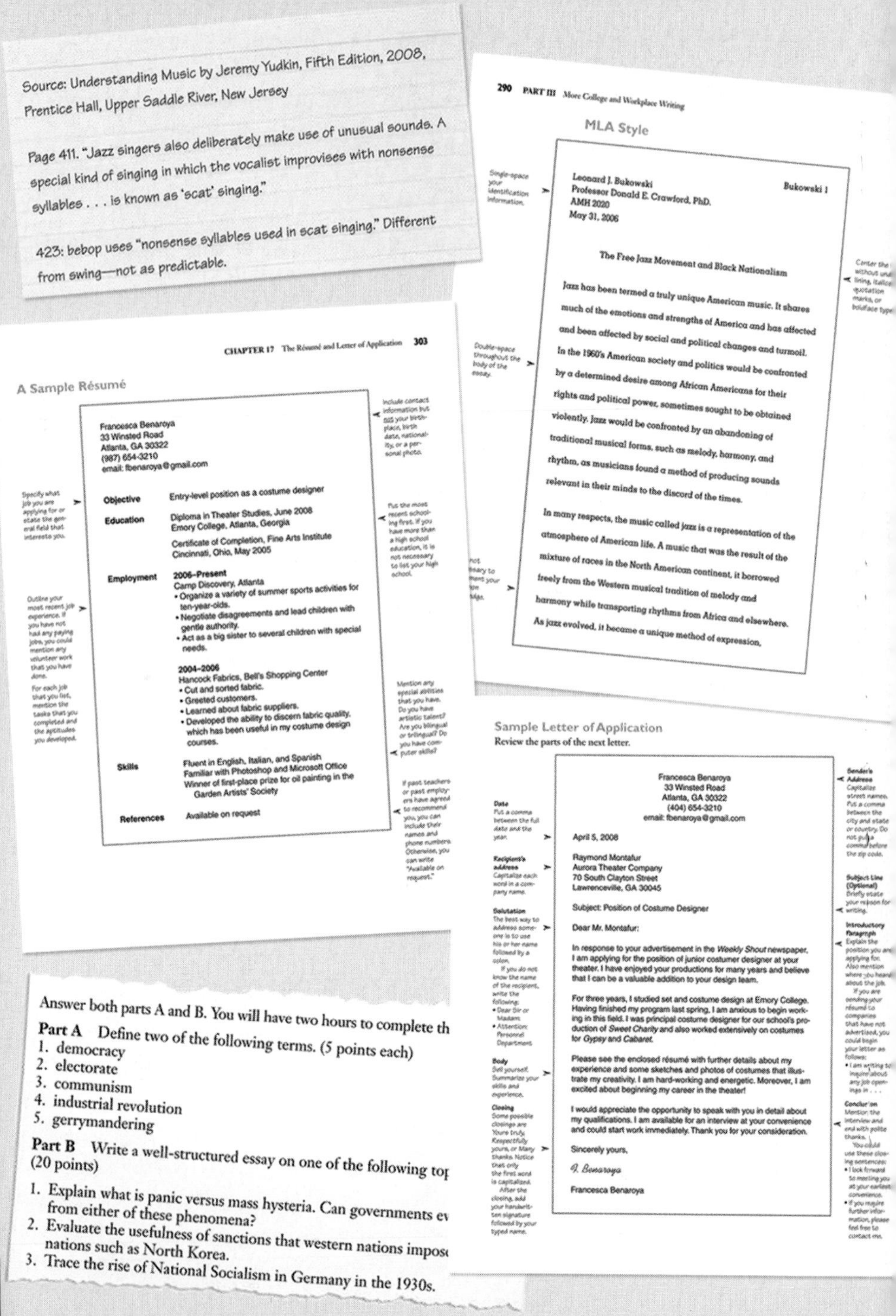

Source: Understanding Music by Jeremy Yudkin, Fifth Edition, 2008, Prentice Hall, Upper Saddle River, New Jersey

Page 411. "Jazz singers also deliberately make use of unusual sounds. A special kind of singing in which the vocalist improvises with nonsense syllables . . . is known as 'scat' singing."

423: bebop uses "nonsense syllables used in scat singing." Different from swing—not as predictable.

290 PART III More College and Workplace Writing

MLA Style

Leonard J. Bukowski Bukowski 1
Professor Donald E. Crawford, PhD.
AMH 2020
May 31, 2006

The Free Jazz Movement and Black Nationalism

Jazz has been termed a truly unique American music. It shares much of the emotions and strengths of America and has affected and been affected by social and political changes and turmoil. In the 1960's American society and politics would be confronted by a determined desire among African Americans for their rights and political power, sometimes sought to be obtained violently. Jazz would be confronted by an abandoning of traditional musical forms, such as melody, harmony, and rhythm, as musicians found a method of producing sounds relevant in their minds to the discord of the times.

In many respects, the music called jazz is a representation of the atmosphere of American life. A music that was the result of the mixture of races in the North American continent, it borrowed freely from the Western musical tradition of melody and harmony while transporting rhythms from Africa and elsewhere. As jazz evolved, it became a unique method of expression.

CHAPTER 17 The Résumé and Letter of Application 303

A Sample Résumé

Francesca Benaroya
33 Winsted Road
Atlanta, GA 30322
(987) 654-3210
email: fbenaroya@gmail.com

Objective: Entry-level position as a costume designer

Education: Diploma in Theater Studies, June 2008, Emory College, Atlanta, Georgia. Certificate of Completion, Fine Arts Institute, Cincinnati, Ohio, May 2005

Employment: 2006–Present, Camp Discovery, Atlanta
• Organize a variety of summer sports activities for ten-year-olds.
• Negotiate disagreements and lead children with gentle authority.
• Act as a big sister to several children with special needs.

2004–2006, Hancock Fabrics, Bell's Shopping Center
• Cut and sorted fabric.
• Greeted customers.
• Learned about fabric suppliers.
• Developed the ability to discern fabric quality, which has been useful in my costume design courses.

Skills: Fluent in English, Italian, and Spanish. Familiar with Photoshop and Microsoft Office. Winner of first-place prize for oil painting in the Garden Artists' Society

References: Available on request

Sample Letter of Application
Review the parts of the next letter.

Francesca Benaroya
33 Winsted Road
Atlanta, GA 30322
(404) 654-3210
email: fbenaroya@gmail.com

April 5, 2008

Raymond Montafur
Aurora Theater Company
70 South Clayton Street
Lawrenceville, GA 30045

Subject: Position of Costume Designer

Dear Mr. Montafur:

In response to your advertisement in the *Weekly Shout* newspaper, I am applying for the position of junior costumer designer at your theater. I have enjoyed your productions for many years and believe that I can be a valuable addition to your design team.

For three years, I studied set and costume design at Emory College. Having finished my program last spring, I am anxious to begin working in this field. I was principal costume designer for our school's production of *Sweet Charity* and also worked extensively on costumes for *Gypsy* and *Cabaret*.

Please see the enclosed résumé with further details about my experience and some sketches and photos of costumes that illustrate my creativity. I am hard-working and energetic. Moreover, I am excited about beginning my career in the theater!

I would appreciate the opportunity to speak with you in detail about my qualifications. I am available for an interview at your convenience and could start work immediately. Thank you for your consideration.

Sincerely yours,

F. Benaroya

Francesca Benaroya

Answer both parts A and B. You will have two hours to complete th

Part A Define two of the following terms. (5 points each)
1. democracy
2. electorate
3. communism
4. industrial revolution
5. gerrymandering

Part B Write a well-structured essay on one of the following top (20 points)
1. Explain what is panic versus mass hysteria. Can governments ev from either of these phenomena?
2. Evaluate the usefulness of sanctions that western nations impose nations such as North Korea.
3. Trace the rise of National Socialism in Germany in the 1930s.

Paraphrasing and Summarizing

CHAPTER 15

CONTENTS

- Integrating Borrowed Information
- Paraphrasing
- Summarizing

When cooking, you combine small amounts of specific ingredients to create an appetizing meal. When writing a research-supported essay, you combine other people's ideas with your own to support your main points.

Integrating Borrowed Information

During your college career, your instructor may ask you to support your essay ideas using quotations, paraphrases, or summaries. These useful strategies strengthen your research paper and make it more forceful and convincing.

A **quotation** permits you to use another person's exact language. A **paraphrase** lets you use your own words to present someone else's essential information or ideas. Finally, a **summary** allows you to use borrowed information by presenting only the main points of one or several works in your own words. A summary is a shortened version of the original work.

All of these strategies are valid ways to incorporate research into your writing, as long as you give credit to the author or speaker.

> "*After all, the ultimate goal of all research is not objectivity, but truth.*"
>
> HELENE DEUTSCH, *psychoanalyst*

Hint **Avoid Plagiarism**

Plagiarism is the act of using—intentionally or unintentionally—someone else's words or images without giving that person credit. Plagiarism is a very serious offense and can result in expulsion from college or termination from work. **Always** acknowledge the source when you borrow material. Here are some ways to avoid plagiarizing someone else's work.

- Do not buy another work and present it as your own.
- Do not use another student's work and present it as your own.
- Do not use someone's exact words or ideas without citing that source.
- Do not make slight modifications to an author's sentences and then present the work as your own.

To avoid plagiarism, keep detailed notes about your sources. Then, when you want to borrow words, phrases, or ideas, you can acknowledge the source.

GRAMMAR LINK

To find out more about using quotations, see Chapter 37.

Paraphrasing

Paraphrasing allows you to support your essay using other people's ideas. By paraphrasing, you can make the ideas of a source clearer in your own paper. In addition, paraphrasing forces you to grasp a text completely, which may be useful for fully understanding the subject of your research paper. Clarifying ideas by paraphrasing may also help when you are studying. When you paraphrase, use only your own words.

How to Paraphrase

- Read the original text carefully and underline any key ideas. You will have to restate the main ideas and supporting details of the text when you paraphrase.
- Use your own words to restate the main and supporting ideas of the original text. To help prevent copying, try not to look at the original source. Use a dictionary and thesaurus to find exact meanings and synonyms of words in the original text.
- Mention the source of the original text. State the author and title.
- Put quotation marks around any words or phrases used from the original source. Words that are specific names or generic words do not have to be put into quotation marks.
- Use approximately the same number of words as the original passage. A paraphrase is a restated version of the original text.

- Do not change the meaning of the original text. Do not include your own opinions.
- Verify that your paraphrase expresses the ideas and intent of the author of the original text.

The next paragraph is from a longer article written by Matt Richtel and appeared in the April 11, 2006, edition of *The New York Times* online edition. Read the selection and paraphrase.

Original Selection

Ms. Vargas works not in a restaurant but in a busy call center in this town, 150 miles from Los Angeles. She and as many as thirty-five others take orders remotely from forty McDonald's outlets around the country. The orders are then sent back to the restaurants by Internet, to be filled a few yards from where they were placed. The people behind this setup expect it to save just a few seconds on each order. But that can add up to extra sales over the course of a busy day at the drive-through.

Effective Paraphrase

On the New York Times Web site, Matt Richtel states that at least thirty-five workers who are employed at a call center near Los Angeles receive take-out food orders from McDonald's restaurants in different parts of the United States. Using the Internet, call center employees e-mail the orders back to the McDonald's restaurants, and then employees serve customers. McDonald's owners believe that this system will save time and increase profits each day.

Unacceptable Paraphrase

As many as thirty-five people take orders from forty McDonald's outlets around the country. They send back the orders to the original McDonald's restaurants. This method is supposed to save a few seconds on each order and add extra sales to each day.

Teaching Tip: For the "Unacceptable Paraphrase," ask students to identify the exact phrases from the original selection.

This paraphrase is unacceptable because it contains exact words from the text without enclosing them in quotation marks.

PRACTICE 1 Read the following selections and answer the questions that follow. The original selection, written by Mike Oliveira, appeared in *The Montreal Gazette* on December 4, 2006, on page D5.

ORIGINAL SELECTION

While Apple has sold 70 million units and has legions of devotees, the iPod has also received unfavorable attention for problems that have been known to kill the pricey gadgets—including screens that break, batteries that fade, damaged headphone jacks that distort sound, and failing hard drives. In rare cases, some iPods were even sold with a virus.

PARAPHRASE A

In the Montreal Gazette, Mike Oliveira writes that iPod sales are in the millions. However, some iPods contain many problems that lead to breakage. Such problems are breaking screens, fading batteries, damaged headphone jacks that distort sound, and failing hard drives. Some iPods even contain a virus.

1. How does this paraphrase plagiarize the original piece of writing?

   The paraphrase slightly modifies or uses exact words from the excerpt: "breaking screens, fading batteries, damaged headphone jacks that distort sound, and failing hard drives. Some iPods even contain a virus."

Teaching Tip: Some students think that they only have to cite the source when they use direct quotations. Remind them that paraphrases and summaries require citations as well.

PARAPHRASE B

Apple computers have sold millions of iPods, but some customers are experiencing difficulties with the popular product. Some iPod users complain that screens fracture, batteries weaken, and headphones do not work. Also, iPod hard drives collapse and some have a virus.

2. How does this paraphrase plagiarize the original piece of writing?

   The paraphrase does not acknowledge the original source.

Summarizing

Summarizing is a vital skill for writing and studying. When you summarize, you condense a text to its key ideas. Reducing a long work to its bare essentials requires that you fully understand the message of the text. It also helps you understand how ideas are organized in a text.

How to Summarize

- Read the original text carefully.
- Underline any key ideas. In a summary, you will only present the main ideas of a text.
- Ask yourself *who*, *what*, *when*, *where*, *why*, and *how* questions. These questions will help you to synthesize the ideas of the original text.
- Restate the essential ideas in your own words. Refer to a dictionary and thesaurus for the meanings of words and for useful synonyms.
- Maintain the original meaning of the text. Do not include your own opinions.

- Mention the author and title of the original source.
- Reread your summary. Verify that you have explained the key message of the text.

PRACTICE 2 The next paragraph is from pages 186–187 of John J. Macionis's textbook *Sociology*. Compare the paraphrase and summary of the original text. Then answer the questions that follow by underlining the appropriate response.

ORIGINAL SELECTION

For decades, the level of personal privacy in the United States has been declining. Early in the twentieth century, when state agencies began issuing driver's licenses, for example, they generated files for every licensed driver. Today, officials can send this information at the touch of a button not only to the police but to other organizations as well. The Internal Revenue Service and the Social Security Administration, as well as government agencies that benefit veterans, students, the unemployed, and the poor, all collect mountains of personal information.

PARAPHRASE

In Sociology, John J. Macionis states that since the recent past, various groups in the United States are getting more information about an individual. At the beginning of the 1900s, government officials started to require that individuals obtain driver's licenses. Therefore, Americans had to give out personal information. Presently, different organizations such as tax agencies and other government departments that provide services for different groups of people have access to a citizen's personal information (186–187).

SUMMARY

According to John J. Macionis in Sociology, more and more organizations in the United States are gaining access to the personal information of individual citizens (186–187).

1. Which is about the same length as the original text?

   paraphrase summary both

2. Which contains only the main idea of the original text?

   paraphrase summary both

3. Which maintains the author's intent of the original text?

   paraphrase summary both

4. Which includes all the details of the original text?

   paraphrase summary both

5. Which mentions the source of the original text?

   paraphrase summary both

Hint **Consider Your Audience**

When you decide whether to paraphrase or summarize, think about your audience.

- Paraphrase if your audience needs detailed information about the subject.
- Summarize if the audience needs to know only general information.

Teaching Tip: To help students write succinct summaries about longer works, ask them to reduce their summaries from a page to a paragraph and, finally, to a sentence. Then ask students to state what words, phrases, and details they removed in each text.

PRACTICE 3 The following essay is from pages 192–193 of *Cultural Anthropology* by Carol R. Ember and Melvin Ember. Read the essay and then write a summary. To make summarizing a longer text a little easier, follow these steps: Answers will vary.

Read the complete article.

- Underline the main ideas in the text.
- Write the summary by answering *who*, *what*, *when*, *where*, *why*, and *how* questions.
- Write a first draft of the summary.
- Remove any unnecessary details.
- Ensure that you have not used the exact words or phrases from the original text.
- Reduce your writing to only a paragraph by revising and condensing your draft.
- Reread your summary to verify that you have stated the essential ideas of the text.

Why Street Gangs Develop

1 The street gangs of young people that we read and hear about so often are voluntary associations. They are a little like age-sets in that the members are all about the same age, but they are unlike age-sets in being voluntary, and they do not "graduate" through life stages together. Nobody has to join, although there may be strong social pressure to join the neighborhood gang. Gangs have a clear set of values, goals, roles, group functions, symbols, and initiations. Street gangs are also often like military associations in their commitment to violence in the defense of gang interests.

2 Violent street gangs are found in many U.S. cities, particularly in poor neighborhoods. But poverty alone does not appear sufficient to explain the existence of gangs. For example, there is plenty of poverty in

Mexico, but gangs did not develop there. In Mexico there was a *palomilla* (age-cohort) tradition; age-mates hung out together and continued their friendship well into adulthood, but there were no gangs as we know them. Mexican American gangs did develop in the barrios of cities such as Los Angeles. When we realize that most youths in poor neighborhoods do not join gangs, it is clear that poor neighborhoods cannot explain gangs. It is estimated that only 3 to 10 percent of Mexican American young people join gangs.

3 But why do some young people join and not others? If we look at who joins a gang, we see that it seems to be those children who are subject to the most domestic stress. The gang "joiners" are likely to come from poor families, have several siblings, and have no father in the household. They seem to have had difficulty in school and have gotten into trouble early.

4 What about gangs appeals to them? Most adolescents in this country have a difficult time deciding who they are and what kind of people they want to be, but young people who join gangs seem to have more identity problems. One 18-year-old said he "joined the gang for my ego to go higher," reflecting a low self-esteem. Those who are raised in female-centered households seem to be looking for ways to show how "masculine" they are. They look up to the tough male street gang members and want to act like them.

5 So, belonging to a gang may make some youths feel as if they belong to something important. This is a kind of psychological adjustment, but is it adaptive? Does being in a gang help such youth survive in a neighborhood where young men are often killed? Or are gang members less likely to survive? We really don't know the answers to those questions.

The Writer's Room Paraphrasing or Summarizing

Writing Activity 1

Choose one of the photos in this textbook and briefly summarize what seems to be taking place in it.

Writing Activity 2

Exchange an essay with a classmate and paraphrase or summarize it.

Writing Activity 3

Summarize the information found in Chapter 19, Becoming a Successful Student.

Writing Activity 4

Summarize the plot of a novel, movie, or television program.

Writing Activity 5

Read one of the essays in this textbook and paraphrase a section of it.

CHECKLIST: PARAPHRASING AND SUMMARIZING

When you paraphrase or summarize, ask yourself these questions.

- ☐ In a paraphrase, have I kept the original intent of the author?
- ☐ In a summary, have I kept only the key ideas?
- ☐ Have I used my own word when paraphrasing or summarizing?
- ☐ Have I mentioned the source when paraphrasing or summarizing?

How Do I Get a Better Grade?

PEARSON mywritinglab

Visit www.mywritinglab.com for audio-visual lectures and additional practice sets about paraphrasing and summarizing.

Get a better grade with MyWritingLab!

The Research Essay

CHAPTER 16

CONTENTS

Before legislators plan new laws, they might examine previous case studies, survey public opinion, and consult with legal experts. In the same way, when you prepare to write a research essay, you look for resources in books, magazines and newspapers, and on the Internet.

Planning a Research Essay

Conducting **research** means looking for information that will help you better understand a subject. Knowing how to locate, evaluate, and use information from other sources is valuable in your work and day-to-day activities. It is also crucial in college writing because, in many of your assignments, you are expected to include information from outside sources. In this chapter, you will learn some strategies for writing a research paper.

> "*Research is the process of going up alleys to see if they are blind.*"
>
> MARSTON BATES, *American zoologist*

Determining Your Topic

In some courses, your instructor will ask you to write a research paper about a specific topic. However, if you are not assigned one, then you will need to think about issues related to your field of study or to your personal interests.

The scope of your topic should match the size of the assignment. Longer essays might have a broader topic, but a short research essay (of three or four pages) must have a rather narrow focus. For instance, you would not write about the history of Spanish art in a short research paper, but you could write about a particular artwork, artist, or issue. To help find and develop a topic, you can try exploring strategies such as freewriting, questioning, or brainstorming. (See Chapter 1 for more information about prewriting strategies.)

Finding a Guiding Research Question

The point of a research essay is not to simply collect information and summarize it; the idea is to gather information that relates directly to your central question. To help you determine your central question, brainstorm a list of questions that you would like your research to answer. For example, Leonard Bukowski wants to write a research essay about something related to jazz, so he asked himself the next questions to narrow his topic.

> What is the history of jazz?
>
> How does jazz tie into social movements?
>
> What are the predecessors to jazz?
>
> What were the major periods in jazz?
>
> What links the jazz greats?

Bukowski's next step is to find a guiding research question that can become the focus of his essay.

> How does jazz tie into social movements?

Gathering Information

Once you know what information you seek, you can begin gathering ideas, facts, quotations, anecdotes, and examples about the research topic you have chosen. Before you begin to gather information, consider how to find it and how to sort the valid information from the questionable information.

Writer's Desk Find a Research Topic

Choose a general topic that you might like to write about.

Topic: ______________________________

Now ask five or six questions to help you narrow the topic.

____

____

____

____

____

____

Decide which question will become your guiding research question, and write it here.

____

____

Consulting Library-Based Sources

Today's technological advances in both print and electronic publishing make it easier than ever to access information. For sources, you can consult encyclopedias, online catalogues in libraries, periodical databases, and the Internet. Here are some tips for finding information about your topic through library resources.

- **Ask a reference librarian** to help you locate information using various research tools, such as online catalogues, CD-ROMs, and microfiches. Before meeting with the librarian, write down some questions that you would like the answers to. Possible questions might be *Can I access the library's online databases from my home computer?* and *Can you recommend a particular online database?*
- **Search the library's online holdings.** You can search by keyword, author, title, or subject. Using an online catalogue, student Lenny Bukowski typed in the keywords *jazz and social movements*. He found the following book about jazz.

Author	▸ Anderson, Iain, 1967–
Title	This is our music : free jazz, the Sixties, and American culture / Iain Anderson.
Published	Philadelphia : University of Pennsylvania Press, c2007.
Description	254 p. : ill. ; 24 cm.
Location	Marvin Duchow Library
Series	▸ The arts and intellectual life in modern America
LC Subject	▸ Free jazz—United States—History and criticism.
Call Number	▸ ML3508 A53 2007
ISBN	9780812239805
Status	Available

Teaching Tip: Some of today's spellings may vary (e.g., *email/e-mail, website/web site/Web site*). Point out how language evolves with technology and how technology often affects how we spell words. Also discuss the importance of using consistent spellings in a single piece of writing. For example, if students choose *website* over *Web site*, they should use that same spelling consistently in an essay.

Notice that the listing gives the call number, which helps you locate the book on the library shelves. If the catalogue is part of a library network, the online listing will explain which library to visit. Because books are organized by topic, chances are good that you will find other relevant books near the one you have chosen.

- **Use online periodical services in libraries.** Your library may have access to *EBSCOhost*® or *INFOtrac*. By typing keywords into *EBSCOhost*®, you can search through national or international newspapers, magazines, or reference books. When you find an article that you need, print it or cut and paste it into a word processing file and then e-mail the document to yourself. Remember to print or copy the publication data because you will need that information when you cite your source.

Searching the Internet

Search engines such as *Google* and *Yahoo!* can rapidly retrieve thousands of documents from the Internet. However, most people do not need as many documents as those engines can generate. Here are some tips to help make your Internet searches focused and efficient.

Choose your keywords with care. Imagine you want information about new fuel sources for automobiles. If you type in the words *alternative energy* in Google's keyword search space, you will come up with over ten million entries (also known as "hits"). Think about more precise terms that could help you limit your search. For instance, if you are really interested in fuel sources for automobiles, you might change your search request to *alternative fuel sources*. Other options might be *alternative car fuel*. To limit the search, type only the keywords that are most relevant to your research question. If you do not find information on your topic, think about synonyms or alternative ways to describe it.

Use quotation marks to limit the search. Remember that you are driving the search engine, and you can control how many hits you get. By putting quotation marks around your search query, you limit the number of sites to those that contain all of the words that you requested. For example, when you input the words *alternative car fuel* into Google without quotation marks, you will have over three million hits. When the same words are enclosed within quotation marks, the number of hits is reduced to about one thousand, and the displayed Web pages are more relevant.

Use bookmarks. When you find information that might be useful, create a folder where you can store the information in a "bookmark" or "favorites" list. Then you can easily find it later. (The bookmark icon appears on the toolbar of your search engine.)

Use academic search engines. Sites such as *Google Scholar* (scholar.google.com) or *Virtual Learning Resources Center* (virtuallrc.com) help you look through academic publications such as theses, peer-reviewed papers, books, and articles. To find more academic sites, simply do a search for "academic search engines."

Conducting Interviews or Surveys

To conduct an **interview,** you can speak to an expert in the field or someone who is directly affected by an issue. If you record the interview, ensure that your subject gives you permission to do so. Remember to plan the interview before you meet the person, and list key questions that you would like answered. Include the person's complete name and qualifications in your research notes.

Another source of information can be a **survey**, which is an assessment of the views of many people. For example, if you are writing about a tuition fee increase, you can survey students to gather their opinions. When you plan your survey, follow some basic guidelines:

- **Determine your goal.** What do you want to discover?
- **Determine the age, gender, and status of the respondents** (people you will survey). For example, in a survey about the legalization of marijuana, you might decide to survey equal-sized groups of males and females or those over and under twenty-five years of age.
- **Decide how many people you will survey.** Try to survey at least twenty people. If you are working with a partner or a team of students, you can increase that number.
- **Determine the type of survey you will do.** Will you survey people using phone, Internet, or written forms? Keep in mind that people are more likely to obscure the truth when asked questions directly, especially if the questions are embarrassing or very personal. For example, if you ask someone whether he agrees or disagrees with legalized abortion, he might present a viewpoint

Teaching Tips: Ask students in pairs or teams to choose a controversial topic. Then, working together, the group can come up with survey questions. Each person on the team can be responsible for surveying a set number of people. When they mention the survey in their essays, they should mention how many people were surveyed. They can also acknowledge that a small survey sample may have limited relevance.

that he thinks you or nearby listeners will accept. The same person might be more honest in an anonymous written survey.

- **Plan your survey questions.** If gender, age, marital status, or job status are important, place questions about those items at the beginning of your survey. When you form your questions, do not ask open-ended, essay-type questions because it will be difficult to compile the results. Instead, ask yes/no questions or provide a choice of answers. Sample questions:

What is your gender? male ____ female ____

How often do you use the public transit system (the bus, subway, or train)?

____ weekdays ____ about once a week
____ rarely or never ____ about once a month

If you want to determine your respondents' knowledge about a topic, include an "I don't know" response. Otherwise, people will make selections that could skew your survey results.

Has Jackson Monroe done a good job as student union leader?

____ yes ____ no ____ I don't know

Writer's Desk Research Your Topic

Using the guiding research question that you developed in the previous Writer's Desk, list some keywords that you can use to research your topic.

____

____

Using the library and the Internet, find some sources that you can use for your research essay. You might also conduct interviews or prepare a survey.

Teaching Tip: Ask students to find a certain minimum number of sources. Request that at least two sources be from the library so that students practice using the library for research.

Evaluating Sources

When you see sources published in print or online, especially when they are attention-grabbing with color or graphics, you may forget to question whether those sources are reliable. For instance, a company's Web site advertising an alternative cancer therapy might be less reliable than an article in a scientific journal by a team of oncologists (doctors who treat cancer).

Newspaper Title
Edition
Date
Page Number
Article Title
Author
The New York Times
"All the News That's Fit to Print"
Late Edition
VOL. CLVI . . No. 53,986
NEW YORK, MONDAY, JUNE 25, 2007
An Empire Builder, Still Playing Tough
Pulling Vast Array of Levers, Murdoch Is Used to Winning
HUSSEIN'S COUSIN SENTENCED TO DIE FOR KURD ATTACKS
Deadly Attack on Peacekeepers in Lebanon
High-Tech Titans Strike Out on Immigration Bill
Can They Really Call the Chainsaw Eco-Friendly?
Japan Adapts to Tuna Shortage: Waiter, There's Deer in My Sushi
THE NEW YORK TIMES INTERNATIONAL MONDAY, JUNE 25, 2007
A3
Tensions Rise as Kosovo Awaits Word on Its Future
By CRAIG S. SMITH and NICHOLAS WOOD
The unlikelihood of a United Nations agreement soon is having repercussions.
TIFFANY & CO.
JUNE IS PEARL MONTH
MIKIMOTO
Brooks Brothers
SteubenGlass
GARDEN PARTY

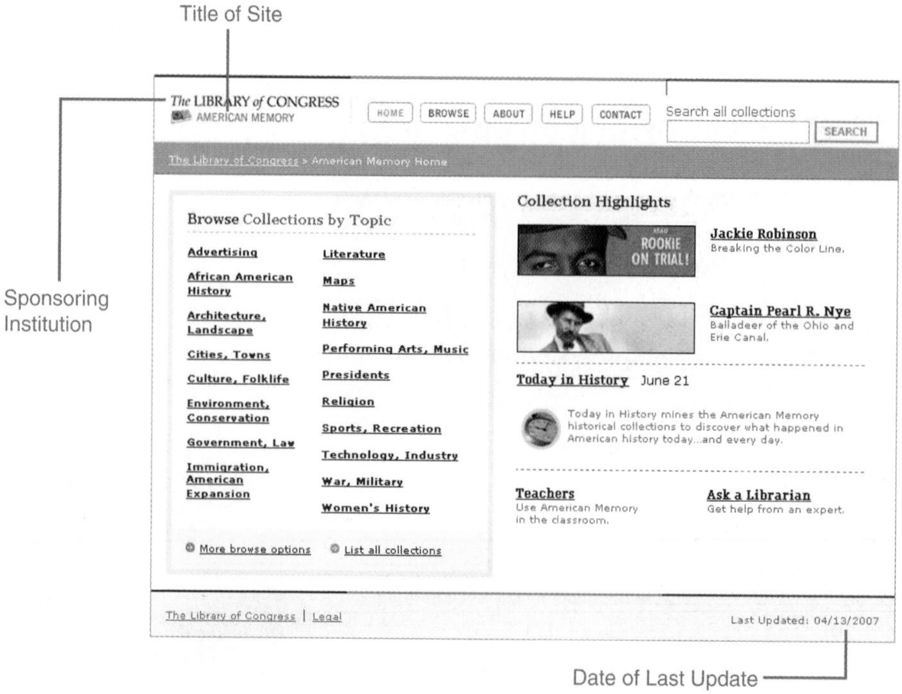

Teaching Tip: Remind students that they must cite sources when they paraphrase, summarize, and quote. Some students mistakenly think it is acceptable to paraphrase or summarize without citing the source.

Hint Avoid Plagiarism

Do not plagiarize. When you use someone else's work without giving that person credit, it is considered stealing, and it is a very serious offense. To eliminate your chances of inadvertently plagiarizing, ensure that your notes contain detailed and clear source information. Then, when you later quote, paraphrase, or summarize another's work, you can cite the source. For more information about plagiarism, paraphrasing, and summarizing, see Chapter 15.

Writer's Desk Take Notes

Use your topic from the previous Writer's Desk. Take notes from the sources that you have found. In your notes, include direct quotations, paraphrases, and summaries. Organize your sources and keep a record of your sources.

Organizing Your First Draft

For research essays, as for any other type of essay, planning is essential. After you have evaluated the material that you have gathered, decide how you will organize your material. Group your notes under the main points that you would like to develop. Then arrange your ideas in a logical order. You might choose to use spatial, chronological, or emphatic order.

Writing a Thesis Statement

After taking notes, plan your thesis statement. Remember that the thesis expresses the main focus of the essay. One way to form the thesis statement is to convert your guiding research question into a statement. For instance, Lenny Bukowski, the student writer mentioned earlier in this chapter, decided to use the following as his guiding question: *How does jazz tie into social movements?* After researching and gathering material on the topic, he then reworked the question to create a thesis statement.

> Jazz musicians abandoned traditional musical forms as they found sounds that echoed the discord of the times.

Creating an Outline

A general **outline** or **plan** will help you organize your ideas. List some of the supporting details that you will insert into your essay. Then, ask yourself the next questions as you evaluate your outline.

- Do I have sufficient supporting examples?
- Is my plan organized in a logical manner?
- Do I need to research more sources?

Leonard's Preliminary Outline

Introduction: Background. Define jazz.

Thesis: Jazz musicians abandoned traditional musical forms as they found sounds that echoed the discord of the times.

Free jazz as representation of American life
- Music transported rhythms from Africa and elsewhere
- Became a unique method of expression for African Americans

Birth of free jazz in 1959
- Was more improvised (Dean, Kofsky page 160)
- Jazz listeners doubted validity of free jazz

Free jazz linked to failure of Civil Rights Movement
- Grew with rise of Black Nationalism (Breitman 45)
- Musicians were often active in radical politics (Shepp 11, Pinkney 65)

Teaching Tip: The sample outline is an informal one. Before students begin their papers, specify if you prefer a more formal format.

An outline also helps you check whether you have any "holes" in your research. If you need more support for certain ideas, do more research and fill in any holes before starting on your first draft. For more samples of essay plans and for reminders about the writing process in general, see Chapters 1–5.

Hint **Inserting Quotations, Paraphrases, and Summaries**

When writing a research paper, remember to smoothly integrate supporting paraphrases, summaries, and quotations. Rather than repeating "Yudkin says" over and over, try to use a variety of verbs when you integrate information from your sources. Here are some examples:

states	suggests	notes	indicates
concurs	reiterates	discusses	mentions

You can use alternate phrasing to introduce a quotation, such as "According to Yudkin" or "A recent survey suggests." You can also begin sentences with the quotations: "Cool jazz was really a subcategory of pop," says Yudkin. Refer to Chapter 15 for more detailed information about paraphrasing and summarizing, and see Chapter 37 for information about punctuating quotations.

Writer's Desk **Make a Preliminary Plan**

Organize your topic and make a plan. In your preliminary plan, include source information. Remember that this is not a final plan. You can add or remove information afterward.

Incorporating Visuals

Visuals—such as charts, maps, graphs, photos, or diagrams—can help to clarify, summarize, emphasize, or illustrate certain concepts in research essays. For example, a graph showing the falling crime rate can be an effective way to support an argument that policing methods have become increasingly successful. Remember to use visuals sparingly and to cite them properly.

Most word processing programs offer templates for many visuals. For example, the toolbar in MS Word allows you to select *Chart* under *Insert* to create line, bar, pie, and other types of charts. Simply input your own data, and the program will create the chart for you. The following charts are standard templates from MS Word.

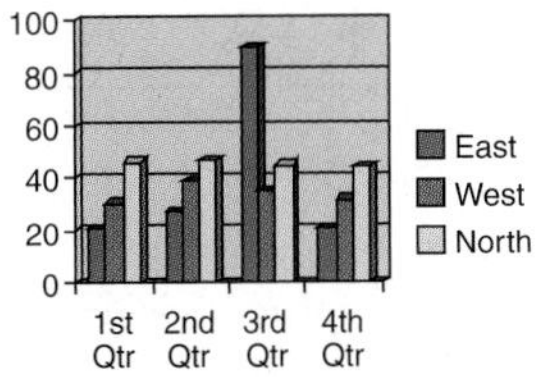

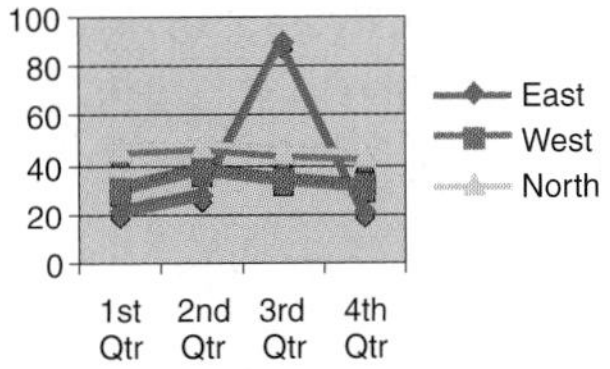

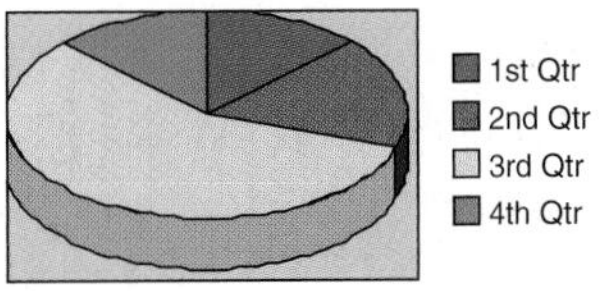

Other visuals can also be useful for illustrating concepts. Often, readers prefer seeing an object or idea in context rather than trying to understand it in writing. Basic diagrams, like the one shown here, can be especially useful for scientific and technical writing.

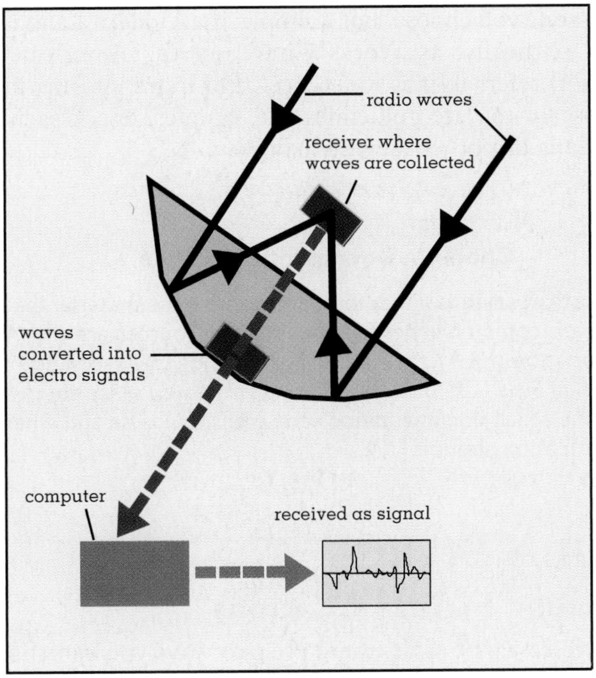

Hint **Using Visuals**

Here are some recommendations for using visuals in an academic research essay:

- Ask your instructor whether you are permitted to use visuals in your essay and, if so, where you need to insert them (in the body of your essay or in an appendix).
- Include a label above each visual to clearly identify it. For example, you can number figures and tables sequentially: *Figure 1, Figure 2*, or *Table 1, Table 2*, and so on.
- Place a caption alongside or under the visual to help the reader understand it.
- Acknowledge the source of any visual that you borrow.
- Explain in the text how the visual supports a specific point. For example, in the body of your paper, you might write *Figure 2 illustrates how the crime rate has fallen steadily since the 1990s.*

Citing Sources

Each time you borrow someone's words, ideas, or images, you must **cite** or credit the source to avoid plagiarizing (see page 260 of Chapter 15). There are two places you need to cite sources in your research essays—in the essay and at the end of it. Use **in-text citations** (also known as **parenthetical citations**) as you incorporate quotations, paraphrases, or summaries. Then, cite the sources in an alphabetized list at the end of your essay. The title of this source list depends on the documentation style you choose. For example, the Modern Language Association (MLA) refers to the list as Works Cited and the American Psychological Association (APA) refers to it as References. For more information about where to find the most up-to-date guidelines and samples, check each organization's Web site: www.mla.org or www.apastyle.org.

Hint **Choose a Documentation Style**

A **documentation style** is a method of presenting the material that you have researched. Three common styles for documenting sources are the Modern Language Association (MLA), the American Psychological Association (APA), and *Chicago Manual of Style* (CMS). Before writing a research essay, check with your instructor about which documentation style you should use and where you can find more information about it.

Using MLA Style

MLA: Including In-Text Citations

In an MLA-style research essay, there are two ways you can show readers that you have borrowed an idea or a quotation from a source.

1. **Enclose the author and page number in parentheses.** Include the last name of the author along with the page number where the material appears. If there is more than one author, write both authors' names in parentheses. Do not use a comma between the name(s) and page reference. Place the final period after the final parenthesis.

    Sometimes a group of rioters will direct their hostility at one person, even if that person has never attacked them or their ideals (Locher 92).

    The consequences of a nuclear attack would be devastating: "Nuclear winter could produce climatic disaster" (Roskin and Berry 236–237).

    If you are using several works by the same author, then you can place a shortened version of the title—perhaps the first two or three words—within the parentheses.

    Martin Luther King attended the rally (Kofsky, Black Nationalism 48).

Hint **Quoting from a Secondary Source**

If your source material includes a quotation, and you do not know the original source of the quotation, then use *Qtd. in* (a shortened form of "quoted in").

> "Our society's fearful of our kids," remarked David York, cofounder of Toughlove International (Qtd. in Schmalleger 533).

2. **Introduce the source in the text and write the page reference in parentheses.** You can mention the author's name in the introductory phrase, with only the page number in the parentheses. Place the final period *after* the parentheses.

    "Violent mobs often take out their anger and frustration on any individual," writes David A. Locher (92).

    According to sociologist David A. Locher, mobs display violent behavior as a way of venting hostility and frustration (92).

Hint **Citing Certain Web Sources**

If you are using a Web-based source, no page number is necessary. If you cannot find the author's name, then put the title of the Web page in parentheses.

> Jazz is not purely American: "Jazz is a musical art form rooted in West African cultural and musical expression and in the African American blues tradition" ("Jazz History").

GRAMMAR LINK

To find out more about writing titles, see pages 540–541 in Chapter 37.

MLA: Making a Works Cited List

An MLA-style Works Cited list appears at the end of a research essay. It gives readers details about each source from which you have borrowed material to write your essay. Works Cited is not the same as a running bibliography, which lists all of the sources you consulted while you were researching your essay topic. In a Works Cited list, only include works that you have quoted, paraphrased, or summarized.

To prepare a Works Cited list, follow these basic guidelines.

1. Write "Works Cited" at the top of the page and center it. Do not italicize it, underline it, or put quotation marks around it.
2. List each source alphabetically, using the author's last name.
3. Indent the second line and all subsequent lines of each entry five spaces.
4. Double-space all lines.

Hint **Name, Title, and Publishing Information (MLA Style)**

Name
Write the author's complete last name and first name.

Title
Add quotation marks around the titles of short works. Underline or italicize titles of longer works such as books, newspapers, or magazines.

Place and Year of Publication
Mention the name of the city and the name of the publisher. MLA does not require the name of the state. If the work is published outside the U.S., add a shortened form of the country name, such as Eng. for England. Also mention the year of publication.

Publisher's Name
Use a shortened form of the publisher's name. Omit *A, An,* or *The* from the beginning, and omit words such as *Co., Corp., Books, Press,* and *Publishers.* The short form for University Press is UP.

Here is an example of a basic Works Cited entry. Notice that you do not underline the final period that follows the title.

Brainard, Shirl. A Design Manual. Upper Saddle River: Prentice, 2006.

Sample MLA-Style Works Cited Entries

The following are a few sample entries for various publications. The *MLA Handbook for Writers of Research Papers* has a complete list of sample entries. As you look at the samples, notice how they are punctuated.

Books

Last name, First name. Title of the Book. Place of Publication: Publisher, Year.

Teaching Tip: Point out specific punctuation in the entries. Students often incorrectly place commas, rather than periods, between items.

ONE AUTHOR

Krakauer, Jon. Into Thin Air. New York: Random, 1999.

TWO OR THREE AUTHORS Write the last name and first name of the first author. Follow with *and*, and then write the first and last name of subsequent authors. If the book is a second, third, or subsequent edition, write just the abbreviated form of the edition after the title.

Bovée, Courtland, and John Thill. Business Communication Essentials. 2nd ed. Upper Saddle River: Prentice, 2006.

FOUR OR MORE AUTHORS Add *et al.*, which means "and others," after the first author's name.

Coon, Dennis, et al. Psychology, A Journey. Scarborough: Thomson, 2003.

BOOK WITH AN EDITOR INSTEAD OF AN AUTHOR Write the editor's name followed by *ed.*

Koppleman, Susan, ed. Old Maids: Short Stories by Nineteenth-Century US Women Writers. Boston: Pandora, 1984.

TWO OR MORE BOOKS BY THE SAME AUTHOR Write the author's name in the first entry only. In subsequent entries, type three hyphens followed by a period. Then add the title.

Angelou, Maya. I Know Why the Caged Bird Sings. New York: Random, 1969.

- - -. Mother: A Cradle to Hold Me. New York: Random, 2006.

A WORK IN AN ANTHOLOGY When your source is a story or article in an anthology, mention the author and title of the article first.

Munroe, Alice. "Boys and Girls." Literature. Eds. R.S. Gwynn and Wanda Campbell. Toronto: Longman, 2003.

If you are using several pieces from the anthology, include separate entries for each piece like the first example that follows. Then add another entry for the anthology itself that looks like the second example.

Munroe, Alice. "Boys and Girls." Gywnn and Campbell 313-326.

Gwynn, R. S. and Wanda Campbell, eds. Literature. Toronto: Longman, 2003.

ENCYCLOPEDIA AND DICTIONARY When encyclopedias and dictionaries list items alphabetically, you can omit volume and page numbers. It is sufficient to list the edition and year of publication.

"Democracy." Columbia Encyclopedia. 6th ed. 2005.

"Legitimate." The New American Webster Handy College Dictionary. 3rd ed. 2003.

Periodicals

Teaching Tip: Point out that there is no punctuation between the magazine or newspaper title and the date.

> Last name, First name. "Title of Article." Title of the Magazine or Newspaper Date: Pages.

ARTICLE IN A MAGAZINE

Foster, Don. "The Message in the Anthrax." Vanity Fair Oct. 2003: 180–200.

ARTICLE IN A NEWSPAPER

Dugger, Celia W. "Clinton Helps Broker Deal for Medicine to Treat AIDS." New York Times 1 Dec. 2006: A9.

EDITORIAL If the editorial is signed, begin with the editor's name. If it is unsigned, begin with the title. Follow the title with the word *Editorial*.

"Tax Freedom Day Is Here." Editorial. Montreal Gazette 27 June 2006: A16.

ARTICLE IN A JOURNAL

Seligman, Martin. "The American Way of Blame." APA Monitor 29.7 (1998): 97.

Electronic Sources

Electronic sources include Web sites, information from subscription services, and reference databases. Electronic communications are frequently updated or moved, so keep track of the date you accessed a site. When using a source published on the Internet, include as much of the following information as you can find. Keep in mind that some sites do not contain complete information. Also, when you write the network address, break the address only at a slash mark.

> Last name, First name. "Title of Article." Title of Site or Online Publication. Date of most recent update. Date you accessed the site <Network Address>.

ARTICLE ON A PERSONAL WEB SITE

Krystek, Lee. "Crop Circles from Outer Space?" Museum of Unnatural Mystery 2006. 16 May 2007 <http://www.unmuseum.org/cropcir.htm>.

ARTICLE IN AN ONLINE PERIODICAL If the site mentions the volume or page reference, include it. If not, include as much information as you can find.

Grossman, Lev, and Richard Lacayo. "All-Time 100 Novels." Time. 2005. 25 Apr. 2007 <http://www.time.com/time/2005/100books/the_complete_list.html>.

GOVERNMENT SITE (OR OTHER SITES WITHOUT AUTHOR INFORMATION) If the author is not mentioned on the site, begin with just the title and include as much information as you can find.

"Dangerous Jobs." US Department of Labor. 1997. 28 May 2006 <http://stats.bls.gov/iif/oshwc/cfar0020.pdf>.

Other Types of Sources

INTERVIEW THAT YOU CONDUCTED

Kumar, Nantha. Personal interview. 14 Aug. 2007.

FILM OR VIDEO Include the name of the film, the director, the studio, and the year of release.

Casablanca. Dir. Michael Curtiz. 1942. DVD. Warner Brothers, 2003.

RADIO OR TELEVISION PROGRAM Include the segment title, the program name, the network, and the broadcast date.

"Global Warming." Nightline. ABC News. 27 June 2006.

SOUND RECORDING Include the name of the performer or band, the title of the song, the title of the CD, the name of the recording company, and the year of release.

Nirvana. "About a Girl." Unplugged in New York. Geffen, 1994.

Hint **Placement and Order of Works Cited**

The Works Cited list should be at the end of the research paper. List sources in alphabetical order of the authors' last names. If there is no author, list the title (but ignore *A*, *An*, or *The*, which may appear at the beginning of the title).

Douglas, Ann. The Feminization of American Culture. New York: Avon, 1977.

Godey's Lady's Book. April 1850. 14 July 2006 <www.history.rochester.edu/godeys>.

Welter, Barbara. Dimity Convictions: The American Woman in the Nineteenth Century. Athens: Ohio UP, 1976.

---. The Woman Question in American History. Hinsdale: Dryden, 1973.

Wiesenthal, Chris. Figuring Madness in Nineteenth-Century Fiction. New York: St. Martin's, 1997.

Teaching Tip: When students look at the list of works in the Hint box, ask them to identify a work without an author's name (*Godey's Lady's Book*). Also ask them what the three hyphens indicate (i.e., it's another work by Welter).

PRACTICE 3 Imagine that you are using the following sources in a research paper. Arrange the sources for a Works Cited list using MLA style.

- An article by David Mamet in Harper's called "Bambi v. Godzilla." The article, published in the June 2005 issue, appeared on pages 33 to 37.
- A book by David Mamet called Boston Marriage that was published by Vintage Books in New York, in 2002.
- A book called Flashback: A Brief History of Film written by Louis Giannetti and Scott Eyman. The book was published by Prentice Hall in Upper Saddle River, New Jersey, in 2006.
- A book called Cultural Anthropology by Serena Nanda. The book was published by Wadsworth in Belmont, California, in 1991.
- An article called "Biography" on the Web site Marilyn Monroe. The site was created in 2006. You accessed the site on May 10, 2007. The Web address is http://www.marilynmonroe.com/about/bio.html. You cannot find the author's name on the site.

Works Cited

"Biography." Marilyn Monroe. 2006. 10 May 2007 <http://www.marilynmonroe.com/about/bio.html>.

Giannetti, Louis and Scott Eyman. Flashback: A Brief History of Film. Upper Saddle River: Prentice, 2006.

Mamet, David. "Bambi v. Godzilla." Harper's June 2005: 33–37.

---. Boston Marriage. New York: Vintage, 2002.

Nanda, Serena. Cultural Anthropology. Belmont: Wadsworth, 1991.

Sample Research Essay

Title Pages and Outlines

Although MLA does not insist on a title page or an outline for a research essay, your instructor may recommend or request one or both. Include the following information on your title page.

Title

Your name

Your course

Professor's name

Date

To prepare a formal outline in MLA style, use the following format.

Thesis: Jazz would be confronted by an abandoning of traditional musical forms, such as melody, harmony, and rhythm, as musicians found a method of producing sounds relevant in their minds to the discord of the times.

I. Free jazz represented American life.
   A. Music transported rhythms from Africa and elsewhere.
   B. It became a unique method of expression for African Americans.

II. Free jazz was born in 1959.
   A. Music was more improvised.
      1. It eliminated musical patterns.
      2. It was called "energy music."
   B. Jazz listeners doubted validity of free jazz.
      1. People couldn't recognize rhythmic patterns.
      2. White listeners rejected free jazz.

III. Free jazz linked to failure of Civil Rights Movement.
   A. Movement grew with rise of Black Nationalism.
      1. Assassination of King provoked furor.
      2. Riots occurred in American cities.
   B. Musicians were often active in radical politics.
      1. Closed ranks and created associations such as Black Artists' Group.
      2. Archie Shepp commented on the black nationalist movement.

MLA Style

Bukowski 1

Leonard J. Bukowski

Double-space your identification information.

Professor Donald E. Crawford

AMH 2020

May 31, 2007

The Free Jazz Movement and Black Nationalism

Center the title without underlining, italics, quotation marks, or boldface type.

Jazz has been termed a truly unique American music. It shares much of the emotions and strengths of America and has affected and been affected by social and political changes and turmoil. In the 1960s, American society and politics would be confronted by a determined desire among African Americans for their rights and political power, sometimes sought to be obtained violently. Jazz would be confronted by an abandoning of traditional musical forms, such as melody, harmony, and rhythm, as musicians found a method of producing sounds relevant in their minds to the discord of the times.

Double-space throughout the body of the essay.

Place your thesis in your introductory paragraph.

In many respects, the music called jazz is a representation of the atmosphere of American life. A music that was the result of the mixture of races on the North American continent, it borrowed freely from the Western musical tradition of melody and harmony while transporting rhythms from Africa and elsewhere. As jazz evolved, it became a unique method of

It is not necessary to document your common knowledge.

expression, particularly for Afro-Americans. The racial inequality so prevalent in American society in the early twentieth century helped form jazz movements.

In 1959, alto saxophonist Ornette Coleman sounded the first notes of a music soon to be called "Free Jazz." Free Jazz soloists cast off the ensemble arrangement structure ("Styles"). It can be considered a form of thematic improvisation with spontaneous variations on a musical theme based loosely or not at all on what had been previously musically stated. It sought to eliminate patterns such as repeating bar sequences, chord- or scale-based harmonics, and fixed pulses (Dean xix). Conversely, Free Jazz could not be termed atonal, lacking a tonal center, according to Kofsky (160). Free Jazz was also called energy music as it completely did away with the reliance on the necessity for the music to "swing." Instead, this music relied on the pure power of playing.

If the source has no author name, put the title in parentheses.

Place the source name and page number in parentheses.

Acknowledge sources of borrowed ideas.

Initially, many jazz listeners doubted the validity of Free Jazz. They could not recognize the tune nor find an easily decipherable rhythmic pattern. To many listeners, it was a cacophony, incomprehensible and frightening. A large core of mainly white listeners soon would turn away from active participation in jazz. Critics, mostly white, who were used to

Bukowski 3

understanding the music form presented, were at a loss. To them, it may have seemed as if the music had gone from ragtime to swing time to no-time. Club owners found patrons leaving en masse when musicians played this new music. Just as Black political movements frightened white America, this new jazz came under vitriolic attack.

Free Jazz grew with the increasing disillusionment among Afro-Americans over the failures of the Civil Rights Movement. It also grew with the rise of Black Nationalism, defined by Malcolm X as

> the tendency for Black people in the United States to unite as a group, as a people into a movement of their own to fight for freedom, justice and equality . . . . This tendency holds that Black people must control their own movement and the political, economic and social institutions of the Black community. (Breitman 45)

Place ellipses to show where irrelevant material has been removed.

With the assassination of Dr. Martin Luther King, the furor in the music and society increased. In 1968, there were 125 riots in American cities, with the most violent in Detroit, Michigan, and Watts, California, where the fury of violence provoked by decades of repression spilled out of the ghettos and affected the entire urban landscape. Tenor saxophonist Archie Shepp,

Bukowski 4

composer of such pieces as "Malcolm, Malcolm, Semper Malcolm," proclaimed,

> The Negro musician is a reflection of the Negro people as a social and cultural phenomenon. His purpose ought to be to liberate America aesthetically and socially from its inhumanity. . . . I think the Negro people through the force of their struggles are the only hope of saving America. . . . (11)

Musicians of the Free Jazz movement were often very active in radical politics. Stokely Carmichael said, "The concept of Black Power rests on a fundamental premise: Before a group can enter the open society, it must first close ranks" (qtd. in Pinkney 65). Musicians of this new jazz sought to do just that. Associations of musicians and creative individuals were formed, among them the Black Artists' Group (BAG) of St. Louis and the Association for the Advancement of Creative Musicians (AACM) from Chicago. These organizations sought to combine music and other art forms to create a sense of racial pride and foster development of unique African American culture. Archie Shepp proclaimed,

Use "qtd. in" to show that the quote appeared in a secondary source and is not the original.

> Some of us are more bitter about the way things are going. We are only an extension of that entire civil

Bukowski 5

> rights–Black Muslim black nationalist movement that is taking place in America. That is fundamental to music. (qtd. in Kofsky 63)

Yet, the rage of the 1960s would fade. Black Nationalist political organizations collapsed from government infiltration or from suppression. The Free Jazz movement would also lose momentum, as many performers would move to Europe, where a more receptive climate existed. Others died: naturally, as did John Coltrane, or violently, as did Albert Ayler. Many turned to more melodic forms of jazz, realizing that the need for income often outweighed the need for totally free expression. An Albert Ayler composition is entitled "Music Is the Healing Force of the Universe." It is through music that the dignity of humanity is reaffirmed and that diverse groups can find a common ground.

Bukowski 6

Works Cited

Ayler, Albert. Music is the Healing Force of the Universe. LP. Impulse, 1969.

Breitman, George. The Assassination of Malcolm X. New York: Pathfinder, 1991.

Dean, Roger. Creative Improvisation. Milton Keynes, Eng.: Open UP, 1989.

Kofsky, Frank. Black Nationalism and the Revolution in Music. New York: Pathfinder, 1970.

Pinkney, Alphonso. Red, Black, and Green: Black Nationalism in the United States. London: Cambridge UP, 1976.

Shepp, Archie. "An Artist Speaks Bluntly." Downbeat 16 Dec. 1965: 11.

"Styles of Jazz Music," A Passion for Jazz. 22 Jan. 2007 <http://www.apassion4jazz.net/jazz_styles2.html>.

Place sources in alphabetical order.

Double-space sources.

Indent the second line five spaces or one-half inch when an entry runs over one line.

Using APA Style

The American Psychological Association (APA) documentation style is commonly used in scientific or technical fields such as social sciences, economics, and nursing. Before you write a research essay for any course, ask your instructor which style he or she prefers.

Hint **APA Web Site**

To get some general information about some basic style questions, you can view the APA's Web site at www.apastyle.org. Use the menu on the left side of the page to direct you to specific style questions and answers.

On the same Web site, there is a link to information about online or "electronic" sources. Because the information about online sources is continually being updated, the site has comprehensive information about the latest citation methods. Visit www.apastyle.org/elecref.html.

APA: Including In-Text Citations

Here are two basic options for inserting parenthetical citations in an APA-style research essay.

1. **Enclose the author(s), the publication year, and the page number(s) in parentheses.** Include the last name(s) of the source's author(s). For more than one author, separate the authors' names using & (the ampersand sign). Follow with the publication year and then the page number or the page range where the material appears, using *p.* or *pp.* Separate the names, date, and page references with commas, and place the final period after the closing parenthesis.

   Sometimes rioters lose control and "take out their anger and frustration on any individual" (Locher, 2002, p. 92).

   A dozen men are responsible for the development of the movie camera (Giannetti & Eyman, 2006, p. 4).

2. **Introduce the source directly in the text.** When you include a short quotation within a sentence, place the publication year in parentheses immediately after you mention the author's name. Present the quotation, and then write the page number in parentheses immediately after it.

   Sociologist David A. Locher (2002) explains, "Violent mobs often take out their anger and frustration on any individual" (p. 92).

   As Giannettti and Eyman (2006) explained, a dozen men are responsible for the development of the movie camera (p. 4).

APA: Making a References List

Similar to the MLA Works Cited list, the APA References list gives details about each source you have used, and it appears at the end of your paper. Follow these basic guidelines to prepare References using the APA format.

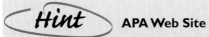

1. Write "References" at the top of the page and center it. Do not italicize it, underline it, or put quotation marks around it.
2. List each source alphabetically, using the last names of the authors.
3. Indent the second line and all subsequent lines of each reference one-half inch from the left margin.
4. Double-space the list.

Hint **Writing the Author, Date, Title, and Place Using APA Style**

Author
On the References page, write the complete last name and use the first and middle initials (if provided). Do not write complete first names.

Date
Put the date in parentheses immediately after the name. If you do not have the author's name, then put the date immediately after the title.

Title
Capitalize the first word of the title, the first word of the subtitle, and any proper nouns or adjectives in Reference lists. Do not add quotation marks or any other special marks around the titles of short works. Italicize titles of longer works such as books, newspapers, or magazines.

Place of Publication
Mention the name of the city and the postal abbreviation of the state or province. If the city is a major city such as New York, no state or province is necessary.

Here is an example of a complete entry for a References list in APA style.

Brainard, S. (2006). *A design manual.* Upper Saddle River, NJ: Prentice Hall.

Books

Carefully review the punctuation of the following example.

Last name, Initial(s). (date). *Title of the book*. City and State of Publication: Publisher.

ONE AUTHOR Reverse the name of the author. Put the complete last name and the first initial.

Krakauer, J. (1999). *Into thin air*. New York: Random House.

TWO OR MORE AUTHORS Reverse the name of each author.

Ciccarelli, S. K., & Meyer, G. E. (2006). *Psychology*. Upper Saddle River, NJ: Prentice Hall.

BOOK WITH AN EDITOR INSTEAD OF AN AUTHOR Put the editor's name followed by (Ed.).

Koppleman, S. (Ed.). (1984). *Old maids: Short stories by nineteenth-century US women writers*. Boston: Pandora Press.

TWO OR MORE BOOKS BY THE SAME AUTHOR Include the author's name in all references. Arrange the works by year of publication, putting the earliest work first.

Angelou, M. (1969). *I know why the caged bird sings*. New York: Random House.

Angelou, M. (2006). *Mother: A cradle to hold me*. New York: Random House.

A WORK IN AN ANTHOLOGY

Munroe, A. (2003). Boys and girls. In R. S. Gwynn & W. Campbell (Eds.), *Literature* (pp. 313–326). Toronto: Pearson Longman.

ENCYCLOPEDIA AND DICTIONARY

Democracy. (2005). In *Columbia encyclopedia* (6th ed.). New York: Columbia University Press.

Legitimate. (2003). In *The new American Webster handy college dictionary* (3rd ed.). New York: Signet.

Periodicals

Last name, Initials. (Year, Month and day). Title of article. *Title of the Magazine or Newspaper, Volume number*, Pages.

ARTICLE IN A MAGAZINE When citing newspapers or magazines, write as much of the following information as is available.

Shreeve, J. (2005, March). Beyond the brain. *National Geographic, 207*, 2–31.

ARTICLE IN A NEWSPAPER

Dugger, C. W. (2006, December 1). Clinton helps broker deal for medicine to treat AIDS. *New York Times,* p. A9.

ARTICLE IN A JOURNAL

Last name, Initials. (Year, Month). Title of article. *Title of Journal. Volume*(Issue), Pages.

Seligman, M. (1998). The American way of blame. *APA Monitor, 29*(7), 97.

Electronic Sources

If the source was published on the Internet, include as much of the following information as you can find. Keep in mind that some sites do not contain complete source information.

> Last name, Initials. (date of most recent update). Title of article. *Title of Site* or *Online Publication*. Retrieved on date, from http://site_address.html.

ARTICLE ON A PERSONAL WEB SITE

Krystek, L. (2006). Crop circles from outer space? *Museum of unnatural mystery*. Retrieved May 16, 2007, from http://www.unmuseum.org/cropcir.htm.

ARTICLE IN AN ONLINE JOURNAL If the site mentions the volume or page reference, include it. If not, put as much information as you can find.

Grossman, L., & Lacayo, R. (2005). All-time 100 novels. *Time*. Retrieved May 25, 2006, from http://www.time.com/time/2005/100books/the_complete_list.html.

GOVERNMENT SITE (OR OTHER SITES WITHOUT AUTHOR INFORMATION) If the author is not mentioned on the site, begin with the title followed by the date, and include as much information as you can find.

Dangerous jobs. (1997). *US Department of Labor*. Retrieved May 28, 2006, from http://stats.bls.gov/iif/oshwc/cfar0020.pdf.

Other Types of Sources

INTERVIEW THAT YOU CONDUCTED In APA style, do not include a personal interview in your References list. In the actual text, just include the parenthetical notation along with the exact date of the communication. For example: (personal communication, June 15, 2008).

FILM OR VIDEO

Curtiz, M. (Director). (2003). *Casablanca* [DVD]. United States: Warner Brothers. (Original movie released 1942)

SOUND RECORDING

Nirvana. (1994). About a girl. On *Unplugged in New York* [CD]. New York: Geffen.

PRACTICE 4 Imagine that you are using the following sources in a research paper. Arrange the sources for a References page using APA style.

- An article by David Mamet in Harper's called "Bambi v. Godzilla." The article, published in the June 2005 issue, appeared on pages 33 to 37.

- A book by David Mamet called Boston Marriage that was published by Vintage Books in New York, in 2002.
- A book called Flashback: A Brief History of Film written by Louis Giannetti and Scott Eyman. The book was published by Prentice Hall in Upper Saddle River, New Jersey, in 2006.
- A book called Cultural Anthropology by Serena Nanda. The book was published by Wadsworth in Belmont, California, in 1991.
- An article called "Biography" on the Web site Marilyn Monroe. The site was created in 2006. You accessed the site on May 10, 2007. The Web address is http://www.marilynmonroe.com/about/bio.html. You cannot find the author's name on the site.

Teaching Tip: When students are writing a References list by hand, they should underline the titles that we show in italics here.

References

Biography. (2006). *Marilyn Monroe.* 2006. Retrieved May 10, 2007, from http://www.marilynmonroe.com/about/bio.html.

Giannetti, L., & Eyman, S. (2006). *Flashback: A brief history of film.* Upper Saddle River, NJ: Prentice Hall.

Mamet, D. (2002). *Boston marriage.* New York: Vintage.

Mamet, D. (2005, June). Bambi v. Godzilla. *Harper's,* pp. 33–37.

Nanda, S. (1991). *Cultural anthropology.* Belmont, CA: Wadsworth.

The Writer's Room Research Essay Topics

Writing Activity 1

Write a research paper about one of the following topics. Ask your instructor what reference style you should use. Put a Works Cited (MLA) or References (APA) page at the end of your assignment.

1. Write about a contemporary issue that is in the news.
2. Write about any issue in your career choice or field of study.

Writing Activity 2

Write a research paper about one of the following topics. First, brainstorm questions about your topic and find a guiding research question. Then follow the process of writing a research essay.

Abortion
Affirmative action
Assisted suicide
Attention-deficit disorder
Body image
Carpal tunnel syndrome
Censorship of the Internet
Consequences of war
Date rape
Election reform
Executive salaries
Fast food
Foreign adoptions
Genetically modified food
Government-sponsored gambling
Health-care reform
Holistic healing
Home schooling
Immigration
Legalization of marijuana
Necessity of military intervention
Prison reform
Privacy and the Internet
Response to terrorism
Same-sex marriage
Sperm-donor rights
Tobacco industry
Violence in the media
Volunteer work
Youth gangs

Teaching Tip:
Pair Work
Before students submit their essays, ask them to exchange essays with partners. Each student should evaluate his or her partner's essay to ensure that sources are cited properly.

CHECKLIST: RESEARCH ESSAY

When you plan a research essay, ask yourself these questions.

- [ ] Have I narrowed my topic?
- [ ] Have I created a guiding research question?
- [ ] Are my sources reliable?
- [ ] Have I organized my notes?
- [ ] Have I integrated source information using quotations, paraphrases, and summaries?
- [ ] Have I correctly documented my in-text or parenthetical citations?
- [ ] Have I correctly prepared and punctuated my Works Cited page or References list?

Teaching Tip:
Please encourage your students to submit their best research essays for possible publication to: <thewritersworld @prenhall.com>.

CHAPTER 17

The Résumé and Letter of Application

CONTENTS

- Preparing a Résumé
- Writing a Letter of Application

When you apply for a job, you generally send a résumé and a letter of application. A résumé is like a professional version of your personal photo album. Each line is a snapshot of your education and work experience.

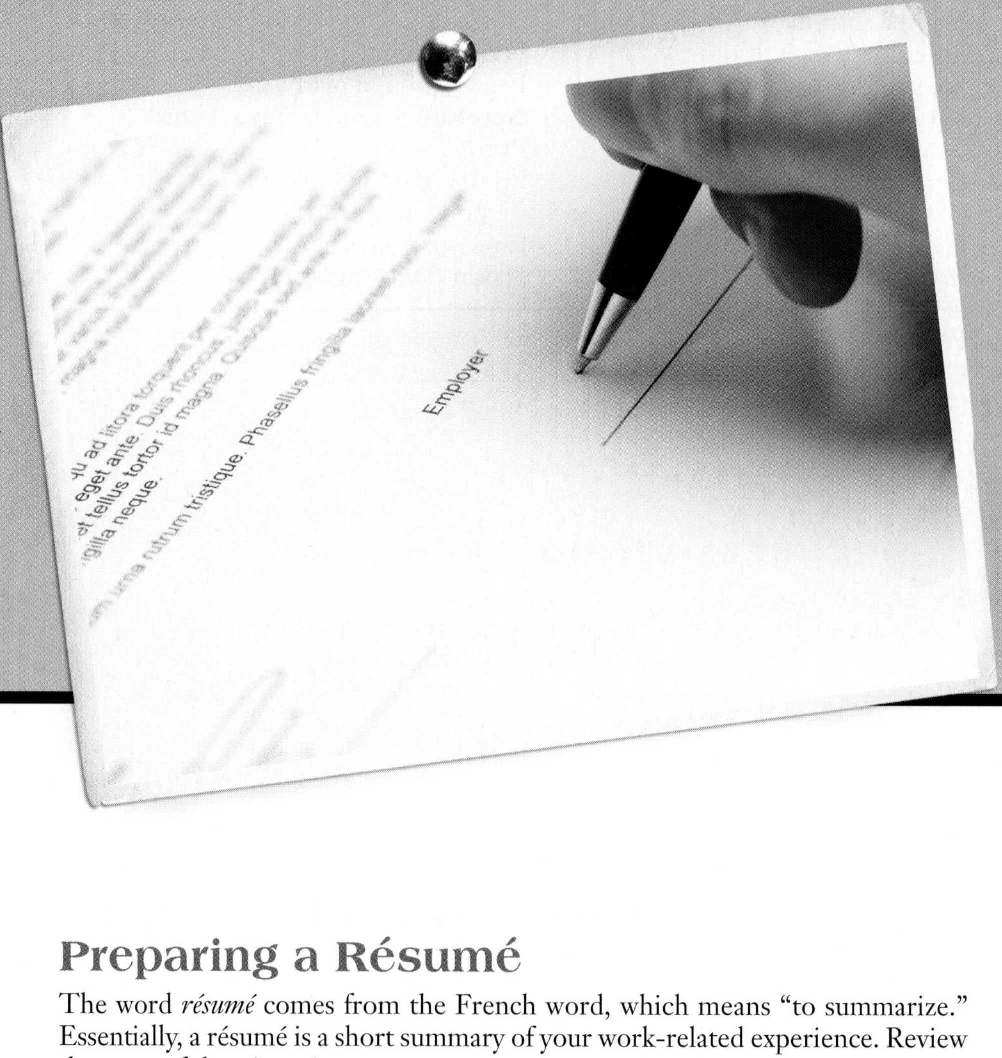

> *"Whenever you are asked if you can do a job, say, "Certainly I can." Then get busy and find out how to do it."*
>
> THEODORE ROOSEVELT, *American politician*

Preparing a Résumé

The word *résumé* comes from the French word, which means "to summarize." Essentially, a résumé is a short summary of your work-related experience. Review the parts of the résumé.

A Sample Résumé

Specify what job you are applying for or state the general field that interests you.

Outline your most recent job experience. If you have not had any paying jobs, you could mention any volunteer work that you have done. For each job that you list, mention the tasks that you completed and the aptitudes you developed.

Francesca Benaroya
33 Winsted Road
Atlanta, GA 30322
(987) 654-3210
email: fbenaroya@gmail.com

Objective Entry-level position as a costume designer

Education Diploma in Theater Studies, June 2008
Emory College, Atlanta, Georgia

Certificate of Completion, Fine Arts Institute
Cincinnati, Ohio, May 2005

Employment **2006–Present**
Camp Discovery, Atlanta
- Organize a variety of summer sports activities for ten-year-olds.
- Negotiate disagreements and lead children with gentle authority.
- Act as a big sister to several children with special needs.

2004–2006
Hancock Fabrics, Bell's Shopping Center
- Cut and sorted fabric.
- Greeted customers.
- Learned about fabric suppliers.
- Developed the ability to discern fabric quality, which has been useful in my costume design courses.

Skills Fluent in English, Italian, and Spanish
Familiar with Photoshop and Microsoft Office
Winner of first-place prize for oil painting in the Garden Artists' Society

References Available on request

Include contact information but not your birthplace, birth date, nationality, or a personal photo.

Put the most recent schooling first. If you have more than a high school education, it is not necessary to list your high school.

Mention any special abilities that you have. Do you have artistic talent? Are you bilingual or trilingual? Do you have computer skills?

If past teachers or past employers have agreed to recommend you, you can include their names and phone numbers. Otherwise, you can write "Available on request."

Hint **Use Parallel Structure**

When you describe your work experience, use parallel action verbs.

Not Parallel: I learned to **greet** customers, **take** inventory, and **handling** cash.

Parallel: I learned to **greet** customers, **take** inventory, and **handle** cash.

PRACTICE 1

ESL Teaching Tip: In some countries, photos are required on résumés. Point out that photos are not required unless the employer specifically requests it.

1. When you write a résumé, in what order should you include the following items? Number them from 1 to 5.

   __3__ experience __4__ special skills __1__ name and address

   __2__ education __5__ references

2. Circle the order in which you should list your work experience.

   a. chronological order (b.) from most recent to most distant

3. Why do you think it would not be a good idea to include a photo, birth date, or birthplace on your résumé? (The answer does not appear in the sample résumé.)

   Employers might discriminate based on appearance, nationality, or age.

Writing a Letter of Application

Include a letter of application with your résumé. Remember to begin each paragraph with a topic sentence that clearly states the main point of the paragraph, and try to keep paragraphs relatively brief.

Hint **Letter Basics**

When you write a letter of application, remember the following points:

- Be brief! Employers may receive large numbers of applications. They will not appreciate long, detailed letters of application. Your letter should be no longer than four short paragraphs.
- Follow the standard business letter format. Most businesses use full block style, in which all elements of the letter are aligned with the left margin. Do not indent any paragraphs. Instead, leave an extra space between paragraphs.
- To make a favorable impression, ensure that your letter is free of grammar, spelling, or punctuation errors. Proofread your letter very carefully before you send it. If possible, ask someone else to look it over for you, too.

Sample Letter of Application

Review the parts of the next letter.

Francesca Benaroya
33 Winsted Road
Atlanta, GA 30322
(404) 654-3210
email: fbenaroya@gmail.com

April 5, 2008

Raymond Montafur
Aurora Theater Company
70 South Clayton Street
Lawrenceville, GA 30045

Subject: Position of Costume Designer

Dear Mr. Montafur:

In response to your advertisement in the *Weekly Shout* newspaper, I am applying for the position of junior costume designer at your theater. I have enjoyed your productions for many years and believe that I can be a valuable addition to your design team.

For three years, I studied set and costume design at Emory College. Having finished my program last spring, I am anxious to begin working in this field. I was principal costume designer for our school's production of *Sweet Charity* and also worked extensively on costumes for *Gypsy* and *Cabaret.*

Please see the enclosed résumé with further details about my experience and some sketches and photos of costumes that illustrate my creativity. I am hard-working and energetic. Moreover, I am excited about beginning my career in the theater!

I would appreciate the opportunity to speak with you in detail about my qualifications. I am available for an interview at your convenience and could start work immediately. Thank you for your consideration.

Sincerely yours,

F. Benaroya

Francesca Benaroya

Sender's Address
Capitalize street names. Put a comma between the city and state or country. Do not put a comma before the zip code.

Date
Put a comma between the full date and the year.

Recipient's address
Capitalize each word in a company name.

Subject Line (Optional)
Briefly state your reason for writing.

Salutation
The best way to address someone is to use his or her name followed by a colon.
If you do not know the name of the recipient, write the following:
- Dear Sir or Madam:
- Attention: Personnel Department

Introductory Paragraph
Explain the position you are applying for. Also mention where you heard about the job.
If you are sending your résumé to companies that have not advertised, you could begin your letter as follows:
- I am writing to inquire about any job openings in . . .

Body
Sell yourself. Summarize your skills and experience.

Conclusion
Mention an interview and end with polite thanks.
You could use these closing sentences:
- I look forward to meeting you at your earliest convenience.
- If you require further information, please feel free to contact me.

Closing
Some possible closings are *Yours truly, Respectfully yours,* or *Many thanks.* Notice that only the first word is capitalized.
After the closing, add your handwritten signature followed by your typed name.

ESL Teaching Tip: Ask students to identify the states mentioned in the list of postal abbreviations. Students could do this as a competition.

ESL Teaching Tip: You can use the sample letter of application as a model. The punctuation and capitalization information is for the benefit of nonnative speakers because in many languages, words such as *street* are not capitalized.

ESL Teaching Tip: Your nonnative speakers may not know the differences between *Mrs., Miss,* and *Ms.* Point out the differences in meaning and in punctuation. Also, mention that in English, the word *dear* can be used in both personal and business letters. You could put the next examples on the board.

Dear Mr. Wong,
Dear Ms. Aziz,
Dear Sir or Madam:
Attention: Human Resources

Hint **Abbreviations for States**

The following two-letter abbreviations are the standard ones used by the U.S. Postal Service (www.usps.com).

- Ten states have two-part names and are abbreviated by the first letter of each word.

  NC, ND, NH, NJ, NM, NY, RI, SC, SD, WV
- Nineteen states are abbreviated by their first two letters.

  AL, AR, CA, CO, DE, FL, ID, IL, IN, MA, MI, NE, OH, OK, OR, UT, WA, WI, WY
- Twelve states are abbreviated by the first and last letter in the state's name.

  CT, GA, HI, IA, KS, KY, LA, MD, ME, PA, VA, VT
- Nine states are abbreviated with two major letters.

  AK, AZ, MN, MO, MS, MT, NV, TN, TX

PRACTICE 2 Answer the following questions. Refer to the sample letter of application if necessary.

1. Where should the date be placed? Circle your response.

   (a.) above the recipient's address   b. below the recipient's address
2. If you do not know the name of the person in human resources, how should you address your letter of application?

   Attention: Human Resources Manager or *Dear Sir or Madam*
3. Should you place a comma at the end of each line in the recipient's address? Yes/(No)
4. In a letter of application, why are the next closings inappropriate?

   a. Bye for now   *too informal*

   b. Please accept my most gracious sentiments   *too stiff and formal*
5. In the sample application letter, why would Francesca avoid mentioning her job at the children's camp?

   She needs to keep her letter short and should include only the most important and relevant information. The job information appears on her résumé.
6. Write the two-letter postal abbreviations for each state.

   a. Ohio *OH*   d. West Virginia *WV*

   b. Maine *ME*   e. Texas *TX*

   c. Vermont *VT*   f. Kentucky *KY*

PRACTICE 3 The next letter contains twelve errors. Correct eight punctuation errors and four capitalization errors.

Dr. Bakar Rahim
33 Winestead road,
Cincinnati Ohio 45001

May 6 2008
Fernanda Martinez
965 Slater street
Chicago Illinois, 65002

Subject, Project Assistant Position

Dear Ms. Martinez

I have received your application for a position as a project assistant. Unfortunately, as a result of unforeseen circumstances, I did not receive the budget to fund this position. Please accept my apologies. Your education and experience appear exemplary.

On a brighter note, next january, I am hoping to receive the funding, which will allow me to begin accepting applications again. At that time, if you are still available, please contact me for a project assistant's position.

Respectfully Yours

Dr. B. Rahim

Dr. Bakar Rahim

ESL Teaching Tip:
In some nations, letters of application are quite detailed, flowery, and overly formal. Remind your nonnative speakers that brevity and clarity are key requirements in American business writing.

ESL Teaching Tip:
In many languages, letter closings are extremely formal and elaborate; therefore, some students may try to directly translate elaborate closings from their native languages. Remind students that conventional closings such as *Sincerely* or *Yours truly* are preferable in American business letters.

ESL

Teaching Tip: Suggest that each student peer edit a partner's letter of application. If you have concerns about nonnative speakers needing some help with certain cultural or English-language conventions, try to pair them with native speakers.

The Writer's Room Résumé and Letter

Find a job listing in the newspaper, at an employment center, or on the Internet. (Some Web sites are monster.com, usajobs.opm.gov, or studentjobs.gov.) Look for a job that you feel qualified for, or find a job that you hope to have one day. Write a résumé and a letter of application.

CHECKLIST: THE RÉSUMÉ AND THE LETTER OF APPLICATION

When you write a résumé or letter of application, ask yourself these questions:

- ☐ Have I used correct spelling and punctuation?
- ☐ In my résumé, have I included my work experience and my education beginning with the most recent?
- ☐ In my letter of application, have I indicated the position for which I am applying and where or how I heard about the job?
- ☐ Is my letter concise?
- ☐ Have I used standard English?

How Do I Get a Better Grade?

PEARSON mywritinglab

Visit www.mywritinglab.com for audio-visual lectures and additional practice sets about the résumé and letter of application.

Get a better grade with MyWritingLab!

Responding to Film and Literature

CHAPTER 18

CONTENTS

- Responding to Film and Literature
- Structuring Your Written Response

Critics who review musical performances are influenced by many factors, including their moods, the performance venues, and the extent of their knowledge about the art form. You take similar elements into consideration when you interpret works of film and literature.

Responding to Film and Literature

As a college student, you are often asked to state your opinion, to interpret issues, and to support your ideas. In some of your courses, your instructors may ask you to write a personal response to a literary work or film. When writing a personal response, you use your knowledge and perspective to connect with the work you are analyzing.

To write a personal response to a literary work or film, remember the basic steps of the writing process (Chapters 1–5). In particular, remember to ask yourself who will read your response and why they will be reading it.

> "*A wide screen just makes a bad film twice as bad.*"
>
> SAMUEL GOLDWYN, *producer*

- **Consider your audience.** Are you writing for a general audience, your classmates, or experts in a particular field? In general, you should use standard English and explain any specific terminology that your readers may not know.
- **Consider your purpose.** What is the goal of your writing? Your specific purpose may be to address issues raised in the literary work or film that you feel are important. For example, you may want to compare your own personal experience to the message of the work you are examining.

Teaching Tip: Reassure students that there are no right answers. Students should focus on supporting their reactions with evidence from the film, novel, or story.

Structuring Your Written Response

A basic written response has four parts: an introduction, a summary, some reactions, and a conclusion.

Introduction

For a story or novel, identify the name, title, publisher, and publication date. For a film, identify the title, director, and date of release. Then give some general background information about the film, story, or novel. For example, you might mention something about the director or author, the type of film or book, or the reception to the film or story.

Summary

Write a **brief** synopsis of the work. Include the main points and do not go into great detail about the work. Summarize the work so that readers can clearly understand the main storyline. At this point, do not make any personal value judgments about the work. Ensure that your summary is factual.

Reactions

Ask yourself the following questions to help you generate supporting ideas.

- What is the main message of the work? Is it relevant to me personally? What lessons, if any, did I learn?
- Did it change my understanding about an issue? Did it move me emotionally?
- Is the subject of the work relevant to any of my academic studies? Did it develop complementary ideas on a particular subject I have studied for a course?
- Did it give accurate, complete, or unbiased information about a subject, or did the author or filmmaker present the information in a slanted way?
- What, if any, is the social or political value of the work? Did it add to a universal understanding of an issue? Will it influence society as a whole?
- Would I recommend the work to other people?

Teaching Tip: Ask students to choose a particular passage, quotation, or scene from a text or film and discuss or write a personal response to it. Ask them: Why did you choose it? What emotions did it arouse in you?

Conclusion

Sum up the main arguments or ideas you presented in the essay. Leave readers with a sense of completion and perhaps encourage them to ponder or consider their own ideas about the work, too.

Hint **Follow the Writing Process**

When preparing your response, remember to follow the writing process. You can try exploring strategies to generate ideas. Organize your ideas and make a plan. Write a first draft and check for unity, adequate support, and coherence. Then edit your written work for errors.

Give specific details to support your ideas and opinions. Include examples as well as direct and indirect quotations. Avoid using vague sentiments such as *I like this* or *I do not like that*. When you finish writing, refer to the checklist at the end of this chapter.

Teaching Tip: Group Work
Ask two or three students to write a personal response to the same work. Then have them discuss their responses with the other students to see the similarities and differences in their responses.

Teaching Tip:
Although the following example is an analysis of a film, students could write a response to a story or novel using the same format.

A Sample Response to a Film

College student Stacy Taylor wrote the following written response to one of her favorite films. Notice how she structured her work.

The Simple Understanding of a Complex Life

"Stupid is as stupid does" is just one of many famous phrases associated with director Robert Zemeckis's 1994 sensation *Forrest Gump*. Novelist Winston Groom and screen writer Eric Roth probably never guessed how Americans would react to their portrayal of the simple-minded Alabamian, Forrest Gump. However, after the film won seven Academy Awards and several Golden Globes, it was clear that Groom's main character had grabbed our emotions from the beginning and never let go. Most viewers can agree that Forrest Gump is a national hero, both in times of war and everyday life. His heartwarming outlook on society gently guided him down a very rocky path that included meeting U.S. presidents, losing loved ones, and even qualifying for the international ping-pong championships.

Introduction
The writer begins with general background information about the film. She also identifies the film's title, release date, and director.

As the film opens, we are introduced to Forrest sitting on a bus bench. Throughout the movie, we see Forrest starting up casual conversations with local strangers. Most of his conversations with his new-found friends end with a life lesson. For example, the first woman he encounters at the bench is an African-American nurse dressed in uniform. He presents a box of chocolates to her and asks if she would like to have one. The woman shakes her head apprehensively, and Forrest replies, "Momma always said 'Life is like a box of chocolates. You never know what you're gonna get.' " He then notices the woman's shoes and tells her, "Momma always says there's an awful lot you can tell about a person by their shoes: Where they're going, or where they've been." In between the scenes on the bench, we learn that Forrest is a heroic character who becomes an Alabama State football star, saves the lives of several men in the Vietnam War, and earns

Summary
The writer briefly describes the film's main events.

Reaction
The writer explains the film's main message.

millions in the shrimp-boat business. The creators do not try to cover up his naïve nature. They treat his mental state as if he has an advantage over the rest of the world. In other words, because he is simple-minded, he does not take everything so seriously, which in turn makes his life happier and more meaningful.

As an audience, we can easily attach ourselves to naïve characters such as Forrest because they are victims of society and vulnerable. The mentally handicapped have frequently been seen in this light, so we tend to pity them or treat them as if they are inferior. In recent years, there have been many films, such as *I Am Sam* and *The Other Sister*, that aim to correct this stereotype by giving accurate portrayals of "real-life" handicaps. *Forrest Gump,* on the other hand, is different. The creators of the film do not try to reinforce stereotypes or realistically portray the mentally handicapped. Instead, the message of the movie is to emphasize the importance of simplicity in today's complex society.

Reaction
The writer discusses the universal values that are expressed in the film. In her reactions, she also supports her ideas and includes direct quotations from the film. Notice how she places the integrated quotations throughout.

An example of Forrest's simple but deep grasp on life is a moment he has with Jenny when they return to his Alabama home toward the end of the movie. They have just finished watching the Fourth of July celebration on TV, and Jenny is walking up the stairs to go to bed. Forrest asks, "Would you marry me? I'd make a good husband, Jenny." Jenny declines his offer, and he continues to say, "Why don't you love me, Jenny? I'm not a smart man, but I know what love is." Forrest's comments show that he may be ignorant about the complex things in life, such as solving economic problems or mastering chemistry, but he has a very basic understanding of what is important. He is a dedicated partner and friend to Jenny throughout his entire life and begins to realize that she is what he longs for, and that dedication is what a strong relationship is built on.

Reaction
The writer evaluates the merit of the work.

Audiences of every age, race, and social class can connect emotionally with this film. If you have not seen the movie, I would highly recommend it. Tom Hanks does a superb job of portraying the main character. The audience is quickly captured by Forrest's gentle nature and finds him to be even more likeable as he continues his heroic journey in a judgmental world. We feel for Forrest when he longs for Jenny, and mourn for him when he loses his best friend, Bubba. Hanks's character comes to warm our hearts by the end of the movie.

Overall, *Forrest Gump* stresses the importance of life, love, and happiness through the eyes of a man who sees things in a very uncomplicated way. Whether it is "stupid is as stupid does" or "life is like a box a of chocolates, you never know what you're gonna get," Forrest always leaves us with something to think about. Are our lives too complicated? Can this slow individual actually know the meaning of life? Forrest appears to be the everyday superhero with childlike qualities and never seems helpless or mistreated by society. Whether he is saving a dozen men from a devastating fate in Vietnam or simply allowing a stranger at a bus stop let down her guard enough to chat with a fellow human being, Forrest Gump is a person we can appreciate and admire.

Conclusion
The writer concludes the essay by restating the main points in the essay.

The Writer's Room Responding to Film and Literature

Write a response to a short story, novel, or film. Remember to include an introduction, a summary, and several paragraphs explaining your reaction to the work.

Teaching Tip: You might suggest particular films or stories. The Writer's Room activities at the end of each section in Chapter 40 offer a few films that you could choose from. Each film has some relation to the themes of the Editing Handbook chapters and the readings in Chapter 40.

CHECKLIST: RESPONSE TO A LITERARY WORK OR A FILM

After you write your response, review the checklist on the inside front cover. Also, ask yourself these questions:

- Have I considered my audience and purpose?
- Have I identified relevant information such as the title, author, and date in the introduction?
- Have I given a short summary of the plot?
- Have I described my reactions to the work?
- Have I avoided using vague statements, such as *I feel that* or *I do not like*?
- Have I integrated specific quotations and examples?
- Have I summed up my main arguments in the conclusion?
- Have I properly cited my sources?

Teaching Tip: Please encourage your students to submit their best responses to a film or literary text for possible publication to: <thewritersworld@prenhall.com>.

How Do I Get a Better Grade?

mywritinglab

Visit www.mywritinglab.com for audio-visual lectures and additional practice sets about responding to film and literature. ***Get a better grade with MyWritingLab!***

Chapter 19 Becoming a Successful Student

CONTENTS

- Preparing for Exams
- Writing Essay Exams

Just as athletes rigorously train to win an important race, successful students follow specific strategies to ace exams.

> "*Being prepared is the best way to reduce exam anxiety.*"
>
> ADELE BERRIDGE, *instructor*

Preparing for Exams

All courses in educational institutions measure how much students understand a subject through different forms of evaluation, including oral presentations and essay exams. Learning and practicing effective study habits early on will help you achieve success in your college courses.

Here are two tips every student should remember:

Do not procrastinate. If you know that an assignment is due on a given date, then give yourself enough time to complete it. You may want to finish the assignment a couple of days ahead of time so that you will have time to reread it with a fresh eye and make any revisions necessary. If you know that you have a test in a couple of weeks, give yourself enough time to study. Do not wait until the last minute and cram because you may be unable to retain the information that you need.

Balance your college, home, and career lives. If you put too much emphasis on your college career, you may feel stressed or anxious about passing or failing. Such stress will not help you to achieve good grades. If you put too much emphasis on your social life, you may realize too late in the semester that you are failing certain courses. Maintain equilibrium in your life so that you remain motivated to achieve success in your studies.

PRACTICE 1 Write a short paragraph explaining what kind of study habits you have. Be honest with yourself and support your description with specific examples. Then read the rest of this chapter to see how you can develop better study skills. Answers will vary.

____

____

____

____

____

____

Take Two Types of Class Notes

Having effective notes will make studying for tests and exams easier. When you take notes, record the primary and secondary ideas of a subject. Always keep notes for each course in a separate binder, or use a binder with dividers so that each subject has its own space. Here are strategies for taking both textbook and lecture notes.

Textbook Notes

- Read the text carefully and underline any key words or phrases.
- Use a dictionary to understand the definitions of unfamiliar words.
- Give a title to your notes. It could just be the chapter of your textbook, or it could be the name of the subject.
- Rewrite all primary and secondary ideas in your own words. (Chapter 15 gives you guidelines on how to paraphrase and summarize.)
- Review your notes to verify that you have understood the key concepts of the text.

Lecture Notes

- Complete all homework and reading assignments before class. Most lecturers use homework reading assignments as a springboard to transmit new concepts.
- Bring your notebook, textbooks, and pens to class. You will need these to take notes and refer to concepts the instructor is explaining.

- Listen carefully. An instructor often gives clues to critical information using statements such as "and most importantly ..." or "remember to consider ...."
- Write only the key words or phrases, and use symbols or abbreviations. You probably will not have time to write complete sentences.
- Ask your instructor to repeat what you do not hear or understand. If you have not caught the information, chances are great that others in your class have not either. If it would be inappropriate to interrupt the lecture, put a mark beside the concept to remind yourself to get clarification from the instructor or a classmate later.
- Date your notes. You will want a record of when you wrote them during the semester. The dates might help you to know what to focus on while you are studying.

Hint **Using Abbreviations**

Many abbreviations we use in English derive from Latin terms. Here are some abbreviations to help you take notes more efficiently.

Abbreviation	English	Latin
e.g.	for example	exempli gratia
etc.	and so on	et cetera
i.e.	in other words	id est
N.B.	important	Nota Bene
vs., v.	against	versus

Keep in mind that these abbreviations are useful for note taking. When you write an essay, use the complete English words, not the abbreviations.

Sharpen Your Study Skills

Here are some guidelines for studying effectively.

Take meaningful notes. Follow the previous note-taking tips to learn how to summarize and synthesize the key concepts of an article, textbook, or lecture.

Review course material. Cramming is an ineffective, short-term strategy for college success. Reviewing your course material *regularly*, perhaps every second day or each week, will ensure that you know your subjects well.

Organize study time. Decide regular study times and write your study plan in your agenda. Be strict with yourself and always spend that time studying. As little as thirty minutes a day could be sufficient to become familiar with the subject matter.

Ask questions. All college instructors are available outside class hours. Make regular appointments with your instructor and prepare questions about concepts that you do not understand. Waiting until the day before your exam will be too late.

Study with a classmate or friend. Set a particular time each week, which will motivate you to study during times when you want to do something else. Ask each other questions on key concepts or proofread each other's written work.

Hint **Predict Exam Questions**

An effective study strategy is to predict possible exam questions.

- Look for important themes in your course outline.
- Study your notes and try to analyze what information is of particular importance.
- Look at previous exams for the course. Determine if any questions or subjects are repeated in more than one exam.

Writing Essay Exams

In many of your courses, you will have to answer exam questions with a paragraph or essay to reveal how well you understand information. Although taking any exam can be stressful, you can reduce exam anxiety and increase your chances of doing well by following some of the preparation and exam-writing strategies outlined in this chapter.

Schedule Your Time

Before you write the exam, find out exactly how much time you have, and then plan how much time you will need to answer the questions. For example, if you have a one-hour exam, and you have three questions worth the same value, try to spend no more than twenty minutes on each question.

Determine Point Values

As soon as you get an exam, scan the questions and determine which questions have a larger value. For example, you might respond to the questions with the largest point value first, or you might begin with those that you understand well. Then go to the more difficult questions. If you are blocked on a certain answer, skip to another question, and then go back to that question later.

Carefully Read the Exam Questions

In an exam question, every word counts. Here are two ways you can read actively.

1. **Identify Key Words and Phrases.** When you read an exam question, underline or circle key words and phrases to understand exactly what you are supposed to do. In the next example of an essay question, the underlined words highlight two different tasks.

   Explain what is meant by neocolonialism and analyze how it influences the economies of rich and poor.

   1. Define the term neocolonialism.
   2. Explain how neocolonialism affects both rich and poor countries.

2. **Examine Common Question Words.** Exam questions direct you using verbs (action words). The following chart gives you several common words that you will find in essay-style questions.

Teaching Tip: Ask students to identify verbs that relate to a specific essay pattern.

Verb	Meaning
describe discuss review	Examine a subject as thoroughly as possible. Focus on the main points.
narrate trace	Describe the development or progress of something using time order.
evaluate explain your point of view interpret justify take a stand	State your opinion and give reasons to support your opinion. In other words, write an argument essay.
analyze criticize classify	Explain something carefully by breaking it down into smaller parts.
enumerate list outline	Go through important facts one by one.
compare contrast distinguish	Discuss important similarities and/or differences.
define explain what is meant by	Give a complete and accurate definition that demonstrates your understanding of the concept.
explain causes	Analyze the reasons for an event.
explain effects	Analyze the consequences or results of an event.
explain a process	Explain the steps needed to do a task.
summarize	Write down the main points from a larger piece of work.
illustrate	Demonstrate your understanding by giving examples.

PRACTICE 2 Write the letter of the correct key word in the space provided.

Topic

1. Explain how the gross national product (GNP) of a country is calculated. ___c___
2. Explain the events that led to the end of World War I. ___e___

Key Word

a. compare and contrast
b. define

3. Illustrate alternative energy sources. __f__
4. Distinguish between universal health care and privatized medicine. __a__
5. Discuss whether euthanasia should be legalized. __d__
6. Explain what utilitarianism is. __b__

c. explain a process
d. argue
e. explain causes
f. give examples

PRACTICE 3 The following sample has been taken from an essay exam. Read the instructions and then answer the questions that follow the sample. Answers will vary.

Answer both parts A and B. You will have two hours to complete the evaluation.

Part A Define two of the following terms. (5 points each)
1. democracy
2. electorate
3. communism
4. industrial revolution
5. gerrymandering

Part B Write a well-structured essay on one of the following topics. (20 points)
1. Distinguish between panic versus mass hysteria. Can governments ever benefit from either of these phenomena?
2. Evaluate the usefulness of sanctions that Western nations impose on nations such as North Korea.
3. Trace the rise of National Socialism in Germany in the 1930s.

1. What is the total point value of the exam? __30 points__
2. Which part of the exam would you do first? Explain why. __Do the essay first because it is worth more points.__
3. How much time would you spend on Part A and on Part B? Why?
__I would spend thirty minutes on Part A and one and a half hours on Part B because Part B is worth more than Part A.__
4. How many definitions and essays should you write?
__only two definitions and one essay__
5. In Part B, which two questions would be answered with an argument essay?
__1__ __2__

Follow the Writing Process

Treat an essay exam as you would any other writing assignment by following the three main steps of the writing process.

Explore Jot down any ideas that you think can help you answer the question. Try the prewriting activities suggested in Chapter 1 of this book, such as brainstorming or clustering. Prewriting will help you generate some ideas for your essay.

Develop Use the exam question to guide your thesis statement and topic sentences. List supporting ideas, organize your ideas using an essay plan or outline, and then write an essay. Remember to include an introduction with a clear thesis statement and to use transitions such as *first*, *moreover*, or *in addition* to link your ideas.

Revise and Edit Read over your essay to verify that all ideas support the thesis statement and to ensure that you have adequate details to support your topic sentences. Also check your spelling, punctuation, and mechanics.

PRACTICE 4 Write thesis statements for the following exam questions. Answers will vary.

EXAMPLE: Discuss the influences of the industrial revolution on class structure.

Thesis statement: *The industrial revolution caused a dramatic change in the means of production and transformed traditional class structure.*

1. Explain your point of view on poverty.

   Thesis Statement ______________________________

   ____

2. Distinguish between a religion and a cult.

   Thesis Statement ______________________________

   ____

3. Analyze the effects of new globalization on world culture.

   Thesis Statement ______________________________

   ____

PRACTICE 5 College student Seokman Chang wrote the following essay for an exam. Read the essay and answer the questions that follow.

1 Throughout human history, there have been migratory movements of people all over the world. The Polynesians journeyed and stayed in the Hawaiian Islands, the Vikings found homes in Great Britain and Ireland,

and the Moguls came and settled in India. Today, the migration trend continues. People migrate to different parts of the world for many reasons and often bring benefits to the host region or country.

2 First, many people go to different countries searching for better work opportunities. For example, many groups of professionals migrate to get higher paying jobs. There are engineers, teachers, lawyers, and computer specialists who have come to this country to broaden their skills and work experience. One day, in a supermarket line, I had a conversation with a woman from China. She and her husband had just arrived in this country. They were both doctors and were preparing to take the qualifying exams. The woman was very excited about being able to continue her career. She felt that she would grow professionally. Unskilled laborers also come to North America because the pay for such jobs is higher than in their homeland. A factory worker usually earns more per hour in an industrialized country than in a developing country. Most skilled and unskilled economic migrants come to new lands seeking a better quality of life.

3 Second, sometimes immigrants leave their homelands unwillingly. They may be forced to leave their homes because of famine or war. For example, many Africans have migrated from one region or country to another for both reasons. There is drought in the sub-Saharan countries and war in Congo, Darfur, Somalia, and other areas. Furthermore, often people are expelled from their homeland. In 1972, the Ugandan dictator Idi Amin expelled the Indian community. They had very little time to pack up and leave. China and other countries have expelled some political activists, while other activists have fled for their lives, claiming political refugee status.

4 Moreover, some people leave their native lands to join family members who have already immigrated. Such cases are especially true of new immigrants. Often first-generation immigrants arrive in the new country alone. When they have settled, they send for their immediate family members. My neighbor came from Vietnam about ten years ago. For the first few years, he was in this country alone. He worked during the day and took night courses. As soon as he got settled, he sent for his parents because they were getting older and had no one to take care of them in Vietnam. Now the family is together again.

5 The receiving country gains many advantages from immigrants. New groups add to the cultural diversity of the country. For example, new immigrants bring their language, culture, and traditions with them. North American cities have a variety of ethnic restaurants, grocery stores, and cultural festivals. In addition, Western countries need immigrants to maintain or increase the population. The birthrates of most developed countries are falling and immigrants are needed to maintain population rates. New immigrants also bring skills that are advantageous to the host

Teaching Tip:

Group Discussion

Ask your nonnative speakers about their first experiences in this country. When did they arrive? Why did they immigrate? What were their first impressions? Also ask your native speakers if they would ever consider moving to another country. If so, which one and why? What adjustments would they have to make?

country. New immigrants perform many varied jobs, from doctors and engineers to fruit pickers and waiters. Immigrants contribute to the economy of the host country.

6 People leave their homelands for a variety of reasons and their adopted countries gain tremendously from migration. The migrant usually finds a more stable and prosperous life. The adopted countries of new immigrants gain tremendously in social and economic areas. A country that is multicultural is vibrant and flourishing. So the next time you eat at your favorite Italian restaurant, dance to Carlos Santana, or debate the policies of Arnold Schwarzenegger, remember that immigration made it all possible.

1. This student essay is an answer to which of the following questions? Circle the best possible answer.
   a. Distinguish the periods of immigration to North America and describe the migrant groups.
   b. Evaluate the current immigration policy of the nation.
   c. Explain why people immigrate and some consequences of their migration.
2. On paper or on the computer, deconstruct this essay by making an informal essay plan. For the details, just use words or phrases.

Thesis Statement: People migrate to different parts of the world for many reasons and usually bring with them benefits to the host region or country.

Topic Sentence 1: First, people go to different countries often searching for better work opportunities.

Details: – engineers, teachers, lawyers, computer specialists, and unskilled laborers
– couple from China

Topic Sentence 2: Second, sometimes immigrants leave their homeland unwillingly.

Details: – war and famine such as in Darfur, Congo, ...
– political refugees such as East Indians from Uganda and political activists

Topic Sentence 3: Moreover, some people leave their native land to join family members who have already immigrated.

Details: – true of new immigrants
– neighbor from Vietnam

Topic Sentence 4: The receiving country gains many advantages from immigrants

Details: – restaurants, food stores, festivals

– helps offset declining population due to low birth rate

– bring skilled and unskilled labor force, which helps the economy

The Writer's Room Essay Exam Topics

1. Predict at least three essay exam questions for one of your courses. Then develop an informal essay plan for one of the questions.
2. Look at an older exam that you completed. Write a paragraph explaining what you should have done to receive a higher mark.

CHECKLIST: AN ESSAY EXAM

As you prepare for your essay exam, ask yourself the following questions.

- ☐ Have I taken clear notes during lectures?
- ☐ Have I reviewed my notes on a regular basis?
- ☐ Have I organized study time?
- ☐ Have I asked my instructor questions when I didn't understand a concept?
- ☐ Have I asked my instructor about the types of questions on the exam?
- ☐ Have I asked my instructor what material the exam will cover?

How Do I Get a Better Grade?

PART IV

Editing Handbook

When you speak, you have tools such as tone of voice and body language to help you express your ideas. When you write, however, you have only words and punctuation to get your message across. If your writing includes errors in style, grammar, and punctuation, you may distract readers from your message, and they may focus, instead, on your inability to communicate clearly. You increase your chances of succeeding in your academic and professional life when you write in clear, standard English.

This Editing Handbook will help you understand important grammar concepts, and the samples and practices in each chapter offer interesting information about many themes. Before you begin working with these chapters, review the contents and themes shown here.

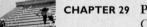

20 CHAPTER

Identifying Subjects and Verbs

CONTENTS

- Identifying Subjects
- Identifying Verbs

Section Theme **CONFLICT**

Is behavior learned or genetic? In this chapter, you will learn about the sources of aggressive behavior.

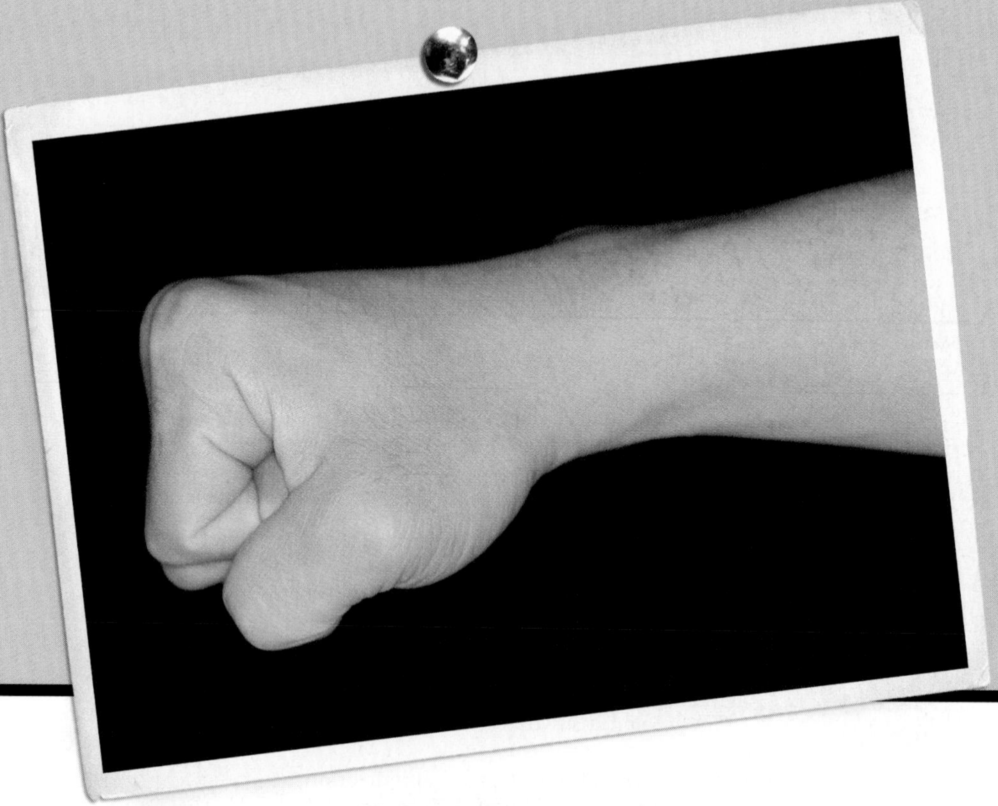

Teaching Tip:
In the Grammar Snapshot, ask students to identify sentences that appear to have no subjects. Ask them who or what the subject is in those sentences.

Grammar Snapshot

Looking at Subjects and Verbs

Psychologist Ken Low has given seminars on dealing with aggression. In the following excerpt from a seminar, he discusses the source of anger. Notice that subjects are in bold and verbs are underlined. Also observe that some sentences have no visible subjects.

> Understand the source of your anger. Examine your feelings of unhappiness. In my case, the **cause** of the unhappiness was my sense of worthlessness. **Everyone** was succeeding, in my mind, and **I** was not. **I** wanted to blame my boss, my parents, or my wife. **I** was prepared to blame anybody and anything outside of myself. **Recognizing** my unhappiness gave me insight into the source of my anger. **I** held a mistaken conviction: the **world** owed me a good life.

In this chapter, you will identify subjects and verbs.

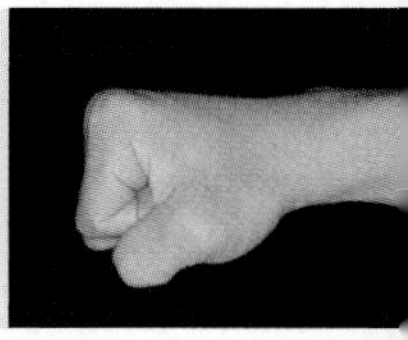

Identifying Subjects

A **sentence** contains one or more subjects and verbs, and it expresses a complete thought. The **subject** tells you who or what the sentence is about. A **verb** expresses an action or state. If a sentence is missing a subject or a verb, it is incomplete. You will use your ability to identify subjects and verbs in the editing process.

- Subjects may be **singular** or **plural**. A subject can also be a **pronoun**. To determine the subject of a sentence, ask yourself who or what the sentence is about. It may be about a person, place, or thing.

  Detective Marcos will interview the suspects.

  Many **factors** cause people to break laws.

  It is an important case.

- A **compound subject** contains two or more subjects joined by *and*, *or*, or *nor*.

  Reporters and **photographers** were outside the prison gates.

- Sometimes a **gerund** (*-ing* form of the verb) is the subject of a sentence.

  Listening is an important skill.

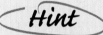

Teaching Tip: The grammar chapters are flexible. You can skip certain chapters or do them in whatever order suits your course syllabus or teaching style. Before working through the grammar chapters, you may wish to ask students to review some key grammar terms in Appendix 1.

Hint **Here and There**

Here and *There* are not subjects. In sentences that begin with *Here* or *There*, the subject follows the verb.

> There are several **ways** to find a criminal.
>
> Here is an interesting **brochure** about the police academy.

ESL Teaching Tip: Remind students that the *-ing* form can be a noun or a verb. Ask them to explain the difference between two sentences: *Relaxing is important. I am relaxing right now.*

How to Find the Subject

To find the subject, ask yourself *who* or *what* the sentence is about. The subject is the noun or pronoun or the complete name of a person or organization.

The **Federal Bureau of Investigation** is a large organization. **It** has branches in every state.

When you are identifying the subject, you can ignore words that describe the noun.

adjectives (pompous and rude) — subject (sergeant)

The pompous and rude **sergeant** left the room.

PRACTICE 1 Circle the subject in each sentence. Sometimes there may be more than one subject.

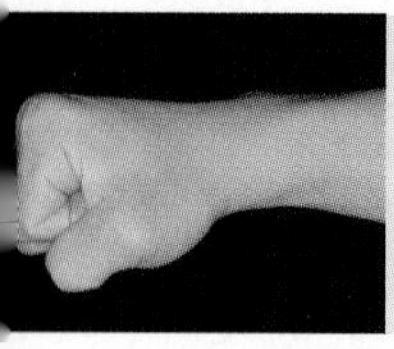

CHAPTER 20

EXAMPLE: A behavioral study examines genetics and behavior.

1. Research psychiatrist Carl E. Schwartz works in the Department of Psychiatry at Massachusetts General Hospital.
2. He conducted a study to determine hereditary factors in behavior.
3. There were over one hundred children in his study.
4. Infants and toddlers were classed into two groups.
5. Objects, strange people, and unfamiliar settings were used to test the children.
6. Talking was not permitted.
7. The outgoing toddlers easily interacted in new surroundings.
8. The inhibited children were more likely to show signs of stress in unfamiliar surroundings.

Teaching Tip: Before doing the grammar sections, ensure that students understand the basic "Parts of Speech" vocabulary. As they do the following activity, they can look at the glossary of terms in Appendix I if they need help. Ask students to write sentences using the following parts of speech: noun, verb, pronoun, adjective, adverb, preposition, conjunction, and interjection.

Prepositional Phrases

A **preposition** is a word that links nouns, pronouns, and phrases to other words in a sentence. It expresses a relationship based on movement or position. A **prepositional phrase** is made up of a preposition and its object (a noun or a pronoun).

Because the object of a preposition is a noun, it may look like a subject. **However, the object in a prepositional phrase is never the subject of the sentence.**

prepositional phrase — subject

With the parents' approval, the **experiment** began.

Common Prepositions

about	among	beside	during	into	onto	toward
above	around	between	except	like	out	under
across	at	beyond	for	near	outside	until
after	before	by	from	of	over	up
against	behind	despite	in	off	through	with
along	below	down	inside	on	to	within

ESL Teaching Tip: Ask nonnative speakers to underline prepositions that they do not understand. They can discuss the meanings of those prepositions with other students in the class.

To help you identify the subject, put parentheses around prepositional phrases. In each of the following examples, the prepositional phrase is in parentheses. Notice that a sentence can contain more than one prepositional phrase.

(In spite of the storm), **they** drove to the hospital.

The **clinic**, (after 1971), expanded greatly.

(In the late 1990s), (during a period of cost cutting), high-tech **cameras** were placed in the room.

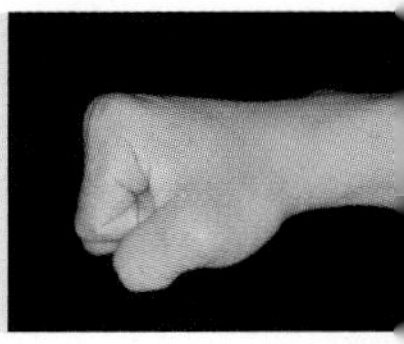

Hint **Using *of the***

In most expressions containing *of the*, the subject appears before *of the*.

subject
Each (of the parents) agreed to participate.

One (of the fathers) was uncomfortable with the process.

PRACTICE 2 Circle the subject in each sentence. Also add parentheses around any prepositional phrases that are near the subject.

EXAMPLE: (For many years), Schwartz has studied genetics and behavior.

1. (In Schwartz's study,) half (of the babies) were classified as shy. The others (in the group) were classified as outgoing. (In unfamiliar surroundings,) the shy and outgoing children reacted differently. (For example), (in the presence of a stranger,) the shy toddlers would freeze. The outgoing toddlers would approach the stranger and interact.

2. The differences (in reactions) occurred in their heart rate, in the dilation of their pupils, and in the levels of the stress hormone, cortisone. Generally, the differences (in the temperament of children) persisted to adulthood.

3. (After the first study,) Carl Schwartz tracked down twenty-two of the original subjects. About one-third (of the uninhibited adults) showed impulsive and aggressive behavior. Some (of the shy children) became extremely shy adults. However, not all outgoing infants become bold or aggressive adults. In fact, most individuals (in the study) did not develop behavioral problems.

Identifying Verbs

Every sentence must contain a verb. The **verb** expresses what the subject does, or it links the subject to other descriptive words.

An **action verb** describes an action that a subject performs.

Detective Rowland attended a seminar. He spoke to some officials.

A **linking verb** connects a subject with words that describe it, and it does not show an action. The most common linking verb is *be*, but other common linking verbs are *appear*, *become*, *look*, and *seem*.

Kim Rossmo is a former detective. His methods seem reliable.

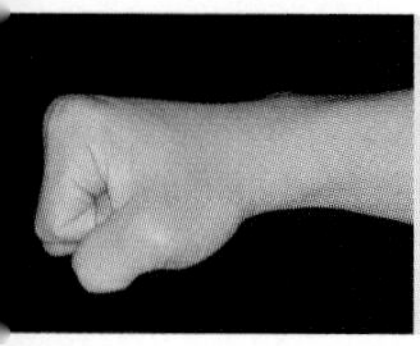

When a subject performs more than one action, the verbs are called **compound verbs.**

In 2003, Rossmo wrote and spoke about his methods.

Helping Verbs

The **helping verb** combines with the main verb to indicate tense, negative structure, or question structure. The most common helping verbs are forms of *be*, *have*, and *do*. **Modal auxiliaries** are another type of helping verb, and they indicate ability (*can*), obligation (*must*), and so on. For example, here are different forms of the verb *ask*, and the helping verbs are underlined.

is asking	had asked	will ask	should have asked
was asked	had been asking	can ask	might be asked
has been asking	would ask	could be asking	could have been asked

The **complete verb** is the helping verb and the main verb. In the following examples, the main verb is double underlined. In **question forms**, the first helping verb usually appears before the subject.

Criminal profiling techniques have been spreading across the continent.

Should the detective have studied the files?

Interrupting words such as *often*, *always*, *ever*, and *actually* are not part of the verb.

Rossmo has often returned to Vancouver.

Teaching Tip:
Draw attention to the hint about infinitives. Students often confuse the infinitive with the main verb.

Hint **Infinitives Are Not the Main Verb**

Infinitives are verbs preceded by *to* such as *to fly*, *to speak*, and *to go*. An infinitive is never the main verb in a sentence.

infinitive
The network wanted **to produce** a show about geographic profiling.

PRACTICE 3 In each sentence, circle the subject and underline the complete verb. Remember to underline the helping verbs as well as the main verbs. You could also place prepositional phrases in parentheses to help you identify the other parts of the sentence.

EXAMPLE: (According to Professor Saundra K. Ciccarelli,) many factors contribute to aggressive behavior.

1. The amygdala is located near the base of the brain. Studies have shown the amygdala's role in fear responses. In a 1939 experiment, the temporal lobe was removed from the brains of several monkeys. The lobe contains the amygdala. After the surgery, the monkeys showed absolutely no fear of snakes and humans. This anecdote illustrates the role of the brain in fearful or aggressive behavior.
2. Why do people harm others? In her book *Psychology*, Ciccarelli discusses the connection between the brain and aggressive behavior. She gives an example of a specific case. In 1966, Charles Whitman shot and killed fourteen people. Before his death in a shootout with police, Whitman wrote a note and asked doctors to examine the state of his brain. In fact, a later examination revealed the presence of a tumor next to his amygdala.
3. There are also chemical links to aggression, according to Ciccarelli. Testosterone, in high levels, has been shown to cause aggressive behavior. Also, certain substances have an impact on the brain. Alcohol affects the amount of some brain chemicals and reduces a person's inhibitions.

CHAPTER 20

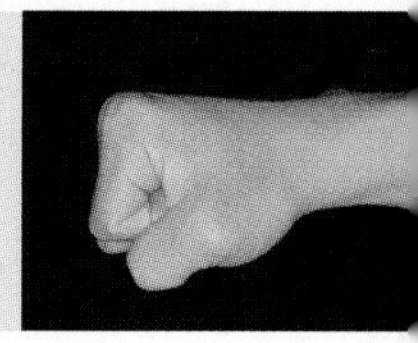

Teaching Tip:
To make the practice more challenging, you can ask students to identify helping verbs (H) and linking verbs (L) as well.

Teaching Tip:
Group Work
Groups of students could practice identifying subjects and verbs by looking at a reading in Part V. They could focus on one or two paragraphs in the reading.

FINAL REVIEW

Circle the subjects and underline the complete verbs in the following sentences. Underline *all* parts of the verb. To avoid misidentifying subjects, you can place prepositional phrases in parentheses.

EXAMPLE: One (of the most interesting influences on behavior) is social roles.

1. Many psychologists and social scientists believe in the importance of social roles on behavior. Thus, children can be influenced by aggressive characters on television. Young adults may be pressured or manipulated by peers. Basically, people can learn to be aggressive.
2. Most interesting of all, people of all ages can modify their behavior due to their social roles. Psychologist Philip Zimbardo demonstrated the importance of social roles in his prison experiment at Stanford University. He recruited about seventy volunteers and gave half of them guard roles and the other half prisoner roles. Many volunteers in the guard roles exhibited violent behavior. Other volunteers in the prisoner roles became meek. Therefore, the behavior of the students changed due to their roles.
3. History is filled with examples of people behaving badly, often during times of conflict. Soldiers, especially, are in stressful situations and fulfill

Teaching Tip:
You can use the final review as a test. Additional practice and test material appears in the Instructor's Resource Manual and on *MyWritingLab*.

Teaching Tip:
To make the final review more challenging, you can ask students to place parentheses around prepositional phrases and write V over main verbs.

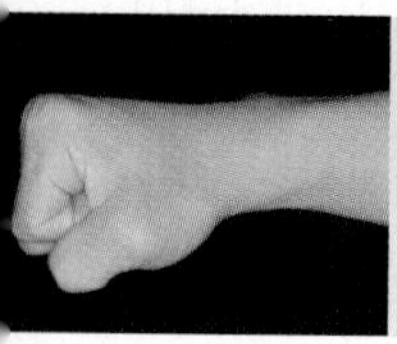

the obligations of their roles. The prison abuse scandal at Abu Ghraib in Iraq is a real-life example. Prison guards beat and humiliated prisoners. Why did the guards act so cruelly? According to psychologists, a uniform and a specific social role have powerful influences on people's behavior.

The Writer's Room Topics for Writing

Write about one of the following topics. After you finish writing, identify your subjects and verbs.

1. List various ways in which social roles influence people's behavior. Support your points with specific examples.
2. Some experts suggest that personality traits are partly inherited. Are your character traits similar to a family member's traits? Compare and contrast yourself with someone else in your family.

CHECKLIST: SUBJECTS AND VERBS

Review this chapter's main points.

- To identify **subjects,** look for words that tell you who or what the sentence is about.
- To identify **verbs,** look for words that do the following:
  - **action verbs** describe the actions that the subject performs.
  - **linking verbs** describe a state of being or link the subject with descriptive words.
  - **helping verbs** combine with the main verb to indicate tense, negative structure, or question structure.
- To identify **prepositional phrases,** look for words that consist of a preposition and its object. Note: the object of a prepositional phrase cannot be the subject.

prepositional phrase — subject — helping verb — verb

In spite of criticism, the police chief has released the suspect.

How Do I Get a Better Grade?

Visit www.mywritinglab.com for audio-visual lectures and additional practice sets about identifying subjects and verbs.

mywritinglab

Get a better grade with MyWritingLab!

Sentence Combining

CHAPTER 21

CONTENTS

- Understanding Key Words
- Making Compound Sentences
- Making Complex Sentences

Section Theme **CONFLICT**

In this chapter, you will read about eyewitness testimony, profiling techniques, and wrongful convictions.

Grammar Snapshot

Looking at Compound and Complex Sentences

The following excerpt is from *Criminal Justice Today* by Frank Schmallager. The underlined sections are called dependent clauses.

> Defendants may choose to be represented in Chinese courts by an attorney, a relative, or a friend, or they may choose to represent themselves. If they desire, a lawyer will be appointed for them. . . . While they work to protect the rights of the defendant, attorneys have a responsibility to the court. Defense lawyers are charged with helping the court render a verdict.

In this chapter, you will identify and write compound and complex sentences.

Teaching Tip: Ask students to look at the underlined clauses in the Grammar Snapshot. Ask them to consider why the underlined clauses are called "dependent."

Understanding Key Words

When you use sentences of varying lengths and types, your writing flows more smoothly and appears more interesting. You can vary sentences and create relationships between ideas by combining sentences.

Before you learn about the types of sentences, it is important to understand some key terms.

A **phrase** is a group of words that is missing a subject, a verb, or both, and is not a complete sentence.

in the morning   acting on her own   the excited witness

Teaching Tip: You might ask students to discuss how a person can be dependent. Help them visualize that an independent person needs no help whereas a dependent person must lean on someone else. They can then apply this visual to sentence structure.

A **clause** is a group of words that contains a subject and a verb. There are two types of clauses.

- An **independent clause** is a complete sentence. It stands alone and expresses one complete idea.

  The victims asked for compensation.

- A **dependent clause** has a subject and a verb, but it cannot stand alone. It "depends" on another clause to be complete. A dependent clause usually begins with a subordinator such as *after, although, because, unless,* and *when.*

  . . . because they had lost a lot of money.

PRACTICE 1 Write S next to each complete sentence. If the group of words is not a complete sentence—perhaps it is a phrase or a dependent clause—then write X in the blank.

Teaching Tip: As an additional activity, ask students to make the incomplete sentences complete in Practice 1.

EXAMPLE: Circumstantial evidence is discounted. S

Although it may be reliable. X

1. Circumstantial evidence is often very reliable. S
2. Blood, for example. X
3. It may match with the DNA of the victim. S
4. Pieces of clothing, hair fibers, and other types of evidence. X
5. Unless somebody altered it. X
6. Such evidence is usually very good. S
7. A credit card may place a criminal at the crime scene. S
8. Although the suspect may have an alibi. X

Making Compound Sentences

Combining Sentences Using Coordinating Conjunctions

A **coordinating conjunction** joins two complete ideas and indicates the connection between them. The most common coordinating conjunctions are *for*, *and*, *nor*, *but*, *or*, *yet*, and *so*.

Complete idea **, coordinating conjunction** complete idea.

The detective collected the evidence, **and** the lab analyzed it.

Review the following chart showing coordinating conjunctions and their functions.

Conjunction	Function	Example
and	to join two ideas	Anna went to school**, and** she became a forensics expert.
but	to contrast two ideas	The courses were difficult**, but** she passed them all.
for	to indicate a reason	She worked very hard**, for** she was extremely motivated.
nor	to indicate a negative idea	The work was not easy**, nor** was it pleasant.
or	to offer an alternative	She will work for a police department**, or** she will work for a private lab.
so	to indicate a cause and effect relationship	She has recently graduated**, so** she is looking for work now.
yet	to introduce a surprising choice	She wants to stay in her town**, yet** the best jobs are in a nearby city.

Teaching Tip:
To help students remember the seven coordinators, suggest that they learn the acronym f.a.n.b.o.y.s.

ESL
Teaching Tip:
This chart is useful for nonnative speakers.

Hint **Recognizing Compound Sentences**

To be sure that a sentence is compound, place your finger over the coordinator, and then ask yourself if the two clauses are complete sentences. In compound sentences, always place a comma before the coordinator.

Simple: The witness was nervous **but** very convincing.

Compound: The witness was nervous, **but** she was very convincing.

PRACTICE 2 Insert coordinating conjunctions in the blanks. Choose from the following list, and try to use a variety of coordinators. (Some sentences may have more than one answer.)

but or yet so for and nor

EXAMPLE: In 1969, the FBI introduced criminal profiling as an investigative strategy, _____***and***_____ it has been quite successful.

1. Kim Rossmo is a renowned geographic profiler, _____*but / and*_____ he is also an excellent detective. In the early 1990s, Detective Rossmo could either work in Canada, _____*or*_____ he could take a job in the United States. The Vancouver Police Department did not try to keep Rossmo, _____*so*_____ he moved south.
2. Rossmo examines the movements of criminals, _____*and*_____ he searches for specific patterns. According to Rossmo, criminals attack places they know, _____*but / yet*_____ they generally don't work in their own neighborhoods. Most people don't want to travel long distances for their jobs, _____*for*_____ they are lazy. Criminals work the same way, _____*so*_____ they stay relatively close to home.
3. Rossmo developed a fascinating mathematical formula, _____*yet / but*_____ many police departments were skeptical about his ideas. He tried to convince others, _____*for*_____ he believed strongly in his computer program. Basically, he inputs the addresses of suspects into a computer, _____*and*_____ he also inputs details about the crime scenes. His program can process a ten-square-mile area, _____*and*_____ it looks for a "hot" area. Suspects may live directly in the center of the hot area, _____*or*_____ they may live within a few blocks.
4. For example, in the late 1990s, there were several sexual assaults in a town in Ontario, Canada, _____*so*_____ Rossmo and his associates created a profile map. One particular suspect's home was compared to the location of the crime scenes, _____*and*_____ it was placed in Rossmo's computer program. Originally, the main offender's name was low on a list of 316 suspects, _____*but*_____ it rose to number 6 on the list after the

Teaching Tip:
Remind students that sentences containing *and, but*, etc. are not necessarily compound. To show the differences between simple and compound sentences, write a few examples on the board (without punctuation), and then ask students how to punctuate each sentence. Here are some examples you could use:

He was held for questioning and asked for a lawyer.

He was held for questioning but didn't ask to phone his lawyer.

He was held for questioning, but he did not ask to phone his lawyer.

You can study criminology or forensics.

You can study criminology, or you can study forensics.

profiling. The suspect did not admit his guilt, ___but / yet___ other evidence tied him to the crime scenes. He was eventually tried and convicted for the crimes, ___so / and___ he went to prison.

Combining Sentences Using Semicolons (;)

Another way to form a compound sentence is to join two complete ideas with a semicolon. The semicolon replaces a coordinating conjunction.

Complete idea ; complete idea.

The eyewitness was certain; she pointed at the suspect.

GRAMMAR LINK

For more practice using semicolons, see Chapter 24, Run-Ons.

Hint **Use a Semicolon to Join Related Ideas**

Use a semicolon to link two sentences when the ideas are equally important and closely related. Do not use a semicolon to join two unrelated sentences.

Incorrect: Some eyewitnesses make mistakes; I like to watch criminal trials.
(The second idea has no clear relationship with the first idea.)

Correct: One eyewitness misidentified a suspect; the witness was not wearing contact lenses that day.
(The second idea gives further information about the first idea.)

PRACTICE 3 Make compound sentences by adding a semicolon and another complete sentence to each simple sentence. Remember that the two sentences must have related ideas. Answers will vary.

Teaching Tip: Advise students to use semicolons sparingly. Some students overuse them.

EXAMPLE: Last year, Eric joined a gang; *he regretted his decision.*

1. Eric rebelled against his parents ______________________________
____

2. Some people don't have supportive families ______________________________
____

3. At age fifteen, I acted like other teens ______________________________
____

4. She didn't commit the crime ______________________________
____

CHAPTER 21

5. His friends tried to influence him ______________________________

____

6. Eric entered the courtroom ______________________________

____

Combining Sentences Using Transitional Expressions

A **transitional expression** links two complete ideas and shows how they are related. Most transitional expressions are **conjunctive adverbs** such as *however* or *furthermore*.

Some Transitional Expressions

Addition	Alternative	Contrast	Time	Example or Emphasis	Result or Consequence
additionally	in fact	however	eventually	for example	consequently
also	instead	nevertheless	finally	for instance	hence
besides	on the contrary	nonetheless	frequently	namely	therefore
furthermore	on the other hand	still	later	of course	thus
in addition	otherwise		meanwhile	undoubtedly	
moreover			subsequently		

ESL Teaching Tip: **Group Work** Ask nonnative speakers to underline transitional words that they do not understand. Then, in groups, those who understand the term can teach the others by using the term in a sentence. Ensure that nonnative speakers are placed in groups with native speakers.

If the second sentence begins with a transitional expression, put a semicolon before it and a comma after it.

Complete idea **; transitional expression,** complete idea

Truscott was not guilty**; nevertheless,** he was convicted.

PRACTICE 4 Combine sentences using the following transitional expressions. Choose an expression from the list, and try to use a different expression in each sentence. Answers will vary.

in fact	~~frequently~~	however	of course	for instance
therefore	moreover	nevertheless	thus	eventually

; frequently, it

EXAMPLE: DNA evidence is useful~~. It~~ has helped clear many innocent people.

1. In the past, many technicians looked at evidence through a
   ; for instance, t
   microscope~~. T~~hey might examine a strand of hair.

2. In the early 1990s, a comparison of hair samples could deliver a
   ; eventually, s
   conviction~~. S~~cientists developed more sophisticated techniques.

3. ; thus, h
   Dr. Edward Blake is a leading authority on DNA evidence~~. H~~e often testifies at trials.

4. ; nevertheless, i
   According to Dr. Blake, microscopic hair analysis is subjective~~. I~~t has secured convictions in many cases.

5. ; in fact, b
   Billy Gregory's hair matched a hair found at a crime scene~~. B~~oth strands of hair appeared identical.

6. ; however, t
   The strands of hair had exactly the same color and width~~. T~~hey were genetically different.

7. ; moreover, h
   In 1993, Gregory was convicted of the crime~~. H~~e was sentenced to life in prison.

8. ; of course, h
   In 2000, a DNA test cleared him~~. H~~e was able to go home.

9. Today, conventional hair comparison evidence is no longer allowed in most
   ; therefore, i
   courtrooms~~. I~~t may become an obsolete science.

Making Complex Sentences

When you combine a dependent and an independent clause, you create a **complex sentence.** An effective way to create complex sentences is to join clauses with a **subordinating conjunction.** "Subordinate" means secondary, so subordinating conjunctions are words that introduce secondary ideas.

If you use a subordinator at the beginning of a sentence, put a comma after the dependent clause. Generally, if you use a subordinator in the middle of the sentence, you do not need to use a comma.

Main idea	**subordinating conjunction**	secondary idea

The police arrived **because** <u>the alarm was ringing</u>.

Subordinating conjunction	secondary idea ,	main idea

Because <u>the alarm was ringing</u>, the police arrived.

Meanings of Subordinating Conjunctions

Subordinating conjunctions create a relationship between the clauses in a sentence.

Subordinating Conjunction	Indicates	Example
as, because, since, so that	a reason, cause, or effect	He paid a lot <u>because</u> he wanted a reliable alarm system.
after, before, since, until, when, whenever, while	a time	<u>After</u> he drove home, he parked on the street.
as long as, even if, if, provided that, so that, unless	a condition	The alarm won't ring <u>unless</u> someone touches the car.
although, even though, though	a contrast	<u>Although</u> the alarm began to wail, nobody looked at the car.
where, wherever	a location	<u>Wherever</u> you go, you will hear annoying car alarms.

Teaching Tip:
Remind students that in most cases there is no comma before *because*.

Teaching Tip:
You might write two short sentences on the board (example: *The defendant won her case. Crowds cheered.*), and ask students to join them with different subordinating conjunctions. Point out that the verb in the sentence would have to change to accommodate some of the conjunctions.

More About Complex Sentences

Complex sentences can have more than two clauses.

¹
<u>Although males commit most violent crimes</u>, ²<u>more and more females engage</u>
³
<u>in violent acts</u> <u>after they have joined gangs</u>.

You can also combine compound and complex sentences. The next example is a **compound-complex sentence.**

complex
<u>Although Alicia is tiny</u>, <u>she is strong</u>, and <u>she is a dedicated police officer</u>.
compound

PRACTICE 5 Add a missing subordinating conjunction to each sentence. Use each subordinating conjunction once. Answers will vary.

although	when	because	since
even though	if	unless	whenever

1. ___When___ a new television program about crime scene investigations is announced, many people watch it. Real-life lawyers and prosecutors get annoyed ___because___ members of the jury expect to see the same expensive, sophisticated crime-solving techniques used in average cases. ___Although___ the members of the jury are not experts, they believe they know a lot about crime investigations because they have picked up tidbits from crime shows.

2. It is very expensive and difficult to get DNA analyses ___unless___ the case is a very high profile and important one. ___Even though___ there is no DNA evidence, the case can still be very strong.

Teaching Tip: You might suggest that students do Practice 5 in pairs.

3. According to actor Robert Blake's defense lawyer, jurors will listen to detailed scientific evidence ___since___ they are used to watching those crime shows on television. The jury will find the defendant guilty ___whenever___ the evidence is solid. ___If___ the jury is unconvinced, the defendant might be released.

PRACTICE 6 Combine the sentences by adding a subordinating conjunction. Use a different subordinating conjunction in each sentence. Properly punctuate your sentences. Answers will vary.

EXAMPLE: He entered the courtroom. Photographers snapped photos.

As he entered the courthouse, photographers snapped photos.

Or *The photographers snapped photos as he entered the courthouse.*

1. Stephen was fourteen years old. He was arrested.

   When Stephen was fourteen years old, he was arrested.

2. He proclaimed his innocence. The police refused to believe him.

   Although he proclaimed his innocence, the police refused to believe him.

3. He was extremely nervous. He appeared to be guilty.

   Because he was extremely nervous, he appeared to be guilty.

4. He was in jail. He finished high school.

   While he was in jail, he finished high school.

5. New evidence surfaced. He was released.

   After new evidence surfaced, he was released.

Teaching Tip:
You can use the final review as a test. Additional practice and test material appears in the Instructor's Resource Manual and on *MyWritingLab*.

Teaching Tip:
Pair Work
You might ask students to do the final review with a partner. They can discuss possible combining options, and they can get ideas from each other.

Final Review

The following paragraphs only contain simple sentences. When sentences are not varied, the essay is boring to read. To give the paragraphs more sentence variety, combine at least fifteen sentences. You will have to add some words and delete others. Answers will vary.

When the *, she*

EXAMPLE: ~~The~~ witness is traumatized~~. She~~ might not remember her assailant's face.

, but how

1. Each day, you may see many faces~~. How~~ many will you remember? You *, and you* might recall the ones you see repeatedly~~. You~~ will forget the others. *; he* Dr. Rod Lindsay works at Queen's University~~. He~~ is an expert on eyewitness testimony. Dr. Lindsay says that it is not easy to remember faces. During a traumatic moment, the brain almost shuts down. *because he* Dr. Lindsay is worried~~. He~~ does not trust the methods used to collect eyewitness testimony.

2. In 1986, the police showed a crime victim a set of six photos~~. She~~ , and she felt a strong pressure to make a choice. One photo looked different than the others~~. It~~ because it was in color. The other photos were black and white. She picked the color photo~~. It~~ , but it was not the guilty man. According to Dr. Lindsay, all photos of suspects should have similar color and lighting to avoid biasing witnesses.

3. The best way to show photos is to show them sequentially. The witness must look at each photo~~. The~~ , and the witness must say "yes" or "no." He or she cannot go back to a previous picture. The witness must compare each photo to his or her memory. Dr. Lindsay contacted thirty-three police departments~~. Only~~ , and only nine showed photos of suspects sequentially.

4. According to experts, more police departments should use the "double blind" procedure. Sometimes, police officers know about the main suspect~~. They~~ ; therefore, they might cue the witness unconsciously. The double blind procedure ensures that the person showing the photos does not know the main suspect. When Dr. Lindsay contacted thirty-three police departments~~. Only~~ , only six used the double blind procedure.

5. Marvin Anderson spent fifteen years in jail~~. He~~ because he was convicted of rape. ~~The~~ When the witness pointed at him during the trial~~. She~~ , she identified him as her rapist. Many years later, DNA evidence cleared Anderson~~. He~~ , and he was released. Today, the lawyers see problems with the ways the photos of suspects were presented to the victim. Also, the officer may have "cued" the victim.

6. According to Dr. Lindsay, many people are wrongfully convicted~~.~~
when witnesses *, but the*
~~Witnesses~~ misidentify them. It is unfortunate~~. The~~ jury tends
even though it
to believe eyewitness testimony~~. It~~ can be seriously flawed.

The Writer's Room **Topics for Writing**

Teaching Tip:
Pair Work
Each student can peer-edit a partner's work. Ask them to look specifically for places where sentences can be combined. Students can also determine whether compound and complex sentences are properly written and punctuated.

Write about one of the following topics. Include some compound and some complex sentences.

1. Do you watch crime shows or read about crime? Describe a crime show, movie, or book.
2. What can people do to reduce the risk of being robbed? List several steps that people can take.

CHECKLIST: COMBINING SENTENCES

When you edit your writing, ask yourself these questions.

- Are my compound and complex sentences complete?

  He was arrested because
  ~~Because~~ of the scandal.
- Are my sentences correctly punctuated?
  - In compound sentences, place a comma before the coordinator.
  - In complex sentences, place a comma after a dependent introductory clause.

  Comma: The case was dismissed, and the suspect was freed.
  Comma: After she was released, she tried to find a job.
  No comma: She tried to find a job after she was released.

How Do I Get a Better Grade?
Visit www.mywritinglab.com for audio-visual lectures and additional practice sets about sentence combining.

mywritinglab

Get a better grade with MyWritingLab!

Sentence Variety

CHAPTER 22

CONTENTS

Section Theme **CONFLICT**

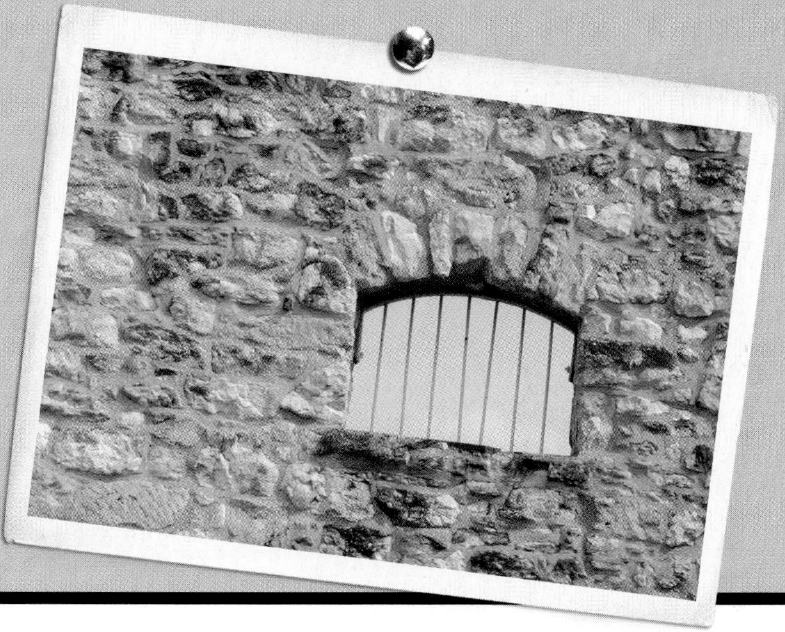

In this chapter, you will read about crime and prisons.

Grammar Snapshot

Looking at Sentence Variety

The next selections from *Crime, A Normal Phenomenon* by sociologist Emile Durkheim were translated from the original French. The first translation sounds choppy because the sentences are short and uniform in length. When the passage is rewritten with sentence variety, it flows more smoothly.

No Sentence Variety

Crime is normal. It exists in all societies. The type of crime may change. The form of crime may change. Everywhere and always there have been criminals.

Sentence Variety

Crime, which is normal, exists in all societies. The type or form of crime may change, but everywhere and always there have been criminals.

In this chapter, you will vary the length and structure of sentences to produce sentence variety.

Teaching Tip: Ask students to discuss how the sentences have been modified in the second version in the Grammar Snapshot.

CHAPTER 22

What Is Sentence Variety?

In Chapter 21, you learned about writing different types of sentences. In this chapter, you will learn to vary your sentences by consciously considering the length of sentences, by altering the opening words, and by joining sentences using different methods.

Teaching Tip: Draw attention to the hint. You might read aloud each selection, and then point out that the second selection is much easier to understand.

Hint **Be Careful with Long Sentences**

If your sentence is too long, it may be difficult for the reader to understand. Also, you may accidentally write run-on sentences. If you have any doubts, break up a longer sentence into shorter ones.

Long and complicated: In his book *Criminal Justice Today,* Frank Schmalleger describes a practice of the ancient Hebrews who sometimes punished a tribe by sending a sacrificial goat into the wilderness, and the goat, which was supposed to symbolically contain the tribe's sins, became the source of the modern word *scapegoat.*

Better: In his book *Criminal Justice Today,* Frank Schmalleger describes a practice of the ancient Hebrews. They sometimes punished a tribe by sending a sacrificial goat into the wilderness. The goat, which was supposed to symbolically contain the tribe's sins, became the source of the modern word *scapegoat.*

PRACTICE 1 Edit each long sentence by breaking it into smaller, more easily understood segments. Each segment must be a complete sentence.
Answers will vary.

1. Many early punishment methods were designed to publicly humiliate criminals, and one of the most common methods was to force an offender to stand in a public square with his or her head and hands secured so that everyone in the community would see that person, and often the local citizens would throw eggs and tomatoes at the offender, but sometimes they would throw rocks which could end the offender's life, so such retribution was permitted by the community, and ultimately citizens had the power to exact extreme punishment if they believed that the criminal deserved it.
2. In the eighteenth century, England sent convicts to the American colonies and to Australia, and the program, which was known as transportation, had two purposes, which included ridding Britain of undesirable criminals but

also of providing a captive force of workers who could help build roads, bridges, and housing for the people who were developing the colonies, so although many criminals had to go on long journeys and would never see their families again, they also had a much better life than they would have had if they had remained in Great Britain's damp and overcrowded prisons, so some may have been grateful for the chance to build a new life in a different country.

Varying the Opening Words

An effective way to make your sentences more vivid is to vary the opening words. Instead of beginning each sentence with the subject, you could try the following strategies.

Begin with an Adverb (*-ly* word)

An **adverb** is a word that modifies a verb, and it often (but not always) ends in *-ly*. *Quickly* and *frequently* are adverbs. Non *-ly* adverbs include words such as *sometimes* and *often*.

> Quickly, the criminal left the scene.

Begin with a Prepositional Phrase

A **prepositional phrase** is a group of words made up of a preposition and its object. *In the morning* and *at dawn* are prepositional phrases.

> On the courtroom steps, the defendant covered his head with his jacket.

Begin with a Present Participle (*-ing* Verb)

You can begin your sentence with a **present participle** or *-ing* word. Only combine sentences using an *-ing* modifier when the two actions happen at the same time.

> Reaching for her identification, she asked the officer why she had been pulled over.

Begin with a Past Participle (*-ed* Verb)

You can begin your sentence with a **past participle**, which is a verb that has an *-ed* ending. There are also many irregular past participles such as *gone*, *seen*, and *known*.

> Shocked, she stepped into the police cruiser.

GRAMMAR LINK

For a list of irregular past participles, see Appendix 2.

PRACTICE 2 Combine the sets of sentences using the indicated words.

EXAMPLE: The attacker was nervous. (-*ly* word)
He grabbed the purse.

Nervously, the attacker grabbed the purse.

1. The bystanders watched the police cruiser arrive. (-*ly* word)
   They were anxious.

   Anxiously, the bystanders watched the police cruiser arrive.

2. The bystanders were relieved. (-*ed* verb)
   They left the scene.

   Relieved, the bystanders left the scene.

3. The officers saw the people leave. (-*ed* verb)
   They were annoyed.

   Annoyed, the officers saw the people leave.

4. One witness gave the officers his name. (-*ly* word)
   He was reluctant.

   Reluctantly, one witness gave the officers his name.

5. The officers looked at the injured woman. (-*ing* verb)
   They felt upset.

   Feeling upset, the officers looked at the injured woman.

6. The guilty man raised his hands. (prepositional phrase)
   He did this with a grin.

   With a grin, the guilty man raised his hands.

Combining Sentences with an Appositive

An **appositive** is a word or phrase that gives further information about a noun or pronoun. You can combine two sentences by using an appositive. In the example, the italicized phrase could become an appositive because it describes the noun *Mr. Zlatko*.

Two sentences: Mr. Zlatko was *a middle-aged male*.
He lost his savings.

You can place the appositive directly before the word that it refers to or directly after that word. Notice that the appositives are set off with commas.

appositive

Combined: A middle-aged male, **Mr. Zlatko** lost his savings.

appositive

Mr. Zlatko, a middle-aged male, lost his savings.

PRACTICE 3 Combine the following pairs of sentences. In each pair, make one of the sentences an appositive. Try to vary the position of the appositive. Answers will vary.

EXAMPLE: The man, ~~was~~ an extravagant spender, ~~. He~~ owed money to many people.

Charles Dickens

1. Charles Dickens, ~~was~~ a British novelist, ~~. He~~ often wrote about Debtor's Prison.
2. Dickens lived in the 1800s, ~~. It was~~ a time when laws were very harsh.
3. His father, ~~was John Dickens.~~ John Dickens, was a poor businessman who often owed money to others.
4. When Charles was twelve years old, his father was taken to Marshalsea Debtor's Prison, ~~. It was~~ an event that changed the life of the boy.
5. The prison, ~~was~~ a filthy, crowded place, ~~. It~~ had no separate sections for males and females.
6. For the next six months, Charles left school, a place where he had been receiving a good education, and went to work in a shoe factory. ~~The school was a place where he had been receiving a good education.~~
7. When he was released from prison, John Dickens, a thinner, tired man, paid for Charles to return to school. ~~John Dickens was a thinner, tired man.~~
8. Charles Dickens, a talented writer, wrote about Debtor's Prison in many of his novels. ~~He was a talented writer.~~

CHAPTER 22

Combining Sentences with Relative Clauses

A **relative pronoun** describes a noun or pronoun. You can form complex sentences by using relative pronouns to introduce dependent clauses. Review the most common relative pronouns.

who whom whomever whose which that

ESL Teaching Tip: Draw attention to the spelling of *which.* It is a word that nonnative speakers commonly misspell.

Which

Use ***which*** to add nonessential information about a thing. Generally use commas to set off clauses that begin with *which.*

The crime rate, **which** peaked in the 1980s, has fallen in recent years.

GRAMMAR LINK

For more information about punctuating relative clauses, refer to Chapter 35.

That

Use ***that*** to add information about a thing. Do not use commas to set off clauses that begin with *that.*

The car **that** was stolen belonged to a police officer.

Teaching Tip: To help students understand essential versus nonessential information, give them the next sentences. Show them that some sentences can still be understandable without the *who* clause, whereas others can't. *The man who robbed me apologized. The man who torched the building was a dentist. Mr. Ray, who has two children, escaped from prison.*

Who

Use ***who*** (*whom, whomever, whose*) to add information about a person. When a clause begins with *who,* you may or may not need a comma. Put commas around the clause if it adds nonessential information. If the clause is essential to the meaning of the sentence, do not add commas. To decide if a clause is essential or not, ask yourself if the sentence still makes sense without the *who* clause. If it does, the clause is not essential.

The woman **who** committed the theft did not use a gun.
(The clause is essential. The sentence would not make sense without the *who* clause.)

The female thief, **who** spent a lot on legal fees, was sentenced to ten years in prison.
(The clause is not essential.)

Hint Using *That* or *Which*

Both *which* and *that* refer to things, but *which* refers to nonessential ideas. Also, *which* can imply that you are referring to the complete subject and not just a part of it. Compare the next two sentences.

> The shirts **that** had stains provided DNA evidence.
> (This sentence suggests that some shirts had no stains.)
>
> The shirts, **which** had stains, provided DNA evidence.
> (This sentence suggests that all of the shirts had stains.)

PRACTICE 4 Using a relative pronoun, combine each pair of sentences. Read both sentences before you combine them. Having the full context will help you figure out which relative pronoun to use. Answers will vary.

EXAMPLE: Sociologist Emile Durkheim ^*, who* was from France~~. He~~ ^*,* believed that deviant behavior can be good for societies.

1. Crime ^*, which* can vary from culture to culture~~. It~~ ^*,* sometimes forces societies to change and adapt.

2. In many countries, people ^*who* express their opinions about the government~~. These people~~ are breaking the law.

3. Last year, some citizens in China ^*who* criticized government policies~~. They~~ were arrested and imprisoned.

4. Some rigid governments ^*that* enact questionable laws~~. Those governments~~ may eventually collapse.

5. Definitions of criminal behavior ^*, which* are agreed on by citizens~~. The definitions~~ ^*,* can change over time.

6. For instance, in the 1960s, Americans ^*who* broke Jim Crow laws~~. They~~ were arrested.

Teaching Tip: The specific distinction between *which* and *that* is complicated, but students sometimes ask to know the difference. Here is another example to help clarify the difference between *that* and *which*. *Bears **that** have white fur live in the Arctic. Bears, **which** have white fur, live in the Arctic.* (The second sentence incorrectly suggests that all bears have white fur.)

CHAPTER 22

7. The activists ^who^ were treated as criminals~~. But they~~ actually helped change society.

8. Durkheim reflects ^that^ ~~about crime.~~ ^s^~~S~~ometimes there are positive consequences to criminal behavior.

9. However, Durkheim also warns people ^that d^~~. D~~eviance beyond a certain level can threaten the social order.

Teaching Tip: Remind students to put commas around *which* clauses. They should also be careful with *who* clauses; they should put commas around *who* clauses that contain nonessential information.

PRACTICE 5 Add dependent clauses to each sentence. Begin each clause with a relative pronoun (*who*, *which*, or *that*). Add any necessary commas.
Answers will vary.

EXAMPLE: The case ___*that involved an adolescent boy*___ was made into a documentary.

1. The boy ___*who was in the store*___ did not commit the crime.
2. His lawyers ___*, who were unpaid,*___ did not have all of the evidence.
3. The jury came to a conclusion ___*that was not accurate.*___
4. The judge sentenced the boy ___*who was innocent*___ to a long prison term.
5. The wrongfully convicted ___*, who might spend years in prison,*___ are sometimes never exonerated.
6. Sometimes mistakes ___*that could have been avoided*___ can change the lives of individuals.
7. The case ___*, which was widely publicized,*___ brought attention to the wrongfully convicted.

Teaching Tip: Draw attention to problems with embedded questions. You might put extra examples on the board. For example, you could write a question such as *How old is he?* or *Why did he plead guilty?*, and then ask the students to make the question embedded by adding *Do you know* or *I wonder.*

Writing Embedded Questions

It is possible to combine a question with a statement or to combine two questions. An **embedded question** is a question that is set within a larger sentence.

Question: How old was the victim?

Embedded question: The detectives wondered how old the victim was.

In questions, there is generally a helping verb before the subject. However, when a question is embedded in a larger sentence, remove the helping verb or place it after the subject. As you read the following examples, pay attention to the word order in the embedded questions.

1. **Combine two questions.**

   Separate: Why **do** people commit crimes? Do you know?
   (In both questions, the helping verb is *do*.)

   Combined: Do you know <u>why people commit crimes</u>?
   (The helping verb *do* is removed from the embedded question.)

2. **Combine a question and a statement.**

   Separate: How **should** society treat young offenders? I wonder about it.
   (In the question, the helping verb *should* appears before the subject.)

   Combined: I wonder <u>how society should treat young offenders.</u>
   (In the embedded question, *should* is placed after the subject.)

Hint **Use the Correct Word Order**

When you edit your writing, ensure that you have formed your embedded questions properly.

Dr. Alvarez wonders why ~~**do**~~ people commit crimes. I asked her what *she thought* ~~**did she think**~~ about the issue.

Teaching Tip: Both native and nonnative speakers make embedded question errors, so draw special attention to the hint.

PRACTICE 6 Edit six errors in embedded questions.

EXAMPLE: The writer explains how *people can* ~~can people~~ become criminals.

1. Many experts wonder why *the crime rate is* ~~is the crime rate~~ so high*.* ~~?~~ Parents may ask how *role models are* ~~are role models~~ a factor. They question how ~~do~~ negative models influence youths. Some blame icons in youth culture. For example, a recent

CHAPTER 22

newspaper report linked the hateful words found in some gangsta rap songs to youth crime.

2. However, it is unclear how ~~can people~~ *people can* only criticize singers or other celebrities from youth culture. In fact, they should really ask why ~~are so many "pillars" of society~~ *so many "pillars" of society are* deviant. Corporate executives have stolen from shareholders, and prominent religious figures have promoted intolerance and hatred. A reporter from San Diego asks why ~~have~~ so many people in highly regarded positions of authority *have* abused their power. Psychologists, sociologists, and criminologists are trying to find answers.

Teaching Tip: You can use the final review as a test. Additional practice and test material appears in the Instructor's Resource Manual and on *MyWritingLab*.

Final Review

The next essay lacks sentence variety. Use the strategies that you have learned in this chapter, and create at least ten varied sentences. Answers will vary.

EXAMPLE: Criminal profilers study crime scenes~~. They believe~~ *, believing* that they can determine the personality of the perpetrator.

1. Two people were at a bus stop. A large man *who* tried to take a woman's purse~~. He~~ was very aggressive. An innocent bystander intervened. He asked the man to leave the woman alone. ~~The~~ *Suddenly, the* thief pushed the bystander~~. This~~ *, which* caused the bystander to fall and crack his head on the pavement. The woman got onto the next bus.

2. The police arrived. ~~The~~ *Thinking that the situation was under control, the* witnesses left the scene. ~~They thought that the situation was under control.~~ Susan Helenchild*,* ~~is~~ a prosecutor~~. She~~*,* has advice for witnesses. ~~They~~ *Remaining at the crime scene, they* should give their names and addresses to police

Without evidence, a
officers. ~~They should remain at the crime scene. A~~ court cannot easily convict a guilty person. ~~The court needs evidence.~~

who
3. A girl ^ arrived after the crime had occurred~~. She~~ was interviewed by the police. She said nothing important. The prosecutor asked the police to
Earlier in the day, the
interview her again. ~~The~~ girl had seen the thief ~~earlier in the day~~. He was drunk and aggressive. In court, the thief claimed to be calm and gentle.
Blaming *, he*
~~He blamed~~ the victim for the crime~~. He~~ called the victim aggressive.
, which *,*
The girl's testimony ^ helped the prosecution~~. Her testimony~~ contradicted the words of the accused.

Officers often wonder why *.*
4. ~~Why do~~ witnesses leave crime scenes~~? Officers often wonder.~~ Sometimes witnesses believe they have nothing useful to add. Helenchild *,* ~~feels~~ frustrated with such witnesses*,*~~. She~~ says that any evidence can help the prosecution. Witnesses should always give contact information to police officers.

The Writer's Room **Topics for Writing**

Write about one of the following topics. Use a variety of sentence lengths.

1. What are some categories of criminals? Classify criminals into different types.
2. Why does criminal life seem exciting to some people? What factors contribute to make crime appealing?

READING LINK

Conflict

The following essays contain more information about law, order, and conflict.

"Little Brother Is Watching You" by Eric Gall (page 93)
"Types of Correctional Officers" by Frank Schmalleger (page 192)
"The CSI Effect" by Richard Willing (page 572)
"Types of Rioters" by David Locher (page 575)
"Naming Good Path Elk" by Kenneth M. Kline (page 580)

CHECKLIST: SENTENCE VARIETY

When you edit your writing, ask yourself the following questions.

☐ Are my sentences varied? Check for problems in these areas:

- too many short sentences
- long sentences that are difficult to follow

  Police departments examine strategies to lower the crime rate because they want to show they are being effective in
  . Sometimes
  the fight against crime ~~and sometimes~~ they present those strategies to the media.

☐ Do I have any embedded questions? Check for problems in these areas:

- word order
- unnecessary helping verbs

  I don't know why ~~do~~ people break the law.

How Do I Get a Better Grade?

Visit www.mywritinglab.com for audio-visual lectures and additional practice sets about sentence variety.
Get a better grade with MyWritingLab!

Fragments

CHAPTER 23

CONTENTS

- What Are Fragments?
- Phrase Fragments
- Fragments with *-ing* and *to*
- Explanatory Fragments
- Dependent-Clause Fragments

Section Theme **URBAN DEVELOPMENT**

In this chapter, you will read about the development of suburbs and cities.

Grammar Snapshot

Looking at Sentence Fragments

In his essay "Every Day Carless," Ewan Schmidt argues for a motorized vehicle–free downtown. The sentence fragments are underlined.

> The downtown core is very quiet each Friday. There are no car horns. No screeching of the brakes. No yelling. No loud motor noises. Because there are no cars. People can walk anywhere they want without worrying about traffic. Even in the middle of the street.

In this chapter, you will identify sentence fragments and write complete sentences.

Teaching Tip: Ask students to guess why the underlined sections are fragments. Also ask how to make each fragment into a complete idea.

What Are Fragments?

A **fragment** is an incomplete sentence. It lacks either a subject or a verb, or it fails to express a complete thought. You may see fragments in newspaper headlines and advertisements (*overnight weight loss*). You may also use fragments to save space when you are writing a text message. However, in college writing, it is unacceptable to write fragments.

Sentence: More and more people are moving to urban centers.

Fragment: In developing countries.

Teaching Tip:
Mention that although some professional writers may use fragments for effect, students should not use fragments in academic writing.

Phrase Fragments

Phrase fragments are missing a subject or a verb. In each example, the fragment is underlined.

No verb: The history of cities. It is quite interesting.

No subject: Ancient civilizations usually had one major city. Specialized in trades.

Teaching Tip:
Native and nonnative speakers often write sentence fragments. Emphasize how important it is to verify that all sentences in their writing express a complete idea. Students may need to review how to identify subjects and verbs. Refer them to Chapter 20.

How to Correct Phrase Fragments

To correct phrase fragments, add the missing subject or verb, or join fragment to another sentence. The following examples show how to correct the previous phrase fragments.

Join sentences: The history of cities is quite interesting.

Add words: Ancient civilizations usually had one major city. **The citizens in that city** specialized in trades.

Hint **Incomplete Verbs**

The following example is a phrase fragment because it is missing a helping verb. To make this sentence complete, you must add the helping verb.

Fragment: Modern cities growing rapidly.

Sentence: Modern cities are growing rapidly.

PRACTICE 1 Underline and correct ten phrase fragments.
Answers will vary.

EXAMPLE: Damascus is one of the world's oldest cities. ~~Founded~~ *It was founded* in the third millenium B.C.

1. The first cities began in ancient civilizations. Mesopotamia, the Indus Valley, and China~~. Those~~ were large ancient civilizations. Ancient cities such as Jericho, Harappa, and Mohenjo-daro had small populations~~.~~ ~~C~~*c*ompared to modern cities. For example, the first cities had only around 150,000 people. Eventually, ancient empires grew. Rome reached a population of one million. Baghdad~~. It~~ exceeded that number.
2. During the Middle Ages, some European cities became powerful city-states. Venice and Genoa even had their own military and maritime institutions. Around that time~~.~~*,* London became the largest city in the world. Paris *was* as populated as Beijing and Istanbul.
3. The Industrial Revolution was an important phenomenon for the growth of cities. In the eighteenth and nineteenth centuries~~. M~~*, m*any people migrated from the countryside to the urban centers. Urbanization led to many social problems. Child labor, low wages, and unsanitary living conditions~~. Those~~ were some common problems. Many reformers worked hard to improve the living conditions~~. Of~~ *of* the urban poor.
4. By the 1930s, the Great Depression raised the unemployment rate. In rural areas~~. Many~~*, many* people had to leave their farms and look for work in the cities. After World War II~~. Economic~~*, economic* prosperity helped to increase the migration to the cities. Most of today's cities are growing and prospering.

Teaching Tip:
Team Work
Ask students to generate the names of book, movie, and song titles. Write some of the titles on the board. Ask students to identify which titles are complete sentences. If all of the titles are fragments, then ask teams of students to create complete sentences out of the fragments.

CHAPTER 23

Fragments with *-ing* and *to*

A fragment may begin with a **present participle**, which is the form of the verb that ends in *-ing* (*running*, *talking*). It may also begin with an **infinitive**, which is *to* plus the base form of the verb (*to run*, *to talk*). These fragments generally appear next to another sentence that contains the subject. In the examples, the fragments are underlined.

***-ing* fragment:** Reacting to urban sprawl. City planners started a new movement in the 1980s and 1990s.

***to* fragment:** Urban designers believe in the new urbanism. To help people live better lives.

How to Correct *-ing* and *to* Fragments

To correct an *-ing* or *to* fragment, add the missing words or join the fragment to another sentence. The following examples show how to correct the two previous fragments.

Join sentences: Reacting to urban sprawl, city planners started a new movement in the 1980s and 1990s.

Add words: Urban designers believe in the new urbanism. **They want** to help people live better lives.

ESL

Teaching Tip: Nonnative speakers may confuse gerunds and progressive verb forms. Point out that gerunds function as nouns.

Hint **When the *-ing* Word Is the Subject**

Sometimes a gerund (*-ing* form of the verb) is the subject of a sentence. In the example, *cycling* is the subject of the sentence.

Correct sentence: Cycling is a great form of exercise in urban areas.

A sentence fragment occurs when the *-ing* word is part of an incomplete verb string or when you mention the subject in a previous sentence. In the example, the fragment is underlined.

Fragment: Many city dwellers get exercise. Cycling on bike paths.

PRACTICE 2 Underline and correct ten *-ing* and *to* fragments.

Answers will vary.

One principle is designing

EXAMPLE: The new urbanism movement has many principles. ~~Designing~~ walkways in neighborhoods.

1. New urbanism is a suburban planning movement~~. To create~~ to create <u>people-friendly neighborhoods</u>. <u>To limit the use of cars</u>~~. Urban~~ , urban planners design self-contained neighborhoods. <u>Believing in the need to curtail urban sprawl</u>~~. Architects~~ , architects pattern areas where people can walk to work and choose recreational activities close to home.
2. The new urbanism movement is a reaction against older suburban areas. After World War II, architects designed suburbs that relied heavily on the use of cars. Therefore, most people living in traditional suburbs have to commute to city centers~~. Creating~~ , creating <u>problems such as traffic congestion and air pollution</u>.
3. <u>Driving to work, school, and shopping areas</u>~~. Suburban~~ , suburban dwellers waste a lot of time traveling in their cars. In addition, urban sprawl creates difficulties for people who cannot drive~~. Limiting~~ , limiting <u>their daily activities</u>. <u>To do errands downtown or at a mall</u>~~. Non~~ , nondrivers must find other means of transport.
4. <u>To answer such concerns</u>~~. Urban~~ , urban designers reconsidered traditional suburban models. Since 1990, the new urbanism movement has become very popular. <u>To improve the quality of suburban life</u>~~. City~~ , city planners design beautiful areas for living, working, shopping, and playing. They hire innovative architects who insert skylights and green spaces in their designs. Presently, there are many communities in North America~~. Using~~ using <u>the principles of the new urban movement</u>.

Explanatory Fragments

An **explanatory fragment** provides an explanation about a previous sentence and is missing a subject, a complete verb, or both. These types of fragments begin with one of the following words.

also	especially	for example	including	particularly
as well as	except	for instance	like	such as

In the examples, the explanatory fragment is underlined.

Fragment: Planners in the 1960s influenced the new urbanism movement. For example, Jane Jacobs.

Fragment: New urbanism planners take into consideration many factors. Especially reducing the use of the automobile.

How to Correct Explanatory Fragments

To correct explanatory fragments, add the missing words, or join the explanation or example to another sentence. The following examples show how to correct the previous explanatory fragments.

Teaching Tip: Ask students to pay particular attention to explanatory fragments, as they are the most common types of fragments.

Add words: Planners in the 1960s influenced the new urbanism movement. For example, Jane Jacobs **was an important authority on urban planning**.

Join sentences: New urbanism planners take into consideration many factors, especially reducing the use of the automobile.

PRACTICE 3 Underline and correct ten explanatory fragments. You may need to add or remove words. Answers will vary.

EXAMPLE: Some new urbanism towns are famous~~. Such as~~ , such as Celebration.

1. New urbanists plan communities with a central downtown area that is walking distance from all neighborhoods. The first community built on the new urbanism principles is Seaside, Florida. It was started in 1981 and became very famous. For example, *The Atlantic Monthly*~~. It~~ featured Seaside on its cover. Robert Davis bought the land to build the community. He

hired many people who followed the principles of the new urbanism philosophy~~. Such~~ *, such* as architects and urban planners.

2. Seaside was relatively easy to build because the area did not have the traditional rules for developing land. For instance, *there were* no zoning regulations. The buildings in the town have uniform designs~~. Particularly~~ *, particularly* the houses. They all have certain features, including porches that must be sixteen feet from the sidewalk. Also, the streets~~. They~~ must be made of bricks so cars cannot speed.

3. There are many other towns~~. Like~~ *like* Seaside. The most famous of these is the one Disney has built in Florida called Celebration. It also has strict rules for conformity. For example, the windows~~. They~~ must be decorated with white or off-white curtains. The houses are built close together. For instance, *they are* only twenty feet apart. In Celebration, if neighbors complain about a barking dog, the dog can be evicted from the town.

4. Many people criticize those types of communities~~. Especially~~ *, especially* regarding the conformity of the design. On the other hand, people moving to those towns hope to live in an ideal community. For example, *they would like* no crime or social problems. However, critics point out that all communities have some social problems.

Dependent-Clause Fragments

A **dependent clause** has a subject and verb, but it cannot stand alone. It literally depends on another clause to be a complete sentence. Dependent clauses may begin with subordinating conjunctions or relative pronouns. The following list contains some of the most common words that begin dependent clauses.

Common Subordinating Conjunctions				Relative Pronouns
after	before	though	whenever	that
although	even though	unless	where	which
as	if	until	whereas	who(m)
because	since	what	whether	whose

ESL Teaching Tip: Nonnative speakers may have trouble distinguishing between complete clauses and fragments that begin with subordinators. They may not be able to distinguish between a transitional word such as *however* and a subordinator such as *although*. Place nonnative speakers with native speakers to do Practice 4.

In each example, the fragment is underlined.

Fragment: In the city, houses are close together. <u>Whereas in the suburbs, houses have large yards.</u>

Fragment: <u>Before William Levitt built Levittown.</u> Many people lived in congested neighborhoods.

How to Correct Dependent-Clause Fragments

To correct dependent-clause fragments, join the fragment to a complete sentence, or add the necessary words to make it a complete idea. You could also delete the subordinating conjunction. The following examples show how to correct the previous dependent-clause fragments.

Delete subordinator: In the city, houses are close together. In the suburbs, houses have large yards.

Join sentences: Before William Levitt built Levittown, many people lived in congested neighborhoods.

PRACTICE 4 Underline and correct ten dependent-clause fragments.
Answers will vary.

EXAMPLE: William Levitt and his brother built Levittown~~. Because~~ [because] of a shortage of affordable housing.

1. In 1948, developer William Levitt built a community in Pennsylvania~~. Which~~ [, which] <u>has been designated the first traditional suburb.</u> Levitt wanted to give returning soldiers the opportunity to participate in the American dream. He called his community Levittown. This town consisted of similarly built single-family homes~~. That~~ [that] <u>attracted young</u>

families. People wanted to escape the crowds of big cities like New York and Philadelphia. Homes in large cities were very expensive~~.~~ *whereas* Levittown contained affordable housing. The community grew to approximately 17,000 houses~~. Which~~ *, which* led to the beginning of urban sprawl.

2. Some people criticized the idea of Levittown~~. Because~~ *because* all of the houses looked similar. Even though the town had four different house styles~~. The~~ *, the* first residents sometimes got lost trying to find their homes. Although it began with the premise of affordable housing for everyone~~.~~*,* Levittown initially discriminated against nonwhites and did not permit them to buy houses in the community. Eventually, Levittown abandoned its "whites-only" policy. In 1957, the first African Americans to buy a house there were Bill and Daisy Meyers~~. Who~~ *, who* had rocks thrown at them by the other residents.

3. Because Levittown is getting older~~. It~~ *, it* has become a more attractive suburb. Many homeowners have remodeled their homes, and the saplings have grown into mature trees. Although many other suburbs have developed~~.~~*,* Levittown remains a model of traditional suburban living.

CHAPTER 23

Final Review

The following paragraphs contain the four types of fragments: phrase, explanatory, *-ing* and *to*, and dependent clause. Correct fifteen fragment errors.

Answers will vary.

EXAMPLE: Tourists have been coming to Tokyo~~. Since~~ *since* World War II.

Teaching Tip:
You can use the final review as a test. Additional practice and test material appears in the Instructor's Resource Manual and on *MyWritingLab*.

1. Tokyo, the world's largest city~~. It~~ *,* was originally called Edo. The Edo warrior family inhabited a marshy region of Japan~~. Where~~ *where* there were a few villages. Eventually, the town of Edo grew. It started to gain prominence in the 1600s. In 1603, Edo warrior Tokugawa Ieyasu became shogun or warlord of the region. He was so powerful that he moved the government from Kyoto to Edo~~. Thinking~~ *, thinking* that he would have more control over politics. He acquired complete control over Japan. Quelling any opposition~~. His~~ *, his* government promoted an isolationist policy. Japan had no contact with other nations~~. Until~~ *until* the nineteenth century.

2. From the seventeenth century to the nineteenth century, Japan was politically stable, allowing Edo's population to grow rapidly to about one million people. Both London and Paris had a smaller population~~. At~~ *at* that time. Edo became the economic center of Japan~~. Prospering~~ *, prospering* greatly due to industry. Also at that time, Japanese society developed a class system. ~~Based~~ *based* on four levels of hierarchy. The samurai or warriors were at the top of the social system.

3. The Tokugawa Ieyasu family's power collapsed by the 1850s~~. Because~~ *because* of corruption within its government. At the same time, the Western powers were pressuring Japan~~. To~~ *to* open trade. England and the United States wanted Japan as a trading post. For example, in 1853, Matthew Perry~~. He~~ forced Japan to open trade relations with America. Japan westernized

after
rapidly~~. After~~ its contact with Europe and America. In 1867, Edo's name was changed to Tokyo.

4. Since the late 1800s~~.~~, Tokyo has modernized like other Western capitals. In 1923, a great earthquake destroyed much of the city, and rebuilding became a priority. Many structures were built~~. Such~~ , such as a subway system in 1927, an airport in 1931, and a port in 1941. After World War II, Tokyo greatly expanded. Today, it is a mega metropolis~~. Inviting~~ , inviting visitors from all around the world.

The Writer's Room Topics for Writing

Write about one of the following topics. Check that there are no sentence fragments.

1. Write about where you live. Describe your neighborhood.
2. What are some similarities and differences between living in a city and living in a suburb?

Patricia Schwimmer (Canadian, b. 1953) "My San Francisco", 1994, Tempera, Private Collection. © Patricia Schwimmer/SuperStock.

Teaching Tip:
Pair Work
Each student can peer edit a partner's work. Ask them to look specifically for sentence fragments.

CHECKLIST: SENTENCE FRAGMENTS

When you edit your writing, ask yourself this question.

☐ Are my sentences complete? Check for the next types of fragments.

- phrase fragments
- *-ing* and *to* fragments
- explanatory fragments
- dependent-clause fragments

Los Angeles and San Francisco are moving closer together~~. Because~~ *because* of the San Andreas fault. The two cities will make the largest urban area in the world~~. If~~ *if* the movement continues.

How Do I Get a Better Grade?

mywritinglab

Visit www.mywritinglab.com for audio-visual lectures and additional practice sets about fragments.
Get a better grade with MyWritingLab!

Run-Ons

CHAPTER 24

CONTENTS

Section Theme **URBAN DEVELOPMENT**

In this chapter, you will read about architects and architecture.

Grammar Snapshot

Looking at Run-Ons

Darius Knightley is a freelance travel writer. The next excerpt about his recent trip to Barcelona contains a sentence error. The underlined error is a run-on.

> Barcelona is a city of contrasts. Visitors see medieval buildings, narrow streets, and grandiose churches they also see grid-like neighborhoods, modernist architecture, and glass and steel places of worship. The modern sections of the city contrast with the older areas.

In this chapter, you will learn to correct run-on sentences.

Teaching Tip:
Ask students to guess why the underlined sentence in the Grammar Snapshot is a run-on. Also have students discuss how to correct the error.

What Are Run-Ons?

A **run-on sentence** occurs when two or more complete sentences are incorrectly joined. In other words, the sentence runs on without stopping.

There are two types of run-on sentences.

CHAPTER 24

1. A **fused sentence** has no punctuation to mark the break between ideas.

   Incorrect: Skyscrapers are unusually tall buildings the Taipei 101 tower is among the tallest.

2. A **comma splice** uses a comma incorrectly to connect two complete ideas.

   Incorrect: The CN Tower is located in Toronto, it is the world's tallest communication structure.

Teaching Tip:
Remind students that run-ons are not necessarily long sentences. For the following sentences, ask students which one is the run-on:

The Eiffel Tower is in Paris, it's an impressive structure.

The Eiffel Tower, which is in Paris, is an impressive structure that is made of steel, and millions of people visit it every year.

PRACTICE 1 Read the following sentences. Write C beside correct sentences, FS beside fused sentences, and CS beside comma splices.

EXAMPLE: Gustave Eiffel was born in 1832 he designed the Eiffel Tower and the Statue of Liberty. FS

1. One of the most recognizable modern structures is the Eiffel Tower, it was built at the end of the eighteenth century. CS
2. The French government wanted to celebrate the centennial anniversary of the French Revolution, which took place in 1789. C
3. The government held a competition it invited architects to submit designs to commemorate the anniversary of the revolution. FS
4. Winners of the competition would have their designs displayed at the World's Fair of 1889. C
5. Many architects submitted designs, Gustave Eiffel's tower design won. CS
6. The tower took twenty-six months to complete it was the tallest structure in the world at that time. FS
7. It was 1,051 feet tall and weighed 70,000 tons. C
8. Many Parisians did not like the look of the tower, they wanted to destroy it. CS
9. But it proved to be a very popular tourist attraction people from all over the world visit Paris and climb the tower. FS
10. In fact, tourism experts consider the Eiffel Tower as the number one tourist attraction in the world. C

Teaching Tip:
If you think the distinction between fused sentences and comma splices is not important, you could ask your students to identify both types of run-ons by writing "RO."

Correcting Run-Ons

You can correct both fused sentences and comma splices in a variety of ways. Read the following run-on sentence, and then review the four ways to correct it.

Run-On: Antoni Gaudi began his career as a secular architect he eventually became very religious.

1. Make two separate sentences by adding end punctuation, such as a period.

   Antoni Gaudi began his career as a secular architect**. He** eventually became very religious.

2. Add a semicolon (;).

   Antoni Gaudi began his career as a secular architect**;** he eventually became very religious.

3. Add a coordinating conjunction such as *for, and, nor, but, or, yet,* or *so*.

   Antoni Gaudi began his career as a secular architect**, but** he eventually became very religious.

4. Add a subordinating conjunction such as *although, because, when, before, while, since,* or *after*.

   Although Antoni Gaudi began his career as a secular architect, he eventually became very religious.

CHAPTER 24

Teaching Tip: To better understand how to correct run-ons, students may need to review types of sentences. Refer them to Chapter 21.

Teaching Tip: Tell students that people often use *coordinator* and *subordinator* as shortened forms of coordinating conjunctions and subordinating conjunctions.

PRACTICE 2 Correct the run-ons by making two complete sentences.

EXAMPLE: Antoni Gaudi designed very interesting works~~, he~~ *. He* is considered to be a genius.

1. Antoni Gaudi was born in 1852 in Tarragona, Spain ~~he~~ *. He* is considered to be Catalonia's greatest architect.

2. Gaudi became a Catholic ~~he~~ *. He* also believed in Catalan nationalism.

3. Gaudi designed the *Sagrada Familia* ~~he~~ *. He* wanted to express his Catholic faith in his work.

4. Nature fascinated Gaudi~~, he~~ *. He* incorporated nature's images into his creations.

5. Classical design used geometric shapes Gaudi's designs mimicked shapes from nature.

6. Gaudi's style evolved from Gothic influences~~, he~~ *. He* created intricate, flowing, asymmetrical shapes.

7. Businessmen in Barcelona commissioned Gaudi to design a modern neighborhood~~, he~~ *. He* constructed many buildings like the Casa Mila.

8. His work used the *trencadis* style ~~this~~ *. This* style involves the use of broken tiles to decorate surfaces.

9. One of Gaudi's most famous designs is Park Guell~~, the~~ *. The* park has dragon-shaped benches and tree-shaped columns.

10. Many people initially laughed at Gaudi's vision ~~eight~~ *. Eight* of his creations are now recognized as World Heritage Sites.

Teaching Tip: Point out that the opening photo in this chapter is a Gaudi design.

Hint Semicolons and Transitional Expressions

Another way to correct run-ons is to connect sentences with a transitional expression. Place a semicolon before the expression and a comma after it.

Example: The construction costs were too high**; therefore,** the town abandoned plans to build city hall.

The design was beautiful**; nevertheless,** it was rejected.

Some common transitional expressions are:

additionally	meanwhile	of course
furthermore	moreover	therefore
however	nevertheless	thus

To practice combining sentences with transitional expressions, see Chapter 21.

PRACTICE 3 Correct the run-ons by joining the two sentences with a semicolon. Answers will vary.

EXAMPLE: I. M. Pei has designed many famous buildings the John F. Kennedy Library is just one.

1. The Louvre Palace is one of the most recognized buildings in Paris, it was built in the Renaissance style for French monarchs.
2. The French Revolution abolished the monarchy the Louvre became a museum.
3. French officials wanted to expand the Louvre, they hired a famous architect to modify the building.
4. I. M. Pei was born in China in 1917 he immigrated to the United States to study architecture.
5. The French government commissioned Pei to enlarge the museum, he designed three pyramids for the entrance.
6. The main pyramid gives light to the underground entrance, it is made of many glass squares.
7. The pyramid is about seventy feet high, it has two smaller pyramids on each side.
8. The pyramids were completed in 1989 many people thought the entrance was unattractive.
9. I. M. Pei is an outstanding architect his innovative designs have won many prizes.

PRACTICE 4 Correct the run-ons by joining the two sentences with a comma and a coordinator (*for*, *and*, *nor*, *but*, *or*, *yet*, *so*). Answers will vary.

EXAMPLE: Arthur Erickson is a Canadian architect *, and* his designs are world famous.

1. The University of British Columbia has many beautiful buildings *, but* Arthur Erickson's Museum of Anthropology is the most beautiful.

Museum of Anthropology

2. The museum rooms are high and spacious *, so* they can house large totems of the northwest First Nations.

3. The museum contains unusual artifacts, *and* its totem pole collection is very interesting.

4. Architect Arthur Erickson considers the environment important *, so* his designs must fit into the landscape.

5. Erickson was an inexperienced architect *, yet* his design won first place in a competition.

6. Many architects entered the competition *, but* Erickson's design was the most innovative.

7. The first-place winner was asked to design Simon Fraser University *, so* Erickson evaluated the surroundings.

8. The site was on top of a mountain *, and* it overlooked the ocean.

9. Erickson could follow the design trend of the time *, or* he could design according to his personal vision.

10. Simon Fraser University fits into the landscape *, and* its buildings are built into the mountainside.

PRACTICE 5 Correct the run-ons by joining the two sentences with a **subordinator.** Use one of the following subordinators: *because*, *before*, *although*, *when*, *even though*, and *although*. If the dependent clause comes at the beginning of the sentence, remember to add a comma. Answers will vary.

EXAMPLE: *Even though* European ideas have influenced African architecture, many indigenous designs reveal beauty and practicality.

1. *Although* African architecture is not that well known, it is very rich and diverse.
2. African architecture was influenced by Arabs *when* they colonized North Africa.
3. *Before* Europeans arrived in the sixteenth century, Islam provided inspiration for architectural design.
4. Until the twenty-first century, there were very few famous African architects *because* African countries were controlled by European powers.
5. *Even though modern* ~~Modern~~ African buildings are beautiful, they are not appreciated as World Heritage Sites.
6. *After the* ~~The~~ Aswan Dam, one of the most famous dams in the world, was constructed in the twentieth century, the Nile River no longer flooded each year.

because

7. The construction of the Aswan Dam was controversial people were concerned about its impact on the environment.

When the ,

8. ~~The~~ Eastgate Centre was built in Harare it became the world's first modern building to use natural cooling methods.

because

9. Modern African architecture is gaining momentum architects are considering the unique needs of Africa.

PRACTICE 6 Use a variety of methods to correct ten run-on errors. Add commas when necessary. Answers will vary.

and

EXAMPLE: Many new buildings are being erected all over China, ^ modern building designs are very popular.

When the ,

1. ~~The~~ Chinese Revolution dominated politics China's government developed policies to minimize class differences. As a result, new buildings were designed for utility with no regard for beauty.

, and

2. Now, China is industrializing at a great rate businesses are asking architects to design practical but beautiful buildings. The National Theatre

yet Even though it

building, for example, is controversial, it is also extremely intriguing. ~~It~~ was designed by French architect Paul Andreu, many people have criticized

and

its design. It is shaped like an egg. It has three halls and a lake, it has a bridge. Another highly discussed building in Beijing is the CCTV tower.

Because it

~~It~~ looks like the letter *Z*, many Chinese think it is an eyesore.

and

3. The cost of building these edifices is very expensive, some members of the public complain that such designs are too foreign. Others believe that

designing interesting buildings is very important[.] China built a fabulous stadium for the 2008 Olympics. The Olympic Stadium is a necessity, [yet] the cost was prohibitive.

4. The Beijing skyline has changed, [but] not everybody has liked the changes. Some say that such change is the price for industrialization. Average citizens are eager for Beijing to join the ranks of the most beautiful cities in the world.

FINAL REVIEW

Correct ten run-on errors. Answers will vary.

Teaching Tip: You can use the final review as a test. Additional practice and test material appears in the Instructor's Resource Manual and on *MyWritingLab*.

EXAMPLE: The construction industry is the largest in the world, [and public] ~~public~~ and private buildings consume a lot of energy.

1. When most people envision cities, they think about houses, roads, and skyscrapers built above ground[;] they do not think about subterranean cities. However, many people use underground public and private buildings every day. In North America, there are at least five hundred public and private underground buildings[. For] ~~for~~ example, the Engineering Library at the University of Berkeley and the Vietnam Veterans Memorial Education Center are only two such subterranean structures. More and more underground structures are being built every day.

2. Some of the oldest underground cities are located in Cappadocia, Turkey[. The] ~~the~~ first underground city in that area was constructed around 2000 BC. Archaeologists believe that at one time, up to twenty thousand

Entrance to tunnels in Cappadocia.

because
people lived in those underground Turkish cities the early Christians used them as a means to escape persecution.

3. Montreal, Canada, contains an extremely large modern underground city.
, and
It was designed by I. M. Pei in the 1960s other architects have contributed to its expansion. It is located downtown and has around 26 miles of tunnels with about 120 exterior access points. More than 500,000 people use the
because
underground city each day they want to avoid Montreal's very cold temperatures in the winter.

4. There are many reasons to build underground. First, underground buildings
. Architects
benefit from better climate control ~~architects~~ say that such buildings can be heated and cooled more efficiently than above-ground buildings. Also,
;
building underground reduces the impact on the environment~~,~~ forests and fields do not have to be cleared. Moreover, the wind, snow, and rain do not
and
erode the walls, well-constructed underground buildings are resistant to fire and earthquakes.

5. Perhaps in the future, there will be more underground public and private
because
buildings~~,~~ they are more environmentally friendly and more energy efficient. Certainly it is time to rethink how urban planners design cities.

The Writer's Room **Topics for Writing**

Write about one of the following topics. Edit your writing and ensure that there are no run-ons.

1. Are there any buildings or areas in your neighborhood, town, or country that you find attractive or unattractive? Describe these buildings and explain why you believe they are beautiful or unsightly.
2. Are there any changes or additions that you would make to the town or city where you live, such as adding a new park or a museum? What suggestions would you make to city planners?

CHECKLIST: RUN-ONS

When you edit your writing, ask yourself this question.

- Are my sentences correctly formed and punctuated? Check for and correct any fused sentences and comma splices.

  One of the most successful architects in the world is Frank Lloyd ~~Wright his~~ *Wright. His* famous house design "Falling Water" is a national monument.

How Do I Get a Better Grade?

mywritinglab

Visit www.mywritinglab.com for audio-visual lectures and additional practice sets about run-ons.
Get a better grade with MyWritingLab!

25 CHAPTER Faulty Parallel Structure

CONTENTS

- What Is Parallel Structure?
- Correcting Faulty Parallel Structure

Section Theme **URBAN DEVELOPMENT**

In this chapter, you will read about landscapes and gardens.

Teaching Tip:
Ask students to guess why the underlined sentences might be called "parallel structure."

Grammar Snapshot

Looking at Parallel Structure

The Royal Botanic Gardens in Kew, England, supports research on conservation of the environment. The following paragraph summarizes one of the conservation schemes in Peru. Review the underlined ideas to see how they are parallel.

The Huarango (*Prosopis pallida*) forests of the south coast of Peru are among the most highly threatened ecosystems on earth. The remaining trees are important primary producers, forming soil, preventing desertification, and providing the only refuge for biodiversity in large areas of hyperarid desert. They also furnish an extraordinary cornucopia of food, forage, and other products used by local people for thousands of years.

In this chapter, you will identify and correct faulty parallel structure.

What Is Parallel Structure?

Parallel structure occurs when pairs or groups of items in a sentence are balanced. Notice how the following sentences repeat grammatical structures but not ideas.

Parallel Nouns: Books, stores, and catalogs give gardeners information.

Parallel Tenses: Gardeners dig and plant in the soil.

Parallel Adjectives: Kew Garden is large, colorful, and breathtaking.

Parallel Phrases: You will find the public garden down the road, over the bridge, and through the field.

Parallel Clauses: There are some gardens that have just trees, and some that have only flowers and plants.

Teaching Tip: Discuss the meaning of *parallel*. You could give the example of parallel bars used in gymnastics. The bars have the same size and shape and are equal distances apart.

Correcting Faulty Parallel Structure

Use parallel structure for a series of words or phrases, for paired clauses, for comparisons, and for two-part constructions. If you see "//" or simply "faulty parallelism" on one of your marked essays, try the following tips for correcting those errors.

Series of Words or Phrases

Use parallel structure when words or phrases are joined in a series.

Not Parallel: The English, the Chinese, and people from Japan create luxurious gardens.

Parallel Nouns: The English, the Chinese, and the Japanese create luxurious gardens.

Not Parallel: I like to read books about gardens, to attend lectures about gardening, and buying plants for my garden.

Parallel Verbs: I like to read books about gardens, to attend lectures about gardening, and to buy plants for my garden.

Paired Clauses

Use parallel structure when independent clauses are joined by *and*, *but*, or *or*.

Not Parallel: I am allergic to grass seed, and ragweed also gives me allergies.

Parallel Word Order: I am allergic to grass seed, and I am also allergic to ragweed.

Not Parallel: The tourists were dazzled, but they also had a feeling of fatigue.

Parallel Adjectives: The tourists were dazzled, but they were also fatigued.

Teaching Tip:
Ask students to describe a beautiful sight in nature and to include many nouns and adjectives in their sentences. Write them on the board. Then the group can ensure that the words are parallel.

Hint **Use Consistent Voice**

When joining two independent clauses with a coordinating conjunction, use a consistent voice. For example, if the first part of the sentence uses the active voice, the other part should also use the active voice.

Not parallel: The bees flew (active) to the flowers, and then the nectar was tasted (passive) by them.

Parallel active voice: The bees flew (active) to the flowers, and then they tasted (active) the nectar.

PRACTICE 1 Underline and correct the faulty parallel structure in each sentence.

The Winter Palace

EXAMPLE: The Hermitage, which was the Winter Palace of the Russian Tsars, has a collection of valuable paintings, rare books, and furniture that is antique.

antique furniture

1. Tsar Peter the Great was cosmopolitan, educated, and he had great determination.

   determined

2. In 1703, Peter created plans and workers were ordered to build a new city.

   ordered workers

3. The Tsar commissioned a summer palace and a palace for the winter.

   winter palace

4. The Tsar designed parks, flower gardens, and he was also creating
   arboretums
   arboretums.

   , and rare
5. The summer garden contains large, exotic trees that are rare.

6. The landscaper, Domenico Trezzini, worked fastidiously, diligently, and
   creatively
   he was creative.

7. Tourists can stroll down paths, over bridges, and ~~walking~~ by marble statues.

8. St. Petersburg is called the "window to the west," "the city of the white nights," and ~~people also view it as~~ "the northern Venice."

Comparisons

Use parallel structure in comparisons containing *than* or *as*.

Not Parallel:	Designing an interesting garden is easier than to take care of it.
Parallel *-ing* Forms:	Designing an interesting garden is easier than taking care of it.
Not Parallel:	The rock garden looks as colorful as the garden where there are roses.
Parallel Noun Phrases:	The rock garden looks as colorful as the rose garden.

Two-Part Constructions

Use parallel structure for the following paired items.

either . . . or	not . . . but	both . . . and
neither . . . nor	not only . . . but also	rather . . . than

Not Parallel:	The lecture on landscaping was both enlightening and of use.
Parallel Adjectives:	The lecture on landscaping was both enlightening and useful.

Not Parallel:	I could either see the bonsai exhibit or going to a film.
Parallel Verbs:	I could either <u>see</u> the bonsai exhibit or <u>go</u> to a film.

PRACTICE 2 Correct ten errors in parallel construction.

EXAMPLE: Cities need parks to create green areas, to prevent overcrowding,
to develop recreational facilities
and <u>people can use them for recreation.</u>

1. During the Industrial Revolution, urban life changed rapidly and
completely
<u>with completion</u>. City planners realized that more people were moving to
immigrants
the cities. Planners, politicians, and <u>people who immigrated</u> saw city life
changing. Urban designers wanted to create green space rather than
to fill
<u>filling</u> cities with concrete buildings.

2. One of the most important advocates of city beautification was Frederick Law Olmsted. He was born in 1822, in Hartford, Connecticut. He not
designed
only promoted urban planning, but he also <u>was designing</u> beautiful city gardens. He and collaborator Calvert Vaux designed New York's Central Park. Olmsted wanted the park to reflect his personal philosophy, so in it
winding paths
he created open spaces, beautiful views, and <u>paths that wind</u>.

3. Olmsted and Vaux designed many other projects. An important design was the Niagara Falls project. At that time, the falls were not completely visible to tourists. Olmsted wanted to create a harmonious landscape,
to conserve the area.
to allow greater tourist accessibility, and <u>conservation of the area</u>

was important to him. Such a park required a great deal of planning. Goat Island separates Canada from the United States. Either the landscapers
could continue
could buy Goat Island or Goat Island was continuing to be an eyesore. Olmsted and Vaux bought the island and restored it.

4. For Olmsted, contributing to the community was more important than
having he planned
to have fame. He designed Mount Royal Park in Montreal, and the 1893 World Fair in Chicago was also planned by him. He was known as much
his respect of
for his sense of beauty as for respecting the environment. Olmsted died in 1903, but thousands of people continue to enjoy his legacy.

Teaching Tip: You can use the final review as a test. Additional practice and test material appears in the Instructor's Resource Manual and on *MyWritingLab*.

Final Review

Correct fifteen errors in parallel construction.

Answers will vary.

EXAMPLE: Walking through Kew Gardens is more relaxing than
reading
to read a book.

1. One of London's most famous sites is the Royal Botanic Gardens.
stone sculptures
Kew Gardens contains flower beds, greenhouses, and there are stone sculptures. In the 1700s, King George III commissioned and was
supported
supporting the garden's expansion. Since then, not only has Kew
has become
been enlarged, but it was becoming a World Heritage site. To visit Kew Gardens, travel over the Thames, along the edge of Kew village, and ~~you must go~~ past the Kew Gardens subway station.

2. Today, at Kew Gardens, botanical research is as important as <u>attracting</u>
   tourism
   <u>people who are tourists</u>. The site is important for storing seeds, cataloguing
   training professional gardeners
   plants, and <u>professional gardeners go there for training</u>. But, modernization is creating problems for Kew. Being so close to London, Kew experiences
   small amounts of rainfall
   air pollution, hot weather, and <u>the rainfall is in small amounts</u>. Even with such problems, Kew is truly beautiful, very innovative, and ~~it is also~~ extremely impressive.

3. Another famous European garden is the Versailles garden near Paris, France. King Louis XIV moved his court from Paris to Versailles in 1682, and he asked the great landscaper Andre Le Notre to design the gardens.
   passionately
   Le Notre worked carefully, intuitively, and <u>with passion</u>. Le Notre not
   he also had to bring water
   only had to plan a garden, but <u>water also had to be brought</u> to the site <u>by</u>
   nor
   <u>him</u>. The original soil was neither rich <u>and it was not</u> fertile.

4. Le Notre succeeded in his design. It is perfectly laid out, adhering to Renaissance principles. The gardens have walkways, fountains, statues, and ~~there are~~ ponds. The gardens reflect the glory of the king, the beauty of
   the creativity of humans
   nature, and <u>human creativity</u>. Le Notre received great fame, honor, and
   wealth
   <u>was wealthy</u>. Millions of visitors visit Versailles to enjoy the gardens, to
   to see
   understand a part of history, and <u>seeing</u> the splendor of the age of Louis XIV.

CHAPTER 25

The Writer's Room Topics for Writing

Choose one of the following topics, and write a paragraph. Make sure your nouns, verbs, and sentence structures are parallel.

1. If you could be anywhere right now, where would you be? Describe that place. Include details that appeal to the senses.
2. What do you do to relax? List some steps.

CHECKLIST: PARALLEL STRUCTURE

When you edit your writing, ask yourself this question.

☐ Are my grammatical structures balanced? Check for errors in these cases:

- when words or phrases are joined in a series
- when independent clauses are joined by *and*, *but*, or *or*
- when you make comparisons

English gardens
We saw Chinese gardens, Japanese gardens, and ~~gardens from England~~.

How Do I Get a Better Grade?

mywritinglab

Visit www.mywritinglab.com for audio-visual lectures and additional practice sets about faulty parallel structure.
Get a better grade with MyWritingLab!

CHAPTER 26

Mistakes with Modifiers

CONTENTS

- Misplaced Modifiers
- Dangling Modifiers

Section Theme **URBAN DEVELOPMENT**

In this chapter, you will read about pollution and other urban issues.

Teaching Tip:
Ask students to guess why the underlined sentences in the Grammar Snapshot are mistakes with modifiers. In the first sentence, car horns are not stuck in traffic, and in the second sentence, the commuters, not the caterpillars, want to get home.

Grammar Snapshot

Looking at Mistakes with Modifiers

Myles Oka, a student in urban planning, wrote about the consequences of urban sprawl. The next excerpt contains some modifier errors.

> Because I live in a suburb, I drive many miles each day to work. Last night, stuck in traffic, car horns blared constantly. Commuters inched their cars slowly like caterpillars wanting to get home. I was stressed and anxious.

In this chapter, you will identify and correct misplaced and dangling modifiers.

Misplaced Modifiers

A **modifier** is a word, a phrase, or a clause that describes or modifies nouns or verbs in a sentence. To use a modifier correctly, place it next to the word(s) that you want to modify.

modifier — words that are modified

> Trying to combat pollution, **city planners** have launched an anti-littering campaign.

A **misplaced modifier** is a word, a phrase, or a clause that is not placed next to the word that it modifies. When a modifier is too far from the word that it is describing, the meaning of the sentence can become confusing or unintentionally funny.

> I saw a pamphlet about littering waiting in the mayor's office.
> (How could a pamphlet wait in the mayor's office?)

Teaching Tip: Ask students how to correct the sentence. The answer is "Waiting in the mayor's office, I saw a pamphlet about littering."

Commonly Misplaced Modifiers

As you read the sample sentences for each type of modifier, notice how the meaning of the sentence changes depending on where the modifier is placed.

Prepositional Phrase Modifiers

A prepositional phrase is made of a preposition and its object.

Confusing: Helen read an article on electric cars in a cafe.
(Who was in the cafe: Helen or the cars?)

Clear: In a cafe, Helen read an article on electric cars.

Participle Modifiers

A participle modifier is a phrase that contains an *-ing* verb or an *-ed* verb.

Confusing: Jamal Reed learned about anti-littering laws touring Singapore.
(Can laws tour Singapore?)

Clear: While touring Singapore, Jamal Reed learned about anti-littering laws.

Relative Clause Modifiers

A modifier can be a relative clause or phrase beginning with *who, whose, which,* or *that.*

Confusing: The woman received a $1,000 fine from the officer who dropped a candy wrapper.
(Who dropped the candy wrapper: the woman or the officer?)

Clear: The woman who dropped a candy wrapper received a $1,000 fine from the officer.

Limiting Modifiers

Limiting modifiers are words such as *almost*, *nearly*, *only*, *merely*, *just*, and *even*. In the examples, notice how the placement of *almost* changes the meaning of each sentence.

> **Almost** all of the citizens took the steps that solved the littering problem.
> (Some of the citizens did not take the steps, but most did.)
>
> All of the citizens **almost** took the steps that solved the littering problem.
> (The citizens did not take the steps.)
>
> All of the citizens took the steps that **almost** solved the littering problem.
> (The steps did not solve the littering problem.)

Hint **Correcting Misplaced Modifiers**

To correct misplaced modifiers, follow these steps:

1. First, identify the modifier.
   Armando saw the oil slick **standing on the pier.**
2. Then, identify the word or words being modified.
   Armando
3. Finally, move the modifier next to the word(s) being modified.
   Standing on the pier, Armando saw the oil slick.

Teaching Tip:
Pair Work
You could suggest that students do Practice 1 in pairs, or do it alone and compare answers with a partner.

PRACTICE 1 Underline and correct the misplaced modifier in each sentence.

who was fined $500
EXAMPLE: The man ^ forgot to flush the public toilet who was fined $500.

from the United Nations

1. Experts^ recognize Singapore as the cleanest city in the world from the United Nations.

who patrol city streets

2. Singaporean police officers^ will immediately arrest litterbugs who patrol city streets.

polluters receive

3. After littering, ~~officers give~~ a $1,000 fine ~~to polluters~~.

wearing a bright yellow vest

4. For a second littering offense, a polluter^ must clean a public area such as a park or school yard wearing a bright yellow vest.

, which caused a large controversy,

5. In 1992, Singapore's new law^ prohibited the importation, selling, or chewing of gum, which caused a large controversy.

6. Because gum was stuck on them, passengers could not close the doors to the subway trains^.

because gum was stuck on them.

that has medicinal purposes

7. In 2004, the law was revised to allow gum^ into the country that has medicinal purposes.

Not seeing the police officer,

8. ^Evangeline dropped her gum on a downtown street not seeing the police officer.

nearly

9. She nearly cleaned the park for^ eight hours on the weekend.

with no litter

10. Singaporeans with no litter are proud of their city^.

Dangling Modifiers

A **dangling modifier** opens a sentence but does not modify any words in the sentence. It "dangles" or hangs loosely because it is not connected to any other part of the sentence. To avoid having a dangling modifier, make sure that the modifier and the first noun that follows it have a logical connection.

Confusing: While eating a candy bar, the wrapper fell on the ground.
(Can a wrapper eat a candy bar?)

Clear: While eating a candy bar, Zena dropped the wrapper on the ground.

Confusing: To attend the conference, a background in environmental work is necessary.
(Can a background attend a conference?)

Clear: To attend the conference, **participants need** a background in environmental work.

Teaching Tip: Point out that the passive voice can cause many modifier errors. If students need more information, refer them to page 423 in Chapter 28.

Hint — Correcting Dangling Modifiers

To correct dangling modifiers, follow these steps:

1. First, identify the modifier.
   When traveling, public transportation should be used.
2. Then, decide who or what the writer aims to modify.
   Who is traveling? **People**
3. Finally, add the missing subject (and in some cases, also add or remove words) so that the sentence makes sense.
   When traveling, people should use public transportation.

Teaching Tip: Students often make modifier mistakes by starting sentences with *Based on, Thankfully, Happily, Sadly,* or *Hopefully.* Ask students to correct the next sentence. *Hopefully, the train arrives on time.*

PRACTICE 2 Underline the dangling modifier in each sentence. Then, rewrite the sentence keeping the modifier. You may have to add or remove words to give the sentence a logical meaning. Answers will vary.

EXAMPLE: Enjoying parks, it is difficult when there is a lot of litter.

It is difficult for people to enjoy parks when there is a lot of litter.

1. Believing it is not garbage, cigarette butts are left on city streets.

Believing it is not garbage, some people leave cigarette butts on city streets.

2. With an unconcerned attitude, the hamburger wrapper ended up on the ground.

   With an unconcerned attitude, Amos threw the hamburger wrapper on the ground.

3. Unhappy with the garbage in the park, a major cleanup took place.

   Unhappy with the garbage in the park, the public cleaned it up.

4. Playing in the sand, there were pieces of glass from broken bottles.

   Playing in the sand, the children found glass from broken bottles.

5. Sitting on a park bench, all sorts of plastic bags drifted by.

   Sitting on a park bench, Makiko saw all sorts of plastic bags drift by.

Teaching Tip: Ask students to complete sentences that begin with the next modifiers: *Putting on her gloves; By refusing to enter; To leave the area clean; Searching for answers.* Tell them to generate a variety of sentences.

6. To understand the effects of littering, the cleanup costs must be examined.

   To understand the effects of littering, city councilors must examine the cleanup costs.

7. Seeing no available trash can, the cigarette butt can be wrapped up and carried.

   Seeing no available trash can, smokers can wrap up and carry cigarette butts.

8. While walking barefoot on the grass, a piece of glass cut Pablo's foot.

   While walking barefoot on the grass, Pablo cut his foot on a piece of glass.

9. The car alarm was wailing while reading my newspaper in the park.

   The car alarm was wailing while I read my newspaper in the park.

10. By thinking about litter, parks can be kept clean.

    By thinking about litter, the public can keep parks clean.

PRACTICE 3 Correct the dangling or misplaced modifiers in the following sentences. If the sentence is correct, write *C* next to it. Answers will vary.

Alicia noticed that
EXAMPLE: Living in Mexico City, ^ the air is extremely bad.

Because Mexico City has
1. ~~Having~~ ^ the highest level of air pollution in the world, people suffer from asthma ~~in Mexico City~~.

Citizens know the dangers of air pollution, which comes
2. ^ ~~Coming~~ mainly from the millions of cars on the streets~~, the dangers of the air pollution are well known~~.

Because Mexico City is situated
3. ^ ~~Situated~~ in a valley surrounded by mountains, pollution gets trapped ~~above Mexico City~~.

4. Living near Ermita subway, Alicia Gutierrez suffers from pollution-related illnesses. *C*

many cars do not have
5. Because they are older models, ^ the latest catalytic converters ~~are not in many cars~~.

In a meeting,
6. ^ Mexico City planners discussed ways to combat the bad air ~~in a meeting~~.

in a state of excitement,
7. Several years ago, ^ Mexico City's mayor introduced the new fuel-efficient buses ~~in a state of excitement~~.

8. Because of the law requiring motorists to leave their cars home one day a week, Luis took a bus to work. *C*

the Finance Department has spent
9. Trying to combat the pollution, ^ at least five billion dollars ~~has been spent~~.

the citizens enjoy much better
10. Appreciating Mexico City's initiatives, ^ ~~the~~ air quality ~~is much better~~.

Final Review

Identify fifteen dangling or misplaced modifier errors in this selection. Then, correct each error. You may need to add or remove words to ensure that the sentence makes sense. Answers will vary.

a young boy found surprising results.
EXAMPLE: Working on his school project, ~~some surprising results were found.~~

In his school project,
1. Emilio discovered that there are many ways to help the environment
Drinking coffee, he
~~in his school project~~. ~~He~~ sat with his parents to discuss energy-saving
in their kitchens
strategies ~~drinking coffee~~. First, there are things people can do to help the environment ~~in their kitchens~~. When using freezer bags or aluminum foil,
people can to
washing ~~ing~~ them ~~can~~ reduce waste. Also, people should use cloth napkins and dishtowels instead of paper products. ~~With airtight lids,~~ Emilio places
with airtight lids
leftover food in plastic containers.

2. Emilio and his parents also discussed tips for other areas of the home.
who want to save energy
Families can take measures in the bathroom ~~who want to save energy~~. For
Emilio turns the faucet off as much as possible while he brushes
example, people should take shorter showers. ~~While Emilio is brushing~~ his teeth~~, it is important to leave the faucet turned off as much as possible~~. People can install a toilet dam to reduce water consumption.

With a smile,
3. ~~For their laundry room,~~ Emilio's parents bought energy-efficient
for their laundry room
appliances ~~with a smile~~. After washing shirts, the family hangs them out
Doing the shopping, they
to dry instead of using a clothes dryer. ~~They~~ also buy phosphate-free detergent ~~doing the shopping~~.

Teaching Tip:
You can use the final review as a test. Additional practice and test material appears in the Instructor's Resource Manual and on *MyWritingLab*.

Teaching Tip:
Pair Work
Because pair work helps both native and nonnative speakers practice their cooperation, negotiation, and communication skills, ask students to do the Final Review with a partner. They can help each other identify modifier errors.

CHAPTER 26

4. When Emilio's father goes to the grocery store, [near his house] he makes sensible decisions about products ~~near his house~~. Trying to do fewer trips and buying in bulk, the [family has reduced] gas consumption ~~is reduced.~~ He buys compact fluorescent lightbulbs [that save energy] at the local hardware store ~~that save energy.~~

5. The family's furnace [, which is very old,] needs to be upgraded~~, which is very old~~. ~~Based on the latest technology,~~ Emilio's parents are planning to buy an energy-efficient heater [based on the latest technology]. Also, watching only one television, ~~there is a reduction in energy consumption and~~ the family spends more time together [and reduces energy consumption]. Using the techniques mentioned above, Emilio's family has managed to reduce its energy consumption by nearly thirty percent.

Teaching Tip: You could suggest that students research their topics.

The Writer's Room **Topics for Writing**

Write about one of the following topics. Proofread your text to ensure that there are no modifier errors.

1. What are some steps that your neighborhood or town could take to combat a littering or pollution problem?
2. What are some types of polluters? Write about three categories of polluters.

CHECKLIST: MODIFIERS

When you edit your writing, ask yourself these questions.

- Are my modifiers in the correct position? Check for errors with the following:
  - prepositional-phrase modifiers
  - participle modifiers
  - relative clause modifiers
  - limiting modifiers

  Wearing overalls, the
  ~~The~~ urban planner surveyed the garbage ~~wearing overalls~~.

- Do my modifiers modify something in the sentence? Check for dangling modifiers.

  the police officer gave
  Throwing the plastic bag onto the street, a hefty fine ~~was given~~ to the tourist.

How Do I Get a Better Grade?

PEARSON mywritinglab

Visit www.mywritinglab.com for audio-visual lectures and additional practice sets about mistakes with modifiers.

Get a better grade with MyWritingLab!

READING LINK

Urban Development

The following essays contain more information about urban issues.

"Friendless in North America" by Ellen Goodman (page 231)
"My African Childhood" by David Sedaris (page 585)
"Living Environments" by Avi Friedman (page 592)
"Nature Returns to the Cities" by John Roach (page 624)

CHAPTER 27

Subject–Verb Agreement

CONTENTS

- Basic Subject–Verb Agreement Rules
- More Than One Subject
- Special Subject Forms
- Verb Before the Subject
- Interrupting Words and Phrases

Section Theme **INTERNATIONAL TRADE**

In this chapter, you will read about cultural differences in the world of international business.

Teaching Tip: Ask students to explain why some of the underlined verbs end in "s" in the Grammar Snapshot. Also ask students to link each verb with its subject.

Grammar Snapshot

Looking at Subject–Verb Agreement

The next excerpt is from "Vacation Policies Around the World," an article that appeared on Jobcircle.com. The subjects and verbs are identified.

> On average, **European employees** get four weeks of vacation. **It** would take the typical American employee fifteen years or longer to attain the same vacation privileges, says **Ann Leeds**, a Hewitt **consultant** who specializes in global benefit practices. And as **job-hopping** becomes more common, fewer **Americans** than ever qualify for such extended vacations.

In this chapter, you will practice making subjects and verbs agree.

Basic Subject–Verb Agreement Rules

Subject–verb agreement simply means that a subject and verb agree in number. A singular subject needs a singular verb and a plural subject needs a plural verb.

GRAMMAR LINK

For more information about the present tense, see Chapter 28.

Simple Present Tense Agreement

Writers use **simple present tense** to indicate that an action is habitual or factual. Review the following rules for simple present tense agreement.

CHAPTER 27

Third-person singular form: When the subject is *he*, *she*, *it*, or the equivalent (*Mark*, *Carol*, *Miami*), add an *-s* or *-es* ending to the verb.

> **Maria Orlon** works as a marketing researcher.

Base form: When the subject is *I*, *you*, *we*, *they*, or the equivalent (*women*, *the Rocky Mountains*), do not add an ending to the verb.

> Many **businesses** rely on marketing research.

Hint ***Be*, *Have*, and *Do***

The verbs *be*, *have*, and *do* have irregular third-person singular forms.

Be:	I am	He is	We are
Have:	I have	She has	They have
Do:	I do	It does	You do

ESL Teaching Tip:

Some nonnative speakers may benefit from the information about *be*, *have*, and *do* because the verbs have an irregular structure and are used differently in other languages. For example, Spanish, Italian, and French speakers may say *I have twenty years old* instead of *I am twenty years old*.

Agreement in Other Tenses

In the past tense, almost all verbs have one past form. The only past tense verb requiring subject–verb agreement is the verb *be*, which has two past forms: *was* and *were*.

> **I** was tired. **Edward** was also tired. That day, **we** were very lazy.

In the present perfect tense, which is formed with *have* or *has* and the past participle, use *has* when the subject is third-person singular and *have* for all other forms.

> The **travel service** has raised its booking fees. Other **agencies** have not raised their fees.

GRAMMAR LINK

For more information about using the present perfect tense, see Chapter 28.

In the future tense and with modal forms (*can*, *could*, *would*, *may*, *might* . . .), use the same form of the verb with every subject.

> **I** will work. **She** will work with me. **We** can work together.

Hint **Use Standard English**

In casual conversations and in movies, you may hear people say *He be cool*, or *She don't have the time*. In professional and academic situations, use the correct forms of *be*, *have*, and *do*: *He is cool* and *She doesn't have the time.*

ESL **Teaching Tip:** The rules for agreement in different verb tenses are particularly useful for nonnative speakers. They may apply certain subject–verb agreement rules to tenses that don't require them.

PRACTICE 1 Underline the correct present tense form of the verbs in parentheses.

EXAMPLE: Many businesses (export / exports) products to other nations.

1. Although several countries (share / shares) the English language, the details in the language and culture (be / is / are) different. Business travelers (learn / learns) about these differences.

2. For example, Americans and Canadians (put / puts) gas in their cars, whereas British citizens (use / uses) petrol. In England, you (do / does) not phone people, you "ring" them. Australians also (use / uses) interesting expressions. A "chalkie" (is / are) a teacher, and a "mozzie" (is / are) a mosquito.

3. In England, class-based traditions (is / are) still strong, and many people (support / supports) the monarchy. Australia, on the other hand, (have / has) a very egalitarian culture. Mr. Ian Wynn (have / has) been an Australian real estate agent for seven years, and he (does / do) not like signs of arrogance. Last spring, when some tourists (was / were) arrogant, Wynn said, "Don't be a tall poppy. The tall poppy (get / gets) its head cut off."

4. Spelling also (differ / differs) among English-speaking nations. In countries where people speak British English, common words such as "flavor" or

"color" (have / has) an *our* ending. For example, "color" (become / becomes) "colour" in Canada and Great Britain.

More Than One Subject

There are special agreement rules when there is more than one subject in a sentence.

And

When two subjects are joined by *and*, use the plural form of the verb.

> Colleges, universities, and trade schools **prepare** students for the job market.

Or / Nor

When two subjects are joined by *or* or *nor*, the verb agrees with the subject that is the closest to it.

> The layout artists or the editor (singular) **decides** how the cover will look.

> Neither the artist nor her assistants (plural) **make** changes to the design.

Hint ***As Well As* and *Along With***

The phrases *as well as* and *along with* are not the same as *and*. They do not form a compound subject. The real subject is before the interrupting expression.

> Japan, China, and South Korea **develop** high-tech computer products.

> Japan, as well as China and South Korea, **develops** high-tech computer products.

PRACTICE 2 Underline the correct verb in each sentence. Make sure the verb agrees with the subject.

EXAMPLE: Japan and China (have / has) interesting types of restaurants.

1. Tokyo and other Japanese cities (have / has) "Maid Cafés."
2. The hostess and the female servers (dress / dresses) in traditional maid uniforms.

3. Recently, in the Otome Road area of Tokyo, a businesswoman and her partner (have / has) opened a Butler Café.

4. Every day, Jin or another waiter (serve / serves) customers.

5. The coffee or the tea (come / comes) on a special tray.

6. The host and the waiters (treat / treats) the customers like British royalty.

7. "Mademoiselle" or "Your Highness" (is / are) said to each customer by the server in the butler uniform.

8. A crumpet as well as a large scone (appear / appears) on each table.

9. Every day, many young and old women (try / tries) to get a table at the Butler Café.

Special Subject Forms

Some subjects are not easy to identify as singular or plural. Two common types are indefinite pronouns and collective nouns.

Indefinite Pronouns

Indefinite pronouns refer to a general person, place, or thing. Carefully review the following list of indefinite pronouns.

Indefinite Pronouns

Singular	another	each	nobody	other
	anybody	everybody	no one	somebody
	anyone	everyone	nothing	someone
	anything	everything	one	something
Plural	both, few, many, others, several			

Singular Indefinite Pronouns

In the following sentences, the verbs require the third-person-singular form because the subjects are singular.

> Almost everyone **knows** about the Free Trade Agreement.

You can put one or more singular nouns (joined by *and*) after *each* and *every*. The verb is still singular.

> Every client **likes** the new rule. Each man and woman **knows** about it.

Plural Indefinite Pronouns

Both, *few*, *many*, *others*, and *several* are all plural subjects. The verb is always plural.

> A representative from the United States and another from Mexico are sitting at a table. Both **want** to compromise.

Collective Nouns

Collective nouns refer to groups of people or things. Review the following list of common collective nouns.

army	class	crowd	group	population
association	club	family	jury	public
audience	committee	gang	mob	society
band	company	government	organization	team

Generally, each group acts as a unit, so you must use the singular form of the verb.

> The company **is** ready to make a decision.

Hint **Police Is Plural**

Treat the word *police* as a plural noun because the word "officers" is implied but not stated.

> The police **have** a protester in custody.

PRACTICE 3 Underline the correct verb in each sentence.

EXAMPLE: The Executive Planet Web site (have / has) tips for business travelers.

1. Each large and small nation (have / has) its own gift-giving rules. For example, Singapore (have / has) strict rules against bribery, and the

ESL Teaching Tip: Nonnative speakers may not understand the indefinite pronoun rule. To help students remember that pronouns such as *everyone* are singular, point out that they end with a singular word (*one*, *body*, or *thing*).

Teaching Tip: If your students have many problems with subject-verb agreement, suggest that they circle the subjects in each sentence and determine whether they are singular or plural.

government (pride / prides) itself on being corruption-free. The police (arrest / arrests) officials who accept a bribe.

2. Specific rules (apply / applies) to gift-giving in Singapore. Certainly, everyone (love / loves) to receive a gift. Nobody (like / likes) to be left out while somebody else (open / opens) a present, so in Singapore, every businessman or businesswoman (know / knows) that gifts must be presented to a group. For example, if somebody (want / wants) to thank a receptionist, he or she (give / gives) a gift to the entire department. The group (accept / accepts) the gift graciously.

3. To be polite, most individuals (refuse / refuses) a gift initially. Some (believe / believes) that a refusal (make / makes) them appear less greedy. If the gift-giver (continue / continues) to insist, the recipient will accept the gift.

4. Singaporeans (do / does) not unwrap gifts in front of the giver. It (imply / implies) that the receiver is impatient and greedy. Everyone (thank / thanks) the gift-giver and (wait / waits) to open the gift in privacy.

5. China, as well as Japan, also (have / has) unusual gift-giving rules. In China, nobody (give / gives) a gift in white or green wrapping paper because those colors are unlucky. In Japan, the number four (sound / sounds) like the word meaning "death," so people do not give gifts that contain four items. To avoid insulting their hosts, business travelers should learn about gift-giving rules in other nations.

Verb Before the Subject

Usually the verb comes after the subject, but in some sentences, the verb is before the subject. In such cases, you must still ensure that the subject and verb agree.

There or Here

When a sentence begins with *there* or *here*, the subject always follows the verb. *There* and *here* are not subjects.

> Here **is** (V) the menu (S). There **are** (V) many different sandwiches (S).

Questions

In questions, word order is usually reversed, and the main or helping verb is placed before the subject. In the following example, the main verb is *be*.

> Where **is** (V) the Butler Café (S)? **Is** (V) the food (S) good?

In questions in which the main verb is not *be*, the subject agrees with the helping verb.

> When **does** (HV) the café (S) **close** (V)? **Do** (HV) students (S) **work** (V) there?

PRACTICE 4 Correct any subject–verb agreement errors. If there are no errors, write C for "correct" in the space.

EXAMPLE: ~~Has~~ *Have* you ever visited Turkey? _____

1. ~~Is~~ *Are* there etiquette rules about greetings? _____
2. ~~Do~~ *Does* each nation have its own rules? _____
3. There ~~be~~ *are* specific rules in each country. _____
4. In Turkey, do older men or women receive preferential treatment? __*C*__
5. If someone enters a room, he or she ~~greet~~ *greets* the oldest person first. _____
6. There ~~be~~ *is* tremendous respect for elders. _____
7. Why ~~is~~ *are* the two women holding hands? _____
8. In Turkey, handholding is a sign of respect and friendship. __*C*__
9. In many companies, there ~~have~~ *has* not been enough attention given to business etiquette. _____
10. On the other hand, there ~~is~~ *are* many business professionals who learn about the customs of their foreign clients. _____

CHAPTER 27

ESL Teaching Tip: Nonnative speakers have particular problems with sentences beginning with *there* because they transfer structures from their other languages. Draw their attention to this rule.

ESL Teaching Tip: Nonnative speakers may add the -*s* ending to the main verb instead of the helping verb in question forms. They may need extra practice with verb agreement in questions.

Teaching Tip: If students have problems with Practice 4, suggest that they underline the subject.

CHAPTER 27

Interrupting Words and Phrases

Words that come between the subject and the verb may confuse you. In these cases, look for the subject and make sure that the verb agrees with the subject.

Some companies [S] in the transportation sector [interrupting phrase] **lose** [V] money.

The manager [S] in my office [interrupting phrase] never **wears** [V] a suit and tie.

> **Hint** — **Identify Interrupting Phrases**
>
> When you revise your writing, place words that separate the subject and the verb in parentheses. Then you can check to see if your subjects and verbs agree.
>
> An employee [S] **(**in my brother's company**)** [interrupting phrase] **annoys** [V] his co-workers.
>
> When interrupting phrases contain *of the*, the subject appears before the phrase.
>
> One [S] **(**of the most common work-related ailments**)** [interrupting phrase] **is** [V] carpal tunnel syndrome.

PRACTICE 5 Identify the subject and place any words that come between each subject and verb in parentheses. Then underline the correct form of the verb. (Two possible verb choices are in bold.)

EXAMPLE: (One) *(*of the most controversial topics in business circles*)* **is** / **are** stress.

1. People (in this nation) **take** / **takes** very few vacation days. Other nations, (including France, England, and Sweden,) **have** / **has** many vacation days. The average employee (in France) **have** / **has** about thirty-nine vacation days annually. The typical American, (according to numerous studies,) only **take** / **takes** fourteen days off each year.

2. Canada, as well as England and France, **legislate / legislates** vacation days. The United States, unlike most industrialized countries, **do / does** not regulate benefits in the private sector. One of the problems caused by a lack of time off **is / are** stress-related illness.

3. Some Americans, according to JobCircle.com, **is / are** beginning to rebel. Workers increasingly **call / calls** in sick when they really **have / has** family responsibilities or other reasons for missing work. Ted Owens, for example, **have / has** a job as a broker in Los Angeles. Each of the workers in Ted Owens's office **admit / admits** to using sick days for other purposes. Most of the workers **have / has** lied to the boss.

Interrupting Words—*Who, Which, That*

If a sentence contains a clause beginning with *who*, *which*, or *that*, then the verb agrees with the subject preceding *who*, *which*, or *that*.

> There is a woman in my neighborhood who **works** as an executive.

Sometimes a complete dependent clause appears between the subject and verb.

> interrupting clause
> The problem, which we discussed, **needs** to be solved.

PRACTICE 6 Correct nine subject–verb agreement errors.

EXAMPLE: Jeff Geissler ~~discuss~~ *discusses* maternity leave in an article for the Associated Press.

1. Elisa Elbert, who works for an accounting firm, is expecting a child. Elisa, like other Australian citizens, ~~receive~~ *receives* up to twelve months of paid leave.

ESL
Teaching Tip:
Nonnative speakers may question how *the United States* can be a singular noun. Point out that although the word is plural, it refers to one nation and is considered singular.

CHAPTER 27

Madhuri Datta, a Canadian, is having her baby next month. Datta, who is due in November, ~~want~~ *wants* to share her paid leave with her husband. According to a recent poll, one of the Canadian government's best laws ~~are~~ *is* the one that permits parents to divide thirty-five weeks of paid parental leave.

2. The U.S. Family and Medical Leave Act, which only ~~cover~~ *covers* workers in large companies, ~~protect~~ *protects* new mothers from losing their jobs. The act, according to a Harvard study, only ~~provide~~ *provides* for twelve weeks of paid leave.
3. One of the Harvard researchers ~~think~~ *thinks* that the United States is out of step with most nations. The study showed that 163 out of 168 nations ~~has~~ *have* some sort of paid parental leave. The United States, along with Papua New Guinea and Swaziland, ~~do~~ *does* not.

Teaching Tip:
You can use the final review as a test. Additional test material appears in the Instructor's Resource Manual and on *MyWritingLab*.

Final Review

Correct fifteen errors in subject–verb agreement.

EXAMPLE: The worker ~~enjoy~~ ***enjoys*** his afternoon nap.

1. ~~Is~~ *Are* afternoon naps beneficial? In Spain, a siesta ~~have~~ *has* been part of the culture for centuries. Many businesses, including shops, restaurants, and offices, close for three hours each afternoon and then ~~opens~~ *open* from 5:00 to 7:00 p.m. During the long break, employees return home and ~~has~~ *have* a siesta. However, this custom is changing.

Mario Carreno (b. 1913/Cuban) La Siesta 1946. Oil on canvas. © Christie's Images/ SuperStock.

2. Some multinational companies that ~~operates~~ operate in Spain remain open for business in the afternoons. One of the reasons ~~are~~ is the companies' desire to increase productivity. To give sleep-deprived Spaniards the siesta that they crave, a new type of business has opened. There ~~is~~ are "siesta shops" throughout Spain. Each shop ~~satisfy~~ satisfies a need.

3. Jose Luis Buqueras, a computer programmer, ~~work~~ works for a British multinational in Madrid, and he has a one-hour lunch break. Luckily for Buqueras, there ~~be~~ are several siesta shops in his neighborhood that ~~offers~~ offer short siestas. If he pays 500 pesetas, he can doze in a darkened room for twenty minutes. One of the attendants ~~massage~~ massages his neck. Then somebody ~~cover~~ covers him with a blanket. Quiet music plays in the background.

4. Although many Spanish citizens no longer enjoy three-hour breaks, they have not given up their afternoon siestas. Perhaps other nations can benefit from Spain's example. According to many medical professionals, a short afternoon nap helps reduce stress. There ~~is~~ are also studies showing that naps reduce heart disease. David Jenkins, a government employee in Ireland, ~~want~~ wants siesta shops to open in his country.

The Writer's Room Topics for Writing

Write about one of the following topics. Proofread your text to ensure that your subjects and verbs agree.

1. Do you have afternoon naps? Explain why or why not. Compare yourself to someone who has, or does not have, frequent naps.
2. Describe a visit that you made to a culturally different restaurant. What happened? Use language that appeals to the senses.

CHECKLIST: SUBJECT–VERB AGREEMENT

When you edit your writing, ask yourself these questions.

☐ Do my subjects and verbs agree? Check for errors with the following:

- present tense verbs
- *was* and *were*
- interrupting phrases

The clients, whom I have never met, ~~is~~ are unhappy with the new ad. It ~~be~~ is too dull.

☐ Do I use the correct verb form with indefinite pronouns? Check for errors with singular indefinite pronouns such as *everybody*, *nobody*, or *somebody*.

Somebody ~~have~~ has to modify the photograph.

☐ Do my subjects and verbs agree when the subject is after the verb? Check for errors with the following:

- sentences containing *here* and *there*
- question forms

~~Do~~ Does she watch commercials? There ~~is~~ are many funny ads on television.

How Do I Get a Better Grade?

Visit www.mywritinglab.com for audio-visual lectures and additional practice sets about subject-verb agreement.

mywritinglab

Get a better grade with MyWritingLab!

Verb Tenses

CHAPTER 28

CONTENTS

- What Is Verb Tense?
- Present and Past Tenses
- Past Participles
- Present Perfect Tense
- Past Perfect Tense
- Passive Voice
- Progressive Forms

Section Theme **INTERNATIONAL TRADE**

In this chapter, you will learn about advertising and marketing.

Grammar Snapshot

Looking at Verb Tenses

The following excerpt is from *Business Ethics* by Richard T. De George. Look at the underlined verbs and try to determine what tense the author has used.

> The growth of giant corporations has tended to make competition in many areas very costly. The growth of supermarkets, which began in the 1940s, has forced most small grocers and vegetable and fruit markets out of business. The prices a supermarket was able to charge were lower than those the small operators could charge for equal-quality goods. The consequence has been the elimination of small grocers.

In this chapter, you will write using a variety of verb tenses.

Teaching Tip:
Ask students questions about the Grammar Snapshot. Which verbs are in the past tense? What is the difference between *was* and *were*? Why do some verbs begin with *has*? You can tell them the answers to these questions appear in the chapter.

What Is Verb Tense?

Verb tense indicates when an action occurred. Review the various tenses of the verb *work*. (Progressive or *-ing* forms of these verbs appear at the end of this chapter.)

Simple Forms

Present	I <u>work</u> in a large company. My sister <u>works</u> with me.
Past	We <u>worked</u> in Cancun last summer.
Future	My sister <u>will work</u> in the Middle East next year.
Present perfect	We <u>have worked</u> together since 2001.
Past perfect	When Maria lost her job, she <u>had worked</u> there for six years.
Future perfect	By 2020, I <u>will have worked</u> here for twenty years.

ESL
Teaching Tip:
Although your native speakers may benefit from the material in this chapter, it is particularly useful for nonnative speakers. They may make errors when they transfer patterns from their languages.

 Use Standard Verb Forms

Nonstandard English is used in everyday conversation and may differ according to the region in which you live. **Standard American English** is the common language generally used and expected in schools, businesses, and government institutions in the United States. In college, you should write using standard American English.

Nonstandard:	He don't have no money.	She be real tired.
Standard:	He <u>does not</u> have <u>any</u> money.	She <u>is really</u> tired.

Present and Past Tenses

Present Tense Verbs

GRAMMAR LINK
For more information about subject-verb agreement, see Chapter 27.

The simple present tense indicates that an action is a general fact or habitual activity. Remember to add *-s* or *-es* to verbs that follow third-person singular forms.

Fact: Our fee **includes** mass mail-outs and pamphlet distribution.

Habitual Activity: Carmen Cruz **takes** drawing classes every Saturday.

PAST	Saturday	Saturday	Saturday	Saturday	FUTURE
▼	▼	▼	▼	▼	▼
	She draws.	She draws.	She draws.	She draws.

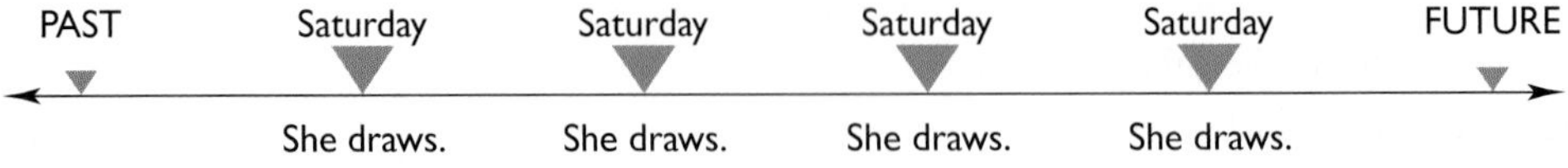

Past Tense Verbs

The past tense indicates that an action occurred at a specific past time. Regular past tense verbs have a standard *-d* or *-ed* ending. Use the same form for both singular and plural past tense verbs.

Yesterday morning, we **discussed** the campaign.

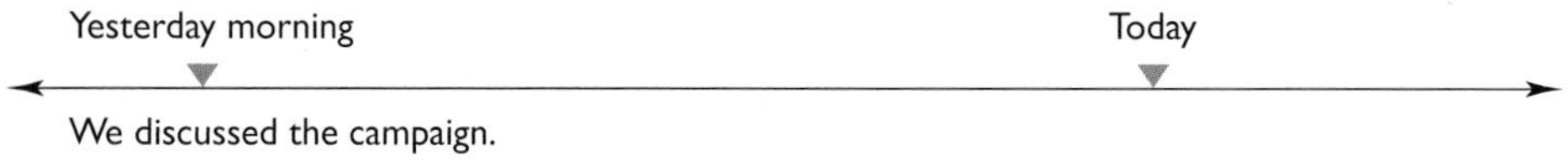

ESL Teaching Tip: The visuals (tense time lines) are for the benefit of your nonnative speakers. In some languages such as Malay, the notion of verb tense does not exist.

PRACTICE 1 Write the present or past form of each verb in parentheses.

EXAMPLE: In the 1960s, some American companies (attempt) ____*attempted*____ to enter the Japanese marketplace.

1. General Mills (produce) ____*produces*____ many food products. Each year, the company (sell) ____*sells*____ products around the world. Sometimes, a product (succeed) ____*succeeds*____ in a foreign marketplace, but occasionally, a product (fail) ____*fails*____.
2. In 2004, Joyce Millet (publish) ____*published*____ an article called, "Marketing in Japan: What History Can Teach Us." To prepare for her article, she (research) ____*researched*____ examples of product failures.
3. In the late 1960s, General Mills (plan) ____*planned*____ to market Betty Crocker cake mixes in Japan. They (try) ____*tried*____ to design a suitable product. Product developers (learn) ____*learned*____ that very few Japanese homes had ovens, so they (need) ____*needed*____ to find a new way to bake the cakes.

At that time, most Japanese homes (contain) ___contained___ a rice cooker, so designers (create) ___created___ a spongy cake mix that worked in a rice cooker.

4. At first, sales of the Betty Crocker cake mix were good, but sales quickly (tumble) ___tumbled___. What was the problem? In the past, most Japanese citizens (believe) ___believed___ that rice was sacred, so they (refuse) ___refused___ to contaminate the rice with cake flavor.

Irregular Past Tense Verbs

GRAMMAR LINK

See Appendix 2 for a list of common irregular verbs.

Irregular verbs change internally. Because their spellings change from the present to the past tense, these verbs can be challenging to remember. For example, the irregular verb *go* becomes *went* when you convert it to the past tense.

The company **sold** the patent. (*sold* = past tense of *sell*)

Consumers **bought** the product. (*bought* = past tense of *buy*)

Be (*Was* or *Were*)

Most past tense verbs have one form that you can use with all subjects. However, the verb *be* has two past forms: *was* and *were*. Use *was* with *I*, *he*, *she*, and *it*. Use *were* with *you*, *we*, and *they*.

The packing box **was** not sturdy enough. The plates **were** fragile.

PRACTICE 2 Write the correct past form of each verb in parentheses. Some verbs are regular, and some are irregular.

EXAMPLE: Long ago, John Pemberton (have) ___had___ a great idea.

1. In 1884, John Pemberton (be) ___was___ a pharmacist in Atlanta, Georgia. He (know) ___knew___ about a successful French product

after they gave formula to their babies. When the women returned home, they did not ~~had~~ *have* enough money to continue buying enough formula. They added too much water to the formula, and the water was often contaminated. Babies who ~~drinked~~ *drank* formula become malnourished. In many villages, the level of infant malnutrition and mortality ~~rised~~ *rose*.

CHAPTER 28

Past Participles

A **past participle** is a verb form, not a verb tense. The past tense and the past participle of regular verbs are the same. The past tense and the past participle of irregular verbs may be different.

	base form	past tense	past participle
Regular verb:	talk	talked	talked
Irregular verb:	begin	began	begun

GRAMMAR LINK

For a list of irregular past participles, see Appendix 2.

Hint **Using Past Participles**

You cannot use a past participle as the only verb in a sentence. You must use it with a helping verb such as *have, has, had, is, was,* or *were.*

	helping verbs	past participle	
The company	**was**	founded	in 1863.
The products	**have**	become	very popular.

ESL Teaching Tip:
For the benefit of nonnative speakers, ask students to quiz each other about past participles. Students could open their books to Appendix 2, and then ask each other to spell irregular past participles. They should highlight the words that they misspell.

Teaching Tip:
You could ask students to identify the helping verbs by circling or underlining them.

PRACTICE 4 In the next selection, the past participles are underlined. Correct ten past participle errors, and write C above correct past participles.

EXAMPLE: The business ethics students have meeted *met* many times to discuss the case.

1. Since 1973, Nestle has faced *C* a lot of criticism for its marketing techniques in Africa. According to critics, Nestle should have knew *known* that the advertising was dangerous and misleading. For instance, by 1980, Nestle had make *made*

hundreds of billboards showing a white woman feeding her child with a bottle. The African women were teached [taught] that good mothers don't breastfeed their children.

2. The method of giving free samples to new mothers was also blamed [C] for the problem. According to critics, a company spokesman has admit [admitted] that the free samples contributed to the drying up of mothers' breast milk. In addition, the color white was weared [worn] by company salespeople when they walked through hospital wards. New mothers could have thinked [thought] that the salespeople were nurses.

3. Nestle's business practices have always being [been] legal. In fact, Nestle has successfully used [C] the same techniques in many wealthy nations. Nonetheless, in 1977, a worldwide boycott of Nestle products was organize [organized] by a group of concerned citizens.

4. Many business students have studied [C] the Nestle case. Technically, Nestle did the same thing in Africa that it has did [done] in the United States for many years. If a marketing technique has work [worked] successfully in wealthy countries, is a company obliged [C] to revise its marketing techniques in less developed countries?

ESL **Teaching Tip:** The present perfect tense is particularly difficult for nonnative speakers because many languages such as Russian and Spanish do not have an equivalent tense.

Present Perfect Tense

(*have* or *has* + past participle)

A past participle combines with *have* or *has* to form the **present perfect tense**.

Kate **has been** a marketing manager for six years.

Since 2001, the products **have sold** extremely well.

You can use this tense in two different circumstances.

1. Use the present perfect to show that an action began in the past and continues to the present time. You will often use *since* and *for* with this tense.

2. Use the present perfect to show that one or more completed actions occurred at unspecified past times.

Mr. Jain **has visited** China four times.
(The time of the four visits is not specified.)

Choosing the Simple Past or the Present Perfect

Look at the difference between the past and the present perfect tenses.

Simple past: In 2002, Kumar Jain **went** to Shanghai.
(This event occurred at a known past time.)

Present perfect: Since 2002, Jain **has owned** a factory in China.
(The action began in the past and continues to the present.)

He **has made** many business contacts.
(Making business contacts occurred at unknown past times.)

ESL Teaching Tip: To practice the first usage of the present perfect, ask students questions that can generate either present perfect or simple past responses. For instance, you can ask the next questions. Student answers will shift from the present to the past to the present perfect.

- Who is your best friend? When did you meet him or her?
- How long have you known your best friend?

To practice the second usage of the present perfect, ask students the next questions.

- Who has traveled to another country?
- How many countries have you visited?
- When did you last go to that country?

Hint — Use Time Markers

When you try to identify which tense to use, look for time markers. **Time markers** are words such as *since, for,* or *ago* that indicate when an action occurred.

Simple past: Three weeks **ago,** Parker launched her new perfume.

Present perfect: **Since then,** her perfume has been selling very well.

ESL Teaching Tip: Encourage nonnative speakers to use time markers in their writing to clarify when events occurred.

PRACTICE 5 Write the simple past or present perfect form of the verb in parentheses.

EXAMPLE: For the last six years, my cousin Mike (be) ___*has been*___ a sales representative.

1. Since the beginning of the twentieth century, many companies (try) *have tried* to create memorable advertisements for their products. Before the 1920s, most ads (be) *were* on billboards and in magazines. Then, in 1922, companies (discover) *discovered* the potential of radio advertising. They (sponsor) *sponsored* radio shows. For example, the Lucky Strike Cigarette Company sponsored a music show. Since then, many companies (sponsor) *have sponsored* artistic and sporting events.

2. In the mid-1920s, radio stations (decide) *decided* to give short time slots to advertisers so that they could promote their products as an alternative to the sponsorship of shows. Ever since, commercials (be) *have been* an effective way for companies to market their products. Most people (see) *have seen* thousands of commercials.

Teaching Tip: As students do Practice 5, remind them to consider the context. If a series of events all occurred in the 1920s, they should use the past tense. If the event has a relationship with the present, and if they see key words such as *since* or *for*, they should use the present perfect.

Teaching Tip:
Pair Work
Give students a topic such as *friends*, *sports*, or *hobbies*, and ask pairs of students to generate sentences that contain the simple past and the present perfect tenses.

Hint **Simple Past or Present Perfect?**

Use the past tense when referring to someone who is no longer living or to something that no longer exists. Only use the present perfect tense when the action has a relationship to someone or something that still exists.

Leonardo da Vinci ~~**has designed**~~ *designed* many products.

PRACTICE 6 Identify and correct ten verb errors.

EXAMPLE: The Coca-Cola Company ~~has begun~~ *began* in 1886.

1. Since 1886, Coca-Cola ~~is~~ has been a familiar product throughout the world. For over a century, the company ~~made~~ has made some very successful marketing decisions. In 1931, Haddon Sunblom ~~has~~ illustrated a Coca-Cola advertisement with a Santa Claus figure that had a white beard, rosy cheeks, and a red suit. Since then, Sunblom's drawing ~~is~~ has been the popular image of the Christmas character.

2. Although the Coca-Cola Company ~~been~~ has been very successful since its inception, occasionally it has made blunders. In 1984, Coca-Cola managers ~~have~~ worried about the increasing popularity of Pepsi. That year, Coke developers modified the original formula and ~~have~~ made the product much sweeter.

3. On April 23, 1985, at a press conference, Coca-Cola's chairman ~~has~~ introduced New Coke by calling it "smoother, rounder, and bolder." Unfortunately, when the product hit store shelves, consumers complained about the taste.

4. On July 29, 1985, the company pulled New Coke from the shelves and reintroduced the original product, calling it Coke Classic. Curiously, Coke Classic ~~is~~ has been very successful since its reintroduction. Since the New Coke fiasco, other companies ~~learned~~ have learned from Coca-Cola's mistake. If consumers love a product, do not modify it!

Teaching Tip:
Pair Work
Ask students to brainstorm sentences explaining how the world has changed since the 1950s. Write some of their sentences on the board and ask students to identify and form the present perfect verbs.

Past Perfect Tense

(*had* + past participle)

The **past perfect tense** indicates that one or more past actions happened before another past action. It is formed with *had* and the past participle.

Mr. Lo **had spent** a lot on research when he launched the product.

Teaching Tip: Ask students to generate other sentences that require the simple past, present perfect, and past perfect tenses.

CHAPTER 28

Notice the differences between the simple past, the present perfect, and the past perfect tenses.

Simple past: Last night, Craig **worked** at Burger Town.
(The action occurred at a known past time.)

Present perfect: He **has owned** the restaurant for three years.
(The action began in the past and continues to the present.)

Past perfect: Craig **had had** two business failures before he bought Burger Town.
(All of the actions happened in the past, but the two business failures occurred before he bought the hamburger restaurant.)

PRACTICE 7 Underline the correct verb form in each sentence. You may choose the simple past tense or the past perfect tense.

EXAMPLE: The Barbosas (were / had been) farmers for ten years when Alex Barbosa decided to sell organic beef.

1. Even though he (never studied / had never studied) marketing, Alex Barbosa decided to promote his organic beef.

2. He printed flyers, and then he (distributed / had distributed) them to private homes.

3. When most residents threw out the flyer, they (did not even read / had not even read) it.

4. The flyer contained a picture that Barbosa (took / had taken) the previous summer.

5. The image of the meat carcass (was / had been) unappealing.

6. After Barbosa received negative feedback about his flyer, he remembered that his daughter (warned / had warned) him about the image.

7. Also, the neighborhood (had / had had) low-income families who could not afford the high price of the organic meat.

8. Finally, in 2005, Barbosa hired a business graduate who (learned / had learned) how to do effective marketing.

9. By December 2006, Barbosa's organic meat (found / had found) a niche in the marketplace.

Passive Voice

(be + past participle)

In sentences with the **passive voice**, the subject receives the action and does not perform the action. To form the passive voice, use the appropriate tense of the verb *be* plus the past participle. Look carefully at the following two sentences.

Active: The boss **gave** documents to her assistant.
(This is active, because the subject, *boss*, performed the action.)

Passive: Several documents **were given** to the assistant.
(This is passive because the subject, *documents*, was affected by the action and did not perform the action.)

Hint **Avoid Overusing the Passive Voice**

Generally, try to use the active voice instead of the passive voice. The active voice is more direct and friendly than the passive voice. For example, read two versions of the same message.

Passive voice: No more than two pills per day should be ingested. This medication should be taken with meals. It should not be continued if headaches or nausea are experienced. Any side effects should be reported immediately.

Active voice: Do not ingest more than two pills per day. Take this medication with meals. Do not continue taking it if you experience headache or nausea. Immediately report any side effects to your doctor.

Teaching Tip:
To help students understand voice, you could write a sentence on the board such as "Workers make shoes in that factory." Then write the word "Shoes" under it, and ask students to generate a sentence that means the same thing as the first sentence, but uses *shoes* as the subject. The students would generate the passive form.

ESL Teaching Tip:
Nonnative speakers—German speakers, for instance—overuse the passive form when they transfer sentence patterns from their own language. Remind students to use the passive voice sparingly.

Teaching Tip: Mention that students should especially avoid the passive voice when writing documents such as resumes, medical labels, ads, leaflets, or instructions.

PRACTICE 8 Complete the following sentences by changing the passive verb to the active form. Do not alter the verb tense.

EXAMPLE: Each department *will be visited* by the supervisor.

The supervisor will visit each department.

1. A funny commercial *was created* by the advertising agency.

   The advertising agency created a funny commercial.

2. The ad *will be seen* by many people.

   Many people will see the ad.

3. A well-known comedian *was hired* by the company.

   The company hired a well-known comedian.

4. Many commercials *are created* by Pedro Guzman.

   Pedro Guzman creates many commercials.

5. Complaints about their commercials *are often ignored* by companies.

   Companies often ignore complaints about their commercials.

Hint **When *Be* Is Suggested, Not Written**

In the passive voice, sometimes the verb *be* is suggested but not written. The following sentence contains the passive voice.

A man **named** Harley Cobb complained about the car company's decision.

↑

(who was)

PRACTICE 9 Underline and correct eight errors with past participles.

EXAMPLE: A problem was find (*found*) with the design.

1. When Apple Computer first developed the Macintosh, a pull-down screen, or window, was include (*included*) in the product. The computer also had a variety of icons for different tasks. For instance, useless files were drag (*dragged*) to a

trash can icon. A year later, Microsoft Corporation introduced its popular

software program name Windows. The software, create in 1988, looked a
named *created*

lot like Apple's software. Apple sued Microsoft for copyright infringement

and argued that Microsoft copied the "look and feel" of Apple software.

2. There are strict rules about copyright. A unique product can be <u>patent</u>.
 patented

 However, people cannot copyright an idea. Therefore, Apple's decision to

 use specific icons could not be <u>protect</u>. Still, Apple argued that its original
 protected

 concept should not have been <u>copy</u>. The case, which lasted for four years,
 copied

 was <u>win</u> by Microsoft.
 won

Progressive Forms
(-*ing* verbs)

Most verbs have progressive tenses. The **progressive tense**, formed with *be* and
the *–ing* form of the verb, indicates that an action is, was, or will be in progress.
For example, the present progressive indicates that an action is happening right
now or for a temporary period of time. The following time line illustrates both
the simple and progressive tenses.

Every day, he **sells** leather wallets. (Simple present)

	sells	sells	sells	sells	
PAST	▼	▼	▼	▼	FUTURE
	Sunday	Monday	Today, he **is visiting** the stores on Main Street. (Present progressive)	Wednesday	

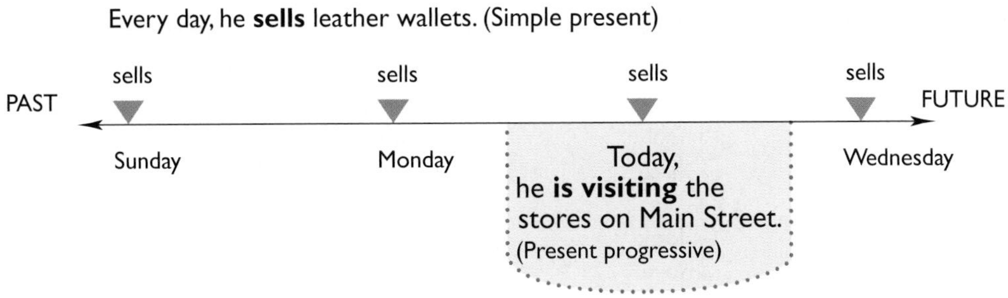

To form the progressive, use the appropriate tense of the verb *be* with the
-ing verb.

Present progressive:	Right now, I **am** <u>working</u>.
Past progressive:	We **were** <u>sleeping</u> when you phoned us.
Future progressive:	Tomorrow, at noon, I **will be** <u>driving</u>.

Teaching Tip:
Point out that the
helping verbs show the
tense.

Present perfect progressive: The receptionist **has been working** since 8:00 A.M.

Past perfect progressive: She **had been speeding** when the officer stopped her.

Common Errors in the Progressive Form

- Do not use the progressive form when an action happens regularly.

  Every day he ~~is complaining~~ *complains* about his job.

- In the progressive form, use the correct form of the verb *be*.

  Right now, Ron ~~be~~ *is* talking with his manager.

- In the progressive form, always include the complete helping verb.

  Right now, the manager ^*is* discussing the problem. They ^*have* been talking for hours.

Nonprogressive Verbs

Some verbs do not take the progressive form because they indicate an ongoing state or a perception rather than a temporary action.

ESL Teaching Tip: Your nonnative speakers may not realize that certain verbs should not take the *-ing* form. Draw their attention to this list.

Examples of Nonprogressive Verbs

Perception Verbs	Preference Verbs	State Verbs	Possession
admire	desire	believe	have*
care	doubt	know	own
hear	feel	mean	possess
see	hate	realize	
seem	like	recognize	
smell*	look	suppose	
taste*	love	think*	
	prefer	understand	
	want		

*Some verbs have more than one meaning and can be used in the progressive tense. Compare the following pairs of sentences.

Nonprogressive	Progressive
He **has** a franchise. (expresses ownership)	He **is having** a bad day.
I **think** it is unethical. (expresses an opinion)	I **am thinking** about you.

PRACTICE 10 Correct one verb error in each sentence.

EXAMPLE: She *had* been working in the store for ten years when she was fired.

1. Ellen Peters was producing and ~~give~~ *giving* away her own fragrances when her sister suggested that she try to market her perfume.

2. These days, Peters *is* negotiating with a cosmetics company that hopes to market her perfume internationally.

3. She *has* been looking for a product name for the last six months.

4. Last May, she ~~be~~ *was* planning to call it Golden Mist when someone told her that "mist" means "manure" in German.

5. While her friends were ~~brainstorm~~ *brainstorming* to help her, one of them suggested the name "Pete," which is a shortened form of Peters.

6. Unfortunately, pétéx ~~is meaning~~ *means* "release of gassy air" in French.

7. Often, companies ~~are having~~ *have* problems with bad translations.

8. For instance, the owner of the Japanese travel agency called Kinki Nippon Tours ~~be~~ *was* complaining about foreign customers who wanted sex tours when a customer told him the English meaning of "kinky."

9. In another case, a Scandinavian vacuum cleaner company ~~was making~~ *made* a mistake when it created the slogan "Nothing sucks like an Electrolux."

ESL Teaching Tip: There are many other examples of names or slogans that translate badly. You might ask students to go to Web sites containing bad translations. (Just type "bad translations" in the search engine, and many sites will appear.) Students could work in groups to repair the poorly translated sentences.

10. Ellen Peters wants her product to sell internationally, so right now she is
working
~~work~~ with a marketing firm to come up with a good product name.

FINAL REVIEW

Underline and correct fifteen errors in verb form or tense.

published
EXAMPLE: The book *Business Ethics* was publish by Prentice Hall in 2006.

CHAPTER 28

Teaching Tip:
You can use the final review as a test. Additional practice and test material appears in the Instructor's Resource Manual and on *MyWritingLab*.

have been
1. Since 1900, many products been defective. In his book *Business Ethics*, Richard T. De George discusses a famous product defect case. In the early
lost or were losing
1970s, American automakers lose market share because smaller Japanese
were
imports be flooding the market.

wanted
2. Lee Iacocca, the CEO of Ford Motor Company, was wanting the company to produce a lightweight, economical car. Engineers developed the Ford Pinto. Because Ford wanted the product on the market quickly, the car was
tested
not test for rear-end impact during the production period. Then, after the
produced
Pintos had been produce, they were put in collision tests, and they failed
hit
the tests. When the Pinto was hitted from behind, a bolt on the bumper sometimes punctured the fuel tank. It could cause an explosion.

3. Ford conducted a study and determined that a small baffle, worth about
placed
$8, could be place between the bumper and the gas tank. The company
made
maked a cost–benefit analysis to compare the cost of adding the baffle against the estimated cost of lawsuits. The company decided that it was less expensive to fight lawsuits than to insert the baffle. For the next seven

years, the design of Ford Pintos did not changed [change]. The company also neglected to offer the baffle to customers.

4. In 1976, Pintos had thirteen explosions from rear-end impacts, which was twice the number of explosions for cars of a comparable size. When it be [was] too late, the Ford Motor Company realized that the lawsuits was [were] much more expensive than the baffle installations.

5. The Pinto was recall [recalled] in 1978. Since 1978, Ford has make [made] much better business decisions. In the late 1970s, the bad publicity from the Pinto case damaged the company's reputation. Since then, Ford tried [has tried] to improve its image.

The Writer's Room Topics for Writing

Write about one of the following topics. Proofread your writing and ensure that your verbs are formed correctly.

1. Write a short paragraph describing a useful product that you own. When and where did you get the product? How is it useful?
2. What are the effects of advertising on consumers? How does the deluge of commercials, spam, billboards, and other advertising affect the population?

CHECKLIST: VERB TENSES

When you edit your writing, ask yourself these questions.

- Do I use the correct present and past tense forms? Check for errors in these cases:
  - verbs following third-person singular nouns
  - irregular present or past tense verbs
  - question and negative forms

  The products that ~~was~~ *were* defective ~~was~~ *were* in his shop.

- Do I use the correct form of past participles? Check for errors in the following:
  - spelling of irregular past participles
  - present perfect and past perfect verbs
  - passive and active forms

  Since the 1970s, some car companies ~~made~~ *have made* bad business decisions.

- Do I use *-ing* forms correctly? Check for the overuse or misuse of progressive forms. Also ensure that progressive forms are complete.

  In 1971, while engineers were ~~design~~ *designing* the Pinto, nobody ~~was wanting~~ *wanted* to make an unsafe car.

How Do I Get a Better Grade?

Visit www.mywritinglab.com for audio-visual lectures and additional practice sets about verb tenses.
Get a better grade with MyWritingLab!

Problems with Verbs

CHAPTER 29

CONTENTS

- Verb Consistency
- Avoiding Double Negatives
- Nonstandard Forms—*Gonna, Gotta, Wanna*
- Problems in Conditional Forms
- Nonstandard Forms—*Would of, Could of, Should of*
- Recognizing Gerunds and Infinitives

Section Theme **INTERNATIONAL TRADE**

In this chapter, you will read about unusual and dangerous jobs.

Grammar Snapshot

Looking at Other Verb Forms

The following excerpt is from a personal letter by Garrett Brice, a student who spent one summer working in a fire tower. Conditional sentences are underlined, and some modals are in bold.

> The strangest job I have ever had was working in a fire tower. Sometimes, I would spend weeks at a time completely alone. I had to alert the base camp if I saw smoke rising in the forest. I brought along a guitar because I wanted to learn how to play it. Probably I **should have tried** harder. Maybe if I had had a teacher with me, I would have learned some songs. As it was, I spent the time playing with my dog, reading, writing, and just watching the birds.

In this chapter, you will identify and write modals, conditionals, gerunds, and infinitives.

Teaching Tip: Ask students to guess why the underlined sentences are called "conditional." Also ask them to look at the modal in bold and consider how such past forms are often misspelled.

Verb Consistency

A verb tense gives your readers an idea about the time that an event occurred. A **tense shift** occurs when you shift from one tense to another for no logical reason. When you write essays, ensure that your tenses are consistent.

Tense shift: Jean Roberts traveled to Santiago, Chile, where she interviews a salon owner.

Correct: Jean Roberts traveled to Santiago, Chile, where she **interviewed** a salon owner.

CHAPTER 29

ESL Teaching Tip: The error mentioned in the Hint box is particularly common among nonnative speakers.

Hint ***Would* and *Could***

When you tell a story about a past event, use *would* instead of *will* and *could* instead of *can*.

couldn't
In 2001, Simon Brault wanted to be an actor. At that time, he can't find a good
would
acting job. To earn extra cash, he will deliver telegrams wearing a costume.

PRACTICE 1 Underline and correct ten tense shifts in the next paragraphs.

decided
EXAMPLE: In the 1990s, Gretta Zahn made a decision. She decides to work as a parts model.

1. Some people have very unusual jobs. In 1992, a modeling agent noticed seventeen-year-old Gretta Zahn's hands. He signed the young girl to a
would
contract, and he said that he will make her famous as a "hand model." During Zahn's modeling years, her jobs were diverse. She soaked her
wore
fingers in dishwashing liquid, wear diamond rings, and demonstrated nail polish.

2. In the 1990s, Zahn's modeling career was lucrative. At the height of her
could *would*
career, she can earn up to $1500 a day. She will start her day at 5:00 a.m.,

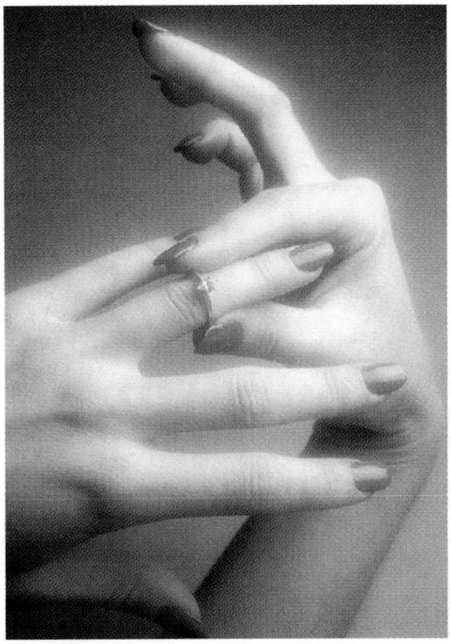

and sometimes she will [would] have to work for fourteen hours. To get a perfect shot, some photographers will [would] take hundreds of pictures of her.

3. Zahn's agent told her that she will [would] need to take special care of her hands. From 1992 to 2000, she cannot [could not] wear jewelry because it would leave tan lines. Also, during those years, she will [would] not do the dishes, and she refused to pump her own gas.

4. In 2000, Zahn gave up modeling. Today, she enjoys gardening, and she likes to wear rings and bracelets. Her hands are no longer flawless, but she did [does] not mind. "I have a life," she says. "I no longer worry about getting a cut or scrape."

Avoiding Double Negatives

A double negative occurs when a negative word such as *no* (*nothing, nobody, nowhere*) is combined with a negative adverb (*not, never, rarely, seldom,* and so on). The result is a sentence that has a double negative. Such sentences can be confusing because the negative words cancel each other.

Double negative: Mr. Lee doesn't want no problems.
(According to this sentence, Mr. Lee wants problems.)

He didn't know nothing about it.
(According to this sentence, he knew something about it.)

Teaching Tip: Discuss with students how the two negative words in the examples cancel each other out.

How to Correct Double Negatives

There are two ways to correct double negatives.

1. Completely remove *one* of the negative forms. Remember that you may need to adjust the verb to make it agree with the subject.

Mr. Lee **doesn't** want ~~no~~ problems.
Mr. Lee ~~doesn't~~ wants **no** problems.

2. Change "no" to *any* (*anybody*, *anything*, *anywhere*).

any
Mr. Lee doesn't want ~~no~~ problems.

PRACTICE 2 Correct five errors with double negatives. You can correct each error in more than one way.

any / have
EXAMPLE: They don't have ~~no~~ openings. OR They ~~don't have~~ no openings.

Have you ever had a strange job? Jordan Woo has had his share of unusual occupations. In 2005, he ~~couldn't find no~~ *couldn't find any or could find no* summer job. Then he saw an ad for a sign holder. For three months, he stood beside a work crew and held up signs to direct traffic. Occasionally, for an hour or two, he ~~didn't have nothing~~ *had nothing or didn't have anything* to do. The crew was working on a rural road, and sometimes there ~~wasn't no~~ *was no or wasn't any* traffic. He was bored, but he kept his job because he ~~didn't have no~~ *had no or didn't have any* better offers. Eventually, when he ~~couldn't take it no more~~ *couldn't take it any more*, he quit.

Nonstandard Forms—*Gonna, Gotta, Wanna*

Teaching Tip: Students often hear these nonstandard forms in movies and on the street, but remind them that these are incorrect forms.

Some people commonly say *I'm gonna*, *I gotta*, or *I wanna*. These are nonstandard forms, so avoid using them in written communication.

- Write "going to" instead of *gonna*.

  going to
  The boss is ~~gonna~~ hire three new cashiers.

- Write "have to" instead of *gotta* or *got to*.

  have to
  We ~~gotta~~ stay open until midnight.

- Write "want to" instead of *wanna*.

  want to
  We ~~wanna~~ keep our jobs.

PRACTICE 3 Underline and correct eight nonstandard verbs.

EXAMPLE: You and I gotta find *[have to find]* a better job.

1. If you wanna *[want to]* find work, there are many job-hunting sites on the Internet. One of the oldest and most established sites is Monster.com. The site was created in 1994. Jeff Taylor owned a job-recruitment agency, and he thought that an Internet site could help his business. He decided that his new site was gonna *[going to]* match job seekers with employers. That year, he created The Monster Board.

2. In 1995, Taylor sold his business because he didn't wanna *[want to]* pass up a great business offer. The new owners said that they were gonna *[going to]* change the name of the Web site. They didn't think that consumers would wanna *[want to]* associate "monster" and work. However, Taylor convinced them to keep the name.

3. In 1999, Monster Board joined with Online Career Center and became Monster.com. When you go on the site, you gotta *[have to]* find your region. Monster posts jobs in twenty-three countries. Then you gotta *[have to]* choose the job category that interests you. If you go on the site, you are probably gonna *[going to]* find interesting jobs in your city or area.

Problems in Conditional Forms

In **conditional sentences**, there is a condition and a result. There are three types of conditional sentences, and each type has two parts, or clauses. The main clause depends on the condition set in the *if* clause.

First Form: Possible Present or Future

The condition is true or very possible. Use the present tense in the *if* clause.

condition (*if* clause) result
If you **ask** her, she **will hire** you.

Teaching Tip: Draw students' attention to the verb tense that is used in each "if" clause.

Second Form: Unlikely Present

The condition is not likely, and probably will not happen. Use the past tense in the *if* clause.

condition (*if* clause) result
If I **had** more money, I **would start** my own business

Note: In formal writing, when the condition contains the verb *be*, always use "were" in the *if* clause.

If Katrina **were** younger, she **would change** careers.

Teaching Tip: In newspapers and articles, students may read, "if I *was*," or "if she *was*," but you can reinforce that this usage is incorrect in academic writing.

Third Form: Impossible Past

The condition cannot happen because the event is over. Use the past perfect tense in the *if* clause.

condition (*if* clause) result
If the business **had closed** in 2002, many people **would have lost** their jobs.

Teaching Tip: Draw attention to this hint. Both native and nonnative speakers make errors with conditional forms.

Hint **Be Careful with the Past Conditional**

In "impossible past" sentences, the writer expresses regret about a past event or expresses the wish that a past event had worked out differently. In the "if" part of the sentence, remember to use the past perfect tense.

if & past perfect tense ⟶ would have (past participle)

had stayed
If the factory ~~would have stayed~~ open, many workers would have kept their jobs.

PRACTICE 4 Write the correct conditional forms of the verbs in parentheses.

EXAMPLE: If the miners (go, not) *had not gone* on strike, their working conditions would have remained unsafe.

1. If you do research on the Internet, you (learn) ___*will learn*___ that truck driving is one of the most dangerous professions. William Roach

is a long-distance trucker, and he took a truck-driving course in 1992. If he (fail) had failed the course, he would never have found his passion.

2. Roach loves driving. "On a highway, with nothing but the road in front of me, I feel alive and free. Even if someone offered me a better job, I (remain) would remain a truck driver." Roach claims that the only drawback is the time he spends away from his family. He says, "If I (be) were able to, I would bring my wife and son with me."

3. In 2003, Roach was late for a delivery. To save time, he took an unfamiliar route. While driving, Roach fell asleep, and his truck rolled into a ditch. If he (have) had had a nap earlier that day, perhaps he (not, have) would not have had the accident. If he (stay) had stayed on the main highway, perhaps the accident (involve) would have involved more vehicles. According to medical professionals, if Roach had been awake during the accident, his injuries (be) would have been more severe. Because he was asleep, his body was relaxed and his injuries were minor.

4. Roach claims that even if he (know) had known about the dangers in truck driving, he would still have chosen to be a long-distance driver. If you could, (you, become) would you become a long-distance driver?

Teaching Tip: Both native and nonnative speakers make these types of errors because many native English speakers do not tend to pronounce the "have" clearly. Draw attention to this rule.

Nonstandard Forms—*Would of, Could of, Should of*

Some people commonly say *would of*, *could of*, or *should of*. They may also say *woulda*, *coulda*, or *shoulda*. These are nonstandard forms and you should avoid using them in written communication. When you use the past forms of *should*, *would*, and *could*, always include *have* with the past participle.

> Dominique Brown is a nurse, but she really loves real estate. She ~~should of~~ *should have* become a real-estate agent. She ~~woulda~~ *would have* been very successful.

PRACTICE 5 Underline and correct nine errors in conditional forms or in the past forms of *could* and *should*.

EXAMPLE: The workers should of *have* stayed home.

1. One of the world's most successful companies began in a small village in Sweden. In 1943, seventeen-year-old Ingvar Kamprad did well in his studies, and his father gave him a gift of money. Kamprad coulda *could have* bought anything he wanted. His mother thought that he shoulda *should have* continued his studies. The young man had other ideas. He decided to create a company called IKEA, and he sold small items through a mail-order catalogue.

2. In 1947, Kamprad decided to add furniture to his catalogue. One day, an employee from IKEA removed the legs from a table so that it would fit into his car trunk. Soon, the company created flat packaging designs. If the employee woulda *had* owned a truck, perhaps IKEA would of *have* continued to sell completely assembled furniture. If that had been the case, the company would not of *have* been so successful.

3. Kamprad's extreme youth helped him in his quest to take chances. Maybe
   had *would have*
   if he <u>woulda</u> been older, he <u>woulda</u> been more conservative. If IKEA
   had not *have*
   <u>would not have</u> changed, perhaps it would <u>of</u> remained a small company.

ESL Teaching Tip: This section on gerunds and infinitives is especially relevant for nonnative speakers because their languages may just have one infinitive form.

CHAPTER 29

Recognizing Gerunds and Infinitives

Sometimes a main verb is followed by another verb. The second verb can be a gerund or an infinitive. A **gerund** is a verb with an *–ing* ending. An **infinitive** consists of *to* and the base form of the verb.

verb + gerund
Edward <u>finished</u> **installing** the carpet.

verb + infinitive
He <u>wants</u> **to take** weekends off.

Some verbs in English are always followed by a gerund. Do not confuse gerunds with progressive verb forms.

Progressive verb: Julie is working now.
(Julie is in the process of doing something.)

Gerund: Julie <u>finished</u> **working**.
(*Working* is a gerund that follows *finish*.)

Some Common Verbs Followed by Gerunds

acknowledge	deny	keep	recall
adore	detest	loathe	recollect
appreciate	discuss	mention	recommend
avoid	dislike	mind	regret
can't help	enjoy	miss	resent
complete	finish	postpone	resist
consider	involve	practice	risk
delay	justify	quit	tolerate

Some Common Verbs Followed by Infinitives

afford	decide	manage	refuse
agree	demand	mean	seem
appear	deserve	need	swear
arrange	expect	offer	threaten
ask	fail	plan	volunteer
claim	hesitate	prepare	want
compete	hope	pretend	wish
consent	learn	promise	would like

Some Common Verbs Followed by Gerunds or Infinitives

Some common verbs can be followed by gerunds or infinitives. Both forms have the same meaning.

begin continue like love start

Elaine likes **to read**. Elaine likes **reading**.
(Both sentences have the same meaning.)

Stop, Remember, and Used to

Some verbs can be followed by either a gerund or an infinitive, but there is a difference in meaning depending on the form you use.

Term	Form	Example	Meaning
Stop	+ infinitive	He often stops to buy gas every Sunday.	To stop an activity (driving) to do something else.
	+ gerund	I stopped smoking five years ago.	To permanently stop doing something.
Remember	+ infinitive	Please remember to lock the door.	To remember to perform a task.
	+ gerund	I remember meeting him in 2004.	To have a memory about a past event.
Used to	+ infinitive	Jane used to smoke.	To express a past habit.
	+ gerund	Jane is used to living alone.	To be accustomed to something.

Prepositions Plus Gerunds

Many sentences have the structure *verb + preposition + object*. If the object is another verb, the second verb is a gerund.

verb + preposition + gerund
I dream **about** traveling to Greece.

Some Common Words Followed by Prepositions plus Gerunds

accuse of	be enthusiastic about	be good at	prohibit from
apologize for	feel like	insist on	succeed in
discourage him from*	fond of	be interested in	think about
dream of	forbid him from*	look forward to	(be) tired of
be excited about	forgive me for*	prevent him from*	warn him about*

*Certain verbs can have a noun or pronoun before the preposition.

CHAPTER 29

PRACTICE 6 Complete the sentence with the appropriate verb. Underline either the gerund or the infinitive form.

1. Do you remember (using / to use) a cell phone camera for the first time? When they first came out, I looked forward (owning / to own / to owning) one. When I first got my phone, I remember (to take / taking) pictures of myself when I accidentally hit the camera button.

2. A few weeks later, I insisted (to buy / buying / on buying) my grandfather a cell phone. I told him that he would need (using / to use) one during emergencies. My grandfather (is not used to speaking / didn't use to speak) on such tiny phones. Each time I visit him, I plan (to show / showing) him how to use it. However, my grandfather is not a technophobe. These days, he (used to work / is used to working) on a computer. He knows how to send e-mails, although he wishes that salespeople would stop (to send / sending) him spam. However, he just can't stand (to use / using / on using) a cell phone.

3. My grandfather is good (to think / thinking / at thinking) up solutions for problems. He wrote a letter to the cell phone manufacturer. He explained

that some older people dislike (to try / trying / of trying) to read the tiny numbers, and they don't want (having / to have) all of the extra features such as Internet links. He succeeded (to get / getting / in getting) a response. In fact, the cell phone company offered my grandfather a job as an advisor for the seniors market. Now, some cell phone companies are excited (to promote / promoting / about promoting) a new larger-model cell phone with large numbers and no extra features.

Teaching Tip: You can use the final review as a test. Additional test material appears in the Instructor's Resource Manual.

FINAL REVIEW

Underline and correct fifteen errors with verbs.

EXAMPLE: Many jobs are gonna [going to] become obsolete.

1. Certain jobs disappear because of advances in technology or changing habits. For instance, if you would have [had] been born one hundred years ago, you would of [have] worn a hat every time you went outside. However, since the 1950s, hats have not been standard attire and, as a result, hatmaking is no longer a popular profession.

2. In 1949, Joseph Wade didn't know nothing [anything] about hats, yet he decided to open a hatmaking business in Boston. Wade created men's felt hats and sold them in his hat store. However, if he would have [had] known what was coming, he woulda [would have] chosen another profession. By 1952, when the ducktail haircuts became popular, young men stopped wearing hats because

they did not wanna [want to] ruin their hair styles. Wade's business eventually closed. He had no idea that hatmaking was gonna [going to] become obsolete.

3. In 1964, Theo Malizia enjoyed to deliver [delivering] milk in his white van. The milk was bottled in glass containers, and it was deposited on the front steps of customers' homes. One day, he hit a pothole, a crate tipped over, and twelve bottles broke. If the bottles would have [had] been made with a less breakable material, they would have been easier to transport. When supermarkets began carrying lighter milk containers, Malizia had to find another job. Home milk delivery wasn't popular no [any] more.

4. In the 1990s, many people thought that any computer-related job would last for life. Carmen Morales took a nine-month course in Web site building in 1999. She thought that she was gonna [going to] earn a good living. Perhaps she shoulda [should have] seen what was coming. New software has become so user friendly that many businesses simply create their own Web sites. Perhaps if Morales would have [had] taken a programming course, she would have found a job more easily. Since September, Morales has been taking some business courses because she wants to be an accountant. "People always gotta [have to] do their taxes, but very few people wanna [want to] do the math," she says. Morales hopes her accounting job will never become obsolete.

READING LINK

International Trade

To find out more about the business world, see the following essays.

"Keep Your Roses" by Melonyce McAfee (page 253)
"I, Telemarketer" by Eugene Henry (page 596)
"The Rich Resonance of Small Talk" by Roxanne Roberts (page 599)
"Google's China Web" by Frida Ghitis (page 603)

CHAPTER 29

The Writer's Room Topics for Writing

Write about one of the following topics. Ensure that your verbs are correctly formed.

1. If you had lived one hundred years ago, what job would you have done? Describe the job using details that appeal to the senses.
2. Examine this photo. What terms come to mind? Define a term or expression that relates to the photo. Some ideas might be *mindless work*, *balancing act*, *glass ceiling*, *success*, *a go-getter*, or *a "suit."*

CHECKLIST: OTHER VERB FORMS

When you edit your writing, ask yourself these questions.

- ☐ Are my verb tenses consistent? Check for errors with the following:
  - shifts from past to present or present to past
  - *can/could* and *will/would*

  When he drove trucks, he ~~will~~ *would* drive when he was tired.

- ☐ Do I use the correct conditional forms? Check for errors in the following:
  - possible future forms (*If I meet . . . , I will go . . .*)
  - unlikely present forms (*If I met . . . , I would go . . .*)
  - impossible past forms (*If I had met . . . , I would have gone . . .*)

  If he ~~would have~~ *had* sold shoes, he would have been successful.

- ☐ Do I use standard verbs? Do not write *gonna*, *wanna*, *gotta*, *shoulda*, etc.

  If you ~~wanna~~ *want to* know the truth about the Free Trade Agreement, you ~~gotta~~ *have to* do some research.

How Do I Get a Better Grade?

Visit www.mywritinglab.com for audio-visual lectures and additional practice sets about problems with verbs.

mywritinglab

Get a better grade with MyWritingLab!

Nouns, Determiners, and Prepositions

30 CHAPTER

CONTENTS

- Count and Noncount Nouns
- Determiners
- Prepositions

Section Theme **FORCES OF NATURE**

In this chapter, you will read about some unusual weather events.

Grammar Snapshot

Looking at Nouns, Determiners, and Prepositions

In her article "Weird Weather: Sprites, Frogs, and Maggots," Pamela D. Jacobson describes unusual weather phenomena. The nouns, determiners, and prepositions are underlined.

> Sprites are barely visible to the naked eye. They sometimes look bluish closest to the clouds, but extend red, wispy flashes upward. Some occur as high as sixty miles above the storm. On images from weather satellites and space shuttles, sprites appear as marvelously complex shapes.

In this chapter, you will identify and write nouns, determiners, and prepositions.

Teaching Tip: Ask students to identify the nouns, determiners, and prepositions in this paragraph.

ESL Teaching Tip: Although your native speakers may benefit from the material in this chapter, it is particularly useful for nonnative speakers.

Count and Noncount Nouns

In English, nouns are grouped into two types: count nouns and noncount nouns.

Count nouns refer to people or things that you can count such as *tree*, *house*, or *dog*. Count nouns have both a singular and plural form.

She wrote three articles about global warming.

Noncount nouns refer to people or things that you cannot count because you cannot divide them, such as *sugar* and *imagination*. Noncount nouns have only the singular form.

The weather is going to turn cold.

Here are some examples of common noncount nouns.

CHAPTER 30

Common Noncount Nouns

Categories of Objects		Food	Nature	Substances	
clothing	machinery	bread	air	chalk	paint
equipment	mail	fish	electricity	charcoal	paper
furniture	money	honey	energy	coal	
homework	music	meat	environment	fur	
jewelry	postage	milk	radiation	hair	
luggage	software	rice	water	ink	

Abstract Nouns

advice	effort	information	progress
attention	evidence	knowledge	proof
behavior	health	luck	research
education	help	peace	violence

ESL Teaching Tip: Nonnative speakers might need some information about noun plurals. Remind students about common irregular plural nouns such as *people*, *children*, *men*, *women*, *teeth*, or *mice*. Ask students what the singular forms of irregular plural nouns are.

Hint **Latin Nouns**

Some nouns that are borrowed from Latin keep the plural form of the original language.

Singular	Plural	Singular	Plural
millennium	millennia	paparazzo	paparazzi
datum	data	phenomenon	phenomena

ESL Teaching Tip: This list is particularly useful for nonnative speakers. Remind them that noncount nouns have no plural form and cannot be preceded by *a* or *an*.

Determiners

Determiners are words that help to determine or figure out whether a noun is specific or general. Examples of determiners are articles (*a*), demonstratives (*this*), indefinite pronouns (*many*), numbers (*three*), possessive nouns (*Maria's*), and possessive adjectives (*my*).

> Gabriel Daniel Fahrenheit manufactured the first mercury thermometer in 1714. Fahrenheit's product was his claim to fame.

ESL Teaching Tip: Nonnative speakers may make mistakes with determiners. For example, Slavic languages do not use *the*, and Latin languages (Spanish, for example) use *the* more frequently than English speakers.

Commonly Confused Determiners

Some determiners can be confusing because you can only use them in specific circumstances. Review this list of some commonly confused determiners.

a, an, the

A and *an* are general determiners and *the* is a specific determiner.

> I need to buy a new winter coat. The winter coats in that store are on sale.

Use *a* and *an* before singular count nouns but not before plural or noncount nouns. Use *a* before nouns that begin with a consonant (*a storm*) and use *an* before nouns that begin with a vowel (*an institute*).

Use *the* before nouns that refer to a specific person, place, or thing. Do not use *the* before languages (*He speaks Italian*), sports (*They watch tennis*), or most city and country names (*Two of the coldest capital cities in the world are Ottawa and Moscow*). Two examples of exceptions are *the United States* and *the Netherlands*.

many, few, much, little

Use *many* and *few* with count nouns.

> Many satellites collect weather information, but few forecasts are completely accurate.

Use *much* and *little* with noncount nouns.

> Much attention is focused on solar power, but North Americans use very little solar energy.

this, that, these, those

This* and *these refer to things that are physically close to the speaker or at the present time. Use *this* before singular nouns and *these* before plural nouns. ***That* and *those*** refer to things that are physically distant from the speaker or in the past time. Use *that* before singular nouns and *those* before plural nouns.

ESL Teaching Tip: If you have many nonnative speakers in your group, you might draw their attention to the differences between *this, that, these,* and *those*.

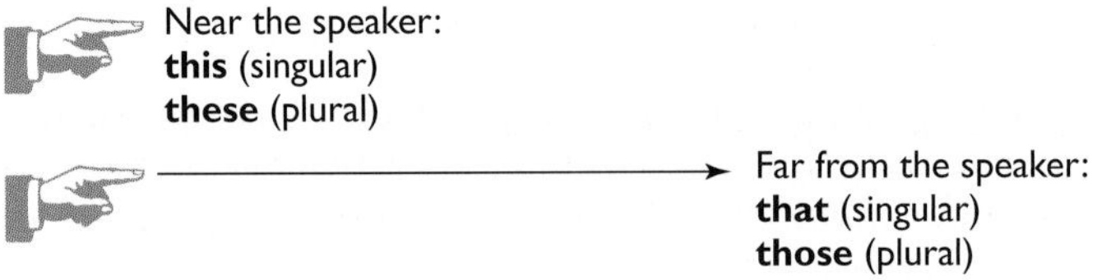

This **book** on my desk and those **books** on that **shelf** are about India. Did you know that in 1861, India had some very wet weather? In that **year**, Cherrapunji received 366 inches of rain. In those **days**, cities had trouble coping with so much rain, but these **days**, they are better equipped.

PRACTICE 1 Underline the determiner in parentheses that best agrees with the noun before it. If the noun does not require a determiner, underline *X*.

EXAMPLE: (The / A / X) driest place on earth is (the / a / X) Arica, Chile.

1. (Much / Many) people all over (the / a / X) world talk constantly about (the / a / X) weather. (Few / Little) phenomena are as exciting as extreme weather. For example, (the / X) tornadoes are seasonal in (the / X) North America. (A / The) tornado lasts about fifteen minutes. In 1967, there were around 115 tornadoes in (a / the / X) Texas. In (this / that) year, meteorologists believed (a / the / X) hurricane caused the numerous tornadoes in the state.

2. (Many / Much) people are fascinated with thunderstorms. (A / An / X) interesting fact about (a / the / X) Empire State Building is that it is struck by lightning around five hundred times per year. During thunderstorms, (the / X) golfers should be very careful. They should spend as (few / little) time as possible outdoors if there is lightning. (A / The) thunderstorm can produce a few hundred megawatts of electrical power.

3. (The / X) United States launched its first weather satellite in 1961. In (these / those) days, satellite pictures amazed weather researchers. Today, (much / many) research is being done by meteorologists about weather patterns. (These / Those) days, satellites gather (a / the / X) information about global weather systems.

Teaching Tip: To practice using determiners correctly, ask students to write different sentences using as many different determiners as possible.

Prepositions

Prepositions are words that show concepts such as time, place, direction, and manner. They show connections or relationships between ideas.

In 1998, northern New York State experienced nearly a week of freezing rain.

Freezing rain fell for a few days.

ESL Teaching Tip: Many nonnative speakers have difficulty with prepositions because they are not easily translated. For example, the Spanish word *en* can be translated as *in, on,* and *at.* Ask students to review the rules carefully.

Prepositions of Time and Place

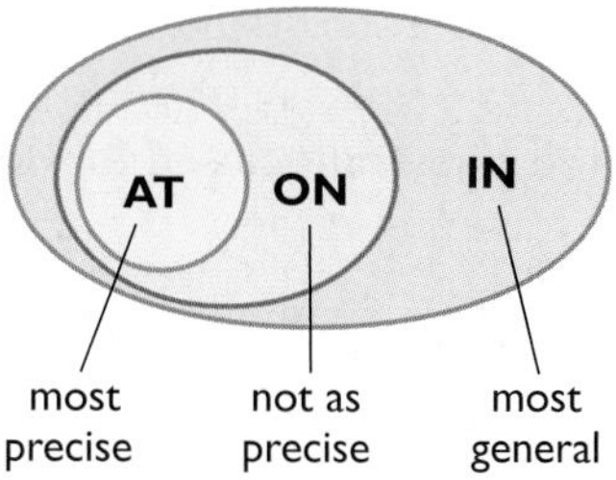

	Prepositions of Time	Prepositions of Place
in	in a year or month (in February)	in a city, country, or continent (in Phoenix)
on	on a day of the week (on Monday) on a specific date (on June 16) on a specific holiday (on Memorial Day)	on a specific street (on Lacombe Ave.) on technological devices (on TV, on the radio, on the phone, on the cell phone, on the computer)
at	at a specific time of day (at 9:15) at night at breakfast, lunch, dinner	at a specific address (at 18 Oriole Crescent) at a specific building (at the hospital)

(continued)

ESL Teaching Tip: Many nonnative speakers confuse these prepositions because they do not necessarily translate from one language to another. Nonnative speakers might have first-language interference problems. Ask them to carefully review the common errors.

CHAPTER 30

	Prepositions of Time	Prepositions of Place
from . . . to	from one time to another (from 10:00 AM to 1:00 PM)	from one place to another (from Fort Lauderdale to Orlando)
for	for a period of time (for five hours)	for a distance (for two miles)

Commonly Confused Prepositions

to versus *at*

Use ***to*** after verbs that indicate movement from one place to another. Use ***at*** after verbs that indicate being or remaining in one place (and not moving from one place to another). Exception: Do not put *to* directly before *home*.

> Each day, Suraya **runs** to the gym, and then she goes home and **sits** at the computer.

for, during, since

Use ***during*** to explain when something happens, ***for*** to explain how long it takes to happen, and ***since*** to indicate the start of an activity.

> During the summer, the restaurant closed for one week because of the heat.
>
> Since 2006, I have been taking skiing lessons during the winter.

PRACTICE 2 Write the correct preposition in the blanks.

EXAMPLE: ___At___ 5:15 A.M. we heard the news.

1. ___Since___ the beginning of human history, people have been trying to predict the weather. Many writers have created almanacs to record weather-related events.

2. ___In___ 1792, ___during___ George Washington's second term as president, *The Old Farmer's Almanac* was published. Robert B.

Thomas was its first editor. ____From____ 8:00 A.M. ____to____ 6:00 P.M., Thomas would work on his magazine. Sitting ____at____ his desk, he developed a successful formula to forecast weather. He had over an 80 percent accuracy rate. Thomas died ____in____ 1846, but people can go ____to____ Dublin, New Hampshire, and view his secret formula ____at____ the *Almanac*'s office.

3. *The Old Farmer's Almanac* has been published each year ____since____ it was first established. ____During____ World War II, the *Almanac* became notoriously associated with a German spy, whom the FBI captured ____on____ Long Island. The spy had the *Almanac* ____in____ his pocket. The U.S. government wanted to discontinue publishing the *Almanac* because it contained information that was useful ____to____ the Germans. After discussing the issue ____on____ the telephone, U.S. officials eventually allowed the *Almanac* to be published again.

ESL Teaching Tip: Other languages often use different prepositions after common verbs. For example, Spanish speakers say *think on* instead of *think about*. Suggest that nonnative speakers identify expressions that they misuse and memorize the correct expressions.

CHAPTER 30

Common Prepositional Expressions

Many common expressions contain prepositions. These types of expressions usually express a particular meaning. The meaning of a verb will change if it is used with a specific preposition. Examine the difference in meaning of the following expressions.

to turn on—to start a machine or switch on the lights
to turn off—to stop a machine or switch off the lights
to turn down—to decline something
to turn over—to rotate
to turn up—to arrive

ESL Teaching Tip: Give students the verbs *put*, *get*, *look*, and *pick*, and ask them to generate as many verb–preposition combinations as possible. In pairs or groups, they can write the meanings next to each expression. This activity is useful for nonnative speakers who may not know all the subtleties in meanings of different expressions.

The next list contains some of the most common prepositional expressions.

accuse (somebody) of	dream of	long for	satisfied with
acquainted with	escape from	look forward to	scared of
afraid of	excited about	participate in	search for
agree with	familiar with	patient with	similar to
apologize for	fond of	pay attention to	specialize in
apply for	forget about	pay for	stop (something) from
approve of	forgive (someone) for	prevent (someone) from	succeed in
associate with	friendly with	protect (someone) from	take advantage of
aware of	grateful for	proud of	take care of
believe in	happy about	provide (someone) with	thank (someone) for
capable of	hear about	qualify for	think about / of
comply with	hope for	realistic about	tired of
confronted with	hopeful about	rely on	willing to
consist of	innocent of	rescue from	wish for
count on	insist on	responsible for	worry about
deal with	insulted by		
depend on	interested in		

PRACTICE 3 Write the correct prepositions in the next paragraphs. Use the preceding list of prepositional expressions to help you.

EXAMPLE: Many people were upset __*about*__ the damage from the storm.

1. In southern Asia, many people look forward __*to*__ the monsoon. The word monsoon comes from the Arabic "mausin," which means "the season of the winds." During the wet season from June to September, India receives an average of 12 inches of rain each month. During the monsoon, people get tired __*of*__ dealing with the rain.

2. Throughout the year, South Asians depend __*on*__ the monsoon. Farmers hope __*for*__ adequate rainfall for their crops. Children love the monsoon because it provides them __*with*__ the opportunity to

play in the rain and the puddles. Although South Asians are often grateful ___for___ a good rainy season, they are also realistic ___about___ nature's forces and think ___about___ possible flooding, transportation delays, and malaria.

Teaching Tip:
You can use the final review as a test. Additional practice and test material appears in the Instructor's Resource Manual and on *MyWritingLab*.

Final Review

Correct fifteen errors in singular nouns, plural nouns, determiners, and prepositions.

EXAMPLE: ~~Much~~ *Many* houses lost ~~electricities~~ *electricity* during the ice storm.

1. One of the most interesting weather ~~phenomenon~~ *phenomena* is an ice storm. Freezing rain coats all surfaces with a heavy layer of ice. ~~On~~ *In* January 1998, Quebec and parts of ~~the~~ New England experienced the worst ice storm of the twentieth century. About 4 inches of freezing rain fell in the region ~~since~~ *for* five days. There were ~~much~~ *many* consequences because of the ice.

2. Over 900,000 households had no electricity for about a week. About 100,000 people had to leave their homes and go ~~at~~ *to* refuge centers. Many people worried ~~of~~ *about* the damage to their homes. Some people stayed at ~~the~~ home, but it was difficult without electricity. Others relied ~~of~~ *on* their neighbors. Also, the authorities were concerned about some people getting hypothermia.

3. The ~~environments~~ [environment] looked like a disaster scene from a science fiction movie. Farmers lost pigs, sheep, and other livestock. Some ~~business~~ [businesses] lost income ~~at~~ [during] that period because they had no electricity to remain open. Citizens received ~~few~~ [little] information from the authorities.

4. Although ~~this~~ [that] time has passed, many friends and neighbors still talk about the ice storm. ~~Those~~ [These] days, it is just a distant memory.

The Writer's Room Topics for Writing

Write about one of the following topics. Proofread your text to ensure that there are no errors in singular or plural forms, determiners, and prepositions.

1. What should people do to prepare for severe weather? List some steps.
2. What are some types of severe weather phenomena? Classify severe weather into three different types.

CHECKLIST: NOUNS, DETERMINERS, AND PREPOSITIONS

When you edit your writing, ask yourself these questions:

- ☐ Do I use the correct singular or plural form of nouns? Check for errors with the spelling of regular and irregular plurals and count and noncount nouns.

  Many children in snow

  ~~Much~~ ~~childrens~~ love to play ~~on~~ the ~~snows~~.

- ☐ Do I use the correct determiners? Check for errors with *a*, *an*, *the*, *much*, *many*, *few*, *little*, *this*, *that*, *these*, and *those*.

  These much the

  ~~This~~ days, there is too ~~many~~ information about ~~a~~ impact of global warming.

- ☐ Do I use the correct prepositions? Check for errors with *in*, *on*, *at*, and *to*, with *for* and *during*, and with prepositional expressions.

  For on

  ~~During~~ three months each winter, the town depends ~~of~~

  at

  tourists who stay ~~to~~ the ski resorts.

CHAPTER 30

How Do I Get a Better Grade?

Visit www.mywritinglab.com for audio-visual lectures and additional practice sets about nouns, determiners, and prepositions.

Get a better grade with MyWritingLab!

CHAPTER 31

Pronouns

CONTENTS

- Pronoun and Antecedent Agreement
- Indefinite Pronouns
- Vague Pronouns
- Pronoun Shifts
- Pronoun Case
- Relative Pronouns

Section Theme **FORCES OF NATURE**

In this chapter, you will read about nature's power.

Teaching Tip:
Ask students to whom *I, its, my, they*, etc. refer to get a sense of how well students understand pronoun reference.

Grammar Snapshot

Looking at Pronouns

The following quote is from the article "The Weather: Friend and Tyrant," in which William Renaurd discusses the effects of weather on people's health. The pronouns are underlined.

> "I can feel a cold weather front coming days ahead of its arrival," says Jane. "My teeth begin to hurt, and my entire lower jaw aches. I've been x-rayed, prodded by dentists, filled with pain-killing drugs, and examined by half a dozen neurologists. They can find no reason for my pain. I've decided that it's the weather and just try to bear it while waiting for the weather to change."

In this chapter, you will identify and write pronouns.

Pronoun and Antecedent Agreement

Pronouns are words that replace nouns (people, places, or things) and phrases. Use pronouns to avoid repeating nouns.

> *They*
> Hurricanes are large tropical storms. ~~Hurricanes~~ commonly form in the Caribbean.

A pronoun must agree with its **antecedent**, which is the word to which the pronoun refers. Antecedents are nouns and phrases that the pronouns have replaced, and they always come before the pronoun. Pronouns must agree in person and number with their antecedents.

> Sarah was late for **her** meeting because **she** drove slowly in the blinding rain.

GRAMMAR LINK

For a list of common collective nouns, see page 403 in Chapter 27.

CHAPTER 31

Hint **Using Collective Nouns**

Collective nouns refer to a group of people or things. The group acts as a unit; therefore, it is singular.

> The organization is very popular. Many people belong to **it.**
>
> The company was fined for polluting. **It** had to pay a large sum of money.

PRACTICE 1 Circle the pronoun and underline its antecedent.

EXAMPLE: Although hurricane names used to be only female, now (they) may also be male.

1. Anna Petrowski works for the World Meteorological Organization (WMO) where (she) helps to select hurricane names.
2. The WMO makes a list of distinctive names because (they) are easier to remember.
3. An Atlantic hurricane can have an English, a Spanish, or a French name because (it) mirrors the nationalities of people that may be affected.

Teaching Tip:
To help students remember singular indefinite pronouns, ask them to look at the word's ending. *Everyone, somebody,* and *nothing* end with singular nouns (*one, body, thing*); therefore, any verb or pronoun related to those words should also be singular.

4. In fact, when hurricanes become famous, the WMO retires their names.

5. The army usually sends its personnel to help with emergency relief during a hurricane.

Indefinite Pronouns

Use **indefinite pronouns** when you refer to people or things whose identity is not known or is unimportant. This chart shows some common singular and plural indefinite pronouns.

Indefinite Pronouns

Singular	another	each	nobody	other
	anybody	everybody	no one	somebody
	anyone	everyone	nothing	someone
	anything	everything	one	something
Plural	both, few, many, others, several			
Either singular or plural	all, any, half (and other fractions), none, more, most, some			

Singular

When you use a singular indefinite antecedent, also use a singular pronoun to refer to it.

Nobody remembered to bring **his** or **her** raincoat.

Plural

When you use a plural indefinite antecedent, also use a plural pronoun to refer to it.

Hurricanes and tornadoes arrive each year, and both have **their** own destructive power.

Either Singular or Plural

Some indefinite pronouns can be either singular or plural depending on the noun to which they refer.

Many meteorologists spoke at the conference. All gave important information about **their** research.

(*All* refers to meteorologists; therefore, the pronoun is plural.)

I read <u>all</u> of the newspaper and could not find **its** weather section.
(*All* refers to the newspaper; therefore, the pronoun is singular.)

Hint **Avoid Sexist Language**

Terms like *anybody, somebody, nobody,* and *each* are singular antecedents, so the pronouns that follow must be singular. At one time, it was acceptable to use *he* as a general term meaning "all people." However, today it is more acceptable to use *he or she*.

Sexist: <u>Everyone</u> should stay inside **his** house during a tornado.

Solution: <u>Everyone</u> should stay inside **his or her** house during a tornado.

Better Solution: <u>People</u> should stay inside **their** houses during a tornado.

Exception: In the men's prison, <u>everyone</u> has **his** own cell.
(If you know for certain that the subject is male or female, then use only *he* or only *she*.)

Teaching Tip: Point out that you can use the male pronoun if the context makes it obvious that only men did that activity. For example, if you write about soldiers in Napoleon's army, you could probably assume that they were all male.

CHAPTER 31

PRACTICE 2 Correct nine errors in pronoun–antecedent agreement by changing either the antecedent or the pronoun. If you change any antecedents, make sure that your subjects and verbs agree. Answers will vary.

EXAMPLE: Some of the workers had ~~his~~ *their* own skis.

1. Everyone should know what to do if ~~they are~~ *he or she is* caught in extreme weather conditions. For example, people should be aware of lightning storms. All need to avoid open spaces, and ~~he~~ *they* should get inside a building. No one should remain in the open because ~~they~~ *he or she* could be struck by lightning. If lightning is nearby, each person who is outside should get into a crouching position but never lie down.

2. In the winter months, snowstorms can be dangerous. Somebody stranded in a blizzard should stay with ~~their~~ *his or her* car. Nobody should wander outside on

CHAPTER 31

~~their~~ *his or her* own during a blinding snowstorm. It is very dangerous if a car gets stuck in a snowbank. One of the most common problems is carbon monoxide poisoning, which happens when snow blocks the back of the car and carbon monoxide gas backs up in ~~their~~ *its* exhaust pipe. To solve this problem, everyone should clear the snow from ~~their~~ *his or her* exhaust pipe.

3. Many have heard ~~his or her~~ *their* weather stations reporting on tornadoes. During a tornado warning, everybody should go into a basement or windowless room in ~~their~~ *his or her* home. Knowing what to do during extreme weather can save people's lives.

Vague Pronouns

Avoid using pronouns that could refer to more than one antecedent.

Vague: My father asked my brother where <u>his</u> umbrella was.
(Whose umbrella? My father's or my brother's?)

Clearer: My father asked my brother where **my brother's** umbrella was.

Avoid using confusing pronouns such as ***it*** and ***they*** that have no clear antecedent.

Vague: <u>They</u> say that thousands of people lost their lives during the 1995 earthquake in Kobe, Japan.
(Who are *they*?)

Clearer: **Government officials** say that thousands of people lost their lives during the 1995 earthquake in Kobe, Japan.

Vague: <u>It</u> stated in the newspaper that the scientific name for a thundercloud is cumulonimbus.
(Who or what is *it*?)

Clearer: **The journalist** stated that the scientific name for a thundercloud is cumulonimbus.

This, that, and ***which*** should refer to a specific antecedent.

Vague: My girlfriend said that the roads were icy. I was glad she told me <u>this</u>.
(What is *this*?)

Clearer: My girlfriend said that the roads were icy. I was glad she told me **this information.**

> **Hint** **Avoid Repeating the Subject**
>
> When you clearly mention a subject, do not repeat the subject in pronoun form.
>
> Thunder ~~it~~ occurs when cold air collides with hot air.

ESL Teaching Tip: Nonnative speakers may mistakenly use double subjects because, in many languages, the subject is repeated in the pronoun form.

CHAPTER 31

PRACTICE 3 The next paragraphs contain vague pronouns or repeated subjects. Correct the nine errors in this selection. You may need to rewrite some sentences. Answers will vary.

The journalist reported
EXAMPLE: ~~They said on television~~ that most tornadoes occur in agricultural areas around the world.

1. Meteorologist Patricia Bowles told her friend Sheila that ~~her~~ *Sheila's* photo of the tornado would appear in the newspaper. ~~They~~ *Meteorologists* say that tornadoes are the most powerful storms on earth. Tornado winds ~~they~~ can often exceed 100 miles per hour. This ^*wind force* can cause a lot of damage to property and sometimes kill people.

2. ~~It~~ *The science article* says that tornadoes form during thunderstorms when cool air moves downward and hot air rises very quickly, creating a funnel effect. When this ^*funnel* touches the ground, it becomes a tornado. The United States ~~it~~ has a "Tornado Alley." This ^*area* consists of Texas, Oklahoma, Kansas, and Nebraska. These states ~~they~~ have more tornadoes than other parts of North America because cold air from Canada meets warm air from the Gulf of Mexico over the flat prairies.

Pronoun Shifts

If your essays contain unnecessary shifts in person or number, you may confuse your readers. They will not know exactly who or how many you are referring to. Carefully edit your writing to ensure that your pronouns are consistent.

Making Pronouns Consistent in Number

If the antecedent is singular, then the pronoun must be singular. If the antecedent is plural, then the pronoun must be plural.

> A **meteorologist** (singular) and ~~their~~ his or her team spend years keeping meticulous records of weather patterns.

> When there are storm **warnings** (plural), ~~it~~ they should be taken seriously.

Making Pronouns Consistent in Person

Person is the writer's perspective. For some writing assignments, you might use the first person (*I*, *we*). For other assignments, especially most college essays and workplace writing, you might use the second person (*you*), or the third person (*he*, *she*, *it*, *they*).

Shifting the point of view for no reason confuses readers. If you begin writing from one point of view, do not shift unnecessarily to another point of view.

> **Many** tourists like to travel, but **they** should be careful. ~~You~~ *They* never know when there will be bad weather. ~~You~~ *They* should always be prepared for emergencies.

PRACTICE 4 Correct five pronoun shift errors.

EXAMPLE: Many people were saddened when they heard that thousands of people had died in the 2001 Indian earthquake. ~~One~~ *They* donated money, clothes, and blankets to the victims.

In 2005, we were traveling in Pakistan. We had just finished our breakfast when ~~you~~ *we* felt the ground moving. Everything in our tenth floor apartment started to shake and fall. We knew we should not panic, but ~~one~~ *we* really didn't know what to do. We knew ~~you~~ *we* had to get out of the high-rise and onto the ground because ~~one~~ *we* could never be certain that the building would remain standing. There were no guarantees that ~~you~~ *we* could make it out in time.

Pronoun Case

Pronouns are formed according to the role they play in a sentence. A pronoun can be the subject of the sentence or the object of the sentence. It can also show possession. This chart shows the three main pronoun cases: subjective, objective, and possessive.

Pronouns

			Possessive	
Singular	**Subjective**	**Objective**	**Possessive Adjective**	**Possessive Pronoun**
1st person	I	me	my	mine
2nd person	you	you	your	yours
3rd person	he, she, it, who, whoever	him, her, it, whom, whomever	his, her, its, whose	his, hers
Plural				
1st person	we	us	our	ours
2nd person	you	you	your	yours
3rd person	they	them	their	theirs

Subjective Case and Objective Case

When a pronoun is the subject of the sentence, use the subjective form of the pronoun. When a pronoun is the object in the sentence, use the objective form of the pronoun.

subject / subject / object

He left the umbrella at work, and **I** asked **him** to bring it home.

Possessive Case

A possessive pronoun shows ownership.

- **Possessive adjectives** come before the noun that they modify.

  She finished **her** research on the polar ice caps, but we did not finish **our** research.

- **Possessive pronouns** replace the possessive adjective and the noun that follows it. In the next sentence, the possessive pronoun *ours* replaces both the possessive adjective *our* and the noun *research*.

  possessive adjective

  She finished **her** research on the polar ice caps, but we did not

  possessive pronoun

  finish **ours**.

Teaching Tip: Remind students that they cannot use "which" unless the clause is set off with commas.

PRACTICE 7 Underline the correct relative pronoun in the parentheses.

EXAMPLE: People (<u>who</u> / which) live in the Arctic are used to harsh weather.

1. Ruth, (who / <u>whom</u>) I met in school, has been my best friend for twenty years.
2. Ruth, (<u>who</u> / whom) is a journalist, recently spent some time on Baffin Island.
3. The people on Baffin Island about (who / <u>whom</u>) Ruth is writing are mostly Inuit.
4. The Inuit (<u>who</u> / whom) are accustomed to extreme weather are active year round.
5. Ruth, (<u>who</u> / whom) loves the sun, sometimes feels depressed during the winter when there is very little daylight.
6. Many people (who / <u>whom</u>) Ruth has interviewed are worried about climate change.

Teaching Tip: You can use the final review as a test. Additional practice and test material appears in the Instructor's Resource Manual and on *MyWritingLab*.

FINAL REVIEW

Correct the fifteen pronoun errors in the next paragraphs.

EXAMPLE: Many people around the world have lost ~~one's~~ *their* relatives and property because of severe weather.

1. In 2004 and 2005, severe weather and natural disasters ~~they~~ caused havoc in the lives of people around the world. ~~They~~ *Scientists* say that forces of nature are

uncontrollable and unpredictable. But with increasingly sophisticated technology, climatologists and ~~there~~ their assistants should be able to improve natural disaster warnings around the world.

Katsushika Hokusai (1760–1849, Japanese) "The Wave", 19th Century, Woodcut print. © SuperStock, Inc.

2. In December 2004, my friend and ~~me~~ I were on holiday in Thailand. At that time, the strongest earthquake in forty years occurred in the Indian Ocean. It caused a tsunami that annihilated cities, villages, and holiday resorts. My friend, ~~whom~~ who is from Indonesia, said that all members of his uncle's family lost ~~his~~ their homes. Many people have suffered more than ~~me~~ I.

3. Some months after the Asian tsunami, New Orleans experienced one of ~~their~~ its worst hurricanes in history. Hurricane Katrina caused the levees to break and flood the city. ~~This~~ The flooding caused severe property damage and loss of life. Almost everybody in New Orleans had to leave ~~their~~ his or her home.

4. Also in 2005, a severe earthquake in the mountainous regions of Pakistan caused death and destruction. ~~They say~~ A newspaper says that around 100,000 people died. I watched television reports of people living in tents and wanted to help them because ~~you~~ I could see they had lost everything. So I collected donations from students at my college, and my brother, to ~~who~~ whom I sent our donations, passed them along to an aid organization in Pakistan.

5. The forces of nature are more powerful than ~~us~~ *we are*. We have no ability to control flooding, hurricanes, or earthquakes. With better warning systems and relief infrastructures, maybe ~~one~~ *we* can reduce the misery caused by natural disasters.

The Writer's Room Topics for Writing

Write about one of the following topics. Proofread your text to ensure there are no pronoun errors.

1. Describe a severe weather event that you or someone you know experienced. What happened? Try to use descriptive imagery.
2. Argue that bicycles should be the only type of vehicle allowed in city centers. Support your argument with specific examples.

CHECKLIST: PRONOUNS

When you edit your writing, ask yourself these questions.

- Do I use the correct pronoun case? Check for errors with the following:
  - subjective, objective, and possessive cases
  - comparisons with *than* or *as*
  - prepositional phrases
  - pronouns following *and* or *or*

  Between you and ~~I~~ *me*, my sister watches the weather reports more than ~~me~~ *I (do)*.

- Do I use the correct relative pronouns? Check for errors with *who* or *whom*.

  My husband, ~~who~~ *whom* you have met, is a meteorologist.

- Do my pronouns and antecedents agree in number and person? Check for errors with indefinite pronouns and collective nouns.

  The bad weather and ~~their~~ *its* aftermath were reported on the news.

- Are my pronoun references clear? Check for vague pronouns and inconsistent points of view.

  ~~They~~ *Scientists* say the weather will change rapidly. I read the report and ~~you~~ *I* could not believe what it said.

How Do I Get a Better Grade?

Visit www.mywritinglab.com for audio-visual lectures and additional practice sets about pronouns.

Get a better grade with MyWritingLab!

32 CHAPTER

Adjectives and Adverbs

CONTENTS

- Adjectives
- Adverbs
- Comparative and Superlative Forms

Section Theme **FORCES OF NATURE**

In this chapter, you will read about environmental issues and alternative energy sources.

Teaching Tip: Ask students to identify the adjectives and adverbs in this paragraph.

Grammar Snapshot

Looking at Adjectives and Adverbs

In his article "Iceland's Ring Road: The Ultimate Road Trip," Mark Sundeen describes aspects of that country's landscape. The adjectives and adverbs are underlined.

> Occasionally an iceberg floated beneath the highway bridge, was carried to sea, then was dashed on the beach by the windswept waves. We walked along the gray strand where the blocks of glacier rocked gently in the tide, and we gathered in our hands the cocktail-size ice cubes that had washed up on shore and flung them back to the sea.

In this chapter, you will identify and write adjectives and adverbs.

Adjectives

Adjectives describe nouns (people, places, or things) and pronouns (words that replace nouns). They add information explaining how many, what kind, or which one. They also help you appeal to the senses by describing how things look, smell, feel, taste, and sound.

> The **young** students convinced their **imposing** principal to start an **important** project on air quality in the schools.

ESL Teaching Tip: Because of first-language transference errors, many nonnative speakers place adjectives after the noun. Remind them that in English, adjectives cannot be placed directly after a noun.

CHAPTER 32

Hint **Placement of Adjectives**

You can place adjectives either before a noun or after a linking verb such as *be, look, appear, smell,* or *become.*

Before the noun: The **nervous** environmentalist gave a suitable speech.

After the linking verb: The biologist was **disappointed**, and he was **angry**.

Problems with Adjectives

You can recognize many adjectives by their endings. Be particularly careful when you use the following adjective forms.

Adjectives Ending in *-ful* or *-less*

Some adjectives end in *-ful* or *-less*. Remember that *ful* ends in one *l* and *less* ends in double *s*.

> The Blue Oceans Club, a **peaceful** environmental organization, has promoted many **useful** projects. Protecting the environment is an **endless** activity.

Adjectives Ending in *-ed* and *-ing*

Some adjectives look like verbs because they end in *-ing* or *-ed*. When the adjective ends in *-ed*, it describes the person's or animal's expression or feeling. When the adjective ends in *-ing*, it describes the quality of the person or thing.

> The **frustrated** but **prepared** lobbyist confronted the politician, and his **challenging** and **convincing** arguments got her attention.

ESL Teaching Tip: Many nonnative speakers make usage errors between *-ing* and *-ed* adjective endings. Draw their attention to this rule.

ESL
Teaching Tip:
In certain languages, adjectives agree in number and gender with the nouns they are describing. Remind students that adjectives are always singular in English.

Hint **Keep Adjectives in the Singular Form**

Always make an adjective singular, even if the noun following the adjective is plural.

> *year*
> Lucia was a forty-five-~~years~~-old woman when she sold her five-thousand-
> *dollar*
> ~~dollars~~ car and rode a bicycle to work.

Adverbs

Adverbs add information to adjectives, verbs, or other adverbs. They give more specific information about how, when, where, and to what extent an action or event occurred. Some adverbs look exactly like adjectives, such as *early*, *late*, *soon*, *often*, and *hard*. However, most adverbs end in *-ly*.

CHAPTER 32

> verb / adverb
> Biologists studied the statistics on climate change **carefully**.

> adverb adverb
> They released the results **quite** quickly.

> adverb adjective
> The **very** eloquent speaker was Dr. Ying.

ESL
Teaching Tip:
Give students a list of adjectives and a noun, and ask them to put the words in the proper order. After students finish, explain about the order of adjectives: determiner (number, etc.); quality; size or shape; age; color; origin; type; noun. Suggestions: (1) wooden, box, beautiful, red, tiny; (2) earrings, Chinese, jade, two, stunning; (3) tall, prisoner, white, elderly, Spanish; (4) shy, girl, Greek, twenty-year-old. Answers: (1) beautiful tiny red wooden box; (2) two stunning Chinese jade earrings; (3) tall elderly white Spanish prisoner; (4) shy twenty-year-old Greek girl.

Forms of Adverbs

Adverbs often end in *-ly*. In fact, you can change many adjectives into adverbs by adding *-ly* endings.

- If you add *-ly* to a word that ends in *l*, then your new word will have a double *l*.

> professional + ly
> The journalist covered the story **professionally**.

- If you add *-ly* to a word that ends in *e*, keep the *e*. Exceptions to this rule are *true–truly* and *due–duly*.)

> close + ly
> Scientists monitor the polar ice caps **closely**.

Hint: Placement of Frequency Adverbs

Frequency adverbs are words that indicate how often someone performs an action or when an event occurs. Common frequency adverbs are *always, ever, never, often, sometimes,* and *usually*. They can appear at the beginning of sentences, or they can appear in the following locations.

- Place frequency adverbs before regular present and past tense verbs.

  Politicians **sometimes** forget the importance of the environment.

- Place frequency adverbs after all forms of the verb *be*.

  She is **often** an advisor for environmental agencies.

- Place frequency adverbs after helping verbs.

  They have **never** donated to an environmental group.

ESL Teaching Tip: Some of your nonnative speakers might find the concept of word order difficult. For example, in Slavic languages, words have case endings, so word order is not as important as in English.

CHAPTER 32

PRACTICE 1 Correct eight errors with adjectives or adverbs.

EXAMPLE: I entered the room ~~quiet~~ *quietly* because the lecture had started.

1. Many people ~~frequent~~ *frequently* debate the issue of climate change. There are two ~~clearly~~ *clear* sources that cause global warming: natural and human. People ~~forget often~~ *often forget* that natural forces have contributed to climate change throughout the history of the world. Scientists know that ice ages have developed and diminished ~~rapid~~ *rapidly*.

2. Global temperature increases ~~naturaly~~ *naturally* for several reasons. For instance, explosions in the sun generate heat that causes the earth's temperature to rise ~~abrupt~~ *abruptly*. Another natural source for global warming is volcanic eruptions. A strong eruption gives off smoke and gases. These elements may ~~act sometimes~~ *sometimes act* as a shield preventing sunlight from entering the

atmosphere. In addition, a minor change in the earth's orbit may *also affect* ~~affect also~~ the earth's temperature. So when debating climate change, keep in mind the natural causes of temperature fluctuations.

Teaching Tip: Native and nonnative speakers often do not use adverb forms correctly. Draw their attention to this explanation.

Problems with Adverbs

Many times, people use an adjective instead of an adverb after a verb. Ensure that you always modify your verbs using an adverb.

The snowstorm developed *really quickly* ~~real quick~~. We had to drive very *slowly* ~~slow~~.

CHAPTER 32

PRACTICE 2 Underline and correct ten errors with adjective and adverb forms.

EXAMPLE: Climate change is a realy *(really)* controversial issue.

1. Human activity contributes great *(greatly)* to global warming. With modernization, lifestyles are changing real quick *(really quickly)*. More people are driving cars, and more industries are consuming largely *(large)* amounts of energy. When humans burn fossil fuels such as gasoline, coal, and oil, gases in the atmosphere that trap heat rise steady *(steadily)*. This condition creates a dangerously *(dangerous)* greenhouse effect, which means that heat cannot escape the earth's atmosphere.

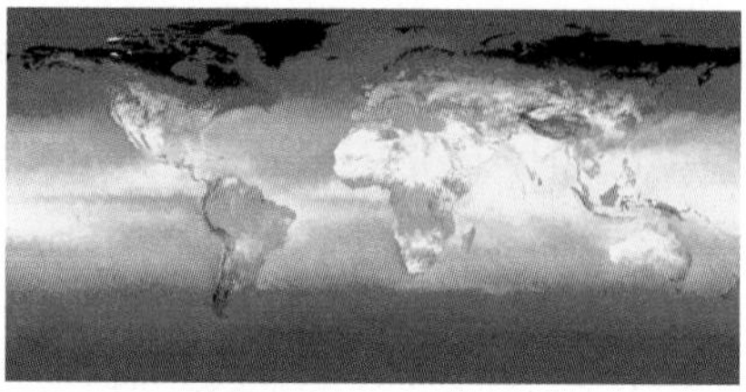

2. There is a general consensus by knowing *(known)* scientists around the world that the earth is experiencing global warming. Rising temperatures could have extreme *(extremely)* profound consequences for future generations. For instance, with melting ice caps, ocean levels could rise dramatical *(dramatically)*. Other areas in the world might experience harmfull *(harmful)* desertification.

Good and Well / Bad and Badly

Good is an adjective, and **well** is an adverb. However, as an exception, you can use *well* to describe a person's health (for example, *I do not feel **well***).

Adjective: We will have **good** weather tomorrow.

Adverb: She slept **well** even though the storm was noisy.

Bad is an adjective, and **badly** is an adverb.

Adjective: The **bad** weather remained during the past week.

Adverb: The meteorologist spoke **badly** during the nightly forecast.

> **Teaching Tip:** Point out to students that they may hear many people use *good/well* and *bad/badly* incorrectly, especially in spoken language. Emphasize that it is important to learn to use these words correctly.

PRACTICE 3 Underline the correct adjectives or adverbs.

EXAMPLE: Generally, public servants who listen (good / <u>well</u>) make (<u>good</u> / well) policies.

1. My biology professor explains subjects (good / <u>well</u>). Yesterday, he spoke about the (<u>bad</u> / badly) effects of greenhouse gases. The sunlight heats the earth's surface really (good / <u>well</u>), but not all of the heat is absorbed. The extra heat is reflected back into the earth's atmosphere, and greenhouse gases prevent this heat from escaping into the atmosphere.

2. The students in my class reacted (good / <u>well</u>) to a personal challenge for reducing global warming. Nobody thought (bad / <u>badly</u>) of the need for taking personal responsibility. They came up with (<u>good</u> / well) ideas to change their lifestyles, including writing a newsletter about the public's need to change (<u>bad</u> / badly) habits. Two (<u>good</u> / well) ways to reduce greenhouse gases are to reduce driving times and to recycle. Most people have (<u>good</u> / well) intentions and know (good / <u>well</u>) that humans must reduce greenhouse gases.

ESL Teaching Tip: Remind your nonnative speakers that the comparative form is often followed by the word *than*.

Comparative and Superlative Forms

Use the **comparative form** to compare two items. Use the **superlative form** to compare three or more items. You can write comparative and superlative forms by remembering a few simple guidelines.

Using *-er* and *-est* endings

Add *-er* and *-est* endings to one-syllable adjectives and adverbs. Double the last letter when the adjective ends in *one vowel* + *one consonant.*

short	short**er** than	the short**est**
hot	hott**er** than	the hott**est**

When a two syllable adjective ends in *-y*, change the *-y* to *-i* and add *-er* or *-est.*

happy	happ**ier** than	the happ**iest**

Using *more* and *the most*

Add *more* and *the most* to adjectives and adverbs of two or more syllables.

beautiful	**more** beautiful than	the **most** beautiful

Using Irregular Comparative and Superlative Forms

GRAMMAR LINK

Farther indicates a physical distance. *Further* means "additional." For more commonly confused words, see Chapter 34.

Some adjectives and adverbs have unique comparative and superlative forms. Study this list to remember some of the most common ones.

good / well	better than	the best
bad / badly	worse than	the worst
some / much / many	more than	the most
little (a small amount)	less than	the least
far	farther / further	the farthest / the furthest

ESL Teaching Tip: Nonnative speakers may have difficulty with irregular forms. Suggest that they memorize irregular comparative and superlative forms.

PRACTICE 4 Fill in the blanks with the correct comparative and superlative forms of the words in parentheses.

EXAMPLE: The problems of global warming are (serious) *more serious* than we previously believed.

1. The international community is trying to deal with one of the (urgent) *most urgent* environmental problems the world is facing.

   Global warming is one of the (debated) *most debated* issues in the scientific community. The Kyoto Protocol is an international agreement made under the United Nations. Nations agreed to reduce their greenhouse gas emissions and prevent the greenhouse effect from becoming (bad) ___worse___ than in previous years.

2. Dr. Anif Mohammed is a famous climatologist. His presentation was (short) ___shorter___ than some of the others, but it was also the (clear) ___clearest___. In fact, he seemed to be the (little) ___least___ nervous speaker at the conference.

ESL Teaching Tip: Native and nonnative speakers sometimes write *more* before a comparative that already has an *-er* ending. Draw their attention to this rule.

Teaching Tip: Ask students if they should use *fewer* or *less* with the following nouns: *sugar, evidence, people, armies, furniture, beliefs,* and *snow.* Then point out that they can only use *fewer* with plural nouns such as *people, armies,* and *beliefs.*

Problems with Comparative and Superlative Forms

Using *more* and *-er*

In the comparative form, never use *more* and *-er* to modify the same word. In the superlative form, never use *most* and *-est* to modify the same word.

> The photographs of the tornado were ~~more~~ better than the ones of the rainstorm, but the photos of the huge waves were the ~~most~~ best in the exhibition.

Using *fewer* and *less*

In the comparative form, use *fewer* before count nouns (*fewer people*, *fewer houses*) and use *less* before noncount nouns (*less information*, *less evidence*).

> Diplomats have **less** time than they used to. **Fewer** agreements are being made.

GRAMMAR LINK

For a list of common noncount nouns, refer to page 446 in Chapter 30.

Hint **Using *the* in the Comparative Form**

Although you would usually use *the* in superlative forms, you can use it in some two-part comparatives. In these expressions, the second part is the result of the first part.

> action / result
> The more you recycle, the better the environment will be.

Teaching Tip: Ask students to think of other sentences using two comparative forms. For example: *The more, the merrier. The more you drink, the better you'll feel, so drink milk with every meal.*

PRACTICE 5 Correct the nine adjective and adverb errors in the next paragraphs.

EXAMPLE: If ~~less~~ *fewer* people drove cars, we would have ~~fewer~~ *less* air pollution.

1. The Amazon rainforest is the ~~most~~ largest in the world. It plays a vital role in regulating the global climate. Forests, such as the Amazon, create ~~more~~ better air quality for humans. Trees and plants remove carbon dioxide from the air and release oxygen into the air. The Amazon rainforest has been experiencing deforestation ~~real~~ *really* rapidly.

Teaching Tip:
Team Work
Place students in teams and ask them to come up with a short advertisement for your college. They should use some comparative and superlative forms in their advertisement.

2. There are several reasons for the Amazon deforestation. The ~~most~~ biggest causes of it are cattle ranching and road construction. Roads provide ~~more~~ greater access for logging and mining companies. Clearing the forest, farmers obtain more land for their cattle.

3. The depletion of the Amazon rainforest is one of the ~~worse~~ *worst* problems for our global climate. ~~Less~~ *Fewer* politicians than environmental activists are concerned with this issue. The more humanity waits to tackle this problem, the ~~worst~~ *worse* it will become. Perhaps over time, governments and the general public will try ~~more~~ harder to save the Amazon rainforest.

Final Review

Correct fifteen errors in adjectives and adverbs.

EXAMPLE: We need to find ~~more~~ better sources of renewable energy.

1. Our society has depended ~~economic~~ *economically* on oil for the past two hundred years. Oil is a nonrenewable energy source. Many politicians have reacted ~~bad~~ *badly* to the suggestion that we need to reduce our reliance on oil. They are concerned about economic progress, which is presently fueled by oil. Yet, ~~worrying~~ *worried* scientists and environmentalists believe that burning fossil fuels is causing temperatures around the world to become ~~more~~ warmer. Because of the threat of global warming, scientists are trying to develop alternative energy sources ~~real~~ *really* quickly.

2. Wind energy is one ~~powerfull~~ *powerful* alternative. Historically, ~~countles~~ *countless* efforts have been made to use wind to power millstones for grinding wheat and running pumps. Today, wind-powered turbines produce electricity 25 percent of the time because winds might not blow ~~strong~~ *strongly* or ~~continual~~ *continually*. Therefore, the wind is not a dependable source of energy.

3. ~~Less~~ *Fewer* people use geothermal energy to heat homes in North America than in some other parts of the world. Nevertheless, it is also one of the ~~most~~ best alternative energy sources. Steam and hot water from under the earth's surface are used to turn turbines ~~quick~~ *quickly* enough to create electricity. Around the world, there are a few areas that have steam or hot water close to the earth's surface, making geothermal energy cost-

Teaching Tip:
You can use the final review as a test. Additional practice and test material appears in the Instructor's Resource Manual and on *MyWritingLab*.

effective. Iceland uses geothermal energy to heat about 80 percent of its buildings.

4. The ~~preceded~~ preceding energy sources are just a few of the alternative approaches that researchers are working on perfecting. These alternatives do not substitute completely for the versatility of oil. Scientists, government officials, and concerned citizens know ~~good~~ well that our society must reduce its dependence on oil. The more money we spend on research, the ~~best~~ better the chances will be to develop and promote energy alternatives.

READING LINK

Forces of Nature

The following essays contain more information about weather and climate issues.

"Weird Weather" by Pamela D. Jacobsen (page 607)

"The Rules of Survival" by Laurence Gonzales (page 610)

"Monsoon Time" by Rahul Goswami (page 617)

The Writer's Room Topics for Writing

Write about one of the following topics. Proofread your text to ensure that there are no adjective and adverb mistakes.

1. Compare two types of transportation that you have owned. Explain which one you prefer.
2. Argue that our government should or should not address the issue of global warming.

CHECKLIST: ADJECTIVES AND ADVERBS

When you edit your writing, ask yourself these questions:

- Do I use adjectives and adverbs correctly? Check for errors in these cases:
  - the placement, order, and spelling of adjectives
  - the placement of frequency adverbs, and the spelling of adverbs ending in *-ly*

- the adjective and adverb form
- the use of *good/well* and *bad/badly*

Magnus Forbes spoke very ~~quiet~~ quietly about the ~~interested~~ interesting article on El Niño at the news conference. He was often asked to speak ~~often~~ on environmental topics. The environmental lobbyist hid his concern ~~real good~~ really well.

Do I use the correct comparative and superlative forms? Check for errors in these cases:

- *more* versus *-er* comparisons
- *the most* versus *-est* comparisons
- *fewer* versus *less* forms

The ~~most~~ quickest tornado trackers take the first photographs.

The organization had ~~less~~ fewer members, but it also has ~~fewer~~ less bad publicity.

How Do I Get a Better Grade?

Visit www.mywritinglab.com for audio-visual lectures and additional practice sets about adjectives and adverbs. ***Get a better grade with MyWritingLab!***

33 CHAPTER Exact Language

CONTENTS

- Using Specific and Detailed Vocabulary
- Avoiding Wordiness and Redundancy
- Avoiding Clichés
- Using Standard English

Section Theme **PLANTS AND INSECTS**

In this chapter, you will read about plants.

Teaching Tip: Ask students to identify the simile in the Grammar Snapshot.

Grammar Snapshot

Looking at Exact Language

In his article "Deep in the Jungle of Suriname," Conger Beasley describes the beauty of a tropical jungle. The descriptive language is underlined.

> The view from the summit over the rippling tree canopy was impressive. The upper parts of the canopy were drenched in sunlight; it's here where the foliage is thickest that the majority of birds and animals range, not down on the floor where the sun rarely penetrates and the air seems to hold its breath like a whale at the bottom of the sea.

In this chapter, you will identify and write exact language.

Using Specific and Detailed Vocabulary

Effective writing evokes an emotional response from the reader. Great writers not only use correct grammatical structures, but they also infuse their writing with precise and vivid details that make their work come alive.

When you proofread your work, revise words that are too vague. **Vague words** lack precision and detail. For example, the words *nice* and *bad* are vague. Readers cannot get a clear picture from them.

Compare the following sets of sentences.

Vague: The flower smelled nice.

Precise: The crimson rose smelled musky sweet.

Vague: The gardener planted some flowers.

Precise: The gardener, Mr. Oliver, planted azaleas, hyacinths, and irises.

> **Hint** **Some Common Vague Words**
>
> The following is a list of some frequently used vague words. Try to find substitutes for overly familiar and vague words: *good, bad, nice, pretty, big, small, great, happy, sad, thing.*

Creating Vivid Language

When you choose the precise word, you convey your meaning exactly. Moreover, you can make your writing clearer and more impressive by using specific and detailed vocabulary. To create vivid language, do the following:

> **WRITING LINK**
>
> You can find more information about appealing to the five senses in Chapter 8, Description.

- **Modify your nouns.** If your noun is vague, make it more specific by adding one or more adjectives. You could also rename the noun with a more specific term.

Vague:	the child	
Vivid:	the angry boy	the tearful and frightened orphan

- **Modify your verbs.** Use more vivid, precise verbs. You could also use adverbs.

Vague:	talk	
More vivid:	bicker	debate passionately

- **Include more details.** Add information to make the sentence more detailed and complete.

  Vague: Some herbs are good for the health.

  Precise: Garlic has antibiotic properties that can fight bacteria and viruses.

Teaching Tip:
Group Work
Ask groups of students to use vivid language to describe the picture at the beginning of this chapter or to describe a photo in this book.

Teaching Tip:
Pair Work
Ask students to peer edit each other's work.

CHAPTER 33

PRACTICE 1 Underline vague words in the following sentences. Then replace them with more precise and detailed vocabulary. Answers will vary.

EXAMPLE: Our town's garden is pretty.

The pond in our town's garden is filled with pink and white water lilies and surrounded by ferns and wild poppies that attract green frogs, mallard ducks, and cardinals.

1. My neighbor likes to garden.
2. She has planted many flowers and plants.
3. There are also vegetables.
4. The herbs she has planted smell nice.
5. She has fun in her garden.

Avoiding Wordiness and Redundancy

Sometimes students fill their writing assignments with extra words to meet the length requirement. However, good ideas can get lost in work that is too wordy. Also, if the explanations are unnecessarily long, readers will become bored.

To improve your writing style, use only as many words or phrases as you need to fully explain your ideas.

The farm was big ~~in size~~.

(*Big* is a measure of size, so it is unnecessary to repeat it.)

Correcting Wordiness

You can cut the number of words needed to express an idea by substituting a wordy phrase with a single word. You could also remove the wordy phrase completely.

because
I don't like gardening ~~due to the fact that~~ I spend most of the time just pulling out weeds.

Some Common Wordy Expressions and Substitutions

Wordy	Substitution	Wordy	Substitution
at this point in time	now, currently	gave the appearance of being	looked like
at that point in time	then, at that time		
big / small in size	big / small	in order to	to
in close proximity	close *or* in proximity	in spite of the fact	in spite of
a difficult dilemma	a dilemma	in the final analysis	finally, lastly
due to the fact	because	past history	past *or* history
equally as good as	as good as	period of time	period
exactly the same	the same	still remain	remain
exceptions to the rule	exceptions	a true fact	a fact
final completion	end	the fact of the matter is	in fact
for the purpose of	for		

PRACTICE 2 Edit the following sentences by crossing out all unnecessary words or phrases. If necessary, find more concise substitutes for wordy expressions.

EXAMPLE: Medical researchers are conducting experiments with herbs ~~in order~~ to examine their medicinal value.

1. Herbs ~~One true fact is that herbs~~ have played an important part in the lives of human beings through the ages.

2. For example, in the past ~~in past history,~~ the Romans put laurel in the crowns of the emperors.

3. The ancient Greeks ate parsley to cure ~~for the purpose of curing~~ stomach aches.

4. During the Middle Ages, mint was popular because ~~due to the fact that~~ people used it to purify drinking water.

5. During ~~The fact of the matter is that during~~ the Middle Ages, people thought that herbs had magical powers.

6. The early settlers in North America grew herbs close ~~in proximity~~ to their houses.

7. At that ~~point in~~ time, the new immigrants also used herbs as medicine.

8. Today, some people believe that herbal medicines are ~~equally~~ as good as synthetic medicines.

Avoiding Clichés

Clichés are overused expressions. Avoid boring your readers with clichés, and use more direct and vivid language instead.

clichés	direct words
In this neck of the woods, she is considered an expert on orchids.	In this area

Other Common Clichés

a drop in the bucket	death trap
add insult to injury	easier said than done
as luck would have it	go with the flow
axe to grind	in the nick of time
better late than never	keep your eyes peeled
between a rock and a hard place	at a loss for words
break the ice	under the weather
calm, cool, and collected	time and time again
crystal clear	tried and true

ESL Teaching Tip:
If you have students who are nonnative speakers, you could discuss the meanings of these and other clichés with the class. You could also place native and nonnative speakers in mixed groups, and ask them to discuss the meanings of the expressions.

Hint Modifying Clichés

To modify a cliché, change it into a direct term. You might also try playing with language to come up with a more interesting description.

Cliché:	She was as happy as a lark.
Direct language:	She was thrilled.
Interesting description:	She was as happy as a teenager whose parents had gone away for the weekend.

CHAPTER 33

PRACTICE 3 Cross out the clichéd expression in each sentence. If necessary, replace it with fresh or direct language. Answers will vary.

Teaching Tip:
Pair Work
Ask students to do this practice with a partner.

greatly impressed
EXAMPLE: I was ~~blown away~~ by my neighbor's garden.

took a chance
1. My neighbor ~~threw caution to the wind~~ and planted some strange plants.

risked
2. She ~~was playing with fire~~ planting a ginkgo tree.

3. When I smelled something putrid, I was sure ~~beyond a shadow of a doubt~~ that it was the ginkgo tree.

Ginkgo leaves

4. ~~To add insult to injury, she~~ She had also planted a corpse flower in her greenhouse.

5. I ~~was at a loss for words~~ did not know what to say when she asked me how I liked her new plants.

6. ~~In the nick of time, my~~ My boyfriend arrived, so I could avoid answering her question.

Using Standard English

Most of your instructors will want you to write using **standard English**. The word "standard" does not imply better. Standard English is the common language generally used and expected in schools, businesses, and government institutions in the United States. **Slang** is nonstandard language. It is used in informal situations to communicate common cultural knowledge. In any academic or professional context, do not use slang.

Slang: Me an' some bros wanted to make some dough, so we worked on a farm picking apples. We made a bit of coin, and our grub was included. It was real cool. On the weekends, we mostly chilled.

Standard American English: My friends and I wanted to make some money, so we worked on a farm picking apples. We were well paid, and our food was included. We had a memorable time. On the weekends, we mostly relaxed.

Teaching Tip: Ask the class to compare contemporary slang with slang from past decades. For example, you might discuss the various ways to say that something is great (e.g., cat's pajamas, swell, groovy, hip, sharp, cool, awesome, wicked, sweet, tight, etc.).

Hint: Reasons to Avoid Slang

Slang changes depending on generational, regional, cultural, and historical influences. For example, one group might say "upset" whereas others might say "freaked out" or "having a fit." You should avoid using slang expressions in your writing because they can change very quickly—so quickly, in fact, that you might think that this textbook's examples of slang are "lame."

PRACTICE 4 Substitute the underlined slang expressions with the best possible choice of standard English. Answers will vary.

EXAMPLE: Over five thousand years ago, the Chinese cultivated roses that were bad. *excellent*

1. The history of roses is sweet. *fascinating*
2. An awesome fact is that the rose is about 35 million years old. *interesting*
3. I was blown away when I learned that there are 150 species of roses. *shocked*
4. Throughout history, famous chicks, such as Napoleon's wife Josephine, cultivated roses. *women*
5. From the eighteenth century onwards, Europeans thought it was tight to grow roses in their gardens. *a wonderful idea*
6. Cultivating a successful rose garden is no cakewalk. *not easy*
7. Roses need a lot of TLC to blossom. *attention*
8. The roses in my garden are fly. *gorgeous*

Final Review

Edit the following paragraphs for twenty errors in wordiness, slang, clichés, and vague language to make the text more effective. Answers will vary.
Wordy, clichéd, and slang expressions are underlined.

1. At this point in time, many people are freaking out about genetically modified foods. Genetic modification (GM) is a technology that lets scientists fool around with the genetic composition of plants.

Teaching Tip:
Group Work
Ask students to work in small groups and construct a short paragraph that incorporates many slang words. In the paragraph, they should describe a conflict. Then ask teams to exchange sheets and rewrite the paragraph using standard English.

Teaching Tip:
Pair Work
Ask students to do Practice 4 with a partner. Go over student answers to make sure that they have not simply replaced one slang word with another.

Teaching Tip:
To help students build vocabulary, ask them to work in pairs and come up with a list of possible substitutions for each slang term, cliché, wordy expression, or vague term in the Final Review.

Teaching Tip:
You can use the final review as a test. Additional practice and test material appears in the Instructor's Resource Manual and on *MyWritingLab*.

Historically, people have always tried to change the characteristics of plants for the purpose of making them more disease-resistant. That process has traditionally been done through hybridization, a tried and true method. That is, two parent plants from the same genus are bred to create an improved hybrid plant. One true fact is that hybrid wheat is hardier than traditional wheat.

2. Today, in North America, hundreds of things that we use daily are genetically modified. In the final analysis, there is great controversy about genetically modified foods. Proponents of this technology say time and time again that food will contain higher levels of nutrition, be resistant to disease, and produce higher yields. In spite of the fact of such arguments, opponents are all fired up about genetically modified foods because they say that there is not enough knowledge about how such foods will affect human health. They believe such foods might become a death trap. For example, will humans who are allergic to peanuts have a reaction if they are eating tomatoes that have been genetically modified with a peanut gene? Furthermore, opponents also believe that the loss of diversity in crops and plants really bites. Another worry is that food production will go into the hands of super-sized agricultural companies who will control growth and distribution of food. Moreover, the bigwigs in this debate stress out about the ethics of mixing genes from species to species.

3. The genetically modified food industry is growing rapidly in size. But it is important to have a healthy and open debate over this issue. Presently, consumers are faced with a difficult dilemma. Most people are in a fog and are unknowingly buying genetically modified foods because such foods lack complete labeling. For example, most cooking oil comes from genetically modified grains. The public should be in the know about this technology. Consumers need to be clued in so that they make the right choices.

CHAPTER 33

The Writer's Room Topics for Writing

Write about one of the following topics. Proofread your text to ensure that you have used detailed vocabulary and avoided wordiness, clichés, and slang.

1. Examine this photo. What are some terms that come to mind? Some ideas might be *family farm*, *agribusiness*, *healthy living*, *back to basics*, *farm aid*, or *green thumb*.
2. Why are fast foods and other unhealthy foods so popular? Think of some reasons.

CHECKLIST: EXACT LANGUAGE

When you edit your writing, ask yourself these questions.

- ☐ Have I used specific and detailed vocabulary? Check for errors with vague words.

  Vague: My son likes to garden.

  Detailed: My fifteen-year-old son, Kiran, is an enthusiastic gardener.

- ☐ Have I used exact language? Check for errors with wordiness, clichés, and slang.

  now
  Julian works in the garden center ~~at this point in time~~.

  evident
  It is ~~as plain as black and white~~ that many people like organic food.

  easy
  The biology exam was ~~a no-brainer~~.

How Do I Get a Better Grade?

Visit www.mywritinglab.com for audio-visual lectures and additional practice sets about exact language.
Get a better grade with MyWritingLab!

Spelling and Commonly Confused Words

CHAPTER 34

CONTENTS

- Spelling Rules
- 120 Commonly Misspelled Words
- Look-Alike and Sound-Alike Words

Section Theme **PLANTS AND INSECTS**

In this chapter, you will read about insects.

Grammar Snapshot

Looking at Spelling

In this excerpt from the article "Songs of Insects," writer Sy Montgomery discusses how insects communicate. Writers often misspell the underlined words.

> If you share this poet's sensibilities, now is the time to fulfill your longing. Though widely loved for its changing leaves and migrating birds, early fall is, in some circles anyway, yet more renowned for the sweetness of its insect voices.

In this chapter, you will identify and correct misspelled words.

Teaching Tip: Ask students to look at the underlined words and discuss the types of spelling errors people make. Then ask students to list other words that they commonly misspell.

Teaching Tip:

Team Work

Put students into teams and give them the following challenge. Ask them to compete with one another to write as many words as possible. Each word must have one of the following combinations of letters: (1) an *ei* vowel combination, (2) an *lly* ending, (3) a double *e*, or (4) a *ght* ending.

Spelling Rules

It is important to spell correctly because spelling mistakes can detract from important ideas in your work. Here are some strategies for improving your spelling skills.

How to Become a Better Speller

- **Look up words** using the most current dictionary because it will contain new or updated words. For tips on dictionary usage, see page 569 in Chapter 40.
- **Keep a record of words that you commonly misspell.** For example, write the words and definitions in a spelling log, which could be in a journal or binder. See Appendix 5 for more information about your spelling log.
- **Use memory cards or flash cards** to help you memorize the spelling of difficult words. With a friend or a classmate, take turns asking each other to spell difficult words.
- **Write out the spelling of difficult words at least ten times** to help you remember how to spell them. After you have written these words, try writing them in a complete sentence.

Six Common Spelling Rules

Memorize the following common rules of spelling. If you follow these rules, your spelling will become more accurate. Also try to remember the exceptions to these rules.

1. **Writing *ie* or *ei*** Write *i* before *e*, except after *c* or when *ei* is pronounced as *ay*, as in *neighbor* and *weigh*.

i before *e*:	ch**ie**f	f**ie**ld	gr**ie**f
ei after *c*:	rec**ei**pt	dec**ei**t	rec**ei**ve
ei pronounced as *ay*:	w**ei**gh	b**ei**ge	v**ei**n

Here are some exceptions:

anc**ie**nt	**ei**ther	n**ei**ther	for**ei**gner	l**ei**sure	h**ei**ght
sc**ie**nce	spec**ie**s	soc**ie**ty	s**ei**ze	th**ei**r	w**ei**rd

2. **Adding *-s* or *-es*** Add *-s* to form plural nouns and to create present-tense verbs that are third-person singular. However, add *-es* to words in the following situations.

- When words end in *-s*, *-sh*, *-ss*, *-ch*, or *-x*, add *-es*.

noun box–boxes **verb** miss–misses

- When words end in consonant *-y*, change the *-y* to *-i* and add *-es*.

    noun baby–babies **verb** marry–marries

- When words end in *-o*, add *-es*. Exceptions are *pianos*, *radios*, *logos*, *stereos*, *autos*, *typos*, and *casinos*.

    noun tomato–tomatoes **verb** go–goes

- When words end in *-f* or *-fe*, change the *-f* to a *-v* and add *-es*. Exceptions are *beliefs* and *roofs*.

    life–lives wolf–wolves

3. **Adding Prefixes and Suffixes** A **prefix** is added to the beginning of a word, and it changes the word's meaning. For example, *con-*, *dis-*, *pre-*, *un-*, and *il-* are prefixes. When you add a prefix to a word, keep the last letter of the prefix and the first letter of the main word.

    i**m** + **m**ature = i**mm**ature mi**s** + **s**pell = mi**ss**pell

    A **suffix** is added to the ending of a word, and it changes the word's tense or meaning. For example, *-ly*, *-ment*, *-ed*, and *-ing* are suffixes. When you add the suffix *-ly* to words that end in *-l*, keep the *-l* of the root word. The new word will have two *-l*s.

    casua**l** + **l**y = casua**ll**y factua**l** + **l**y = factua**ll**y

4. **Adding Suffixes to Words Ending in *-e*** If the suffix begins with a vowel, drop the *-e* on the main word. Some common suffixes beginning with vowels are *-ed*, *-er*, *-est*, *-ing*, *-able*, *-ent*, and *-ist*.

    bak**e**–baking creat**e**–created

    Some exceptions are words that end in *-ge*, which keep the *-e* and add the suffix.

    outrag**e**–outrag**e**ous manag**e**–manag**e**able

    If the suffix begins with a consonant, keep the *-e*. Some common suffixes beginning with consonants are *-ly*, *-ment*, *-less*, and *-ful*. Some exceptions are *acknowledgment*, *argument*, and *truly*.

    sur**e**–sur**e**ly awar**e**–awar**e**ness

ESL Teaching Tip: Many languages have words that look like English words but are spelled differently. You might ask your nonnative speakers to keep a list of such words. For example, English: *occupation*, *comfortable*. Spanish: *ocupacion*, *confortable*. Also point out that look-alike words may have different meanings. For example, in German, the word *bald* means *soon*.

CHAPTER 34

5. **Adding Suffixes to Words Ending in *-y*** If the word has a consonant before the final *-y*, change the *-y* to an *-i* before adding the suffix. Some exceptions are *ladybug*, *dryness*, and *shyness*.

   pretty–prett**i**est   happy–happ**i**ness

   If the word has a vowel before the final *-y*, if it is a proper name, or if the suffix is *-ing*, do not change the *y* to an *i*. Some exceptions are ***daily***, ***laid***, and ***said***.

   employ–employed   apply–applying   Levinsky–Levinskys

6. **Doubling the Final Consonant** Double the final consonant of one-syllable words ending in a consonant-vowel-consonant pattern.

   ship–shi**pp**ing   swim–swi**mm**er   hop–ho**pp**ed

   Double the final consonant of words ending in a stressed consonant-vowel-consonant pattern. If the final syllable is not stressed, then do not double the last letter.

   refer–refe**rr**ed   occur–occu**rr**ed   happen–happened

ESL Teaching Tip: Nonnative speakers may be confused as to why a word such as *beginning* doubles the *n* but *happening* doesn't. Say the following words out loud and ask students to guess which words require a double consonant: *preferred, offered, altered, opened, delivered, occurred.*

120 Commonly Misspelled Words

The next list contains some of the most commonly misspelled words in English.

absence
absorption
accommodate
acquaintance
address
aggressive
already
aluminum
analyze
appointment
approximate
argument
athlete
bargain
beginning
behavior
believable
business
calendar
campaign
careful
ceiling
cemetery
clientele
committee
comparison
competent
conscience
conscientious
convenient
curriculum
definite
definitely
desperate
developed
dilemma
disappoint
embarrass
encouragement
environment
especially
exaggerate
exercise
extraordinarily
familiar
February
finally
foreign
government
grammar
harassment
height
immediately
independent
jewelry
judgment
laboratory
ledge
leisure
license
loneliness
maintenance
mathematics
medicine
millennium
minuscule
mischievous
mortgage
necessary
ninety
noticeable
occasion
occurrence
opposite
outrageous
parallel
performance
perseverance
personality
physically

possess	reference	surprise	vacuum
precious	responsible	technique	Wednesday
prejudice	rhythm	thorough	weird
privilege	schedule	tomato	woman
probably	scientific	tomatoes	women
professor	separate	tomorrow	wreckage
psychology	sincerely	truly	writer
questionnaire	spaghetti	Tuesday	writing
receive	strength	until	written
recommend	success	usually	zealous

Teaching Tip: Ask students to highlight words that they commonly misspell. Then ask them to exchange their lists with a partner. The partner can then ask the student to spell the difficult words.

PRACTICE 1 Edit the next paragraphs for twenty misspelled words.

EXAMPLE: Some insects have an incredible amount of ~~strenght~~ *strength*.

CHAPTER 34

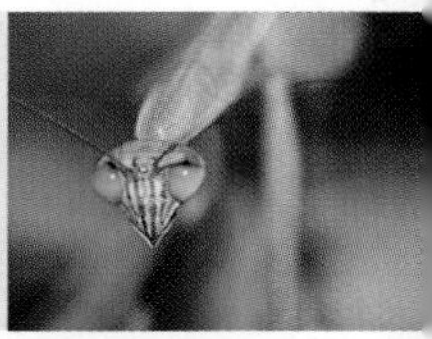

1. Throughout history, humans have either been fascinated or repulsed by insects. In fact, humans have ~~developped~~ *developed* a close connection to insects and recognize the power and importance of insects for sustaining life. For example, insects pollinate plants and aerate soil. Without such help, the ~~enviroment~~ *environment* would suffer. Thus, human cultures have ~~acknowleged~~ *acknowledged* insects through art, literature, and religion.

2. First, the ancient Egyptians honored different insects. The dung beetle or scarab was ~~definatly~~ *definitely* an important religious symbol. The Egyptians called it Khepera, the god of virility and rebirth. They ~~beleived~~ *believed* that he was ~~responsable~~ *responsible* for pushing the sun along the horizon. To honor Khepera, the Egyptians wore scarab amulets as precious ~~jewlry~~ *jewelry* and buried them in pots and ~~boxs~~ *boxes* with the dead. The ancients thought that the scarabs helped the dead who were

~~enterring~~ entering the afterlife. Furthermore, ancient Egyptian kings took the name of Khepera when they became rulers. For example, Tutankhamen's royal name was Neb Kheperu Ra.

3. Another insect, the cricket, was valued in Chinese culture. The Chinese kept both singing and fighting varieties. Singing crickets were ~~expecialy~~ especially crucial to farmers. They knew it was time to plow when crickets and other insects began to wake and sing. Wealthy ~~ladyes~~ ladies and palace concubines kept crickets as pets in cages. People surmised that the crickets represented the women ~~themselfs~~ themselves, who had very little status in the community. Fighting crickets were also very popular, and many people lost much of their savings ~~beting~~ betting on cricket fights.

4. Western artists are also fascinated with insects. There are many fables that feature different ~~speceis~~ species as the main characters. In modern literature, insects play a ~~noticable~~ noticeable role. For example, in Franz Kafka's *Metamorphosis*, the main character turns into a giant cockroach. Insects are common symbols in modern film. Jiminy Cricket is Pinocchio's ~~conseeince~~ conscience. In the movie *The Fly*, a scientist is ~~unaturaly~~ unnaturally transformed into a six-foot human fly. ~~Flys~~ Flies and other insects can also symbolize human fear and repugnance.

5. Humans and insects have had a ~~truely~~ truly unique relationship for many millennia. Different cultures have integrated insects into the fields of art, music, religion, and history. Indeed, some people say that the teeny creepy crawlers are survivors and will ~~surly~~ surely outlive humans.

Look-Alike and Sound-Alike Words

Sometimes two English words can sound the same but have different spellings and meanings. These words are called **homonyms**. Here are a few commonly confused words and basic meanings. (For more specific definitions for these and other words, consult a dictionary.)

accept	to receive; to admit	We must accept the vital role that insects play in our culture.
except	excluding; other than	I like all insects except ants.
allowed	permitted	We were not allowed to view the exhibit.
aloud	spoken audibly	We could not speak aloud, so we whispered.
affect	to influence	Pesticides affect the environment.
effect	the result of something	Scientists are examining the effects of pesticides on our health.
been	past participle of the verb *to be*	He has been to the Imax film about caterpillars.
being	present progressive form (the *-ing* form) of the verb *to be*	She was being kind when she donated to the butterfly museum.
by	preposition meaning *next to*, *on*, or *before*	A bee flew by the flowers. By evening, the crickets were making a lot of noise.
buy	to purchase	Will you buy me that scarab necklace?
complement	to add to; to complete	The film about the monarch butterfly was a nice complement to the exhibit.
compliment	to say something nice about someone	The film was informative and the director received many compliments.
conscience	a personal sense of right or wrong	After spraying pesticides, the gardener had a guilty conscience.
conscious	to be aware; to be awake	He made us conscious of the important role insects play in our society.

Teaching Tip: Ask students to look at the list and highlight the words that they commonly confuse.

CHAPTER 34

PRACTICE 2 Underline the correct word in the parentheses.

EXAMPLE: Many people (by / buy) clothes made out of silk.

1. Silk has (been / being) produced (by / buy) the Chinese for at least four thousand years. The silkworm is actually a caterpillar that eats nothing (accept / except) mulberry leaves, grows quickly, and then encircles itself

into a cocoon of raw silk. The cocoon contains a single thread around 300 to 900 yards in length, so it's not surprising that it takes about 2,000 cocoons to make one pound of silk. (Been / Being) very (conscious / conscience) of the long and intense silk-making process, most people (accept / except) the high cost of the material.

2. The Chinese valued silk and guarded the secret of its making carefully. In ancient China, only the emperor and his family were (allowed / aloud) to wear silk garments. Sometimes, members of royalty wore the fabric as a (complement / compliment) to their regular clothes. Of course, less fortunate people admired the emperor's beautiful clothes and always (complimented / complemented) him.

3. By the fifth century, the secret of silk-making had been revealed to Korea, Japan, and India. How did the secret get out? Legend says that a princess with no (conscious / conscience) smuggled out silkworm larvae to Korea by hiding them in her hair. The emperor was outraged (by / buy) the actions of the princess, and there was great debate about her treachery.

everyday	ordinary or common	Swatting mosquitoes is an everyday ritual of camping.
every day	each day	Every day, I check my roses for aphids.
imminent	soon to happen	The journalist reported that the arrival of locusts in parts of Africa was imminent.
eminent	distinguished; superior	Professor Maurice Kanyogo is an eminent entomologist.
imply	to suggest	The entomologist implied that he received a large grant.
infer	to conclude	His students inferred that they would have summer jobs because of the grant.
its	possessive case of the pronoun *it*	The worker bee went into its hive.
it's	contraction for *it is*	It's well known that the queen bee is the largest in the colony.

knew	past tense of *to know*	I knew that I should study for my test on worms.
new	recent or unused	But my new book on honey making was more interesting.
know	to have knowledge of	The beekeepers know that there has been a decline of bees in recent years.
no	a negative	There were no books on beekeeping in the library.
lose	to misplace or forfeit something	Do not lose the mosquito repellent.
loose	too baggy; not fixed	You should wear loose clothes when camping.
loss	a decrease in an amount; a serious blow	Farmers would experience a loss if there were no bees to pollinate crops.
peace	calmness; an end to violence	The peace in the woods was wonderful.
piece	a part of something else; one item in a group of items	The two pieces of amber had insects in them.
principal	director of a school; the most important item in a group; main	The principal of our school is an expert on beetles. They are his principal hobby.
principle	rules or standards	Julius Corrant wrote a book about environmental principles.
quiet	silent	The crickets remained quiet this evening.
quite	very	They usually make quite a noise.
quit	stop	I would like them to quit making so much noise.

CHAPTER 34

PRACTICE 3 Identify and correct ten word choice errors.

EXAMPLE: I need some ~~piece~~ *peace* and quiet.

1. I am reading a book on pollination by professor Zoe Truger, an ~~imminent~~ *eminent* entomologist who specializes in butterfly behavior. ~~Its~~ *It's* very interesting. On ~~it's~~ *its* cover, there is a beautiful photograph of a butterfly. ~~Everyday~~ *Every day*, during the summer, thousands of monarch butterflies are found in southern Canada, their summer home. As autumn arrives, these butterflies know that migration to warmer climates is ~~eminent~~ *imminent*.

2. The ~~principle~~ principal of Jake's school took the students on a nature walk to look for earthworms. The students were very ~~quite~~ quiet when the guide told them there are 2,700 species of earthworms.

3. Did you ~~no~~ know that beekeeping is one of the world's oldest professions? Some beekeepers may ~~loose~~ lose their businesses because bees are dying due to pesticide overuse. Citizens need to ~~quite~~ quit spraying their fields, parks, and gardens with pesticides.

taught	past tense of *to teach*	I taught a class on pollination.
thought	past tense of *to think*	I thought the students enjoyed it.
than	word used to compare items	There are more mosquitoes at the lake than in the city.
then	at a particular time; after a specific time	He found the termite nest. Then he called the exterminators.
that	word used to introduce a clause	They told him that they would come immediately.
their	possessive form of *they*	They wore scarab amulets to show their respect for the god Khepera.
there	a place	The ant colony is over there.
they're	contraction of *they are*	The ants work hard. They're very industrious.
to	part of an infinitive; indicates direction or movement	I want to hunt for bugs. I will go to the hiking path and look under some rocks.
too	also or very	My friend is too scared of bugs. My brother is, too.
two	the number after *one*	There were two types of butterflies in the garden today.
where	question word indicating location	Where did you buy the book on ladybugs?
were	past tense of *be*	There were hundreds of ladybugs on the bush.
we're	contraction of *we are*	We're wondering why we have this infestation.

who's	contraction of *who is*	Isabelle, who's a horticulturist, also keeps a butterfly garden.
whose	pronoun showing ownership	Whose garden is that?
write	to draw symbols that represent words	I will write an essay about the common earthworm.
right	correct; the opposite of the direction left	In the right corner of the garden, there is the compost bin with many worms in it. You are right when you say that earthworms are necessary for composting.

PRACTICE 4 Identify and correct sixteen word choice errors.

EXAMPLE: ~~Their~~ *There* are many different types of hobbies.

1. ~~Their~~ *There* are both professional and amateur beekeepers. Beekeepers wear special clothes, but even with protective gear, ~~there~~ *they're* usually stung at least once while practicing ~~there~~ *their* profession. Some beekeepers have a greater resistance to stings ~~then~~ *than* others have. All of them know ~~than~~ *that* there is a small danger of death from anaphylactic shock because of a bee sting. A person ~~whose~~ *who's* interested in beekeeping should know the risks. ~~Than~~ *Then* he or she can make the ~~write~~ *right* choice about beekeeping as a hobby.

2. We recently read ~~to~~ *two* books on ladybugs. We went to the library ~~were~~ *where* an expert ~~thought~~ *taught* us about ladybugs. The expert, ~~who's~~ *whose* bug collection was on display, said each ladybug controls pests because it eats around 5,000 aphids in its lifetime. Ladybugs eat other pests, ~~to~~ *too*. We ~~where~~ *were* extremely surprised when we heard that information. ~~Were~~ *We're* going to do more research on ladybugs. I will ~~right~~ *write* an e-mail to the expert asking for more information.

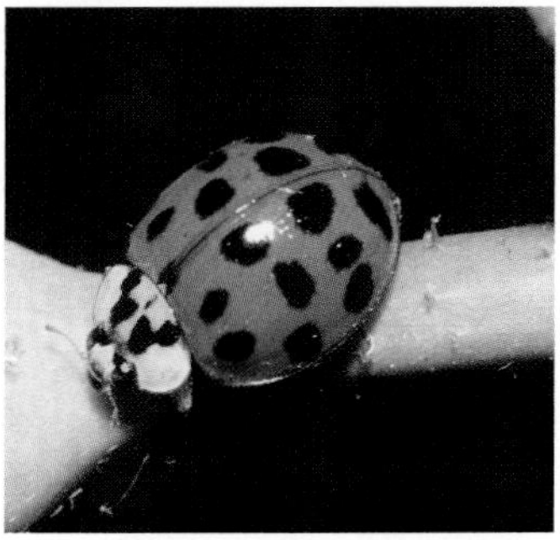

Teaching Tip:
You can use the final review as a test. Additional practice and test material appears in the Instructor's Resource Manual and on *MyWritingLab*.

Teaching Tip:
Pair Work
Ask students to do this activity in pairs.

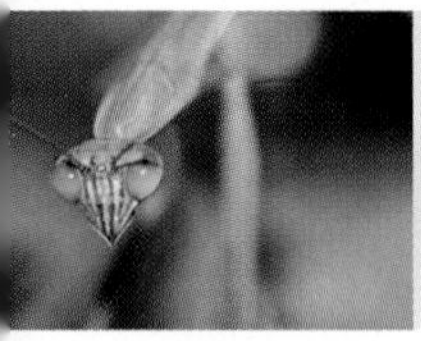

Final Review

Correct the twenty spelling errors and mistakes with commonly confused words in the essay.

EXAMPLE: The bee ~~carrys~~ *carries* pollen grains from one plant to another.

1. Around the world, ~~unatural~~ *unnatural* causes such as climate change, pollution, and human activities are threatening the ~~enviroment~~ *environment*. Forests are ~~expecialy~~ *especially* vulnerable to these pressures because of ~~loging~~ *logging*, increasing pests, and global warming. Conserving biodiversity is important to protect forests.

2. Biodiversity, a contraction of the words *biological diversity*, means that a variety of plants, animals, and microorganisms coexist in an ecosystem. Today, ~~imminent~~ *eminent* scientists concerned with species' extinction refer to the ~~necesity~~ *necessity* of maintaining biodiversity on our planet. Scientists are ~~conscience~~ *conscious* of the value of each species. ~~Argueing~~ *Arguing* for conserving biodiversity, scientists believe that if species become extinct, ~~than~~ *then* their ecosystem will become unstable.

3. Insects are crucial to sustain the biodiversity of an ecosystem and are the most diverse life form on earth. Currently, there are approximately 800,000 identified species of insects, all of which are ~~usefull~~ *useful* in balancing the ecosystem. For example, they pollinate plants, and they eat other insects and plants. ~~Their~~ *They're* also important to the global economy. For

instance, insects are used for honey production, silk making, and agricultural pest control. If an insect species becomes extinct, ~~they're~~ *there* will be a variety of consequences on the remaining species in the ecosystem, such as an increase in predatory insects or a ~~lost~~ *loss* of another species higher on the food chain. Such a change in the ecosystem would have an ~~eminent~~ *imminent* effect on all life forms.

4. Most people think that insects are troublesome and should be eradicated. Of course, insects such as ~~mosquitos~~ *mosquitoes* carry diseases, including malaria and West Nile virus, which are ~~harmfull~~ *harmful* to human health. But ~~its~~ *it's* important to keep in mind that most insects provide important services for the natural world, ~~to~~ *too*. ~~Were~~ *Where* there are insects, there is a thriving ecosystem. Extinction of an insect species will have a serious ~~affect~~ *effect* on nature, so the next time you are tempted to swat a fly or step on an ant, you might think twice.

CHAPTER 34

The Writer's Room **Topics for Writing**

Write about one of the following topics. Proofread your text to ensure there are no spelling and commonly confused word errors.

1. Discuss types of insects that are particularly annoying, repulsive, or frightening.
2. Are laws banning the use of pesticides on lawns a good idea? Explain your ideas.

READING LINK

Plants and Insects

The following readings contain more information on plants and insects.

"Living Among the Bees" by Lucie Snodgrass (page 132)

"Songs of Insects" by Sy Montgomery (page 621)

"Nature Returns to the Cities" by John Roach (page 624)

CHECKLIST: SPELLING RULES

When you edit your writing, ask yourself these questions.

- [ ] Do I have any spelling errors? Check for errors in words that contain these elements:
  - *ie* or *ei* combinations
  - prefixes and suffixes

    Dragonflies *lovely* *Their*
    ~~Dragonflys~~ are ~~lovly~~. ~~There~~ wings are transparent, but

    their
    ~~they're~~ bodies are a variety of colors. They eat other

    mosquitoes
    insects such as ~~mosquitos~~.

- [ ] Do I repeat spelling errors that I have made in previous assignments? I should check my previous assignments for errors or consult my spelling log.

How Do I Get a Better Grade?

PEARSON mywritinglab

Visit www.mywritinglab.com for audio-visual lectures and additional practice sets about spelling and commonly confused words.

Get a better grade with MyWritingLab!

Commas

CHAPTER 35

CONTENTS

Section Theme
HUMAN DEVELOPMENT

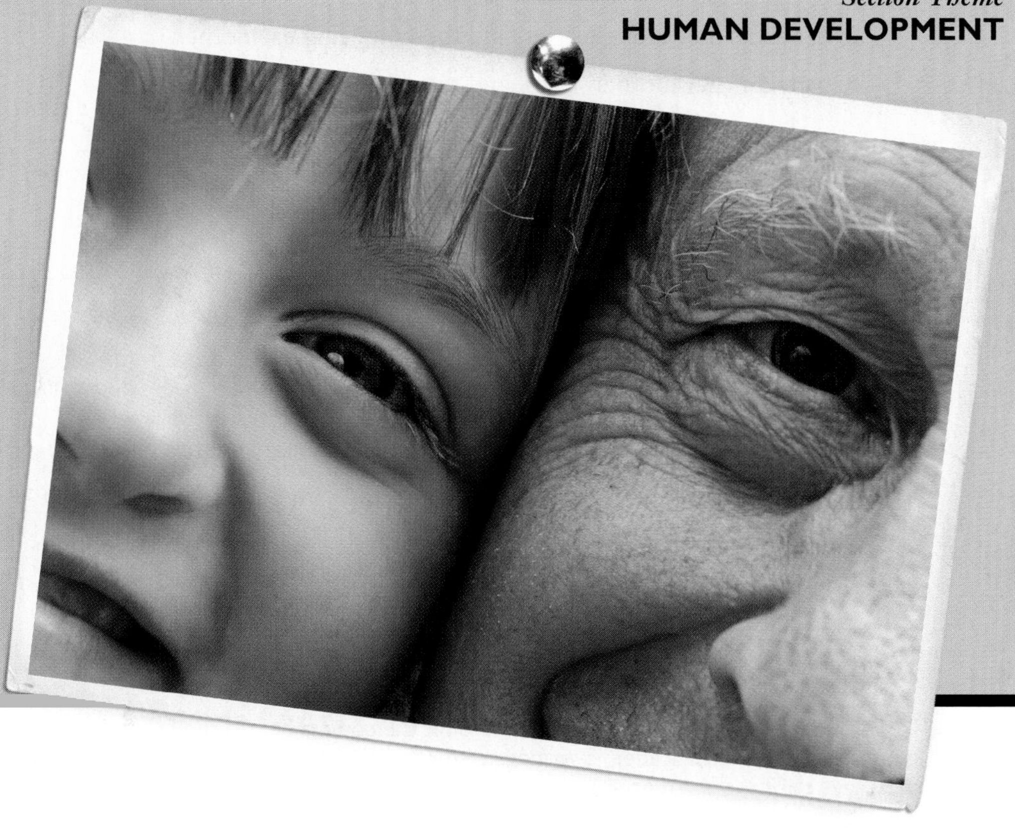

In this chapter, you will read about life stages.

Grammar Snapshot

Looking at Commas

On an episode of the *ABC News* program *Primetime*, Connie Chung interviewed citizens from Yuzuri Hara, Japan, a small mountainous village two hours outside of Tokyo. In the excerpt that follows the commas are highlighted.

> Mr. Takahashi attributes his smooth skin, even after working fifty years in the sun, to sticking to the local traditional diet. The skin on his arms felt like a baby's, and the skin on his legs barely had a wrinkle. Some of what Mr. Takahashi eats is on the menu every day at a hotel in Yuzuri Hara. The innkeeper, Mrs. Ishi, is eighty and looks pretty good herself.

In this chapter, you will learn to use commas correctly.

Teaching Tip:
Ask students to identify why commas are used in the Grammar Snapshot. Many students have the mistaken notion that commas simply indicate a pause while speaking. You might mention that they actually separate and help identify distinct ideas.

Teaching Tip: Ask students who cries in each sentence. In the first sentence, the mother cries, and in the second sentence, the baby cries. Another example is the sentence *Jason watches plays and laughs.* Ask students to suggest how commas can change the meaning of the sentence.

What Is a Comma?

A **comma (,)** is a punctuation mark that helps identify distinct ideas. There are many ways to use a comma. In this chapter, you will learn some helpful rules about comma usage.

Notice how comma placement changes the meanings of the following sentences.

The baby hits, her mother cries, and then they hug each other.

The baby hits her mother, cries, and then they hug each other.

Commas in a Series

Use a comma to separate items in a series of three or more items. Remember to put a comma before the final "and."

Unit 1	,	unit 2	,	and	unit 3
			,	or	

Canada, the United States, and Mexico have psychology conferences.

The experiment required patience, perseverance, and energy.

Some teens may work part time, volunteer in the community, and maintain high grades at school.

Hint **Comma Before *and***

There is a trend, especially in the media, to omit the comma before the final *and* in a series. However, in academic writing, it is preferable to include the comma because it clarifies your meaning and makes the items more distinct.

PRACTICE 1 Underline series of items. Then add fifteen missing commas.

EXAMPLE: Some psychological studies are simple, obvious, and extremely important.

1. Mary Ainsworth was born in Ohio, attended the University of Toronto, and worked in Uganda. She became an expert in the childhood development

field. Ainsworth's most significant research examined the attachment of infants to their caretakers.

2. Ainsworth designed an experiment called The Strange Situation. She measured how infants reacted when the primary caretaker left the room a stranger entered and the primary caretaker returned. She determined that children have four attachment styles. They may be secure avoidant ambivalent or disoriented.

3. Secure children may leave their mother's lap explore happily and return to the mother. Avoidant babies are not upset when the mother leaves do not look at the stranger and show little reaction when the mother returns. Ambivalent babies are clinging unwilling to explore and upset by strangers. Disoriented infants react oddly to their mother's return. They look fearful avoid eye contact and slowly approach the returning mother.

Commas After Introductory Words and Phrases

Place a comma after an **introductory word** or **phrase**. Introductory words include interjections (*well*), adverbs (*usually*), or transitional words (*therefore*). Introductory phrases can be transitional expressions (*of course*), prepositional phrases (*in the winter*), or modifiers (*born in Egypt*).

Introductory word(s)	,	sentence.

Introductory word: Yes, the last stage of life is very important.

Introductory phrase: After the experiment, the children returned home.

Feeling bored, he volunteered at a nearby clinic.

PRACTICE 2 Underline each introductory word or phrase. Then add twelve missing commas.

EXAMPLE: Before leaving home adolescents assert their independence.

1. In *Childhood and Society* Erik Erikson explained his views about the stages of life. According to Erikson there are eight life stages. In his opinion each stage is characterized by a developmental crisis.

2. In the infancy stage babies must learn to trust others. Wanting others to fulfill their needs babies expect life to be pleasant. Neglected babies may end up mistrusting the world.

3. During adolescence a young man or woman may have an identity crisis. Confronted with physical and emotional changes teenagers must develop a sense of self. According to Erikson some adolescents are unable to solve their identity crisis. Lacking self-awareness they cannot commit to certain goals and values.

4. In Erikson's view each crisis must be solved before a person develops in the next life stage. For example a person may become an adult chronologically. However that person may not be an adult emotionally.

Commas Around Interrupting Words and Phrases

Interrupting words or phrases appear in the middle of sentences, and while they interrupt the sentence's flow, they do not affect its overall meaning. Some interrupters are *as a matter of fact*, *as you know*, and *for example*. Prepositional phrases can also interrupt sentences.

Sentence,	interrupter,	sentence.

The doctor, for example, has never studied child psychology.

Adolescence, as you know, is a difficult life stage.

The child, with no prompting, started to laugh.

Hint **Using Commas with Appositives**

An appositive gives further information about a noun or pronoun. It can appear at the beginning, in the middle, or at the end of the sentence. Set off an appositive with commas.

beginning
A large hospital, the Mayo Clinic has some of the world's best researchers.

middle
Gail Sheehy, a journalist, has written about life passages.

end
The doctor's office is next to Sims Wholesale, a local grocery store.

PRACTICE 3 The following sentences contain introductory words and phrases, interrupters, and series of items. Add the missing commas. If the sentence is correct, write C in the space provided.

EXAMPLE: Erik Erikson, a child development expert, wrote about his identity crisis. _____

CHAPTER 35

1. Erik Erikson, during his youth, had an identity crisis. _____
2. At age sixteen, he learned about his past. _____
3. His mother admitted that Erik was the result of an extramarital affair. __C__
4. He felt surprised, confused, and angry. _____
5. At that time, he did not know his birth father. __C__
6. Erikson's mother, a Danish woman, had moved to Germany. _____

Teaching Tip:
Pair Work
Ask students to do Practice 3 in pairs. By working together, they can share their understanding of the comma placement rules.

7. His adopted father a pediatrician named Theodore Homburger was Jewish. _____

8. Erikson felt confused about his nationality his religion, and his genealogy. _____

Teaching Tip:
Read the next sentences aloud and ask students to identify the ones that require a comma. *The old man tumbled, and someone helped him up. The old man tumbled and broke his hip. The little mouse scampered into its hole but was unable to carry in some cheese. The little mouse tried to enter the hole, but he couldn't fit the cheese into the tiny space.*

9. In the early 1920s, Erikson went to Vienna. __C__

10. Erikson, at a conference met Anna Freud._____

11. Anna Freud Sigmund Freud's daughter, analyzed Erikson._____

12. Using psychoanalysis she helped him resolve his identity crisis._____

Commas in Compound Sentences

In compound sentences, place a comma before the coordinating conjunction (*for*, *and*, *nor*, *but*, *or*, *yet*, *so*).

Sentence	, and	sentence.

Adulthood has three stages, **and** each stage has its particular challenge.

Carolina lives with her mother, **but** her sister lives on her own.

She goes to school, **yet** she also works forty hours a week.

Hint **Commas and Coordinators**

To ensure that a sentence is compound, cover the conjunction with your finger and read the two parts of the sentence. If one part of the sentence is incomplete, then no comma is necessary. If each part of the sentence contains a complete idea, then you need to add a comma.

No comma: Ben still lives with his parents **but** is very self-sufficient.

Comma: Ben still lives with his parents, **but** he is very self-sufficient.

PRACTICE 4 Edit the next paragraphs and add ten missing commas.

EXAMPLE: She is not an adult yet she is not a child.

1. Adulthood is another stage in life but the exact age of adulthood is unclear. Some cultures celebrate adulthood with high school graduation ceremonies and others celebrate with marriage. Some people define adulthood as the moment a person has full-time work and is self-sufficient yet many people only become independent in their thirties.

2. Various cultures treat early adulthood differently. Irene Berridge has a culturally mixed background. Her mother is German and her father is British. She was encouraged to leave home and get an apartment at age nineteen. Today, twenty-one-year-old Irene washes her clothing at a laundromat and she does her own cooking. She has a part-time job and she splits the bills with her roommate. Irene, an independent woman, admits that she often misses her family.

3. Alexis Khoury's parents are recent immigrants from Greece and they want their daughter to stay home until she marries. Alexis is thirty-one years old and she sometimes feels embarrassed to be living at home. She does not feel like an adult and her parents encourage her dependence. However, Alexis will respect her parents' wishes and she will not leave home until she has found a life partner.

Commas in Complex Sentences

A **complex sentence** contains one or more dependent clauses (or incomplete ideas). When you add a **subordinating conjunction**—a word such as *because*, *although*, or *unless*—to a clause, you make the clause dependent.

Teaching Tip: Read the next sentences aloud and ask students to identify the ones that require a comma. *Although you are very sweet, I won't date you. Britney shaved her head even though she loved her glorious long hair. The thirty-year-old man moved into an apartment when he was able to afford it. When Latisha found a good job, she moved into a larger apartment.*

dependent clause — independent clause

After Jason graduated from college, he moved out of the family home.

Using Commas After Dependent Clauses

If a sentence begins with a dependent clause, place a comma after the clause. Remember that a dependent clause has a subject and a verb, but it cannot stand alone. When the subordinating conjunction comes in the middle of the sentence, it is generally not necessary to use a comma.

Dependent clause, main clause.

Comma: When I find a better job, I will move into an apartment.

Main clause dependent clause.

No comma: I will move into an apartment when I find a better job.

PRACTICE 5 Edit the following sentences by adding or deleting commas.

CHAPTER 35

EXAMPLE: Although thirty-year-old Samuel Chong lives at home, he is not ashamed.

1. When he examined the 2001 census, Mark Noble noticed a clear trend.
2. Although most people in their twenties lived on their own, about 40 percent of young adults still lived with their parents.
3. In 1981, the results were different/ because only 25 percent of young adults lived at home.
4. After examining the statistics, Noble determined several causes for the shift.
5. Because the marriage rate is declining, fewer people buy their own homes.

6. When the cost of education increases, people cannot afford to study and pay rent.

7. Other young adults stay with their parents because the rents are so high.

8. Because these conditions are not changing, many young adults will likely continue to live with their parents.

Using Commas to Set Off Nonrestrictive Clauses

Clauses beginning with *who*, *that*, and *which* can be restrictive or nonrestrictive. A **restrictive clause** contains essential information about the subject. Do not place commas around restrictive clauses. In the following example, the underlined clause is necessary to understand the meaning of the sentence.

No commas: The local company that creates computer graphics has no job openings.

A **nonrestrictive clause** gives nonessential or additional information about the noun but does not restrict or define the noun. Place commas around nonrestrictive clauses. In the following sentence, the underlined clause contains extra information, but if you removed that clause, the sentence would still have a clear meaning.

Commas: Her book, which is in bookstores, is about successful entrepreneurs.

Hint **Which, That, and Who**

Which Use commas to set off clauses that begin with *which.*

The brain, **which** is a complex organ, develops rapidly.

That Do not use commas to set off clauses that begin with *that.*

The house **that** I grew up in was demolished last year.

Who If the *who* clause contains nonessential information, put commas around it. If the *who* clause is essential to the meaning of the sentence, then it does not require commas.

Essential: Many people **who** have brain injuries undergo subtle personality changes.

Not essential: Dr. Jay Giedd, **who** lives in Maryland, made an important discovery.

GRAMMAR LINK

For more information about choosing *which* or *that*, see Chapter 22, Sentence Variety.

Teaching Tip:

To illustrate the difference between an essential and a nonessential clause, write the next sentences on the board. Then ask students to explain how the meaning changes when the *who* clause is set off with a comma.

- *My brother who works as a nurse will move to France.* (You have more than one brother, thus the *who* clause is essential.)
- *My brother, who works as a nurse, will move to France.* (You have one brother, thus the *who* clause contains extra information about that brother.)

PRACTICE 6 Edit the following sentences by adding twelve missing commas.

EXAMPLE: The neurologist whom I have never met made an exciting discovery.

1. Twenty years ago, scientists thought that the brain stopped changing in late childhood. They believed that after children reached twelve years of age their brains would stop growing. In 1997, a team of doctors who specialized in brain research made an exciting discovery. Neuroscientist Dr. Jay Giedd who works at the National Institute of Mental Health realized that brain cells have a growth spurt just before puberty and continue growing well into adulthood. Scientists discovered that myelin which connects brain cells increases during adolescence. However, not all parts of the brain receive myelin at once, and the last region to receive it is the frontal lobe.

2. The frontal lobe, which is responsible for rational decision making stops an individual from making impulsive choices. For example imagine that you are driving your car. When another car cuts you off the primitive part of your brain wants to hurt the other driver. The frontal lobe helps you to think about alternatives. Thus, you may simply accept that all drivers make mistakes.

3. According to specialists the delay in receiving myelin to the frontal lobe affects many teens, and they may have trouble curbing their impulses. They may react quickly violently or irrationally, and they are more likely than people in other age groups to engage in risky behavior. When the frontal lobe has fully developed people generally become less impulsive.

Final Review

Edit this essay by adding seventeen missing commas and removing three unnecessary commas.

EXAMPLE: If people want to have longer lives, they can exercise, eat well, and avoid risky behavior.

1. In 350 BC, Aristotle wrote an essay about life spans. Everybody has a maximum life span and nothing can be done to prolong that span. Until recently scientists agreed with Aristotle. They would argue that today's life expectancies are about as high as they can possibly get. However a group of researchers believes that human life expectancy will increase significantly in the future.

2. Dr. James Vaupel a researcher at Duke University, believes that our life spans can be extended significantly. He gives a concrete example. In 1840, Swedish women had the world's longest life expectancy and the average Swedish woman lived to age forty-five. Today, Japanese women, who live to an average age of eighty-five have the world's longest life expectancy. This huge increase in life expectancy was partly due to the decrease in infant mortality. In 1800, about 25 percent of babies died in the first year of life. Surgery vaccines and antibiotics have helped to lower the childhood death rates. Also,

Teaching Tip: You can use the final review as a test. Additional practice and test material appears in the Instructor's Resource Manual and on *MyWritingLab*.

GRAMMAR LINK

For information about comma usage in business letters, see Chapter 17, The Résumé and Letter of Application.

because they have access to new medical interventions people over age sixty-five are living longer. Still, only about 2 percent of the population lives to one hundred years of age.

3. According to Dr. Vaupel, today's babies will have much longer life expectancies than their parents had and half of all newborns could live to one hundred years of age. Dr. Aubrey De Grey, a professor at Cambridge University believes that human life expectancy will increase to five hundred years or more. Certainly, there are very promising discoveries on the horizon. Cures for cancer, and heart disease will help increase life expectancy. Also, because so many women delay childbirth the period of human fertility may lengthen which could have an eventual impact on life expectancy.

4. Some experts disagree with Vaupel and De Grey. Leonard Hayflick, discovered that human cells divide and reproduce about fifty times before slowing down and stopping. The longest average life span humans can attain in Hayflick's view is 120 years of age. However, some research labs are experimenting with ways of increasing the life spans of cells. For example scientists have isolated a part of the chromosome that shrinks with age. If scientists find a way to slow down cell aging the results could significantly increase life expectancies of all humans.

5. A very long life expectancy, would force humans to rethink life stages. When would childhood end? Would you want to live to 150 years of age or more?

The Writer's Room Topics for Writing

Write about one of the following topics. After you finish writing, make sure that you have used commas correctly.

1. What problems could occur if the human life expectancy gets a lot longer? Think about the effects of an increased life expectancy.
2. Which life stage is the most interesting? Give anecdotes to back up your views.

CHECKLIST: COMMAS

When you edit your writing, ask yourself these questions.

- Do I use commas correctly? Remember to use commas in the following situations:
  - between words in a series of items
  - after an introductory word or phrase
  - around an interrupting word or phrase

    The conference will be in Santa Fe, San Francisco, or Phoenix.

    Beyond a doubt, many psychologists will attend.

    The key speaker, in my opinion, is extremely interesting.

- Do I use commas correctly in compound and complex sentences? Remember to use commas in the following situations:
  - before the coordinator in a compound sentence
  - after a dependent clause in a complex sentence
  - around nonrestrictive clauses

    She will discuss brain development, and she will present case studies.

    When her presentation ends, participants can ask questions.

    The questions, which must be short, are about the brain.

CHAPTER 35

How Do I Get a Better Grade?

Visit www.mywritinglab.com for audio-visual lectures and additional practice sets about commas.

mywritinglab

Get a better grade with MyWritingLab!

36 CHAPTER Apostrophes

CONTENTS

Section Theme **HUMAN DEVELOPMENT**

In this chapter, you will read about artistic ability and creativity.

Man Reclining, 1978, Fernando Botero, Private Collection.

Teaching Tip:
Ask students what the long forms of the contractions are in this Grammar Snapshot.

Grammar Snapshot

Looking at Apostrophes

In an interview with Diane Sawyer for *ABC News*, musician Paul McCartney discusses his art show and his initial feelings about painting. Review the highlighted words.

> The way I was brought up, in the working class, only people who went to art school painted. It wasn't for us to paint. We didn't ride horses. They did. You know, we'd we ride bikes if we were lucky. I would've felt like I was a bit uppity to paint, you know. "Oh, you're painting now, are you?"

In this chapter, you will learn to use apostrophes correctly.

What Is an Apostrophe?

An **apostrophe** is a punctuation mark showing a contraction or ownership.

Emma **Chong's** art gallery is very successful, and **it's** still growing.

Apostrophes in Contractions

To form a **contraction**, join two words into one and add an apostrophe to replace the omitted letter(s). The following are examples of common contractions.

1. **Join a verb with *not*.** The apostrophe replaces the letter "o" in *not*.

is + not = isn't
are + not = aren't
could + not = couldn't
do + not = don't
does + not = doesn't
has + not = hasn't
have + not = haven't
should + not = shouldn't
would + not = wouldn't

Exception: will + not = won't, can + not = can't

2. **Join a subject and a verb.** Sometimes you must remove several letters to form the contraction.

I + will = I'll
I + would = I'd
he + is = he's
he + will = he'll
Joe + is = Joe's
she + has = she's
she + will = she'll
Tina + is = Tina's
they + are = they're
we + will = we'll
who + is = who's
who + would = who'd

Exception: Do not contract a subject with the past tense of *be*. For example, do not contract *he* + *was* or *they* + *were*.

CHAPTER 36

ESL Teaching Tip: Nonnative speakers may incorrectly use apostrophes in past tense contractions of *be*. Draw their attention to the exception.

Hint **Common Apostrophe Errors**

Do not use apostrophes before the final -s of a verb or a plural noun.

Mr. Garcia ~~want's~~ *wants* to open several ~~gallery's~~ *galleries*.

In contractions with *not*, remember that the apostrophe replaces the missing *o*.

He ~~does'nt~~ *doesn't* understand the problem.

ESL Teaching Tip: Nonnative speakers have difficulty with apostrophes. You could remind students that although they are learning about contractions, they should avoid using them in academic or formal writing except to show ownership.

PRACTICE 1 Edit the next sentences for fifteen apostrophe errors. Each word counts as one error.

EXAMPLE: Making a great work of art isn't a simple process.

1. ~~Whos~~ Who's a great artist? Why do some people have amazing artistic abilities whereas others ~~do'nt~~ don't? Researchers in biology, sociology, and psychology haven't unlocked the keys to human creativity. However, ~~expert's~~ experts in each field have proposed theories about creativity.

2. Sigmund Freud proposed that creativity is an occurrence of the subconscious. If ~~someones~~ someone's in pain, he or she may create an artwork to relieve the suffering. Near the end of his life, Freud changed his mind. He said that he ~~didnt~~ didn't believe that suffering was a prerequisite to creativity.

CHAPTER 36

3. Neurologists look inside the brain to answer questions about creativity. ~~Theyve~~ They've said that the left portion of the ~~brains~~ brain's responsible for logical processing and verbal skills. The right ~~sides~~ side's responsible for artistic, abstract thinking. In the past, neurologists ~~did'nt~~ didn't believe that the left side of the brain had an impact on creative impulses, but recent brain ~~scan's~~ scans have shown that both sides of the brain are used in creative thinking.

4. ~~Whats~~ What's the source of creativity? Maybe ~~its~~ it's never going to be understood. What everybody ~~know's~~ knows for certain is that artistic talent ~~isnt~~ isn't evenly distributed. Some people ~~are'nt~~ aren't as talented as others.

Hint **Contractions with Two Meanings**

Sometimes one contraction can have two different meanings.

I'd = I had *or* I would **He's** = he is *or* he has

When you read, you should be able to figure out the meaning of the contraction by looking at the words in context.

Joe's working on a painting. **Joe's** been working on it for a month.
(Joe is) (Joe has)

ESL Teaching Tip:

Pair Work

Ask students to work in pairs generating sentences that contain at least six apostrophes. Pair up native and nonnative speakers, if possible. The team with the most apostrophes in a sentence wins. As an additional activity, ask teams to exchange sheets. Students should then write out the long form of contractions on another team's sheet.

PRACTICE 2 Look at each underlined contraction, and then write out the complete words.

EXAMPLE: They weren't ready to start a business. *were not*

1. Rachel Wood's very happy with her sculpture. *Wood is*
2. She's been a professional artist since 2002. *She has*
3. She's an extremely creative woman. *She is*
4. I wish I'd gone to art school. *I had*
5. I'd like to be an artist, too. *I would*

CHAPTER 36

Apostrophes to Show Ownership

You can also use apostrophes to show ownership. Review the following rules.

Possessive Form of Singular Nouns

Add -*'s* to the end of a singular noun to indicate ownership. If the singular noun ends in *s*, you must still add -*'s*. Add *'s* to singular nouns ending in *s* if you pronounce the *s* (*boss's*). If you would not pronounce the final *s*, add only an apostrophe (*Moses'*).

Lautrec's artwork was very revolutionary.

Morris's wife is a professional dancer.

Possessive Form of Plural Nouns

When a plural noun ends in *-s*, just add an apostrophe to indicate ownership. Add *-'s* to irregular plural nouns.

Many **galleries'** Web sites contain images from their exhibits.

The **men's** and **women's** paintings are in separate rooms.

Possessive Form of Compound Nouns

When two people have joint ownership, add the apostrophe to the second name. When two people have separate ownership, add apostrophes to both names.

Joint ownership: Marian and **Jake's** gallery is successful.

Separate ownership: **Marian's** and **Jake's** studios are in different buildings.

PRACTICE 3 Write the possessive forms of the following phrases.

EXAMPLE: the sister of the doctor — *the doctor's sister*

1. the brush of the artist — *the artist's brush*
2. the brushes of the artists — *the artists' brushes*
3. the lights in the studio — *the studio's lights*
4. the room of the child — *the child's room*
5. the rooms of the children — *the children's rooms*
6. the entrances of the galleries — *the galleries' entrances*
7. the photo of Ross and Anna — *Ross and Anna's photo*
8. the photo of Ross and the photo of Anna — *Ross's and Anna's photos*

Hint **Possessive Pronouns Do Not Have Apostrophes**

Some contractions sound like possessive pronouns. For example, *you're* sounds like *your*, and *it's* sounds like *its*. Remember that the possessive pronouns *yours*, *hers*, *its*, and *ours* never have apostrophes.

> The conference is on ~~it's~~ *its* last day.
>
> The document is ~~your's~~ *yours* and not ~~her's~~ *hers*.

PRACTICE 4 Correct nine errors. You may need to add, move, or remove apostrophes.

1. Many ~~artist's~~ *artists'* paintings are unique. Have you ever heard of Fernando Botero? The Colombian ~~painters~~ *painter's* work has been exhibited in the Museum of Modern Art in Washington. Several of his ~~painting's~~ *paintings* have also appeared in New York galleries. His painting "Man Reclining" appears at the beginning of this chapter.

2. Botero's paintings usually contain images of people. What makes his work unique is ~~it's~~ *its* humor. He makes generals, religious figures, and dictators look like children. ~~Theyre~~ *They're* small and bloated, and the images are filled with color.

3. Another great artist is Georgia O'Keeffe. ~~Its~~ *It's* not difficult to recognize an artwork that is ~~her's~~ *hers*. ~~Shes~~ *She's* known for her paintings of white bones, bull skulls, and flowers. In many art galleries, ~~youll~~ *you'll* find her artwork.

Apostrophes in Expressions of Time

If an expression of time (*year, week, month, day*) appears to possess something, you can add *-'s*.

Alice Ray gave two **weeks'** notice before she left the dance company.

When you write out a year in numerals, an apostrophe can replace the missing numbers.

The graduates of the class of **'99** hoped to find good jobs.

However, if you are writing the numeral of a decade or century, do not put an apostrophe before the final *-s*.

In the **1900s**, many innovations in art occurred.

PRACTICE 5 Correct ten errors. You may need to add, move, or remove apostrophes.

EXAMPLE: Octavio Cruz ~~doesnt~~ *doesn't* have a studio.

1. In the summer of 2000, Octavio Cruz did a ~~years~~ *year's* worth of painting. He felt incredibly inspired. In the early ~~1990's,~~ *1990s* ~~hed~~ *he'd* sold some artworks, but his paintings were uninspired, and he had trouble becoming motivated. Then, in 1999, he was in a car accident. He spent three ~~week's~~ *weeks* in a hospital. Since then, ~~hes~~ *he's* been extremely creative. His wife's astonishment is evident: "~~Hes~~ *He's* a different man," she says. "His paintings are so much more vivid and colorful."

2. Cruz has been studied by a neurologist, Dr. Wade. The ~~doctors~~ *doctor's* theory is that ~~Cruzs~~ *Cruz's* injury "disinhibited" his right brain, thus allowing him to become more creative. Many other ~~peoples~~ *people's* stories are similar to Cruz's. In fact, since the ~~1970's,~~ *1970s* scientists have recognized that certain brain injuries can stimulate creativity.

Final Review

Edit the next paragraphs and correct fifteen apostrophe errors. You may need to add, remove, or move apostrophes.

EXAMPLE: What is an ~~artists~~ *artist's* motivation to create?

Donald Martin, after Van der Weyden (20th Century American), "Portrait", Airbrush on wood. © Donald C. Martin/ SuperStock.

1. In 1982, Dr. Teresa Amabile made an interesting study in creativity. For ~~Amabiles~~ *Amabile's* study, she divided ~~schoolgirl's~~ *schoolgirls* into two groups. Both ~~groups~~ *groups'* rooms were filled with collage material, including colored paper, paste, and construction paper. The doctor chose collage-making because it ~~doesnt~~ *doesn't* require drawing skills.

2. Both groups were invited to an "art party" in separate rooms. The first ~~groups~~ *group's* goal was to create art to win a prize, such as a toy. The doctor offered toys to the three best artists. Thus, the ~~childrens~~ *children's* motivation to create was to win the exciting prize. The girls in the second group ~~didnt~~ *didn't* have to compete for a prize. They were simply told that three ~~name's~~ *names* would be randomly drawn for prizes.

CHAPTER 36

3. The ~~doctors~~ *doctor's* hypothesis was that a ~~persons~~ *person's* creativity would lessen if he or she were motivated by a reward. Amabile asked local artists and art critics to judge the collages when the children ~~werent~~ *weren't* in the room. The ~~judges~~ *judges'* scores for the first group were consistently lower than those for the second group. Thus, the ~~doctors~~ *doctor's* hypothesis was correct. A reward, such as money or a prize, ~~isnt~~ *isn't* helpful to the creative process. When people create art for ~~arts~~ *art's* sake, they tend to be more imaginative.

Teaching Tip:
You can use the final review as a test. Additional practice and test material appears in the Instructor's Resource Manual and on *MyWritingLab*.

The Writer's Room Topics for Writing

Write about one of the following topics. After you finish writing, make sure that you have used apostrophes correctly.

1. Describe the work of a painter, illustrator, photographer, or sculptor that you like. Explain what is most interesting about that artist's work.
2. Define a term or expression that relates to this photo. Some ideas might be *creativity*, *graffiti*, *art*, *vandalism*, or *beauty*.

CHECKLIST: APOSTROPHES

When you edit your writing, ask yourself these questions.

- Do I use apostrophes correctly? Check for errors in these cases:
  - contractions of verbs + *not* or subjects and verbs
  - possessives of singular and plural nouns (*the student's* versus *the students'*)
  - possessives of irregular plural nouns (*the women's*)
  - possessives of compound nouns (*Joe's and Mike's cars*)

  shouldn't Wong's
  You ~~should'nt~~ be surprised that Chris ~~Wong'~~ going to exhibit his paintings.

  Chris's
  ~~Chris'~~ artwork will be on display next week.

- Do I place apostrophes where they do not belong? Check for errors in possessive pronouns and present tense verbs.

  looks its
  It ~~look's~~ like the gallery is moving ~~it's~~ collection to Houston.

CHAPTER 36

How Do I Get a Better Grade?

Visit www.mywritinglab.com for audio-visual lectures and additional practice sets about apostrophes.

mywritinglab

Get a better grade with MyWritingLab!

Quotation Marks, Capitalization, and Titles

CHAPTER 37

CONTENTS

- Quotation Marks
- Using Quotations in Research Essays
- Capitalization
- Titles

Section Theme **HUMAN DEVELOPMENT**

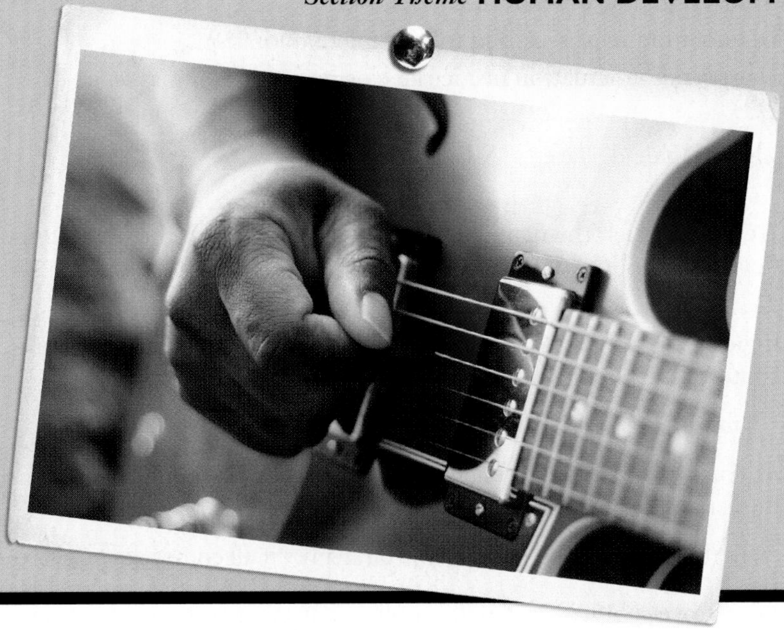

In this chapter, you will read about artists and musicians.

Grammar Snapshot

Looking at Quotation Marks

This excerpt is translated from Paul Gauguin's book, *Avant et Apres*. It recounts when Vincent Van Gogh cut off part of his own ear. Notice that the quotation marks and some capital letters are highlighted.

The man in the bowler hat harshly questioned me: "Well, sir, what have you done to your friend?"

"I don't know," I replied.

"But you know that he is dead," he said.

I would not wish such a moment on anyone, and it took me a while before I could think. My heart pounded, and I was choking with anger and pain. I felt everyone's eyes staring at me. I stammered, "Sir, let's go upstairs and discuss it there."

In this chapter, you will learn how to use direct quotations correctly. You will also learn about capitalization and title punctuation.

Teaching Tip: Discuss how the quotations are punctuated in the Grammar Snapshot.

Teaching Tip: You might mention that Van Gogh cut off a portion of his ear after having a drunken fight with his house guest, Paul Gauguin.

Teaching Tip: If you teach research in your course, you may wish to add to this discussion by explaining how using quotations and documenting them properly will help students avoid plagiarism. They can find more information about summarizing and paraphrasing in Chapter 15.

Quotation Marks (“ ”)

Use **quotation marks** to set off the exact words of a speaker or writer. When you include the exact words of more than one person in a text, then you must make a new paragraph each time the speaker changes. If the quotation is a complete sentence, punctuate it in the following ways.

- Capitalize the first word of the quotation.
- Place quotation marks around the complete quotation.
- Place the end punctuation inside the closing quotation marks.

Oscar Wilde declared, “All art is useless.”

Generally, attach the name of the speaker or writer to the quotation in some way. Review the following rules.

Teaching Tip: Students often use a colon instead of a comma to introduce quotations. Remind them to use commas after phrases.

1. **Introductory Phrase** When the quotation is introduced by a phrase, place a comma after the introductory phrase.

   Pablo Picasso said, “Art is a lie that makes us realize the truth.”

2. **Interrupting Phrase** When the quotation is interrupted, place a comma before and after the interrupting phrase.

   “In the end,” says dancer Martha Graham, “it all comes down to breathing.”

3. **End Phrase** When you place a phrase at the end of a quotation, end the quotation with a comma instead of a period.

   “Great art picks up where nature ends,” said Marc Chagall.

   If your quotation ends with other punctuation, put it inside the quotation mark.

   “Who is the greatest painter?” the student asked.

   “That question cannot be answered!” the curator replied.

Teaching Tip: Point out that a colon appears before a quotation only when the quotation is preceded by a complete sentence. Remind students to use commas after phrases.

4. **Introductory Sentence** When you introduce a quotation with a complete sentence, place a colon (:) after the introductory sentence.

   George Balanchine explains his philosophy about dance: “Dance is music made visible.”

5. **Inside Quotations** If one quotation is inside another quotation, then use single quotation marks (‘ ’) around the inside quotation.

   To her mother, Veronica Corelli explained, “I am not sure if I will succeed, but you’ve always said, ‘Your work should be your passion.’ ”

Hint **Integrated Quotations**

If the quotation is not a complete sentence, and you simply integrate it into your sentence, do not capitalize the first word of the quotation.

> Composer Ludwig Von Beethoven called music "the mediator between the spiritual and the sensual life."

Susan Valadon (1867–1938 French) "Portrait of Madam Coquiot", 1915. Oil on canvas. Musée du Palais Carnoles, Menton, France. © Artists Rights Society (ARS), New York.

PRACTICE 1 In each sentence, the quotation is set off in bold. Add quotation marks and periods, commas, or colons. Also, capitalize the first word of the quotation, if necessary.

EXAMPLE: Professor Wayne Johnson asks, "~~w~~W**here are the great female artists?**"

1. Art student Alex Beale says **the lack of great female artists throughout history is puzzling**
2. Professor Aline Melnor states **one must consider the conditions for producing art**
3. **Art schools did not accept women** she points out.
4. **Until a hundred years ago, the only alternative to family life for women was the convent** proclaimed writer and feminist Germaine Greer.
5. **Suzanne Valadon** says historian Maria Sage **went from being an artist's model to being an artist**
6. Historian Andre Villeneuve writes that sculptor Camille Claudel was **the mistress of Auguste Rodin**
7. Germaine Greer shows the connection between female and male artists **the painter Rosa Bonheur learned about art from her father, who was also an artist**

8. **In the twentieth century, the numbers of female artists exploded** declared gallery owner Jon Sidell.

9. Angel Trang told her mother **I know that I shouldn't have drawn on the walls, but you always say Express yourself**

10. Louise Otto-Peters has a strong opinion about women in the arts **women will be forgotten if they forget to think about themselves**

PRACTICE 2 Correct ten punctuation errors in the next dialogue.

EXAMPLE: She told me. "Your future is in your hands".

Jamilla was concerned about her son, "I don't understand why you are leaving college".

Omar looked at her and replied: "I need to try and make it as a musician."

"How will you make a living in the arts" she asked?

He replied, "I do not need to earn a lot of money to be happy."

"You're being very naïve." Jamilla retorted.

Shocked, Omar said, "I'm simply following your advice. You always say, "Find work that you love." "

"Perhaps you have to take some chances" his mother responded, "and learn from your own mistakes."

Omar stated firmly, "my decision will not be a mistake!"

CHAPTER 37

Using Quotations in Research Essays

Use quotations to reveal the opinions of an expert or to highlight ideas that are particularly memorable and important. When quoting sources, remember to limit how many you use in a single paper and to vary your quotations by using both direct and indirect quotations.

Direct and Indirect Quotations

A **direct quotation** contains the exact words of an author, and the quotation is set off with quotation marks.

> A shopping tip from Consumer 4 Kids Reports states, "The name brands are always displayed up front when you first walk into the department."

An **indirect quotation** keeps the author's meaning but is not set off by quotation marks.

> A shopping tip by the Consumer 4 Kids Reports states that name-brand clothes are always put on view at the front of the clothing department.

Teaching Tip: Ask students to read "My African Childhood" in Chapter 40. They can highlight direct and indirect quotations.

Integrating Quotations

Short Quotations

Introduce short quotations with a phrase or sentence. (Short quotations should not stand alone.) Read the following original selection, and then view how the quotation has been introduced using three common methods.

> The selection, written by Mary Lou Stribling, appeared on page 6 of her book Art from Found Materials.

Original Selection
Picasso is generally acknowledged as being the first major artist to use found objects in his paintings. About the same time, however, a number of other artists who were active in the Cubist movement began to make similar experiments. The collages of Braque and Gris, which were made of printed letters, newspapers, wallpaper scraps, bottle labels, corrugated cardboard, and other bits of trivia, are especially notable.

Phrase Introduction
In Art from Found Materials, Mary Lou Stribling writes, "Picasso is generally acknowledged as being the first major artist to use found objects in his paintings" (6).

Teaching Tip: Point out that the page number is in parentheses.

Sentence Introduction
In her book Art from Found Materials, Mary Lou Stribling suggests that Picasso was not the only artist to use found objects in his work: "About the same time, however, a number of other artists who were active in the Cubist movement began to make similar experiments" (6).

Integrated Quotation

In Art from Found Materials, Mary Lou Stribling reveals that artists incorporated everyday objects into their paintings, including "wallpaper scraps, bottle labels, corrugated cardboard, and other bits of trivia" (6).

Hint **Words That Introduce Quotations**

Here are some common words that can introduce quotations.

admits	concludes	mentions	speculates
claims	explains	observes	suggests
comments	maintains	reports	warns

The doctor **states,** "______________________"

"______________________," **observes** Dr. Hannah.

Dr. Hannah **speculates** that ______________________.

Long Quotations

If you use a quotation in MLA style that has four or more lines (or in APA style, more than forty words), insert the quotation in your research paper in the following way.

- Introduce the quotation with a sentence ending with a colon.
- Indent the entire quotation about ten spaces from the left margin of your document.
- Use double spacing.
- Do not use quotation marks.
- Cite the author and page number in parentheses after the punctuation mark in the last sentence of the quotation.

Review the next example from a student essay about art history that uses MLA style. The quotation is from page 132 of Germaine Greer's The Obstacle Race. The explanatory paragraph introduces the quotation and is part of an essay.

Much great art has been lost due to a variety of factors:

> Panels decay as wood decays. Canvas rots, tears, and sags. The stretchers spring and warp. As color dries out it loses its flexibility and begins to separate from its unstable ground; dry color flakes off shrinking or swelling wood and drooping canvas. (Greer 132)

Teaching Tip: You can direct students to Chapter 16 for a discussion of MLA and APA citation styles.

Teaching Tip: Point out that the sample quotation would be double spaced in a research essay.

Hint **Using Long Quotations**

If your research paper is short (two or three pages), avoid using many long quotations. Long quotations will only overwhelm your own ideas. Instead, try summarizing a long passage or using shorter quotations.

Using Ellipses (. . .)

If you want to quote key ideas from an author, but do not want to quote the entire paragraph, you can use **ellipses**. These three periods show that you have omitted unnecessary information from a quotation. Leave a space before and after each period, and if the omitted section includes complete sentences, add a period before the ellipses.

The original selection, written by Jeremy Yudkin, appeared in his book Understanding Music on page 446. Notice how the quotation changes when the essay writer uses ellipses.

Original Selection
In his early years, Elvis Presley symbolized something very important for American youth. He was the symbol of freedom and rebellion. His unconventional clothes, the messages of his music, and especially his raw sexuality appealed to the new and numerous groups of American teenagers. The spirit of rebellion was in the air.

Quotation with Omissions
In his book Understanding Music, Jeremy Yudkin describes the impact of Elvis: "In his early years, Elvis Presley symbolized something very important for American youth. . . . The spirit of rebellion was in the air" (446).

Teaching Tip: Point out that the ellipses are preceded by a period in the example because a complete sentence was omitted.

PRACTICE 3 Read the following selection and then use information from it to write direct and indirect quotations. The selection, written by David G. Martin, appeared on page 567 of his book Psychology.

Until fairly recently, up to the early or mid-nineteenth century, events that could not be explained were often attributed to supernatural causes. Human behavior that was bizarre was thought to be the work of demons. Demonology is the study of the ancient belief that mental disorders are caused by possession by demons. Autonomous evil beings were thought to enter a person and control his or her mind and body.

1. Make a direct quotation. Answers will vary.

2. Make an indirect quotation. Answers will vary.

Capitalization

Remember to capitalize the following:

- the pronoun *I*
- the first word of every sentence

My brothers and **I** share an apartment.

There are many other instances in which you must use capital letters. Always capitalize in the following cases.

- **days of the week, months, and holidays**

Thursday	June 22	Labor Day

Do not capitalize the seasons: summer, fall, winter, spring.

- **titles of specific institutions, departments, companies, and schools**

Microsoft	Department of Finance	Elmwood High School

Do not capitalize general references.

the company	the department	the school

- **names of specific places such as buildings, streets, parks, cities, states, and bodies of water**

Eiffel Tower	Times Square	Los Angeles, California
Sunset Boulevard	Florida	Lake Erie

Do not capitalize general references.

the street	the state	the lake

- **specific languages, nationalities, tribes, races, and religions**

Greek	Mohawk	Buddhist	a French restaurant

- **titles of specific individuals**

General Franklin	the President	Doctor Blain
Professor Sayf	Prime Minister Blair	Mrs. Robinson

If you are referring to the profession in general, or if the title follows the name, do not use capital letters.

my doctor	the professors	Ted Kennedy, a senator

- **specific course and program titles**

Physics 201	Marketing 101	Advanced German

If you refer to a course, but do not mention the course title, then it is not necessary to use capitals.

He is in his math class. I study engineering.

- **the major words in titles of literary or artistic works**

The Miami Herald	*Prison Break*	*The Lord of the Rings*

- **historical events, eras, and movements**

World War II	Post-Impressionism	Baby Boomers

ESL Teaching Tip:
You might ask nonnative speakers to list some instances where capitalization rules in their languages differ from those in English. For example, in Spanish and Italian, you do not capitalize the days of the week or the months. Other languages such as Hindi and Mandarin have no capital letters at all!

Hint **Capitalizing Computer Terms**

Always capitalize the following computer terms.

Internet	Netscape	World Wide Web	Microsoft Office

CHAPTER 37

PRACTICE 4 Add twenty missing capital letters to this selection.

EXAMPLE: Mozart was born in ~~s~~Salzburg, Austria.

1. Erich Schenk describes the life of Wolfgang Amadeus Mozart in his book <u>Mozart and ~~his~~ His ~~times~~ Times</u>. Mozart, born on ~~january~~ January 27, 1756, was a gifted musician who composed his first pieces at age five. By the age of thirteen, he had written a ~~german~~ German and an ~~italian~~ Italian opera. In Salzburg, his employer

was ~~p~~Prince-~~a~~Archbishop Colloredo. Then, in Vienna, he wrote compositions for ~~e~~Emperor ~~j~~Joseph II. At that time, Austria was a part of the ~~h~~Holy ~~r~~Roman ~~e~~Empire.

2. Mozart's best-known works include *~~t~~The ~~m~~Marriage of ~~f~~Figaro* and *~~t~~The ~~m~~Magic ~~f~~Flute*. Mozart, a ~~c~~Catholic, died mysteriously at the age of thirty-five, and his body was put into a communal grave, which was the common practice for the poor in Vienna at that time. His final resting place is near a river called the ~~d~~Danube.

Titles

Place the title of a short work in quotation marks. Underline (or italicize, if you are using a computer) the title of a longer document.

Short Works		**Long Works**	
short story:	"The Lottery"	**novel:**	*The Grapes of Wrath*
chapter:	"Early Accomplishments"	**book:**	*The Art of Emily Carr*
newspaper article:	"The City's Hottest Ticket"	**newspaper:**	*The New York Times*
magazine article:	"New Artists"	**magazine:**	*Rolling Stone*
Web article:	"Music Artists Lose Out"	**Web site:**	*CNET News.com*
essay:	"Hip-Hop Nation"	**textbook:**	*Common Culture*
TV episode:	"The Search Party"	**TV series:**	*Lost*
song:	"Mouths to Feed"	**CD:**	*Release Therapy*
poem:	"Howl"	**anthology:**	*Collected Poems of Beat Writers*

Capitalizing Titles

When you write a title, capitalize the first letter of the first word and all the major words.

__T__o __K__ill a __M__ockingbird "**S**tairway to **H**eaven"

Do not capitalize the word ".com" in a Web address. Also, do not capitalize the following words, unless they are the first word in the title.

articles	a, an, the
coordinators	for, and, nor, but, or, yet, so
prepositions	of, to, in, off, out, up, by, . . .

Hint **Your Own Essay Titles**

In essays that you write for your courses, do not underline your title or put quotation marks around it. Simply capitalize the first word and the main words.

Why Music Is Important

PRACTICE 5 Add twelve capital letters to the following selection. Also, add quotation marks or underlining to five titles.

EXAMPLE: The magazine *~~f~~[F]orbes* featured successful female entrepreneurs.

1. The singer known as Pink was born Alecia Moore on ~~s~~[S]eptember 8, 1979. During her teen years, she regularly performed at Club ~~f~~[F]ever near ~~g~~[G]irard ~~s~~[S]treet in Philadelphia. One ~~s~~[S]aturday night, after her five-minute slot, a representative from MCA ~~r~~[R]ecords spotted her and asked her to audition for the band Basic ~~i~~[I]nstinct.

2. After some time playing in bands, Pink decided to become a solo artist. Her first CD, called *Can't ~~t~~[T]ake ~~m~~[M]e ~~h~~[H]ome*, was released in 2000. It was a double-platinum hit, and spun off three singles. Pink then went on to record Patti LaBelle's hit song "Lady Marmalade" with three other artists. In the ~~a~~[A]pril 2006 issue of *Rolling Stone*, Barry Walter reviewed Pink's fourth CD *I'm Not Dead*. He had particular praise for her song "Stupid ~~g~~[G]irls."

CHAPTER 37

Teaching Tip: You can use the final review as a test. Additional practice and test material appears in the Instructor's Resource Manual and on *MyWritingLab*.

Final Review

Identify and correct twenty-five errors. Look for capitalization errors. Also ensure that titles and quotations have the necessary capital letters, quotation marks, punctuation, and underlining.

EXAMPLE: The marketing manager said, "Each generation is distinct."

1. People who belong to a generation may have wildly different life experiences. Nonetheless, as Ted Rall points out in his book Marketing Madness, "you are more likely to share certain formative experiences and attitudes about life with your age cohorts".

2. In the last century, each generation was anointed with a title. F. Scott Fitzgerald named his cohorts when he wrote the book The Jazz Age, which described 1920s flappers who frequented jazz clubs. Tom Brokaw, in his book The greatest generation, discussed people who came of age in the 1930s. Born between 1911 and 1924, they grew up during the Great depression. However, perhaps the best-known spokesperson for a generation is Douglas Coupland.

3. Douglas Coupland was born in 1961 and raised in Vancouver, british Columbia. Even as a young student at Sentinel secondary school, Coupland knew that he would be an artist. When he got older, he took Sculpture classes at Vancouver's Emily Carr institute of Art and design. He also studied at the European Design Institute in italy. As a sculptor,

Coupland had some success and, in ~~n~~November 1987, he had a solo show called "The ~~f~~Floating ~~w~~World" at an art gallery in Vancouver.

4. Most know Coupland from his second career. While writing a comic strip for the magazine *Vista*, Coupland was approached by St. Martin's ~~p~~Press and asked to write a guidebook about his generation. Instead, he wrote a complete novel called *~~g~~Generation X.*

5. Coupland's novel, which describes the generation that came of age in the 1970s and 1980s, is filled with original terminology. For instance, Coupland writes~~:~~, "Clique maintenance is the need of one generation to see the generation following it as deficient so as to bolster its own collective ego~~".~~." One chapter in his book is called, "Our Parents ~~h~~Had ~~m~~More." On page 27, a character has a mid-twenties breakdown that occurs because of "~~A~~an inability to function outside of school or structured environments coupled with a realization of one's essential aloneness in the world."

6. Every current generation has unique characteristics. Music, clothing, and slang words help define a generation. What name will define the youths who are growing up today?

CHAPTER 37

The Writer's Room Topics for Writing

Write about one of the following topics. Include some direct quotations. Proofread to ensure that your punctuation and capitalization is correct.

1. List some characteristics of your generation. What political events, social issues, music, and fashion bind your generation?
2. List three categories of art. Describe some details about each category.
3. Examine the photograph. What do you think the people are saying to each other? Write a brief dialogue from their conversation.

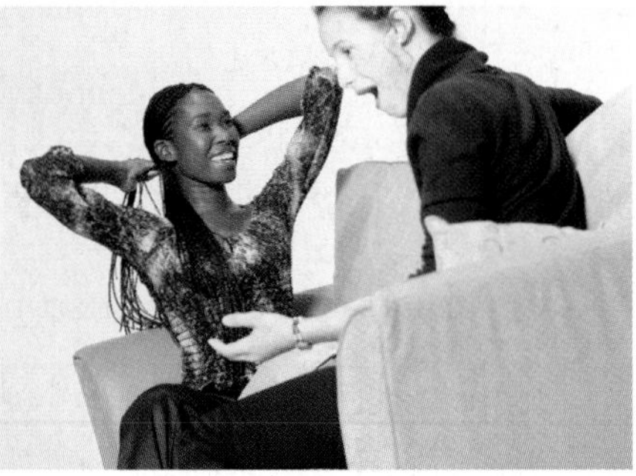

CHECKLIST: QUOTATION MARKS

When you edit your writing, ask yourself these questions.

- Are there any direct quotations in my writing? Check for errors with these elements:
  - punctuation before or after quotations
  - capital letters
  - placement of quotation marks

  "Art is making something out of nothing and selling it," said musician Frank Zappa.

- Do my sentences have all the necessary capital letters?

  Munch's greatest works were painted before World ~~war~~ War II.

- Are the titles of small and large artistic works properly punctuated?

  Edvard Munch's painting was called ~~The sceam.~~ <u>The Scream</u>.

CHAPTER 37

How Do I Get a Better Grade?

Visit www.mywritinglab.com for audio-visual lectures and additional practice sets about quotation marks, capitalization, and titles.

mywritinglab

Get a better grade with MyWritingLab!

Numbers and Additional Punctuation

CHAPTER 38

CONTENTS

- Numbers
- Additional Punctuation

Section Theme **HUMAN DEVELOPMENT**

In this chapter, you will read about photography and photographers.

Grammar Snapshot

Looking at Numbers and Hyphens

This excerpt is taken from *History of Photography and the Camera* by Mary Bellis. Abbreviations, numbers, and hyphenated words are in boldface type.

> Nitrate film is historically important because it allowed for the development of roll films. The first flexible movie films measured **35-mm** wide and came in long rolls on a spool. In the **mid-1920s**, using this technology, **35-mm** roll film was developed for the camera. By the late **1920s**, **medium-format** roll film was created. It measured **six** centimeters wide and had a paper backing making it easy to handle in daylight. This led to the development of the **twin-lens-reflex** camera in **1929**.

In this chapter, you will learn about using numbers and punctuation such as hyphens.

Teaching Tip: Ask students if they know why certain words need hyphens. Also, point out that numbers may appear as both figures and words.

Numbers

When using numbers in academic writing, follow these rules:

- Spell out numbers that can be expressed in one or two words.

  We spent **eighteen** days in Mexico City.

  There were **forty-seven** people waiting for another flight.

  The airline had room for **four hundred**.

  That day, **thousands** of people cleared customs.

Teaching Tip: The rules presented about numbers apply to academic essays. The rules are not the same in fields such as business management, accounting, math, and so on.

- Use numerals with numbers of more than two words.

  The manager booked rooms for **358** guests.

- Spell out fractions.

  Only **one-third** of the residents have their own homes.

- When the sentence begins with a number, spell out the number. If the number has more than two words, do not place it at the beginning of the sentence.

  Three hundred people were invited to the gallery.

  There were **158** guests.

- Spell out *million* or *billion* if the word appears in a sentence.

  There were about four **million** residents in the surrounding suburbs.

- Use numerals when writing addresses, dates, times, degrees, pages, or divisions of a book. Also use numerals with prices and percentages. However, write out the word "dollar" or "percent."

  A yearly subscription costs **29** dollars, which is about **15** percent less than the cover price.

Hint **Several Numbers in a Sentence**

When writing two consecutive numbers, write out the shorter number.

We used **two 35-mm** rolls of film.

Be consistent when writing a series of numbers. If some numbers require numerals, then use numerals for all of the numbers.

The gallery guests consumed **300** appetizers, **8** pounds of cheese, and **120** glasses of wine.

PRACTICE 1 Correct any errors with numbers in the next sentences.

EXAMPLE: She was just ~~9~~ *nine* years old when she picked up a camera.

1. Photographer Moyra Davey has ~~six~~ *6* cameras, 184 rolls of film, and ~~thirty-three~~ *33* different lenses.
2. She has worked professionally as a photographer for ~~10~~ *ten* years.
3. A small art gallery exhibited ~~25~~ *twenty-five* of Davey's photos.
4. ~~40~~ *Forty* people came to the opening.
5. Davey would like to publish her photos and sell each book for ~~one hundred and twenty nine~~ *129* dollars.
6. She wants to self-publish ~~20~~ *twenty* 168-page books.

GRAMMAR LINK

For practice using semicolons, see Chapters 21 and 24.

Teaching Tip: Students can practice using semicolons more extensively in Chapter 21, Sentence Combining, and Chapter 24, Run-Ons.

Additional Punctuation

Semicolon (;)

Use a semicolon

- between two complete and related ideas.

  The photograph was stunning; Sherman was very pleased.

- between items in a series of ideas, if the items have internal punctuation or are very long.

  Sherman's works were exhibited in Birmingham, Alabama; Fort Worth, Texas; Toronto, Ontario; and London, England.

Teaching Tip: Because semicolons in a series are rarely used, and the semicolons can often be replaced by commas, this chapter introduces students to the idea but does not include related exercises. However, if you want students to practice using semicolons in a series, you can ask them to construct sentences that would need such semicolons. They can brainstorm sentences in pairs.

Colon (:)

Use a colon

- after a complete sentence that introduces a quotation.

  The photographer Henri Cartier Bresson stated his view: "Photographers are dealing with things that are continually vanishing."

- to introduce a series or a list after a complete sentence.

  The new museum includes the work of some great photographers: Ansel Adams, Cindy Sherman, Edward Weston, Alfred Stieglitz, Dorothea Lange, and Annie Leibowitz.

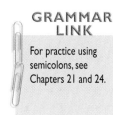

- to introduce an explanation or example

  The tiny sculpture is outrageously expensive: it costs $2.5 million.
- after the expression "the following."

  Please do the following: read, review, and respond.
- to separate the hour and minutes in expressions of time.

  The exhibit will open at 12:30 P.M.

Hyphen (-)

Use a hyphen

- with some compound nouns. (Note that *compound* means "more than one part.") The following nouns always require a hyphen.

sister-in-law	mother-in-law	show-off

- when you write the complete words for compound numbers between twenty-one and ninety-nine.

twenty-five	ninety-two	seventy-seven

- after some prefixes such as *ex-*, *mid-*, or *self-*.

self-assured	mid-December	ex-husband

- when you use a compound adjective before a noun. The compound adjective must express a single thought.

one-way street	well-known actor	thirty-year-old woman

There is no hyphen if the compound adjective appears after the noun.

The street is one way.	The actor was well known.	The woman is thirty years old.

CHAPTER 38

Hint **Nonhyphenated Compound Adjectives**

Some compound adjectives never take a hyphen, even when they appear before a noun. Here are some common examples.

World Wide Web	high school senior	real estate agent

Dash (—)

You can use a dash to set off information that you want to emphasize. Use dashes sparingly.

Marge Stranton raised her camera to take the picture, but it was too late—the moment had passed.

Parentheses ( )

You can use parentheses to set off incidental information such as a date or abbreviation. Use parentheses sparingly.

> Lange's photo of the migrant mother, which was taken during the height of the Depression era (1936), has become an enduring image.
>
> The United Press Photographer's Association (UPPA) was founded in 1946.

Hint Using Abbreviations

Sometimes you will not want to repeat the name of an organization over and over in an essay. To use abbreviations correctly, mention the complete name of an organization the first time you mention it, put the abbreviation in parentheses immediately after the full name, and then use only the abbreviation throughout the rest of the essay.

> The North Atlantic Treaty Organization (NATO) supports an international security agreement that was signed in 1949 in Washington, DC. Today, NATO's headquarters are in Brussels, Belgium.

There are two types of abbreviations: **initialisms** and **acronyms**. When saying an initialism, pronounce each of the first letters of an organization's title individually. Examples are IBM, FBI, and CIA. When saying an acronym, pronounce it as a full word. Examples of acronyms are NATO (pronounced "nay-toh") and WHO (pronounced "hoo").

CHAPTER 38

PRACTICE 2 Add either a colon, hyphen, dash, or a set of parentheses to each sentence.

EXAMPLE: Dorothea Lange rushed home and printed the photos—a decision that would change her life.

1. Florence Thompson and her husband, Cleo, were living in Merced Falls, California, when there was a tragedy : the Crash of 1929.

2. A couple of years later, the Merced Falls Mill (MFM) lost business and let go many of the employees.

3. Many ~~laid off~~ laid-off workers, including the Thompson family, left Merced Falls and went from town to town looking for work.

4. Cleo's short life (1899 to 1931) ended in a tiny cabin near Feather River.

thirty-two-year-old

5. Cleo was a ~~thirty two year old~~ man when he died.

:

6. Florence decided to keep her children with her "I made a promise to Cleo to see his six kids raised, and by God I'm going to keep that promise!"

:

7. In the back of her truck were Florence's possessions a small stove, a few pieces of clothing, some blankets, and a canvas tent.

;

8. Florence and her children took many low-wage jobs they struggled and rarely had enough to eat.

9. Florence and the other migrant workers stooped over in fields to pick the
:
following items strawberries, peas, corn, and asparagus.

10. One day, Florence was in a tent by the highway waiting for her son to
—
return a day that would make her famous.

Teaching Tip: You can use the final review as a test. Additional practice and test material appears in the Instructor's Resource Manual and on *MyWritingLab*.

Final Review

Identify and correct any errors in numbers, semicolons, colons, hyphens, dashes, or parentheses. Write C next to correct sentences. (Note: You can see the photograph <u>Migrant Mother</u> on the first page of this chapter.)

ten-year-old

EXAMPLE: The ~~ten year old~~ truck broke down. _____

1. In 1936, Dorothea Lange had joined the Farm Security Administration
( )
FSA and was traveling around Nipomo Valley in California. _____

2. On a warm day in March, Lange was driving home when she saw a sign for a migrant camp. __C__

3. Lange described what happened that day: “I saw and approached the hungry and desperate mother, as if drawn by a magnet.” _____

4. Sitting in her ~~dust covered~~ dust-covered canvas tent, Florence Thompson was holding her baby, and her children were crowded around her. _____

5. Florence Thompson described their encounter: “She just took my picture. She did not ask me my name.” __C__

6. The next day, Lange delivered the photos to a popular San Francisco newspaper. __C__

7. The ~~front page~~ front-page story described the migrant workers and their suffering. _____

8. Immediately, concerned citizens sent 184 tins of food, ~~forty~~ 40 tents, and 3 boxes of tools to the migrant camp. _____

9. Some doctors came to the camp to care for the sick, and some local employers offered jobs. __C__

10. However, Florence Thompson was not there to see the outpouring of generosity because her ~~brother in law~~ brother-in-law had brought her to his home. _____

11. Her ~~12 year old~~ twelve-year-old son, who was staying in town with his uncle, had seen his mother’s face on the front page of the newspaper. _____

READING LINK

Human Development

The following essays contain more information about human development and creativity.

“Out of Sight” by Ryan Knighton (page 112)
“Do You Have What It Takes to Be Happy?” by Stacey Colino (page 149)
“On Genius” by Dorothy Nixon (page 169)
“The Dating World” by Naomi Louder (page 212)
“Raunch Culture” by Ariel Levy (page 629)
“Twixters” by Betsy Hart (page 632)
“The Untranslatable Word ‘Macho’” by Rose del Castillo Guilbault (page 635)
“Medicating Ourselves” by Robyn Sarah (page 638)

12. He ran to his uncle in a panic: “My mother has been shot!” _____

13. An ink stain appeared on the photo~~,~~; the boy thought it was a bullet hole in his mother’s head. _____

14. The photo—an iconic image of the Depression—has been reproduced in ~~1000s~~ thousands of books and magazines. _____

15. The compassionate photographs of Dorothea Lange (1895–1965) have influenced modern documentary photography. _____

The Writer’s Room Topics for Writing

Write about one of the following topics. Proofread for errors in numbers or punctuation.

1. Describe a personal photograph that you cherish. When was the photo taken? What is in the photo? Why is it so compelling?
2. Compare two art forms. For example, you could compare a photograph and a painting.

CHECKLIST: NUMBERS AND PUNCTUATION

When you edit your writing, ask yourself these questions.

- Are there any numbers in my writing? Check that your numbers are consistently written, and verify that you have used words rather than numerals when necessary.

  Lange took ~~1000s~~ thousands of photographs.

- Are my semicolons, colons, hyphens, dashes, and parentheses used in a correct and appropriate manner?

  She brought the following supplies~~,~~: a camera, a ~~well used~~ *well-used* chair, and a camera stand.

How Do I Get a Better Grade?

Visit www.mywritinglab.com for audio-visual lectures and additional practice sets about numbers and additional punctuation.

Get a better grade with MyWritingLab!

CHAPTER 39 Editing Practice

To conquer Mount Everest, climbers meet the physical and mental challenges through practice and training. To write good essays, students perfect their skills by revising and editing.

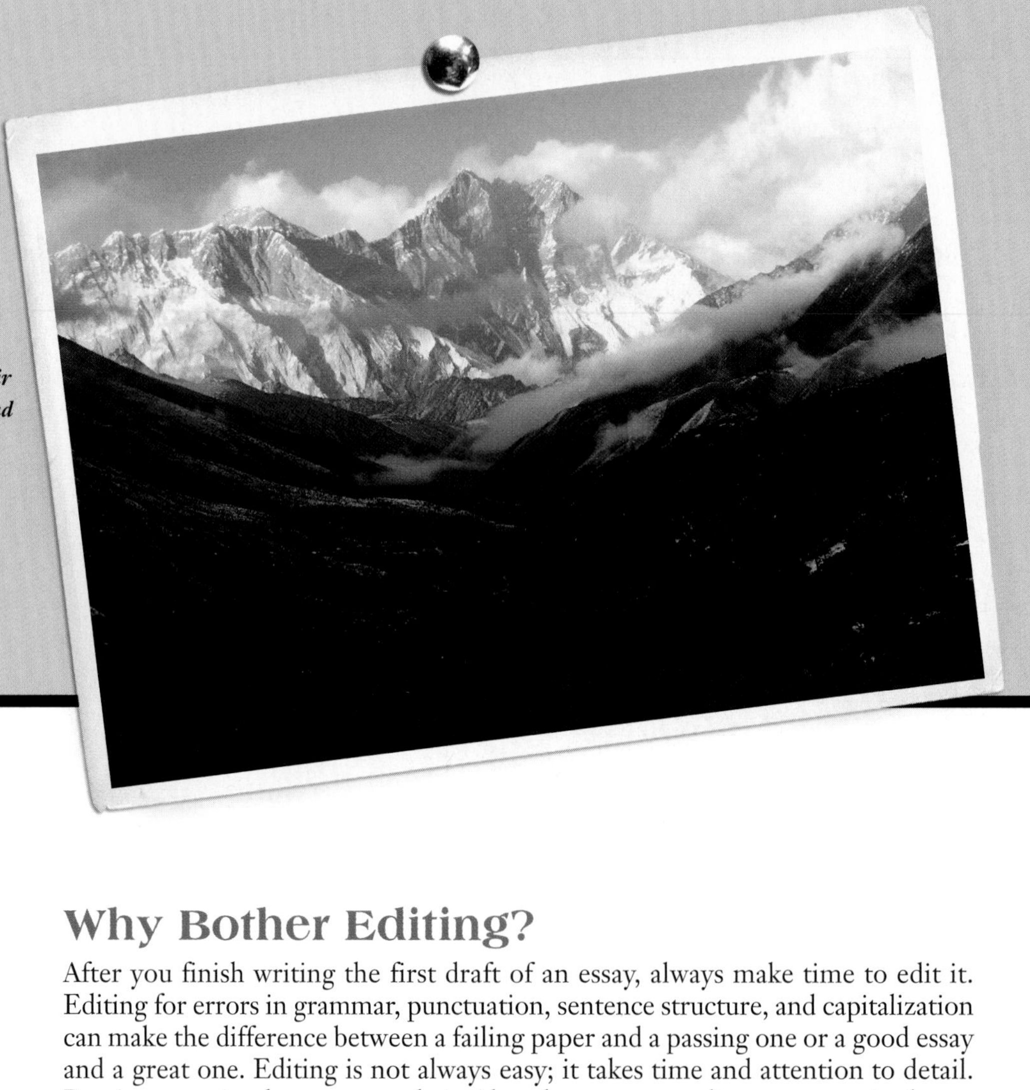

Why Bother Editing?

After you finish writing the first draft of an essay, always make time to edit it. Editing for errors in grammar, punctuation, sentence structure, and capitalization can make the difference between a failing paper and a passing one or a good essay and a great one. Editing is not always easy; it takes time and attention to detail. But, it gets easier the more you do it. Also, the more you edit your essays (and your peers' essays, too), the better your writing will be, and the less time you will need to spend editing!

PRACTICE 1 EDIT AN ESSAY

Correct fifteen errors in this student essay. An editing symbol appears above each error. To understand the meaning of each symbol, refer to the revising and editing symbols on the inside back cover of this book.

Climbing Everest

Tibetans
//
1 The Nepalese and Indians name it Sagarmatha, and people from Tibet call
M
cap
it Qomolangma. The rest of the world knows it as mount Everest. In 1852, a
geological survey of the Himalayan mountain range identified the highest peak as
"Peak XV." By 1865, the British named the peak "Everest" after a surveyor named
Sir George Everest. For mountain climbers, Everest became a challenge as soon
was
shift
as it is named the highest peak in the world.

its
sp
2 By 1921, Tibet opened it's borders to the outside and gave climbers easy access
to Everest. The first Europeans to attempt to climb Everest were George Mallory
. U
ro
and Andrew Irvine in 1924~~, u~~nfortunately, they both perished in the attempt.
Many other unsuccessful endeavours were made to reach the Everest summit.
Then in 1953, Edmund Hillary, a New Zealander, and Tenzing Norgay, a Nepalese
Sherpa, became the first climbers to reach the top of the world at 29,028 feet
heroes
sp
above sea level. Both men became world-famous heros. In addition, in 1978, two

Teaching Tip: Practices 1 and 2 contain editing symbols and codes that are found at the back of the book. The practices can help students get used to more formal editing techniques. If you use different symbols or codes, tell your students about them before they begin these editing practices.

Austrian climbers, Reinhold Messner and Peter Habeler, reached the Everest summit without the aid of supplemental oxygen. Two years later, Messner again

It was a solo . . .
frag

attained the summit without extra oxygen. A solo climb.

have reached
vt

3 Since 1921, around 2,200 mountaineers reached the summit; others have paid

attempt
sp

a great price. About 185 climbers have died in the attemt. There is a graveyard on the ascent to the summit. Mountaineers see the remains of corpses, tents, and

oxygen bottles
//

bottles that were filled with oxygen. The dead remain on Everest. Even if climbers

they
shift

wanted to carry the corpses down, you could not because of the altitude.

ad

4 The popularity of climbing the world's ~~most~~ highest peak has become so great that critics call Everest just another tourist trap. Many climbers set up businesses

businessman
pl

as guides. A Nepalese businessmen is planning to develop a cyber café at the base

is
agr

camp, and some snowboarders want to surf down from the summit. There are also a lot of trash on the summit trail. Nonetheless, Everest still catches the

people
pl

imagination of persons all over the world.

PRACTICE 2 EDIT AN ESSAY

Correct fifteen errors in this student essay. An editing symbol appears above each error. To understand the meaning of each symbol, refer to the revising and editing symbols on the inside back cover of this book.

The Man Who Discovered King Tutankhamen

1 Howard Carter's persistence helped him make a great contribution to the

history of human civilization. Carter was born in 1874 near London, England. He

seventeen
sp
became interested in Egyptology at the age of 17, when he was working in Egypt

site
wc
on an archaeological sight. His job was to trace drawings and inscriptions. Howard

Carter discovered one of the greatest archaeological finds in history: the tomb of

King Tutankhamen.

,
p
2 At the age of twenty-five Carter became the first inspector general for

monuments in Upper Egypt. He was responsible for supervising digs around the

Kings, which
frag
area of the Valley of the Kings. Which had a great number of tombs. He became

fascinated
ad
very fascinating by the story of the young pharaoh, King Tutankhamen, and he

absolutely
sp
was absolutly certain that the tomb was located in the general area of the

Valley of the Kings.

3 For excavations, Carter received funding from Lord Carnarvon, a wealthy
Carter's
sp
patron of many digs. From 1914–1922, Carnarvon funded Carters search for the
legendary tomb of King Tut. By 1922, Lord Carnarvon became frustrated at the
lack of success and decided that he would only support the search for one more
really
ad
year. Carter got real lucky when, one morning, one of his workers tripped over a
rock. When
ro
flat rock, when Carter went to see what it was, he realized that it was the top of a
staircase.

,
p
4 Carter was elated by the discovery but his workers had a completely different
reaction. They were convinced that the tomb had a curse on it. Whoever broke
superstition and . . .
frag
the door seal was doomed for death. Carter ignored the superstition. And went
inside the tomb. Inside he found everything intact and spent the next ten years
in
wc
cataloguing his find. Some people continued to believe at the curse and blamed
it for the death of six workers. Eventually an urban legend formed called the
exaggerated
sp
Mummy's Curse, which exagerated the power of the curse. Carter never believed
any died
wc shift
in no curse, and he dies of natural causes at the age of sixty-six.

PRACTICE 3 EDIT A FORMAL LETTER

Correct twelve errors in this formal business letter.

George Bates

S W
5672 Manet ~~street~~ ~~west~~

Lazerville, TX 76202

August 15, 2008

Customer Service

S
The Furniture ~~store~~

1395 Division Street

Denton, TX 76205

Subject: Desk

M
Attention: Sales ~~manager~~

A ,
I bought a desk from your store on ~~august~~ 13 ^ 2008, and the store delivered it
T
~~thursday~~ morning. After the delivery people had left, I discovered a large
It's
scratch on the surface of the desk. ~~Its~~ also lopsided. Since I have always
,
found your products to be of excellent quality ^ I would like to have a
replacement desk delivered to my home and the damaged desk taken
a
away. If you do not have replacement desk of the same model, then I would
like to have a full reimbursement.

.
Thank you very much for your cooperation in this matter~~,~~ I look forward to
receiving my new desk.

sincerely,
Yours ~~sincerly,~~

George Bates

George Bates

PRACTICE 4 EDIT AN ESSAY

Correct twenty errors in the following essay.

Discovering Venice

1 My brother and ~~me~~ I are spending this summer in one of the most beautiful ~~city~~ cities in the world. Venice, Italy~~. It~~ is unique because it is composed of a number of small islands in the Adriatic ~~sea~~ Sea. It has over one hundred canals and over four hundred bridges. One of Italy's must-see places, Venice has an intriguing history.

2 Venice was founded in the fifth century by Romans escaping the ferocious Gothic ~~tribes. According~~ tribes, according to legend. In the tenth century, Venice became a city of wealthy merchants who profited from the Crusades. By the twelfth century, after its successful war against Genoa, Venice had become a powerful city-state, trading with the Byzantines, the Arabs, and many others.

3 One of ~~it's~~ its most famous citizens was the explorer Marco Polo (1254–1324), a businessman who was one of the first ~~europeans~~ Europeans to reach China. ~~Him~~ He and his father spent about twenty-four years in China and ~~was~~ were reputedly friends and confidants of Kublai Khan, the emperor of China. Polo may have brought back noodles from ~~China. Which~~ China, which have become the basis for ~~italian~~ Italian pasta.

4 When the Polos returned from China, they recounted the adventures they had had. The citizens of Venice did not believe them. Even today, scholars differ about ~~weather~~ whether Marco Polo actually reached China. Some say it was highly ~~unlikly~~ unlikely because he did not mention things such as chopsticks, tea, or Chinese script. Others think that Polo reached China because he talked about paper money and the Chinese postal system.

5 Venice has been written about in many works of fiction. For example, Shakespeare's Merchant of Venice is set in ~~this~~ that city. Shakespeare also set the first part of his tragedy Othello in Venice. In fact, the first scenes of the Shakespearean tragedy ~~takes~~ take place in the Duke's palace. Another famous book, Thomas Mann's Death in Venice, takes place on a Venetian island that is popular among tourists.

6 My brother has traveled more than ~~me~~ I have, and he says that of all the cities he's seen, Venice is his absolute favorite. If I ~~would have known~~ had known how fascinating the city is, I would have visited it a long time ago.

PRACTICE 5 EDIT A WORKPLACE MEMO

Correct ten errors in the following excerpt from a memo. Answers will vary.

To: Career development faculty members

From: Maddison Healey

Re: Internships

I'm ~~gonna~~ going to take this opportunity to remind you that ~~their~~ there are financial resources to ~~hiring~~ hire two new interns for the Career ~~development~~ Development Program. If anyone wishes to participate in this collaboration, please let Danielle or ~~I~~ me know. The current deadline for applying to the internship program is the beginning of ~~april~~ April. The internship program provides valuable mentoring to college students. ~~Treating an intern with respect, it is very important.~~ It is important to treat interns with respect. If you hire an intern, you are responsible for training ~~them~~ him or her. Also, you must provide constructive feedback to the intern and to the college administrator. For those who are interested, please let me know as ~~quick~~ quickly as possible.

PRACTICE 6 EDIT A SHORT ARTICLE

Correct fifteen errors in the next selection. Answers will vary.

Forget What Your Fifth Grade Teacher Taught You

1 The solar system no longer has nine ~~planets, on~~ planets. On August 24, 2006, the International Astronomical ~~union,~~ Union which has a voting membership of about 2,500 scientists, met in Prague. It decided to demote Pluto from a planet to a dwarf planet. The astronomers said that Pluto does not exhibit the same characteristics as the other major planets. According to scientists, a planet must orbit the sun, it ~~must be having~~ must have a spherical shape, and it must have a clear orbit. ~~Unfortunatly,~~ Unfortunately, Pluto's orbit overlaps Neptune's orbit, so it does not meet the third criterion for a planet.

2 At the ~~begining~~ beginning of the twentieth century, ~~much~~ many astronomers suspected the possibility of another planet in the solar system. In 1930, while working for the Lowell Conservatory in Flagstaff, Arizona, astronomer Clyde Tombaugh took photographs of a sphere that was composed mainly of ~~ices~~ ice and rocks. It also had a satellite, Charon, orbiting it. ~~Evenutaly,~~ Eventually this sphere was named the ~~nineth~~ ninth planet in the solar system.

3 Scientists were very ~~exciting~~ excited about the discovery. People from all over the world suggested names for the new planet. The scientists from the observatory received so many suggestions that they had difficulty choosing one. An eleven-~~years~~year-old girl from Oxford, England, suggested the name Pluto. Venetia Burney was interested in Greek and Roman mythology, and Pluto is the Roman name

for Hades, the Greek God of the Dead. She ~~was giving~~ *gave* her suggestion to her grandfather, who then wired it to the Lowell Observatory.

4 The scientific community and the public have had a mixed reaction to the declassification of ~~Pluto. As~~ *Pluto as* a planet. Some refuse to accept it. But I wonder why ~~are they~~ *they are* resistant. Perhaps teachers don't ~~wanna~~ *want to* change astronomy textbooks. Maybe humans feel particularly wary when the scientific community "revises" what it once asked them to accept as fact.

PART V

Reading Strategies and Selections

In this chapter, the essays are organized according to the same themes used in the grammar chapters. The predominant writing pattern of each essay is shown in parentheses.

From Reading to Writing

CHAPTER 40

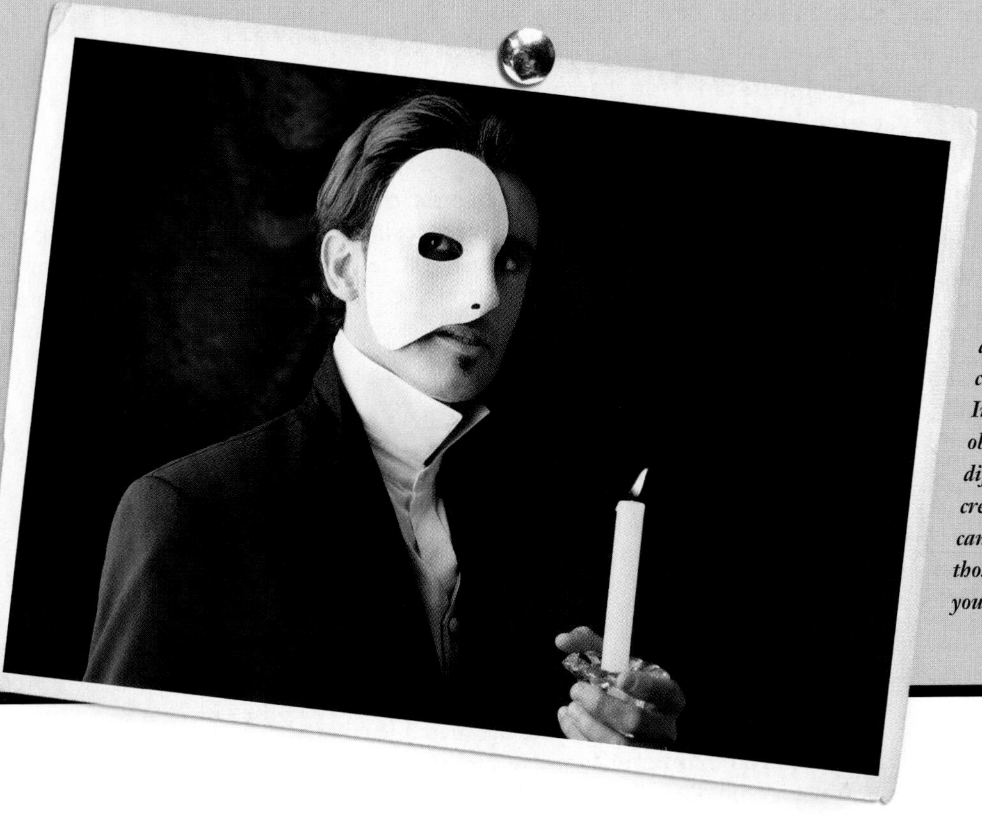

Aspiring actors study ordinary people, psychological profiles, and the work of other actors to fully develop the characters they play. In the same way, by observing how different writers create their work, you can learn how to use those techniques in your own writing.

Reading Strategies

The reading strategies discussed in this chapter can help you develop your writing skills. They can also help you become a more active reader. You will learn about previewing, finding the main and supporting ideas, understanding difficult words, and recognizing irony. When you read, you expand your vocabulary and learn how other writers develop topics. You also learn to recognize and use different writing patterns. Finally, reading helps you find ideas for your own essays.

> *"You don't have to burn books to destroy a culture. Just get people to stop reading them."*
>
> Ray Bradbury, Author

Previewing

Previewing is like glancing through a magazine in a bookstore; it gives you a chance to see what the writer is offering. When you **preview**, look quickly for the following visual clues so that you can determine the selection's key ideas:

- Titles or subheadings (if any)
- The first and last sentence of the introduction
- The first sentence of each paragraph
- The concluding sentences
- Any photos, graphs, or charts

Finding the Main Idea

After you finish previewing, read the selection carefully. Search for the **main idea**, which is the central point that the writer is trying to make. In an essay, the main idea usually appears somewhere in the first few paragraphs in the form of a thesis statement. However, some professional writers build up to the main idea and state it only in the middle or at the end of the essay. Additionally, some professional writers do not state the main idea directly.

Hint: Making a Statement of the Main Idea

If the reading does not contain a clear thesis statement, you can determine the main idea by asking yourself *who, what, when, where, why*, and *how* questions. Then, using the answers to those questions, make a statement that sums up the main point of the reading.

Making Inferences

If a professional writer does not state the main idea directly, you must look for clues that will help you to **infer** or figure out what the writer means to say. For example, the next paragraph does not have a topic sentence. However, you can infer the main idea. Underline key words that can lead you to a better understanding of the passage.

> Algie Crivens III was 18 and fresh out of high school in 1991 when he was sentenced to twenty years in prison for a murder he did not commit. He spent the next eight-and-a-half years consumed with educating himself while his appeals crawled through the courts. Crivens is nothing if not energetic; he tends to speak in paragraphs, not sentences. While in prison, he channeled this energy into earning an associate's degree in social science and a bachelor's in sociology. He also took courses in paralegal studies and culinary arts. His fellow prisoners used to ask how he could spend so much time reading. But, to him, reading was a way to escape the boredom of prison life.
>
> —From "Righting a Wrong" by Liliana Ibara

PRACTICE 1 Ask yourself the following questions.

1. What is the subject of this text?

   a young man who has been wrongfully convicted

2. What points can you infer that the writer is making? *You can infer that the legal system sometimes makes mistakes, and that prisoners are not necessarily unmotivated, unintelligent, uneducated, or lazy.*

Finding the Supporting Ideas

Different writers use different types of supporting ideas. They may give steps for a process, use examples to illustrate a point, give reasons for an argument, and so on. Try to identify the author's supporting ideas.

Highlighting and Making Annotations

After you read a long text, you may forget some of the author's ideas. To help you remember and quickly find the important points, you can highlight key ideas and make annotations. An **annotation** is a comment, question, or reaction that you write in the margins of a passage.

Each time you read a passage, follow these steps:

- Look in the introductory and concluding paragraphs. Underline sentences that sum up the main idea. Using your own words, rewrite the main idea in the margin.
- Underline or highlight supporting ideas. You might even want to number the arguments or ideas. This will allow you to understand the essay's development.
- Circle words that you do not understand.
- Write questions in the margin if you do not understand the author's meaning.
- Write notes beside passages that are interesting or that relate to your own experiences.
- Jot down any ideas that might make interesting writing topics.

Here is an example of a highlighted and annotated passage from an essay titled "Sprawl Fallout" by Patricia L. Kirk.

1 For suburbanites who spend hours in traffic each day commuting to city jobs, the concept of urban sprawl is more than a euphemism batted around by city planners. Many commuters know the psychological tolls of their long, slow journeys—irritation, anxiety, less time at home—but the negative impacts might be broader than most realize.

2 Urban sprawl—a phenomenon that results in people living far from their workplaces—has been linked to asthma, obesity, and just plain foul

< What is a euphemism?
< General background for the introduction
< Main point suggests urban sprawl is not good.
< Definition of sprawl

Shows the effects of sprawl

Traffic jams drive me crazy.

moods. In one study, people with long commutes reported more headaches, ➢ stomach problems, and fatigue than people with shorter drives. Irritability from long commutes was also shown to transfer to job performance, ➢ resulting in lower productivity.

Understanding Difficult Words

When you come across an unfamiliar word in a passage, do not stop reading to look up its definition in the dictionary. First, try using context clues to figure out the term's meaning on your own. If you still do not understand the word, circle it to remind you to look up its meaning in the dictionary when you have finished reading through the passage. You can keep a list of new vocabulary in the "Vocabulary Log" at the end of this book on page 651.

Using Context Clues

Context clues are hints in the selection that help to define a word. To find a word's meaning, try the following:

- **Look at the word.** Is it a noun, a verb, or an adjective? Knowing how the word functions in the sentence can help you guess its meaning.
- **Look at surrounding words.** Look at the entire sentence and try to find a relation between the difficult word and those that surround it. There may be a **synonym** (a word that means the same thing) or an **antonym** (a word that means the opposite), or other terms in the sentence that help define the word.
- **Look at surrounding sentences.** Sometimes you can guess the meaning of a difficult word by looking at the sentences, paragraphs, and punctuation marks surrounding it. When you use your logic, the meaning becomes clear.

In most cases, you can guess the meaning of a new word by combining your own knowledge of the topic with the information conveyed in the words and phrases surrounding the difficult word.

PRACTICE 2 Can you define the words *strewn*, *emanate*, or *haven*? Perhaps you are not quite sure. Looking at the words in context makes it much easier to guess the definitions of the words.

> When I arrived in my hometown, I was baffled by the changes in my old neighborhood. Garbage was **strewn** across front lawns, paint peeled on the graying wooden homes, and roofs sagged. The auto body shop on the corner **emanated** horrible fumes of turpentine and paint, forcing me to cover my nose when I passed it. I wondered what had happened to my former safe **haven**.

Now write your own definition of the words as they are used in the context.

strewn ___scattered___ emanated ___gave off___ haven ___refuge___

Hint **Cognates**

Cognates (also known as word twins) are English words that may look and sound like words in another language. For example, the English word *responsible* is similar to the Spanish word *responsable*, although the words are spelled differently.

If English is not your first language, and you read an English word that looks similar to a word in your language, check how the word is being used in context. It may or may not mean the same thing in English as it means in your language. For example, in English, *sensible* means "to show good sense," but in Spanish, *sensible* means "emotional." In German, *bekommen* sounds like "become" but it really means "to get," and the German word *gift* means "poison" in English. If you are not sure of a word's meaning, you can always consult a dictionary.

ESL Teaching Tip: Draw your nonnative speakers' attention to the cognates hint. Then, ask them to brainstorm a list of words in their native languages that look like English words. They should determine if the words have similar or different meanings in both languages. Using Spanish as an example, some words that Spanish speakers may misuse—because the meanings in English and Spanish are different—are *actually, animator, embarrassed, costume, cruise, deception, resume,* and *sensible*. For instance, although *actual* means "real" or "genuine" in English, it means "current" or "present" in Spanish.

Using a Dictionary

If you cannot understand the meaning of an unfamiliar word even after using context clues, then look up the word in a dictionary. A dictionary is useful if you use it correctly. Review the following tips for proper dictionary usage:

- **Look at the dictionary's front matter.** The preface contains explanations about the various symbols and abbreviations. Find out what your dictionary has to offer.
- **Read all of the definitions listed for the word.** Look for the meaning that best fits the context of your sentence.
- **Look up root words, if necessary.** For example, if you do not understand the word *unambiguous*, remove the prefix and look up *ambiguous*.

Here is an example of how dictionaries set up their definitions:

Word-Break Divisions
Your dictionary may indicate places for dividing words with heavy black dots.

Stress Symbol (′) and Pronunciation
Some dictionaries provide the phonetic pronunciation of words. The stress symbol lets you know which syllable has the highest or loudest sound.

Parts of Speech
The *n* means that *formation* is a noun. If you do not understand the "parts of speech" symbol, look in the front or the back of your dictionary for a list of symbols and their meanings.

for•ma′•tion / fôr′māshən/ *n* 1, the process of shaping. 2, that which is shaped. 3, formal structure or arrangement, esp. of troops.

From *The New American Webster Handy College*, A Signet Book, 2000.

Determining Connotation and Denotation

A **denotation** is the literal meaning for a word that may be found in the dictionary. For example, the dictionary definition of *mother* is "a female parent." A **connotation** is the implied or associated meaning. It can be a cultural value

Teaching Tip: Discuss how terms such as *abandoned* carry emotional weight.

judgment. For instance, the word *mother* may trigger feelings of comfort, security, anger, or resentment in a listener, depending on that person's experience with mothers.

Authors can influence readers by carefully choosing words that have specific denotations. For example, review the next two descriptions. Which one has a more negative connotation?

Terry left his family. Andrew abandoned his family.

Teaching Tip: Ask students to discuss how certain words and phrases show a bias. Also ask them to rewrite one of the passages using a more neutral tone.

PRACTICE 3 Read the next passages and underline any words or phrases that have strong connotations. Discuss how the words support a personal bias. Answers will vary.

1. Furthermore, in too many states, welfare keeps flowing while the kids are in jail, or middle-class parents continue to claim children as tax deductions even as the state pays for their upkeep in detention facilities. We must demand that parents reimburse the state for housing their failures.

   from "Enough Is Enough" by Judy Sheindlin

2. There is no question about whom Ms. Politkovskaya held responsible in years of unflinching reporting from Chechnya: the Russian Army and Mr. Putin himself. When he finally got around to acknowledging her death yesterday, it was in a cold-blooded statement that the authorities "will take every step to investigate objectively the tragic death of the journalist Politkovskaya."

   from "Another Killing in Moscow" (*The New York Times* editorial)

3. Rohe could have chosen to give a substantive speech detailing why she believes "pre-emptive war is dangerous and wrong"—or as she so categorically put it, how she "knows" that it is. Instead she took the easy way out by insulting the speaker and throwing out some leftist chestnuts about the still missing Osama bin Laden and weapons of mass destruction. But the former would have required her to grapple with ideas; she chose to take potshots.

   from "The Real Meaning of Courage" by Linda Chavez

Recognizing Irony

Irony is a technique that some writers use to make a point. When an author is being ironic, he or she says one thing but really means the opposite. When the author uses an ironic tone, he or she does not intend the reader to interpret the words literally. Sarcasm is a type of verbal irony.

EXAMPLE: The charred burger lay in a grease-soaked bun. "That looks wonderful," he muttered.

PRACTICE 4 Read the next selection from an essay called "The Greatest Player" by Gary Lautens. Then answer the questions.

Occasionally, I run into sports figures at cocktail parties, on the street, or on their way to the bank. "Nice game the other night," I said to an old hockey-player pal.

"Think so?" he replied.

"You've come a long way since I knew you as a junior."

"How's that?"

"Well, you high-stick better for one thing—and I think the way you clutch sweaters is really superb. You may be the best in the league." He blushed modestly. "For a time," I confessed, "I never thought you'd get the hang of it."

"It wasn't easy," he confided. "It took practice and encouragement. You know something like spearing doesn't come naturally. It has to be developed."

"I'm not inclined to flattery but, in my book, you've got it made. You're a dirty player," I continued. . . . "There isn't a player in the league who knows as many obscene gestures."

How is the selection ironic? What does the author really mean?

The speaker appears to applaud hockey violence. The author really intends to criticize hockey violence.

From Reading to Writing

After you finish reading a selection, you could try these strategies to make sure that you have understood it.

Summarize the reading. When you summarize, you use your own words to write a condensed version of the reading. You leave out all information except for the main points. You can find a detailed explanation about summaries in Chapter 15.

Outline the reading. An outline is a visual plan of the reading that looks like an essay plan. First, you write the main idea of the essay, and then write down the most important idea from each paragraph. You could make further indentations, and under each idea, include a detail or example.

Analyze the reading. When you read, look critically at the writer's arguments and evaluate them, point by point. Also analyze how the writer builds the argument and ask yourself questions such as *Do I agree? Are the author's arguments convincing?* Then, when you write your analysis, you can break down the author's explanations and either refute or agree with them, using your own experiences and examples to support your view.

Teaching Tip:
To reinforce the link between reading and writing, you might assign students a particular reading and have them make an outline of that reading. Then point out that all prose—student essays, research papers, workplace memos—also need clear writing plans.

Write a response. Your instructor may ask you to write about your reaction to a reading. These are some questions you might ask yourself before you respond in writing.

- What is the writer's main point?
- What is the writer's purpose? Is the writer trying to entertain, persuade, or inform?
- Who is the audience? Is the writer directing his or her message at someone like me?
- Do I agree or disagree with the writer's main point?
- Are there any aspects of the topic to which I can relate? What are they?

After you answer the questions, you will have more ideas to use in your written response.

Reading Selections

Teaching Tip: After each reading there are questions about vocabulary, comprehension, structure, and critical thinking.

Theme: Conflict

READING 1

The CSI Effect

Richard Willing

Richard Willing is a journalist for *USA Today*. In the next article, he discusses the impact of crime scene shows on courtrooms across the nation.

1 Television shows such as *CSI* (Crime Scene Investigation) are affecting action in courthouses by, among other things, raising jurors' expectations of what prosecutors should produce at trial. Prosecutors, defense lawyers, and judges call it "the *CSI* effect," after the crime-scene shows that are among the hottest attractions on television. The shows feature high-tech labs and gorgeous techies. By shining a glamorous light on a gory profession, the programs also have helped to draw more students into forensic studies.

2 The programs also foster what analysts say is the mistaken notion that criminal science is fast and infallible and always gets its man. That's affecting the way lawyers prepare their cases, as well as the expectations that police and the public place on real crime labs. Real crime-scene investigators say that because of the programs, people often have unrealistic ideas of what criminal science can deliver.

3 Many lawyers, judges, and legal consultants say they appreciate how *CSI*-type shows have increased interest in forensic evidence. "Talking about science in the courtroom used to be like talking about geometry—a

real jury turnoff," says jury consultant Robert Hirschhorn of Lewisville, Texas. "Now that there's this obsession with the shows, you can talk to jurors about scientific evidence and just see from the looks on their faces that they find it fascinating."

4 But some defense lawyers say *CSI* and similar shows make jurors rely too heavily on scientific findings and unwilling to accept that those findings can be compromised by human or technical errors. Prosecutors also have complaints: They say the shows can make it more difficult for them to win convictions in the large majority of cases in which scientific evidence is irrelevant or absent. "The lesson that both sides can agree on is, what's on TV does seep into the minds of jurors," says Paul Walsh, president of the National District Attorneys Association. "Jurors are going to have information, or what they think is information, in mind. That's the new state of affairs."

5 Lawyers and judges say the *CSI* effect has become a phenomenon in courthouses across the nation. For example, in Phoenix, jurors in a murder trial noticed that a bloody coat introduced as evidence had not been tested for DNA. The jurors alerted the judge. The tests were unnecessary because, early in the trial, the defendant admitted his presence at the murder scene. The judge decided that TV had taught jurors about DNA tests but not enough about when to use them.

6 Juries are sometimes right to expect high-tech evidence. Three years ago in Richmond, Virginia, jurors in a murder trial asked the judge whether a cigarette butt found during the investigation could be tested for links to the defendant. Defense attorneys had ordered DNA tests but had not yet introduced them into evidence. The jury's hunch was correct—the tests exonerated the defendant, and the jury **acquitted** him.

acquitted: pronounced not guilty

7 The *CSI* effect also is being felt beyond the courtroom. At West Virginia University, forensic science is the most popular undergraduate major for the second year in a row, attracting 13 percent of incoming freshmen this fall. In June, supporters of an Ohio library drew an overflow crowd of 200-plus to a luncheon speech on DNA by titling it "CSI: Dayton." The Los Angeles County Sheriff's Department crime lab has seen another version of the *CSI* effect. Four technicians have left the lab for lucrative jobs as technical advisers to crime-scene programs. "They found a way to make science pay," lab director Barry Fisher says.

8 The stars of crime shows often are the equipment—DNA sequencers, mass spectrometers, photometric fingerprint illuminators, scanning electron microscopes. But the technicians run a close second. "It's 'geek chic,' the idea that kids who excel in science and math can grow up to be cool," says Robert Thompson, who teaches the history of TV programming at Syracuse University. "This is long overdue. . . . Cops and cowboys and doctors and lawyers have been done to death."

9 Some of the science on crime shows is state-of-the-art. Real lab technicians can, for example, lift DNA profiles from cigarette butts, candy wrappers, and gobs of spit, just as their Hollywood counterparts do. But some of what's on TV is far-fetched. Real technicians don't pour caulk into knife wounds to make a cast of the weapon. That wouldn't work in soft tissue. Machines that can identify cologne from scents on clothing are still in the experimental phase. A criminal charge based on "neuro-linguistic programming"—detecting lies by the way a person's eyes shift—likely would be dismissed by a judge.

10 Real scientists say the main problem with crime shows is this: The science is always above reproach. "You never see a case where the sample is degraded or the lab work is faulty or the test results don't solve the crime," says Dan Krane, president and DNA specialist at Forensic Bioinformatics in Fairborn, Ohio. "These things happen all the time in the real world."

Comprehension and Critical Thinking

1. Find a word in paragraph 2 that means "cultivate or advance." *foster*
2. What is the meaning of *exonerated* in paragraph 6?
   a. convicted b. determined (c.) exempted
3. Underline the thesis statement; that is, find a sentence that sums up the main idea of the essay.
4. In which paragraphs are there examples of the following:

   Anecdotes: *paragraphs 5, 6*

   Statistics: *paragraph 7*

   Expert opinions: *paragraphs 3, 4, 7, 8, 10*
5. What can you infer, or guess, after closely reading paragraph 6?
   a. The defendant left a cigarette butt at the crime scene.
   (b.) The defendant did not leave a cigarette butt at the crime scene.
   c. The DNA proved that the defendant was at the crime scene.
6. What do lawyers and judges appreciate about crime-scene shows?

   These days, jury members are interested in crime scene evidence, and they like to hear about science in the courtroom. CSI-type shows have helped create an interest in forensic evidence.
7. What problems do crime-scene shows cause for lawyers? Think of at least two answers.

   Juries expect crime scene evidence, even when it is not necessary or possible to obtain. They trust crime scene evidence too much. They don't realize that evidence can be flawed.

8. Crime-scene shows glamorize forensic science. How might the reality of life as a forensic scientist be different from what is shown on TV?

   TV shows make the job look exciting, but in reality, it is probably a very depressing and gory line of work. Also, cases are not as easy to solve as is shown on television.

9. How are crime-scene shows great for science "geeks?"

   The shows make people who are interested in science look attractive and exciting.

10. Why do real scientists object to crime-scene shows?

    The shows make the science look easy and "above reproach." In reality, lab tests can be faulty or useless.

WRITING TOPICS

Write about one of the following topics. Remember to explore, develop, and revise and edit your work.

1. Think about another type of television series or movie, and describe how it influences viewers. For example, you might choose soap operas, medical dramas, or mobster movies.
2. What causes people to break laws?

Teaching Tip: The suggested topics give students the opportunity to practice cause and effect writing. Specify whether students should write a paragraph or an essay.

READING 2

Types of Rioters

David Locher

David A. Locher is an author and college professor at Missouri Southern State College. The next excerpt about rioters is from his book *Collective Behavior*.

1 In March of 1992, Los Angeles was a city with a long history of conflict between racial groups. That year, a videotape of Rodney King being brutally beaten was shown over and over again on local, regional, and national television news reports. What almost no one realized at the time was that they were seeing an edited tape. KTLA, the Los Angeles television station that first acquired the videotape, edited out the first few seconds of the video because it was blurry. Most reporters, together with the public, saw only the edited, sixty-eight-second version of the video. They were not aware of the missing thirteen seconds, which apparently showed Rodney King charging at the police officers. The vast majority of Americans who saw the televised video believed that the beating had

been totally unprovoked and that the officers were therefore guilty. The untelevised thirteen seconds were enough to convince many jurors that the beating was at least partially provoked. Legally, they believed that the beating was excessive but not sufficient grounds for conviction in a court of law.

2 The videotape created a presumption throughout the country that the officers would be found guilty. When the not guilty verdict was announced, it led to the South-Central Los Angeles riot, which was the bloodiest, deadliest, most destructive riot in modern American history. At the time the riots were beginning, no one blamed the prosecutors; most blamed the jury and the system itself. The generalized belief throughout much of the country and shared by the rioters was that guilty verdicts could not have been reached, no matter what. Participants believed that legal justice was beyond their reach, but revenge was right at hand.

3 In all riots, there are categories of participants. Five categories can be labeled ego-involved, concerned, insecure, curious spectators, and ego-detached exploiters. Each category of participant may be operating under a different generalized belief, and possibly even a different set of structural strains.

Ego-Involved

4 Ego-involved participants feel a deep connection to the concerns expressed. In Los Angeles, the ego-involved participants were the ones who felt the most empathy for Rodney King, the most hatred for the LAPD, and the most outrage over the verdicts. They fully accepted the generalized beliefs and believed that it was up to them to do something. These individuals placed themselves into the position of responsibility. They threw bricks or started fires because they believed that doing so would produce real change and that their violent actions were the only way to produce that change. Ego-involved participants actually started the riot. Anger, outrage, and disappointment drove their actions. They believed that those actions were necessary, desirable, or unavoidable.

Concerned

5 Concerned riot participants are not so personally involved. They have a more general interest in the event. The concerned participants were those who took part in the rioting, but who focused their attention on following the lead of others. They accepted the generalized belief and engaged in riotous actions, but they did so as much out of empathy with the other rioters as empathy for Rodney King. These individuals helped the ego-involved start fires, break windows, and so on. Under only slightly

different circumstances, they could just as easily have followed leaders in a peaceful march. In Los Angeles, the concerned participants were acting out of hatred of the system or of authority in general. They followed the lead of the ego-involved but did not choose the course of action themselves.

Insecure

6 Insecure participants just want to be a part of something or are afraid of missing out. They may not have any understanding of the riot's causes. In this sense, they may get confused. They see others throwing objects and smashing windows, and they engage in the same behavior themselves. However, it could be that the ego-involved and concerned participants are all attacking a particular building because of what it represents, while the insecure simply smash whatever is handy. Insecure riot participants revel in the power that they feel by taking part, and they seek safety in numbers.

7 In the South-Central riot, the insecure participants went along with the actions of the others because it made them feel powerful. They were standing up to authority, spitting in the eye of society, and all from the relative safety of a large and anonymous crowd. Individuals who would never think of talking back to a police officer suddenly felt secure enough to throw rocks at them. The meek became powerful; the tame became dangerous. These participants turned the violence away from symbols of authority and toward anyone or anything that stood in the path of the crowd.

Spectators

8 In any form of collective behavior, there may be those who want to watch the actions of participants but do not wish to get directly involved. Photographs and videotaped segments of the Los Angeles riots frequently reveal more people standing around watching the action than participants. At one point during the riot, Reginald Denny, a truck driver who was passing through the area, was pulled out of his truck and nearly beaten to death by rioters. There were many more people watching the attack on Denny than there were actually hitting him. For spectators, the riot was simply an exciting form of entertainment.

9 Spectators are important for several reasons. In a deadly riot, they can frequently become targets for the hostile participants. They may also get caught up in the excitement and decide to join the action. They may take the side of participants against police. Sometimes social control agents force them into action. Social control agents usually do not attempt to distinguish between spectators and active participants. Circumstances often make it impossible for them to do so. In Los Angeles, many

spectators joined in the looting, and the police, soldiers, and guardsmen made no real attempt to distinguish between active participants and spectators. Everyone on the streets not wearing a uniform was perceived as a riot participant and treated accordingly. This sort of treatment sometimes outrages spectators to the extent that they become active in resisting social control.

Ego-Detached Exploiters

10 The ego-detached participant does not care about the issues that drive a riot. They do not accept the generalized belief shared by many other participants. They might not even know why the riot started in the first place. None of these issues matter to the ego-detached. They only want to exploit the conditions created by the riot for their own personal gain. An individual who throws a brick at a policeman might be driven by outrage over the verdicts (ego-involved), by a general hatred of the police (concerned), or by a sense of power and group identity (insecure). An individual who throws a brick at a store window to steal a television is driven by the desire for a free TV. Looting is an act of exploitation by those who are detached from the strain and generalized belief of the riot. Looters use the circumstances created by the riot to gather as many material goods as possible for themselves. No deep sense of outrage over a legal injustice drives an individual to steal a freezer. The exploiter uses the chaos, confusion, and temporary lack of social control to acquire commercial goods for free. They carry out their own personal agendas under cover of the collective episode.

11 The Los Angeles riot was literally taken over by exploiters. The pattern of destruction reveals that the targets changed within the first few hours. Rioters first attacked buildings that symbolized authority or individuals who, through their race, symbolized those with authority. By nightfall, however, they started attacking liquor stores. Before long, any business was fair game. If it could be moved, it was stolen. If it couldn't be moved, it was destroyed. The actions of the exploiters are not difficult to pick out in Los Angeles: they removed any object with any potential value before setting fire to each building. This is not the action of social revolutionaries; it is the action of greedy individuals looking to score. The passion of the ego-involved and concerned participants may fade out within a brief period of time, but the greed of the exploiters does not go away. Only the return of effective social control or the absence of anything to steal ends looting.

12 By the time a riot as big as the South-Central riot has begun, the ego-involved participants may be dramatically outnumbered by those from other categories. This may make the entire event seem pointless or

illogical to outside observers. "If they are so mad at the LAPD, why are they burning down their own houses?" was a common question asked by many Americans during the 1992 riot. These critics were overlooking the simple fact that many of the riot participants were not deeply concerned with the issues that caused the riot in the first place. Insecure participants blindly following the crowd and exploiters using the breakdown of social order for their own material gain can vastly outnumber those who actually care about the issues that caused the riot to begin in the first place. Spectators might outnumber all participants combined.

Comprehension and Critical Thinking

1. What does Locher mean by a *generalized belief* in paragraph 4?

   widely accepted belief that may or may not be based on facts
2. What is the meaning of *revel* as it is used in paragraph 6?
   a. feel drunk (b.) enjoy c. abuse
3. Which three types of rioters are likely to be most violent toward others?

   ego-involved, concerned, and insecure
4. Which type of rioter simply wants to benefit materially from the riot?

   ego-detached exploiters
5. Using your own words, briefly sum up the main characteristics of each type of rioter.

   Ego-involved: *feel empathy and connected to the cause, have strong beliefs about the issue, believe they can change things*

   Concerned: *have a general interest in the cause, accept generalized belief, follow others, want to join in*

   Insecure: *don't want to miss something, confused, don't really understand the issues, want to feel powerful, might become violent*

   Spectators: *watch but don't want to get involved, might become targets, might join in*

   Ego-detached exploiters: *don't care about issues, want to steal or get something out of the riot, are motivated by greed*
6. Locher used emphatic order to organize his essay. Specifically, how does he organize the types of riot participants?

   from most involved in the issue to most destructive and self-involved
7. Does Locher feel that the riots were justified? You will need to infer, or read between the lines.

   No. The core reason to start the riots was based on incomplete media reporting, thus the generalized belief may have been flawed.

Teaching Tip:
The suggested topics give students the opportunity to practice classification writing. Specify whether students should write a paragraph or an essay.

Teaching Tip:
Ask students to discuss the first writing topic. They can divide the first writing topic into mainstream journalism, tabloid journalism, and specialty or highbrow journalism. They can categorize the ways in which news is transmitted: newspapers, magazines, Internet, and so on. Finally, they can choose to categorize a specific type of medium, such as the magazine, according to its subject matter. For example, different magazines might focus on fashion, finance, music, or hard news.

8. Although this is mainly a classification essay, it also touches on causes and effects of the Los Angeles riot. Briefly sum up some of the main causes and effects. Answers will vary.

   Causes: *a history of conflict among racial groups, faulty media reporting, and a sense in certain communities that justice cannot be obtained*

   Effects: *an underprivileged community was destroyed, an innocent bystander was nearly murdered, racial tensions increased, and exploiters and looters benefited*

9. The author starts this essay by telling an anecdote. Why is this anecdote crucial to the main focus of the essay?

   It gives the reason for the subject of the essay. It links a theoretical subject to a real event. It is the running example in the essay to explain the types of rioters.

10. Who is the audience for this essay? Look closely at the tone and vocabulary.

    It is an academic audience such as students in criminology.

WRITING TOPICS

Write about one of the following topics. Remember to explore, develop, and revise and edit your work.

1. What are some types of media reports? Divide media reporting into at least three categories.
2. When an event such as a celebrity divorce, a terrorist attack, or a sports scandal occurs, how do you react? Does one topic excite your interest more than others? Discuss at least three types of audiences for media reporting.

READING 3

Naming Good Path Elk

Kenneth M. Kline

Kenneth M. Kline, an African American man of Lakota-Sioux descent, describes an initiation ceremony that he took part in during his adolescence. He looks back at the lessons he learned about giving.

1 I stand at the top of Morningside Park in New York City and stare down at Harlem's legendary brownstones. I come to this spot whenever I'm melancholy. Here, with the warm afternoon sun massaging my skin, I consider my life. Trying to survive as a freelance journalist has only meant

that I am out of work. Six months ago, I lost my uptown apartment, and creditors are showing no mercy. My name is so tarnished I begin to think that my only escape is to change it. As far as I'm concerned, my good name is dead.

2 Just then, a strong wind blows up from the park, quenching the hot, humid afternoon. It takes me back to a summer I spent at Camp Flying Cloud in the remote mountains around Plymouth, Vermont. I was eleven in 1974 and one of fifty boys living in teepees and dressing in loincloths at the Native-American camp.

3 That was my first year at the camp, and I was eager to learn about the Native-American blood that flowed in my African-American veins, courtesy of both my grandmothers. I'd been at the camp for two weeks when Medicine Rainbow, the camp director, announced that we would begin our first naming ceremony of the summer at that night's powwow. In the tradition of the Lakota Sioux, those selected for the naming quest would trek into the wilderness and spend three days in strict silence at a place called Blue Ledges on the edge of a mountain. There we would meditate on the names we had been given and how they would shape our lives.

4 Everyone was excited about the ceremony—except me. I had something on my mind. Earlier that week, while playing stickball, I'd lost my balance trying to score and crashed into the goalie. "Look out, you moron!" he'd yelled, spewing derogatory comments about my dark skin. I dusted myself off and, before I could stop myself, drop-kicked him, the way I'd learned in karate school. He crumpled like a house of cards, then walked away crying. Ever since that scuffle, he'd become a target for teasing by other campers.

5 On the night of the powwow, I worried that the scuffle might have tarnished my reputation—that any name I received would reflect the fight. The evening began with the lighting of a large bonfire. <u>As the tall flames bowed</u> and flickered in the summer breeze, a camper named Running Bull Thunders marched in, holding a long Indian pipe. He was followed by four other campers in ceremonial garments. Bells around their ankles rang with each step as Running Bull Thunders offered a ritual in gratitude to <u>Mother Earth and the Four Winds for blessing us</u>. Then he seated himself before the drum at the fire's edge and began to beat softly: Boom-boom! Boom-boom! It was our signal to begin the powwow, our late-night dance around the campfire, singing traditional songs. Our voices and footsteps echoed in the night as <u>tall spruce and pine trees danced</u> alongside us in the firelight.

6 When the drumming stopped, we grew silent in anticipation. Suddenly a shadow broke away from the group. Known as the Stalker, he walked lightly to the fire and unrolled a red quilt with Native-American

designs. Then, a shadow among shadows, he moved among us, an eagle feather between his fingers. He chose ten campers to be given names that night, and I was one of them.

7 The Stalker's strong hands clasped my arms as he whispered instructions in my ear. I was to take the eagle feather and sit cross-legged on the quilt. I held my breath as he came up behind me and daubed red paint on my temples. "Here is a boy who follows a good path like an elk crossing the woods," he told the gathering. "He is quiet and strong, always giving and helping others, and is eager to learn. For this, he shall be known as Good Path Elk." Turning solemnly to me, he added, "You must never say your name unless you become lost. Speaking your Indian name will bring a power to help you find your way."

8 Had I heard right? Had he seen me earlier in the week fighting on the stickball field? Now a chill came into the night air, and it was time for the giveaway ceremony, in which a camper volunteers to give something in friendship. Burning Eagle, an older boy I admired for his skill with Indian crafts, got to his feet. He held a woolen vest decorated with leather and seashells. Stitched on the back was an elk. "To Good Path Elk," he said, walking up to me. "This is for your naming." I was overwhelmed. I couldn't say thank you, because of the rule of silence, but I embraced him warmly.

9 The next morning, preparing to leave for Blue Ledges, I decided to take materials with me to make a pair of leggings. We newly named campers hiked over steep woodlands and crossed rivers until we came to a clearing of rocks beside a stream. From there we could see the mountains stretching into the distance. That was Blue Ledges.

10 I felt on top of the world. I settled on a cool rock upstream from our campsite to work on my leggings. As I stitched, a gentle breeze from the mountainside seemed to whisper my Indian name: Good Path Elk. Good Path Elk. I looked up from my work to watch an eagle gliding high above the valley, and a strong sense of confidence filled me.

11 At the next naming ceremony, ten more campers were chosen, among them the goalie I had drop-kicked. His name was to be Forest Talker, because he liked to talk to the plants and the trees. As I thought about the quest he and the others would begin the next morning, I had an idea. I ran back to my teepee for the leggings I had made on my quest.

12 "I'd like to give my leggings to Forest Talker," I said as the giveaway ceremony began. "This is for your naming." The stillness of the night magnified the sound of wood crackling in the fire. I stared at Forest Talker: "With these I apologize for drop-kicking you."

13 A few days later, Forest Talker approached me. He said, "Thanks, Good Path Elk. Those were nice leggings. Want to play a game of stickball?"

14 Now, years later, I look out over Harlem, the sun polishing my skin as it did at Blue Ledges, the strong wind on my face reminding me of new beginnings. Suddenly I understand: There's no need to change my name. Instead I will find something to give, some way to use my life to help others. Through giving, I will find the strength to face all my challenges because in the end giving and receiving are the same. I take a deep breath of the wind as it climbs over the park, and in that moment I think I can still hear it—the wind at Blue Ledges, whispering my Indian name.

Comprehension and Critical Thinking

1. Find an adjective in paragraph 4 that means "offensive" and "insulting."

   derogatory

2. What is the meaning of *daub* in paragraph 7?
   a. increase b. remove (c.) smear; apply
3. What is the author's mood at the beginning of the essay? Explain your answer.

   He feels upset about his lack of career success and his financial difficulties.

4. In paragraph 1, Kline says "As far as I'm concerned, my good name is dead." Why does he feel this way?

   He has no credit rating, and his name as a journalist is not valued.

5. Why did Kline drop-kick another boy?

   During the heat of a stickball game, the other boy had made derogatory comments about Kline's skin color.

6. Personification is the act of attributing human characteristics to something that is inanimate. Underline two examples of personification in paragraph 5.
7. Why was the author prepared to forgive the boy who had insulted him? You will need to infer, or read between the lines.

   He felt ashamed for using violence, and he saw that his actions resulted in the other boy being teased. Thus, he felt compassion for the other boy. He also felt like he should live up to his native name.

8. The author deviates from chronological order to recount his tale. Describe the order of events and explain how the order is significant.

   The time moves from the present, to the past, and back to the present. Because the author feels depressed in the present, he remembers a moment in the past that helps him to re-evaluate his present mood.

9. How does the author change after remembering his naming ceremony?

He felt lost and worthless. The memory reminds him that his native name implies "giving and helping others." This memory helps him focus on what he can do for others instead of focusing on what he hasn't done or doesn't have.

Teaching Tip: The suggested topics give students the opportunity to practice narrative writing. Specify whether students should write a paragraph or an essay.

WRITING TOPICS

Write about one of the following topics. Remember to explore, develop, and revise and edit your work.

1. Write about your name. You could write about the following: the meaning of your name, the story of how your parents named you, the evolution of your feelings about your name, and so on.
2. Have you ever done something that you feel ashamed about? Narrate what happened. Describe how you have changed since it happened.

Teaching Tip: Photo writing topic 1 can generate a cause and effect essay, and writing topic 2 can lead to a classification essay.

The Writer's Room Images of Conflict

The previous three readings, and Editing Handbook Chapters 20–22, deal with issues related to conflict. The following activities continue developing that theme.

Teaching Tip: The film prompts may appeal particularly to auditory and visual learners. You might assign film viewing as homework or, depending on your college's viewing policies, show a film to the whole class. If the suggested films do not appeal to your group of students, choose one (or ask students to choose one) that addresses the theme and then adapt the writing prompt as needed.

Writing Activity 1: Photo Writing

1. The photo depicts a couple that is clearly having problems. What are the reasons for conflicts in personal relationships?
2. What types of couples do you know? Think of several different categories of couples.

Writing Activity 2: Film Writing

1. *Remember the Titans* is about racial conflicts in small-town Virginia. In *The Fight Club*, a young man deals with his inner demons. Choose one of these films and describe the steps the main character takes to overcome adversity.
2. In *The Departed*, two young men become police officers in a department where they must play vastly different roles. Officer Billy Costigan goes undercover to infiltrate the mob, while mobster Colin Sullivan becomes a police officer. Compare and contrast the main characters.
3. View a film that deals with conflict such as *Crash*, *Clueless*, *Taxi Driver*, *Friday Night Lights*, *The DaVinci Code*, or *The Shawshank Redemption*, and discuss the causes or effects of the main character's decisions.

Teaching Tip: The film writing prompts encourage students to use process, comparison and contrast, and cause and effect writing.

Theme: Urban Development

READING 4

My African Childhood

David Sedaris

David Sedaris is an award-winning essayist and humorist. In the following essay, excerpted from his collection *Me Talk Pretty One Day*, Sedaris contrasts his own childhood with that of his friend who lived in Africa.

1 When Hugh was in the fifth grade, his class took a field trip to an Ethiopian slaughterhouse. He was living in Addis Ababa at the time, and the slaughterhouse was chosen because, he says, "it was convenient." This was a school system in which the matter of proximity outweighed such petty concerns as what may or may not be appropriate for a busload of eleven-year-olds. "What?" I asked. "Were there no autopsies scheduled at the local morgue? Was the federal prison just a bit too far out of the way?"

2 Hugh defends his former school, saying, "Well, isn't that the whole point of a field trip? To see something new?"

3 "Technically yes, but . . ."

4 "All right then," he says. "So we saw some new things." One of his field trips was literally a trip to a field where the class watched a

wrinkled man fill his mouth with rotten goat meat and feed it to a pack of waiting hyenas. On another occasion, they were taken to examine the bloodied bedroom curtains hanging in the palace of the former dictator. There were tamer trips, to textile factories and sugar refineries, but my favorite is always the slaughterhouse. It wasn't a big company, just a small rural enterprise run by a couple of brothers operating out of a low-ceilinged concrete building. Following a brief lecture on the importance of proper sanitation, a small white piglet was herded into the room, its dainty hooves clicking against the concrete floor. The class gathered in a circle to get a better look at the animal that seemed delighted with the attention he was getting. He turned from face to face and was looking up at Hugh when one of the brothers drew a pistol from his back pocket, held it against the animal's temple, and shot the piglet, execution-style. Blood spattered, frightened children wept, and the man with the gun offered the teacher and bus driver some meat from a freshly slaughtered goat.

5 When I'm told such stories, it's all I can do to hold back my feelings of jealousy. An Ethiopian slaughterhouse. Some people have all the luck. When I was in elementary school, the best we ever got was a trip to Old Salem or Colonial Williamsburg, one of those preserved brick villages where time supposedly stands still and someone earns his living as a town crier. There was always a blacksmith, a group of wandering patriots, and a collection of bonneted women hawking corn bread or gingersnaps made "the old fashioned way." Every now and then you might come across a doer of bad deeds serving time in the stocks, but that was generally as exciting as it got.

6 Certain events are parallel, but compared with Hugh's, my childhood was unspeakably dull. When I was seven years old, my family moved to North Carolina. When he was seven years old, Hugh's family moved to the Congo. We had a collie and a house cat. They had a monkey and two horses named Charlie Brown and Satan. I threw stones at stop signs. Hugh threw stones at crocodiles. The verbs are the same, but he definitely wins the prize when it comes to nouns and objects. An eventful day for my mother might have involved a trip to the dry cleaner or a conversation with the potato chip deliveryman. Asked one ordinary Congo afternoon what she'd done with her day, Hugh's mother answered that she and a fellow member of the Ladies' Club had visited a leper colony on the outskirts of Kinshasa. No reason was given for the expedition, though chances are she was staking it out for a future field trip.

7 Due to his upbringing, Hugh sits through inane movies never realizing that they're often based on inane television shows. There were no pokerfaced sitcom Martians in his part of Africa, no oil rich hillbillies

or aproned brides trying to wean themselves from the practice of witchcraft.[1] From time to time a movie would arrive packed in a dented canister, the film scratched and faded from its slow trip around the world. The theater consisted of a few dozen folding chairs arranged before a bed sheet or the blank wall of a vacant hangar out near the airstrip. Occasionally a man would sell warm soft drinks out of a cardboard box, but that was it in terms of concessions.

8 When I was young, I went to the theater at the nearby shopping center and watched a movie about a talking Volkswagen. I believe the little car had a taste for mischief, but I can't be certain, as both the movie and the afternoon proved unremarkable and have faded from my memory. Hugh saw the same movie a few years after it was released. His family had left the Congo by this time, and they were living in Ethiopia. Like me, Hugh saw the movie by himself on a weekend afternoon. Unlike me, he left the theater two hours later, to find a dead man hanging from a telephone pole at the far end of the unpaved parking lot. None of the people who'd seen the movie seemed to care about the dead man. They stared at him for a moment or two and then headed home, saying they'd never seen anything as crazy as that talking Volkswagen. His father was late picking him up, so Hugh just stood there for an hour, watching the dead man dangle and turn in the breeze. The death was not reported in the newspaper, and when Hugh related the story to his friends, they said, "You saw the movie about the talking car?"

9 I could have done without the flies and the primitive theaters, but I wouldn't have minded growing up with a houseful of servants. In North Carolina, it wasn't unusual to have a once-a-week maid, but Hugh's family had houseboys, a word that never fails to charge my imagination. They had cooks and drivers, and guards who occupied a gatehouse, armed with machetes. Seeing as I had regularly petitioned my parents for an electric fence, the business with the guards strikes me as the last word in quiet sophistication. Having protection suggests that you are important. Having that protection paid for by the government is even better, as it suggests your safety is of interest to someone other than yourself.

10 Hugh's father was a career officer with the US State Department, and every morning a black sedan carried him off to the embassy. I'm told it's not as glamorous as it sounds, but in terms of fun for the entire family, I'm fairly confident that it beats the sack race at the annual IBM picnic. By the age of three, Hugh was already carrying a diplomatic passport. The rules that applied to others did not apply to him. No tickets, no arrests, no

[1]Sedaris is referring to *My Favorite Martian*, *The Beverly Hillbillies*, and *Bewitched*, popular television shows in the 1960s.

luggage search: He was officially licensed to act like a brat. Being an American, it was expected of him, and who was he to deny the world an occasional tantrum?

11 They weren't rich, but what Hugh's family lacked financially they more than made up for with the sort of exoticism that works wonders at cocktail parties, leading always to the remark, "That sounds fascinating." It's a compliment one rarely receives when describing an adolescence spent drinking **Icees** at the North Hills Mall. No fifteen-foot python ever wandered onto my school's basketball court. I begged, I prayed nightly, but it just never happened. Neither did I get to witness a military coup in which forces sympathetic to the colonel arrived late at night to assassinate my next-door neighbor. Hugh had been at the Addis Ababa teen club when the electricity was cut off and soldiers arrived to evacuate the building. He and his friends had to hide in the back of a jeep and cover themselves with blankets during the ride home. It's something that sticks in his mind for one reason or another.

Icees: Iced drinks

12 Among my personal highlights is the memory of having my picture taken with Uncle Paul, the legally blind host of a Raleigh children's television show. Among Hugh's is the memory of having his picture taken with Buzz Aldrin on the last leg of the astronaut's world tour. The man who had walked on the moon placed his hand on Hugh's shoulder and offered to sign his autograph book. The man who led Wake County schoolchildren in afternoon song turned at the sound of my voice and asked, "So what's your name, princess?"

13 When I was fourteen years old, I was sent to spend ten days with my maternal grandmother in western New York State. She was a small and private woman named Billie, and though she never came right out and asked, I had the distinct impression she had no idea who I was. It was the way she looked at me, squinting through her glasses while chewing on her lower lip. That, coupled with the fact that she never once called me by name. "Oh," she'd say, "are you still here?" She was just beginning her long struggle with Alzheimer's disease, and each time I entered the room, I felt the need to reintroduce myself and set her at ease. "Hi, it's me. Sharon's boy, David. I was just in the kitchen admiring your collection of ceramic toads." Aside from a few trips to summer camp, this was the longest I'd ever been away from home, and I like to think I was toughened by the experience.

14 About the same time I was frightening my grandmother, Hugh and his family were packing their belongings for a move to Somalia. There were no English-speaking schools in Mogadishu, so, after a few months spent lying around the family compound with his pet monkey, Hugh was sent back to Ethiopia to live with a beer enthusiast his father had met at a cocktail party. Mr. Hoyt installed security systems in foreign embassies.

He and his family gave Hugh a room. They invited him to join them at the table, but that was as far as they extended themselves. No one ever asked him when his birthday was, so when the day came, he kept it to himself. There was no telephone service between Ethiopia and Somalia, and letters to his parents were sent to Washington and then forwarded on to Mogadishu, meaning that his news was more than a month old by the time they got it. I suppose it wasn't much different than living as a foreign-exchange student. Young people do it all the time, but to me it sounds awful. The Hoyts had two sons about Hugh's age who were always saying things like "Hey, that's *our* sofa you're sitting on" and "Hands off that ornamental stein. It doesn't belong to you."

15 He'd been living with these people for a year when he overheard Mr. Hoyt tell a friend that he and his family would soon be moving to Munich, Germany, the beer capital of the world. "And that worried me," Hugh said, "because it meant I'd have to find some other place to live."

16 Where I come from, finding shelter is a problem the average teenager might confidently leave to his parents. It was just something that came with having a mom and a dad. Worried that he might be sent to live with his grandparents in Kentucky, Hugh turned to the school's guidance counselor, who knew of a family whose son had recently left for college. And so he spent another year living with strangers and not mentioning his birthday. While I wouldn't have wanted to do it myself, I can't help but envy the sense of **fortitude** he gained from the experience. After graduating from college, he moved to France knowing only the phrase "Do you speak French?"—a question guaranteed to get you nowhere unless you also speak the language.

fortitude: strength

17 While living in Africa, Hugh and his family took frequent vacations, often in the company of their monkey. The Nairobi Hilton, some suite of high-ceilinged rooms in Cairo or Khartoum: these are the places his people recall when gathered at a common table. "Was that the summer we spent in Beirut or, no, I'm thinking of the time we sailed from Cyprus and took the *Orient Express* to Istanbul."

18 Theirs was the life I dreamt about during my vacations in eastern North Carolina. Hugh's family was hobnobbing with chiefs and sultans while I ate hush puppies at the Sanitary Fish Market in Morehead City, a beach towel wrapped like a hijab around my head. Someone unknown to me was very likely standing in a muddy ditch and dreaming of an evening spent sitting in a clean family restaurant, drinking iced tea and working his way through an extra-large seaman's platter, but that did not concern me, as it meant I should have been happy with what I had.

19 Rather than surrender to my bitterness, I have learned to take satisfaction in the life that Hugh has led. His stories have, over time,

kumbaya: The title of a spiritual song popular in the 1960s that was thought to have African ties and symbolized peace, harmony, and unity among people.

become my own. I say this with no trace of a **kumbaya**. There is no spiritual symbiosis; I'm just a petty thief who lifts his memories the same way I'll take a handful of change left on his dresser. When my own experiences fall short of the mark, I just go out and spend some of his. It is with pleasure that I sometimes recall the dead man's purpled face or the report of the handgun ringing in my ears as I studied the blood pooling beneath the dead white piglet. On the way back from the slaughterhouse, we stopped for Cokes in the village of Mojo, where the gas-station owner had arranged a few tables and chairs beneath a dying canopy of vines. It was late afternoon by the time we returned to school, where a second bus carried me to the foot of Coffeeboard Road. Once there, I walked through a grove of eucalyptus trees and alongside a bald pasture of starving cattle, past the guard napping in his gatehouse, and into the warm arms of my monkey.

Comprehension and Critical Thinking

1. What is the meaning of *inane* in paragraph 7?
   a. fascinating b. serious (c.) ridiculous
2. Find a word in paragraph 7 that means "to reduce" or "to stop."

   wean
3. Underline the thesis statement. Remember that it may not be in the first paragraph.
4. Look in paragraph 4 and underline examples of imagery that appeal to hearing, taste, and sight. Answers will vary.
5. How were the author's school field trips different from Hugh's?

   Hugh saw bloody and frightening things, such as animals getting slaughtered or the bloody curtains of a dictator. David's field trips were to American historical sights.
6. What nationality is Hugh? Look carefully at paragraph 10.

   He is American because his father worked for the US State Department.
7. Briefly describe the author's childhood. Give a few details.

   He had a typical middle-class upbringing that included having pets, going to movies, and watching television. His daily existence was safe and secure.

8. In paragraph 13, the author describes the summer he spent with his grandmother, and in paragraph 14, he describes Hugh's year with the Hoyt family. What are some similarities and differences in their experiences?

   They both felt lonely, ignored, and perhaps neglected. They were both toughened by the experience. However, the narrator probably knew that his grandmother did care about him at one time, whereas Hugh was truly unimportant to the Hoyts.

9. In paragraph 4, the author describes Hugh's trip to a slaughterhouse. In paragraph 8, he describes Hugh's trip to a theater, and in paragraph 11, he discusses a military coup that Hugh witnessed. What do the anecdotes about Hugh's childhood have in common?

   Each event has an undercurrent of horror and violence.

10. The author uses humor to describe his friend's childhood. How does humor affect the reader's perception of events?

    He makes Hugh's childhood seem so exotic by using humor, but the events described are about death and violence.

11. On the surface, the author appears to envy Hugh's childhood. What is he also suggesting?

    Hugh's childhood was often filled with violence and loneliness whereas the author's childhood, although dull, was filled with love and security.

12. Think about the title. Why does Sedaris call this essay "My African Childhood"?

    Sedaris appropriates his friend's childhood memories. He wishes that he had lived the African childhood.

Writing Topics

Write about one of the following topics. Remember to explore, develop, and revise and edit your work.

1. Interview an older family member or friend about his or her childhood. Then write an essay comparing and contrasting your childhood with his or hers.
2. Reflect on how you were parented. How do you parent your own children, or how would you like to parent your future children? Compare and contrast your parenting style with the style of the people who raised you.

Teaching Tip:
The suggested topics give students the opportunity to practice comparison and contrast writing. Specify whether students should write a paragraph or an essay.

READING 5

Living Environments

Avi Friedman

Avi Friedman is professor at the McGill School of Architecture. In the following article, which appeared in *The Montreal Gazette*, Friedman reflects on designing an appropriate house for the individual needs of families.

1 When invited to design a home, I first like to know what kind of dwellers my clients are. In our first meeting, I ask them to take me on a guided tour of their current residence and describe how each room is used—when and by whom. Walking through hallways, scanning the interior of rooms, peeping into closets, looking at kitchen cupboards, and pausing at family photos have helped me devise several common categories of occupants.

2 The "neat" household regards the house as a gallery. The home is spotless. The placement of every item, be it hanging artwork, a memento on a shelf, or furniture, is highly choreographed. The color scheme is coordinated and the lighting superb. It feels as if one has walked into an *Architectural Digest* magazine spread. Recent trends, professional touches, and carefully selected pieces are the marks of the place.

3 The "utilitarian" family is very pragmatic. They are minimalists, believing that they get only what they need. Environmental concerns play an important role in buying goods. The place, often painted in light tones, is sparsely decorated with very few well-selected items. Souvenirs from a recent trip are displayed and some photos or paintings are on the wall. They will resist excess consumption and will squeeze as much use as they can from each piece.

4 The home of the "collector" family is stuffed to the brim. It is hard to find additional space for furniture or a wall area to hang a painting. Books, magazines, and weekend papers are everywhere. Newspaper cutouts and personal notes are crammed under magnets on the fridge door. The collector family seems to pay less attention to how things appear and more to comfort. Stress reduction is a motto. Being an excessively clean "show house" is not a concern. Placing dirty breakfast dishes in the sink and the morning paper in the rack before leaving home is not a priority as long as things are moving along.

5 Of course, these are only a few household types, but at the end of a house tour, I have a pretty good idea about my clients. More than the notes that I take during a meeting, these real-life images tell me all about my client's home life and desired domestic environment. When I began practicing, I quickly realized house design is about people more than

architecture. As hard as I might try, I will never be able to tailor a new personality to someone by placing them in a trendy style, one that does not reflect who they really are. I can attempt to illustrate options other than their current life habits and decorating choices. But in the end, when they move into their new place, they will bring along their old habits.

6 My experience has taught me some homeowners have been trying hard to emulate lifestyles and décors that are really not theirs. The endless decorating shows on television and the many magazines that crowd supermarket racks provide a tempting opportunity to become someone else. Some homeowners are under constant pressure, it feels, to undergo extreme makeovers and borrow rather than mature into their natural selves. They search for a readymade packaged interior style rather than discovering their own.

7 I am often at a loss when clients ask me what style I subscribe to, or solicit advice on the style they are to adopt. I reply that styles are trendy and comfort is permanent, and that they should see beyond the first day of occupancy into everyday living. Sipping a freshly brewed coffee on the back porch on a summer Sunday and letting the morning paper litter the floor while watching a squirrel on the tree across the yard is a treasured moment. It will never be able to fit into a well-defined architectural style. Home design needs to create the backdrop for such opportunities. It is these types of moments that make us enjoy life.

8 If someone wants to read, why not have a wall of books? Does someone love listening to music? Then a music room or corner should be created, even if it is not trendy. Does someone want to interact with the children? He or she might add a hobby space, even if it is outdated and cannot be found in most magazines.

9 Referring to technological advances, the renowned French architect Le Corbusier once described the home as a "machine for living." It is partially true. Home is the site where mundane and utilitarian activities take place. It is also where special moments, uniquely ours, are created and treasured.

Comprehension and Critical Thinking

1. Find a four-word expression in paragraph 4 that means "completely filled."

   stuffed to the brim

2. Find a word in paragraph 6 that means "to copy."

   to emulate

3. Underline the thesis statement.
4. Underline the topic sentences in paragraphs 2–7.

Teaching Tip: The film prompts on the next page may appeal particularly to auditory and visual learners. If the suggested films do not appeal to your group of students, choose one (or ask students to choose one) that addresses the theme and then adapt the writing prompt as needed.

Teaching Tip: The film writing prompts on the next page encourage students to use comparison and contrast, process, illustration, and descriptive writing.

5. Paragraph 8 is missing a topic sentence. Which sentence best expresses the main idea of that paragraph?
   a. People can create a music room in their homes.
   b. Everybody should think about his or her likes and dislikes.
   c. People should create spaces in their homes to accommodate their personal interests.
   d. Hobby rooms and bookshelves can help make a home feel very unique.
6. How does Friedman assess the needs of families when designing a house?

   He takes a tour of the house and asks family members how they use each room. He also looks in the closets and cupboards and looks at family photos to get an idea of the family's lifestyle.
7. What are the three categories of households that Friedman describes in this article?

   He classifies them into the "neat," "utilitarian, and "collector."
8. In your own words, describe the characteristics for each type of household.

   The neat household is highly organized and spotless. It looks as if it is a model for Architectural Digest. *The utilitarian household has minimal possessions, and its objects are very practical. The collector household is usually very full of objects.*
9. a. What influences families when they choose a design for their homes?

   They are influenced by television and magazine makeovers.

   b. Does Friedman think that such influences are positive or negative? Explain your answer.

   He thinks the influences might be negative because people feel pressured to do home makeovers. They emulate styles that are not really their own.
10. According to Friedman, what is the most important factor that home design should take into consideration?

    Home design should allow families to enjoy moments of leisure and relaxation, such as drinking coffee and reading the newspaper on a porch.

WRITING TOPICS

Teaching Tip: The suggested topics give students the opportunity to practice classification writing. Specify whether students should write a paragraph or an essay.

Write about one of the following topics. Remember to explore, develop, and revise and edit your work.

1. Use a different classification method to describe types of living environments.
2. Friedman writes, "Home is the site where mundane and utilitarian activities take place. It is also where special moments, uniquely ours, are created and treasured." Write about different categories of special or memorable moments.

The Writer's Room — Images of Urban Development

Teaching Tip:
Photo writing topic 1 can generate an illustration essay, and writing topic 2 can lead to a descriptive essay.

The previous two readings, and Editing Handbook Chapters 23–26, deal with issues related to urban development. The following activities continue developing that theme.

Writing Activity 1: Photo Writing

1. What are the advantages and disadvantages of living in an apartment? You can think about financial, safety, and comfort issues.
2. Describe your ideal living environment. What would that place look like?

Writing Activity 2: Film Writing

1. In *The Truman Show*, Truman Burbank believes that he is living in an ideal town. Compare the world Truman lives in with a real neighborhood.
2. In *The Commitments* and *Hoop Dreams*, inner-city youths plan their escapes from their urban environments by focusing on music or sports. Choose one of those films and describe the process the main character(s) goes through to make his or her dream come true.
3. Films can tell us a lot about the country where they were made. Choose a foreign film and explain what the film shows us about that nation.
4. View a film that deals with urban, suburban, or country life, such as *Clockwork Orange*, *Pleasantville*, *Babel*, *Jungle Fever*, or *Erin Brockovich*. Describe the environment that the main characters reside in.

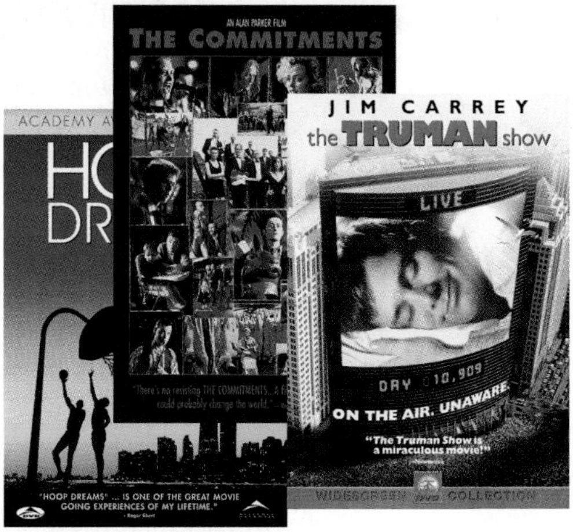

Theme: International Trade

READING 6

I, Telemarketer

Eugene Henry

Journalist Eugene Henry is a frequent contributor to Canadian newspapers. He spent nine months as a telephone salesman. In the following essay, Henry describes his experience.

1 It's a familiar experience: The phone rings, and you find yourself listening to a telemarketer. Depending on your resolve, you might end the unwanted communication in ten or twenty seconds—maybe as long as a minute for the weak-willed or those with especially good manners. Either way, the call usually comes as an annoying interruption in your busy life. However, there's a whole world on the other end of your phone cord, a world in which telemarketing is not one of life's interruptions, but life itself. In late 2003, I became part of that world when I became a telemarketer.

2 Montreal is North America's call-center capital, and despite the impression one gets from investigative news reports, many are perfectly respectable employers. Some even recruit at career fairs—which is where, fresh out of university, I came across a promising-looking outfit that offered me a modest signing bonus and a respectable salary. The firm was part of a large, publicly traded telemarketing company based in the United States, with call centers in twenty-six countries. The size was comforting: It meant I wouldn't have to worry about working at the sort of fly-by-night operation that ends up being raided by the police.

3 During my training, I learned more than I ever wanted to know about cable television packages. Our goal was to sell premium movie channels to existing cable customers, and this would become my professional mission over the next few months.

4 Workers at a call center are divided into a day shift and a night shift, and everyone works from a desk with a computer and a phone in a large, colorless room. The work isn't pleasant, and the days go by slowly.

5 The pressure to sell is intense. Telemarketers who don't make quota tend to disappear. Someone you've worked with for a while and talked with on breaks or at lunch will one day simply stop showing up. They are usually fired, though sometimes they quit.

6 I almost lost my own job in November, shortly after I started. There was an incentive prize of fifty dollars for the employee with the best "conversion"—the ratio of sales to calls—which is a lot of money for a telemarketer. I wasn't a bad salesman, mainly because I didn't push. (A casual manner on the phone works better than someone who sounds desperate or aggressive.) But to win the fifty dollars, I knew I needed to

cheat. So I put down people who rejected my pitch as wrong numbers, which meant they would be kept out of my conversion ratio, artificially boosting it. Unfortunately, a "quality assurance monitor"—the big brothers of the call center—discovered my ruse. It was grounds for immediate dismissal, but my sales were decent, so they kept me on.

7 Others weren't so lucky. Over our Christmas break, almost all of my colleagues were laid off. We were all supposed to return from our Christmas break on January 5; instead, Human Resources called most of us on January 4 to instruct us not to come in the next day.

8 I felt guilty about surviving the **purge**. Most telemarketers are hard-luck cases who live on the margins of the job market. In other words, the people who lost their jobs needed the work more than I did. I didn't have a family to feed—like my single-mother colleague who had no way to pay the bills that had piled up over the holidays.

purge: elimination of employees

9 As March and April wore on, I fell in love with one of the "big brothers." Kelly was a twenty-six-year-old graphic designer. We had a lot to talk about—mostly how she'd rather be designing things, and I'd rather be writing things.

10 I found that being in a secret relationship with the person monitoring your calls helps make telemarketing easier. I had carte blanche to slack off. I even started writing at my desk between calls. Kelly told me there was nothing to worry about, as long as I made enough sales to pass under the radar of her managers. It was a high-stakes sacrifice on her part: She could have lost her job if anyone found out she was cutting someone slack on the floor.

11 Despite Kelly's help, May, which would become my last full month on the job, was a difficult one. The cable company was trying to move everyone to digital, and so we were schooled on the superiority of digital television technology. The job meant calling retired people who had no idea what digital was. Notwithstanding their ignorance, it was our job to "increase their bill a few dollars" so they could enjoy digital splendor.

12 One guy on the floor found an effective strategy. Salman, a Pakistani Muslim, had recently arrived in Montreal by way of Florida. His strategy for selling digital was to find "specialty channels" that he knew would catch old people's interest. There were a few channels that focus on Christian programming, and Sal found it amusing that he, of all people, had so much success pitching them to pensioners. "It's easy," he told me. "All you have to do is sell Jesus. Jesus sells himself."

13 By the end of May, I'd been on the job nine months, and I'd had enough. I asked Human Resources how to quit. They told me to write a notice and give it to my team manager. When I actually did this, everyone seemed surprised. Apparently, I'm among the small minority of telemarketers who actually give two weeks' notice. Consistent with the disposable employment ethos that governs the profession, many simply stop showing up.

14 Nine months may not seem like a long time. But I think I learned more during that period than I did during four years of university. Certainly, I learned to be more respectful when the phone rings and I hear a stranger's voice. The next time you talk to a telemarketer, think about a polite "no thanks" instead of the all-too-common expletive or hang-up. Sometimes that's enough to get a telemarketer through the day with at least a half-smile on his or her face.

Comprehension and Critical Thinking

1. Find a word in paragraph 6 that means "reason" or "justification."

   grounds

2. In paragraph 6, what is the meaning of *ruse*?

   trick; method of cheating

3. Why did Henry take a job as a telemarketer?
   a. He wanted to work with his girlfriend.
   b. At a job fair, a company made him a good offer.
   c. He thought that he would be very good in sales, and he wanted to have a career in telemarketing.
4. Which statement is not true about paragraph 6?
   a. Henry wanted to win a $50 prize.
   b. Henry lied and pretended that people who did not want to buy from him were really wrong numbers.
   c. Henry's supervisor did not discover that Henry was cheating.
   d. Henry did not lose his job because his sales were quite good.
5. What is Henry's special sales technique?

   He is casual. He doesn't push customers.

6. What is ironic about Salman's sales pitch? See paragraph 12.

   Salman, a Muslim, was successful at selling "Jesus" to Christian subscribers.

7. Why were Henry's employers surprised when he gave two weeks' notice?

   Most telemarketers just stop coming to work. They don't bother informing Human Resources.

8. Henry says that he learned more at his job "than at four years of university," but he does not state explicitly what those lessons are. Read between the lines and explain some positive and negative lessons that he learned.

   He learned that if he is good enough at a job, he can break the rules. He learned to cultivate relationships to his advantage. He learned that people don't like to be pushed. He learned to be more compassionate to people who do telemarketing jobs.

9. How does the author conclude his essay?
   (a.) suggestion b. quotation c. prediction
10. What is the author's attitude toward his job? You will have to make inferences.

    He is condescending about the work. He doesn't really need the job, and he describes people who do it as "hard-luck cases."

Writing Topics

Write about one of the following topics. Remember to explore, develop, and revise and edit your work.

1. Write about a memorable job that you had in the past. Describe your experiences and explain what you learned.
2. Have you ever had a workplace romance, or do you know someone who has? What happened?

Teaching Tip:
The suggested topics give students the opportunity to practice narrative writing. Specify whether students should write a paragraph or an essay.

READING 7

The Rich Resonance of Small Talk

Roxanne Roberts

Roxanne Roberts is a staff writer for the *Washington Post*. In the next article, she muses about the importance of small talk.

1 I talk too much. The good news is that I can enter a room full of strangers, walk up to anyone, and start yammering away. The bad news is . . . well, you can guess that I bore people. All things considered, this has worked out pretty well. In my sixteen years as a social reporter for a newspaper, I've marched up to presidents, movie stars, and kings and felt unafraid to make small talk, otherwise known as the mother's milk of party coverage. I have an advantage, of course, in that I have a press pass and a notebook.

2 But small talk is a big deal for everyone; it is one of those essential social skills that separate the men from the boys. The ability to connect in short, casual conversations can make or break careers, friendships, and romances—it's how we gather information, and hopefully, make a favorable impression. There are only three golden rules for small talk: First, shut up and listen; second, when in doubt, repeat Rule 1; third, get others to talk about themselves.

3 First, Rule 1 and Rule 2 take a lifetime for the average extrovert or egomaniac to master. To listen that intently, to focus with every muscle, takes not only great skill but also great discipline, which is why mere mortals fall short. It is so easy to respond to a casual comment by unwittingly turning the spotlight back on yourself: "You're going to Italy?

We stayed at this great little place outside of Florence." It seems so natural—your small talk might be helpful, witty, and even relevant, but you're nonetheless talking instead of listening—and you can never learn anything while talking, except that you talk too much.

4 In the meantime, there are a few other tricks for small talk with strangers and acquaintances. For example, introduce yourself by name, even if you think they know it. "I don't think we've met. I'm Queen Elizabeth II." It's gracious, it's efficient, and it's smart. It's very awkward when someone starts a conversation with "Remember me?" and you don't. Second, ask simple questions. "What do you think of the [party, conference, cheese puffs]?" Then listen. When you run into a casual acquaintance, ask what he or she has been doing lately. Then listen. Ask follow-up questions based on the answers. If you are genuinely interested, most people will be surprised and flattered. Resist the temptation to display your own special brand of brilliance, and when you catch yourself doing so, shift the focus back. Later on, when the relationship has evolved beyond small talk, you can strut your fabulousness.

5 Furthermore, mastering the art of small talk is important for drawing shy people into a conversation. If this is done right, they walk away thinking *you're* great. "A great small talker is someone who has three to four open-ended questions that make the person open up," says Ann Stock, former White House social secretary for the Clintons and currently the vice president of the Kennedy Center. "It ignites something in them that makes them start talking. After that, you ask leading questions."

6 Use your body language. There's nothing worse than chatting with people who simultaneously scan the room for someone more important. Give someone your full and real attention during your conversation. Face him or her directly, and look in his eyes. Never underestimate small talk—even though many people dread it or think it's silly, boring, or superficial.

7 Once in a rare while, someone comes along who innately gets it and turns a brief, casual moment into a truly memorable encounter. Former president Bill Clinton is a genius at it. In the course of two minutes, he can lock eyes with a person, ask a seemingly simple question, and make a person feel like the center of the universe. Clinton's remarkable memory for names and faces means he can meet someone and—months or years later—ask about his or her family or golf game. People are shocked and delighted.

8 Another legendary master at the art of small talk was the late Pamela Harriman, Democratic fundraiser, ambassador to France, and the woman

once called the "greatest courtesan of the century"—a nod to her many high-profile lovers. What set her apart was her laser-like ability to make anyone feel like the most important person in the room. She wanted to know everything about the people she met. She hung on every word and seldom talked about herself. She made people feel like brilliant, under-appreciated jewels. "She had the power to make people want to talk with her," William Pfaff wrote in the *International Herald Tribune* shortly after her death in 1997. "She was—or certainly made herself seem to be—interested in everyone with whom she spoke, and in what they had to say. She, in turn, had something intelligent to say to them." She was not, he wrote, an intellectual or particularly sophisticated in matters of international relations. She knew enough to ask the right questions. But mostly she let others do the talking: "The willingness to listen is seduction itself—certainly to vain men, and in the world in which she functioned, all men are vain."

9 Finally, consider the famous story about British Prime Minister Benjamin Disraeli and his great political rival, William Gladstone. Legend has it that a lady was taken to dinner one evening by Gladstone and the next by Disraeli. When asked her impression of the two men, she replied, "When I left the dining room after sitting next to Mr. Gladstone, I thought he was the cleverest man in England. But after sitting next to Mr. Disraeli, I thought I was the cleverest woman in England."

Comprehension and Critical Thinking

1. What is the meaning of *nod to* in paragraph 8?
   a. acknowledgment of
   b. an indication of agreement
   c. falling asleep
2. Underline the thesis statement.
3. Why does the author begin the introductory paragraph with the first-person pronoun *I*, but use third-person pronouns for the rest of the essay?

   The initial anecdote arouses the reader's interest.
4. Why does the author think that learning the art of small talk is important?

   Small talk allows people to advance their careers, make friends, and make a favorable impression on others.

5. Using your own words, list at least five pieces of advice the author gives to master the art of small talk.

   Introduce yourself, listen to others, get others to talk about themselves, ask open-ended questions, and let people know they are the focus of your attention.

6. According to Roberts, why is it difficult for people to follow the first rule of small talk?

   It is difficult because people have a tendency to bring the conversation around to themselves. People want to demonstrate their knowledge.

7. Why does the author use Bill Clinton and Pamela Harriman as examples to support her thesis?

   Both Clinton and Harriman were experts at small talk.

8. How are Clinton's and Harriman's strategies for making small talk similar?

   Both of them had the ability to make others feel "important"—as if they were "the center of the universe."

9. How are Clinton's and Harriman's strategies for making small talk different?

   Clinton impressed people with his ability to remember names and faces. He also remembered details about people. Harriman had the ability to make people feel valued, like "under-appreciated jewels."

10. How is the anecdote in the concluding paragraph a good support for mastering the art of small talk?

   Disraeli made the lady feel as if she were the focus of his attention, thereby demonstrating that he had mastered the author's rule 3. Therefore, it is better to make people feel they are as important, if not more important, than you.

Teaching Tip: The suggested topics give students the opportunity to practice process writing. Specify whether students should write a paragraph or an essay.

Writing Topics

Write about one of the following topics. Remember to explore, develop, and revise and edit your work.

1. Explain steps that people can take to have better relationships with their life partners.
2. Describe a process people can go through to make their guests feel more comfortable. You can discuss houseguests, dinner guests, or party guests.

READING 8

Google's China Web

Frida Ghitis

Frida Ghitis is a journalist, businesswoman, and writer who authored *The End of Revolution: A Changing World in the Age of Live Television*. In the next essay, Ghitis examines the role that Google and other Internet providers play in supporting China's severe censorship laws.

1 A few years ago, I walked into an Internet room in Tibet's capital, Lhasa. There were no Chinese soldiers in the room and no visible government censors nearby. A sign on the wall, however, reminded Web users that even after entering the stateless world of the Web, China's all-seeing eye had not disappeared. "Do not use Internet," the warning instructed crassly, "for any political or other unintelligent purposes."

2 Since then, China's ruling regime has perfected the science of controlling what the Chinese can read or write on the Internet to such a degree that it has become the envy of tyrants and dictators the world over. We might have expected that from a regime that has proven it will do whatever it takes to stay in power. What we never expected was to see Google, the company whose guiding motto reads "Don't be evil," helping in the effort. Google's decision to help China censor searches on the company's Chinese website is not only a violation of its own righteous-sounding principles, and it's not just an affront to those working to bring international standards of human rights for the Chinese people. No, Google's sellout to Beijing is also a threat to every person who has ever used Google anywhere in the world.

3 Google saves every search, every e-mail, every fingerprint we leave on the Web when we move through its Google search engine, or its Gmail service, or its fast-growing collection of Internet offerings. Google knows more about us than the **FBI** or the **CIA** or the **NSA** or any spy agency of any government, and nobody regulates it. When a company that holds digital dossiers on millions of people decides profits are more important than principles, we are all at risk. Google will now participate actively in a censorship program whose implications, according to Harvard's Berkman Center for Internet and Society, "are profound and disturbing." The Chinese government blocks thousands of search terms—including censorship.

FBI: Federal Bureau of Investigation

CIA: Central Intelligence Agency

NSA: National Security Agency

4 To be fair, Google is hardly alone in its decision to capitulate to Beijing's rulers in order to gain a Web share of China's 1.3 billion inhabitants. The country's tantalizing market has tested the ethics of many

Western corporations—and almost all have failed the test. That is particularly true in the Internet business. Just last year, Yahoo helped Beijing's Web goons track down the identity of a Chinese journalist who wrote an e-mail about the anniversary of the 1994 Tiananmen Square massacre—a massacre of thousands of Chinese democracy advocates perpetrated by the same regime whose efforts Google now abets. The journalist, Shi Tao, was sentenced to ten years in prison. Reporters Without Borders labeled Yahoo an "informant" that has "collaborated enthusiastically" with the Chinese regime. Microsoft, too, plays by the dictatorship's rules. Bloggers on MSN's service cannot type words such as "democracy" or "freedom." Internet users cannot read or write about anything that even hints of opposition to the ruling Communist Party. Even pro-Western commentary can trigger a block. And forget anything about Tibet or the Dalai Lama. Chinese bloggers, incidentally, must all register and identify themselves to authorities.

5 Neither Yahoo nor Microsoft claims to have higher ethical standards than the competition. The often-stated desire to "do good" and make the world a better place was one of the traits that endeared Google to the public. It was one of the reasons we trusted them to guard the precious and valuable contents of their thousands of servers. Now Google has become a company like all others, one with an eye on the bottom line before anything else. The company has decided to help China's censors even as it fights a request for records from the US Justice Department's investigation of online child pornography. Skeptics had claimed Google was resisting the request to protect its technology, rather than to protect users' privacy. That explanation now sounds more plausible than ever.

6 We've long known about China's disdain for individual freedoms. But Google, we hardly knew you. It's definitely time to rethink that Gmail account and demand some safeguards from a potentially dangerous company. Perhaps here, too, we will need to heed the Tibetan cybercafé warning, "Do not use Internet for any political or unintelligent purposes."

Comprehension and Critical Thinking

1. Find a word in paragraph 4 that means "to give in to."

   to capitulate

2. The verb *abet* in paragraph 4 means

   a. hurt b. encourage (c.) help or assist

3. Underline the thesis statement.
4. In your own words, explain the author's main point.

   The author states that because Google is accepting China's policy of censorship, it is a threat to everyone's freedom.

5. How does the author introduce the text?
   a. general background
   b. historical background
   (c.) anecdote
   d. contrasting position
6. Why is the author so upset about Google's actions in China? Give at least two reasons. Answers will vary.

   Google contradicts its own motto "Don't be evil" by doing something unethical.

   Google's policy could encourage censorship in other countries.

   Google puts profits before consumer rights.
7. According to the author, how are Google's policies in China hypocritical?

   Google is being hypocritical because it yields to the Chinese government about censorship but will not give information about child pornography sites to the American government.
8. Examine paragraph 4. Is the author acknowledging the opposing position? Explain your answer.

   She says that Google is not the only international company to agree to the Chinese government policies. She gives examples of Yahoo and Microsoft. However, the author does not really justify the actions of Google or other companies; therefore, it does not really address the opposition's arguments.
9. Why do western businesses agree to participate in the violation of personal freedoms in China?

   China has a huge market, over one billion people. Big corporations can earn a lot of money if they can access Chinese markets.
10. In which paragraphs does the author use an anecdote to support her point of view? *1, 3*
11. Name two informed sources that the author quotes.

    Harvard's Berkman Center for Internet and Society, and Reporters Without Borders.
12. What is the author's predominant tone?

contemplative	<u>outraged</u>	lighthearted	sarcastic
humorous	friendly	casual	supportive

Teaching Tip: The suggested topics give students the opportunity to practice argument writing. Specify whether students should write a paragraph or an essay.

WRITING TOPICS

Write about one of the following topics. Remember to explore, develop, and revise and edit your work.

1. Take the opposite position to the author, and argue that Google has every right to act as it does in China.
2. Argue that the censorship rules should (or should not) be more severe. Consider censorship of the Internet, music, film, or television.

The Writer's Room Images of International Trade

The previous two readings, and Editing Handbook Chapters 27–29, deal with issues related to work and international trade. The following activities continue developing that theme.

Teaching Tip: Photo writing topic 1 can generate an argument essay, and writing topic 2 can lead to a process essay.

Teaching Tip: The film prompts may appeal particularly to auditory and visual learners. If the suggested films do not appeal to your group of students, choose one (or ask students to choose one) that addresses the theme and then adapt the writing prompt as needed.

Writing Activity 1: Photo Writing

1. Advertisers actively market products to the youngest and most vulnerable members of our society. Should advertising aimed at children be banned?
2. How can parents teach their children about finances? What steps should parents take to teach their children about financial responsibility?

Writing Activity 2: Film Writing

1. In *The Devil Wears Prada*, Andrea, a young journalist, works for the ruthless fashion magazine editor, Miranda Priestley. What are the causes of the boss's behavior? What are the effects of the boss's cruelty on her employees?
2. In the comedy *Office Space*, the central character, Peter Gibbons, feels disillusioned with his job. *Wall Street* portrays the greed and corruption of the financial business. Explain what one of the films suggests about modern office life.
3. View another film that deals with work, advertising, or international trade such as *The Firm*, *The Pursuit of Happyness*, *Jerry McGuire*, *Blood Diamonds*, *Jungle Fever*, or *Erin Brockovich*. Describe the process that the film's main character goes through.

Teaching Tip: The film writing prompts encourage students to use cause and effect, argument, and process writing.

Theme: Forces of Nature

READING 9

Weird Weather

Pamela D. Jacobsen

Pamela D. Jacobsen is a journalist who writes for *The Christian Science Monitor*. In the next article, she reflects on some strange weather phenomena.

1 How's this for a weather forecast? "Temperatures in the low 70s tonight, with a slight chance of raining frogs. Thunderstorms tomorrow, with ball lightning and perhaps a few elves." Frogs from the sky? Ball-shaped lightning and elves? Can that be right? It can. There are several types of weird weather that confound us.

2 We've all heard the old saying "It's raining cats and dogs," yet we don't expect a downpour of small mammals. But frogs, fish, maggots, and even beer cans have fallen with rain. Falling frogs and fish can occur "with any tornado or waterspout that goes over a body of water with frogs and fish," says Marcin Szumowski. He's an assistant professor at the Desert Research Institute in Reno, Nevada. Swirling winds moving over bodies of water can suck up small creatures or light objects. They may be carried for many miles before falling as odd rain. On July 12, 1873,

Scientific American reported that a storm in Kansas City, Missouri, had blanketed the city with frogs.

3 Another strange weather phenomenon is ball-shaped lightning. The ancient Greeks reported seeing strange glowing balls moving across the sky. The luminous globes are called ball (or globe) lightning. Sometimes ball lightning is the size of a baseball, but it can be up to six feet across. Dr. Szumowski says ball lightning is generally "red, or red and yellow, changing to white, and disappearing with a loud bang." It may also leave a bad smell behind. (The odor is believed to be caused by ozone.) It usually lasts for only twenty seconds or so, but it can linger for many minutes. Ball lightning travels in weird ways. Eyewitnesses describe it moving parallel to the ground. It may also descend vertically from clouds or bounce! It can hiss, too. While it's very startling, it does little damage. Scientists don't exactly know what ball lightning is or why it acts the way it does. It may be glowing plasma (electrically charged gas) trapped in a series of magnetic fields.

4 Whirling dust and whirling fire are a third puzzling weather occurrence. Dust devils are swirling columns of air full of sand and debris. Columns can be 3,000 feet tall and from three to several hundred feet in diameter. They most often occur at midday in arid regions when the ground temperature is at least 68 degrees Fahrenheit hotter than the air directly above. When dust is picked up by the swirling air, a dust devil is seen. They are like mini-tornadoes but with important differences. Tornadoes develop underneath thunderstorms whereas dust devils form when the weather is clear, hot, and dry. Sometimes, a dust devil picks up more than sand. According to Szumowski at the Desert Research Institute, dust devils may also suck up flames from a nearby forest fire. It doesn't happen often, but when it does, it creates "a spectacular image of a rotating fire rope."

5 Elves are the latest of the strange weather phenomena to be documented. Elves look like huge bluish or white disks or cone-shaped light coming from the top of a thunderstorm. Some grow to be 250 miles or more in diameter, and they can extend 60 miles into the air. Elves may be produced when electromagnetic pulses move through the ionosphere, which is the atmospheric layer containing electrically charged air. The pulses could come from radio waves within the lightning flashes themselves. Elves last less than 1/1000th of a second. Like those impish creatures in fairy tales, they are gone in the blink of an eye!

6 The next time you look at the sky, consider the mysterious weather incidents that can occur. Sometimes reality is stranger than fiction.

Comprehension and Critical Thinking

1. Circle a word in paragraph 1 that means "mystify."
2. Circle a word in paragraph 3 that is the opposite of "dull" or "dark."
3. Underline a cliché in paragraph 5. Suggest a standard alternative for the cliché.

   quickly
4. Underline the thesis statement.
5. List the four different types of weird weather phenomena described in this article.

   a rain of small mammals and fish; ball-shaped lightning; whirling dust and fire; and elves
6. How is it possible for living creatures to fall from the sky?

   According to the article, winds blowing over bodies of water can pick up fish and small mammals and carry them for many miles.
7. How can whirling fires occur?

   Dust devils suck up flames from forest fires.
8. What type of support does the author use to back her thesis? (You can choose more than one answer.)

   (a.) expert opinion (b.) facts (c.) examples d. statistics
9. Throughout history, what have people probably attributed weird weather events to? Answers will vary.

   Probably many people throughout history have attributed such events to supernatural powers.
10. Generally, what causes the weird weather events described in the essay?

    The events are always caused by a set of unusual natural occurrences.

Writing Topics

Write about one of the following topics. Remember to explore, develop, and revise and edit your work.

1. How does the weather in different places affect people's lifestyles? Support your response with examples.
2. What are some inventions that humans have developed to deal with different types of weather? Give examples of specific inventions and the weather conditions that they deal with.

Teaching Tip: The suggested topics give students the opportunity to practice illustration writing.

Teaching Tip: Some possible inventions could be air conditioners, fireplaces, humidifiers, fans, windshield wipers, umbrellas, insulation in walls, weather-specific clothing, and new types of heating sources such as geothermal energy.

READING 10

The Rules of Survival

Laurence Gonzales

Laurence Gonzales won the National Magazine Award in 2001 and 2002. His work has appeared in such publications as *Harper's*, *National Geographic Adventure*, and *Smithsonian Air and Space*, just to name a few. The next excerpt is from his latest book, *Deep Survival*.

1 As a journalist, I've been writing about accidents for more than thirty years. In the last fifteen or so years, I've concentrated on accidents in outdoor recreation, in an effort to understand who lives, who dies, and why. To my surprise, I found an eerie uniformity in the way people survive seemingly impossible circumstances. Decades and sometimes centuries apart, separated by culture, geography, race, language, and tradition, the most successful survivors—those who practice what I call "deep survival"—go through the same patterns of thought and behavior, the same transformation and spiritual discovery, in the course of keeping themselves alive. It doesn't seem to matter whether they are surviving being lost in the wilderness or battling cancer; the strategies remain the same.

2 Survival should be thought of as a journey, a vision quest of the sort that Native Americans have had as a rite of passage for thousands of years. Once people pass the precipitating event—for instance, they are cast away at sea or told they have cancer—they are enrolled in one of the oldest schools in history. Here are a few things I've learned about survival.

Stay Calm

3 In the initial crisis, survivors are not ruled by fear; instead, they make use of it. Their fear often feels like (and turns into) anger, which motivates them and makes them feel sharper. Aron Ralston, the hiker who had to cut off his hand to free himself from a stone that had trapped him in a slot canyon in Utah, initially panicked and began slamming himself over and over against the boulder that had caught his hand. But very quickly he stopped himself, did some deep breathing, and began thinking about his options. He eventually spent five days progressing through the stages necessary to convince him of what decisive action he had to take to save his own life.

Think, Analyze, and Plan

4 Survivors quickly organize, set up routines, and institute discipline. When Lance Armstrong was diagnosed with cancer, he organized his fight against it the way he would organize his training for a race. He read

everything he could about it, put himself on a training schedule, and put together a team from among friends, family, and doctors to support his efforts. Such conscious, organized effort in the face of grave danger requires a split between reason and emotion in which reason gives direction and emotion provides the power source. Survivors often report experiencing reason as an audible "voice."

5 Steve Callahan, a sailor and boat designer, was rammed by a whale, and his boat sunk while he was on a solo voyage in 1982. Adrift in the Atlantic for seventy-six days on a five-and-a-half-foot raft, he experienced his survival voyage as taking place under the command of a "captain" who gave him his orders and kept him on his water ration, even as his own mutinous (emotional) spirit complained. His captain routinely lectured "the crew." Thus under strict control, he was able to push away thoughts that his situation was hopeless and take the necessary first steps of the survival journey: to think clearly, analyze his situation, and formulate a plan.

Celebrate Every Victory

6 Survivors take great joy from even their smallest successes. This attitude helps keep motivation high and prevents a lethal plunge into hopelessness. It also provides relief from the unspeakable strain of a life-threatening situation.

7 Lauren Elder was the only survivor of a light plane crash in the High Sierra. Stranded on a 12,000 foot peak, one arm broken, she could see the San Joaquin Valley in California below, but a vast wilderness and sheer and icy cliffs separated her from safety. Wearing a wrap-around skirt and blouse but no underwear, with two-inch heeled boots, she crawled "on all fours, doing a kind of sideways spiderwalk," as she put it later, "balancing myself on the ice crust, punching through it with my hands and feet." She had thirty-six hours of climbing ahead of her—a seemingly impossible task. But Elder allowed herself to think only as far as the next big rock. Once she had completed her descent of the first pitch, Elder said that she looked up at the impossibly steep slope and thought, "Look what I've done! Exhilarated, I gave a whoop that echoed down the silent pass." Even with a broken arm, joy was Elder's constant companion. A good survivor always tells herself, "Count your blessings—you're alive."

Enjoy the Survival Journey

8 It may seem counterintuitive, but even in the worst circumstances, survivors find something to enjoy, some way to play and laugh. Survival can be tedious, and waiting itself is an art. Elder found herself laughing

out loud when she started to worry that someone might see up her skirt as she climbed. Even as Callahan's boat was sinking, he stopped to laugh at himself as he clutched a knife in his teeth like a pirate while trying to get into his life raft. And Viktor Frankl ordered some of his companions in **Auschwitz** who were threatening to give up hope to force themselves to think of one funny thing each day. Singing, playing mind games, reciting poetry, and doing mathematical problems can make waiting tolerable, while heightening perception and quieting fear.

Auschwitz: a Nazi concentration camp

Never Give Up

9 Yes, you might die. In fact, you will die—we all do. But perhaps it doesn't have to be today. Don't let it worry you. Forget about rescue. Everything you need is inside you already. Dougal Robertson, a sailor who was cast away at sea for thirty-eight days after his boat sank, advised thinking of survival this way: "Rescue will come as a welcome interruption of . . . the survival voyage." One survival psychologist calls that "resignation without giving up. It is survival by surrender."

10 Survivors are not easily discouraged by setbacks. They accept that the environment is constantly changing and know that they must adapt. When they fall, they pick themselves up and start the entire process over again, breaking it down into manageable bits. When *Apollo 13*'s oxygen tank exploded, apparently dooming the crew, Commander Jim Lovell chose to keep on transmitting whatever data he could back to mission control, even as they burned up on re-entry. Elder and Callahan were equally determined and knew this final truth: If you're still alive, there is always one more thing that you can do.

Comprehension and Critical Thinking

1. What is the meaning of *precipitating* in paragraph 2?
   a. ending b. unexpected (c.) initiating or beginning
2. In paragraph 7, what is the meaning of *pitch*?
   a. throw (b.) slope c. tone
3. How does the author introduce the text?
   (a.) general background
   b. historical background
   c. anecdote
   d. contrasting position
4. In this process essay, the author describes the experiences of several survivors. Briefly explain what challenge the following people faced.

   Aron Ralston: *His hand was trapped in a boulder, and he had to decide how to free himself.*

Teaching Tip: For question 3, the introduction also has elements of historical background information.

Lance Armstrong: *He had to deal with cancer.*

Lauren Elder: *She survived a light plane crash and had to descend a snowy peak.*

Viktor Frankl: *He survived being incarcerated in a concentration camp.*

Dougal Robertson: *He was cast away at sea for thirty-eight days.*

5. a. What do most of the stories of survival have in common? What kinds of threats were they surviving?

   Most of the people were surviving a force of nature or a natural process (cancer). They were dealing with a great physical or psychological threat.

   b. How is Frankl's journey different from those of the others mentioned in the essay?

   Frankl had to survive a situation in which others (Nazis) were deliberately trying to harm him and his companions at Auschwitz.

6. This process essay also uses elements of narration and cause and effect. What are some of the effects of positive thinking while in a dangerous situation?

   When people keep their spirits up and refuse to give up hope, it helps them deal with the issues they are facing. They think of creative solutions.

7. What is the author's specific purpose?

   He wants to inform readers about how others have survived, and teach them about survival techniques.

8. Who was likely the targeted audience for this essay?
   a. an academic or intellectual audience
   b. children
   (c.) a general audience

   Give some reasons for your choice.

   The writing style appears too casual to be written for experts, and it might scare children.

9. What lessons does this essay have for the reader?

   It shows how resilient the human spirit is. It reminds us that we can get through our ordeals if we follow the survival steps of staying calm, analyzing the situation, celebrating small successes, and so on.

10. Using your own words, explain why it is important to enjoy the survival journey.

    It helps make the situation tolerable and keeps people's spirits up.

Teaching Tip: The suggested topics give students the opportunity to practice process writing. Specify whether students should write a paragraph or an essay.

WRITING TOPICS

Write about one of the following topics. Remember to explore, develop, and revise and edit your work.

1. Describe a difficult physical ordeal that you or someone you know went through. What happened? What steps were taken to get through the ordeal?
2. Explain the steps people should take when they have an emotional crisis. For example, how can they survive a breakup, a public humiliation, or the loss of a friend?

READING 11

Into Thin Air

Jon Krakauer

John Krakauer is a mountaineer and writer. In his memoir, *Into Thin Air*, Krakauer recounts the tragic tale of the 1996 Mount Everest climbing expedition in which he participated. During this expedition, many people who were Krakauer's climbing companions died when a sudden ferocious storm engulfed them. The next reading is an excerpt from Krakauer's best-selling book.

1 The literature of Everest is rife with accounts of hallucinatory experiences attributable to hypoxia and fatigue. In 1933, the noted English climber Frank Smythe observed "two curious looking objects floating in the sky" directly above him at 27,000 feet: "[One] possessed what appeared to be squat underdeveloped wings, and the other a protuberance suggestive of a beak. They hovered motionless but seemed slowly to pulsate." In 1980, during his solo ascent, Reinhold Messner imagined that an invisible companion was climbing beside him. Gradually, I became aware that my mind had gone haywire in a similar fashion, and I observed my own slide from reality with a blend of fascination and horror.

2 I was so far beyond ordinary exhaustion that I experienced a queer detachment from my body, as if I were observing my descent from a few feet overhead. I imagined that I was dressed in a green cardigan and wingtips. And although the gale was generating a windchill in excess of seventy below zero Fahrenheit, I felt strangely and disturbingly warm.

3 At 6:30, as the last of the daylight seeped from the sky, I'd descended to within 200 vertical feet of Camp Four. Only one obstacle now stood

between me and safety: a bulging incline of hard, glassy ice that I would have to descend without a rope. Snow pellets borne by 70-knot gusts stung my face; any exposed flesh was instantly frozen. The tents, no more than 650 horizontal feet away, were only intermittently visible through the whiteout. There was no margin for error. Worried about making a critical blunder, I sat down to marshal my energy before descending further.

4 Once I was off my feet, inertia took hold. It was so much easier to remain at rest than to summon the initiative to tackle the dangerous ice slope; so I just sat there as the storm roared around me, letting my mind drift, doing nothing for perhaps forty-five minutes.

5 I'd tightened the drawstrings on my hood until only a tiny opening remained around my eyes, and I was removing the useless, frozen oxygen mask from beneath my chin when Andy Harris suddenly appeared out of the gloom beside me. Shining my headlamp in his direction, I reflexively recoiled when I saw the appalling condition of his face. His cheeks were coated with an armor of frost, one eye was frozen shut, and he was slurring his words badly. He looked in serious trouble. "Which way to the tents?" Andy blurted, frantic to reach shelter.

6 I pointed in the direction of Camp Four, and then warned him about the ice just below us. "It is steeper than it looks!" I yelled, straining to make myself heard over the tempest. "Maybe I should go down first and get a rope from camp—." As I was in midsentence, Andy abruptly turned away and moved over the lip of the ice slope, leaving me sitting there dumbfounded.

7 Scooting on his butt, he started down the steepest part of the incline. "Andy," I shouted after him, "it's crazy to try it like that! You're going to blow it for sure!" He yelled something back, but his words were carried off by the screaming wind. A second later he lost his purchase, flipped ass over teakettle, and was suddenly rocketing headfirst down the ice.

8 Two hundred feet below, I could just make out Andy's motionless form slumped at the foot of the incline. I was sure he'd broken at least a leg, maybe his neck. But then, incredibly, he stood up, waved that he was O.K., and started lurching toward Camp Four, which at the moment was in plain sight, 500 feet beyond.

9 My backpack held little more than three empty oxygen canisters and a pint of frozen lemonade; it probably weighed no more than sixteen or eighteen pounds. But I was tired and worried about getting down the incline without breaking a leg, so I tossed the pack over the edge and hoped it would come to rest where I could retrieve it. Then I stood up and started down the ice, which was as smooth and hard as the surface of a bowling ball.

10 Fifteen minutes of dicey, fatiguing **crampon** work brought me safely to the bottom of the incline, where I easily located my pack, and another

crampon: steel spikes attached to the soles of mountain climbing boots to create a better grip on ice and prevent slipping.

ten minutes after that I was in camp myself. I lunged into my tent with my crampons still on, zipped the door tight, and sprawled across the frost-covered floor too tired to even sit upright. For the first time I had a sense of how wasted I was: I was more exhausted than I'd ever been in my life. But I was safe.

Comprehension and Critical Thinking

1. In paragraph 1, *protuberance* means
   (a.) a bulge   b. a disturbance   c. a bird
2. Which word in paragraph 4 means "inactivity"?
   inertia
3. What type of narrator is telling this story?
   (a.) first-person narrator   b. third-person
4. What can you infer or guess about his personality? Answers will vary.
   He is courageous, reckless, and strong. He also has great mental endurance and physical endurance.
5. In your own words, sum up the story in a couple of sentences. Remember to answer who, what, when, where, why, and how questions.
   In 1996, Krakauer, while descending to Camp Four on Mount Everest, got caught in a violent storm and nearly lost his life.
6. Describe the author's physical and mental state at the beginning of the essay.
   He was freezing cold and almost hypothermic. He was exhausted and hallucinating.
7. What were some obstacles that the narrator faced during his descent to Camp Four?
   He faced a lack of oxygen, fatigue, severe weather, mental exhaustion, hallucinations, and fear.
8. This excerpt contains examples of imagery (description using the senses). Give examples of imagery that appeal to touch, sight, and hearing. Answers will vary.
   touch: a windchill in excess of seventy below zero; hard glassy ice; snow pellets . . . stung my face
   sight: the tents . . . only intermittently visible through the whiteout; his cheeks were coated with an armor of frost
   hearing: he was slurring his words; his words were carried off by the screaming wind

9. Which organizational method does the author use in this essay?
   (a.) time order b. space order c. emphatic order
10. The author uses dialogue in this essay. What is the purpose of the dialogue?

    The dialogue involves the reader in the author's experience by making the experience more vivid.

Writing Topics

Write about one of the following topics. Remember to explore, develop, and revise and edit your work.

1. Have you or someone you know participated in a risky activity? What happened? Include descriptive details that appeal to the senses.
2. In Krakauer's story, he describes his reactions during a challenging moment from his past. Think about a time when you felt extremely excited, ashamed, or moved. Where were you and what were you doing? Describe what happened and include descriptive details.

Teaching Tip: The suggested topics give students the opportunity to practice descriptive writing. Specify whether students should write a paragraph or an essay.

READING 12

Monsoon Time

Rahul Goswami

Rahul Goswami is a journalist for *Orientation: Middle East*. In the following essay, he reminisces about the weather in his homeland. Pay closs attention to the descriptive details.

1 My father used to tell me about the monsoon in Bangladesh. He was born in Handiyal, a village in the north-central district of the country. Behind his parents' house was a river, the Padma, a part of the immense water system that crisscrosses Bangladesh. Big even during the sweltering dry months, the Padma would become an inland ocean at the height of the monsoon. My father would talk about the river swelling day after day as the rain drove down. He loved the monsoon, despite the inevitable annual floods, the misery, and the hardship.

2 Years later, I moved to Dubai, where I lived until just recently. It is a modern metropolis—built on the edge of the great Arabian sand sea—glittering with glazed glass and proud of its impeccably maintained highways. It scarcely ever rains here. On perhaps five days a year, a few millimeters of rain will reluctantly descend. More frequent are the sandstorms, which clog drains that are tested no more than annually. This past year was my first full one in Dubai and the first time in my life I have missed an entire monsoon.

squalls: sudden violent gusts of wind

archipelagos: groups of small islands

3 By June in India, when the first wet **squalls** explode over Bombay [Mumbai], one has been anticipating the rain for a month and more. Then in July, the massive, heavy cloud systems have settled immovably over the subcontinent, and they let fall torrents of rain, day after day. Indoors a patina of moisture coats everything, clothes will not dry, and head colds make one miserable. Outside, the city struggles with its everyday routines. Suburban trains do not run, their tracks submerged under feet of muddy water. City drains, routinely untended and choked with tons of garbage, refuse to do their work. Housing colonies turn into **archipelagos**. Mosquitoes assume fearsome proportions.

4 By August, the monsoon has dulled the world. Trees appear a uniform drab green, the sea stays gray and forbidding, and the city stinks. When, in September, the rains have at last weakened into ineffectual evening drizzles, one is relieved.

5 The monsoon season has, I discovered, a rhythm that the mind and body grow accustomed to. In Dubai last June, when the temperature reached 48° Celsius, I would catch myself glancing at the sky, wondering idly if there was a hint of interesting cloud. My rational self knew there could not be a monsoon here, but the subconscious would not be denied. Some mornings I would awake in my darkened, air-conditioned room and imagine rain drumming on the window. It was an illusion that persisted several seconds into wakefulness, and even after I rose I would resist drawing the curtain aside, preferring instead to retreat to the even darker bathroom. Then I'd tell myself there is no rain, and I'd lace my shoes and step outside into the pitiless heat of Arabia.

6 Late in July, I noticed that the illusions persisted at work, too. With the window blinds down and the central air-conditioning humming along at a cool 22° Celsius, I occasionally caught myself wondering whether I'd find a cab that would be willing to drive me home in the rain. After all, it must be raining outside by now. At these times it took some courage to walk into the passageway between the office suites, face the window, stare at the Dubai skyline carelessly shimmering in the late evening sun, and remind myself that the monsoon lay on the other side of the Indian Ocean.

7 The sounds of rain would still visit, sometimes surprising, always comforting, while outside Dubai still blazed with heat and light. August slipped into September and as the body readjusted itself, the mind played along. As the Gulf's fall months began, the harsh absence of monsoon faded. I no longer looked for that high and lonely cloud in the sky. The time for rain had passed, and I wondered whether next year my longing would be the same.

Comprehension and Critical Thinking

1. Define *monsoon*.

   a season of heavy rains in Asia
2. Circle a word in paragraph 3 that means "violent flow or downpour."
3. In paragraph 3, the author uses the word *patina*. What does it mean?

   a layer
4. What are some effects of the author's decision to move to Dubai?

   He finds himself longing for his homeland.
5. Using your own words, sum up the main idea of the essay.

   When Rahul Goswami moves to Dubai, he realizes how much he misses the rhythm and comfort of the monsoon season.
6. What impression does the writer give of Dubai? Using your own words, describe that place.

   large city surrounded by sand with very clean highways. There are occasional sandstorms.
7. What impression does the writer give of Mumbai during the monsoon season? Using your own words, describe what the city is like.

   constant rain; clothing is humid, trains don't work because of mud covering the tracks
8. What is the dominant impression in Goswami's essay? Circle the letter of the best answer.

   a. joy b. tension (c.) homesickness d. anger e. despair
9. The writer appeals to more than one sense. Give an example for each type of imagery. Answers will vary.

   sight: *trees appear a uniform drab green; a patina of moisture coats everything*

   hearing: *rain drumming on the window; the central air-conditioning humming along*

   smell: *the city stinks; city drains [are] choked with tons of garbage*
10. Monsoons disrupt everyday life with intense and unending rainfall. Moreover, the extreme humidity is unpleasant. Why would the author prefer the chaos and rain of his homeland over the dryness and order of Dubai? To answer this question, you will have to make inferences.

    Answers will vary. *Humans tend to feel nostalgic about their birthplaces, even when they grow up in harsh or uncomfortable surroundings.*

Teaching Tip:
Discuss question 10. Although this essay is predominantly descriptive, it also compares and contrasts Dubai and Mumbai. Ask students to consider the key differences between the two cities. Why would the author prefer the chaos and rain of his homeland over the cleanliness, order, and dryness of Dubai? Discuss what the birthplace represents.

Perhaps the homeland or birthplace is associated with innocence and security. People idealize their birthplaces.

Teaching Tip: The suggested topics give students the opportunity to practice descriptive writing. Specify whether students should write a paragraph or an essay.

WRITING TOPICS

Write about one of the following topics. Remember to explore, develop, and revise and edit your work.

1. Which season do you like the most? Describe that season using vivid imagery.
2. Describe an extreme weather phenomenon that you lived through. What happened? Include descriptive details that appeal to the senses.

The Writer's Room Forces of Nature

The previous four readings, and Editing Handbook Chapters 30–32, deal with issues related to the forces of nature. The following activities continue developing that theme.

Teaching Tip: Photo writing topic 1 can generate an illustration essay, and writing topic 2 can lead to an argument essay.

Writing Activity 1: Photo Writing

1. What is your attitude toward nature? Can you distinguish one tree from another, for example? Describe your relationship with the natural world. Support your main point with detailed examples.
2. Explain why it is or is not important to teach children about the natural world.

Teaching Tip: The film prompts may appeal particularly to auditory and visual learners. If the suggested films do not appeal to your group of students, choose one (or ask students to choose one) that addresses the theme and then adapt the writing prompt as needed.

Writing Activity 2: Film Writing

1. Films such as *A Perfect Storm* and *The Titanic* describe a tremendous force of nature. Choose one of the films and compare or contrast the attitudes of two different characters toward the disaster.
2. In *Cast Away*, a FedEx executive must survive a crash landing on a deserted island. Describe the actions he takes to survive physically and emotionally.
3. View another film that deals with the forces of nature such as *Alive*, *Twister*, or *Earthquake*. Explain why people enjoy such films. Why do people enjoy viewing extreme events in nature?

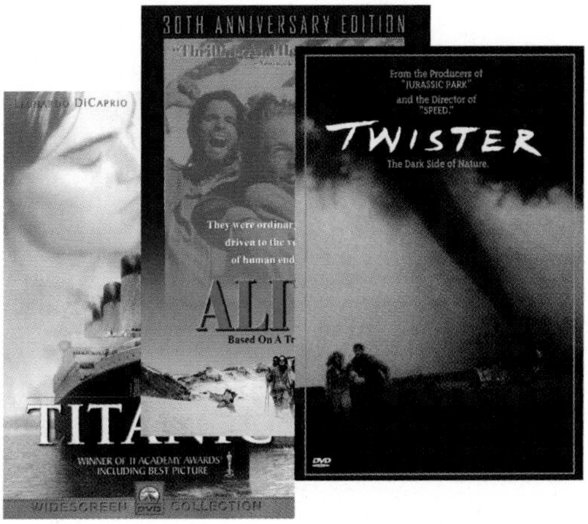

Teaching Tip: The film writing prompts encourage students to use comparison and contrast, illustration, and argument.

Theme: Plants and Insects

READING 13

Songs of Insects

Sy Montgomery

Sy Montgomery is a naturalist and writer. She has written many articles about animals and their environments. In the next article, Montgomery reflects on the methods of communication by insects .

1 In his poem "Conversational Insects," H. I. Phillips has a confession to make:

I long to interview the little Insects,
and get the drift of what they're driving at:
To chat with Wasps and Crickets
In bushes, trees and thickets
And understand the language of the Gnat.

2 If you share this poet's sensibilities, now is the time to fulfill your longing. Though widely loved for its changing leaves and migrating birds, early fall is, in some circles anyway, yet more renowned for the sweetness of its insect voices.

3 The insects' songs tell of longing and pursuit, rivalry and battle. If the song of the autumn field cricket suddenly becomes louder, more rapid, and higher pitched, he's located a lady and is calling to her. If his calls soften, she has come to him and is ready to mate. (Unlike grasshoppers, the

female cricket usually mounts the male.) If he encounters a rival, he chirps more loudly and the chirps get longer and less rhythmic. A vicious battle may ensue—so vicious that cricket fights were the entertainment extravaganza of the Sung dynasty in 10th-century China. The victors earned the title *shou lip*—"conquering cricket"—and were ceremoniously buried in little silver caskets when they died of old age.

4 Some insect songs convey information people can use. Because the insect's metabolism speeds up with the heat, the hotter the weather, the faster the chirping. The male snowy tree cricket, which begins singing in September and continues until the killing frost, tracks temperatures so accurately that, in 1897, Tufts College professor A. E. Dolbear developed a measurement formula accurate to within one degree Fahrenheit: count the number of chirps in 15 seconds and add 39.

5 Songs may have X-rated lyrics. Some species of grasshoppers, for instance, explicitly announce the moment of copulation with a distinct, sharp noise just before the male leaps onto the back of the female—a sound that one **entomologist** interprets as the **orthopteran** equivalent of "Oh, boy!" and terms it "the shout of triumph."

entomologist: a scientist that specializes in insects

orthopteran: another term for insects with folded hind legs

6 The autumn songs of these hopping insects are among the most lovely and lyrical sounds of the natural world, appreciated around the globe. For centuries, the Japanese have given one another gifts of singing insects. These tiny pets were so popular around 1820 that fishermen and peasants used to sell them in pushcarts door-to-door. Today, autumn *suzumushi* (bell crickets) and *kirigirisu* (grasshoppers) are sold in nearly every post office in Japan. In Africa, the songs of crickets are said to have magic powers. And perhaps they do. Henry David Thoreau described the song of one species as "a slumberous breathing," an "intenser dream." Nathaniel Hawthorne, describing the autumn music of the snowy tree cricket, wrote, "If moonlight could be heard, it would sound like that."

7 If it takes some effort for us to listen for insect song, it is because the songs are not meant for us; they are meant for creatures that wear their skeletons on their outsides and whose ears are on their elbows. Members of the grasshopper family, including crickets, locusts, and katydids, hear with small disks near one of the front leg joints. On the inside of the hind leg, grasshoppers have a comb-like structure with a row of teeth. They rub this comb against a ridge on the wing to produce a sound. And these songs are perfect for their purposes. Over the relatively long distances that these little animals must travel to find one another, looks mean nothing; songs call out the identity of the musician. For this reason, entomologists can sometimes better classify these insects by their songs than by their appearance.

8 Most autumn-singing insects prefer to perform on warm mornings, afternoons, and early evenings. But if you listen carefully, you may be able

to hear one or another singing almost anytime. The greenish yellow marsh meadow locust prefers to sing on hot, quiet forenoons from moist ditches and grassy banks. At night, in areas that have been spared aerial spraying, listen for the katydids. They'll be squawking from the lindens, elms, and maples where cicadas sang during summer days.

Comprehension and Critical Thinking

1. What is the meaning of *pitch* as it appears in Paragraph 3?
   a. throw   b. slope   (c.) tone
2. Circle a word in paragraph 5 that means "overtly" or "clearly."
3. How is the author's introduction unusual?

   Sy Montgomery begins her essay with a poem.
4. According to the author, why is autumn the best season to appreciate singing insects?

   Singing insects make the most noise during the autumn.
5. In your own words, list some messages that singing insects communicate to each other.

   A singing insect can communicate when it has located a mate, when it is battling with a rival, and when it is procreating.
6. What do singing insects communicate to humans?

   They communicate temperatures very accurately.
7. How do people in different cultures value singing insects?

   The Japanese give singing insects as gifts, and the Africans think the singing insects have magical powers. The American writer, Nathaniel Hawthorne, shows his appreciation for insects by comparing their songs to moonlight.
8. What type of singing insect is the author mainly describing?

   members of the grasshopper family
9. The author uses examples to support her main point, but she also describes a process. How do singing insects make their sounds?

   They rub a comb-like structure against a ridge on the wing to produce sound.
10. What is the main idea of this essay?

    Not only are insect songs wonderful to hear, but they can also teach us how some insects communicate with each other.

Teaching Tip:
If students are unable to come up with ideas for writing topic 1, ask them to think about sunsets, a full moon, a starry night, or a thunderstorm. They can also think about places such as a canyon, valley, lake, river, or mountain. Or perhaps they have heard birds singing in the trees or marveled at a fluttering butterfly.

Teaching Tip:
The suggested topics give students the opportunity to practice illustration writing. Specify whether students should write a paragraph or an essay.

Writing Topics

Write about one of the following topics. Remember to explore, develop, and revise and edit your work.

1. List some elements in nature that inspire you or move you. Support your essay with examples.
2. How is your personality similar to certain birds, mammals, or insects? Give examples to support your main point.

READING 14

Nature Returns to the Cities

John Roach

John Roach is a writer for *National Geographic*, and he has written many articles about nature. In the next essay, he describes animal life in our concrete jungles.

1 The concrete jungle isn't just for people anymore. Thirty years of good environmental stewardship combined with wildlife's innate ability to adapt has given rise to a resurgence of nature in America's urban centers. In New York City, raccoons have walked through the front door and into the kitchen to raid the refrigerator. In southern California, mountain lions have been seen cooling off under garden sprinklers and breaking into homes near Disneyland. In Chicago, beavers gnaw and fell trees and snarl traffic. In her book *Wild Nights: Nature Returns to the City,* Anne Matthews describes such incidents as she explores the resurgence of wildlife in New York and other cities. "Thirty years of environmental protection and absence of hunting [in cities] have allowed animal populations to soar," she notes.

2 The implications of the wildlife resurgence in cities vary. People may marvel at the presence of a falcon nest on the twenty-seventh floor of New York Hospital. On the other hand, some people were literally sickened to death in the fall of 2000 by the West Nile virus, which had been carried to the city by migrating birds and transmitted to mosquitoes, which passed it on to humans.

3 Overcrowded cities and urban sprawl have put more people and wild animals in close proximity than at any other time in American history, says Matthews. Encounters between these two groups are beginning to exceed what scientists call the cultural carrying capacity, defined in *Wild Nights* as "the moment humans stop saying 'Aww' and start calling 911." This change in the nature of the relationship between people and wildlife, says Matthews, is forcing people to reconsider their ethical and practical role as top predator.

4 Nature's return to U.S. cities has resulted in part from passage of the Clean Air Act in 1970 and the Clean Water Act in 1972. These laws of environmental protection that helped make air safer to breathe and water safer to drink also made cities more hospitable to wildlife, according to Matthews. After being cleaned up, New York Harbor is now home to booming populations of blue crabs and fiddler crabs, which in turn attract thousands of long-legged wading birds such as herons and egrets. With the air now cleaner, owls have flocked in growing numbers to the suburbs in search of easy prey: pets such as schnauzers, chihuahuas, and cats. In parts of the South and Midwest, forests that were logged in the nineteenth century have grown back over the last hundred years, allowing animal populations to recover. Car collisions with moose are now common along Interstate 95, the main East Coast traffic corridor. Crocodiles, who were all but erased by development pressure in Florida, are now breeding at four times their normal rate in the cooling canals of Florida's nuclear power plants.

5 Some creatures, such as rats, never really left the city. Today, an estimated 28 million rats—which are non-native, like much of the city's human population—inhabit New York. The greater New York area is home to eight million people, which means there are more than three rats to every person. Matthews explains how it happened. "Rats are smart," she writes. "Although a fast-forward version of natural selection has made rats in many big cities immune to nearly all conventional poisons, they still may press one pack member into service as a taster; if the test rat dies, the others resolutely avoid the bait."

6 Matthews says the strong adaptive ability of non-native species has begun to change the definition of wilderness. Rats were introduced into U.S. cities in the 1700s after arriving as stowaways on merchant ships. Zebra mussels, which have caused major problems in the Great Lakes by clogging intake pipes, were imported in the ballast water of international ships. "The most important thing is to realize that a city is wilder than we tend to imagine and the land we think of as untouched or wild really isn't," says Matthews. "There has been so much human interference and reshaping that we really don't know what a pristine planet is." Matthews thinks people should not try to undo the effects of this increased interference with wildlife, but to improve their understanding of it and continue to make room for nature in their lives.

7 Matthews says it's crucial that people consider what kind of world they want their grandchildren to inherit, and act to ensure that such a world will exist. One immediate concern is what the impacts of global warming will be in fifty years. Citing the results of computer models showing future conditions if no action is taken to mitigate global warming,

Matthews says much of New York will be under water, as sea levels rise three feet. New Orleans, Louisiana, already eight feet below sea level, might become the next Atlantis. What can we do? "What you can do is as small as don't use air conditioning as much, don't use your gas-guzzling [sport utility vehicle], walk more," says Matthews. "On the macro level, urge your congressperson to do something about environmental issues."

Comprehension and Critical Thinking

1. In paragraph 1, circle a word that means "reappearance."
2. Define *prey*. Look in paragraph 4 for context clues.

   The animal that another animal kills, usually for food.
3. Underline the thesis statement.
4. What are at least two reasons the author gives for animals returning to urban environments?

   Urban sprawl causes humans and wildlife to confront each other more often.

   The Clean Air and Clean Water Acts made cities more hospitable to wildlife.

   Some animals adapt well to city life (rats, for instance).
5. What are at least three effects of wildlife in cities?

   New viruses such as the West Nile virus infect humans. People become afraid of the animals. The animals become a nuisance (rats and raccoons, for instance). Animals such as beavers damage structures. People have car collisions with animals.
6. In paragraph 4, the author implies that
   a. The Clean Air and Clean Water Acts did not help the environment.
   b. The Clean Air and Clean Water Acts were quite effective in helping to improve the quality of the air and water.
   c. Logging practices are much more detrimental to the environment today than they were in the past.
   d. Many dangerous predators such as crocodiles now roam the cities.
7. What is Matthews's opinion about abundant wildlife in the city?

   She believes that people should accept the new reality because, throughout history, humans and animals have interacted.
8. What is Matthews's definition of wilderness in paragraph 6?

   She says that there is really no such thing as a pristine, untouched wilderness because of human interference.

9. Although this is mainly a cause and effect essay, there are also elements of process. Which paragraph gives the readers clear steps to take to help the environment? 7

10. What incorrect assumption or belief do many people today have about the relationship between wildlife and cities?

    People assume that humans and wildlife are distinct and do not really interact, when in fact they have always been living together. There have never been animal-free cities.

Writing Topics

Write about one of the following topics. Remember to explore, develop, and revise and edit your work.

1. Describe your own experiences with wildlife in your home, yard, or neighborhood. What causes or caused the bird, animal, or insect to invade your area? How does it or how did it affect you and your neighbors?
2. Do you have a pet in your home? Why or why not? Describe the causes or effects (or both) of your decision about having pets.

Teaching Tip: The suggested topics give students the opportunity to practice cause and effect writing. Specify whether students should write a paragraph or an essay.

The Writer's Room Plants and Insects

The previous two readings, and Editing Handbook Chapters 33 and 34, deal with issues related to insects and animals. The following activities continue developing that theme.

Teaching Tip: For photo writing question 1, brainstorm some environmental disasters. Some specific examples are the Love Canal, *Exxon Valdez* oil spill, Chernobyl, Bhopal-Union Carbide gas leak, and mad cow disease. Some general examples are oil spills, chemical spills, nuclear hazards, ozone depletion, smog, and so on. Students may also need to research their topic.

Writing Activity 1: Photo Writing

1. Choose one environmental disaster. What are the causes of the disaster, or how have governments and the public responded to it?

Teaching Tip: For photo witing question 2, discuss why the eagle has become an important symbol in the United States. What does the eagle represent? Why did forefathers choose the eagle as a symbol? If students can't answer those questions, suggest that they do some research.

Teaching Tip: Photo writing topic 2 can generate an illustration essay, and writing topic 2 can lead to a cause and effect essay.

2. Insects, animals, and birds are symbolic to various cultures. Choose some nature symbols and explain what they represent to a specific culture. You can write about your own or other cultures. (You might want to research this topic on the Internet.)

Teaching Tip: The film prompts may appeal particularly to auditory and visual learners. If the suggested films do not appeal to your group of students, choose one (or ask students to choose one) that addresses the theme and then adapt the writing prompt as needed.

Teaching Tip: The film writing prompts encourage students to use process, argument, and definition or classification.

Writing Activity 2: Film Writing

1. *March of the Penguins* is a documentary about the activities of a group of penguins in Antarctica. Most of us are not experts in the mating habits of Emperor penguins. How does the filmmaker help a general audience relate to his film?
2. The documentary *An Inconvenient Truth* deals with humans and their impact on the environment. What is your opinion about environmental activism? Does it annoy you, or do you support it? Argue for or against the value of environmental activism.
3. *Arachnophobia* and *The Birds* deal with human fears of insects and birds. Write a definition essay about phobias. You might describe different categories of fears that people have.

Theme: Human Development

READING 15

Raunch Culture

Ariel Levy

Ariel Levy, a contributing editor at *New York Magazine*, is the author of *Female Chauvinist Pigs: The Rise of Raunch Culture*.

1 Some version of a sexy, scantily clad temptress has been around through the ages, and there has always been a demand for smut. But whereas this was once a guilty pleasure on the margins—on the almost entirely male margins—now, strippers, porn stars, and Playboy bunnies have gone mainstream, writing best-sellers, starring in reality television shows, and living a life we're all encouraged to emulate. Prepubescent girls wear thong-style underpants while their mothers drive off to the gym for pole-dancing classes after lunch. A few weeks ago, Anita Roddick, founder of the Body Shop, hit out at what she called "pimp and ho chic." I prefer to call it "raunch culture," and it's everywhere. Men and women alike have developed a taste for kitschy, slutty stereotypes of female sexuality. We don't even think about it any more; we just expect to see women flashing and stripping and groaning everywhere we look.

2 Not so long ago, the revelation that a woman in the public eye had appeared in any kind of pornography would have destroyed her reputation. Think of Vanessa Williams, crowned the first black Miss America in 1983, and how quickly she was dethroned after nude photos surfaced in *Penthouse*. She managed to make a comeback as a singer, but the point is that being exposed as a porn star was something she needed to come back from. Now, it's the comeback itself.

3 Paris Hilton was just a normal blonde New York socialite, an heiress with a taste for table-dancing, before she and her former boyfriend Rick Solomon made a video of themselves having sex. Somehow, the footage found its way on to the Internet and was distributed worldwide, after which Paris Hilton became one of the most marketable celebrities in the world. Since the advent of the sex tapes, Hilton has become famous enough to warrant a slew of endorsement deals. There is a Paris Hilton jewelry line (belly-button rings feature prominently), a perfume, and a string of nightclubs called Club Paris set to open in London, New York, Atlanta, Madrid, Miami, and Las Vegas. Her debut CD—the first single is entitled "Screwed"—has been released. Paris Hilton isn't some disgraced exile of our society. On the contrary, she has become our mascot, the embodiment of our collective fixations—blondness, hotness, richness, anti-intellectualism, and exhibitionism.

4 Raunch culture is not essentially "progressive"; it is essentially commercial. It isn't about opening our minds to the possibilities and mysteries of sexuality. If we were to acknowledge that sexuality is personal and unique, it would become unwieldy. Making sexiness into something simple and quantifiable makes it easier to explain and to market. If you remove the human factor from sex and make it about stuff—big fake boobs, bleached blonde hair, long nails, poles, thongs—then you can sell it. Suddenly, sex requires shopping: you need plastic surgery, peroxide, a manicure, and a mall.

5 There is a disconnection between sexiness, or "hotness," and sex itself. As Paris Hilton told Rolling Stone, "My boyfriends always tell me I'm not sexual. Sexy, but not sexual." And any fourteen-year-old who has downloaded her sex video can tell you that Hilton looks excited when she is posing for the camera, bored when she is engaged in actual sex. (In one tape, Hilton took a cellphone call during intercourse.) She is the perfect sexual celebrity for this moment because our interest is in the appearance of sexiness, not the existence of sexual pleasure.

6 "Hotness" has become our cultural currency, and a lot of people spend a lot of time and a lot of money trying to acquire it. Hotness is not the same thing as beauty, which has been valued throughout history. Hot can mean popular. Hot can mean talked about. But when it pertains to women, hot means two things in particular: sexually available and saleable. These are the literal job criteria for our role models: strippers and porn stars. These are women whose profession is based on faking lust and imitating actual female sexual pleasure and power. If we're all trying to look like porn stars these days (and we are), we're imitating an imitation of arousal. It's a long way from sexual liberation.

7 This is not a situation foisted upon women. In the West, in the twenty-first century, we have opportunities and expectations that our mothers never had. We have attained a degree of hard-won (and still threatened) freedom in our personal lives; we are gradually penetrating the highest levels of the workforce; we get to go to college and play sports and be secretaries of state. But to look around, you'd think that all us women want to do is to rip off our clothes and shake our butts in men's faces.

8 So why do we go in for raunch culture? Why, when the feminist movement was supposed to have freed us from stereotypes, have we deliberately embraced them again?

9 The freedom to be sexually provocative or promiscuous is not enough freedom; it is not the only "women's issue" worth paying attention to. Let's face it: we are not even free in the sexual arena. We females have simply adopted a new norm, a new role to play: lusty, busty exhibitionists. There

are other choices. It's ironic that we call this "adult" entertainment, when reducing sexuality to implants and polyester underpants is really pretty adolescent.

Comprehension and Critical Thinking

1. What is the meaning of *foisted* in paragraph 7?
   a. determined (b.) imposed c. carried
2. According to the author, what is the new definition of *hot*?
   popular, sexually available, and saleable
3. Using your own words, describe *raunch culture*.
   It is a culture that idolizes sexually explicit or promiscuous stereotypes about females.
4. Underline the topic sentences in paragraphs 3, 4, and 5. Remember that the topic sentence may not be the first sentence in the paragraph.
5. In paragraph 4, what type of definition is the topic sentence?
   a. category b. synonym (c.) negation
6. According to the author, how has our society changed regarding sexuality?
   In the past, society used to marginalize pornography or provocative sexuality, but now pornography is embraced and idolized.
7. In the author's view, why is Paris Hilton a raunch culture icon?
   She is "hot" but not really sexual; she is linked to pornography; and she "embodies collective fixations" because she is a blond, rich, anti-intellectual exhibitionist.
8. In paragraphs 2 and 3, the author juxtaposes—places side by side or contrasts—examples of Vanessa Williams and Paris Hilton. What is the purpose of such a juxtaposition?
   These two examples show how the general public's attitude toward sex has changed. Sex is no longer taboo and almost anything is acceptable. What was pornographic in the recent past is now considered acceptable behavior.
9. In paragraph 8, the author asks two rhetorical questions (questions to which no answer is required). What is the purpose of these rhetorical questions?
   The author wants the readers to consider their own opinions.

Teaching Tip:
The suggested topics on the next page give students the opportunity to practice definition writing. Specify whether students should write a paragraph or an essay.

Teaching Tip: Discuss writing topic 1 with the students. For instance, students can think of new terms to describe people who habitually use MySpace or Facebook. They can think about cell phone addicts and come up with an interesting term to describe them, or they can invent a word to describe those who never complete college because they keep changing programs. Students can also think about another predominant feature of our culture and give it a name. For example, they could argue that we have become a Voyeur Culture, a Disposable Culture, or a Binge-and-Purge Culture. Encourage students to be creative.

Teaching Tip: You can give students an argument-writing topic. Who is more responsible for creating raunch culture: men or women? Write an argument essay giving your opinion.

10. Using your own words, sum up the author's opinion of raunch culture. You may need to infer, or read between the lines.

    Women have supported and even helped spread a raunch culture that objectifies women. Raunch culture belittles women and makes them appear as nothing more than sex objects.

Writing Topics

Write about one of the following topics. Remember to explore, develop, and revise and edit your work.

1. Think about new types of behavior in our society, and invent a term that defines that phenomenon. Write a definition essay and provide specific examples.
2. Think of a popular term that is widely used, and write a definition essay about that term. For example, you could define *chick flick* or *shock jock*.

Twixters

Betsy Hart

Betsy Hart is a journalist for the Scripps Howard News Service. In the next essay, she examines adults who do not want to grow up.

1 Meet the Twixters: "Michelle, Ellen, Nathan, Corinne, Marcus, and Jennie are friends. All of them live in Chicago. They go out together three nights a week, sometimes more. Each of them has had several jobs since college; Ellen is on her seventeenth." They are all ages twenty-four to twenty-eight. They don't own homes, they are not married, and they don't have kids. Most telling: They don't want to own homes, be married, or have kids. As one Twixter, charming twenty-seven-year-old Matt—who took six and a half years to graduate from college—put it, "I do not ever want a lawn . . . I do not want to be a parent. I mean, hell, why would I? There's so much fun to be had while you're young." Ah, out of the mouths of babes. Why would he want such things, indeed? He's still a child, just in a man's body. It used to be that our culture presented adulthood as something valuable, so there was prestige in attaining it. Now we teach our children to fear adulthood—and so they stay children.

2 All of this comes from the current *Time* magazine cover story, "They Just Won't Grow Up." Well put. *Time* reports, "Everybody knows a few of them—full-grown men and women who still live with their parents, who dress and talk and party as they did in their teens, hopping from job to job

and date to date, having fun but seemingly going nowhere." Ten years ago, they might have been called, well, losers. But not anymore. There are just too many of them. As *Time* puts it, "This is a much larger phenomenon, of a different kind and a different order." Now, the age from eighteen to twenty-five—and often much later—is seen as a distinct phase in life.

3 Some sociologists who observe this trend say growing up is just harder than it used to be. They are wrong. The problem is, growing up is easier and cushier than ever. And so, the 20 percent of all twenty-six-year-olds who live with their parents—you read right, one-fifth, typically rent-free or heavily subsidized—don't want to go. (How does one put a price on someone doing or helping you with the laundry, anyway?) No one is making them leave the family nest. It's incredibly cushy there, and why in the world would they go through the hard work of building their own nest when they have access to a much fancier one ready-made?

4 The idea that this is all about finances is silly. We're living in a great economy. And the Twixters are such big spenders, on eating out, new cars, and flat-screen TVs, that advertisers are now targeting these adult adolescents, seeing them as something of a gold mine. The Twixters have money. They just want to spend it on the fun toys and leisure activities.

5 Fewer young adults want to take a job they are not crazy about, one that isn't "meaningful enough," or perhaps live in an efficiency apartment and do their laundry down the street, while saving and working for something better. It is more fun to live better now, often at someone else's expense: mom and dad's.

6 Look, I'm not suggesting there should not be a place in the family nest for young adults during a trauma. Sure, parents should help those who are truly getting on their feet—meaning they are working, paying rent, helping around the house—and making plans to move on. I do know some young adults who move in with their parents to help take care of them. It might even be that some generations enjoy living together as equals. I'm just lamenting the adults who want to stay kids, whether they are living with mom and dad or not—and the parents who not only encourage it but subsidize it.

7 Growing up, becoming an adult, and taking on adult responsibilities brings joy and satisfaction and disappointment and heartache and even fun. As a culture, the less we encourage that transition, the more we encourage young adults to stay in their "it's all about me" cocoon. The real problem? If we as a culture make it easy for these young adults to have no real responsibilities either for themselves or to others, we rob them of a tangible way to be plugged into and connected to their community and their world—and something bigger than just themselves.

Comprehension and Critical Thinking

1. Find a verb in paragraph 6 that means "mourning or grieving."
   lamenting
2. Find a word in paragraph 7 that means the opposite of "elusive and vague."
   tangible
3. What are the main characteristics of a Twixter?
   A Twixter is an adult (between ages 18–25) who lives at home and refuses to take on adult responsibilities.
4. Underline the thesis statement.
5. The author is defining a Twixter, but she is also making an argument. What is her point of view?
   Parents should encourage their adult children to be independent. Adult children should accept responsibility, give more to their communities, and stop being selfish.
6. What is the author implying in paragraph 3?
   a. It is society's fault that some people never grow up.
   (b.) Parents contribute to the problem of Twixters by making home too comfortable.
   c. Young adults can't easily move out because it is too expensive these days.
7. What is the author's main point in paragraph 4?
   a. Twixters have a lot of money.
   b. Twixters spend a lot of money on games and toys.
   c. Our economy is doing extremely well.
   (d.) Twixters would rather spend money on themselves than move out of their parents' home.
8. According to the auhor, how does delayed adulthood hurt the Twixters?
   They remain selfish, and they do not connect with the community. They miss out on the joys and sense of accomplishment that accompany adult responsibilities and relationships.

Teaching Tip: The suggested topics give students the opportunity to practice definition writing. Specify whether students should write a paragraph or an essay.

Teaching Tip: As an additional writing topic, you can ask students to write an argument essay explaining why people should leave home before they turn age twenty. You might also ask students to explain the ideal age or time of life for people to leave the family home.

Writing Topics

Write about one of the following topics. Remember to explore, develop, and revise and edit your work.

1. Choose a term that refers to a particular type of adolescent or young adult and write a definition essay about that term. For example, you might write about *rappers*, *punks*, *skaters*, or *jocks*, or you can define a new term that people in your area use.
2. Define adulthood. What are the main characteristics of an adult?

READING 17

The Untranslatable Word "Macho"

Rose del Castillo Guilbault

Rose del Castillo Guilbault is a journalist and the Editorial Director of the ABC affiliate station, KGO-TV, in San Francisco, California. In this essay, Castillo compares how two cultures define the term *macho*.

1 What is *macho*? That depends which side of the border you come from. Although it's not unusual for words and expressions to lose their subtlety in translation, the negative connotations of *macho* in this country are troublesome to Hispanics.

2 Take the newspaper descriptions of alleged mass murderer Ramon Salcido. That an insensitive, insanely jealous, hard-drinking, violent Latin male is referred to as macho makes Hispanics cringe. *"Es muy macho,"* the women in my family nod approvingly, describing a man they respect. But in the United States, when women say, "He's so macho," it's with disdain.

3 The Hispanic *macho* is manly, responsible, hardworking, a man in charge, and a patriarch. He is a man who expresses strength through silence, or what the Yiddish language would call a *mensch*.

4 The American *macho* is a chauvinist, a brute, uncouth, selfish, loud, abrasive, capable of inflicting pain, and sexually promiscuous. Quintessential *macho* models in this country are Sylvester Stallone, Arnold Schwarzenegger, and Charles Bronson. In their movies, they exude toughness, independence, and masculinity. But a closer look reveals their machismo is really violence masquerading as courage, sullenness disguised as silence, and irresponsibility camouflaged as independence.

5 If the Hispanic ideal of *macho* were translated to American screen roles, they might be Jimmy Stewart, Sean Connery, and Laurence Olivier. In Spanish, macho ennobles Latin males. In English, it devalues them. This pattern seems consistent with the conflicts ethnic minority males experience in this country. Typically, the cultural traits other societies value don't translate as desirable characteristics in America.

6 I watched my own father struggle with these cultural ambiguities. He worked on a farm for twenty years. He laid down miles of irrigation pipe, carefully plowed long, neat rows in fields, hacked away at **recalcitrant** weeds, and drove tractors through whirlpools of dust. He stoically worked twenty-hour days during harvest season, accepting the long hours as part of agricultural work. When the boss complained or upbraided him for minor mistakes, he kept quiet, even when it was obvious the boss had erred.

recalcitrant: unmanageable

7 He handled the most menial tasks with pride. At home he was a good provider, helped out my mother's family in Mexico without complaint, and was indulgent with me. Arguments between my mother and him generally had to do with money or with his stubborn reluctance to share his troubles.

He tried to work them out in his own silence. He didn't want to trouble my mother—a course that backfired because the imagined is always worse than the reality.

8 Americans regarded my father as decidedly un-macho. His character was interpreted as nonassertive, his loyalty as a lack of ambition, and his quietness as ignorance. I once overheard the boss's son blame him for plowing crooked rows in a field. My father merely smiled at the lie, knowing the boy had done it, but didn't refute it, confident his good work was well known. But the boss instead ridiculed him for being "stupid" and letting a kid get away with a lie. Seeing my embarrassment, my father dismissed the incident, saying, "They're the dumb ones. Imagine, me fighting with a kid." I tried not to look at him with American eyes because sometimes the reflection hurt.

9 Listening to my aunts' clucks of approval, my vision focused on the qualities America overlooked. "He's such a hard worker. So serious, so responsible." My aunts would secretly compliment my mother. The unspoken comparison was that he was not like some of their husbands, who drank and womanized. My uncles represented the darker side of macho.

10 In a patriarchal society, few challenge their roles. If men drink, it's because it's the manly thing to do. If they gamble, it's because it's how men relax. And if they fool around, well, it's because a man simply can't hold back so much man! My aunts didn't exactly meekly sit back, but they put up with these transgressions because Mexican society dictated this was their lot in life.

11 In the United States, I believe it was the feminist movement of the early seventies that changed macho's meaning. Perhaps my generation of Latin women was in part responsible. I recall Chicanos complaining about the chauvinistic nature of Latin men and the notion they wanted their women barefoot, pregnant, and in the kitchen. The generalization that Latin men embodied chauvinistic traits led to this interesting twist of semantics. Suddenly a word that represented something positive in one culture became a negative prototype in another.

12 The problem with the use of macho today is that it's become an accepted stereotype of the Latin male. And like all stereotypes, it distorts truth. The impact of language in our society is undeniable. And the misuse of macho hints at a deeper cultural misunderstanding that extends beyond mere word definitions.

Comprehension and Critical Thinking

1. Find a word in paragraph 2 that means "contempt." *disdain*
2. Underline the thesis statement.
3. What is the author comparing and contrasting in this essay?

   She is contrasting the English-American view of macho with the Hispanic view of macho.

4. What connotations does the word *macho* have in Latin culture?

   It has positive connotations of somebody who is responsible, hardworking, and respected.

5. What connotations does the word *macho* have in American culture?

   It has negative connotations of someone who could be chauvinistic, uncouth, loud, or selfish.

6. According to the author, why do men like Jimmy Stewart, Sean Connery, and Laurence Olivier better exemplify the word *macho* than men like Sylvester Stallone or Charles Bronson?

   The former are noble as in the Latin definition of macho, whereas the latter are sullen, irresponsible, and violent as in the American definition of macho.

7. In paragraph 8, the author writes that she tried not to look at her father "with American eyes." In her opinion, how did Americans view her father?

   They judged him as weak, nonassertive, and ignorant.

8. According to the author, does the word *macho* in Latin cultures only have a positive connotation? Explain your answer.

   Macho also has a negative connotation. Macho men can behave badly by drinking too much or womanizing, and their wives cannot do anything about it.

9. How did the meaning of the word *macho* evolve in Latin communities in North America?

   It was initially positive. The feminist movement, as well as the generation of Latin women in the 1960s and 1970s, helped change the meaning of the word. The word became associated with chauvinism.

10. Although the predominant pattern in this essay is comparison and contrast, the author also uses definition and narration. How do they help develop her central argument?

    She needs to define the terms to be able to compare adequately, and the narration provides examples to prove her point.

Writing Topics

Write about one of the following topics. Remember to explore, develop, and revise and edit your work.

1. What are some stereotypes of your nationality, religion, or gender? Compare the stereotypes with the reality.
2. Compare and contrast two people in your life who have very different personalities.

Teaching Tip:
The suggested topics give students the opportunity to practice comparison and contrast writing. Specify whether students should write a paragraph or an essay.

READING 18

Medicating Ourselves

Robyn Sarah

Robyn Sarah is a poet and a writer. Her work has appeared in *The Threepenny Review*, *New England Review*, and *The Hudson Review*, and she is a frequent contributor to *The Montreal Gazette*. In the next essay, Sarah reflects on society's overreliance on medication.

1 It is hard to pick up a magazine these days without finding an article attacking or defending some pharmaceutical remedy for syndromes of mood or behavior. These drugs are in vogue because they have shown themselves spectacularly effective for a range of conditions, though their exact workings are not well understood and their long-term effects are not known. Yet for all the noise we continue to hear about, say, Ritalin, for children with attention deficit disorders and related learning or behavior problems—or Prozac and the new family of anti-depressants prescribed to the stressed and distressed of all ages—the real debate on pharmaceuticals has yet to begin.

2 The enormous strides science has made in understanding brain chemistry have precipitated a revolution no less significant than the "cyber-revolution" now transforming our lives. The biochemical model has brought relief to many suffering individuals and families, removing devastating symptoms and lifting blame from parents whose contorted responses to a child's **anomalous** behavior were once mistaken for its cause. But the very effectiveness of corrective pharmacology engenders an insidious imperative: we can, therefore we must. The realization that we can chemically fine-tune personalities—that we may be able to "fix" what were once believed innate flaws of character—has staggering implications for our understanding of morality, our standards for acceptable behavior, our mental pain threshold, and our expectations of self and others.

anomalous: unusual

3 The medication debate should not be a matter of "whether or not," but of where to stop. Mental illness is real and can be life-threatening. But when is something truly a disorder, and when are we **pathologizing** human difference, natural human cycles and processes? How do we decide what needs fixing, and who should decide? These are not simple matters.

pathologizing: making a disease of

4 During my own school years, the boy who today would be prescribed Ritalin used to spend a lot of time standing in the hall outside the classroom. His "bad boy" reputation dogged him year to year and became part of his self-image. He learned to wheel-and-deal his way out of trouble by a combination of charm and **subterfuge**; he learned to affect a rakish persona to mask what anger he might feel about his **pariah** status. But in spite of his often superior intelligence, anything else he learned in school was hit-and-miss. Such "bad boys" rarely lasted beyond the second year of high school.

subterfuge: evasion

pariah: outcast

5 Defenders of Ritalin point out that in making it possible for such a child to focus and sustain attention, to complete tasks and take satisfaction from them, the stimulant breaks a cycle of disruptive behavior, punishment, anger, and acting out. Begun early, Ritalin can prevent the battering of self-esteem such children undergo in school; introduced later, it allows a child to rebuild self-esteem. These are powerful arguments for a drug that, when it works, can effect what seems a miraculous transformation in a "problem child," giving him a new lease on life in a system that used to chew him up and spit him out.

6 But Ritalin is not a benign drug, and many are alarmed at the frequency and casualness with which it is prescribed (often at the school's prompting) for a disorder that has no conclusive medical diagnosis. Some argue that children who may simply be high-spirited, less compliant, or more physically energetic than the norm are being "drugged" for the convenience of teachers and smooth classroom functioning. Others wonder if the frequency of **ADD** and **ADHD** diagnoses says more about the state of schools than it does about the state of children. Do our schools give children enough physical exercise, enough structure and discipline, or enough real challenge? A proliferation of troublemakers can be an indication of something wrong in the classroom—witness any class with an inexperienced substitute teacher. Pills to modify the behavior of "disturbers" may restore order—at the cost of masking the true problem.

ADD: attention-deficit disorder

ADHD: attention-deficit hyperactivity disorder

7 Something similar may be going on as diagnoses of depression and other disorders proliferate, especially among groups in the throes of life change (adolescent, mid-life, or geriatric). Just as physical pain is our body's way of alerting us to a problem, psychic pain can be a response to our changed position in the world. Psychic pain might indicate that we should reorient ourselves by reassessing and rebuilding our primary relationships. If I swallow a pill to conceal my existential problems—an "equanimity" pill—I may be easier to live with, but I may also be masking the need for some fundamental work to be done, some exercise of the spirit. Giving a boost to my brain chemistry might help me do this work, but it is just as likely to take away the urgency to do it.

8 I am myself no stranger to depression, but in eschewing the chemical solution, I have begun to sense I am swimming against the tide. For a while, I felt all the worse because so many of my peers, with lives no less complicated than mine, seemed to be handling mid-life pressures better than I was. Slowly it emerged that several had taken antidepressants at some point "to get over a rough spot." Some are still taking them.

9 The arguments are seductive. Why make things harder for ourselves, and why inflict our angst on others, when there is an alternative? One father I know, the stay-at-home parent of small children, told me he put himself back on Prozac (originally prescribed for migraines) because under stress he tended to be irritable, and things were more stressful with

a new baby in the house. His irritability was not something he wanted to inflict on his children. Who could fault him for such a decision?

10 If we can really smooth our rough edges by popping a pill, why not make life pleasanter for our loved ones and associates by popping a pill? If a pill can make saints of us all, where is the virtue in resisting this pill? But the effect may be to mask how many people would otherwise be doing "badly," which not only induces the unmedicated to bash themselves for their human frailties, but blinds us all to societal ills that may explain why so many of us get depressed.

11 The new pharmaceutical culture could stigmatize the unmedicated. It could make us all less tolerant of our frailties and those of others. It could keep us reconciled to the values that have put us in the pressure cooker to begin with: the worship of youth and success, the pursuit of comfort and expediency, and a model of wellness based on uninterrupted productivity.

12 Shall we lose the sense of what it is to be unique, struggling, evolving souls in the world, and instead use designer drugs to make ourselves smooth-functioning cogs of an unexamined societal machine? Aldous Huxley predicted it in 1932, in his Utopian novel *Brave New World*. Remember the drug *soma*? It has "the advantages of Christianity and alcohol; none of their defects [. . .]. Anyone can be virtuous now. You can carry half your morality around in a bottle." Huxley's book, on the high school reading list a generation ago, enjoys that same place today. But I am beginning to think the satire may have been lost on us. Perhaps it was too late for the message even when he wrote it. With our complicity, his vision gets closer every day.

Comprehension and Critical Thinking

1. In paragraph 7, what does *proliferate* mean? increase
2. Define the word *stigmatize* in paragraph 11. brand, isolate, label
3. In your own words, restate the thesis statement.

   The overuse of new medications influences our behavior, our values, and our expectations.
4. In which paragraph(s) does the author acknowledge an opposing viewpoint?

   paragraphs 2, 5, and 10
5. Which strategies does the author use to support her argument? There is more than one answer.
   - (a.) fact
   - (b.) anecdote
   - c. quotations from informed sources
   - d. statistics
   - (e.) logical consequences

For each type of support that you have identified, underline a sentence from the text. Answers will vary.

6. Using your own words, list at least four of the author's main arguments.

   Behavior modification drugs may only hide the problem, not cure it.
   Perhaps children misbehave in schools because of the structure of the school day.
   Overprescribing drugs may not allow people to deal with the causes of their problems. Those who do not take any medication may feel deficient or even marginalized in a society that favors the use of medication.
   In certain circumstances, taking medication to modify behavior makes people less unique.

7. The author suggests some causes of overmedicating in our culture. What are they?

   It provides a simple solution for mental disorders, it lifts blame from parents, it controls children's behavior, and people have great confidence in science.

Teaching Tip: Ask students to infer the answers to questions 7 and 8.

8. What are some of the effects of using medication to modify behavior problems?

   People do not examine their behavior; sightly eccentric behavior becomes unacceptable.

9. How does the author conclude her essay?
   a. suggestion (b.) prediction c. call to action

10. Why does the author quote Aldous Huxley in her concluding paragraph?

   Huxley predicted a world in which people use drugs to alter personality differences to control behavior.

Writing Topics

Write about one of the following topics. Remember to explore, develop, and revise and edit your work.

Teaching Tip: The suggested topics give students the opportunity to practice argument writing. Topic 2 is a research essay topic. Students should review Chapter 16.

1. Argue for the use of mood-altering drugs.
2. Argue that vaccinations should or should not be mandatory. You will have to do some research and support your points with the opinions of experts. See Chapter 16 for information about writing a research essay.

The Writer's Room Human Development

The previous four readings, and Editing Handbook Chapters 35–38, deal with issues related to human development. The following activities continue developing that theme.

Teaching Tip: Photo writing topic 1 can generate a comparison and contrast essay, and writing topic 2 can lead to a process essay.

Teaching Tip: The film prompts may appeal particularly to auditory and visual learners. If the suggested films do not appeal to your group of students, choose one (or ask students to choose one) that addresses the theme and then adapt the writing prompt as needed.

Teaching Tip: The film writing prompts encourage students to use process, argument, and definition writing.

Writing Activity 1: Photo Writing

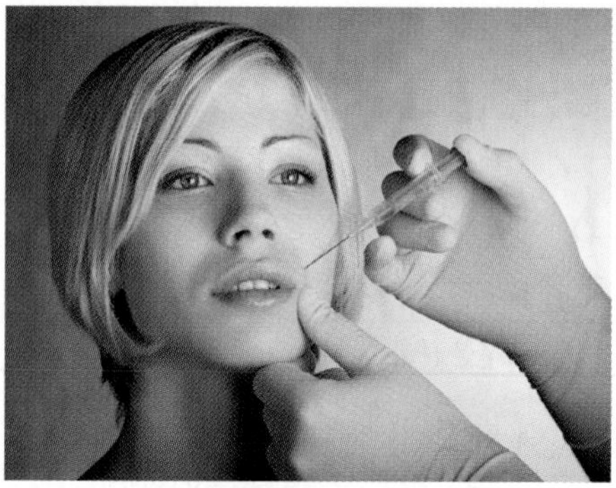

1. Compare how two different people or cultures view aging. You might need to search for information on the Internet.
2. What are some of the mental and physical processes people go through to keep looking or feeling young?

Writing Activity 2: Film Writing

1. The movies *Billy Elliot* and *Frida* describe the journey of an artist. Choose one of the films and describe the process that the main character goes through.
2. The film *Mean Girls* depicts a group of high school girls. What does the film suggest about adolescence? Why is that stage of life so difficult? Give examples from the film to support your point.
3. In films such as *Mean Girls*, *Billy Elliot*, and *Bend It Like Beckham*, the main characters deal with intense pressure from friends, peers, and family. Write a definition essay about one of the following terms: *peer pressure*, *parental pressure*, *success*, *failure*, *courage*, or *adolescence*. Give examples from one of the films to support your point.

Appendix 1
Grammar Glossary

The Basic Parts of a Sentence

Parts of Speech	Definition	Some Examples
Noun	Names a person, place, or thing.	singular: woman, horse, person plural: women, horses, people
Verb	Expresses an action or state of being.	action: look, make, touch, smile linking: is, was, are, become
Adjective	Adds information about the noun.	small, pretty, red, soft
Adverb	Adds information about the verb, adjective, or other adverb; expresses time, place, and frequency.	quickly, sweetly, sometimes, far, usually, never
Pronoun	Replaces one or more nouns.	he, she, it, us, ours, themselves
Preposition	Shows a relationship between words (source, direction, location, etc.).	at, to, for, from, behind, above
Determiner	Identifies or determines if a noun is specific or general.	a, an, the, this, that, these, those, any, all, each, every, many, some
Conjunction	Coordinating conjunction: Connects two ideas of equal importance. Subordinating conjunction: Connects two ideas when one idea is subordinate (or inferior) to the other idea.	but, or, yet, so, for, and, nor although, because, even though, unless, until, when
Conjunctive adverb	Shows a relationship between two ideas. It may appear at the beginning of a sentence, or it may join two sentences.	also, consequently, finally, however, furthermore, moreover, therefore, thus
Interjection	Is added to a sentence to convey emotion.	hey, yikes, ouch, wow

How Do I Get a Better Grade?

mywritinglab

Visit www.mywritinglab.com for audio-visual lectures and additional practice sets about parts of speech.
Get a better grade with MyWritingLab!

Appendix 2
Irregular Verbs

Irregular Verb List

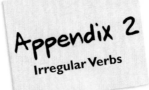

Base Form	Simple Past	Past Participle	Base Form	Simple Past	Past Participle
arise	arose	arisen	eat	ate	eaten
be	was, were	been	fall	fell	fallen
bear	bore	borne / born	feed	fed	fed
beat	beat	beat / beaten	feel	felt	felt
become	became	become	fight	fought	fought
begin	began	begun	find	found	found
bend	bent	bent	flee	fled	fled
bet	bet	bet	fly	flew	flown
bind	bound	bound	forbid	forbade	forbidden
bite	bit	bitten	forget	forgot	forgotten
bleed	bled	bled	forgive	forgave	forgiven
blow	blew	blown	forsake	forsook	forsaken
break	broke	broken	freeze	froze	frozen
breed	bred	bred	get	got	got, gotten
bring	brought	brought	give	gave	given
build	built	built	go	went	gone
burst	burst	burst	grind	ground	ground
buy	bought	bought	grow	grew	grown
catch	caught	caught	hang	hung	hung
choose	chose	chosen	have	had	had
cling	clung	clung	hear	heard	heard
come	came	come	hide	hid	hidden
cost	cost	cost	hit	hit	hit
creep	crept	crept	hold	held	held
cut	cut	cut	hurt	hurt	hurt
deal	dealt	dealt	keep	kept	kept
dig	dug	dug	kneel	knelt	knelt
do	did	done	know	knew	known
draw	drew	drawn	lay	laid	laid
drink	drank	drunk	lead	led	led
drive	drove	driven	leave	left	left

Base Form	Simple Past	Past Participle	Base Form	Simple Past	Past Participle
lend	lent	lent	slit	slit	slit
let	let	let	speak	spoke	spoken
lie[1]	lay	lain	speed	sped	sped
light	lit	lit	spend	spent	spent
lose	lost	lost	spin	spun	spun
make	made	made	split	split	split
mean	meant	meant	spread	spread	spread
meet	met	met	spring	sprang	sprung
mistake	mistook	mistaken	stand	stood	stood
pay	paid	paid	steal	stole	stolen
put	put	put	stick	stuck	stuck
prove	proved	proved / proven	sting	stung	stung
quit	quit	quit	stink	stank	stunk
read	read	read	strike	struck	struck
rid	rid	rid	swear	swore	sworn
ride	rode	ridden	sweep	swept	swept
ring	rang	rung	swell	swelled	swollen
rise	rose	risen	swim	swam	swum
run	ran	run	swing	swung	swung
say	said	said	take	took	taken
see	saw	seen	teach	taught	taught
sell	sold	sold	tear	tore	torn
send	sent	sent	tell	told	told
set	set	set	think	thought	thought
shake	shook	shaken	throw	threw	thrown
shine	shone	shone	thrust	thrust	thrust
shoot	shot	shot	understand	understood	understood
show	showed	shown	upset	upset	upset
shrink	shrank	shrunk	wake	woke	woken
shut	shut	shut	wear	wore	worn
sing	sang	sung	weep	wept	wept
sink	sank	sunk	win	won	won
sit	sat	sat	wind	wound	wound
sleep	slept	slept	withdraw	withdrew	withdrawn
slide	slid	slid	write	wrote	written

[1]*Lie* can mean "to rest in a flat position." When *lie* means "tell a false statement," then it is a regular verb: *lie, lied, lied*.

Appendix 3

Verb Tenses

ESL Teaching Tip:
This time line will be useful for your nonnative speakers. It visually explains when to use the different verb tenses.

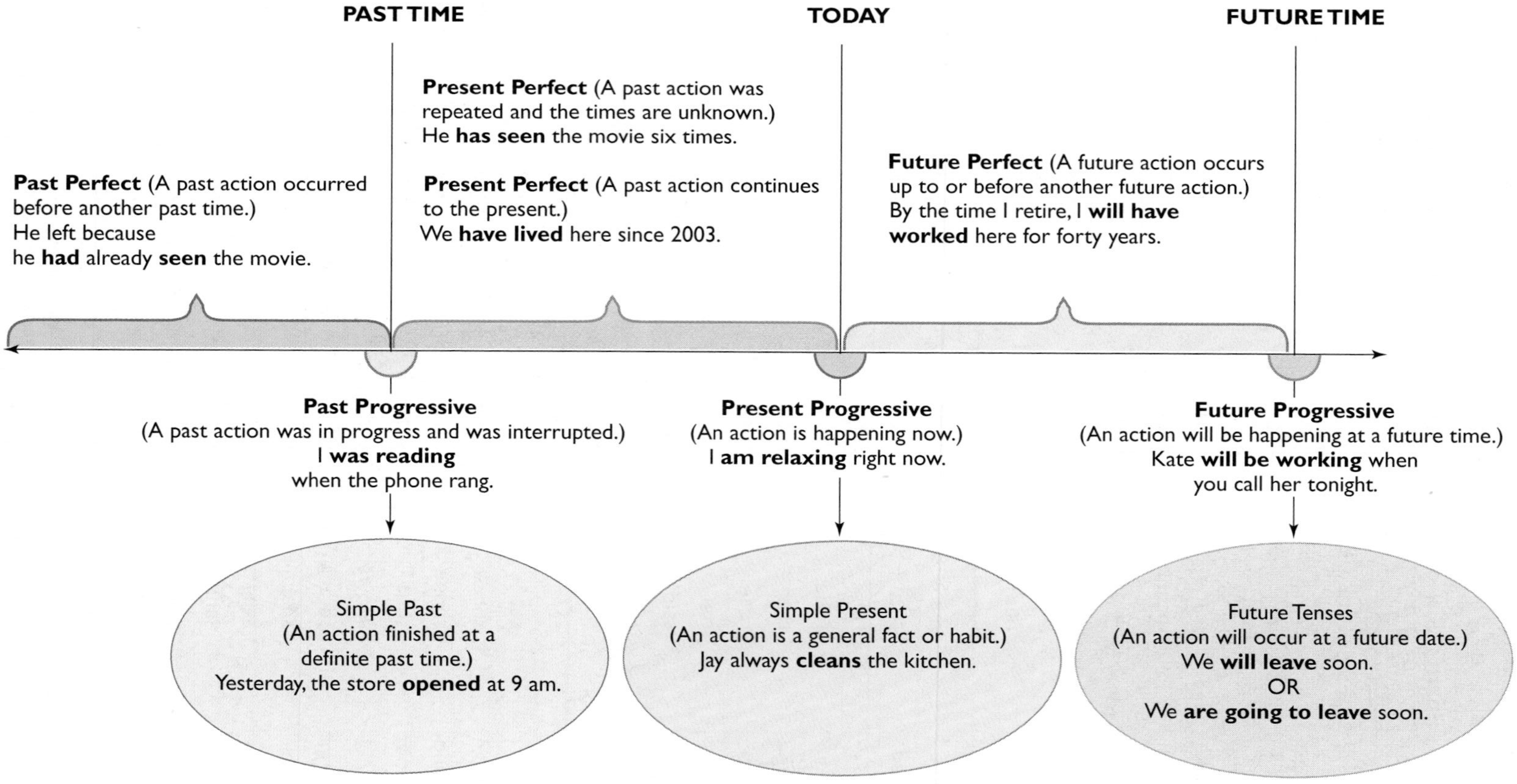

PAST TIME
TODAY
FUTURE TIME
Past Perfect (A past action occurred before another past time.)
He left because he **had** already **seen** the movie.
Present Perfect (A past action was repeated and the times are unknown.)
He **has seen** the movie six times.
Present Perfect (A past action continues to the present.)
We **have lived** here since 2003.
Future Perfect (A future action occurs up to or before another future action.)
By the time I retire, I **will have worked** here for forty years.
Past Progressive
(A past action was in progress and was interrupted.)
I **was reading** when the phone rang.
Present Progressive
(An action is happening now.)
I **am relaxing** right now.
Future Progressive
(An action will be happening at a future time.)
Kate **will be working** when you call her tonight.
Simple Past
(An action finished at a definite past time.)
Yesterday, the store **opened** at 9 am.
Simple Present
(An action is a general fact or habit.)
Jay always **cleans** the kitchen.
Future Tenses
(An action will occur at a future date.)
We **will leave** soon.
OR
We **are going to leave** soon.

Appendix 4
Combining Ideas in Sentences

Making Compound Sentences

A.

Complete idea

, coordinator
, for
, and
, nor
, but
, or
, yet
, so

complete idea.

B.

Complete idea ; complete idea.

C.

Complete idea

; transitional expression,
; however,
; in fact,
; moreover,
; therefore,
; furthermore,

complete idea.

Making Complex Sentences

D.

Complete idea

subordinator
although
because
before
even though
unless
when

incomplete idea.

E.

Subordinator
Although
Because
Before
Even though
Unless
When

incomplete idea , complete idea.

Appendix 5

Spelling, Grammar, and Vocabulary Logs

In the first few pages of your writing portfolio or copybook, try keeping three "logs" to help you avoid repeating errors and improve your writing.

Spelling Log

The goal of keeping a spelling log is to stop repeating errors. Every time you misspell a word, record both the mistake and the correction in your spelling log. Then, before you hand in a writing assignment, consult the list of misspelled words.

EXAMPLE:

Incorrect	Correct
finaly	*finally*
responsable	*responsible*

Grammar Log

The goal of keeping a grammar log is to stop repeating errors in sentence structure, mechanics, and punctuation. Each time a writing assignment is returned to you, identify one or two repeated errors and add them to your grammar log. Next, consult the grammar log before you hand in new writing assignments in order to avoid making the same errors. For each type of grammar error, you could do the following:

1. Identify the assignment and write down the type of error.
2. In your own words, write a rule about the error.
3. Include an example from your writing assignment.

EXAMPLE: *Cause and Effect Essay (Mar. 10)* *Fragment*

Sentences must have a subject and verb and express a complete thought.

Also, an overbearing parent~~. That~~ can cause a child to become controlling.

Vocabulary Log

The vocabulary log can provide you with interesting new terms to incorporate in your writing. As you use this book, you will learn new vocabulary. Keep a record of the most interesting and useful words and expressions. Write a synonym or definition next to each new word.

EXAMPLE: *ubiquitous means widespread*

Spelling Log

Grammar Log

Vocabulary Log

Credits

TEXT:

Page 9: *Meatless Days*, Sara Suleri, University of Chicago Press. Copyright © 1989 by The University of Chicago Press. Reprinted with permission; **pp. 9–10:** Reprinted by permission of the European Food Information Council; **p. 10:** *Sociology*, 11e, John J. Macionis, Prentice Hall © 2007, p. 95; **p. 46:** From *Newsweek*, January 30, 2006 © 2006 Newsweek, Inc. All rights reserved. Used by permission and protected by the copyright Laws of the United States. The printing, copying, redistribution or retransmission of the material without express written permission is prohibited. The credit shall accompany the first or last page of the article and if the article and if the article is reprinted in digital format on a website. User shall provide a link to (www.newsweek.com); **pp. 47–48:** *The New World of International Relations*, 6e, Michael G. Roskin and Nicholas O. Berry, Pearson Education © 2005; **p. 48:** *The Twenty-First-Century Campus: Where Are The Men?*, John J. Macionis, *Sociology*, Pearson Education; **p. 55:** "Phishing," Mike Musgrove, *The Washington Post*, Oct. 22, 2005; **p. 55:** Reprinted with permission of Dorothy Nixon; **p. 83:** Reprinted with permission of the Portland Bolt & Manufacturing company; **pp. 83–84:** Reprinted with permission; **pp. 89–91:** Reprinted with permission; **pp. 93–94:** Reprinted with permission; **pp. 101–103:** Reprinted with permission; **pp. 110–111:** Reprinted with permission; **pp. 113–115:** Excerpted from "Out of Sight" by Ryan Knighton. Copyright © 2005 by Ryan Knighton. Reprinted by permission of the author. Ryan Knighton's memoir *Cockeyed*, is available in the US from PublicAffairs Books; **p. 119;** Reprinted by permission of John Crossely, http://www.americansouthwest.net; **pp. 121–122:** Reprinted with permission; **pp. 130–131:** Reprinted by permission of Natalia McDonald; **pp. 132–134:** Reprinted with permission of Lucie L. Snodgrass; **pp. 140–141:** Reprinted by permission of Tony Ruiz; **pp. 147–148:** Reprinted with permission; **pp. 149–151:** "Do You Have What It Takes to Be Happy?", Stacey Colino, *Shape Magazine*, May 2005; **p. 157:** Reprinted with permission of the Center for Educational Networking, an education information networking effort of the Michigan Department of Education, www.cenmi.org; **pp. 158–159:** Reprinted by permission of Lindsey Davis; **pp. 167–168:** Reprinted with permission; **pp. 169–170:** Reprinted by permission of Dorothy Nixon; **pp. 178–179:** Reprinted with permission; **pp. 189–190:** Reprinted with permission; **pp. 192–194:** "Types of Correctional Officers," Frank Schmalleger, PhD, *Criminal Justice Today*, Prentice Hall, pp. 500–502; **pp. 201–202:** Reprinted with permission; **pp. 209–210:** Reprinted with permission; **pp. 212–213:** Reprinted with permission; **p. 219:** Courtesy of the Canadian Safety Council; **pp. 219-221:** Reprinted with permission; **pp. 228-229:** Reprinted with permission; **pp. 231–232:** © 2006, The Washington Post Writers Group, Reprinted with Permission; **pp. 239–240:** Reprinted with permission; **pp. 250-251:** Reprinted with permission; **pp. 253–255:** © Slate.com and Washngtonpost.com. Newsweek Interactive. All rights reserved; **p. 261:** Copyright © 2006 by The New York Times Company. Reprinted with permission; **p. 262:** Copyright © 2006 by The Gazette; **p. 263:** *Sociology*, 11e, John J. Macionis, Prentice Hall © 2007, pp. 186–87; **pp. 264–265:** "Why Street Gangs Develop," Carol R. Ember and Melvin Ember, *Cultural Anthropology*, Prentice Hall, pp. 192–193; **pp. 289–295:** Reprinted with permission of Leonard J. Bukowski; **pp. 311–313:** Reprinted with permission of Stacy Taylor; **pp. 321–322:** Reprinted with permission; **p. 380:** http://www.rbgkew.org.uk/sihort/tropamerica/peru/index.htm, Royal Botanic Kew; **p. 535:** *Art from Found Materials*, Mary Lou Stribling, p. 6; **p. 536:** *The Obstacle Race*, Germaine Greer, 2001, p. 132; **p. 537:** *Understanding Music*, Jeremy Yudkin, 2002, Pearson, p. 446; **p. 537:** *Psychology*, David G. Martin, p. 567; **p. 545:**

2007 by Mary Bellis http://inventors.about.com/library/inventors/blphotographytwo.htm). Used with permission of About, Inc., which can be found online at www.about.com. All rights reserved; **p. 566:** Reprinted with permission of The Chicago Reporter; **pp. 567 & 568:** *Science & Spirit*, May/June 2004. Reprinted with permission of Helen Dwight Reid Educational Foundation. Published by Heldref Publications, 1319 Eighteenth St., NW, Washington DC 20036-1802. Copyright © 2004; **p. 569:** excerpt from *The New American Webster Handy College Dictionary*, Philip D. Morehead and Andrew T. Morehead. A Signet Book, Penguin © 2000; **p. 571:** Reprinted by permission of Jackie Lautens; **pp. 572–574:** "CSI Effect Has Juries Wanting More Evidence", Richard Willing, *USA Today*, August 5, 2004. Reprinted with permission of the Copyright Clearance Center; **pp. 575–579:** "Types of Rioters," David A. Locher, *Collective Behaviors*, pp. 121–128; **pp. 580–583:** *Essence* © 1997; **pp. 585–590:** From *Me Talk Pretty One Day* by David Sedaris. Copyright © 2000 by David Sedaris. By permssion of Little Brown & Company; **pp. 592–593:** Reprinted with permission of Avi Frideman; **pp. 596–598:** Reprinted with permission of Eugene Henry; **pp. 599–601:** © 2004, The Washington Post, reprinted with permission; **pp. 603–604:** "Google's China Web," Frida Ghitis, *Boston Globe*, January 26, 2006. Reprinted with permission of the Copyright Clearance Center; **pp. 607–609:** Reprinted by permission of Pamela D. Jacobsen; **pp. 610–612:** Copyright © 2007 Laurence Gonzales; **pp. 614–616:** From *Into Thin Air* by Jon Kraukauer, copyright © 1997 by Jon Kraukauer. Used by permission of Villard Books, a divison of Random House, Inc.; **pp. 617–618:** Reprinted with permission of Rahul Goswami; **pp. 621–623:** Reprinted with the permission of The Massachusetts Society for the Prevention of Cruelty to Animals. www.mspca.org; **pp. 624–626:** Reprinted with permission of The National Geographic Society; **pp. 629–631:** Reprinted with permission of Ariel Levy; **pp. 632–633:** Reprinted with permission of the Scripps Howard News Service; **pp. 635–636:** "The Untranslatable Word 'Macho'", Rose Del Castillo Guibaullt, *San Francisco Chronicle*, 2005, Reprinted by permission of the Copyright Clearance Center; **pp. 638–640:** Reprinted with permission of Robyn Sarah.

PHOTOS:

Page 3: Photos.com; **p. 16:** Courtesy of www.istockphoto.com; **p. 17:** Courtesy of www.istock.photo.com; **p. 32:** Courtesy of www.istockphoto.com; **p. 44:** Courtesy of www.istockphoto.com; **p. 61:** Courtesy of www.istockphoto.com; **p. 62:** Courtesy of www.istockphoto.com; **p. 63:** Courtesy of www.istockphoto.com; **p. 65, top:** Courtesy of www.istockphoto.com; **p. 65, mid:** Pixtal/Superstock Royalty Free; **p. 68:** Courtesy of www.istockphoto.com; **p. 81:** Photos.com; **p. 96:** Courtesy of www.istockphoto.com; **p. 98:** Milos Jokic/Shutterstock; **p. 117:** Courtesy of www.istockphoto.com; **p. 118:** Courtesy of www.istockphoto.com; **p. 136:** Courtesy of www.istockphoto.com; **p. 138:** Courtesy of www.istockphoto.com; **p. 153:** Courtesy of www.istockphoto.com; **p. 155:** Courtesy of www.istockphoto.com; **p. 173:** Photos.com; **p. 175:** Photos.com; **p. 196:** Purestock/Superstock Royalty Free; **p. 198:** Courtesy of www.istockphoto.com; **p. 215:** Photos.com; **p. 217:** Courtesy of www.istockphoto.com; **p. 234:** Courtesy of www.istockphoto.com; **p. 236:** Photos.com; **p. 256:** Courtesy of www.istockphoto.com; **p. 259:** Photos.com; **p. 260:** Photos.com; **p. 267:** Photos.com; **p. 302:** Courtesy of www.istockphoto.com; **p. 309:** Courtesy of www.istockphoto.com; **p. 314:** Courtesy of www.istockphoto.com; **p. 326:** Photos.com; **p. 333:** Courtesy of www.istockphoto.com; **p. 341:** Comestock/Superstock Royalty Free; **p. 345:** Courtesy of www.istockphoto.com; **p. 346:** Photos.com; **p. 349:** Underwood Photo Archives/SuperStock, Inc.; **p. 356:** Courtesy of www.istockphoto.com; **p. 357:** Photos.com; **p. 361:** Courtesy of www.istockphoto.com; **p. 366:** Steve Vidler/SuperStock, Inc.; **p. 367:** Patricia Schwimmer (Canadian, b. 1953) "My San Francisco", 1994,Tempera, Private Collection. © Patricia Schwimmer/SuperStock; **p. 369:** Courtesy of www.istockphoto.com; **p. 374:** Richard Cummins/SuperStock, Inc.; **p. 378:** Michele Burgess/SuperStock, Inc.; **p. 379:** Richard Cummins/SuperStock, Inc.; **p. 380:** Courtesy of www.istockphoto.com; **p. 382:** Yoshio Tomii/SuperStock, Inc.; **p. 385:** Hidekazu Nishibata/SuperStock, Inc.; **p. 388:** Photos.com; **p. 396:** Courtesy of www.istockphoto.com; **p. 398:** Courtesy of www.istockphoto.com; **p. 408:** Mario Carreno (b. 1913/Cuban) *La Siesta* 1946. Oil on canvas. © Christie's Images/SuperStock; **p. 410:** Photos.com; **p. 411:** Photos.com; **p. 429:** Ritu Manoj Jethani/Shutterstock; **p. 431:** Courtesy of www.istockphoto.com; **p. 433:** Robert Llewellyn/SuperStock, Inc.; **p. 442:** SuperStock, Inc.; **p. 444:** Courtesy of www.istockphoto.com; **p. 445:**

Courtesy of www.istockphoto.com; **p. 453:** Photos.com; **p. 454:** Superstock Royalty Free; **p. 456:** Photos.com; **p. 464:** Donna and Steve O'Meara/Superstock Royalty Free; **p. 469:** Katsushika Hokusai (1760–1849, Japanese) "The Wave", 19th Century, Woodcut print. © SuperStock, Inc.; **p. 472:** Courtesy of www.istockphoto.com; **p. 476:** Pixtal/Superstock Royalty Free; **p. 480:** Tony Linck/ SuperStock, Inc.; **p. 484:** Courtesy of www.istockphoto .com; **p. 489:** Shutterstock; **p. 493:** Courtesy of www .istockphoto.com; **p. 495:** Courtesy of www.istockphoto .com; **p. 499:** SuperStock, Inc.; **p. 505:** Charles Marden Fitch/SuperStock, Inc.; **p. 509:** Courtesy of www .istockphoto.com; **p. 519:** Photos.com; **p. 522:** The Bridgeman Art Library International; **p. 529:** Donald Martin, after Van der Weyden (20th Century American), "Portrait", Airbursh on wood. © Donald C. Martin/ SuperStock; **p. 530:** Photos.com; **p. 431:** Courtesy of www.istockphoto.com; **p. 533:** © 2007 Artists Rights Society (ARS), New York; **p. 544:** Photos.com; **p. 545:** Courtesy of the Library of Congress; **p. 554:** Photos.com; **p. 565:** Courtesy of www.istockphoto.com; **p. 584:** Courtesy of www.istockphoto.com; **p. 595:** Courtesy of www.istockphoto.com; **p. 606:** Courtesy of www .istockphoto.com; **p. 620:** Courtesy of www.istockphoto .com; **p. 628:** Courtesy of www.istockphoto.com; **p. 642:** Courtesy of www.istockphoto.com.

Index